DATE DUE

WITHDRAWN

C=8.7

(13)

LT=12/8/11

OP 3/17

BY THE AUTO EDITORS OF CONSUMER GUIDE®

THE COMPLETE HISTORY OF
FORD
MOTOR COMPANY

BEEKMAN HOUSE
New York

Louis Weber, President
Publications International, Ltd.
3841 West Oakton Street
Skokie, Illinois 60076

Permission is never granted for commercial purposes.

Manufactured by CGP Delo, Ljubljana, Yugoslavia
h g f e d c b a

ISBN: 0-517-64147-X

This edition published by Beekman House, Distributed
by Crown Publishers, Inc., 225 Park Avenue South, New
York, New York 10003

Author: Richard M. Langworth and the Auto Editors of
CONSUMER GUIDE®

The editors gratefully acknowledge the Ford Motor Company Photomedia Department for its generous and timely assistance with historical photography. In addition, Karl Zahm provided many otherwise unobtainable photos from his personal collection, while photographers Bud Juneau, Vince Manocchi, and Doug Mitchel shot many of the superb photos found within this book.

Special thanks to the owners of the cars featured in the color sections for their enthusiastic cooperation: Andrew Alphonso (1958 Edsel Pacer), Lynn Augustine (1956 Ford Fairlane), Ken Baker (1967 Ford Mustang), Dan and Barbara Baltic (1950 Ford), Art Banducci (1911 Ford), Dan Bergeron (1970 Mercury Cougar convertible), Rod and Claudia Buerke (1963 Mercury Meteor), Jerry Butak (1966 Ford Thunderbird), Kenneth Coleman (1962 Ford Galaxie 500), Ed Coughlin (1965 Ford Shelby GT), Mike Cowles (1960 Edsel Ranger convertible), Ted Davidson (1959 Ford Thunderbird), Dave Doyle (1951 Ford Country Squire station wagon), Gary Emerson (1968 Ford Mustang CS), Jerry Emery (1939 Lincoln Zephyr), Edsel Ford (1959 Edsel Ranger), Frank Gonsalves (1926 Ford), Jack Harbaugh (1931 Lincoln), Charles Hilbert (1958 Ford Fairlane 500), Harold Hofferber (1936 Lincoln Zephyr), Philip and Nancy Hoffman (1941 Lincoln Zephyr), Tom Howard (1953 Ford Crestline), Robert M. Jarrett (1940 Ford coupe), Jay B. Jonagan (1954 Mercury Monterey), Jack Karleskind (1970 Mercury Cougar), George Lyons (1965 Ford Mustang), Jerry H. Magayne (1959 Ford Galaxie 500), Bud Manning (1952 Mercury Monterey), Vince Manocchi (1964 Ford Galaxie 500 XL), Stephen M. McCarthy (1951 Lincoln Cosmopolitan), Dan McCormick (1958 Lincoln Premiere), Glenn Moist (1969 Ford Torino Talladega), Randall Mytar (1956 Continental Mark II), Len Nowasel (1955 Ford Thunderbird), Alan C. Parker (1955 Ford Fairlane), Robb D. Petty (1957 Continental Mark II), Dick Pyle (1934 Ford), Roger Randolph (1961 Ford Galaxie 500), Larry and Annis Ray (1956 Ford Customline), Henry Rehm (1941 Ford), Joseph H. Risner (1967 Ford Fairlane), Herb Rothman (1959 Ford Thunderbird), George Sampson (1929 Ford and 1940 Ford convertible), John F. Stimac, Jr. (1932 Ford), Mike and Marge Tanzer (1964 Ford Thunderbird), Unique Motors (1948 Ford Sportsman), James and Susan Verhasselt (1957 Mercury Turnpike Cruiser), Ron Voyles (1969 Ford Torino Talladega—white), Bob Ward (1949 Mercury), Rick Wassell (1970 Ford Mustang), Gerald Wuicket (1937 Ford), Harry Wynn (1941 Lincoln Continental and 1942 Lincoln Zephyr), Andrew and Phyllis Young (1965 Mercury Comet Caliente), Bob Zarnosky (1948 Lincoln).

CONTENTS

INTRODUCTION

Henry Ford, founder of Ford Motor Company and the driving force behind the firm and its products for more than four decades, made an extraordinary impact on the American scene. Several of his most notable accomplishments—the Model T, institution of mass-production methods, and his wage-price practices—revolutionized industry and society as a whole, not just in America but around the world.

A true folk hero, Ford was an appealing figure to millions of his fellow citizens. He was viewed as one who succeeded through his own creativeness, hard work, and by supplying a product to meet the public's desires, rather than manipulating money or people. He also was admired, despite his great wealth, for having retained the common touch. Asked on his 50th birthday to cite the greatest handicap of the rich, he replied: "For me, it was when Mrs. Ford stopped cooking." Regarded as an industrial superman and widely believed to typify American civilization and genius, he nevertheless reminded many people of an earlier, simpler time.

Ford was a late starter. For him, life began at 40. Born in 1863, he was unknown outside Detroit until 1901, when his racing exploits put his name on the sports pages. He made two false starts as an auto manufacturer before founding Ford Motor Company in 1903. But within a decade, he had become fabulously wealthy and the auto industry's dominant figure. In the process, he also gained a measure of national prominence. In 1914, at age 51, he became an overnight international celebrity by more than doubling the wages of most of his workers. Ford's prime extended into his late 60s, and perhaps would have lasted longer had it not been for the Great Depression. Even so, he remained vigorous, continuing to guide and personify his company well into his 70s.

Controversial, paradoxical, and always colorful, Henry Ford was an endlessly fascinating enigma. An idealistic pioneer in some respects, he was a cynical reactionary in others. He had a selfish, mean, even cruel streak, yet he was often generous, kindly, and compassionate. He was ignorant, narrow-minded, and stubborn, yet at times he displayed remarkable insight, vision, open-mindedness, and flexibility. His mercurial, chameleon-like personality baffled his associates. "History," he once proclaimed, "is more or less bunk." He then proceeded to build Greenfield Village, a repository of Americana. He constructed the world's biggest factory, yet delighted in building hydro-electric plants that employed as few as 11 workers. He did not believe in organized charity, yet gave millions to good works. The list goes on and on.

How, one must ask, could a man like this rise to such greatness? Part of the answer is that Ford possessed several outstanding qualities. He had native intelligence and common sense, even though the latter occasionally failed him; an intuitive mind that leaped beyond the present; a special engineering talent that combined creativity with practicality; a remarkable memory; a missionary's zeal; and a lifelong capacity for hard work—especially thinking, which he termed "the hardest work there is." He shunned the conventional vices. He also had, or made, his share of good luck. His entry into automaking and the introduction of his Model T were both perfectly timed. He was teamed, by accident, with James Couzens, who contributed enormously to Ford Motor Company's early success.

His personal life also played a part. Ford married a woman who understood and complemented him well. Clara Bryant, like Henry, was born on a farm in the Dearborn area. Three years younger than her husband, she was convinced from the time they were wed, in 1888, that he would accomplish great things. Ford called her "The Believer." Clara encouraged and stood by him for a remarkable 59 years.

Henry and Clara had but one son, Edsel, born in 1893. Edsel grew up with the Ford company and, although named president of the firm in 1919, would always remain in his father's shadow. Competent and respected, he gradually gained responsibility for styling, sales, and advertising—but never labor relations, engineering, or manufacturing. Edsel and his wife Eleanor Clay (born in 1896 into a socially prominent Detroit family) had four children between 1917 and 1925: Henry II, Benson, Josephine, and William Clay. Henry II administered the company from 1945 until his retirement as chairman in 1980. Benson served as vice-president and general manager of Lincoln-Mercury Division in 1948-55 and as chairman of Ford's Dealer Policy Board from 1956 until his death in 1978. William Clay Ford served as the company's vice-chairman.

Fourth-generation Fords (including Edsel II, son of Henry II, and William Clay's son, William Clay Jr.) are now rising within the company, but it's unclear whether any of them will ever rise to run it. The Ford family still holds a controlling 40 percent of the voting shares, and can thus install one of its own at will. But the stakes are too high to promote any but the most highly qualified person to the post of president or chairman. Henry II has said many times that family members will have to *earn* higher positions, just like anyone else.

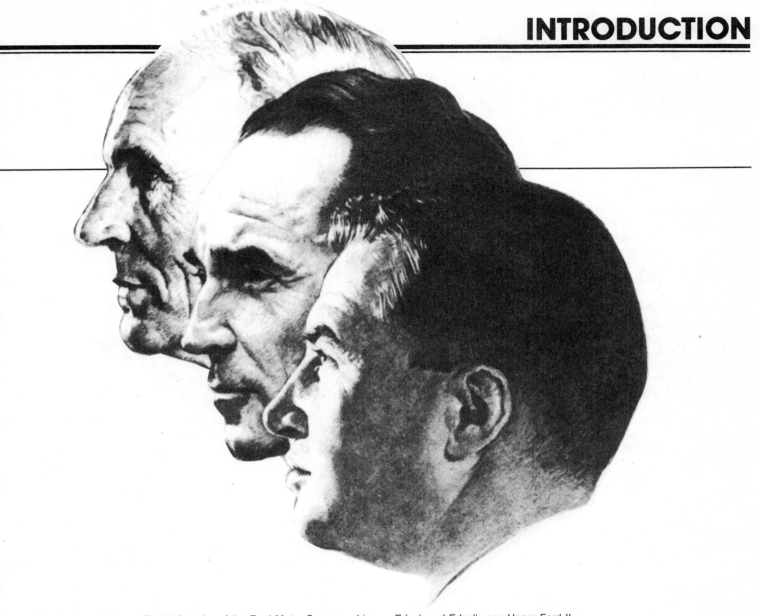

The Ford dynasty: Henry Ford I, founder of the Ford Motor Company, his son Edsel, and Edsel's son Henry Ford II.

As for Henry Ford Senior, he left a magnificent legacy. Idolized by many Americans during his lifetime, he remains a legendary figure to this day. Millions drive vehicles bearing his name; additional millions see the name "Ford" daily on cars and trucks and in advertisements. The company invariably invokes his memory during anniversaries and milestone celebrations despite the mutterings of a few executives that "ancient history and Model T talk don't sell cars." But it can scarcely ignore its founder, so closely intertwined is its history with his life.

Among the more tangible reminders of the Ford legacy are an estimated 300,000 surviving Model Ts, much larger numbers of Model As and early Ford V-8 models, and lesser numbers of Mercurys, Lincolns, Lincoln-Zephyrs and Continentals, all produced during the auto magnate's lifetime. Many of these cars have been viewed in museums by millions of people; many others are displayed in parades and tours and at old-car meets. Most of these carefully preserved vehicles, whether owned by individuals or museums, seem likely to outlast the massive plants in which they were built.

As the years pass and our vision of the man blurs somewhat, it is likely that Henry Ford will be best remembered for his singular contribution to the industrial revolution. By promoting high-volume production, low prices, and universal consumption, he became the key figure in a process much more far-reaching than putting a car in every garage. He and his Model T, and the mass-production methods actually helped remold the world.

Of his company, Ford said to Edsel one day, "We'll build this as well as we know how, and if we don't use it, somebody will. Anything that is good enough will be used." Because of its founder, the Ford Motor Company today has as rich and valuable a heritage as any commercial organization on earth, perhaps richer than any other. Henry Ford obviously built well.

1896-1902

In the winter of 1895-96, a hopeful 33-year-old inventor named Henry Ford struggled to build his first car. On June 4, 1896, he drove this "quadricycle," as he called it, through the streets of Detroit. But the little vehicle's initial run went unreported in the local newspapers, Ford having neither publicly announced a demonstration nor making a photograph or description of his car available to any publication.

Ford sold his first car, then turned to building a second. The work went slowly, and was carried on pretty much anonymously. The first reference to Henry Ford in an automotive context appeared in the November 1898 edition of *Horseless Age* under the heading "Minor Mention":

"Henry Ford, of Detroit, Mich., chief engineer of the Edison Electric Light Co. of that city, has built a number of gasoline vehicles which are said to have been successfully operated. He is reported to be financially supported by several prominent men of the city who intend to manufacture the Ford vehicle. From Mr. Ford himself, no information can be gleaned regarding his vehicles or his plans for their manufacture."

Ford's second car (the *Horseless Age* item had overstated the number built) was working in the summer of 1899, and led to his first press interview and an accompanying photo feature in the July 29th edition of the Detroit *Journal*. A week later, largely on the strength of a successful demonstration Henry had given to a wealthy Detroit lumberman, the Detroit Automobile Company was orga-

A young, and somewhat formal-looking, Henry Ford.

nized. Ford was given a small share of stock in the concern and named its superintendent.

In early February 1900, Ford again demonstrated his car's capabilities, this time to a reporter for the Detroit *News-Tribune*. Normally shy with strangers, Ford was at home behind the tiller, as loquacious as a snake-oil salesman. The rollicking three-column story that followed—headlined "Swifter Than A Race-Horse It Flew Over The Ice Streets"—provides the first inkling that Ford would one day have an easy way with the press.

Whatever their virtues, the cars produced by the Detroit Automobile Company did not sell. Ford apparently wanted to improve the model, but the company's stockholders vetoed the suggestion. The firm slowly ground to a halt in late 1900.

Ford and his assistants spent the spring and summer of 1901 building a race car. By fall, a trim, light, 26-horsepower machine was ready. Its first test came at the Grosse Pointe race track, near Detroit, on October 10. On hand were several of the nation's outstanding drivers, including Alexander Winton. Ford's machine was entered in the 10-mile sweepstakes event, where Winton was heavily favored. The champion's sales manager, Charles B. Shanks, was so confident of his employer's victory that he had already picked the prize: a beautiful punch bowl that he thought would look good in the bay window of the Winton dining room.

Henry Ford sits atop his first Quadricycle, circa 1898.

A 1901 Detroit, built by the Detroit Automobile Company, of which Henry was superintendent.

Winton and Ford were the only starters in the main contest. (A third competitor, Pittsburgh millionaire William N. Murray, who owned one of the fastest cars in the country, withdrew because of mechanical difficulties.) Winton was on the inside, and his deftness in rounding curves enabled him to open up a 1/5-mile lead at the three-

Henry Ford at the wheel of his first racer, 1901.

mile mark (Ford had to shut off power and run wide on each curve). By the halfway point, however, Ford was picking up lost ground on the straightaways, and by the sixth lap had improved his position perceptibly. As the crowd urged Ford on, Winton began to have trouble with overheated bearings. Shanks, riding with him, drenched the bearings with oil, but to no avail. Ford shot ahead on the eighth lap and swept across the finish line well ahead of the faltering champion. His average speed: 43.5 miles per hour.

This victory brought Henry Ford national attention, which in turn provided the impetus for formation of a new company. A number of prominent Detroiters, including several former stockholders in the Detroit Automobile Company, had seen the triumph and were fired by the commercial possibilities of the Ford machine. Accordingly, they organized the Henry Ford Company on November 30, 1901, the name itself a tribute to Ford's newly won reputation. Henry was given a one-sixth share in the new firm and the post of chief engineer. But his continued preoccupation with racing quickly produced friction between him and other stockholders, so he left after only three months, taking with him a $900 settlement and the uncompleted drawings for a new racing car. The company agreed to discontinue the use of his name.

By early May 1902, Ford had joined forces with Tom Cooper, a former bicycle champion who also had racing fever. With Cooper's money and Ford's know-how, they

9

built two 80-horsepower monsters, dubbed "Arrow" and "999," the latter for the record-breaking New York Central train. "There was only one seat," Ford would recall later. "One life to a car was enough. I tried out the cars. Cooper tried out the cars. We let them out at full speed. . . . Going over Niagara Falls would have been [easy] after a ride in one of them." Neither Ford nor Cooper had the nerve to drive the cars in competition. Cooper, however, said that he knew a man "who lived on speed, that nothing could go too fast for him." A wire to Salt Lake City secured the services of one Barney Oldfield, then a professional bicycle rider. Oldfield had never driven a car, but said he would try anything once. He learned quickly, and proved fearless.

Oldfield was primed for the five-mile Manufacturers' Challenge Cup, scheduled for the Grosse Pointe track on

The second Ford "Quadricycle," built in 1898.

Birthplace of the Ford car—a little brick shed on Bagley Avenue in Detroit, Michigan.

October 25, 1902. Four drivers started, Winton and Shanks among them. Oldfield opened up the "999" immediately, was never headed, and defeated runner-up Shanks by a lap. His time was 5 minutes, 28 seconds—not quite the mile-a-minute pace he had said he would aim for a year earlier, but an American record nevertheless. Once again, Ford's name resounded in the press, and Oldfield was launched on his career as one of America's greatest race drivers.

The victory also marked the end of Ford's preoccupation with racing. For purposes of advertising, he would set a world's speed record two years later, and his cars would race until 1912. But with his reputation firmly established, he was now able to turn to his life's work, putting a "family horse" on the market.

Meantime, on August 20, 1902, Ford and Alexander Y. Malcomson, a Detroit coal dealer, signed an agreement to develop a commercial automobile. In November they carried their partnership a step further by organizing The Ford & Malcomson Company, Ltd., and offering shares for sale. They secured 10 investors within a year, and on June 16, 1903 the Ford Motor Company was incorporated with paid-in capital of $28,000. Henry Ford, who contributed his patents, his engine, and his knowledge to the new enterprise, was awarded a 25.5-percent interest.

An 1899 Detroit Automobile Company delivery van.

The 1896 "Quadricycle," Henry Ford's first car, which he drove publicly on June 4, 1898.

This 1901-02 Ford experimental car had two cylinders.

1903

Ford Motor Company was launched with a minimum of fanfare, and made no apparent attempt to win publicity for itself or the car it was putting on the market. Detroit's three daily newspapers were unaware of the firm's incorporation until three days after the fact. Even then, the news was buried in brief stories on their back pages. *Horseless Age* devoted a few lines to a rumor that the "Ford Automobile Company will build a factory at Pontiac." *Motor Age* told its readers—in one paragraph—that the company would place a "Fordmobile" on the market. *Cycle and Automobile Trade Journal* ran a longer, more factual story since, by coincidence, its June issue featured the automotive industry in Detroit. *Automobile* and *Automobile Topics* ignored the new firm completely.

Of course, even if the fledgling concern had tried to garner press notice, it undoubtedly wouldn't have received much. Ford was but one of 15 Michigan companies and one of 88 firms in the nation introducing automobiles in 1903, and neither the amount of its capitalization nor its prospects for success were particularly noteworthy.

The first production Ford car, the Model A, had the great merits of simplicity, lightness, and efficiency. Its principal innovation was a two-cylinder opposed engine that developed eight horsepower and, on good roads, could produce speeds up to 30 mph. Wheelbase of the little runabout measured just 72 inches. As in most other horseless carriages of the period, the steering wheel was on the right. The driver opened no door, but simply slid into his seat, his whole body in full view. There were no running boards and the car stood high off the street, so the passenger had to contend with a small, sharp, sometimes slippery carriage step. The transmission, then often called the "change-gear," was of the planetary type, with two speeds forward and one reverse. Both ignition and throttle were adjusted by hand, the former getting its spark from two sets of six dry-cell batteries. The tonneau or backseat attachment was slipped on and off from the rear. The complete car weighed only 1250 pounds, in line with Henry Ford's insistence that weight had no relation to strength. "The car that I designed was lighter than any car that had yet been made," he later declared. "It would have been lighter had I known how to make it so."

"This new, light touring car fills the demand for an automobile between a runabout and a heavy touring car," declared an early advertisement. "It is positively the most perfect machine on the market, having overcome all drawbacks such as smell, noise, jolt, etc. common to all other makes of auto carriages." Such boasts notwithstanding, a great many faults had to be eliminated. Radiators, for example, were so inadequate that the engine got hot enough to boil its cooling water even when the car was run in high gear on a level road. The first carburetors were inefficient, and there were brake problems. The splash lubrication system needed excessive amounts of oil, the circulating pump was inefficient, and the spark plugs became dirty because oil leaked past the piston rings. Transmissions provoked complaint because their bands slipped. But every early auto manufacturer had such difficulties. Ford tinkered and replaced, and after six months the Model A was running smoothly.

The soon-to-be famous Ford script was used as the new company's symbol right from the start. It was provided by one of Henry Ford's first associates, C.H. Wills, who would later build the Wills St. Claire car. As a boy of 15 or 16, Wills had earned money by making calling cards, which he lettered in flowing script. When the company first grappled with advertising, nobody was satisfied with the appearance of the name Ford. Wills rummaged an attic for his old printing outfit, and wrote out F-O-R-D in its now-familiar style. Immediately accepted, the design endured until the post-World War II era, when it was replaced by block letters. It was revived in the 1960s, framed in an oval against a blue background, and is in worldwide use today.

From the outset, Ford Motor Company could be distinguished from most new automakers of 1903—and, indeed, from many established companies—in that it made money. It netted a total of $36,957 within its first 3½ months, and paid a 10-percent dividend on November 21. Sales were quite respectable: 1708 units for the calendar year. The flow of dividends would continue unabated for the next 23 years and at a phenomenal rate in most of them. In 1903, however, profits were overshadowed by legal entanglements. Ford was the target of litigation, the celebrated Selden case, whose outcome would affect the pocketbook of everyone who made, sold, or bought an automobile in America.

The Selden suit was filed in 1903 by George B. Selden, a Rochester, New York attorney, and the Electric Vehicle Company. Selden had obtained a patent for a "road carriage" covering all gasoline-powered vehicles designed since 1879 and manufactured, sold, or used in the United States in the 17 years ending 1912. In 1899, Selden had assigned the patent to a firm that became the Electric Vehicle Company, and by March 1903, most auto companies had been intimidated into acknowledging the patent's validity. By that summer, 26 firms had formed the Association of Licensed Automobile Manufacturers and struck a deal with the patentholders, agreeing to pay them a royalty of 1.25 percent of the price of each car sold. The Association had the privilege of selecting those manufacturers to be licensed and those to be sued. The latter, presumably, were to be put out of business.

In February and again during the summer of 1903, Henry Ford and his associates approached the ALAM's acting president about obtaining a license for their fledgling company. They were rebuffed, the ALAM executive expressing a lack of confidence in Ford's ability to meet the Association's manufacturing standards and thus qualify as a creditable member of the auto industry. Undeterred, Ford continued to produce and sell cars. Soon the ALAM warned that the company, its dealers, and customers were subject to prosecution for patent infringement. Ford, in turn, promised his buyers protection. "Our Mr. Ford made the first Gasoline Automobile in Detroit and the third in the United States," the firm's advertising inaccurately proclaimed. "Our Mr. Ford also built the famous '999' Gasoline Automobile, which was driven by Barney Oldfield in New York on July 25, 1903, a mile in 55⁴/₅ seconds, on a circular track, which is the world's record. Mr. Ford, driving his own machine, beat Mr. Winton at Grosse Pointe track in 1901. We have always been winners."

Not surprisingly, the patentholders sued Ford, and by 1907, all the evidence had been submitted in court. At that point, both sides began an all-out effort to curry public favor. The fireworks centered around the two main exhibits. The Seldenites had constructed a motor buggy to demonstrate that a car built to the patent's specifications would run. Ford insisted the Selden buggy would start only when facing downhill, and demonstrated a machine with an engine resembling one patented by an Englishman in 1869 to refute Selden's claim to originality. Ford also claimed its car traveled four times as far and as fast as the Selden machine, and daringly offered to race a Selden car over 50 miles—giving it a 45-mile head start.

Finally, in 1909, the federal district court in New York ruled in favor of Selden. Henry Ford appealed. "The patent," he said, was "a freak among alleged inventions," and he offered a bond to each buyer, backed by the $12 million assets of his firm and its bonding company. To the Detroit *Free Press*, which echoed the sentiments of many a reader, Ford's stand was heroic. "There's a man for you, a man of

The first production Ford car, a 1903 Model A.

backbone," declared an editorial entitled "Ford the Fighter." "Of the case behind him, the lawyers were more able to talk, but as a human figure he presents a spectacle to win the applause of all men with red blood; for this world dearly loves the fighting man, and needs him, too, if we are to go forward."

The appellate court's decision was handed down on January 9, 1911. This time the victory went to Ford, and it was total. Dozens of telegrams and letters poured into the Ford offices, from opponents as well as friends. Every automobile man in the country had the name "Ford" on his lips. For the first time in his life, Henry Ford was front-page news in Detroit and in the trade press. He was lauded on all sides as a giant-killer, a symbol of revolt against monopoly, a magnificent individualist. The victory was of tremendous advertising value to the firm and its then-current Model T. As Ford himself later said, "No one factor publicized the company and its products as effectively as the company's role in liberating an industry."

1904

Ford Motor Company entered the 1904-05 selling season—that is, the year beginning in autumn and running through the ensuing spring and summer—with three new models. The Model A gave way to the improved, 1250-pound Model C runabout, selling at $800 ($900 with tonneau). A new touring car, the 1400-pound Model F, was priced at $1000. Both had Ford's original, but now revised, two-cylinder opposed engine. In an effort to reach wealthy people, the company now introduced a heavier, faster, four-cylinder touring car, the Model B, at $2000.

The firm was moving away from, not toward, the $500 car Henry Ford wanted to sell, and this disturbed him. But all these newcomers were better than the original Model A. The Model C had 10 horsepower, the Model F had 12, both through greater bore and stroke. Wheelbases were six and 12 inches longer, respectively, than the A's; and paint was more attractive. The Model B, with 24 horsepower, could be pushed to a speed of 40 mph. It also boasted storage batteries instead of dry cells, a 15-gallon fuel tank, and a weight of 1700 pounds. The Model C and F did well; demand for the Model B was weaker. Ford production in both 1904 and 1905 lagged behind its first-year pace: 1695 and 1599 units, respectively.

Ford vehicles were first exhibited at auto shows in New York, Chicago, and five lesser cities in early 1904. From 1905 to 1910, the company exhibited under the auspices of a small group of manufacturers not licensed under the Selden patent. After winning the Selden case in 1911,

The 1904-05 12-horsepower Ford Model F sold for $1200.

Henry Ford refused to exhibit in New York City under the aegis of successor associations, a policy he maintained all the way through 1940. The company did participate in trade association shows outside New York in 1911-12, then began introducing its new models at private showings in New York and other key cities.

Numerous nonautomotive shows and expositions also attracted the company during its early years. It displayed three cars in 1904 at the Louisiana Purchase Exposition in St. Louis, and cutaway chassis and engines operated by electricity were featured at industrial shows several years later. Henry Ford's personal interest in rural life was reflected in a Model T exhibit at the New York Land Show (for farmers) in 1911-12.

Before establishing branches and dealerships throughout the country, the Ford company sent out "missionary mechanics" to aid and appease complaining customers. Later, under the watchful eye of sales manager Norval Hawkins, dealers had to provide top-notch service facilities in order to obtain and retain their franchises. Clean, neat places of business, pleasing show windows, and attractive cars for demonstrations were required. Branch roadmen took photographs of dealerships, inside and out, to satisfy the home office that its conditions were being met. Snapshots were taken of managers and salesmen to ensure their correct and businesslike appearance. Roadmen also kept a constant watch over their franchisees' financial condition and their standing in the community, comparing them with dealers handling other makes.

Early Ford agents were also told to keep their garages and stockrooms separate from sales and display areas so that prospective consumers would not be able to see cars being ripped apart for repairs—or hear owner complaints. Chains could not be advertised or sold for fear this would suggest the possibility of breakdowns, and at least one branch ordered that malfunctioning cars be towed in only after nightfall, so as to reduce the impact of this "very bad advertisement." Nobody, including customers and visitors, was permitted to smoke in a Ford dealership. Tipping was not tolerated, and acceptance of a gratuity brought instant dismissal. Fresh, clean signs—not faded or soiled ones that "invite breaking of rules"—had to be posted prominently throughout the premises. Strong efforts were made to induce dealers to buy standardized Ford letterheads and outdoor and window signs. Hawkins and James Couzens frequently lectured factory, branch, and dealer personnel to be on their best business behavior at all times, to answer letters promptly, and to "see callers right off."

This concern with customer relations was well founded. Within less than a decade of its incorporation, Ford had grown a vast dealer network, which meant more of its personnel had contact with the public than those of any other automobile or manufacturing company. In fact, Ford probably had more sales outlets (some 7000) and personnel than the rest of the industry combined.

In January 1904, Henry Ford returned to racing to promote the Model B. As a spectacular stroke was needed to

Ford's Model C replaced the "A" for 1904-05. It weighed 1250 pounds and sold for $800-$950.

give the new car nationwide publicity, Ford announced he would break the world's record for the timed mile with an engine practically identical to the production Model B's. The test was to be made on the cinder-covered ice of Lake St. Clair, northeast of Detroit. On January 9, Ford unofficially ran the distance in 36 seconds, 10 full seconds under the world's record. On January 12, with official timers on hand, he repeated the run in 39.4 seconds (91.37 mph). It was, said the Detroit *Tribune*, "the wildest ride in the history of automobiling. . . . Humped over his steering wheel, the tremendous speed throwing the machine in zigzag fashion across the 15-foot roadway, Ford was taking chances that no man, not even that specialist in averted suicide, Barney Oldfield, had dared to tempt."

Ford was very much aware of the dangers but, as he wrote later, having come this far, there seemed no way out. "The ice seemed smooth enough, so smooth that if I had called off the trial we should have secured an immense amount of the wrong kind of advertising. But [it] was seamed with fissures, which I knew were going to mean trouble the moment I got up speed. There was nothing to do but go through with the trial, and I let the old

'Arrow' out. At every fissure the car leaped into the air. I never knew how it was coming down. When I wasn't in the air, I was skidding, but somehow I stayed top side up and on the course, making a record all over the world."

Automobile people everywhere were astounded by Ford's performance, "so sensational that even the most enthusiastic supporters of American speed machines admitted that they would like to see further proof before accepting the figures." Under the headline "Ford's Mile Raises the Dander of the Track Champion," the Detroit *Tribune* pictured Barney Oldfield as green with envy. Dominique Lamberjack, the French champion, flatly stated such a feat was impossible. A Detroit newspaper, after thoroughly considering the question, decided it was unlikely that any car would ever travel a faster mile. Discounting wire reports, eastern officials of the American Automobile Association insisted on seeing affidavits signed by the six timers and two surveyors before even considering the record. The group's chairman then said that if it were authentic, it would be put in a special "made on ice" category, which brought the wrath of Detroit newspapers.

Ford turned to racing to promote the Model B cars, setting a speed record of 91.37 mph on January 12, 1904.

On January 20, 1904, Ford's record was made official. Seven days later, William K. Vanderbilt, on the sands of Ormond Beach, Florida, eclipsed it with a run of 39 seconds flat.

The Model B profited little from Ford's daring and the ensuing controversy. The press persisted in confusing the rebuilt Arrow with the 999, even though Ford personally visited the sports desk of each Detroit paper to see that the Model B received its full due.

Ford apparently didn't race again in 1904. The following year, he attempted to regain the mile speed record on the beach at Cape May, New Jersey, in a new racer, but could not break 41 seconds. The car was rebuilt, and Ford announced in 1906 that it would do the mile in 30 seconds (120 mph). Despite this claim, he failed to break 40 seconds in exhibitions at Ormond Beach.

Meanwhile, the company's racers were achieving success on midwestern and eastern tracks. This year a daring mechanic, Frank Kulick, set light-car records that would stand for more than half a dozen years for one, three, four, and five miles. Between 1904 and 1907, Ford racers proved themselves almost invincible in their class, and

frequently won contests with larger vehicles in open competition. Probably the most publicized victory was a 24-hour speed-endurance contest won by Kulick and a co-driver over eight other cars at the Michigan State Fairgrounds in mid-1907. Ford ads called the race "the swiftest, maddest driving ever witnessed" and claimed world's records for distances covered in one, eight, and 24 hours. The company also promoted races among its test drivers and customers on a private track in Highland Park, Michigan, in 1907. Held on alternate Saturdays, these contests proved popular drawing cards for Detroit-area motorists.

Although racing enjoyed wide popularity in most years before World War I, it came in for considerable criticism between 1905 and 1907. Accidents had become commonplace, and six drivers were killed in 1907 alone. Henry Ford and his company had abandoned racing by fall, the founder for good, the firm for almost two years. Kulick, in testing a new racer, went off the Michigan State Fair track at full speed, narrowly escaping death. Shaken by the accident, Henry Ford declared that until the industry could agree on limiting the speed and power of racing

1905

vehicles, he and his company would forego the sport. He suggested that maximum engine displacement be restricted to 250 cubic inches as a way to permit engineers to show the superiority of their designs and to bring about sane racing. The suggestion fell on deaf ears. Machines with engines of up to 600 cid continued to ply American tracks and, with the exception of Barney Oldfield and the Locomobile and Thomas companies, most of the leading drivers and sponsors continued to race.

Ford apparently had another reason to quit racing: his cars had virtually run out of competition in their low-price, lightweight category. In explaining the move, *Ford Times* grumbled with considerable justification: "After we had beaten all the one- and two-lungers and other low-priced cars, what good would victory do us?"

Nonetheless, Ford's decision was sharply criticized by dealers, who had come to rely heavily on the racing prowess of the Ford car in their advertising. Since 1904, many dealers had entered contests themselves. Now they felt the need to intensify their efforts in order to keep pace with the competition. *Ford Times,* fully aware of racing's promotional value, sympathetically chronicled all Ford victories so that dealers could list them in their ads. The publication also devoted considerable attention to Ford's racing triumphs in Europe, where branches were not bound by the policy.

The Ford model trio continued basically unchanged this year. However, production now shifted from Henry's original plant on Mack Avenue, a converted wagon shop, to a new factory on Piquette Avenue, 10 times larger. The main building (a power plant, paint shop, and testing house stood near it) occupied a site 402 by 56 feet and stood three stories tall. It would be Ford's principal manufacturing facility until superceded by the Highland Park facility in 1910.

The Piquette plant not only produced a variety of pre-T Fords but was also where the Model T was conceived and first built. Ironically, a Michigan Historical Commission marker designates Highland Park as "The Home of the Model T," while the older factory remains unmarked. The Piquette plant, later used for E-M-F and Studebaker production, still stands.

The Mack plant, destroyed decades ago by fire, was located in what is now the heart of Detroit's black community. Today, a smaller-scale reproduction, ordered by Henry Ford, stands in Dearborn's outdoor historical museum, Greenfield Village. Another, mobile replica was built by

Henry Ford sits in the Arrow (to the left), the record-setting race car he campaigned in 1904-05.

1905-07

Metro Detroit Ford Dealers for the company's 75th anniversary in 1978, and appeared in many parades. No historical marker designates the Mack site.

1906-1907

The four-cylinder Model N, progenitor of the Model T, was introduced for the 1906-07 selling season. Much better than its predecessors, it was, in fact, one of the best-designed cars yet seen in the United States. A compact, 1050-pound vehicle powered by a 15-horsepower four-cylinder engine, it could go 45 mph and deliver up to 20 miles per gallon. And its price was right: $600. If still reminiscent of the buggy in the lines of its folding top and two-passenger body, the Model N was nevertheless trim and dashing. Its engine was placed in front under a nickeled hood. Two handsome nickeled lamps adorned the radiator, and there were two more on the dashboard. Wheels were nestled under short mudguards, and the short fenders were brightly polished. Comparing favorably in appearance with the smarter models of its day, the N offered remarkable value for the money.

With all this, the N was greeted with a burst of enthusiasm, reflected by a prodigious jump in sales. From just under 1600 cars the previous year, Ford's calendar 1906 output soared more than five-fold, to 8729. "This car," declared the *Cycle and Automobile Trade Journal*, "is distinctly the most important mechanical traction event of 1906."

Besides the N, Ford introduced two other new light models during this period: the slightly costlier Model R—"a car of more pretentious appearance," as the company put it—and the Model S, a further refinement. Both were even better-looking than the N and had slight differences:

a footboard instead of a small carriage step and a mechanical oiler instead of a force-feed unit. The Model S also had a single-seat tonneau at the rear. The N, R, and S all disappeared from Ford showrooms as the first of the Model Ts arrived. As the last pre-T model, the S was the last Ford with right-hand drive.

Meantime, Ford introduced the six-cylinder Model K, a slightly improved replacement for the Model B, weighing a ton and priced at $2800. The very idea behind the K divided Henry Ford and his chief partner. Alexander Malcomson was a strong advocate of high-priced luxury cars, while Henry wanted a $500 product for the masses. This, plus Malcomson's sizable investment in a rival auto company, led to a split. In July 1906, Ford bought Malcomson's quarter-interest in the Ford company and became its president, succeeding banker John S. Gray, who died that month.

Ford and James Couzens also bought out three other shareholders in 1906-07, by which time Henry owned 58.5 percent of the company, Couzens 11 percent. Henceforth, Ford could, if he wished, have the last word on every matter concerning what was now definitely his company.

The 1906 model lineup stayed essentially the same into

One of the two most famous automobile slogans of all time, Ford used the above line off and on into the '40s.

Henry Ford behind the wheel of a 1906-07 Model K. Sign in the window lists factories in Detroit and Walkerville, Ontario.

The Model K listed for $2800 and weighed over a ton. Pictured here is the chassis of the six-cylinder beast.

This 1907 Model R was a slightly up-market Model N.

The big Model K Runabout was a slow seller in 1907.

Women took to driving early, here in a 1907 "K" Touring.

A 1907 Model R, "a car of more pretentious appearance."

1907, but Ford still struggled unsuccessfully to sell the big Model K. Company policy seemed designed to force the car on the market. For example, applications for new franchises were not accepted unless an applicant agreed to order at least one Model K, and discounts of up to 20 percent were allowed. The firm also tried to insist that agents accept one K for every 10 Ns. But it was all to no avail: the car simply didn't sell. At year's end, those that remained had to be cleared at $1800, a $1000 chop off the original list price. Despite this, Ford's total calendar year output took a vertical leap to 14,887 cars, remarkable for an auto company not even five years old.

One of Ford's most famous and enduring slogans, "Watch the Fords Go By," emerged in 1907, and would be used from time to time in company advertising through the early 1940s. It originated with either advertising manager E. LeRoy Pelletier or traffic manager W.S. Hogue. *Ford Times*, after Pelletier's departure, credited the phrase to Hogue, who was said to have shouted it at a race in which Fords were whizzing by the competition.

These words were a familiar sight on many of the "all-Ford" trains that puffed out of Detroit to all parts of the country. They were also seen on a mammoth electric sign erected atop Detroit's Temple Theater in 1908. Though

other Ford slogans and the company's "winged pyramid" trademark pushed it aside within a few years, "Watch the Fords" became one of the two best-known automobile slogans of all time (Packard's "Ask the Man Who Owns One" is the other).

Numerous takeoffs on this phrase have also appeared over the years. J.T. Flynn wrote an article entitled "Watch the Ford Myths Go By" for *New Republic* in 1937. Al Pearce, appearing for Ford on radio the same year, called his show "Watch the Fun Go By." Ford sponsored a radio newscast during the World War II years titled "Watch the World Go By." A 1940 cartoon showing Henry and Edsel Ford whizzing by labor leader John L. Lewis was captioned "Watch the Fords Go By." So was a 1944 editorial that equated Henry Ford's 1942 and 1944 predictions that the war would end in a few months with his 1931 statement that "prosperity is here, but only a few realize it." *Broadcasting-Television* magazine ran a 1949 article titled "Watch the UN Go By," concerning the company's sponsorship of United Nations telecasts. The slogan also inspired the headline for a 1963 *Newsweek* story on Henry Ford II's luxurious new yacht, and found expression in the form of "Watch the Fords Go Back" for a 1972 *Business Week* magazine article on recalls.

1908-1909

Although a latecomer compared to most competitors, Ford Motor Company had nevertheless managed eight models—A, B, C, F, K, N, R, and S—by this, its sixth year in business. It had also carved out a solid market niche, selling 6398 cars for the fiscal year ending July 31, 1908, and netting over $1.1 million for the 15 months ending December 31. Ford was now one of the "Big Four" sellers and perhaps four rungs from the top of the profit ladder.

As the company introduced its ninth model, competition was still formidable, and the dark cloud of the Selden suit hung ominously on the horizon. But with the Model T, Ford abruptly left the pack. Over the next 18 years it would dominate U.S. car sales, accounting for more than half the industry's total output in 1918-19 and 1921-25. Profits soared accordingly. In 1911-15, 1918, and again in 1921, Ford earned more than all other automakers combined.

On March 18, 1908, advance catalogs describing the Model T were sent to Ford dealers throughout the nation. They evoked an immediate and enthusiastic response. "We must say it is almost too good to be true," a Detroit dealer wrote to headquarters, "and we have rubbed our eyes several times to make sure we were not dreaming." Averred a Pennsylvania agent: "It is without doubt the greatest creation in automobiles ever placed before a people, and it means that this circular alone will flood your factory with orders." Several dealers told the company they were hiding the information, because they feared it would be impossible to sell older models on hand if word of the Model T got out. "We have carefully hidden the sheets away and locked the drawer, throwing the key down the cold-air shaft," declared an Illinois agent.

The 1200-pound Model T was introduced on October 1, 1908, and is thus technically a 1909 model in line with the auto industry's practice of dating cars by their model or style year rather than actual year of manufacture. The T's essential note was utility, not beauty, yet its very homeliness had an appealing honesty. Its compact body, set on a wheelbase of 100 inches, stood high off the road, yet the car's sheer ungainliness somehow gave the impression of a lithe toughness. The inline four-cylinder engine, ample fuel tank (10 gallons for the touring model), and stout wheels and springs suggested an ability to travel far and wide with utter reliability.

Because it may be unfamiliar to those too young to remember it first hand, let's briefly describe the car that once was as common as goggles and duster coats on the rugged, rutted roads of early 20th-century America. The Model T used a side-valve, three-main-bearing engine

with the cylinders cast *en bloc*. Displacement was 176.7 cubic inches, compression ratio 4.5:1, output just 20 horsepower. "It will run," as one contemporary wag put it, "on almost anything from gasoline to a good grade of kerosene." That's maybe a shade optimistic, but octane level certainly didn't matter to a Tin Lizzie. Lubrication was via a combination of gravity and splash systems. Cooling was by means of a thermosyphon system (except on the first 2500 cars, which had water pumps). The sturdy chassis featured a beam axle and transverse leaf spring at the front—and the very same arrangement at the rear. Mr. Ford saw no need for a different suspension layout or geometry at each end of his "Universal Car." Initial body styles comprised the usual open touring car, a two-door landaulet with fabric rear roof section, a two-seat roadster, and a more formal, sedan-like model called town car.

The key to making the thing move was Ford's patented

A further refinement of the Model N, an '08 Model S.

Special-bodied Model T (1909?) looks tall as a house.

The Model T was Ford's ninth model in six years. Although no one knew it in 1907, it would soon dominate the industry.

planetary transmission, built in unit with the engine. The tail end of the transmission housing had a ball-and-socket joint that received the ball front of the driveshaft and took the driving thrust (along with radius rods) from the rear wheel bearings. On all except the earliest cars built, the transmission was controlled with what one writer termed "the three most famous pedals in the world." These were marked "C," "R," and "B"—presumably to prevent novice drivers from forgetting. Pedal "C" (clutch) worked a band, located inside the transmission, that engaged one of the two forward speeds. Pedal "R" (reverse) was connected to a similar reverse band. Pedal "B" (brake) operated a band that simply stopped the driveshaft from rotating and thus more or less brought the car to a halt. The gas tank was under the front seat.

The Model T had several attention-getting features. Its steering apparatus was on the left, a departure with far-reaching consequences because of the Model T's ultimately huge production volume. Within a few years, every other manufacturer in the United States would follow suit. The three-point engine mounting, as yet a novel idea, was especially important in an era of bad roads. It avoided the distortion of the engine base common with two-point mounting, and was also soon adopted by other manufacturers. The detachable cylinder head was yet another valuable innovation. Many automakers ridiculed it, asserting that it was impossible to cast a separate cylinder head that wouldn't leak. But within a half-dozen years they were following Ford's example. The arc springs afforded no luxurious ride cushion, but freed body and chassis from the racking torsional stress then common in cars. The T's improved version of the Ford planetary gearbox got away from heavy stick clutches and stripped gears in a period when countless Americans didn't know how to shift and the metal in transmissions was soft. The simple, ingenious magneto replaced the dry cells of early cars. Built into the engine, it supplied current for ignition and lamps. "Every time the flywheel revolves," said the company, "you get a series of sparks." The magneto required few subsequent modifications. Sturdy vanadium steel, borrowed from the N, R, and S, was used for crankshafts, axles, gears, and springs. All this, plus the fact that the T was to sell for only $825 and up, gave Ford considerable justification for claiming: "No car under $2000 offers more, and no car over $2000 offers more except in trimmings." Here was an Aladdin's lamp that only had to be rubbed vigorously to produce a long career of industrial growth, fame, and prosperity.

Still, early Model Ts had many faults. One weak point was the rear axle bearings, initially made of babbitt metal. Continued pounding on bad roads elongated them, and they consequently required frequent replacement. Roller bearings were substituted by 1910. The transmission bands gave constant trouble, for their linings easily burned out until a better material was employed. Owners complained that front and rear wheels were of different sizes, which necessitated carrying double sets of tires and tubes. The touring car rear seat was too narrow at first. Riveting improvements were needed and made. Cranking the Model T, especially in cold weather, was a source of innumerable broken arms and endless profanity. The company suggested that owners with cold garages attach an electric light to a long cord and keep it burning under the hood to keep the engine warm.

Owners also quickly learned that no two Model Ts were quite alike. Mastery of any one involved a high degree of courage, skill, intuition, and luck. Despite its superior dependability and simplicity, the Tin Lizzie was devastatingly eccentric, with more character than any other car ever known. Buying one was to embark on a great adventure.

So was driving. After checking fuel level (by peering into the tank), the driver fired up with a few healthy cranks on the starter handle. (An electric starter became an option in 1919.) Once the engine was chugging, it was time to adjust the spark using a lever on the left side of the steering column. Dyed-in-the-wool T-drivers took pride in knowing precisely where to set the spark and throttle levers before starting and how to adjust the choke just so. "We all had to know the hand-cranking procedure, with the choke wire by the radiator," remembers longtime aficionado Robert Bateman. "Your left toes knew the pressure and angle to hold it in Neutral while you released the handbrake-cum-clutch neutralizer. The idea was to shove in the pedal to get to low speed as fast as possible, because a slow application wore out the bands. When you judged the speed sufficient for the load and grade you eased back into High, controlling the gas lever at the same time."

Bateman makes it sound easy. The complete Model T shifting drill is extremely complicated for the first-time driver. A newcomer, who may not appreciate that Lizzie isn't just another car, will invariably push the right pedal to accelerate and the left to declutch—with predictable results. It usually took at least a year of practice, John Keats once wrote, before the Model T pilot "could get into High without bounding down the road looking like a frog with St. Vitus' dance and sounding like a canning factory with something wrong with it."

Braking in a Model T is also an interesting exercise, which new drivers attempt only because . . . well, a T is so unbreakable (no pun intended). If it does hit anything, chances are it will just bounce off. To stop, you would ostensibly stomp on the "B" pedal, but this rarely does more than slow the pace a little. The aforementioned left handbrake/declutch lever is usually needed, and it doesn't hurt to jab the "R" pedal on occasion, either.

The seating position in any Tin Lizzie is towering. The commanding view allows you to look *down* on the car's hood from a perch that is level with the roofs of most cars built after 1955 or so. Roadholding, given the rudimen-

tary suspension, is quite good. A Model T really isn't fast enough (only 35-40 mph tops) to put it to a severe test, which it would undoubtedly fail in a hurry. With four turns lock-to-lock, the steering is acceptably quick even by modern standards. The only steering reduction is a planetary gearset under the steering wheel. The lower end of the steering shaft has a bolt-on lever that pushes or pulls a rod working on the tie rod, located between the spindle arms.

Hills present a special challenge. Usually the Model T driver would approach one either flat out (with a running start) or—to make it to the top of steeper grades—in Reverse. There were two reasons for this. First, Reverse was geared higher (4:1) than Low (3:1). Second, the gravity-feed gas tank was placed higher than the carburetor. Unless the tank were full, the car would stall going forward up a grade of one-in-five or steeper. And there was a reason for *that*. The gravity/splash lube system was not fully effective at such angles. Ford had placed the gas tank so as to eliminate the chance of oil starvation on steep grades!

The T's introductory publicity was perhaps the most energetic yet seen from an American manufacturer. News releases, photographs, and sketches were sent to the press on an unprecedented scale, and the response proved commensurate with the effort. *Horseless Age* and *Motor Age* magazines each published eight photos or diagrams of the car, along with highly complimentary stories. *Motor World* ran four large pictures and called the T "a credit to the genius of Henry Ford." A record amount of literature went to dealers, who sent back a torrent of orders by mail, telegraph, telephone, and personal visits. Branch managers, called to Detroit in September, demanded 15,000 cars for their requirements alone. Immediately thereafter, ads appeared in trade journals, prompting a flow of urgent orders from general dealers. Ads were also placed in national weekly magazines. "If we were flattered by the reception the trade tendered the T," stated the company's employee/dealer magazine, *Ford Times,* "and surely no

Frank Kulick drives a 1909 "T" in New York-Seattle race.

FORD MOTOR CARS

Illustrating Four Positions of the Model T Touring Car with Top

Serviceable and of very pleasing appearance from every view point

WATCH THE FORDS GO BY

Topping up a "T" for comfortable all-weather driving.

some years showing more than a 100-percent increase over the one before. America's involvement in Word War I broke the upward spiral in 1917-19. But then came the T's heyday: six years in which domestic sales passed the one-million mark, and one in which they topped two million.

The T's sturdy dependability, plus the urging of a thousand dealers and a host of enthusiasts, induced Henry Ford to approve an official factory entry for a New York-to-Seattle race in the spring of 1909. Mining magnate Robert Guggenheim, who had arranged the cross-country run to promote the Alaska-Yukon-Pacific Exposition, imposed rigid requirements. Competitors had to check in at 30 points; could obtain new parts only in Chicago and Cheyenne, Wyoming; and were forbidden to travel on railroad tracks.

Of the 14 vehicles entered, only five—two Model Ts, an Acme, a Shawmut, and an Italia—responded to the starting gun. The Fords reached St. Louis some two hours ahead of the nearest rival, and remained together until reaching Idaho. Then Ford No. 1, driven by Frank Kulick and advertising manager H.B. Harper, forged ahead with a nine-hour lead. But they got lost twice because of misdirections and fell a day and half behind. In the meantime, Ford No. 2 headed straight for Seattle, arriving amid the cheers of 200,000 people. The trip had taken 22 days and 55 minutes. The Shawmut arrived 17 hours later, followed several hours after that by Ford No. 1. The Acme reached Seattle a week later; the Italia had withdrawn at Cheyenne.

This race was widely reported, and Ford lost little time in capitalizing on the high public interest in it. Harper's booklet, *The Story of the Race,* was distributed to dealers by the tens of thousands. A large-scale newspaper and magazine advertising campaign trumpeted the achievement, and flailed the many manufacturers who had refused to enter the contest. The winning car was displayed at hundreds of dealerships during a 6000-mile swing from Seattle to Los Angeles to New York, reaching the last city in time to be exhibited at the Hudson-Fulton celebration.

But the boom of Ford's victory drums was soon silenced. Five months after the race, the judges discovered that the crewmen of Ford No. 2 had violated the rules by changing the engine en route. First prize was thus awarded to the Shawmut. But Ford lost only a moral victory; the propaganda hay had been reaped long before.

A historical footnote: Ford reenacted the race for publicity purposes in 1959. A 1909 Ford stopped in 85 cities along the original route, and was seen by tens of thousands of people. William Clay Ford, a company vice-president and youngest grandson of Henry Ford, greeted the car and escorting vehicles at the future site of the 1962 Seattle World's Fair. According to the company's northeast regional office, which had major responsibility for it, the promotion was "the most important and successful program carried out by this office in recent years." Interestingly, none of Ford's press releases, nor a film of the expedition released in 1962, mentioned the disqualification of the erstwhile winning Model T.

announcement ever received so glorious an acknowledgement . . . much more were we elated by the response from the consumer. The 'ad' [in the national magazines] appeared on Friday; Saturday's mail brought nearly 1000 inquiries. Monday's response swamped our mail clerks, and by Tuesday night the office was well nigh inundated. There isn't a state in the Union that has not registered its approval of the Model T and the Ford Policy." Branches and local agencies also beat the drums as never before, buying unusually large amounts of newspaper space to advertise the new Ford.

Once loosed, the cascade of orders continued unchecked. By winter of 1908, demand was running so far ahead of production that the company could insist that it would supply Ts only to those dealers who had sold off all their old models on hand, "rationing" heretofore unheard of in the auto business. By May 1, 1909, sales were so far ahead of production that the company had to stop taking orders for nine weeks. The grand total rose from 10,202 units in the transition 1908 calendar year to a very healthy 17,771 for all of 1909.

Model T sales then literally skyrocketed for a decade,

1910

This year's Model T was virtually unchanged from previous versions. The exception was a new body style, the racy Torpedo roadster, with a long steering column and a more rakish windshield angle to suggest speed. And it *was* relatively fast, at least quicker than any other production Model T. Public acceptance of all Fords brought another sharp jump in calendar year output: 32,053, a gain of nearly 50 percent.

Throughout its life, the Model T was known almost as much for the plant in which it was built as for its qualities as a car. This was the mammoth factory in Highland Park, Michigan, then a community of 4120, surrounded by the city of Detroit. Designed by Detroiter Albert Kahn, America's greatest industrial architect, it was the world's largest auto factory and Michigan's largest building un-

der one roof. It was also the most aesthetically pleasing factory of its day in architecture, cleanliness, and arrangement. Measuring 865 feet long by 75 feet wide, the four-story building had more than 50,000 square feet of glass, which led some to call it the "Crystal Palace." Ford publicists spared little effort in touting Highland Park as "the wonder of the automobile world," the "largest single manufacturing institution in the world," and that it maintained the "largest machine shop in the world." A photograph showing some 12,000 of the 16,000 employees in front of the factory was run by many newspapers, accompanied by stories stating the picture was the "largest specially posed photo ever taken and [is] far and away the most expensive, considering the employees' time and loss of production."

As time went on, the plant's size (the entire complex including a foundry covered 60 acres by 1913) evoked less interest than its production feats. To the Boston News Bureau, Ford's 1912 output (over 78,000) was "remarkable" and the 1913 tally (over 168,000) "simply phenomenal." Executives of other car companies, realizing that

Following its return to racing in 1909, the Model T notched many victories. Here, a 1910 model on the Munsey Tour.

size alone could not account for such prodigious numbers, hastened to Highland Park to examine the techniques that made it all possible. They were generous in their praise. Karl Neumaier, general manager of Germany's famed Benz Company, told the press: "The Ford plant is the most remarkable in the world; it is the very best in equipment and method." Louis Renault, head of the French automobile firm bearing his name, declared this facility "the best organized in the country" and said that he was "very much impressed by the ingenuity displayed in the manufacturing of cars."

The advent of mass production, begun with the Model T, is generally regarded as the greatest achievement of Henry Ford and his company. It certainly received a tremendous amount of public notice beginning in 1914. For much of the world, Henry became a symbol of the process and its rewards, something of a messiah to those impressed by bigness, vast quantities of goods, and the higher standard of living mass production made possible. Conversely, he was a devil to those who deplored the "triumph" of machine over man, huge industrial operations, and product uniformity. Yet even many of these detractors drove Model Ts.

Engineering societies, business organizations, and dealer groups began visiting Highland Park as early as 1910 to see the "magic methods" about which they had read or heard. Two years later, *Ford Times* reported that "the reception business is being systematized and soon will be able to handle four or five crowds a day." A 24- to 30-man guide corps was organized, and a concerted effort was made to encourage plant visits. The promotional efforts were evidently successful, the *Christian Science Monitor* reporting that "the competent corps of guides" had escorted "thousands of persons" through the plant in 1912. By early spring of 1914, an average of 150 guests were touring the factory each day. By this time the company's newly organized Motion Picture Department—which featured the factory in a nationally distributed newsreel, believed to be the first ever made in an industri-

What better way to tour than in a 1910 Model T Touring?

al plant—was filming visiting celebrities to provide exclusive material for its "Ford Animated Weekly" newsreel.

After the announcement of the five-dollar-a-day wage in early 1914, the Highland Park complex became "a national landmark and a new Niagara Falls," a place to be seen by every visitor to Detroit. William Howard Taft thought the place "wonderful, wonderful," and Roger W. Babson, president of the Babson Statistical Organization, said his visit was as a pilgrimage to a shrine. His view was shared by William Bausch, head of Bausch & Lomb Company, who, with 19 business friends, traveled the 320 miles to Michigan just to see the Ford factory. Approximately 100,000 persons visited Highland Park during 1915, and the figure more than doubled in two years. The plant and Model T manufacturing thus became a major Midwest tourist attraction.

Following its return to racing in 1909, Ford resumed full-scale competition the following summer. Dealers were delighted; within a few months, many were reporting that the move had greatly stimulated sales. Frank Kulick was again a consistent winner, *Motor Age* magazine ranking him as one of America's top drivers in 1910-11. Two other pilots helped the Ford cause. R.P. Rice, manager of the Seattle branch, dominated Northwest tracks and held the Seattle-to-Portland road race record from 1910 to 1912. E. Roger Stearns, a Los Angeles dealer, was California's top driver in 1910, ousting Barney Oldfield (who had also resumed racing) and other leading professionals.

The Model T was handicapped in competition by its low price and good power-to-weight ratio. In order to compete with the heavier, higher-powered cars whose defeat would count for something, the 950-pound Ford would have been required in certain meets to carry several hundred pounds of dead weight and cost hundreds of dollars more. On principle, Henry refused to bow to such demands just to meet classification requirements, for he regarded the T's lightness and low cost as its chief attributes. In a contest open to it, the little 20-horsepower stock chassis proved a match for the heaviest, most powerful vehicles in the land. As a matter of fact, the firm was supremely

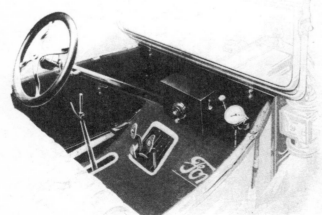

The Model T cockpit was touted for its simplicity.

confident that Kulick, "The Pride of the Company," could defeat anyone. When rain postponed an exhibition between Kulick and Barney Oldfield, who had a specially built, 200-horsepower Benz, *Ford Times* was keenly disappointed: "Such is fate, and the honors that would have come to Ford were postponed for another meeting."

1911

This year saw the first use of sheetmetal in Model T bodies. Up to now they had been made entirely of wood, though aluminum had been used for some in 1909. Construction now changed from all-wood to sheetmetal over wood framing. All 1911 models also received new metal runningboards stamped with "Ford" script, and

steering wheel diameter grew to 15 inches, presumably for better leverage and less steering effort. There were also several minor mechanical changes.

Prices started on what would become a long, downward spiral. The touring was cut from $950 to $780, the roadster dropped from $900 to just $680, and even the town car, the most expensive offering, took a price tumble, from $1200 to $960. These reductions had a predictable effect on sales, which were more than double the 1910 total. Calendar year output climbed to 69,762 units, setting another record for the third year in a row.

Through 1914, Ford made a curious and vain effort to establish its indomitable little rattletrap as something of a prestige item. Press releases boasted of English aristocrats who owned Model Ts, and stories appeared around the country under such headlines as "'Swells' Own Fords." *Ford Times* pointed out that two Russian grand dukes and 19 princes owned them, and that President Wilson had bought one for use at his summer home. Company publicists arranged for show business celebrities

For 1911, the Model T Touring was reduced from $950 to $780; this price cut would be followed by many more over the years.

Although the Ford Flivver took on many guises, one of its most pleasant was in the form of the sporty 1911 "Torpedo."

like Eddie Foy, Billie Burke, and Henrietta Crossman to be photographed in Tin Lizzies as testimonials. Similarly, dealers were asked to furnish pictures of well-known customers and their cars against backgrounds of "fine-looking residences."

But in the long run, the campaign was doomed. Henry Ford was hardly selling an automobile for the elite. "I will build a motor car for the great multitude," he stated early in his career, "constructed of the best materials, by the best men to be hired, after the simplest designs that modern engineering can devise . . . so low in price that no man making a good salary will be unable to own one and enjoy with his family the blessing of hours of pleasure in God's great open spaces." In view of the times and the embryonic auto market, Henry could not have conceived a more intelligent marketing approach, nor could he have a more appealing message for consumers. The Model T, of course, was the embodiment of his vision. It was designed primarily for farm and family use. Utility, not stylish beauty, was its hallmark. Besides, the T's very inexpensiveness— and it would be even less expensive as time went on— subverted the company's efforts to sell the car on the basis of snob appeal.

If not a prestige item, the Model T *was* a hill climber *par excellence.* Certainly on a pound-for-pound basis, there is considerable evidence to support the *Ford Times* contention that it was "the greatest hill climber ever built." With no real rivals in the low-price class, the T carried off honors time and time again against the most expensive

and powerful of automobiles.

During what we might call the hill-climbing era of the automobile's early years, virtually every navigable summit in the country was scaled, some with monotonous frequency. A victory in one of the more important events definitely boosted a car's prestige. Ford consequently focused on the "name" contests, especially the event in Algonquin, Illinois, where it scored notable victories from 1910 to 1912. Meantime, dealers and owners carried the Ford banner in innumerable minor climbs.

Some dealers were so eager to demonstrate the Model T's capabilities that they advertised for competition. A typical notice was posted by a Columbia, South Carolina, agent: "CHALLENGE—Regardless of price, and including Steamers, July 5th, '09, The Ford Model T cleaned up every automobile sold in Columbia in a Hill Climb. If you want to make a little more sport for Labor Day, the Ford is ready." Between contests, many dealers drove their Fords up and down a variety of near-perpendicular surfaces. A Model T climbed Ben Nevis, Britain's highest mountain, in 1911, receiving widespread publicity in Great Britain and the United States. Before thousands of spectators, the company's Nashville dealer drove his car up the 66 steps of the Tennessee capitol building. The Duluth agent covered a $100 bet by climbing three flights of courthouse steps in a Model T, and a Los Angeles dealer used dynamite to blast his way in and out of the Grand Canyon.

Ford never quite worked up the enthusiasm for reliability-endurance runs that it had for racing and hill climbs.

Model T sales for 1911 more than doubled, reaching 69,762 units. Among the most popular models was the Touring Car.

Perhaps it regarded the former as being too tame. "Endurance runs," complained *Ford Times,* "are that only in name; in actuality they are joy rides that accomplish nothing except a holiday for the contestants and advertising orders for the newspapers." The magazine also complained that many of the contestants who finished with perfect scores had cheated, and suggested that each car be

Dusty driver competes in the 1911 Glidden Tour.

equipped "with a moving picture machine and a talking machine to see what the driver and observer are up to." Despite all this, the company, some of its branches, and many of its dealers participated in hundreds of contests during 1907-12. Fords were frequent winners in their class, and occasionally showed up well in the sweepstakes competition of important tours. For example, a Model T finished second in the 1910 Munsey Tour, and a team of three Fords ranked fourth ahead of Cadillac, Marathon, and Flanders, in the prestigious Glidden Tour of 1911. Perhaps the T's greatest victory came in Russia, where it was the only car out of 45 European and two American entries to earn a perfect score in a 1954-mile test conducted by the Imperial War Department. Czar Nicholas II personally inspected the winning T and recommended Fords for the Russian army.

Ford dealers often conducted special endurance tests and stunts to show that their cars could withstand the roughest treatment. A Rochester, New York dealer sponsored January tours over hundreds of miles of snow-covered roads. Others loaded Model Ts with a dozen or so persons for a "parade" down Main Street. This sort of stunt reached its climax in 1911, when a flivver carrying 34 boys, who weighed a combined 3492 pounds, was driven around Payne, Ohio.

A Wichita dealer started a craze by introducing autopolo, played with two Model T chassis as field cars and two touring cars as goaltenders. "Endurance runs, speed races, hill climbs and all other contests are mere parlor games in comparison," the enthusiastic agent assured the company. The Wichita team staged exhibitions all over the country, concluding with a match in Madison Square Garden.

Meanwhile, Ford and its ace driver, Frank Kulick, bowed out of track racing at the Michigan State Fair in September of this year. In an exhibition mile, Kulick defeated some of the sport's biggest names and broke the track record in the process. Immediately afterward, a delighted Henry Ford pressed a $1000 bill into his hand.

The victory marked Kulick's last appearance on a race track. However, he figured in two more events before his retirement. In January 1912 he drove the second "999" over the measured mile in 33.4 seconds on the ice of Lake St. Clair, the fastest anyone had run on ice since Henry's 1904 effort. During the summer of 1912, he made "the automobile world stand aghast" by winning the celebrated Algonquin Hill Climb in record-breaking time. His performance so embarrassed big-car manufacturers that, in 1913, none would enter the contest unless Kulick and his machine were barred. But a boycott was avoided when it was announced that Kulick and the Ford company were finished with competition.

Ford didn't sponsor a racing entry again until 1935. Its dealers, with a few exceptions, also abandoned racing between 1912 and the mid-1930s. Private owners and auto accessory firms, however, entered Model Ts in hundreds of races in the 'teens and '20s. During this period, Model Ts—particularly the so-called Fronty-Fords equipped with the powerful Frontenac cylinder head—dominated the country's small-town dirt tracks. In 1923, three Fronty-Fords qualified for America's premier race, the Indianapolis 500 Memorial Day classic. To the delight of race referee Henry Ford and to the surprise of the racing fraternity, each of the Ts was still running at the finish. The fastest of them, averaging 82.58 mph, captured fifth, an exceptional showing for an inexpensive modified stock car. The machine-gun blast of the racing Fords was heard less often after introduction of the Model A in 1927, although Ts continued to compete on dirt tracks into the 1930s.

The promotional value of hill climbs and reliability runs underwent a slow decline between 1910 and 1913, then rapidly fell off as most all cars became powerful enough to whisk up almost any hill and easily cover routes between distant points. Economy runs survived much longer, but were never as popular as other contests during the early years, and Fords entered only a handful of them. Winning performances in these were based on a fuel-to-weight ratio that the company regarded as unfair for its light, economical car. Its recommendation that weight should not be a criterion in economy runs elicited no response among contest sponsors.

Ford's successful participation in racing and the more practical forms of competition convinced many motorists that the Model T was spirited, dependable, and economical to operate. It did much to propel the Tin Lizzie to commanding sales leadership.

1912

The most notable change in this year's Model T was availability of what we'd now call an option: separate front doors for the ubiquitous touring, thus changing its name to "Fore-Door." After a brief life, the Torpedo Runabout was discontinued. New to the line was a Commercial Runabout featuring a flat rear deck for cargo, something like that of a modern pickup truck, and equipped with a detachable "mother-in-law" bucket seat. Output rose again in this final year before the advent of the mass-

Licensed in New York, this 1911 Coupe looks ready to go.

Ford sits at the helm of a circa 1912 "Fore-Door" Touring.

Although the Torpedo Runabout was discontinued this year, the 1912 Runabout filled in for it nicely.

production assembly line at Highland Park. The total for the 12 months was 78,440 units.

By this time, Henry Ford was convinced that price cuts were by far the most important factor in merchandising the Model T. He often said that he gained 1000 new customers for every dollar he cut the price, and justified his practice by relating T prices to mounting sales figures. In spite of prodigious production increases, the company could scarcely meet demand.

Ford's price cuts were generously reported in newspapers and magazines. Wire services, which rarely carried automotive news, flashed stories highly favorable to Ford following the 1912 and 1913 reductions. *Harper's Weekly*, after weighing the contribution of these to the T's success, agreed that Henry "has thought out the best advertisement, and made the deepest, most sensational appeal to human nature he could have made."

Along with the price cuts, Model T advertising in 1912-16 emphasized the company's "winged pyramid" trademark. This was described by advertising manager Glen Buck as "a happy combination of two of the oldest Egyptian symbols: the pyramid symbolizing strength and stability, the scarab wings symbolizing lightness and grace." The symbol literally permeated the Ford organization for several years. "Here is the new sun of the Ford advertising system," rhapsodized Buck in one of many articles extolling the trademark. "It shall be the 'blazing flag' around which the Ford forces shall rally."

More than half the space in some Ford ads was devoted to reproductions of the new emblem. Dealers were ordered to have it painted on their sales windows and strongly urged to use trademarked letterheads. After October 1912, all Model T number plates bore the emblem. Within a year of introduction, it was "widely established all over

Front view of the 1912 Runabout pictured on page 31.

the world," according to one latterday expert, and was of "enormous value" to the company. It was used consistently until late 1916 when, for some reason, the firm's Operating Committee questioned whether it should be continued. The question was referred to Henry who, according to secretary Ernest G. Liebold, abolished the symbol after being told that "scarab is another name for dung beetle."

The Model T was the only car built before World War II subjected to market research. The firm first surveyed public opinion in early 1912, when 1000 Model T owners (a sample of one percent) were asked, "Just what reason or reasons were foremost in your choice of a Ford car?" Twelve respondents indicated low price as the primary factor, 39 pointed to the sound ignition system, 108 referred to low maintenance cost, and 842 reported that they had purchased on the recommendation of other owners. The same question was asked in a poll of 2000 owners in the fall, but the results have been lost.

The company soon abandoned its pioneering work in market research, ironic in view of what would happen much later with development of the Edsel. If Henry didn't actually say, "The public can have any color it wants so long as it's black," at least it expressed his attitude about customer opinion in the years when the Model T dominat-

Low price and word of mouth were stated reasons for purchasing a Ford in 1912; 78,440 people did just that.

1913

Note the high-mounted front bumper on this '12 Runabout.

This year's Model Ts were the last available in a choice of colors. Not until 1926 would Ford offer an alternative to black. Once more, Lizzie showed almost no change, but one difference again concerned the touring car, which now came without a separate tonneau. It also sported front doors instead of the previous cut-outs, but appearances were deceiving. The driver's door was actually fixed, embossed in such a way as to make it look like it opened, the reason being that the outboard handbrake hindered access on that side.

In August, the first mass-production automobile assembly line began experimental operation at Ford's Highland Park factory. As an event in industrial history, it would have tremendous significance. It would not only make Henry Ford the "father" of the automobile industry as we know it today but would also change the face and pace of the nation. The Model T was the first car built by the thousands, not one at a time, on a moving assembly line with sequentially placed work stations. Thus, it was also

ed the market. Ford was ultimately compelled to answer demand for more colorful, more stylish cars in the mid-1920s, but the firm would not resume its public opinion research until the late 1940s.

A winter shipment of 1913 Model Ts to a New York dealer paused just long enough to have this picture snapped.

Model Ts were put to all kinds of work from the beginning; here a 1913 farm truck (with commercial conversion).

one of the earliest cars to employ the principle of interchangeable parts pioneered by Henry Leland's Cadillac. These factors and simple design enabled the Model T to be sold at very low prices well within the reach of a vast number of Americans who had never been able to afford a car before. And that, of course, is the main reason why automobiles became universal.

Small-scale assembly methods and standardized parts were in use well before this time, both at Ford and elsewhere. The idea of a moving production line was probably first conceived by Ransom Eli Olds, whose cars were once the country's number-one sellers. But it was Henry Ford who perfected the idea. Toward the end of their life, the Models N and S had been built by means of a "sequential floor plan" in which machines and manpower were strategically located to "add" to each car as it proceeded on its orderly way through the Piquette Avenue factory. As author Beverly Rae Kimes has noted: "A hundred cars a day could be easily built that way. But Henry Ford was thinking bigger. What was needed to build thousands was *movement*, continuous and carefully timed movement

throughout the production procedure. . . . It was not until the move to the newer and larger Highland Park plant in 1910 that the idea could be given full attention and the awkward beginnings made." Henry Ford later attributed the idea to foreman William C. Klann, who was inspired by "the overhead trolley that the Chicago meat packers used in dressing beef."

At first, parts were moved around the factory on conveyors. Ultimately, the notion was expanded to having not only assemblies but partially completed cars move slowly past workers. The process was refined through several stages, and by October 1913 it had yielded staggering results: Ford's assembly time was cut in half—and would soon be halved again. Thus, from 78,440 cars in 1912, output zoomed to 168,220 in 1913, then shot past the half-million mark just three years later. Through mass production, Ford factories built more than 15 million Model Ts between 1907 and 1927, a single-model record that would stand until the 1960s when it was surpassed by another car of universal popularity, the Volkswagen Beetle.

In 1913-14 some people thought what was termed the

This 1913 Model T carries a special pickup body on the Runabout chassis—Ford always stressed customer service.

cycle car, a miniature runabout seating two people, might make a dent in Model T sales. Henry decided something should be done about that. Accordingly, he built a smaller Model T, neat and streamlined. His son Edsel showed much interest in its construction. When it was completed, Henry said to him: "Now you take it down and park it in front of the Pontchartrain Hotel." Edsel obeyed. A curious throng gathered, saw the name "Ford," and concluded Henry was about to bring out a cycle car. That ended the cycle-car threat.

As in other years, Model T promotion was closely tied to current events. For example, when trouble with Mexico was anticipated this year, company publicists recommended that every American battleship be equipped with Model Ts to enable the Marines "to charge on Mexico City from Vera Cruz in record time." The idea was hailed in metropolitan papers all over the country. Model Ts actually participated in a Mexican border skirmish in 1917, the episode inspiring a juvenile novel, *Charge of the Model Ts*. The board of directors also appointed one of its members to arrange for a Ford to be the first automobile to pass

Even a Ford could look elegant, like this 1913 Town Car.

1914

through the Panama Canal. The mission must have been unsuccessful though, for the company never published an account of any such milestone.

The Model T had more slang names than any other car ever built. Of course, it's still known today as the Tin Lizzie or flivver, but over the years has had at least 48 other nicknames, each of which enjoyed brief popularity. Here's a rundown: T-bone, Detroit Disaster, Michigan Mistake, Flapper Flivver, Chicken Coup, Bone Crusher, Bouncing Betty, Cattle Hack, Fresh Air Taxi, Galloping Snail, Prince of Snails, Graf Zep's Uncle, Henry's first go-car, Lazy Lulu, Leaping Lena, My Lizzie of the Valley, Navigatin' Nancy, Noah's Ark, Old Faithful, Passion Pot, Puddle Jumper, Road Louse Exterminator, Rough Rider, Satan's Nightmare, Silly Symphony, Spirit of Bumps, Spirit of Detroit, Spirit of Jolts, Spirit of St. Vitus, Madame Elizabeth, Henrietta Elizabeth Van Flivver, Henry VII (capacity four gals), Gilda Gray—shimmy expert, September Morn, Toonerville Trolley, A-Cute Digestion, Little Asphalt Annie, Little Bo-Creep, Rolls Rough, Tacks Collector, United Parts of America, Baby Lincoln, Lincoln's Baby, Lincoln's Relation, and the Missing Link in Lincoln.

For this and the next 11 years, the Model T would be sold in only one color: black. The main reason was the particular kind of black favored by Henry Ford: an enamel that dried more quickly than other paints and thus helped speed up production. So, fashion notwithstanding, it was "any color you like, as long as it's black." Calendar year output set another all-time record at over 308,000 units, about 100,000 more than the rest of the American industry combined.

The 1914s would also be the last Ts to carry the acetylene gas lamps, cherrywood dashboard, and straight rear fenders of the 1909 original. A minor appearance change brought rounded bottom corners on the doors, which enabled Lizzie to shed a little of her "antique" look. Base price now stood at $490, and would drop another $50 in 1915.

As Henry Ford and James Couzens became rich, paid

As of 1914 the Model T came in any color as long as it was black. Note the new "turtle deck" on this Runabout.

higher salaries and bonuses to executives, and gave the public ever cheaper Model Ts, they began to ask themselves, "What of our workers?" Their answer was the celebrated "five-dollar workday," inaugurated on January 12 this year. Besides the new higher basic wage, the work day was reduced from the usual 10 hours to eight, and a third shift was added at Highland Park to make up the difference. This announcement, coming in the midst of a mild, worldwide depression, was immediately flashed to every corner of the globe. Forty years later, the London *Economist* called it "the most dramatic event in the history of wages." In 1959 the distinguished French intellectual, Father R.L. Bruckberger, went further: "I consider that what Henry Ford accomplished in 1914 contributed far more to the emancipation of workers than the October Revolution of 1917. . . . He took the worker out of the class of the 'wage-earning proletariat' to which Ricardo and Marx had relegated him and . . . made every worker a potential customer."

Ford and Couzens regarded the five-dollar daily wage as "the greatest revolution in the matter of rewards for . . . workers ever known" and were aware that it would be of great advertising value. Yet they vastly underestimated

its immediate worldwide impact. The announcement was easily the biggest news story ever to come from Detroit. The statement was issued in mid-morning. By noon, cables and telegrams from wire services and newspapers were pouring in from all over the globe. By the following morning, every daily paper in the country and thousands more abroad had carried the story. Over seven days, the New York City press alone devoted 52 columns—most of it front-page space—to the profit-sharing plan and to Ford.

Many newspapers hailed the five-dollar day as an economic second coming. The Cleveland *Plain Dealer* editorialized that it "shot like a blinding rocket through the dark clouds of the present industrial depression." The New York *Sun* described it as "a bolt out of the blue sky flashing its way across the continent and far beyond." The New York *Herald* called it "an epoch in the world's industrial history." Some papers were so impressed that they made a special point of publicizing the Model T. The East Boston *Free Press* suggested that, "When you see [Ford's] modest little car running by, take your hat off." The Cleveland *News* ran a large photo of a Model T touring car under the headline, "The Car Humanitarian Henry Ford's Making."

With this "ocean of publicity," Ford was the best-known

Base price of a 1914 "T" listed at $490, the last year for acetylene lights, even on this "hack."

manufacturer in the world by mid-1914. One newspaper even predicted that Henry would become "one of the best-known men that America has ever produced," and that his name would "be famous until the sun takes its first chill." Henry enjoyed the headlines. In fact, he quickly developed a strong, lifelong appetite for publicity that would help sell Model Ts and later, Model As and V-8s.

This was also the year when the Model T figured in one of the most striking sales promotions in business history. It was Ford's offer of July 3 to return $40-$60 to each flivver customer should sales exceed 300,000 units in the following year. Coupled with this was a $60 across-the-board price cut and a promise not to cut prices again until August 1, 1915.

Unfortunately, the refund was announced at one of the least propitious times imaginable: the start of World War I. Metropolitan newspapers, particularly on the eastern seaboard, buried the story while their front pages screamed about the outbreak of hostilities in Serbia and the Kaiser's ultimatum to Russia. *The New York Times,* in an editorial entitled "Well Devised But Ill Timed," apolo-

gized for putting the rebate news on page five, conceding that it deserved as much publicity as Ford's widely heralded five-dollar workday.

Nevertheless, the announcement appeared in virtually every newspaper in the nation, and received rave notices in the smaller dailies and country weeklies. The reaction was exactly what sales manager Norval Hawkins had anticipated when he proposed the idea to Henry Ford, and in many communities during the rebate year, the best Ford salesmen were those who had bought Model Ts after August 1914.

As promised, the company announced sales figures on August 1, 1915. It sold exactly 308,213 automobiles the previous year, and accordingly set the per capita amount at $40, about nine percent of the average purchase price. "Profit sharing" checks totaling nearly $15.5 million were duly mailed to most every American hamlet, town, and city during the next few months. Many newspapers, acknowledging that the refund "was a game in which Ford had everything to win and nothing to lose" (except the money), congratulated the company on its "sales-promo-

While 1914 was the last year for the straight rear fenders, the "T" now sported rounded door bottoms.

tion genius" and its customers on their good fortune in climbing aboard the "rebate wagon." The checks, later called "the most virile crop of goodwill seeds ever planted," naturally made hundreds of thousands of friends for the Model T, Henry Ford, and Ford Motor Company.

On the eve of World War I, the Model T was selling at an annual rate of 250,000 units and had attained a worldwide reputation enjoyed by no other car. "While the Constitution may follow the flag, or the flag the Constitution, all depending on the viewpoint with reference to the foreign policy of the United States," reported the Indianapolis *Star*, "the Ford Motor Company has beaten out both the flag and the Constitution in carrying civilization into the wild places of the world." Here are a few examples. Twenty Model Ts were used in the construction of the Amur River Railroad in Siberia. Thirty Indian princes rode in Model Ts, interspersed with elephants, camels, and horses, at the Delhi coronation of King George V. A Model T was delivered to the Tasha Lama of Urga after a 700-mile trip across the Gobi desert. A T won the Johannesburg-Bereeniging race in South Africa. French troops used Ts in pursuit of brigands in Morocco. By mid-1914, more than 550,000 Model Ts were on roads the world over, traveling 10 million miles daily. "A car that is seen as often as the Ford must be right," declared *Ford Times* with some justification, "or its very presence would kill it."

Lizzie's prodigious numbers were, in fact, an advertising asset. Every car bore the name "Ford" in bold script on the radiator. And thanks to its distinctive design, a Model T was recognizable a half-mile away. In a day when every automobile purchase and virtually all out-of-town trips were reported in the "personals" section of small-town newspapers, Fords were naturally mentioned thousands of times. A few samples: "W.H. Judd is now riding around in a new Ford car, which he recently purchased. These are a very neat little car. . . ." "Our genial and efficient mail carrier now delivers the mail on his route in a stylish and comfortable runabout of the Ford make whenever the conditions of the roads will permit." "R.E. Rice is sporting a fine Ford runabout which he purchased from Agent Fred Scott of Coalton." "Mr. and Mrs. John Inglebrecht and children, of near Jefferson City, drove over to Eldon Saturday in their Ford to visit Mr. and Mrs. R.J. Rush." Sometimes, the publicity backfired. The Elgin (Illinois) *Courier* reported that "The funeral of William Kiel, who was killed last Friday from being tipped in the Ford automobile, which he and Joy Seyle were driving, was held Sunday."

The Model T inspired more than 60 melodic tributes, with "The Little Ford Rambled Right Along," written this year, perhaps the most popular. Many of the titles attempted to capitalize on contemporary Model T jokes. Typical were "I Didn't Raise My Ford to Be a Jitney," "It's a Rambling Flivver," and "Let's Take a Ride on the Jitney Bus." Others had a more romantic flavor. "The Packard and the Ford" suggested that Mr. Packard and Miss Flivverette marry and give birth to a Buick, while "The Scan-

dal of Little Lizzie Ford" depicted a demure T garaged with a rakish, low-slung sports car. "On the Old Back Seat of the Henry Ford" promised that the moon would smile on couples spooning in flivvers.

The Model T also formed the theme for a serious musical composition, "Flivver Ten Million," which "created a furore" when performed by the Boston Symphony Orchestra and attracted a record crowd at New York's City College Stadium when played by the New York Philharmonic. Written by T.S. Converse, a professor of music at Harvard, the 14-minute "joyous epic" described the assembling of the 10-millionth Model T (announced by a motor horn, full blast) and followed its wandering across the country. After a necking party and a joyride (interrupted by a collision), "Phoenix Americanus," according to the program note, "righted and shaken, proceeds on his way with redoubled energy, typical of the indomitable spirit of America." At first, Boston Symphony conductor Serge Koussevitzky protested against some of the honks, rattles, squeaks, and crashes in the score, but Converse insisted they were essential. The composer's judgment was upheld by favorable reviews in the Boston *Transcript* and *The New York Times*.

The last Model T songs were suggested by the car's demise in 1927. "Henry's Made a Lady Out of Lizzie," which alluded to the new Model A, of course, and "Poor Lizzie, What'll Become of You Now?" were typical of the nostalgic ditties.

1915

Two new body types were added to the Model T stable this year. One was the Center Door sedan, a high, upright closed model with full-length bodywork, three windows per side, and a pair of doors located slightly behind the center point of the wheelbase. The other was the

Note the rounded rear fenders on the 1915 Town Car/Taxi.

All 1915 Fords, like this "Coupelet," featured a hand-operated Klaxon horn and brass electric headlamps.

The Runabout for 1915 cost but $390 fully equipped.

Coupelet, a two-seat convertible replacing the Coupe. The previous bulb horn and acetylene gas headlamps were replaced on all models by a hand-operated Klaxon horn and brass electric headlamps powered by the magneto. Also, the former straight-topped rear fenders were now curved, though front fenders remained as before and, without exception, were lipped. Hood louvers and an un-braced windshield also appeared for the first time, and wire wheels were offered as an accessory. Base price for the most popular model, the touring, stood at a sensationally low $440. Production passed the milestone half-million mark for the calendar year.

The one-millionth Ford rolled off an assembly line in September but went unnoticed, much to Ford Motor Company's chagrin. It was really the firm's fault. Lamented *Ford Times*: "With twenty-five assembly plants . . . and with a big factory in Detroit assembling so many Ford

New for 1915 was the Center Door sedan, whose doors were located just behind the center point of the wheelbase.

cars a day, we passed the million mark without knowing it."

The milestone car was presented by Henry Ford to one of his favorite dealers, Stanley Roberts of Toledo, who had requested it. Roberts displayed and raced it at numerous northwestern Ohio county fairs; it was later wrecked with his brother at the wheel. A 1983 search for the vehicle, or old-timers' recollections of it, conducted in cooperation with the Toledo *Blade*, turned up nothing.

A highlight of Model T promotion this year was a striking demonstration of automobile production at San Francisco's Panama-Pacific Exposition, where 18-25 cars were built each day on a model assembly line operating on a three-hour "shift." Easily the most popular industrial demonstration at the fair, the exhibit received nationwide publicity and was seen by huge crowds. In recognition of its contribution, it was awarded a special gold medal.

The millionth Ford was built in September, 1915.

1916

Big changes were in store for the Model T, but most of them would have to wait until the middle of this year. The initial 1916s were the last Model Ts with the dinky brass radiator, of which only 800 were made. The brass headlamps and horn—the "brassies" so highly prized by T enthusiasts today—were phased out in favor of pressed-steel equivalents—painted black, of course. The small boxlike hood remained, but was now fashioned of steel instead of aluminum. No new body styles appeared. The 56-inch tread width was standardized in all parts of the country. Previously, cars sold in the South were delivered with a 60-inch tread to match the width of the ruts on roads in that part of the country.

If the Tin Lizzie's looks seemed nearly constant, so did Henry's practice of cutting prices nearly every year. Au-

gust brought another round of reductions. This time, the touring was lowered by $80 to $360, the little runabout went from $390 to an unbelievable $345, and the Center Door sedan dropped by $95 to $545. Another Ford constant, rising production, also continued, hitting a new calendar year high of nearly 735,000 units.

The 1914-20 period was the heyday of the "Ford joke," similar to the Jeep and Volkswagen Beetle jokes of a later era. Ford jokes were as much a part of everyday conversation as shoptalk and office gossip, sports talk or interest in the weather, and were as likely to be heard over tea at a church social as over a beer at the corner saloon. To vaudeville monologists they were the staff of life, to toastmasters a rock of refuge in time of need. Salesmen opened solicitations with them, clergymen punctuated sermons with them, and physicians carried them as part of their pharmacopeia of cheer. For these half-dozen years they were as universal and innumerable as America's time-honored jokes about mothers-in-law, Pat and Mike, and the farmer's daughter. Not surprisingly, scores of Ford joke books appeared, and some sold in the tens of thou-

Only 800 Model Ts for 1916 carried the brass radiator; after that black paint would have to do.

Most了...

sands. Most were cheap paperbacks hawked for five, 10, or 15 cents, but some featured contributions by the nation's leading humorists and cartoonists, including Ring Lardner, Irvin S. Cobb, Bud Fisher, Chic Jackson, and H.T. Webster.

While it's impossible to determine the exact origins of the Ford joke, it was a logical evolution of the general automotive humor that became a stock-in-trade of vaudeville performers after about 1902. Essex, Saxon, and even the high-priced Pierce-Arrow were among the targets during the early years. One gag that always brought a laugh at Franklin's expense was the description of a buck-toothed girl: "She wouldn't be so bad-looking, only she's got Franklin teeth. They're air cooled."

Another view, shared by advertising manager Charles A. Brownell, was that competitors started Ford jokes in the Model T's early days. "It's not a car," rival salesmen allegedly told potential buyers, "it's just a Ford." Some of the company's 1907 advertising supports this opinion: "The Ford 4-cylinder ($600) runabout owes half its unparalleled popularity to the misrepresentation of jealous rivals." Another ad stated: "Had you ever noticed that it is a weakness inherent in disciples to disparage their leader? Some makers affect to discount the achievements of FORD." Vanadium steel was criticized by many manufacturers who, until the alloy was adopted as armor plating on American warships, predicted that Ford's "flimsy contraption" would soon fall apart. There was also what some termed an organized "mud-slinging propaganda campaign." "The best wits were hired to write the material," noted the Ft. Atkinson (Wisconsin) *Union*, "and many were the editors who were caught by it. It came in a blank envelope, apparently from nowhere, and usually had concealed somewhere a thrust at the 'Tin Lizzie,' coupled with a cute story."

One source of the quips and gibes was undoubtedly the self-consciousness of Ford owners. By joking about the car's small size, its low price, and so on, they "could laugh off any joshing the owner of a bigger and higher-priced car might be disposed to give him."

Certainly the Model T's very cheapness and versatility must have encouraged many jokes. Almost everyone knew that more than half the pieces in a Ford engine sold for a dime or less. News stories frequently told of a stationary Model T powering motors that ran everything from newspaper presses to water pumps. The car's toughness was also widely discussed. A Texan abandoned his T to escape Mexican bandits, who hacked and burned it into a wreck that the owner later retrieved and drove away. Another Ford, although buried for six years in the muck of a California riverbed, still had gas in its tank and ran "as good as new" after starting wires were installed. Another true story concerned the Ford whose engine had been removed to pump water and whose body was drawn by a burro. The moral, as the press was quick to point out, was: "You may dissect a Ford, but you cannot kill it."

Such tales made the public feel a Model T could do most anything—hence the countless jokes which, though bordering on the ridiculous, had a trace of plausibility. No doubt many of those who invented or repeated them fully shared the opinion expressed by crusader Ida Tarbell in 1915: "I have never in all the world . . . seen so much to cause me to laugh and weep, to wonder and rejoice, as I have at the Ford."

Many accessory manufacturers generated additional jokes by their advertising. While Ford's own ads proclaimed the Model T to be as flawless as any car ever made, gadget and parts makers catering to T owners spent huge sums to convince the public that their wares made for a much better-performing, easier-riding, more powerful, more economical car. Ford owners were told that their cars drove like trucks and that a certain kind of shock absorber would make them ride like Pullmans. They were assured that by buying a $2.50 crankcase support they could actually save $20, for otherwise the crankcase would surely break and entail a $22.50 repair bill. The difficulty of starting a Model T was emphasized in ads suggesting that old-fashioned blowtorches should be replaced by special firetraps built into the intake manifold. Finally, every one of the T's potential rattles—and there were many—could be countered by "anti-rattler" devices claimed to silence offending parts. (Of course, like the factory parts, the anti-rattlers eventually worked loose too, adding to the clatter.) It's doubtful whether any consumer product in history had its real and imaginary shortcomings so thoroughly exposed as the Model T. That such publicity should add fuel to the Ford joke craze is hardly surprising.

Ford jokes followed several patterns. Perhaps the most numerous were those concerning the Model T's diminutive size. Postmen were reportedly upset over the rumor that Ts were to be delivered by mail. A garbage collector bemoaned how tricky it was to sort dead cats, broken bottles, and Fords. A patron who asked for Model T tires at a large department store complained of being directed to the "Rubber Band Department." The Model T's loose-jointed qualities inspired much "shake and rattle" humor. Henry Ford was reputedly a better evangelist than Billy Sunday because he had shaken hell out of more people than Sunday ever saw. Asked if his car always made a racket, a T owner innocently replied, "Oh no, only when it's running."

The belief that Fords were made entirely of tin prompted the "Tin Lizzie" jokes. Question: "What time is it when one Ford follows another?" Answer: "Tin after tin." The Ford company planned to produce cars without doors, but would furnish can openers. A man hitched his dog to his balky flivver, then was arrested for tying a tin can to a dog. A farmer, knowing that the Ford company needed lots of tin, shipped a battered tin roof to Detroit and later received a letter stating, "While your car was an exceptionally bad wreck, we shall be able to complete repairs and return it by the first of the week."

Another joke theme involved the T's social inferiority. Question: "Why is a Ford like a bathtub?" Answer: "Because you hate to be seen in one." A Ford reportedly ran over a chicken, which got up saying, "cheep, cheep, cheep." Henry Ford, when offered $1.50 after repairing a farmer's stalled car, refused, saying he had all the money he wanted. "You're a liar," retorted the farmer, "because if you had plenty of money, you'd take some of it and buy yourself an automobile!"

Counterbalancing such ridicule were jokes that testified to the Model T's sturdy dependability. A man wanted to have his Ford buried with him, for it had always gotten him out of every hole he had ever been in. Owners of Cadillacs, Pierce-Arrows, and Packards carried Fords in their toolboxes—to pull the big cars when they bogged down. A Ford was like a motion to adjourn: it was always in order. One Model T accidentally left the plant without an engine but ran for a month anyway—on its reputation.

Other jokes—inspired by Dearborn's mass-production techniques, five-dollar workday, 40-dollar rebate, and other departures from convention—complimented the company. In order to avoid fire risks, said one story, Ford was shipping Model Ts in asbestos crates, because the cars came off the line so fast their metal was smoking. Although two flies could "manufacture" 48,876,552,154 new flies in six months, they didn't have anything on two Ford factories. A Ford assembly line worker dropped his wrench and, before he could pick it up, 20 Model Ts had passed by. The company planned to retail its cars at grocery stores and would paint them yellow, rather than black, so that they could be hung outside and sold in bunches like bananas.

Most Ford owners enjoyed these gags, and were among the more inveterate spinners of them. Even if some of the puns rubbed them the wrong way, "they could," as one of the joke books pointed out, "always pat their pocketbook, let in the clutch, and ride serenely on their way, proud of their possession and confident of their good judgment."

However, there were those who never quite got used to the incessant teasing. In 1920 a long-suffering Englishman, in a widely reprinted letter to a British motor publication, expressed the anguish that this dissident minority had experienced over the years: "In our opinion it is quite time that we Fordists should strongly protest against the jokes and insults which have been hurled at us. For years we have been the stock joke of the vermillion-proboscis-tinted 'comedian'; sneered at by the nut whose sole ambition in life soared to the height of his socks matching his coachwork, and the glossiness of his hair equaling a seal emerging from the water; held in contempt by the chauffeur of a big 'six,' doubtless because a Ford has passed him on the hill; treated with brusqueness by many a garage man—such has been the experience of most of us.

"I took delivery of my earliest Ford ten years ago, and at the first garage at which I stopped I was strongly advised to have fitted a tray under the chassis. Innocently I asked the reason. 'So that it will pick up the nuts,' came the reply. I have lost count of the number of times people have told me that they would not be found dead in a Ford.

"But what angers me most is when we are classed as a God-forsaken, poverty-stricken lot. 'He has to put up with a Ford because he cannot spring enough to buy a car.' That is what I frequently hear. Could anything be more insulting? Could anything be more remote from the truth?

"Many a Fordist could buy up a majority of these revilers; many a Fordist is their intellectual superior; many a Fordist possesses more gentleness and character. Therefore, should these lines reach the eye of a Ford scoffer, I will tell him plainly that he is a snob. And a snob of the worst order."

Advertising men were asked constantly whether the Ford joke helped or hindered Model T sales. Until the early 1920s, most of them agreed that "every knock was a boost," that the jibes unquestionably made the car all the more popular. When asked to place a value on the company's stock as of 1913, a New York investment banker testified in 1927 that the jokes were "an important asset," and that any manufacturer with a sense of humor would have welcomed them. Newspaper editorials echoed this view.

Henry Ford pesonally delighted in the jokes and, according to his advertising manager, told more of them than anyone in the country. His favorite was the one about the man who wanted to be buried with his T. Some publications, knowing he had a fresh joke for every reporter, even credited Henry with concocting the best of them during his leisure moments. Toastmasters invariably bantered the Model T at banquets at which Ford was a guest, and no one enjoyed the witticisms more than the head man himself. He did not, however, as rumor often had it, subsidize publication of Ford joke books, although he often made a considerable show of buying them. "The jokes about my car sure help to popularize it," Henry once remarked. "I hope they never end."

But all good things must come to an end, even bad jokes. After the early 1920s, Chevrolet, Dodge, Hudson-Essex, and Willys-Overland all moved rapidly to the fore. The Model T was an anachronism by then, and the Ford jokes began to boomerang too often to be an asset. Now, owners realized their critics were in dead earnest, and fewer of them could laugh off the barbs. The nationwide Keith-Albee vaudeville organization, perhaps the country's leading arbiter of street-corner humor, mandated that Ford jokes be banned from the stage because they weren't funny anymore. Advertising experts also sensed the change, suggesting that Ford ought "to give the T prestige and to take the joke out of the car." A number of company executives, including Edsel Ford, agreed. In 1923, after a lapse of several years, the company resumed Model T advertising on a broad scale, aggressively promoting the car as "a quality product" with "a high social standing." For practical purposes, then, the Ford joke died with the Model T. Its Model A successor, introduced in December 1927, was too highly regarded to be funny. "With her," observed the New York *Sun*, "he who goes to josh remains to praise."

The Ford joke lingered on for many years, however. In 1953, for example, an owner of a 1909 Model T was fined for speeding. His widely reported courtroom comment was in keeping with the best Tin Lizzie tradition: "It was only hitting on three. If it had been hitting on all four, I doubt you would have caught me."

1917

Changes in this year's Model T were striking—so much so that the New York *World*, next to a photo of the much-modified 1917 model, was compelled to assure readers, "Yes, it's a Ford." To be sure, it *did* seem almost like a new Lizzie—comelier and sturdier—and it generated considerable excitement. In Chicago, a stampeding crowd broke down the window of a showroom where the car had been put on display.

The hood was now almost streamlined. The radiator,

necessarily recast, was larger and had a more pleasing shape. It also had a separate shell made of pressed steel that gave it greater strength than the old one-piece construction, simplified repair, and enhanced cooling capacity. Set higher, the radiator blended nicely into the rounded hood, which in turn swept back to the cowl more gracefully. Crowned, curved fenders were the—dare we say it?—crowning touch. Brass trim had given way to black enamel or, for radiator and hubcaps, shining nickel plate. Early Model Ts were easily spotted by their squarish hoods and brass radiator caps, and had become as much a part of every day Americana as baseburner stoves and kerosene lamps. Now, the Ford owner need scarcely blush as he passed other cars. "This comparatively tremendous advance in styling," as historian Leslie R. Henry would later write, "served to set the pattern for most of the succeeding decade."

The more stylish '17s caused something of a business blight among those companies that had done well selling crowned fenders, V-shaped radiators, and other embellishments to style-sensitive Model T owners. "More Class for Your Ford," advertised one such firm. "Makes It Look

Note the "streamlined" hood on this 1917 "T" Roadster.

Like a $1000 Car." But dealers were delighted, and the trade-in value of older models significantly declined.

Early this year, Ford Motor Company halted paid Model T advertising and would not buy another line of space (not counting tractors and Lincoln cars) until 1923. This was in line with a policy established back in 1910 whereby advertising expenditures (or lack thereof) were prorated according to the number of orders on hand. Thus, advertising manager Charles A. Brownell wrote to branch managers in February: "Today we have instructed our advertising agency to wire immediate discontinuance of all Ford advertising. This is done because we are now from 40,000 to 50,000 cars behind orders, and it is simply a waste to continue advertising when production is behind." Similar messages went out the following May and November. Almost all national magazines were dropped from the schedule after 1914, and motoring magazines were omitted starting in 1916, when the company spent only $6000 on advertising, mostly tiny newspaper ads.

Henry's attitude toward paid advertising explained his firm's policy; he felt most of it was unnecessary. While conceding that it was "absolutely essential to introduce good, useful things," he argued that it was "an economic waste" for products already on the market. "If you really have a good thing," he often pointed out, "it will advertise itself."

Ford also liked to say that "our best advertising is free advertising" and that he would rather have a news story on the front page than have to pay for space. Ad executives were at a loss to refute him on this point for, as *Printers' Ink* lamented in 1926, the auto magnate had for years found it "a simple matter to break into the front pages of newspapers almost at will." The magazine, whose view was naturally not a detached one, believed that such publicity was largely worthless, for it "does not tell the full story of the Ford car to buyers [or] firmly fix it in the consciousness of the buying public." Others, however, were convinced that the Model T profited from the industrialist's activities. Indeed, much of its success was owed to the "Ford" name constantly appearing in headlines.

The chief reason the company could afford to forego advertising for six years was continued strong demand for the Model T. The flivver enjoyed a seller's market even before America entered World War I, and production cutbacks during the conflict contributed to a shortage well into 1920. Sales fell off alarmingly during the winter of 1920-21, but bounced back so vigorously the following spring that the company had to strain its capacity for two years to meet demand. This situation embarrassed advertising types, "some of whom," said *Printers' Ink*, "would have felt inclined to chip in if Ford had passed the hat, just to get away from the task of trying to answer reactionaries who pointed to Ford's nonadvertising success."

But the fact was that although Ford Motor Company itself did not advertise, its dealers did. Indeed, the irascible Henry, despite his claim that advertising was "an economic waste," actually required dealers to run ads under terms of their contracts. For many years, dealers handled their own advertising. Then, in late 1916 at the company's suggestion, outlets in larger cities began "clubbing together." Full-page ads listing dealers' names appeared in metropolitan dailies, with cost shared according to the number of cars sold by each agent. A number of dealers balked at this policy, claiming that Ford was using them "to pay its bills." Others, because they thought the investment was sensible as well as necessary, went along without objection. From 1917 to 1923, Ford dealers bought space at the annual rate of $3 million, a figure which, in the company's view, placed Ford among the nation's largest advertisers. Strictly speaking, the firm spent only a few thousand dollars a year on materials for those dealers who would use them.

Ordinarily, Ford Motor Company didn't concern itself with a dealer's choice of media or copy appeals. However, the company did insist that its trademark signature, the famous Ford script used continuously since 1903, appear in all local advertising. It also strongly reprimanded dealers who resorted to unfair practices. Referring to an ad that showed a broken down competitive car over the caption, "Sell it and buy a Ford," Brownell angrily told branch managers: "This is an unwholesome type of advertising which has long since been taboo, and we certainly feel that Ford dealers have enough good things to say about our cars without knocking the other fellow."

1918

Again this year, Ford made no design changes in the Model T. The Town Car, despite having achieved popularity as a taxi, was phased out. So was the Coupelet. Americans, it seemed, were not yet ready for this concept, which might be considered an ancestor of the modern targa-top body style. Total output for the calendar year dropped by nearly 200,000 units to some 436,000 cars, reflecting wartime production cutbacks.

World War I would end late in the year and the T had played a big part, cited for "gallantry in action" in a number of battlefield dispatches. Ten machine-gun-laden Lizzies were used to drive Germans from an entrenched position on the Marne, and the sturdy little car was the only vehicle that could get through to wounded men during the first days of fighting in the Argonne Forest. "Without a doubt the best car for the advance [ambulance] work is the Ford car," ran a 1918 medical report published more than 60 years later in *Antique Automobile* magazine. "It is small, light, easy to run, easy to maintain, simply constructed, economical in the consumption of gas, does not take much road space, and can be handled by one man when necessary. . . . I am firmly convinced that the Ford

Ford vehicles, such as the Model TT stake truck, played a big part in World War I, which ended in late 1918.

ambulance . . . can operate in any place where troops go
. . . . In no case have I known where a Ford was blocked for
more than a few minutes. On account of this fact, should
the car accidentally run into a hole, it may be literally
lifted out."

In Africa, the T saved a detachment of British soldiers
from starvation by providing motive power for flatboats.
General Edmund Allenby attributed the success of the
Palestine campaign to "Egyptian laborers, camels, and
Ford cars." According to newscaster Lowell Thomas, then
lecturing on the Middle Eastern campaign, Allenby rode
in a Rolls-Royce, but always had a Ford on hand as a kind
of insurance.

"Hunka Tin," a parody on Rudyard Kipling's "Gunga
Din," brought down vaudeville houses after its publication in the *American Field Service Bulletin*, and was used
in Ford dealers' advertising all over the country. Cited by
Printers' Ink as the most effective product advertising to
emerge from the war, the poem concluded with a rattling
stanza fully worthy of its subject:

    Yes, Tin, Tin, Tin,
    You exasperating puzzle, Hunka Tin,
    I've abused you and I've flayed you
    But by Henry Ford who made you,
    You are better than a Packard, Hunka Tin.

The unchanged 1918 Fords, shown here at an auto show.

1919

Though Model T styling remained unchanged, this year introduced an electric starter and demountable rims as new optional equipment items. Initially available on closed cars only, they were extended to all models by June.

Hand cranking the Model T had always been irksome, as related by auto writer Murray Fahnestock in 1924: "Mr. Smith . . . climbs in by the right-hand door (for there is no left-hand door by the front seat), sets the spark and throttle levers in a position like that of the hands of a clock at ten minutes to three. Then . . . he gets out to crank. Seizing the crank in his right hand (carefully, for a friend of his once broke his arm cranking), he slips his left forefinger through a loop of wire that controls the choke.

He pulls at the loop of wire, he revolves the crank mightily, and as the engine at last roars, he leaps to the trembling running board, leans in, and moves the spark and throttle to twenty-five minutes of two. Perhaps he reaches the throttle before the engine falters into silence, but if it is a cold morning, perhaps he does not. In that case, back to the crank again and the loop of wire."

This year also marked the only time during the Model T's long life that Henry talked of building another car. He did so to soften up his fellow stockholders before buying them out. The automaker loathed stockholders, equating them with drones and parasites—people who "gave nothing but money to an enterprise." Deciding they had to go, he took the first step on December 30, 1918, by submitting his resignation, effective the following day, as president of Ford Motor Company "to devote my time to building up other organizations with which I am connected." His son Edsel was elected president; Henry retained his seat on the board.

Vacationing in California, Ford next told a reporter

Unchanged style-wise, this 1919 Model T high body coupe could finally be ordered with an electric starter.

that he intended to build a new and better car that would undercut the Model T (by now, selling at an average $466) by $100-$200. The new vehicle would be built and marketed by a concern other than Ford Motor Company. His old company? "Why, I don't know exactly what will become of that," he said vaguely. The story was page-one news across the country. "The new car is well advanced, for I have been working on it while resting in California," Ford said later. Speculation mounted as to what he would do next. One of the wire services reported that Harvey Firestone would be his partner in a $200 million venture. *Printers' Ink* speculated the new car would be called the "Flivv Junior," while the Washington *Herald* was sure it would be named "Flivverette."

Within two weeks, Henry's loose comment had gotten out of hand, and many Ford dealers began to panic. Edsel was forced to write them a soothing letter: "A new car may be manufactured, but [it] could not possibly be designed, tested out, manufactured and marketed in quantities under two or three years' time." He admonished deal-

ers to stop worrying about the new car and to get busy selling Model Ts.

Company stockholders were also worried—concerned that Henry would actually carry out his threat and thereby depress the value of their holdings. They were thus softened up for the calls made by financial agents acting secretly on Henry's behalf. The buyout, completed by July of this year, cost him $105 million, $60 million of which he borrowed, though he knew the price was reasonable. When his stock-purchasing emissaries told him they had completed their mission, he reportedly "danced a jig all around the room" and immediately abandoned plans—assuming he ever really had any—for a Model T rival. Thus ended what would be the most adroit "acting" performance of his entire career.

But coming up with the money wouldn't be easy. Because of curtailed civilian production during World War I, Henry anticipated unprecedented demand and high prosperity for his firm in the postwar era. The Ford company, which had sold from one-third to one-half of America's

Ford Model Ts were always popular as commercial vehicles, such as this 1919 roadster/pickup.

cars up to the end of the war, built a record-breaking 750,000 units—40 percent of national production—in model year 1919. But an economic slump began in mid-1920, and auto sales, including Ford's, began falling. Now it was Henry who was concerned. By April 1921 he needed $25 million to pay off his 1919 loan; he also owed from $18-$30 million in taxes, and he was determined to pay $7 million in employee bonuses in January 1921. Yet in the summer of 1920 he had just $20 million in cash to meet all his obligations.

To maintain production and income, Henry decided to fall back on a familiar ploy: reduce prices so drastically as to shake up the industry and startle the nation. Over the objections of key executives, he instituted more price cuts on September 21, 1920, ranging from $105 to $180 on his five models, which had been priced from $525 to $975. The reductions, averaging $148, were, in percentage terms, the largest in industry history. Again, a Ford announcement was front-page news. Not untypically, the Sidney (Delaware) *Record*'s three-deck headline read, "Henry Fires a Bomb," "Just Like Him," "The Ford Is The Thing and Everybody Can Afford to Buy a Ford." Several papers suggested that the industrialist be made "general manager" of the nation, since he alone had demonstrated the courage and ability to give people relief from inflation.

The rest of the industry was incensed. Representatives from several firms—including General Motors, Dodge, Maxwell-Chalmers, Hupp, Hudson, Essex, and Paige—met in Detroit and solemnly announced that prices should not be lowered, because buyers would then expect further reductions and all buying would cease. Such statements only made Henry's halo glow brighter. Though reluctant, a number of rivals led by Franklin, Studebaker, and Willys-Overland found it expedient to follow Ford's lead. By October 9, some 23 automakers had lowered prices, 28 had not.

For a time it appeared that Ford's pricing strategy might succeed, as more than 100,000 Model Ts were sold in October. In November, however, sales fell approximately 10 percent; in December they sank to less than 50 percent of the November figure. Ford produced 78,000 Model Ts—some 35,000 more than dealers could sell—during the first 24 days of December, then closed its plants "for inventory," promising to reopen January 5, 1921. But the hiatus actually extended to February 1. Meanwhile, rumors that Ford was in financial straits spread throughout the country. Many were genuinely alarmed at the automaker's plight, and Model T owners "rallied like bees" to a suggestion by the chief of the Columbus, Ohio, Western Union bureau that each lend Henry $100 to tide him over.

Ford declined all such offers, recalled workers, and in February assembled 35,000 Model Ts from stock on hand. These cars, along with 30,000 unconsigned vehicles produced in late 1920, were immediately shipped to dealers. As was then industry practice, dealers had to pay for the cars upon arrival or forfeit their franchises. In most instances they went to their bankers, got the money they

needed, and watched demand gradually use up the excess supply. Instead of borrowing money himself, Henry had, in effect, forced his dealers to borrow for him. Fortunately for all concerned, the recession proved short-lived, and by the spring and summer of 1921, Model Ts were again being built and sold at a record-breaking rate. Henry had outwitted Wall Street and finagled his way out of trouble. His stature as a folk hero reached new heights.

1920

It was quite a step up into this 1920 Model T coupe.

Model T greeted the Roaring '20s by switching from wood to composition steering wheels, enlarged from 15 to 16-inch diameter. Calendar year production fell sharply from the 1919 level of about 820,000 to 419,517.

Throughout the Twenties, Ford dealers would make considerable use of sales promotion films. A sales representative later reported that in Pound, Wisconsin, a village of 400, more than 2000 people flocked in from the surrounding area to view films at the Ford dealership every Wednesday night. The Bridgeboro, New Jersey dealer showed movies in a nearby grove to an eager audience of 1800-2000 farmers each week. Many branches and dealers kept specially equipped Model Ts and projectionists on the road. "We've given more than 40 shows with an average of 200 to 250 on hand," reported the dealer at Silsbee, Texas, "and are creating goodwill by the bushel." A number of dealers reported that these were the first motion pictures many people had ever seen. Besides dealer showrooms, they sometimes were shown in prospective

The 1920 Model T switched from wood to composition steering wheels, enlarged from 15- to 16-inch diameter.

buyers' homes and, in many small towns, on the sides of billboards or buildings. Of course, they were silent movies. "Talkies" were still a few years away.

From 1920 on, Henry Ford did far more than run the "Model T Company." Indeed, he developed America's first vertically integrated, highly diversified industrial empire. His company mined coal, iron ore, and lead; owned timber lands, sawmills, dry kilns, a wood distillation plant, a rubber plantation, and a series of "village industries"; operated a railroad, blast furnaces, coke ovens, foundries, steel mills, and lake and ocean fleets; produced glass, artificial leather, textiles, gauges, paper, and cement; built airplanes; farmed 10,000 acres; and made Fordson tractors and Lincolns in addition to Model Ts. It also prospected for oil, bought dolomite lands with magnesium production in mind, took steps to produce abrasives, bought acreage in the Florida Everglades for planting

Model Ts could handle anything, including Michigan winters!

This 1920 "T" Ice Cream Truck served Californians.

rubber trees, and experimented with power generating by burning coal at the mine and making charcoal iron. These various activities received wide attention during the 1920s, and contributed to the popular belief that Henry Ford had a daring and highly original mind, virtually unique technical skills, and a ceaseless devotion to mankind.

1921

Again this year, the Model T itself didn't change but its production figures did, which must have been a relief to Ford accountants. From the depressed level of 1920, calendar year output more than doubled to nearly 904,000 units, a new record.

This was the year that saw the emergence of Ford Days in hundreds of small communities throughout the country. Town merchants, at the instigation of the local dealer, would set aside a day and invite every Model T owner or driver in the surrounding area to come in. Businesses offered them special bargains, and a carnival atmosphere prevailed as Main Street was taken over for parades, band concerts, vaudeville performances, dancing, queen crownings, and Model T and athletic contests. Prizes were awarded to contest winners and owners of the cars carrying the most produce, the most children, the five prettiest girls, and so on. Model Ts turned out by the thousands for Ford Days and virtually took over some towns, inasmuch as drivers of other cars were usually fined if their vehicles appeared on the streets. These events continued until 1931, and Model Ts continued to make up a large proportion of the participants even after production ceased.

This year saw continuation of an unofficial consumer boycott against the Model T, a dubious first for the American industry. It came in response to a notorious, 91-week anti-Semitic campaign launched in 1920 by Henry Ford's weekly magazine, the *Dearborn Independent*. Ford, whose anti-Semitism stemmed more from ignorance than deep-seated bigotry or malice, believed that Jews wanted to gain control of the nation's finances, commerce, and politics at the expense of Christians, and thought he was performing a great service by exposing it. Jews thought otherwise, of course. Although no Jewish organizations or groups declared a formal boycott of the Model T, many Jewish firms and individuals stopped buying Fords nonetheless. So did some others doing business with Jewish concerns and dependent on their goodwill. Jews in Hartford, Connecticut, staging a 400-car parade in honor of Dr. Chaim Weizmann and Albert Einstein, ordered "Positively no Ford machines in line."

Ford's branch managers and dealers, particularly those in cities with large Jewish populations, complained bitterly about the sales resistance and economic pressure prompted by the *Independent* campaign. The manager of the second-ranking dealership in the New York branch even went so far as to suggest that everybody would be happier if Ford put the money for the anti-Semitic articles into making better cars. Some dealers were threatened with eviction by Jewish landlords, but got little sympathy from Ford's personal secretary. In reply to a Minnesota dealer urging the articles be stopped, he suggested that dealers should own their own buildings so as not to be vulnerable to such pressure. Ford himself was similarly unmoved. His stock answer: "If they want our product, they'll buy it."

It's difficult to determine the number of Model T sales lost to this situation. Though sales dropped sharply in the last half of 1920, the main reason was a general economic decline that affected the entire industry. Then Ford sales reached new highs as the economy improved in 1921-23. Unquestionably, some Jews condemned Ford's actions but still bought his products. As Will Rogers pointed out, the boycott "may not be a complete success yet—but it will be as soon as someone learns how to make a cheaper car." At this point the Model T was definitely a better buy than any competitor. But it wouldn't be by the mid-'20s, and Henry would learn he could no longer be complacent when he launched a second anti-Semitic campaign.

As impulsively as he had begun, Ford ordered the articles discontinued in January 1922. The reasons are not altogether clear. One possibility is that his New York manager finally convinced him of the difficulty of selling Model Ts in areas with large Jewish populations. Another is that Henry was swayed by William Fox, president of Fox Film Corporation, who threatened to show choice footage of Model T accidents in his newsreels if Ford persisted in attacking the character of Jewish film executives and their motion pictures. In any event, Henry called off the campaign, although he retracted nothing. Indeed, he later boasted that the articles had opened the minds of

The 1921 Model T Runabout listed for $370 early in the season, but dropped to $325 at mid-year.

many Americans to possible evils.

In 1924, the *Independent* launched a second series of anti-Semitic articles under the general title "Jewish Exploitation of Farmer Organizations." Henry thought that a Jewish group was trying to gain control of American wheat farming. One of those he attacked, Aaron Sapiro, a prominent Chicago attorney, filed a million-dollar suit against him—but not the *Independent*—for defamation of character. Ford settled out of court in July 1927, and published both a personal apology to Sapiro and a formal retraction of all past attacks on Jewish people. His motives for this were complex. An important factor was undoubtedly the critical changeover from Model T to Model A production at a time when much of the sales force was complaining that Jewish hostility hurt business.

After this, many Jews resumed buying Ford products.

But they were alienated again in 1938 when Ford, on his 75th birthday, accepted the Grand Cross of the Supreme Order of the German Eagle, the highest honor Hitler's Third Reich could bestow on a foreigner. An accompanying citation observed that the medal was given to recognize him as a pioneer of motorcars for the masses. But his acceptance of the award, plus other anti-Semitic and pro-Nazi accusations against him, led to an active and effective boycott of Ford products in the years just before World War II by Jews and other Americans unsympathetic to his views. The resulting sales slump was particularly acute in the company's eastern sales region, which had the largest Jewish population in the country. As region manager W.K. Edmunds wrote in 1944: "Mr. Edsel Ford understood this situation thoroughly, and just prior to the time we discontinued making automobiles, he had alloted us a special fund [approximately $50,000] to be used for sales promotion and advertising in this area to improve our sales and counteract the existent antagonism." A company-conducted investigation also revealed that in Hollywood, "Jewish interests . . . agreed to ban all Ford units from their studio lots and forbade employees and stars to buy Ford products." The report added: "A few stars are in a position to disregard the order, but many sales are being lost."

To this day, many older Jews and their descendants have not forgiven Henry Ford. A dwindling number of elderly Jews still will not buy Ford products, and are critical of those who do. Since the late '40s, however, almost all Jews have been gratified by the friendliness of the Ford family and company toward the Jewish community. "The new generation of Fords," declared an influential Jewish editor in 1970, "looks back at the era of their grandfather with a sense of deep regret, rejecting whatever smacked of prejudice and of anti-Semitism."

Henry Ford and Thomas Edison on a camping trip.

1922

The trusty T again stayed the same this year except that the Center Door Sedan, with its distinctive oval rear window, was discontinued due to declining sales. The door's position made entry/exit awkward, and the model was considered top-heavy, slow, and expensive.

The T scored its most highly publicized hill climb victory in this year's fourth annual world's championship contest at Pikes Peak near Colorado Springs, Colorado. It was an achievement with rags-to-riches overtones worthy of the T. The winner was a 21-year-old small-town Nebraskan, Noel E. Bullock, who had driven up the mountain only once before the race. His car, named "Old Liz," was unpainted and hoodless, "home brewed" by the youth in a blacksmith's shop in 1918. Though publicly ridiculed by several competitors as a "tin can" and a "cross between a

Leland-run Lincoln went into receivership in late 1921; Henry Ford moved in and bought it in February, 1922.

Signing the Lincoln take-over: *(standing)* Henry Ford and Henry Leland, *(seated)* Edsel Ford and Wilfred Leland.

kiddie-car and a pushmobile," it bested the elite of road racing and many of the highest-priced makes in America. Bullock planned to flash up Pikes Peak again in 1923, but was blacklisted nine days before the event for participating in a non-sanctioned dirt-track race in South Dakota. No other Model T ever won on the mountain.

The "Lizzie Label" craze, humorous comments painted on flivvers, reached its height during the early and mid-1920s. The Label flourished particularly around land-grant colleges, where small-town smart alecks and country clowns had an abundance of dilapidated Model Ts for "canvases." While the exact origin of Lizzie Labels is obscure, they were likely popularized by *Judge,* a widely quoted satirical weekly that gave this peculiar folk art the dignity of humorous literature by paying five dollars each for the best of them.

Like the Ford jokes, Lizzie Labels had certain discernible patterns. Many were borrowed quotations, such as "Abandon hope, all ye who enter in" and "I do not choose to run." Others were more contemporary sayings, such as "Barnum was right," and "Our booz 'em friend." Another group parodied advertising slogans and the titles of songs, plays, and movies. Some were in the form of notices, like "Quiet please, violent ward" (on hood) or "Night calls by

appointment only." Another theme was the wisecrack: "Follow us, farmer, for haywire"; "You may pass me, big boy, but I'm paid for"; "Heck of the Resperus." Sex was perhaps the most prevalent theme: "Girls, watch your step-ins" and "For fastidious flappers" are examples.

There was little laughter at Lincoln Motor Company in January of this year. The firm had been in receivership since November 1921, and was still up for sale at a court-decreed price of $8 million. But there was one fellow in Detroit who could easily afford it: Henry Ford. On the surface it seemed an unlikely amalgam—the father of the Tin Lizzie selling an automobile that cost 10-15 times more—but actually it was entirely in character. Ever the canny businessman, Henry was undoubtedly intrigued by the prospect of competing at opposite ends of the market, and he took advantage of the opportunity by buying Lincoln in February. "We have built more cars than anyone else," he told the press in announcing his acquisition. "Now we are going to build a better car than anyone else."

It would take a man with Ford's determination to get hold of Lincoln anyway. The company was heavily in debt; the state of Delaware, where it had been incorporated, tried to block the sale; and the U.S. government had a bill for $4.5 million in back taxes (later revised to $500,000).

But Ford persisted, with strong urging from his son Edsel. The Lelands didn't. That father-and-son team left for good less than six months after the Ford takeover. The proximity of such strong figures as Henry Leland and Henry Ford just couldn't last.

One reason was the Lelands' fear that Ford would lower their high standards, but it proved groundless. Lincoln's mechanical excellence would be maintained, while its styling would be considerably improved under the aegis of Edsel Ford, who soon began enlisting the services of other great coachbuilders to supplement Brunn and Judkins.

The Ford takeover and Lincoln's meager resources precluded many changes in this year's Model L, though Ford did manage to get production up. Of the 5767 units completed for the calendar/model year, 5512 were Ford-built, a fact soon to be proclaimed on Lincoln radiator badges for

a time. After the Lelands left, however, Ford engineers tackled the cars' tendency to overheat by fitting a cooler-running cylinder head. They also phased in a revised timing chain and sprocket, and switched from cast-iron to aluminum cylinders.

In typical Ford fashion, Lincoln's 1922 prices were cut in a search for sales. Standard-body models, styled by Brunn, began with a basic seven-seat touring car that now listed at $3800; other styles ranged to $4900. Custom bodies proliferated, with Judkins and Brunn fielding a variety of sedans, berlines, limousines, and coupes at $4600-$7200. Most of this year's production employed the longer, 136-inch-wheelbase chassis. The 130-inch platform was in its last season, offered with only six Lincoln-built open and closed bodies.

To no one's surprise, Ford immediately began a public-

Lincoln Before Ford

Lincoln and Cadillac had the same founder, Henry Martyn Leland, the stern puritan long remembered as "Master of Precision." But the real founder of these two long-familiar prestige marques was none other than that master of mass production, Henry Ford. Had it not been for the failure of his Detroit Automobile Company (see *1896-1902*), there might not have been a Cadillac. And had it not been for Cadillac, there might not have been a Lincoln—or a Ford Motor Company to acquire it.

Leland, a Vermonter born in 1843, was already learning about interchangeable parts as an 18-year-old apprentice mechanic to the Springfield, Massachusetts Federal Arsenal. He continued to demonstrate solid proficiency as a toolmaker in Springfield and, later, for Colt Firearms and Brown & Sharpe. Inevitably, he brought these principles to Ford's derelict Detroit Automobile Company, which he took over in 1902. Reorganized by the following year as Cadillac, the firm issued a low-price car that, although completely fresh, was remarkably similar in concept and appearance to Ford's forthcoming Model A. It even used that designation. But the little one-lunger was a success, and Cadillac began climbing the ladders of both price and production. Three years after introducing its first four-cylinder model in 1905, Cadillac won Britain's coveted Dewar Trophy when three of its Model T runabouts ran perfectly after being com-

pletely disassembled, then reassembled from a pile of mixed-up parts.

That may not seem like much when you can buy an exact duplicate of your car's double-reverse swivel-widget at a nearby store, but this modern convenience stems directly from Leland's fetish for quality, precision, and complete interchangeability. Before him, cars were assembled entirely by hand, one at a time, from parts individually crafted and then fitted to each other. Thanks largely to Cadillac's 1908 achievement, automakers soon recognized the value of standardized parts, thus paving the way for Henry Ford and his mass-production miracle that would put the world on wheels.

With this, Leland's first marque might deservedly have been named for him, instead of the French explorer who founded Detroit in 1702. Then again, maybe it's as well that it wasn't, because Cadillac and Leland wouldn't be together long. The year Cadillac won the Dewar Trophy, mercurial mogul William C. Durant was forming General Motors. Cadillac became part of it in 1909. Durant promised Leland and his son Wilfred that they'd receive "no directions from anyone," and until 1916, they didn't. But then Durant regained control of GM, having been ousted from power six years before, and a conflict arose. America was engaged in World War I, and Leland wanted to build airplane engines. Durant, a pacifist like Henry Ford, refused. Appalled by this "unpatriotic" attitude, the Lelands resigned from Cadillac, organized Lincoln Motor Company in 1917 (named for "Honest Abe," Henry Le-

land's lifelong hero), and took part in the Liberty aero-engine project. Ironically, Durant was soon forced to face facts and bring Cadillac into the program as well. He tried to get the Lelands back, but Henry and Wilfred were unmoved. Still, as Cadillac historian Maurice D. Hendry has written, their "work had been so well done that [Cadillac] never faltered."

With the signing of the Versailles Treaty in late 1919, the Lelands again thought about cars. They had to. Whereas World War II would prove a bonanza for defense contractors, many of the Detroit firms that had aided the nation in World War I emerged laden with debt and excess equipment, plus thousands of dependent employees—6000 in Lincoln's case. For Henry and Wilfred, a return to automaking was the obvious peacetime pursuit.

Accordingly, they reorganized Lincoln Motor Company on January 26, 1920. A stock issue realized $6.5 million after they announced their intention to offer a new, high-quality car, the best their art and science could conceive. That was also enough to bring in a thousand orders, many on the strength of the Leland name alone. In 1920, that was about all it took.

Thus it was that the first Lincoln, a seven-passenger touring car, rolled out of the firm's Detroit factory on September 14 of that year. Designated Model L, the new line spanned chassis with wheelbases of 130 and 136 inches, plus torque-tube drive and Alemite lubrication fittings. Power was supplied by a 357.8-cubic-inch L-head V-8 rated at 81 brake horsepower. Leland technical expertise was evident in its unique "fork and

ity and advertising campaign to promote Lincoln as a car of the highest quality. At auto shows and in hotel lobbies, Lincoln exhibits (frequently called the Lincoln Salon Petite) strove to create an aura of snob appeal. "Guests," many of whom had been sent engraved invitations, were greeted by "doormen and other attendants appropriately uniformed and carefully schooled in the proprieties." They were then escorted to the display, "a picture of exquisite appointments, floral decorations, and perfumed fountains, further enhanced through artistic lighting effects." "Charmingly costumed" pages and tuxedo-clad salesmen, each of whom wore a white carnation, were on hand to serve, while liveried drivers waited outside to demonstrate the "chauffeur-driven equipage."

Ford spent more than $400,000 on Lincoln advertising during 1923-24. Much of that went to 10 "class" maga-zines such as *Vogue, Vanity Fair, Town & Country, Spur,* and *Motor Life.* Aside from print advertising, Lincoln's leading sales-promotion medium was a monthly motoring magazine simply called *The Lincoln.* Introduced in December 1922, it was aimed at "people of taste and culture," with little of the "hard sell" copy found in *Ford Times.* The periodical was sent to Lincoln owners and prospective buyers, as well as to "many of the finest clubs" in the country. Circulation stood at 70,000 by 1924.

Lincoln was not an outstanding sales success in its early years as a Ford Motor Company product, an average of 7000 cars being retailed annually between 1922 and 1930. Packard and Cadillac, competing at the same price level, usually outsold Lincoln by more than three to one, while Pierce-Arrow marketed almost as many units despite considerably higher prices.

blade" connecting rods, one forked rod straddling another on the same crank. Other novel features included automatic spark advance, a 60-degree included cylinder bank angle instead of the usual 90 degrees, a crankshaft running in five rather than three main bearings, and parts tolerances within 0.0005-inch. The last, as *Automobile Quarterly* recorded, was "not surpassed for many years."

But the Lelands weren't content with just a rugged and reliable platform, so each engine was carefully checked on a dynamometer, then mated to its chassis for extensive road testing from 4 mph to wide-open throttle. The finished product was said to require no break-in, another unheard-of achievement that wouldn't be widely duplicated for a long time to come.

Body choices initially comprised eight Lincoln-built styles typical of the Twenties—touring, roadster, phaeton, coupe, sedan, limousine, brougham, and cabriolet—plus special open and closed types respectively supplied by Brunn and Judkins, two sterling coachbuilders. The least expensive offering was the standard factory-built seven-seat touring at $4600, though it wasn't difficult to spend upwards of $7000 for a custom-body example.

Nevertheless, the Model L proved a sales disappointment. Price was less to blame than appearance, which was high, wide, and anything but handsome. The styling had been entrusted to one of H.M.'s sons-in-law whose previous design work had been in ladies' millinery. It showed. Then too, 1920 wasn't a particularly good year for getting into the

Out of 5767 Lincolns, 5512 were Ford-built in 1922 (sedan shown).

car business. A recession was setting in, and auto sales were tailing off as the economy retreated from its early postwar boom. As a result, Lincoln built only 834 cars for the model year (which coincided with the calendar year in this period) and the duplicate 1921 line recorded just 2318 units. By contrast, Cadillac's respective totals were 19,790 and 11,130 units. By November 1921, Lincoln was in receivership.

But the paths of the two automaking Henrys were about to cross once more. This time, though, it was Ford who would ride to the rescue.

Aerial view of the Lincoln factory, 1922.

1923

T his year brought the first major Model T appearance alterations in nearly five years. Most obvious were bodies set lower on their chassis, and higher radiators. Two new closed styles were offered, two- and four-door sedans. The latter was predictably marketed as the "Fordor," a play on the name Ford; the former was called "Tudor" for consistency, though the spelling had nothing to do with England.

Both of the new sedans and the familiar Coupe featured a large, rectangular rear window, thus improving visibility astern, while rotary window regulators, cowl ventilator, and square fuel tanks were adopted across the board. The Coupe's rear compartment was now formed integrally with the rest of the body. The Runabout retained its detachable rear compartment that permitted it to be easily converted into a "pickup delivery." Open cars

had new tops that could be erected or folded by one person, and their windshields were set at a more jaunty angle, with the upper section pivoted at the top of the frame.

Though production would set another record this year—over 1.8 million units—the Model T was looking decidedly old-fashioned, and becoming more so all the time. This partly explains why Ford now resumed Model T advertising. During the previous six years, the company had bought no ad space at all, leaving individual dealers to carry the ball instead. But this left much to be desired in that sales pitches were neither uniform nor consistently seen in all parts of the country. As a result, Edsel Ford announced the reestablishment of an advertising department in August, following a conference with branch managers.

Ford was one of the nation's biggest ad buyers in the mid-1920s, spending nearly $15 million between September 1923 and October 1926. About eight percent of the total budget was scheduled for women's and "prestige" magazines, as the advertising staff sought to imbue the Tin Lizzie with "an atmosphere of 'Pride of Ownership' . . . of class and quality." As with prewar attempts to es-

Model Ts looked different for 1923 with higher radiators and bodies set lower on the chassis.

tablish the Model T as a prestige item, this aspect of the campaign met with little success. In fact, a Ford now likely evoked less pride of ownership among women and prestige-conscious men than any car on the market.

Henry Ford's basic dislike of advertising again surfaced in June 1926, when he told dealers to fend for themselves once more. From mid-1926 until the Model A's introduction in late 1927, the company bought virtually no advertising space. Dealers in many metropolitan areas again banded together, retained advertising agencies, and resumed campaigns on a local basis.

Lincoln's outstanding stock now belonged entirely to Ford, which had always been a family owned company (it wouldn't go public until well after World War II). Now advertised as "all Ford," the cars were not all-new, but there were signs that they were beginning to evolve. Edsel Ford, now entering his prime and having been named Lincoln's president, began indulging his taste for elegant styling in an effort to rid the make of its reputation for ungainly looks. Providing able assistance was a talented general manager, Ernest C. Kanzler. By the end of the year, Lincoln had produced 7875 cars and was operating

Delivery "Direct to the Home" in a Ford Model TT.

Posing in 1922 or 1923, "Honest Abe" is flanked by Will Rogers (left) and Henry Ford.

in the black for the first time in its history.

Though production was accelerating, Edsel and Kanzler continued the Lelands' insistence on quality. Thus, Lincolns were still delivered in the famous dust sheet, the factory warning that seven men were required to remove it lest the paint be scratched. (This no doubt amused Ford dealers, who were used to shoveling Model Ts out the door by the boxcar-load.) But there were important mechanical changes this year: Houdaille hydraulic shock absorbers, optional four-wheel (instead of two-wheel) brakes, laminated safety glass throughout, vibration-free windshield frames.

Edsel's concern with Lincoln design was now manifestly evident. The old-fashioned painted headlamp shells returned on early 1923 production, but nickel-plated drum-type shells became standard after April. Fleetwood, Brunn, and Judkins were now supplying custom bodies in increasing number and variety, and Edsel had contracted with the new firm of LeBaron to create more. This was the beginning of an elegant new automotive combination destined to be famous: the LeBaron Lincoln.

LeBaron was not a person but a thing, the invention of two young coachbuilders, Ray Dietrich and Tom Hibbard. The title of their company sprang from an architect Hibbard knew whose name "had a nice ring to it." Dietrich picked their place of business—2 Columbus Circle in New York City—for much the same reason.

Dietrich had first met Edsel Ford at the 1922 New York Auto Salon. Recalling his vivid personality in 1974, he said Edsel was "a brilliant man, one of the true giants of the industry. But he was also a quiet and considerate man. And while he knew exactly what he wanted, he knew how to get the best out of you and when to give you your head on a project." Between Dietrich, Hibbard, and Roland Stickney, LeBaron's talented watercolor artist, Lincoln at last began evolving designs that were smooth, elegant, and up-to-date—exactly what the old Leland bodies were not.

This Touring was one of 1.8 million Ts built for 1923.

Eleanor and Edsel Ford pose next to a new Lincoln.

1924

Lizzie turned "sweet sixteen" this year. Ford celebrated by building its 10-millionth Model T, which left the Highland Park assembly line on June 15. The milestone flivver led parades through most towns and cities along the Lincoln Highway (New York to San Francisco) and along Route 66 (Chicago to Los Angeles). Several million people are estimated to have seen the vehicle, which was "greeted" by governors and mayors at each stop along the route. The tour was documented in a film entitled "Fording the Lincoln Highway," which was widely exhibited in the mid-'20s.

The 11-millionth Ford was presented to the Prince of Wales during his visit to Highland Park in October of this year. Afterward, the Prince spent time at Fair Lane, the Ford family estate in Dearborn. A photo taken there of Henry, posed with son Edsel and the Prince, served as a model for a life-size statue of the automaker installed in front of Dearborn's Henry Ford Centennial Library in 1974. Stated sculptor Marshall Fredericks: "This pose, the thoughtful look, represents him in the best way. I like to see him thinking."

Though there were no physical changes in the evergreen T, Henry was sharpening his pencil for another price reduction, announced in December. The figures were astonishing: an unheard of $260 for the Runabout and a mere $290 for the Touring, both all-time lows. Despite the bargain rates, Ford made an average of $50 per car and netted a $100 million total profit for 1923-24.

Meanwhile, the competition was preparing to put an end to the Model T's incredible market domination. General Motors, reorganized after the 1920 recession by Pierre duPont and Alfred Sloan, was readying a Chevrolet only slightly more costly than the Ford yet far more modern and better-looking. It would take some time to halt the Model T juggernaut, but it's interesting to note that 1923 would be the peak year for Ford sales. From 1925 on, the trend would be inexorably downward.

Lincoln's main mechanical change this year was a revised camshaft designed to promote smoother valve operation. A minor point was the practical new spark-setting marks set into the clutch rings and flywheels. But the main news again was styling. Though the cars weren't radically different, the whole was a sum of much improved parts. These included new, wider, and much smoother-looking fenders for all models except the Judkins coupe, and vertical instead of horizontal radiator shutters, with thermostatic control to open and close them according to water temperature. While a taller radiator on an already tall car would seem a negative influence, it worked amazingly well here, allowing body engineers to create a smooth, flowing hoodline.

Notable too was the absence of "Ford-built" identification. Now radiator badges read simply "Lincoln." "The idea, of course," said Edsel Ford, "is to underscore the individuality and exclusivity of this automobile."

Exclusive it was, but there was a growing number of people able to afford Lincoln in an improving economy. Production again topped 7000 units, and Kanzler added 311,000 square feet to the Lincoln factory's floor space.

A view of the chassis of a circa 1924 Model T.

The Model TT Side-Screen Delivery, a 1924 offering.

A rare 1924 Ford, the Model T "Cotton Beverly."

A closed '24 delivery van, useful in Detroit.

1925

For only the second time in its long history, Lizzie was treated to a major facelift, at least by Ford standards. Included were larger fenders and newly optional nickel-plated radiator shell. Balloon tires were offered as a new accessory at $25 apiece and, when fitted, made this year's T look almost modern. Another new extra was a factory-installed, hand-operated windshield wiper. Still in force were the price cuts instituted in late 1924. Continuing as the most expensive model in the line was the Fordor sedan at $680. Next came the Tudor priced at $580, followed by the Coupe at $520. The two open cars, Runabout and Touring, remained at $260 and $290, respectively.

By this time, the sliding-gear selective transmission, usually with three speeds forward, was coming into more general use. Ford dealers, finding the Model T's planetary unit increasingly difficult to sell, clamored for a change.

So did many T owners. But Henry clung to the old gearbox like a kid with a well-used toy. In fact, he seemed to have something of a prejudice against sliding-gear transmissions. In 1910, a Ford test driver hit a telephone pole with a vehicle equipped with one of the new gearboxes, and it seemed the transmission was partly to blame. "Mr. Ford was tickled to death," recalled an associate. "He was glad it was smashed up, and he never had anything to do with [the sliding-gear transmission] until we came to the Model A."

When the first in a series of Stickney renderings for LeBaron Lincolns appeared in the house organ *The Lincoln,* Edsel Ford asked his New York office director, Gaston Plantiff, to see if they could actually be built. "LeBaron advises convertible sedan is $3600 for one body with standard fenders and $3300 for 10 bodies," Plantiff replied, later adding, "LeBaron works up some wonderful color work . . . especially on the cabriolet and sedan. I believe we could sell quite a few of them."

They did. A LeBaron sedan had already appeared in the 1924 line, but now, reveling in the new Lincoln styling, LeBaron vastly expanded its offerings with at least 10 different styles. Among them was a dramatic, dual-cowl sport phaeton first shown at the Chicago Salon, a magnificent car in tan and black, upholstered in pigskin.

The "TT" roadster/pickup was popular in 1925.

Police departments loved the '25 Side-Screen Delivery.

A 1925 Runabout appears ready for an afternoon's fun.

Edsel, meanwhile, had convinced Ray Dietrich to move to Detroit where he set up Dietrich, Inc., which for a time was under contract almost exclusively to Lincoln. Dietrich sedans, berlines, broughams, and a collapsible cabriolet now vied with the work of Ray's former firm (by now run by Ralph Roberts) for the attention of Lincoln customers—along with the equally elegant creations of Locke, Holbrook, Hume, Judkins, Brunn, and Fleetwood (the last still producing for chassis other than Cadillac). Even Walter Murphy, the great California coachbuilder whose badge never adorned the early upright Lincolns, produced a custom: an impressive town cabriolet for Mrs. Rudolph Spreckles, with swept-back front fenders and ornate carriage lamps.

The Twenties were starting to roar now, and so was Lincoln: Production rose to a record 8380 units. All cars now came with standard front and rear bumpers and dashboard-mounted fuel gauges. A novel but ill-conceived feature was the Electro-Fogger, which was supposed to aid damp-weather starting by injecting a fuel/air mixture into the carb. But it didn't work very well and was made an option for 1926, then dropped a few years later.

Lincoln's crowning touch this year was a new leaping greyhound mascot commissioned by Edsel from the famous Gorham silversmiths. It would remain a Lincoln trademark through the late 1930s.

Lincolns had taken on a more modern look by 1925.

1926

Slumping sales prompted Ford to spruce up the Model T even more this year. For the first time in more than a decade, closed versions were available in colors other than black, reflecting development of new lacquer paints that dried fast enough to match the Highland Park line rate. Chassis were lowered on all models, and fuel tanks were relocated to the cowl area except on Fordor sedans. The nickel-plated radiator shell was now standard on closed cars, optional for the Touring and Runabout. Inside, steering wheel diameter was enlarged once more, to 17 inches. Wire wheels were a new accessory, and complemented the balloon tires introduced for 1925. Finally, open cars were at last equipped with an opening left front door; no more sliding in from the passenger's side or hopping over the driver's-side gunwale.

When finished in one of the new hues—named Gunmetal Blue, Highland Green, Phoenix Brown, and Fawn Gray—the faithful Tin Lizzie reminded one of a prim but made-up spinster out on a fling. But this and other recent alterations made no difference: The Model T was on its last legs. In 1921-26, Ford accounted for more than half the cars and trucks sold in the United States. The firm's best sales year before 1955 was 1923, when it sold more than two million cars. But by now, the Model T was just plain outdated next to the competition.

The T's greatest assets—low price and a reputation for utility and sturdiness—had served it well in an era of poor roads and equally unsophisticated yet higher-priced rivals. But during the mid-1920s, as hard-surfaced highways fanned across the nation and mechanically sound cars became more commonplace, these selling points began to pale. Furthermore, although Ford had cut prices $100 since 1922, Chevrolet had slashed prices $140, Overland $300, Maxwell $490, and Dodge $890.

More important, public tastes were changing. Rising affluence and new values made many buyers—especially women, who had come to have more influence in car sales—increasingly style-conscious and interested in more comfort and conveniences. Many men insisted on the latest mechanical innovations and more speed and power than Ford had. The Model T had little style; convenience features and mechanical refinements, if they could be had at all, cost extra.

Sensing the shift in attitudes, a number of manufacturers instituted extensive consumer research programs. General Motors surveyed hundreds of thousands of motorists to find out what they liked and didn't like, then skillfully designed and effectively promoted its new models accordingly. Noting Ford's inactivity in this area, one magazine correctly opined: "It is difficult to imagine Henry Ford asking one motorist for advice, let alone taking it." Ford, perhaps the only automaker to conduct formal market studies before World War I and once so attuned to

"The Torque Tube Drive"—An Original Ford Idea

This 1926 Tudor came in colors other than black!

Edsel Ford is at the wheel of this milestone Ford.

the public's needs, stubbornly ignored the winds of change.

But even Henry couldn't ignore the sales figures. From 1924 to 1925, Ford dropped from 1,870,000 to 1,675,000 units while Chevrolet advanced from 280,000 to 470,000. In response, Henry cut prices twice this year. But for the first time in Model T history, these trumps failed to boost sales, and 1926 deliveries were almost 400,000 units below the previous year's figure. Meanwhile, Chevrolet gained an additional 260,000 customers.

By early summer, it was clear to almost everyone in the Ford organization—except Henry and a few other executives also wearing blinders—that the Model T was failing. Despite an improved market, sales in the April-June period were 154,000 units below the comparable 1925 total—a fact not lost on the press. Noting Chevrolet's 33-percent increase and its plan to expand production capacity to a million units annually by 1927, many observed that the Model T's dominance was being seriously threatened for the first time in almost two decades.

Speculation began immediately as to how Henry would turn things around. First reports were that he would replace the four-cylinder T with a six-cylinder car. When he denied this, it was next rumored that Ford would bring out a "Sheik Car" (à la Rudoph Valentino) to satisfy female demands for more style. Again Ford said no, remarking that he had already given the Model T colors and a nickel-plated hood. "Yes," a New York dealer was quoted, "you can paint up a barn, but it will still be a barn and not a parlor." More rumors popped up for the rest of the year and into 1927: Ford would replace the T's planetary transmission with a selective-gear unit; he would add a fourth speed; he would adopt a new carburetor capable of 30 mpg; he would produce an eight-cylinder model priced under $1000; he would enter the medium-price field with a car named Edison; he would build a super-flivver, a two-cylinder car with as much power as a four. Invariably, Ford was asked to comment on these rumors and, invariably, he denied them all. The Model T, he said, would endure.

Lincoln set its second consecutive production record but slipped badly against Cadillac and Packard, which had also been prospering. Its peak penetration against these rivals had come in 1924, when it sold at 40 percent of Cadillac's rate and 50 percent of Packard's. But the opposition had been pulling away, and Lincoln's volume would be only 15 percent of theirs by 1928. This was largely due to the aging Model L, which had still not entirely shed its boxy Leland lines. A new design was clearly needed, but it wouldn't appear for another five years. As it turned out, 1926 would be the production high-point for Lincoln in this decade.

Mechanical specifications were again little changed

"Jazz Age" youth relax beside a '26 Sports Touring.

this year. There was a new steering wheel, fixed instead of tiltable, slightly larger in diameter, and made of handsome black walnut. Engine modifications were limited to a new distributor cam "for more efficient high-speed running," and a centrifugal-type air cleaner. Factory-body models still began at around $4000, but coachbuilt wares expanded with creations by American, Babcock, Derham, Lang, Murray, Waterhouse, and Willoughby—the last two destined to supply some of the make's most popular custom bodies. In Detroit, Ray Dietrich had now evolved his famous coupe-roadster, a really elegant two-seater (if enormous on the 136-inch wheelbase) with smoothly tapered body lines, rumble seat, and twin, rear-mount spare tires. Dietrich sold 263 at about $5500 each, while Murray built 150 copies of a similar Dietrich-designed model priced $1000 less.

If these production figures seem low, remember that this was the heyday of custom and semi-custom coachwork. Bodies were relatively easy to remove from chassis—indeed, some owners alternated winter/summer between closed/open bodies on one chassis—and most coachbuilders were geared to miniscule, even one-of-a-kind output. Thus, Brunn built only three of its Lincoln-based five-passenger sedans and open limousines this year, Dietrich only two of his broughams and collapsible cabriolets.

While producing 10 six-passenger landaulets was a monumental order for a company like Willoughby, larger coachbuilders now issued semi-customs in quantities of 20-30 to 100-200. This tactic was conceived by free-thinkers like Ray Dietrich. Whereas the "individual custom" was a costly ground-up creation reaching upwards of $7000, the semi-custom was a kind of limited edition, though few were ever alike. Dietrich, for example, offered options like disc, wire, or wooden wheels; various seat and/or folding-top treatments; and styling variations like side- or rear-mounted spares. The semi-custom was thus distinctive but cost as little as $5000, thousands less than a one-off. "The full custom became too expensive for most clients," Ray Dietrich remembered, "but it was still up-

Henry Ford leans on the wheel of the Fordson tractor.

Lincoln sales for the Twenties peaked in 1926.

per-upper class for a few. When people called me in New York and asked to speak to 'Mr. LeBaron,' I would give them a phony French accent and say, 'Ah yez, Madame, how can I eessist?' Whereas when they phoned me in Detroit about a semi-custom, I was just Ray Dietrich!"

1927

Ford's Model T reached the end of its long road this year. Despite all the cosmetic freshening of the last 10 years, the last Lizzie to roll out the door really wasn't that much different than the first one built in late 1908. That was one of her problems, of course, the thing that ultimately did her in, but it's also one of the many reasons why we remember the Model T with such affection some 60 years later. Cars built during this final year were equipped with the previously optional wire wheels as standard, replacing the old wood-spoke "artillery" types, and maroon and green were added to the color chart.

In mid-February, Henry Ford admitted for the first time that he needed a new car. While acknowledging he had given some thought to its design, he refused to name an introduction date, claiming that "a statement at this time on the matter . . . might do serious injury to my competitors." A fresh crop of rumors at once sprang up. By early spring it was commonly assumed that the new model would be faster and have a sliding-gear transmission. It would appear soon; some said as early as late June. But Ford was silent. Competitors complained this was responsible for a mild sales slowdown as prospects postponed buying until they saw what Ford had in mind. "The result is getting on everyone's nerves," said an Ohio newspaper, "as Ford himself probably realizes." Henry soon gave in.

On the evening of May 25, 1927, Ford Motor Company confirmed that it would indeed build a new car.

As if to punctuate the announcement, the 15-millionth Model T rolled off the Highland Park assembly line the following afternoon, May 26. The occasion was marked in an appropriately simple manner. There were no bands, no bunting, no speeches. With Edsel at the wheel and his father beside him, the car led a motorcade of company officials and 15 reporters and cameramen to the Dearborn Engineering Laboratory. On the plaza in front of the building, under gray skies, were Ford's earliest automobiles and the first Model T. For the benefit of motion-picture cameramen, Henry drove both of the older cars around the plaza. The ceremony was over.

Most newspapers and magazines commented on the Model T's demise and what its successor would be like. There were, as the Louisville *Times* predicted, "acres of humorous writing devoted . . . to 'hunky Elizabeth, chunky Elizabeth, spunky Elizabeth Ford.'" The Baltimore *Sun* remarked: "Since the Model T makes as much noise as any 10 other cars and the new Ford cannot possibly be noisier than the old, life will be pleasanter, we will all live longer."

Nevertheless, most of the press regarded this as a momentous event and treated it with a certain solemn sentimentality. To the New York *Herald-Tribune*, the T's passing was "The End of an Epoch." The Dayton *News* said a "world institution" was being "Retired with Honors." The Roanoke *News* spoke for many: "It will be long before America loses its affectionate, if somewhat apologetic, remembrance of the car that first put us on wheels. We probably wouldn't admit it to anyone, but deep in our hearts we love every rattle in its body."

Of course, many were reluctant to see Lizzie go. Hearst newspaper executive Arthur Brisbane, on adding a new Ford sedan and truck to the several he already owned, wired Henry that he should keep one plant running indefinitely to make half a million Model Ts a year; he thought they could easily be sold at higher prices by mail order. A Ford dealer in Newark, "believing in the great merit of the Model T and the continued demand for same," sought to arrange for its manufacture and/or assembly in

Henry Ford and Thomas Edison circa 1926-27.

New Jersey. Newark citizens, he assured the company, would finance the scheme. Soon after the May 25 announcement, many owners began taking better care of their Tin Lizzies, eager to prolong their lives. One elderly lady of means in Montclair, New Jersey, purchased and stored away seven new Ts so that she would not be without one for the rest of her life. A man in Toledo bought six, and only wore out the last of them in 1967.

Time would only increase affection and respect for "the first log cabin of the motor age." Archibald Henderson, writing in 1930, was typical in declaring that the Model T's impact was "greater by far than that of the telegraph, the telephone, rural free delivery, the phonograph, the radio, or electric light and power." E.B. White and Richard Lee Strout, in their classic 1936 epitaph "Farewell, My Lovely," said "it was hard-working, commonplace, heroic . . . the miracle God had wrought. And it was patently the sort of thing that could only happen once." To Philip Van Doren Stern, writing in 1955, the Model T "was, as no car before or since has been, truly the people's car . . . part of the fabric of American life, celebrated in song and legend and folklore." In 1959, *Fortune* magazine reported that 100 of the world's leading designers, architects, and design teachers ranked the T as the 82nd "best designed mass-produced product of modern times" (higher than all other Ford cars except the 1940 Lincoln Continental, which ranked sixth, and the 1955 Thunderbird, rated 41st). In 1974, the T was voted "the world's greatest motorcar" by readers of *Motor Trend* magazine.

That the T helped to change America's psychology, manners, and mores as well as the national economy is beyond question. No other single device did more to induce people of a provincial mind to begin thinking in regional and national terms. None did more to knit together different parts of the county, state and, ultimately, the nation.

Ford produced 15,007,033 Model Ts in the United States through May 31, 1927, the figure and date often cited for total output and the end of production. But the company assembled 477,748 additional Ts during the summer of 1927. Ford of Canada had built another 747,259 Tin Lizzies, Ford of England an estimated 250,000. For several decades, automotive historians and journalists believed that the T's production mark would stand unchallenged. "No other model was ever produced in such numbers," asserted Allan Nevins and Frank Ernest Hill in their 1957 book *Ford: Expansion and Challenge 1915-1933,* "and it is safe to say that on this score alone its record will never be matched." But Germany's Volkswagen, amid much fanfare, produced its 15,007,034th Type 1 Beetle on February 17, 1972, and smashed the T's worldwide production record the following year. For decades, the Lizzie shared honors with the Rolls-Royce Silver Ghost (1907-27) as the car with the longest life span. During the 1960s and '70s, however, several European models, including the Beetle, Citroën 2CV, and Fiat's 1100, exceeded the T's production life.

Millions of Model Ts would prove as durable as flivver

The beginning of the changeover to the Model A Ford.

jokes and legend said they were. In March 1927, nearly 19 years after the first one was made, 11,325,521 Lizzies were still registered in the United States. Despite its cheapness, the T lasted longer on the average (eight years) than other cars (6.3 years) because of its low-cost replacement parts, ease of repair, and Ford's vast dealer network. The number of Ts in daily use declined rapidly with the end of production, but 5,432,000 still plied the nation's highways in late 1931; in 1941, an estimated 600,000-800,000. In 1948, when R.L. Polk and Company made the last actual count, 73,111 Model T cars and trucks were still registered. Many additional Ts were unlicensed, of course, stored in garages and farm buildings, while others could be found rusting where they had stopped running years before. In 1953, Ford estimated the number of surviving flivvers at 100,000. In 1971, automotive historian Leslie R. Henry, taking into account subsequent large-scale T restoration, put the number at 300,000. "If an antique buff finds a 'T' frame with a serial number on it," he noted, "he's got enough to start building a car."

Many of the Lizzie's 4830 parts and some accessories are still readily available from old-car parts houses, some new old stock, others newly made reproductions from companies cashing in on the steady demand. The Sears-Roebuck catalog, which once devoted more space to T parts and gadgets than to men's clothing, listed engine gaskets as late as 1975, though perhaps more for sentimental than

River Rouge plant; iron ore in one end, a Ford out the other.

business reasons. Today, every restored or restorable Model T sells for many times its original purchase price; even "basket cases" cost more than they did when new.

Amazingly, a few Ts remain in daily service, and invariably make headlines when stolen or involved in accidents. The Windmiller family of Columbus, Ohio, still hauls produce for its farm in a truck it bought new in 1916. Samuel Treon, of Red Cross, Pennsylvania, continues to drive the flivver his foster father bought the same year. "There's no end of offers for it," he observes, "but I just say it's not for sale." Ernest Duhachek continually used a 1917 truck on his farm near Newman Grove, Nebraska, until his retirement in 1974. He bought the chassis for $495, then added cab, seat, and cargo box.

Two international organizations serve Model T owners today: the Model T Ford Club International, founded in 1952 and one of the oldest old-car enthusiast groups, and the Model T Ford Club of America, established in 1966. The former, headquartered in Chicago, Illinois, has 53 chapters whose members own more than 10,000 Ts. The latter has 66 chapters and 6000 members, many of whom also own more than one Lizzie. Both organizations publish bimonthly magazines that keep alive flivver knowledge and lore. Virtually every old-car museum in the country displays at least one Model T. The Henry Ford Museum displays one of the first, the 15-millionth T, and several historically significant flivvers. Several individuals have impressive T collections, among them Cecil

Church of Harrisburg, Illinois, who houses his in a wooden replica of an early Ford dealership.

To this day, the Model T continues to generate considerable attention. Since 1948 it has been given full chapters in at least 15 books, and has been the subject of six fiction and seven nonfiction works, not to mention a few movies and dozens of reprint owner and service manuals, parts catalogs, and sales brochures. In 1953, the Tin Lizzie was a focal point of Ford Motor Company's 50th anniversary celebration. It was again heavily publicized in 1958, the 50th anniversary of its introduction; in 1963, when Ford marked the centennial of its founder's birth; and during the company's 75th anniversary in 1978.

Ford and others still employ the Model T on occasion to make advertising points. On introducing its Pinto subcompact for 1971, Ford ran ads signed by chairman Henry Ford II, who declared it "the new Model T. The first Model T stood for sensible, simple motoring; it was lively and easy to handle and fun to drive, and this new version of the Model T stands for the same things." It would even be available in "Model T Black." The campaign's early TV commercials showed a Model T being overtaken on the road by its successor, the Model A, and a Pinto. Rival automakers like VW and a few nonautomotive companies have also invoked the T, invariably complimenting it and, in effect, saying "me too." One recent example: "What do the Apple personal computer and the Model T have in common? Ease of operation and affordability."

Over the years, "Model T" has been used as a way of saying "old-fashioned." The instances are too numerous to list. It also comes up when durable, inexpensive, or widely accepted products are discussed. Persian lamb has been called "one of the great 'Model Ts' of the fur industry, seemingly fashionable forever," while Douglas Aircraft's DC-3 and Ford's trimotor airplane have been referred to as "the Model T of aircraft." The term has also become associated with simplicity, success, even quality. For example, a 1979 United Press International story said that the cooling plant for the Three Mile Island nuclear reactor "will use the same natural circulation process Henry Ford used to cool the Model T engine." The Detroit *Free Press* reported at about the same time that the owner of a local shirt-printing company aspires to be "the Henry Ford of T-shirts" and is well on his way "to becoming Mr. Model T." An ad for a Japanese typewriter boasted the machine is "jam-packed with quality like the Model T Ford and just as simple to repair." Such is the memory of the Tin Lizzie that it has become part of America's thinking and vocabulary.

Nowadays, owning a Model T, especially one with brass fittings, is positively stylish. Many old-car buffs would own no other antique. Others go to inordinate lengths to find an example like the one they knew as young adults or children. Perhaps more than any other object from our past, the Model T has a special niche in American hearts. Most older citizens had their first experience in automobiling when they rode in or drove a flivver. Today, the sight of one bobbing along warms them like a ray of sunshine. They smile, and some yell "get a horse!" If the car is pulled up at the curb, they may reminisce with the owner about the "good old days" and perhaps recall a Ford joke or two. If asked to take a spin, they'll immediately climb in. If invited to drive, many accept, eager to prove they still remember how to manipulate the T's pedals and levers. Younger people are similarly moved.

In the end, the Model T outlived its usefulness, but it hasn't been outlived by time. It has become almost immortal, as much a part of this country's heritage as the Fourth of July, a mixture of folk legend and nostalgic affection tinged with bittersweet humor. Few cars, let alone one so humble, can claim as much.

For Lincoln, 1927 was a disappointing year. The luxury-car market may have been expanding at the same pace as the stock market, but Lincoln's share was falling noticeably. Packard had introduced a new Eight at mid-decade, and Cadillac was still improving its V-8. These two continued to slug it out for leadership in the quality field while Lincoln floundered. This year's volume dropped to 7141 units, the lowest since 1922, despite a host of updates: teardrop-shaped nickel-plated headlamps with dual filaments (instead of the old tilt-types) controlled by a dashboard switch; combination tail/brake/backup lights; rubber instead of linoleum runningboard surfaces; oval-shaped central instrument cluster; and one-inch lower ride height for all models. Four-wheel brakes were now standard instead of optional, and Lincoln advertised "six-wheel brakes," referring to a handbrake operating on the two rear drums. There was a lighter-weight clutch system of more efficient design, and a key-lock to immobilize the steering wheel and ignition. Prices took a leap upward. The bare chassis now cost $3500, and the cheapest complete model was the stubby, $4600 four-passenger, two-window sedan by Locke. Some of the more luxurious full customs cost more than $8000—over $110,000 in today's money.

Competing full-tilt in an age of unprecedented opulence, Lincoln spared no expense on its promotional materials, which were magnificent. The deluxe catalog contained automotive interpretations of historical art and design by the make's best-known coachbuilders. Included were the "Egyptian" by Judkins (a berline upholstered in a needlepoint design of papyrus and lotus flowers), the "Oriental" by LeBaron (a gold, black, and bright red coupe), the "Colonial" by Willoughby (a cabriolet trimmed in floral-pattern broadcloth), and the "Roman Club" by Dietrich (done up with ribbed cloth).

This year's most memorable Lincoln was undoubtedly the Dietrich two-passenger convertible coupe that was sent to challenge the Europeans at several *Concours d'Elegance* in summer. It won three gold medals, at Paris, Milan, and Monte Carlo. The last also presented Ray Dietrich with what he remembered as "a loving cup big enough to swim in." If 1927 wasn't one of Lincoln's most profitable years, it certainly established Henry Leland's once-ugly duckling as a serious purveyor of automotive elegance to American gentry.

1928

As the curtain fell on America's most successful wheeled invention, the whole world wondered what "old Henry Ford" was going to do. About to turn 64, yet trim and youthful from a well-disciplined daily routine, he was still in the prime of his extraordinary life. His handsome 34-year-old son, Edsel, was showing great promise of following in his father's footsteps, having succeeded him as company president in 1918. There was nearly $250 million cash on hand, and total assets of the far-flung Ford empire stood at just under a billion dollars. But the ingenious Model T, the very foundation of this fantastic success, had run its course. As his company entered 1927 and sales continued to sink, it was all too clear that Henry would have to work another miracle to bring forth a replacement.

Even as rumors of the Model T's demise swept the nation, the "wizard of motors" was already burning the midnight oil. He had steadfastly resisted the notion that the Model T was really finished. But if it was, he wanted something just as revolutionary to take over.

For several years, Henry had been tinkering with different engines that might someday power such a car. Among them was the "X-8," with four cylinders facing up, as in a V-type configuration, and four facing down where the oil pan would ordinarily be. It also had roller main bearings, a combination starter/generator, and a supercharger built into the flywheel. For Ford, this radical design would be a logical successor to the T's legendary four-cylinder powerplant. It was also a chance to be a step ahead of competitors rather than bring out another inline four or six. Unfortunately, extensive engineering and

The new-generation Ford: a 1928 Model A business coupe.

Henry and Edsel Ford study a model of the giant complex built on the River Rouge outside of Detroit.

testing showed the X-8 far too complex for easy mass production, too heavy, and too prone to lower spark plug fouling by dust and mud. By the end of 1926, his hopes dashed that it would ever be practical, Henry reluctantly ordered development work stopped.

Now, as Henry and a handful of his most trusted aides contemplated the Model T's inevitable end, they began a top-secret rush to develop its successor along conventional lines. Edsel was closer to dealers and the sales department, and had presented the arguments to his father. What was urgently needed was a car that would appeal to the same customer as in the halcyon days of the Model T—and that could beat the best of the competition, namely Chevrolet, Essex, and Plymouth. It would have to be faster, smoother, more durable, and must have the features buyers were demanding.

One thing was certain: It would need a conventional select-shift transmission. Urban owners, especially, preferred such a gearbox, and dealers had long complained of lost sales due to the Model T's old pedal-operated planetary transmission. People were becoming more particular, roads were getting better, and there were more women drivers. The well-informed buyer was less inclined to lay out cash for a car that required a pedal held down hard just to select low gear or reverse. Though Henry staunchly defended this patented device and other features of his

hallowed Model T, he nevertheless understood the language of sales. After great deliberation, he finally gave the order to proceed with a design that would be entirely new from top to bottom, fender to fender.

But first, Henry faced the challenge of closing his plants and scrapping the well-oiled Model T production lines to retool. For one thing, it meant losing incredible sums of money. For another, the grade-school-educated motor king had a well-known disdain for engineers, preferring his own seat-of-the-pants approach. This, plus the Model

The 1928 Model A roadster/pickup listed at $445.

T's long-running success, had left him remarkably shy of engineering and styling staff to handle the tremendous amount of work the transition would involve. What he did have was a disciplined manufacturing operation led by one of the toughest, smartest men in the business.

Charles Sorensen had been top man at Ford Motor Company—apart from Henry and Edsel—for a long time. Starting in 1905 as a pattern maker, the tall Dane had always been a good idea man, and when given a role in management had been one of the key figures in developing the moving Model T assembly line. A stern taskmaster with dynamo energy, he was the mainspring of the company's amazing expansion, creating new manufacturing and assembly techniques, building new plants at home and abroad, and carrying out Henry's orders with rapid-fire precision.

From the very beginning of the secret new-car project, Sorensen and another top production expert, Peter E. Martin, were part of the inner circle. By the time the idea had pretty well crystalized, three engineers had joined the group, selected quietly from the random projects that were always in progress around Dearborn. In charge of the new car's overall design was Eugene Farkas, former head of the X-8 project and a longtime Ford engineer who had played a major role in developing the Fordson tractor. Assisting him would be Frank Johnson, chief engineer at the Lincoln plant, and Lawrence Sheldrick, a young engineer who had caught Henry's eye on another assignment.

By inclination, Henry Ford was a chassis man. Intensely practical, he cared far more about how a car ran than how it looked. Edsel, on the other hand, was concerned more about appearance (he had a natural eye for it), comfort, and features. He also knew the marketing wisdom of updating models every year, something his father had stubbornly resisted with the Model T.

Partly because he was impressed with the job his son had done with Lincoln, but mainly because he was occupied with chassis ideas, Henry gave Edsel responsibility for the new car's body design. Assisting him would be amiable veteran Joe Galamb, a highly respected member of the Ford engineering staff who, for all intents and purposes, was the styling department. The Polish-born designer had laid out the first Model T and, when he wasn't called upon to make an occasional sheetmetal change on it, had charge of experimental engineering.

Edsel was known as the first-class gentleman, and he and Galamb hit it off from the start. Young Ford would outline what he had in mind; Galamb would interpret it in sketches and clay models that the pair would then discuss in great detail. Initially, they favored a scaled-down Lincoln, with the same finely sculptured lines, rounded corners, just the right amount of nickel trim, nicely turned door handles, and a comfortable, well-appointed interior. "He [was quite critical] of the interior," Galamb would recall, "and the instrument work. When we made the first body sample, Edsel was very particular about the trimming and the material. He knew what he wanted and insisted that we get it." But while Edsel knew

what he wanted, nothing was approved without his father's critical—and often creative—contribution.

An example of the cut-and-try engineering that characterized all of Henry Ford's cars was the way the height of the first prototype bodies was decided. All-round production man W.C. Klann was in on the project by now. "The sample bodies were being built at the Highland Park plant," he recalled in a 1956 interview. "I built six bodies there . . . they were always under lock and key. We would bring the panels down [to Engineering] and assemble them and get the height of our seat cushions. Well, Henry Ford wanted to fit himself and Sorensen; Edsel Ford wanted to fit Mr. Martin and himself." Klann related how the elder Ford insisted he should be able to get in and out without knocking his hat off. The shorter Edsel supported Galamb's first drawings, which called for a lower profile. Naturally, Henry won out, and Klann made up a prototype 1½ inches taller. Said Klann: "When Henry Ford saw it, it looked like an old hayrack. He said, 'Scrap that. It looks terrible!' So it remained the same as before."

First styling efforts involved the coupe and Tudor sedan. By March 1927, work was far enough along that a contract for a special set of body stampings was quietly given to the Murray Corporation of America. It may have been Henry's nature to leak a clue now and then, and secrets are hard to keep in Detroit. In any event, it was the first tangible evidence that the Fords were working on a new model. The next morning, the press speculated that, besides refined body lines, the new mystery Ford would probably be introduced with a select-shift transmission and modern distributor ignition.

Henry instantly sparked a wave of national excitement in May 1927 by casually announcing what he'd been planning all along: to shut down the entire Ford system to retool. "We began work on this model several years ago," he told the press with some truth. "In fact, the idea of a car to succeed the Model T has been in my mind much longer than that. But the sale of the Model T continued at such a pace that there never seemed to be an opportunity to get the new car started."

The shutdown would have enormous impact on a national economy in which Ford built nearly half the automobiles. Thousands of workers at 36 assembly plants were immediately laid off, the Model T accessory business went into a tailspin, many suppliers and parts houses went broke, and only the strongest Ford dealers managed to survive. Meantime, thousands of buyers decided to wait. As their salesrooms gathered dust, dealers could do little but wring their hands in frustration. Some of the more optimistic ones put up big colorful posters: "We are taking orders for the new car . . . speed, pick-up, flexibility, beauty, comfort, stamina, coming soon!" But as summer wore into autumn, then into winter, the new Ford was nowhere in sight.

Back in Dearborn, Henry and his team were working night and day toward a tough, spirited, smartly fashioned automobile the average man could afford. In design, it was already so new that it had been christened "Model A," significantly echoing the designation of the first Ford in 1903.

Engineer Harold Hicks, who was transferred from airplane work to help on the new car's engine and chassis details, was awed by Henry's driving ambition and the way he could get the best from his staff. As an engineer, he was even more impressed with Ford's uncanny ability to shortcut extensive development time by being a bear for simplicity: "I remember that they had too many bolts holding the carburetor together. Henry Ford said to me, 'Cut those bolts down!' I had the Zenith company get out a design in which two bolts held the carburetor together. I felt quite proud that they had reduced it from about 14 little screws down to two bolts. I showed him the design. With his characteristic trait he said, 'Two is too many! Make it just one bolt!' So the carburetor came out with just a simple bolt down through it."

Lincoln-like styling was a hallmark of the Model A.

Henry often made up for his technical and educational shortcomings by overwhelming a problem with men and machines. Theodore Gehle recalls how this even rubbed off on Henry's chief lieutenant. Gehle worked in Ford's Pressed Steel Department as the first Model A bodies were painfully taking shape in mid-1927. "Mr. Sorensen said, 'Now you go down . . . and you just live there until you get the first bodies out. When you see daylight for the first bodies, why, you let me know.' . . . The quarter panel was what was holding up the bodies most, and fenders were second." An experienced Ford production man, Gehle worked virtually around the clock trying to straighten out the kinks. Finally he reported to Sorensen that he wasn't having much luck, but he had an idea: "I suggest you [order] Pressed Steel to run off 100 sets of stampings, the best they can make. Some of these are going to be horrible. Then [order] the Body Plant to build

100 bodies with these sets of stampings. They will probably have to be scrapped, but it will give them knowledge. By relaying information back and forth [between departments] maybe out of the next 100 bodies you may get a good one." Gehle was amazed that the headstrong Sorensen went along with it: "These first 100 bodies were assembled and scrapped. On the next 100 bodies we saved about 10. From there we started Model A production, the bodies having been the bottleneck."

The bottlenecks proved almost countless. Starting at the end of May 1927, thousands of toolmakers, die and pattern makers, and millwrights had been hired or recalled to begin the massive overhaul that would have to be completed in record time, often without final plans and in many cases requiring duplicates for installation in the various assembly plants. In some departments, engineers and their assistants would work in relays, 24 hours a day, just correcting mistakes and designing and redesigning the special tools needed.

The Highland Park plant, once described as "the most productive piece of ground on earth," had to be gutted to the walls. Most manufacturing and all car assembly operations for that territory were transferred to Ford's new showcase factory complex rising on the banks of the River Rouge near Dearborn. Giant machines weighing as much as 240 tons had to be completely redesigned or rebuilt. Thousands of smaller tools and precision instruments had to be manufactured. Since the Model A would be composed of about 6800 different parts—compared to fewer than 5000 on the Model T—a multitude of new manufacturing sources had to be developed. Engines, some body stampings, rear axles, and brakes were among parts to be made at the Rouge plant. Shock absorber parts would come from Buffalo; bumpers from Chicago; wood body parts from the Ford lumber mills at Iron Mountain, Michigan; wood floorboards from a supplier in Vancouver, Washington; wheels from Hamilton, Ohio, and Memphis; glass from Dearborn and New Jersey; radiators from the big Ford plant at Green Island, New York.

To supply the wide variety of smart new body types being drawn up by Edsel and Galamb, the company would contract with outside firms for most stampings and built-up bodies. Briggs Manufacturing Company, a longtime supplier that also built custom coachwork for other automakers, was assigned to tool and produce the new Model A coupe. Major contracts were also signed with Murray and the Edward G. Budd Manufacturing Company. Briggs would come to specialize in pressings for sedan, coupe, victoria, and panel delivery bodies, as well as furnishing completely built and trimmed cabriolet bodies. Murray did much the same, plus assembly and finish on the wood-bodied station wagon introduced for 1929. Budd would become an invaluable source for special stampings and commercial bodies.

By mid-August, the Fords were sufficiently satisfied with their progress that Edsel promised the press that the new car would be available within the next few weeks. "Tests already made show that it is faster, smoother, more rugged, and more beautiful than we had hoped for in the early stages of designing," he said. "Experiments have been made with a wide variety of color schemes and body designs, and all these have been decided upon." As it turned out, reporters had to wait a few months for their first official peek. Had they been watching the gates at the Ford engineering laboratory, they might have noticed that experimental cars, thinly disguised Model Ts, had been leaving there on road tests since early spring. By the end of October, as many as 150 prototypes with hand-built chassis had been driven at night over Ford's only test track, the streets and countryside of Dearborn.

In the late afternoon of Thursday, October 20, 1927, after nearly a year's effort and millions of dollars, the first Model A engine approved for full production was built at Dearborn. Its number was ceremoniously hand stamped by Henry Ford as his son, Sorensen, Martin, and two long-time employees, August Degener and Charles Hartner, looked on. The next day, the engine was installed in a chassis rolling slowly down the pilot assembly line, and the tired auto magnate had his first real opportunity to stand back and assess his latest creation.

If the Model T chassis had been a paragon of mechanical simplicity, the Model A's was ideal. True, Henry retained the familiar layout of his beloved flivver. Single, semi-elliptic transverse springs straddled the front and rear axles buggy-style; the "wishbone" radius rod, acting as a front-end stabilizer, was plain to see; and the overall spindly appearance seemed the same at first glance. But every suspension piece, from the spring perches and 21-inch welded wire wheels to the featherlight frame and forged axles, had been completely and ingeniously redesigned for extra strength and nimbleness. And for the first time on a Ford, shock absorbers and rod-operated four-wheel brakes were incorporated for safer, smoother going.

Though still an L-head type, the cast-iron four-cylinder engine was totally new. Rated at 40 brake horsepower, it ran a 3⅞-inch bore and 4¼-inch stroke for a 200.5 cubic-inch displacement. It was thus twice as powerful as the Model T powerplant, lighter, and considerably more efficient. And, sure enough, it was no longer bolted to a heavy, complex, planetary transmission but a modern three-speed-with-reverse gearshift unit driving through a dry, multiple-disc clutch.

As predicted, engineers had also adopted a modern, less costly battery and ignition system that did away with a lot of engine compartment clutter. Instead of the old time-honored magneto ignition, with its four vibrator coils and a maze of wires running from dash to spark plugs, there were just two wires between engine and dash: the high-tension from the coil to the distributor, and the low-tension lead to the ignition switch. A modern, specially designed distributor was now mounted atop the cylinder head, gear-driven by a vertical shaft off the center of the camshaft, with its tail end driving the oil pump. The moulded plastic cap with a pair of winged extensions would give the Model A distributor a character all its own. The wings encased the spark plug leads, connected via simple brass straps secured with round finger nuts.

Assisting the smartly styled fin-and-tube radiator for cooling was a centrifugal water pump and two-blade fan, driven off the front crankshaft pulley by a V-belt that also drove the "powerhouse" generator on the engine's left side. And, to please the stylists, the respected engine crank handle that had always dangled below the Model T radiator could now be removed and stowed away.

As he watched that Tudor sedan body being tried on that first chassis, Henry Ford may have felt special pride in his ingenious fuel system. Unfortunately, though the 1926-27 T had used something similar, it would prove to be one of the new car's most controversial features (insurance companies blindly labeled it explosion-prone). The gas tank was simply part of the cowl, forming the roll over the front body from below the windshield to the hood belt-line, and was filled by unscrewing a knurled cap on top. Fuel fed by gravity to the Zenith double-venturi carburetor, flowing first through a handy in-line sediment bulb. The cowl was designed in such a way that, on the engine side, it formed the firewall and mount for the hood and, on the driver's side, held the instrument panel.

Shock absorbers and bumpers came standard on the "A".

Less than a week after the first Model A was completed, production had inched upward as assembly problems were doggedly worked out. By November 1, 1927, the rate was about 20 a day. Two days later, selected Ford dealers and members of the press were at last invited to have their first look. Describing early Model A assembly line action, veteran auto journalist Fay Leone Faurote would write: "I stood and watched the men for a time. The job is new to them and they 'make haste slowly.' There are stops for fittings. Stops for minor parts and minor adjustments. In fact, the assembly line is just now crawling. But with each new machine a slightly faster pace is evidenced."

Arthur Hatch, Ford's Chicago branch manager in 1927, reminisced in his retirement years about some of the trials and tribulations of starting Model A production at his plant: "Finally, we got a car assembled and I took it out for a spin. I actually blocked the whole city of Chicago with the crowds that developed to see Henry Ford's 'well-kept secret.' . . . We got into production and the next morning my wife calls me at my office. 'I've stalled,' she said. 'The car won't run! I've frozen my feet and hands trying to get it started!' She no more than hung up than I began to get calls from Ford dealers all over Chicago. They were complaining that the new cars wouldn't run. So I went out in the plant and the superintendent said, 'There must be something wrong with the engineering . . . the cars are being put together right.' I called the Ford operator in Detroit and said, 'Get me Sorensen!' Sorensen came on and I said, 'I've just blown the whistle. Shut the whole plant down. My wife is stuck in the park. I've got 300 calls this morning that people are stuck all over town!' Sorensen said, 'Don't leave the office! You stay right there! I'll fly six of our people over there that were supposed to have designed this automobile. Are you sure you're right?' I said, 'I'm dead sure!'"

In Dearborn, Henry himself took one of the newly assembled cars to have lunch at home with wife Clara. When he got back in, it wouldn't start. The same thing happened to Sorensen. "Mr. Ford sent out an order at once to stop production," Hatch recalled. "It didn't take them long to find the problem. It was in the regulator which controlled the cutout between the battery and engine so it [the battery] wouldn't overcharge. He had all the assembly plants ship the faulty regulators—they cost about $4.50 each—back to Detroit, where he made his engineers pile them in a big heap. I went down there and he had them piled up higher than the roof of the engineering laboratory. He'd lead you out and say, 'Look at those things. Look at all the dummies I've got around here!'"

The production problems continued, but Henry wouldn't sell the Model A until it was right. At the end of November, Edsel cautioned the press that it was "doubtful that the new Ford would be available to purchasers before the first of the year." He projected it would be months before the factories could turn out Model As on "anything like a peak production schedule," noting that the company had only shipped about 500 cars up to that time. Asked who was getting those first cars, Edsel let it slip that none were being sold but were, at that very moment, speeding to different parts of the country for the forthcoming introductory shows.

So the stage was set. On the morning of Thursday, December 1, 1927, readers of 2000 daily newspapers across the nation found a full-page advertisement that read in part: "We believe the new Ford car is as great an improvement in motor car building as the Model T was in 1908." So wrote Henry Ford in a $2 million blitz that hit the day before his long-awaited Model A went on sale. "In appearance, in performance, in comfort, in safety, in all that goes to make a good car, it will bear out everything I have said here. . . ."

News spread like wildfire that the car would be shown in major cities the next day, and hundreds of thousands lined up for a look. In New York City, people began gathering outside Ford's big Broadway showroom at 3 a.m. By midday, the crowd had grown so large that the manager had to move the display to Madison Square Garden. "Ex-citement could hardly have been greater," remarked the New York *World*, "had Pah-wah, the sacred white elephant of Burma, elected to sit for seven days on the flagpole of the Woolworth Building."

It was easily the greatest new-model introduction in history, rivaling even Lindbergh's transatlantic flight as the top news story of the decade. In the U.S. alone an estimated 10 million people flocked to see the Model A in the 36 hours after its unveiling. Some 100,000 descended on Detroit showrooms the first day, mounted police had to be called out to control the crowds in Cleveland, and an over-eager mob in Kansas City nearly burst the walls of Convention Hall.

Merrell "Mo" Jordan was an Illinois teenager when the Model A arrived, and would later run a successful dealership in California: "You couldn't get near the car on introduction day. My dad owned the Ford agency, but that didn't help me. I remember the long lines of people waiting to take a ride. We had a special route laid out that ended by crossing a plowed field. That first car would do 50 in second, and I swear to this day that it was a faster model than the later ones." As a wide-eyed youngster, Jordan knew everything that went on at his dad's dealership—or thought he did. Noting that those first Model A demonstrators were taken into the shop and worked on all night, he will always believe that they were doctored to go faster. The mechanics were probably just trying to keep them running.

The Model A was surprisingly quick, 5 to 25 mph in a little more than eight seconds and up to 65 mph tops (against 43 mph for the T). Much of that acceleration, which compared favorably with that of even the best sixes and eights, could be attributed to modifications worked out by Harold Hicks, and to the use of aluminum pistons. The car was so quick that, the day after its introduction, the state of Massachusetts declared that, for safety's sake, it would "require all Model T drivers accustomed to the planetary transmission to take a test before they can operate the new models."

As for looks, the Model A was not sensational by standards of the day, but it had plenty of natural charm. From the shape and contour of its nickel radiator shell to the sweeping hoodline, to the body details and the way the large, full-crowned fenders hugged the wire wheels, the family resemblance with Edsel's elegant Lincolns was obvious. By borrowing some of the big car's finesse and incorporating a longer wheelbase and a higher beltline that reduced window height, the designers had fashioned a lower, much prettier car than the tall, boxy Model T.

Initially, the A was offered in five body styles: Tudor sedan, coupe, sports coupe, roadster, and phaeton. The closed cars wore a smart cadet-type sunvisor, rounded roof corners, and fabric top coverings. All bodies were nicely enhanced by the ample use of reveals to carry the contrasting paint and pinstriping. Naturally, Edsel's artistic eye had selected the four basic shades of Niagara Blue, Arabian Sand, Dawn Gray, and Gunmetal Blue.

Inside, the instrument panel was the epitome of form and function. Shaped roughly like a diamond and finished in satin-nickel, the main cluster was mounted to the back of the cowl/fuel tank and contained a direct-acting float-operated fuel gauge. The 80-mph speedometer was set off at the bottom of a vertical oval, with ignition switch at the left, ammeter to the right. In the center was an instrument lamp. As on the Model T, spark and throttle levers were mounted on the steering column, but their quadrants were now eliminated. An accelerator pedal on the floor supplemented the customary hand throttle. A combination fuel regulator and choke rod extending directly from the carburetor was handily positioned on the panel's lower right. Surrounding the horn button at the lock nut of the hard-rubber steering wheel was the headlight switch, controlled by a multi-position lever. Several grades of fine cloth upholstery were standard in the various closed models, with door panels, pleated door pockets, and side walls trimmed in the same material. Open cars came with imitation leather trim. Roadster and phaeton doors opened by means of an internal lever, as they did not have external door handles in 1928. Windows in all models were crank-operated.

All this in a basic Tudor selling for $495, against a comparable Chevrolet at $585 and the Whippet at $535, was the attraction that had all those folks standing in line. A bonus was an impressive list of standard equipment that now included Houdaille shocks all around, combination tail/stop light, front and rear bumpers, windshield wiper, speedometer, swing-type one-piece ventilating windshield, and a Spartan horn.

It's an auto seller's dream when customers literally break down the doors, but Henry had laid down the law: none of the early demonstrators were to be sold. While the company worked to increase production through December, dealers were only allowed to take deposits on future deliveries as they fended off every kind of offer for the one or two "bolt-down" cars they had. Everyone, it seemed, from grocery clerks to politicians wanted to be the first to have one, but couldn't for love or money.

The record is a bit hazy, but the honor of being the first Model A owner probably belongs to Thomas A. Edison. The famous inventor was invited to drive the first car off the Kearney, New Jersey assembly line on December 19, and it was immediately turned over to him as a gift from his good friend Henry Ford. Michigan Senator James Couzens—one of Ford Motor Company's original founders—got the first car delivered in Washington D.C. It carried serial number 35, the same as his original 1903 Model A, and was also a gift from Henry.

Officially publicized by the company as Model A "Purchaser Number One" was swashbuckling movie idol Douglas Fairbanks, who bought a sport coupe as a Christmas present for his equally famous wife, actress Mary Pickford. As arranged by Edsel, it was delivered on December 26 from a Beverly Hills dealer where it had been a demonstrator. "America's Sweetheart" thanked him by sending a photographed pose with the car, signing it "Mary Pick-a-Ford."

Henry concluded he had spent $100 million in bringing

out the Model A. But while dealers had taken orders for 727,000 of them at the beginning of 1928, deliveries still amounted to only a trickle, and it would take another full month for dealers to get even one of each model for display. "We probably gave back half our deposits eventually," said long-time dealer John Eagal. "People would wait five, six, or seven months and then buy something else. In fact, delivery took so long that we never did locate some of the buyers to give back their money!"

One of the main production hangups was controversy over the new single-system rod-operated brakes. Motor vehicle departments in several states had objected to the design, in which both the foot and emergency brakes worked off the same pressure. The first cars had the emergency brake lever to the left of the driver, but the ruckus over the safety issue got so loud that Henry ordered a redesign. By the end of January, some Ford plants had started building cars with the lever mounted in front of the gearshift and independent of the foot brakes. By the middle of the year, all Model A cars and Model AA trucks would have the modification.

As time dragged on, a confident Henry Ford urged dealers to be patient. "The new car is coming along fine," said a letter released in mid-February. "You can't get a great plant overhauled and converted from one type product to another in a day. It is easy to design a car. It is a tremendous task to get into shape to produce it right in every detail and great quantity."

But slowly, week by week, Model As finally began appearing on American roads, and it soon became quite fashionable to be seen in one. New York Governor Franklin D. Roosevelt bought a roadster for use at his Hyde Park estate. Actress Dolores Del Rio gadded about Hollywood in her chic sport coupe. Will Rogers and movie producers Cecil B. DeMille and Louis B. Mayer bought Tudors to run around in. Billie Dove, Wallace Beery, Lon Chaney, and Lillian Gish were other celebrities who couldn't resist the Model A craze.

Unlike the Model T, the Fords had decided to make more features, colors, and accessories available on the increasingly popular Model A. They also decided to build more passenger and commercial body styles as well. A new Fordor sedan was in full production by May, and nearly every month for the balance of the year saw other new models, culminating with the December 13 introduction of the elegant Town Car. Another of Edsel's creations, it featured a separate chauffeur's compartment, luxurious interior, and more formal styling, intended for well-heeled customers who liked to ride in style but didn't want to appear overly wealthy. Actress Joan Crawford preferred her Lincoln away from Hollywood, but bought one of the first of the spiffy Town Cars just to be one up on all the other Model As.

Lincoln's major mechanical change this year was a more powerful, 384.7-cubic-inch V-8, with bore increased ⅛-inch to 3.50 inches (stroke remained at 5.00 inches). Also new were higher, 4.8:1 compression, larger valves with conical springs, reshaped combustion chambers,

For 1928, Lincoln sported a more powerful 384.7-cubic-inch V-8 that was capable of providing a 90 mph top speed.

counterweighted crankshaft, and an engine oil filter. Chassis changes included a lighter rear axle and revised steering-tube bearings. For all that, several sources suggest no resultant change in brake horsepower, which obviously doesn't make sense. However, a contemporary *Used Car Red Book* listed the larger engine as developing 99 bhp, up from the previous 90. More important were its smoother high-speed running behavior and prodigious torque. If asked, this year's Model L would walk away from a dead stop in high gear with ease. And as George Dammann has written: "The new engine was capable of pushing the car along at an easy 90 mph [despite the fact that] the speedometer only read to 80 mph." This was impressive indeed for a car weighing over two tons and neither low nor particularly streamlined.

This year's most distinguished Lincoln was probably the massive, 4840-pound Locke tonneau-cowl sport phaeton. Priced at a relatively modest $4600, it carried four passengers—five with the rear seat armrest removed—in utter luxury. With its attractive price and smooth good looks, it accounted for 226 sales.

Less distinguished was Lincoln's total 1928 production of only 6362 units, a mere 15 percent of Cadillac's 36,600. Obviously, mechanical refinements would not be enough, and Edsel Ford now initiated work on a Model L replacement that he hoped to release in 1930.

1929

By the beginning of this year, all Ford assembly plants were working full steam—and were still behind the steamrolling demand for the Model A. A thousand boxcars a day moved in and out of both the Highland Park

The dapper 1929 Model A Sport Coupe could top 65 mph.

plant and the Rouge facility to supply the mammoth assembly system as production soared beyond 100,000 units monthly. In January alone the company built 159,786 units worldwide, setting a pace that would make this its biggest production year before 1949.

At the height of the Model A buying binge, in spring, rail shipments proved too slow, so Ford sent one of its freighters, the *Lake Benbow*, on an emergency rush with parts for the West Coast. Loaded at Chester, Pennsylvania, it sailed via the Panama Canal.

The 1929 models debuted with little fanfare, probably because they weren't outwardly much different from the '28s. What parts and sheetmetal had been modified dur-

ing the previous year were designed to fit the newer cars, so it was common to see late-1928s with 1929-model parts and early 1929s with leftover 1928 items. The most noticeable change to open cars (and the commercial truck/pickup) was the appearance of external door handles. There were many other subtle differences, but one sure way to tell them apart is the sportier trim and colors on the '29s.

The Model A cabriolet bowed at the New York Auto Show on January 16, and the millionth Model A was built on February 4. A closed-quarter Town Sedan and a wood-bodied station wagon were added to the line April 25. Ford was on a roll now. On July 24, less than 18 months after

This '29 Standard Roadster was Ford's price leader.

The closed-quarter Town Sedan had an elegant look to it.

A quail hood ornament graces this '29 Standard Roadster.

For summer fun, a 1929 Model A DeLuxe Phaeton.

Ford built more woody wagons than anyone else.

The workaday pickup gained a large following.

the first Model A was completed, the 2-millionth, a cabriolet, came off the line.

The world-shattering stock market crash that broke suddenly in October would dampen Ford sales somewhat. But Henry Ford saw a positive side to the economic chaos that followed: falling wages and materials costs created a good opportunity to expand operations. It was his philosophy that providing new construction jobs and lowering his prices were ways he could help ease the general slump. Thus, brand-new Ford assembly plants were opened in 1930 at Long Beach, California; Seattle, Washington; Buffalo, New York; and Edgewater, New Jersey.

Further efforts were made to modernize the aging Lin-

coln Model L this season. The radiator was completely reshaped, emerging taller, narrower, and with more vertical louvers, while chrome replaced nickel plating as bright trim. Side-mounted spare tires were now found on most models, so beltlines were more prominent, enabling lowness to be emphasized through paintwork and striping. A water temperature gauge joined the fuel gauge on the dash. Mechanical alterations were confined to higher operating oil pressure, a more powerful starter-generator, and rubber engine mounts for quieter running and lower vibrations. Production recovered slightly, ending the year at 7672 units, but was still far off the Cadillac and Packard pace at only about a fifth their volume.

This '29 roadster struts Lincoln's sleeker look.

Lincoln five-passenger convertible sedan for '29.

A two-passenger coupe, with body by Judkins.

Lincoln's four-passenger Town Sedan for 1929.

The three-window, four-passenger Town Sedan by Lincoln.

The 1929 Lincoln Aero-Phaeton, with body by LeBaron.

1930

Arriving the first week of January, this year's Model A attracted almost as much buyer attention as the debut 1928 edition, though the crowd was quieter and smaller, estimated at just over nine million. Rumors had been flying for some time that major changes were in store, and Ford watchers weren't disappointed. A higher, smoother hood-to-body line gave all models a more pleasing appearance via elimination of the prominent cowl stanchion (first adopted on the 1929 cabriolet), and a switch to smaller, 19-inch-diameter wheels and larger tires gave a more up-to-date stance. Also new was Ford's first use of stainless-steel brightwork, encompassing radiator shell, a new cowl finish strip, and headlamp, cowl lamp, and tail-lamp buckets and the doors. Rounding out the style updates were more generous fender shapes and roomier interiors. Colors and trim selections were again upgraded per established policy.

By this time, the Model A's reputation for taking hard knocks had become almost legendary—like the tales told about the banged-up 1930 roadster that faithfully carried champion rodeo rider Alice Sisty from show to show. Before awe-struck crowds, it served as the barrier over which she jumped her matched pair of horses in the daring "Auto Roman Standing Jump." The Model A was also becoming popular with the budding "hot rod" set on the dry lakes of California, where names like Riley, Winfield, and Cragar were pioneering some great new speed equipment, thus setting the stage for the next generation of backyard mechanics and weekend racers.

More testimony to the Model A's fortitude came in February from an almost humorous accident near Spokane, Washington. Two city officials were hurrying across frozen Fernan Lake in a 1929 coupe to greet Army aviators, who had just landed after completing a subarctic test

flight, when they suddenly hit a layer of thin ice. The passengers managed to bail out in time, but the poor Ford sank quickly to the bottom. Twelve days later, the ice had hardened enough that a crew could bring a tow truck to the spot, where a square was cut through the 14-inch-thick floe. The coupe was located with a grappling hook and hauled to the surface. After water was drained from body, crankcase and fuel tank, it was towed to the Ford garage in nearby Coeur d'Alene, Idaho, and given fresh oil, gasoline, and a new battery. The only mechanical work deemed necessary was cleaning spark plugs, fuel bowl, and distributor. The Model A dutifully fired up and was driven back to Spokane, a little soggy but good for many more miles.

Despite the economic downturn, this would be another banner year for Ford. In late summer, however, some serious holes began showing up in the once-predictable sales patterns. On August 16 it was announced that, because of strong demand, production at the Chicago plant would be increased by 5000 cars per month. Four days later, assembly was drastically cut back at Louisville, Kentucky, because sales in that region were off 33 percent. It was an early symptom of the faltering economy and a contracting car market.

But Ford had other problems. The main one was the competition, especially Chevrolet, which had not been idle during the Model A boom. Chevy engineers had been hard at work on a new six-cylinder engine throughout 1928, and it was available that Christmas in a smart line of cars priced only $100 above comparable Fords. The 1929 Chevys were just right for a market that wanted something a little different, backed by a strong advertising campaign intended to win four-cylinder (mainly Ford) buyers over to the "smoother smoothness of the six-cylinder car." Sales of America's second most popular make rocketed to over a million units in just eight months, and Chevy continued whittling away at Ford's lead this year.

Lincoln's Model L replacement was way overdue, but no one had counted on the Depression, which would blunt its expected sales surge. In fact, Ford's prestige make

The 1930 Model A DeLuxe coupe sold for $540.

The 1930 phaeton featured 19-inch wheels.

The Model A lent itself to special bodywork, as demonstrated by this rakish dual-cockpit phaeton.

wouldn't exceed 4000 units annually until 1936, and then only because of a very different, much cheaper Lincoln.

Meantime, the aging L was trimmed of several custom-body offerings for this, its final season, including the Willoughby landaulet and Holbrook cabriolet. The Brunn cabriolet remained, but saw a mere 44 copies. LeBaron, however, had a new convertible that sold 100 units, far more than the factory's old-fashioned club roadster (12) or Locke's version of same (15). The latter was this year's cheapest coachbuilt Lincoln at $4500. Of course, Ford was deliberately holding the line, so prices failed to top $7500 except on the most luxurious closed customs. Other

changes included adoption of worm-and-roller steering and color-matched fenders. It's important to note that not every buyer thought this "modern" look appropriate. A number of 1930 Model Ls were ordered with the traditional black fenders as God and Henry Leland no doubt intended.

Of this valedictory L, the British magazine *The Autocar* recorded: "It is indeed difficult to realise [sic] that Henry Ford, associated primarily with an entirely different type of vehicle, is behind the car. There have been considerable improvements in the bodywork [which is now] extremely smart in appearance but has simple, businesslike lines."

Another view of the 1930 phaeton pictured above.

It cost $4400 to buy a 1930 Lincoln Town Sedan.

The 1930 Lincoln seven-passenger limousine weighed in at 5190 pounds and sold for $4900; only 329 were built.

In another contemporary issue, the editors found a Model L "town carriage" about as fast as a 150-horsepower Isotta-Fraschini Super Sports.

So old though it was, the Model L went out in style. As historian Maurice D. Hendry affectionately observed, the Lincoln owner "knew he had a car that could outrun a Cadillac, a Packard, or a Pierce-Arrow . . . a car whose design required no major change (excepting front brakes) in a period that saw Cadillac, Packard, and Pierce forced to make numerous fundamental changes. His choice was more exclusive than Cadillac or Packard, more advanced than Pierce-Arrow, more secure an investment than a Peerless, more practical than a Duesenberg. The L's historical stature is simply stated, but of awe-inspiring significance: the legacy of Leland, the foundation of Lincoln."

1931

This year's Model A debuted amidst widening economic gloom and increased competition. Changes were confined to a redesigned radiator shell with painted indentation, a restyled instrument panel, and one-piece runningboard splash aprons. As usual with Ford model changeovers, any old parts that fit the new cars were bolted on until stock was used up, so it wasn't unusual for early '31s to have, say, the old two-piece splash aprons. In

March came a distinctive new cabriolet and Fordor/Town Sedan with a noticeably different roofline, the racy "slant-windshield" design first seen on the bustleback Victoria sedan of late 1930. It was brought through in production by moving the front roof header back a bit and

A 1930 Model A DeLuxe interior beckons.

As top of the line, the 1931 Model A convertible sedan listed at $640 and weighed 2360 pounds. Production was 5072.

leaning the windshield stanchions to meet it.

Another styling innovation appeared in June with the arrival of a new convertible sedan. This sporty, all-season five-passenger two-door also featured the slant windshield, as well as unique, fixed side window frames that left the full door and rear-quarter glass available for fending off the elements even with the canvas top lowered. The roof folded away neatly over the body, behind the back seat, covered by a tailored boot. Offered only in DeLuxe trim, the new model came with genuine leather up-

Third most popular '31 Model A was the DeLuxe Roadster with 56,702 built. It sold for $475.

Much sought after now is the 1931 "A" Victoria.

The '31 DeLuxe Roadster shown here with top up.

The '31 DeLuxe Town Sedan could be had for $630.

A milestone Model A, with Henry Ford at the helm.

holstery in a fancy dark tan.

This year's promotional highlight was the nationwide tour of the 20-millionth Ford, a Fordor sedan that rolled out the Rouge door on April 14. After an official send-off from Henry and Edsel Ford, it went to New York where Governor Franklin Roosevelt's wife, Eleanor, took it for a short spin. Then, accompanied by a flock of other new Fords, it headed west for whirlwind publicity stops at hundreds of welcoming dealers. Along the way, it paid a visit to Andy Gump comic strip creator Sidney Smith, received the checkered flag at the Indianapolis Motor Speedway, was inducted into the Sioux tribe, and became the first private car to descend to the bottom of Hoover Dam. It also passed through various state capitals, picking up specially minted "20,000,000" license plates and gubernatorial signatures in its logbook. Other notables signing in were World War I hero Sergeant Alvin C. York, explorer Admiral Richard E. Byrd, and husband-and-wife film stars Douglas Fairbanks and Mary Pickford. Fairbanks also drove the car in Los Angeles' 150th anniversary parade. On its return to Dearborn, the milestone Model A went on display in Henry Ford's new museum and was honored as the most widely traveled and photographed car in America.

But no amount of publicity could prop up Ford sales, which ended the year at just a third of the 1.5 million units retailed in 1929. Rumors abounded in the trade that Henry was working on a small V-8 to counter Chevrolet's six, some saying it would be put in a new car to replace the faltering Model A and named "Edison" in honor of his longtime friend.

On July 29, the day before his 68th birthday, Henry decided something had to be done. In the face of plunging sales he laid off 75,000 workers and closed 25 of his 36 U.S. assembly plants until the situation showed some kind of improvement. But privately, the wily auto baron had something up his sleeve. He knew it was all over for four-cylinder cars, and he was well along with the Model A's replacement.

This year brought the first new Lincoln since Henry Leland's 1920 original. Designated Model K (why they went alphabetically backwards is not known), it boasted a more powerful engine and a massive new chassis. In effect, this was Lincoln's bridge between the Twenties and Thirties. It also represented the thinking of a new generation of engineers.

When the Lelands left Lincoln shortly after the Ford takeover, their ingenious engine designer, Frank Johnson, left too—and ended up at Cadillac. But after chief engineer Thomas Little departed Dearborn in 1927, a desperate Edsel Ford again turned to Johnson, signing him to update Lincoln specifications. As a result, the Model K retained its predecessor's narrow-angle (60-degree) V-8, with the same displacement and bore/stroke dimensions. Also retained were the fork-and-blade connecting rods and cast-iron crankcase and three-piece block, traditional Leland-Lincoln touches that allowed adwriters to dwell lovingly on the new car's "precision-built" nature.

Where Johnson sought new horizons was the chassis, which was really planned for a V-12 due in 1932. A tremendous affair fully nine inches deep, it featured six crossmembers and cruciform bracing. Like the final version of the "L" chassis, the Ks employed torque-tube drive, floating rear axle, worm-and-roller steering, Houdaille hydraulic shock absorbers, and mechanical brakes, but wheelbase was up nine inches, to 145. A peaked radiator announced a much longer hood, punctuated by twin-trumpet horns and bowl-shaped headlamps. With the greater

wheelbase and reduced ride height of its new chassis, the K was thus noticeably longer, lower, and sleeker than the L—just what the sales force, and Edsel Ford, wanted. It also offered a superior ride and greater stability, while more power—now rated at 120 bhp—afforded faster acceleration and a higher top speed.

Naturally, the new line was replete with the work of Lincoln's familiar coachbuilders. Brunn built cabriolets and broughams, Dietrich sporty open cars and a handsome sedan, Judkins its berline, LeBaron its convertible, Willoughby its limousine and panel brougham. Standard bodies comprised five-seat coupe and sedan, seven-passenger sedan and limousine, two- and three-window Town Sedans, seven-place sport tourer, and phaetons with single and dual cowls. But whether custom- or factory-bodied, these Lincolns were the best-looking yet. Prices ranged from $4400 for the coupe or standard phaeton to around $7400 for the "basic" Brunn all-weather

Only 86 two-passenger coupes were built by Judkins on the 1931 Lincoln K chassis. They sold for $5200.

The 1931 Lincoln Model K Town Sedan sold for $4600. The seven-passenger sedan cost $300 more.

The LeBaron 2-4 passenger convertible roadster for 1931 saw production of 275 units. It listed at $4700.

brougham and Willoughby panel brougham.

Alas, production remained in the doldrums—no surprise, given the worsening economy—just 3556 units for the model/calendar year. Lincoln also built 47 miscellaneous specials and 61 standard chassis in 1931 as well as six long-wheelbase chassis, three at 150 inches and another three with 155 inches between wheel centers.

Only 77 copies of model 202A were built for '31.

The Model AA dump truck made for a faithful workhorse.

1932

In the summer of 1930, on returning from a trip to Germany, Henry Ford sent three of his most gifted experimental engineers to a small rustic building deep within his Greenfield Village showplace in Dearborn. He housed them in the replica of Thomas Edison's Ft. Myers, Florida laboratory, authentic right down to the old steam engine of the type the prolific inventor had used, with overhead shafts and belts. One of the men, 28 year-old engineer Emil Zoerlein, had been in on a number of Ford's pet projects.

"There are two more fellows working back there," Henry told Zoerlein. "What you work on and what you see back there I want you to keep to yourself and not say a word to anybody about it. We are designing a V-8 engine. What do you know about electricity?" "I think I know quite a lot about it," replied Zoerlein. "Then," said Ford, "I'd like to have you work on the ignition system for this engine—the generator and starter and so forth. You work along with those two boys back there."

Zoerlein found colleagues Carl Schultz and Ray Laird already at the drawing board, pondering rough sketches they'd made of Henry's suggested ideas for a small V-8 that could, in theory, be mass-produced. "Schultz had already made a layout . . . showing a box [distributor] in front with about the same position and shape as we finally developed," Zoerlein recalled in a 1972 interview. "I worked with him to get the basic configuration first of all. We designed a distributor with two pairs of breaking points and a four-lobe cam for an eight-cylinder engine.

Ford has long been known for its station wagons—this 1932 Model B, on a 106.5-inch wheelbase, shows why.

. . . It was the same principle as the Model K Lincoln . . . except for a new housing."

Looking to Lincoln was understandable, given Ford's growing experience with the make's large, precision-built V-8. But using a smaller version of that engine was scotched by high manufacturing costs. As a low-price car, the Ford was built in huge volume and had a simple four-cylinder engine cast and machined in one piece. One reason the big Lincoln sold for 10 times as much was the labor-intensive production methods dictated by its V-8's complexity. The block, for example, had to be cast and machined in pieces, and the whole engine was carefully bench-assembled.

Of course, the V-8 was nothing new in 1930. The French Antoinette had such an engine way back in 1900, and Rolls Royce had one running in 1905. But just as he'd tinkered with the X-8 for the Model T's intended replace-ment, Henry Ford again wanted something truly revolutionary. The most radical aspect of this new project would be to do what the experts said couldn't be done: produce a *low-cost* V-8 car.

Initially, Ford told no one what he was up to, not Charles Sorensen, his closest aide, nor even son Edsel. Instead, he casually directed his three engineers for nearly a year. While Zoerlein experimented with the new engine's electrical system, Schultz and Laird wrestled with the real puzzle: designing the complex V-8 block so that it could be cast in one piece.

Making life difficult for engineers was one of Henry's more peculiar habits, but it stemmed from a belief that overcoming obstacles often prompts new discoveries. This explains why his V-8 was devised under relatively primitive conditions when his fully equipped Engineering Laboratory sat just a few hundred yards away. Eventually,

Henry Ford's revolutionary V-8 bowed in 1932.

The V-8 emblem marks this '32 roadster a model 18.

The 1932 DeLuxe five-passenger V-8 phaeton sold for $545, $50 more than the equivalent four-cylinder Model B.

The V-8 convertible sedan: Ford's costliest 1932 model.

Ford's new V-8 also powered this '32 roadster.

the team was allowed to recruit Herman Reinhold, head of the pattern shop, with whose help they secretly built molds and then cast the first experimental block at the Rouge foundry. The result was deemed satisfactory, and by early 1931 it was machined and fitted for running at the Greenfield Village workshop.

"We didn't have any instruments in our Ft. Myers lab whatsoever," Zoerlein recalled. "We didn't even have an electric motor. . . .I asked Mr. Ford if we could set one up. At that time we only had direct current, which was supplied by a generator driven by a steam engine at one end of the shop. The steam engine also drove an overhead line shaft [that] provided power via belts to the various shop tools. Mr. Ford said he didn't want any electrical motors in this building even if direct current was available. He didn't give me any reason for that, and I didn't ask for it."

Because of the antiquated equipment they had to work

with, the team faced another problem: how to test their engine. Henry wouldn't allow any bolts or nails in the planking of his cherished Edison building, so the trio had to devise a wooden test stand. This they braced on the floor by running wood beams to the ceiling in such a way that it was forced to stay in position without nailing directly into either surface.

Then, the moment of truth. "We put a pulley on the back end of the engine and ran it up to the steam-powered transmission shaft to get it started by belt drive," Zoerlein remembered. "We were so busy getting [things] set up that it wasn't until the last moment . . . that we noticed that we lacked a carburetor. We sent one of the engineers running and he came back with one that we stuck on. . . .The engine started and the whole building shook. As it ran, it would drive the line shaft and the steam engine, to give it load, until the belt slipped off. We were

The V-8 DeLuxe roadster sold for $500 even.

At $600, the Victoria came only in DeLuxe form.

With 65 horses, this '32 roadster was unbeatable.

The DeLuxe three-window coupe weighed 2477 pounds.

very happy, because before starting the thing, we didn't know whether it would run forwards or backwards!"

While that experimental V-8 ran not only backwards at times but very rough, Henry was sufficiently pleased that he invited Edsel and production bosses Sorensen and Martin out for a look in June 1931. Also brought in was Lawrence Sheldrick, who had exhibited such talent in the Model A's development that he now headed the Ford Engineering Department. Edsel was easily convinced of the new engine's potential, but the others flatly declared that a 90-degree block with right-angle crank throws simply could not be cast in one piece at mass-production speeds—and that attempting to do so was a good way to go broke. Henry listened impatiently to their arguments, then groused: "Anything that can be drawn up can be cast!" With that, he ordered them to get the V-8 into production.

By early August, Henry was personally working full

bore on the project, just as he had to perfect the Model T and Model A. On through the fall, more people were brought to the task of engineering, casting, and testing the blocks. For every success there were a hundred failures, from core shifts to pinholes. Still, Ford was convinced he was on the right track. In fact, by the first week of December, he was so sure that he decided to stop producing the Model A to concentrate on a V-8-powered replacement.

Thus began a $300-million race to solve the casting problems so the new car could be introduced without undue delay. As one industry veteran said much later: "It was an awful gamble. There isn't a man in the business today who would—let alone could—make that bet."

A foundry worker recalled: "We were scared because of the rush." I worked night and day. We even forgot to go home, right through Christmas season. One day . . . we

Despite the tranquil scene depicted here, all Ford "Deuces" (1932 models) became an instant hit with hot rodders.

had exactly 100-percent scrap. Everything was wrong. Not one engine came out right. Just think of this: there were 54 separate cores in that mold—54 sand cores that had to stay put exactly right for the valve sections and cylinders and everything in that engine block."

As the Rouge shops raced to ready the new engine, Edsel and Joe Galamb teamed again to style a full line of open and closed bodies for it. Once more they took their cue from the imposing Model K Lincolns that so embodied Edsel's artistic taste. Their objective was a smaller-scale adaptation incorporating the same sculptured lines and fine detailing. Body design was coordinated with a new chassis being developed under Henry Ford's close supervision by engineers Eugene Farkas and Emery Nador. Also heavily involved were body suppliers Briggs, Murray, and Budd, who fine-tuned the approved stampings in anticipation of fat production contracts.

Farkas contributed the major chassis innovation, his design proving both novel and functional. It originated in an idea first sketched by Galamb, whereby the side rails functioned like traditional runningboard splash aprons. Farkas cleverly developed this so that the actual production rails were stamped out extra deep and with a long contour on their outer faces. With the body installed, they would provide a natural enamel finish between the underbody and runningboards. The methodical Hungarian also had the task of designing a conventional fuel tank, which was to be relocated from above the driver's knees, as in the Model A, to the rear. Ford gas tanks had been up front since 1926, a feature that had drawn a lot of criticism due to largely unproved allegations that it constituted a fire hazard. As with the frame, Farkas and Galamb designed

the tank so that it neatly formed the enameled sheetmetal to finish out the detail at the lower rear body.

But while all this was going on, Ford's great plants lay mostly idle. Their only serious activity by the end of 1931 was making replacement parts and assembling Model AA commercial vehicles, which continued to find a ready market. As this near sequel to the events of mid-1927 unfolded, the entire Ford organization edged closer to the brink of financial disaster. Its cash flow had all but dried up, its trained labor force had been largely laid off, and already hard-pressed dealers were either struggling to stay alive selling parts and used cars—or going broke. Compounding the losses from having no cars to sell was the new model's enormous tooling expense. "The cost was incredible," recalled a V-8 production man. "If it wasn't for Henry Ford's great personal wealth, the company could have gone broke in casting that engine."

Quickly realizing the gravity of the situation, Charlie Sorensen set aside his reservations about the new engine's casting complexities, rolled up his sleeves and pitched in. Armed with his knowledge of pattern making (as noted, his first job at Ford 27 years earlier), he barked orders, made changes, and drove his employees relentlessly. The last stubborn problems were soon solved, largely through his personal initiative, for which he soon became known far and wide as "Cast Iron Charlie."

Confident that he could now actually mass-produce and sell his low-price V-8 car, Henry began promoting it after months of rumor and speculation. As he told the press on February 11: "I have just got back my old determination to get the price of an automobile down to the mark where the public can buy it." Besides introducing the new V-8 line within weeks, he said his company would also offer a four-cylinder version to satisfy those who had written in, urging that a "Four" be continued. What he *didn't* say was that it was also a hedge in case the V-8 failed.

Full details came together on March 9, 1932, when the first V-8 model authorized for production was driven off the assembly line. By the 29th, every dealer had at least one car for display. Finally, on April 2, the public saw the wizard of Dearborn's latest mechanical marvel.

Though many Americans were out of work, nearly six million turned out for their first look at the long-awaited Ford V-8. It was a subdued crowd, but one nevertheless enchanted with the idea that they could now buy a Ford with twice the usual number of cylinders. From a distance, the '32 didn't seem all that different from the Model A, but closer inspection revealed it to be all-new from radiator cap to taillight. Edsel and all who'd helped him could rightfully feel proud, for this was far and away the best-looking Ford yet—an opinion soon confirmed by the nation's youth, who would covet the '32s for hot rodding above all other cars.

No wonder. Here was the first Ford that could boast both performance and beauty. As an impressed newsman wrote after the San Francisco preview: "In the new Ford car the eye is caught by the bright beauty of the rustless-steel headlamps, and travels along the bead on the side of the hood toward the rear of the car [that gives] the impression of an arrow in flight. The bodies are fresh and modern, from the gracefully rounded V-type radiator to the rear bumper. The convex lamps, full-crowned fenders and long, low running boards harmonize with the balance of the design."

For a Ford, the interior was almost as revolutionary as the exterior. While the light switch remained at the horn button, as on the Model A, the key and ignition switch were sensibly combined in a single anti-theft unit at the steering column bracket. With the ignition toggle "Off" and the key removed, the steering gear locked the front wheels for parking. It was a wonderful idea (still in use today), though it took getting used to. The uninitiated were forever removing the key before stopping, thus running into all sorts of locked-up trouble—sometimes literally. Instruments, including an 80-mph speedometer, were grouped in a handsome, engine-turned oval trimmed with a stainless bead strip and mounted in a mahogany-color panel. Sunvisors were hinged to move out of the way, while the top-hinged windshield opened out on a pair of adjustable swing arms. Following now-customary Ford practice, fine wool, mohair, and leather upholstery were offered. Also per tradition, fenders on all models were dipped in black enamel, while bodies came in a fair choice of colors, with contrasting reveals and pinstriping. Models numbered no fewer than 14, arrayed in Standard and DeLuxe series at prices from $460 to $650.

Under the hood sat the ingenious flathead V-8. Its twin four-cylinder banks were cast together with the crankcase and flywheel housing, which allowed a short, powerful crankshaft. As a result, the 65-horsepower, 221-cubic-inch engine took up about the same space as the old four had in the Model A. Up front was a single belt, adjusted by turning a nut (1932 only) on the generator post mount, driving a pair of water pumps and a combination generator/fan off the crank pulley. The aluminum intake manifold was topped by a Detroit Lubricator carburetor, and a fuel pump that worked by way of a pushrod operating off the camshaft. Engine pans were initially made of cast aluminum, later stamped steel.

This compact powerplant was mounted on rubber in a double-drop frame of all-new design. Suspension was by Ford's familiar, twin transverse leaf springs, but the rear one was now behind the differential, which helped lower frame height by nearly two inches from the Model A's. That and the smaller new 18-inch-diameter wire wheels gave the V-8 chassis better handling, the car a smarter road-hugging appearance. The front axle was "stabilized" via a radius-rod wishbone, a Ford feature since the Model T. A system of rods and levers operated the four-wheel mechanical brakes. Shock absorbers were by Houdaille. At the rear, the gas tank neatly formed the underbody finish. Above was the spare tire mount, which also served as a frame member. The transmission was a three-speed with synchronized second and high.

A thoughtful-looking Edsel Ford in the Thirties.

Catering to "four-banger" believers was an improved version of the Model A engine. There were sound business reasons for it. One was the persistent—and as-yet unpublicized—problem of casting perfect V-8 blocks. Another was the high number of buyers who needed a lot of convincing that an eight could be as cheap to run as a four. Of course, the four-cylinder cars were assembled on the same line as the V-8s, since they shared bodies and basic running gear. Their only noticeable difference was lack of V-8 emblems on headlamp bar and hubcaps, the latter bearing "Ford" script instead. For parts identification purposes, the 1932 V-8s were designated Model 18 and the fours Model B, but the latter somehow prevailed for the entire line, and the first V-8s are still erroneously termed Model B to this day.

Nicely tooled and beautiful though it was, Ford's fast new V-8 proved terribly tough to sell. Aside from arriving near the very depths of the Depression, when consumer dollars were scarce and competition from other makes doubly fierce, it had an unproven engine about which buyers were either wary, uninformed, or both. Typical of the reactions were "Twice the cylinders take twice the gas!" and "Cylinders layin' on a slant like that will wear out on the down side!" Rural folk were among the most skeptical, brushing off the V-8 as a passing fad that could never replace the trusty four.

Some doubters weren't far off the mark. Within days of taking to America's roads, the V-8s began earning a reputation as oil guzzlers. Then it was discovered that oil in the pan would surge away from the crankshaft bearings in hard turns, causing engine seizure. Worse yet, pinholes were found in many of the early blocks, prompting a widespread dealer recall for engine replacements.

All this naturally worried Henry Ford, so while his engineers hurried to correct problems, he directed his outlying branches to begin sponsoring reliability events in an effort to counter the mounting bad publicity. The most widely reported was staged this summer in California's Mojave Desert, where veteran racer Eddie Pullen, driving a stock Ford V-8 Victoria over a 32-mile course, logged 33,301 miles in 33 days without engine failure—and averaged 20 miles per gallon.

"After the first run of orders, we had some very difficult selling of the V-8," recalled long-time Stockton, California Ford dealer John Eagal. "With the excessive oil consumption on the early deliveries, it was a hard thing to explain to customers . . . and hurt the V-8 cars more than anything else. It was during this period also that Ford lost the [sales] lead to Chevrolet. With the engineering problems, production lagged behind. . . . The dealers couldn't get cars and the salesmen became discouraged. Chevrolet simply out-produced Ford."

Thus, what should have been a great new-car launch was just a mediocre one. Even lending a fleet of V-8s as official cars for the Indianapolis 500 failed to generate much response. With sales sluggish and dealers going broke in droves as business conditions worsened, word finally came down from Dearborn: get the V-8 into the public's hands—fast.

To accomplish that, dealers began staging "Ford Open Air Salons" this summer, carnival-style shows that attempted to generate buyer interest via demonstration rides, movies about Ford assembly, lectures on the V-8's finer points, and similar activities. As an example, the Marysville, California event was held at a lighted peewee golf course so customers could come in after dark. Besides

For 1932, Ford Tudor sedans and coupes outsold the Fordor sedans, of which only 36,649 were built.

Lincoln's glory days arrived in 1932 with the debut of the Model KB V-12, here a Dietrich Convertible Sedan.

a selection of new models for prospects to try, the local dealer brought in Eddie Pullen's Victoria, fresh from its Mojave run. The 1932 Michigan State Fair was chosen for the company's own "Open Air" exhibit. Alongside a modest cluster of tents shading a display of new cars and trucks was a graded and fenced half-mile oval track so visitors could sample the "smooth" V-8. By fair's end, 63,000 visitors had taken test rides.

But the nation's economy was still plummeting, and no amount of stimulation seemed to reverse the industry-wide sales slump. Toward the end of the year, the V-8 managed to regain some of its lost momentum and was outselling the four-cylinder Ford by nearly nine to one. Nevertheless, most of the firm's assembly plants were down to a four-day week by the first of August, operating at just a fraction of total capacity.

Then, on November 7, 1932, the company issued a terse statement with some somber news: "As the situation has stood, we have been operating plants two or three days a week, getting out from 50 to 100 cars a day at each plant. This is neither good from a manufacturing point of view, nor does it provide workers with a liveable wage. We are, therefore, for the time being, concentrating our production at points where shipping factors are more advantageous."

In other words, Ford was gearing down. Over the next two months it closed all but six of the 30 plants that had been operating that summer. Production now stood at its lowest point since 1914, presenting Henry with another in what would become a series of yearly challenges to stimulate the market.

At the other end of the spectrum, Lincoln offered two distinctly different series for the first time. The previous

Model K became this year's Model KA, riding the old, 136-inch wheelbase and powered by the familiar 385-cid V-8, albeit with a rated 125 bhp, up five. But though dimensionally the same as the old "L," the KA chassis was structurally equal to that of the new KB. Body offerings were trimmed, furnishings simplified, and prices cut to as little as $2900. Nevertheless, the KA was a full-fledged luxury car, not a middleweight, Lincoln's bid for the eight-cylinder Packard/Cadillac segment, which was hardly the low-rent district. Still, its V-8 wasn't as smooth as rival engines or Pierce-Arrow's, and only 2132 KAs were built for the model/calendar year.

Designated Model KB, the new senior series was Dearborn's reply to the multi-cylinder juggernauts of Marmon and, again, Cadillac and Packard. Riding the long, 145-inch chassis and packing the planned V-12 designed by

Note the door: a "Double-Entry" Sport Sedan by Brunn.

Frank Johnson at Edsel Ford's direction, it offered better performance than the KA yet actually cost *less* and offered a wider choice of bodies. Equally capable of being a magnificent, around-town car or fast, open-road tourer, it was an extraordinary machine, far above the typical car of its day, with performance as impressive as its appearance.

Displacing 448 cubic inches on decidedly undersquare bore/stroke dimensions (3.25 × 4.50 inches), the KB powerplant delivered 150 horsepower at 3400 rpm with 5.2:1 compression and a large dual-downdraft Stromberg carburetor. The crankshaft ran in seven main bearings, unique for V-12s at the time. Valves were enormous, measuring no less than two inches across the heads. Roger Huntington described this as "a massive, rugged engine with unusual breathing potential. . . .But maybe there was *too much* breathing potential. You have to maintain

high gas velocities through carburetor venturis, ports, and valves to get good throttle response and high torque at low speeds. This means *smaller* carbs and valves. Big sizes help you only at high speeds. So, when Ford engineers were told to take some cost out of the twelve for 1933, they looked at the entire performance picture with an eye to making the engine smoother and more flexible as well as less expensive." The result would be a smaller and more efficient V-12.

As was now expected of Lincoln, the debut KB body menu encompassed the cream of early-Thirties coachbuilders. Murphy, the great California house, contributed what many thought were the most impressive: a four-passenger dual-cowl sport phaeton and a dashing two-seat sport roadster. Each sold for about $4500 complete, remarkably low for a period custom, though traditional builders like Brunn and Willoughby continued to offer

This 1932 KB dual-cowl phaeton weighed 5600 pounds.

Even in the Depression, the Lincoln V-12 coupe sold for $4400.

Edsel Ford sits at the wheel of this Lincoln KB sport roadster, of which Murphy built only three in 1932.

Dietrich bodied 17 coupes for Lincoln in 1932.

Ford's V-8 DeLuxe Roadster had 75 bhp for 1933.

formal closed models priced well over $7000.

Of course, this was hardly a good time for multi-cylinder giants from any make. Most of their former clientele had been decimated by the Depression. Of the few who still had money to buy, most opted for something much less extravagant. Thus, the KB saw only 1515 units, while Lincoln's total volume barely topped 3600.

And things were going to get a lot worse.

1933

For Henry Ford, changing models every year was "the curse of the industry." In the summer of 1932 he was barely beyond the ordeal of his multi-million-dollar V-8 launch when he had to start revamping the design for 1933. Badgered by bad news from all sides and falling further behind Chevrolet in the sales race, he realized at last that if he couldn't sell his V-8s on performance alone, he'd have to try a combination of speed and sporty good looks.

Ever the motor and chassis man, Henry worked on improving the V-8's running gear while his quietly artistic son Edsel and stylist Joe Galamb rushed to create a new look. This time, though, they'd get invaluable assistance from body suppliers Briggs, Murray, and Budd, which were accomplished enough by now to provide clients like Ford with ideas and mockups expressing the latest, most fashionable styling.

Though cars were becoming more streamlined on the drawing boards, there was still no technology to produce them. Thus, the design Edsel approved for 1933 wasn't the teardrop shape it might have been. But it *was* more graceful, with the sort of racy, low-slung lines characteristic of the early and mid-1930s, the remarkable era that pro-

duced some of America's all-time classic automobiles.

Thanks to a strike at Briggs, plus the usual problems associated with getting out a second new design in as many years, Ford's 1933 line, designated Model 40, didn't bow publicly until February 9, about three months behind the rest of the industry. But it was beautifully executed, as one journalist summarized: ". . . With much roomier bodies, [this year's Ford V-8 has] entirely new and decidedly attractive appearance. . . .Its beauty is enhanced by the rakish angle of the radiator grille which coincides with those of the windshield, hood, and door lines. Fenders are of modern design, with wide skirts, and their construction eliminates the need for the old splash aprons below the radiator and above the running boards. Wire spoke wheels have been reduced to 17-inch in [diameter], and [full-width] bumpers front and rear are styled with a painted horizontal stripe and a slight dip in the center." Not mentioned here was the new 112-inch wheelbase, longest in Ford history.

With most of its block problems ironed out by now, the V-8 was treated to several changes that boosted horsepower to 75, up 10. Included were aluminum cylinder heads, higher compression, and improved cooling and ignition.

The '33 Ford Victoria V-8 sold for $595.

More surprising was a stiffer new X-type frame, still with transverse springing. Aided by axles stabilized with radius rods, it afforded great flexibility over rough roads and an exceptionally soft ride. Once again, buyers could opt for less expensive, four-cylinder alternatives, now designated Model C. Like their 1932 counterparts, they were easily identified by the lack of V-8 emblems on hubcaps.

In all, the '33 Fords were brilliant. Unfortunately, they never achieved the success they deserved, thanks to the late introduction and lack of any real price advantage or publicity buildup. Together with Ford's long-standing policy that prohibited his dealers—now 9000 strong—from using high-pressure sales tactics like most rivals, these factors enabled high-rolling Chevy to lead the low-price field by another commanding margin—and Plymouth to move up a notch to third. Even so, Ford's calendar year sales ended some 100,000 units ahead of 1932.

The Model 40s took to the road amidst signs that the V-8 was catching on at last, especially among the nation's leadfoots. Dirt track and speedboat racers were among the first to discover that, with only a few simple modifications, a Ford V-8 could outperform most everything else its size and weight. In fact, its success on amateur and professional racing circuits from the Detroit River to Pikes Peak would set off a flathead speed craze that continues to this day. Stock-car drivers in particular had found that by stripping the runningboards, fenders, and top from a regular V-8 roadster, and making a few chassis adjustments, they could beat just about anything on the dirt tracks. At this year's running of the nationally famous Elgin (Illinois) Road Race in August, stunned onlookers watched as seven stripped Fords took the first seven places against a highly touted pack of Chevrolets, Plymouths, and Dodges. The winner, in a '33 roadster, was

Beautiful then and now: the '33 Ford DeLuxe roadster.

Ford churned out 220,225 Fordor sedans for 1933-34.

The '33 Fords rode a longer 112-inch wheelbase, V-8 horsepower increased to 75, and the styling was new.

1932 Indy 500 champion Fred Frame, who led the field over the tricky 8.5-mile course for 203 miles at an average 88.22 mph. It proved a tremendous tonic for Ford sales. Two months later, Henry Ford invited his suppliers to Detroit for a special Exposition of Progress, and Frame's car was the featured attraction.

Encouraged by this happier turn of events, Henry began directing Model 40 refinements for the coming year. At the same time, he started planning a major presence for his company at the Century of Progress world's fair in Chicago, and began stepping up advertising and promotion.

Lincoln also came in for a dramatic style change this year. Radiators were smartly raked, with chrome grilles covering the vertical shutters and, at the bottom, newly concealed horns. Louvers replaced vents on the hoodsides, fenders were skirted, and front bumpers slightly vee'd. As

in 1932, the main visual distinction between the two series was the color of their enameled radiator badges: red on KA, blue on KB. The latter, though, still offered the usual custom bodies—actually more semi-custom by now—from all the customary coachbuilders save Murphy.

There was less distinction under the hood, as the KA abandoned its V-8 for a smaller-bore (3.00-inch), 381.7-cubic-inch version of the KB V-12. However, it boasted improved fuel economy, plus greater flexibility thanks to smaller ports, carburetor throttle passages, and valves (reduced from the KB's two-inch diameter to 1.0625 inches). It thus stands as one of Lincoln's more elegantly engineered powerplants. Though it produced the same gross horsepower as the old V-8, a rated 125 bhp, it delivered more torque at low and medium crank speeds than the KB unit, a classic case of *smaller* valves, ports, and carb bores actually improving overall performance. As

Every leadfoot in America loved the V-8, as evidenced by these race-ready, fenderless 1933 Fords.

Fords, light in weight, also competed in economy runs.

The 1933 Ford V-8 station wagon sold for $640.

For 1933, all Lincolns were powered by a V-12: 125 horsepower on the KA series, 150 on the larger KBs.

Roger Huntington concluded: "When you can simplify and cut cost in a design at the same time . . . that's good engineering."

Aside from a slight bore increase for '34, this V-12 would remain in production as standard big-Lincoln power right on through 1940. And in all that time it would see only one other significant change: the adoption of hydraulic valve lifters for 1937. Most reviewers have given it the highest marks as Lincoln's best prewar combination of precision manufacturing, cost-effectiveness, and efficiency.

Otherwise, this year's Lincoln line was basically a 1932 rerun. The KB's 448-cid engine was unchanged, as were chassis assignments and running gear specifications for both series. Five special chassis were built this year, including a one-off with a lengthy 155 inches between wheel centers. Lincoln also built another small batch of so-called "miscellaneous special" cars, 19 in all.

With the Depression now bottoming out, Lincoln production was almost too meager for industry statisticians to record. The total 1703 units was the lowest since the make's first year in business, and just barely enough to beat faltering Franklin. In industry rank, Lincoln stood 25th.

Of course, most rivals were in similar straits. Cadillac's tally was only 3173 units, Pierce's just 2298. Packard, mainly on the strength of its small Eight, was slightly healthier at 4803 units. Still, the picture was pretty grim for Ford's flagship. Most of this year's sporting KB custom bodies saw no more than eight or nine copies each. The highest-volume customs were the Brunn cabriolet at 105 units and the factory's own limousine at 110.

The rear door opening was enlarged for this Ford taxi.

Judkins bodied this '33 Lincoln KB two-window berline.

1934

On December 6, 1933, Henry and Edsel hosted reporters at the best publicized event of its type since the onset of the Depression: a Dearborn preview of the nicely updated 1934 Fords, designated Model 40A. Held a month earlier than other automakers' press shows, it was praised almost as much for the cars as for the fact that this was the first time Henry had ever served an alcoholic beverage at a company function. And as the beer and cigarettes were passed around, the scribes seemed enthusiastic indeed.

This was reflected in the flattering reviews that soon followed. Said *Automotive Industries:* "Changes in the appearance of the attractive car include new hood, radiator and grille lines, a new instrument panel, and luxurious new upholstery treatment. The curve in the grille has been eliminated, and there is a new ornament surrounding the radiator cap. Hubcaps and the spare tire-lock cover are also new, as is the V-8 insignia on the grille. The fashionable bodies have the new 'clear vision' ventilating system similar to that in the new Lincoln cars." The last referred to a redesigned window-winding mechanism that first moved the front door glass rearwards to a "vent" position before lowering it vertically. Because it required a design change to the door window frame, this year's closed bodies differ slightly from 1933's in that respect.

The most noticeable interior change for '34 was deletion of the engine-turned instrument panel insert in favor of a plain painted dash of similar layout. New accessories for 1933 had included either a glove compartment-type or ashtray-mounted radio, dual wipers, and heater. To these was now added a beautifully cast radiator cap in the image of a running greyhound much like Lincoln's mascot. And for the first time in Ford history, body-color fenders were available at no charge.

On the mechanical side, the V-8's Detroit Lubricator carburetor was replaced by a better-engineered Stromberg dual-downdraft instrument that boosted horsepower to 85, a gain of 10 bhp. Other engineering changes were minor fit and wear improvements to existing hardware, but one item was missing: the four-cylinder engine. With growing public acceptance and the worst of its reliability problems long since solved, the versatile 221-cubic-inch flathead V-8 would be Ford's mainstay through 1940, though not its sole powerplant.

With all the good press and the company's renewed interest in promotion, sales began taking off once people had a chance to drive the '34s. Among the new model's earliest champions were police officials who used its explosive speed to chase crooks—and the crooks who stole new Fords to outrun them. Infamous bank robber Clyde Barrow was one unabashed admirer who took time from his criminal pursuits to praise V-8 virtues by writing to a surprised Henry Ford. Postmarked Tulsa, Oklahoma, and dated April 10, 1934, his letter read:

Dear Sir:

While I still have got breath in my lungs I will tell you what a dandy car you make. I have drove [*sic*] Fords exclusively when I could get away with one. For sustained speed and freedom from trouble the Ford has got ever [*sic*] other car skinned, and even if my business hasn't [*sic*] been strictly legal it don't hurt anything [*sic*] to tell you what a fine car you got in the Ford V-8.

Yours truly,
Clyde Champion Barrow

As fate would have it, Clyde and his wife Bonnie would meet their maker in a 1934 Ford sedan, gunned down in a sheriff's ambush.

May 26 saw the opening of Ford's exhibit at the Century of Progress in Chicago, the firm's most ambitious undertaking of this kind. Sprawled over an 11-acre landscaped site fronting Lake Michigan, it was dominated by the magnificent gear-shaped Rotunda building. Along the lakeshore ran a 0.4-mile "Roads of the World" where visitors could ride over short reproduction stretches of historic world thoroughfares. Inside the Rotunda and an adjoin-

This 1934 Ford DeLuxe Fordor could be had for $615.

Note the heavier grille surround on the '34 Ford.

Top-down fun with V-8 go: the $525 DeLuxe Roadster.

After hitting rock bottom in 1933, most automakers began to see a recovery this year, including Lincoln and Ford. The latter improved from about 335,000 units to nearly 564,000 in model/calendar year volume to regain first place, besting archrival Chevrolet by about 12,000 cars. With a total of 2431 units, Lincoln's gain was modest to be sure, but it must have convinced Edsel Ford that the worst was over.

One reason Lincoln gained at all was this year's engine rationalization, where one of two different V-12s was picked to carry on as the make's sole powerplant—and the more elegant one at that. We refer, of course, to Frank Johnson's remarkable KA V-12 of 1933, which now came in for a 1/8-inch bore increase, to 3.13 inches, for total displacement of 414 cubic inches, plus aluminum cylinder heads with higher, 6.38:1 compression to take advantage of the new 70-octane Ethyl gasoline. The result was brilliant: 34 fewer cubic inches but the same 150 brake horsepower as the older, thirstier KB unit, plus equal rigidity and smoothness despite three fewer main bearings. All this was dictated mainly by production economics in an era of hard times and slow sales, but it was a happy development nonetheless, with all the power and smooth flexibility that any luxury-car buyer could want.

Otherwise, this was a year of minor advances and some retrenchment for Lincoln. The KA and KB series continued on their respective wheelbases of 136 and 145 inches. Chassis construction remained essentially the same aside from an extra crossmember on the KB. Styling changes were strictly evolutionary, but attractive. Radiator shells were now painted body color, and shutters returned to replace louvers on the hoodsides. Smaller headlamps arrived with a new "asymmetric" beam arrangement (the

ing industrial wing was a dazzling display of Ford's latest automaking technology, plus supplier exhibits, live demonstrations of parts manufacturing, and displays of antique models and the newest Ford cars and trucks. As a centerpiece, three fully equipped V-8 Victorias were hung as on a chandelier from one 17-inch-diameter wheel, to show the strength of its welded steel spokes.

It was Ford's greatest show ever, and few would forget the sights and sounds, the free souvenirs, and the beauty of the cars. The 1934 models seemed to have just the right blend of ingredients, something that would assure their place in the hearts of car fans everywhere as among the classiest Fords of all time.

With Franklin Roosevelt now firmly in charge at the White House, it began to seem as if "happy days" might be here again after all—or at least just around the corner.

The 145-inch wheelbase Lincoln KB seven-passenger limousine for 1934, by Judkins, cost $5700. Only 27 were built.

1935

A convertible sedan by Dietrich cost $5600 in 1934.

The convertible Victoria by Brunn also went for $5600.

A dwindling number of automakers fought for a dwindling number of sales in the mid-'30s, and cars had to be updated each year if a company hoped to survive the fiercest competition ever. Ford was no exception. Besides, the annual model change was becoming recognized as an effective way to boost sales, as General Motors already knew. Ford had inaugurated a two-year design cycle in 1933 that it would maintain for the rest of the decade. Thus, this year's line received a revised frame and newly styled bodyshells, enough to justify a new series designation: Model 48.

"Greater Beauty, Greater Comfort, and Greater Safety" was the theme for '35. Styling was more rounded, with longer and wider bodies, more steeply raked windshields, narrower radiators, and smaller, 16-inch-diameter wheels. The result was sleeker and more obviously streamlined, though not nearly so radical as the Chrysler/DeSoto Airflow, launched the previous year and destined to remain a sales disaster.

Engineering refinements included a beefed-up frame and rear axle, better mechanical brakes, nicer steering, and new "easy-action" clutch. The 221-cubic-inch flathead V-8 remained at 85 bhp, as it would through 1940, but got a new camshaft and improved crankcase ventilation. Springing was still via single semi-elliptic leafs mounted transversely at each end, an archaic arrangement that would persist at Dearborn for the next 13 years. This and the use of mechanical brakes were two areas in which Ford was glaringly behind the times, but old Henry refused to believe that *any* of his ideas were outdated.

This year brought a significant body change not strictly prompted by styling: built-in trunks on Tudor and Fordor sedans. The '34 Victoria two-door had been a step in this direction, though its trunk didn't have much space, and was awkward to reach because the bottom-hinged lid

left unit could be dipped but not the right), and metal spare tire covers provided a more streamlined appearance. Sedans and limousines gained sloping tails, fairly radical for the mid-Thirties luxury class. Like Pierce, Packard, and Stutz, however, Lincoln was reluctant to abandon the graceful "oh gee" fender sweep so characteristic of the Classic era, and would retain it through 1935.

Retrenchment was evident in this year's markedly reduced number of KB custom bodies. Brunn returned with its usual four offerings and Judkins with its previous three, but Dietrich, Willoughby, and LeBaron were down to just one apiece: respectively, convertible sedan (25 built), limo (77 built), and convertible roadster (45 built). Factory coachwork now accounted for the bulk of KB production, no surprise all things considered. This mainly comprised long sedans and limousines plus a score of seven-passenger touring cars, the last body style fast-vanishing throughout the industry.

Predictably, the cheaper KA continued to outsell the posh KB, this year by a margin of some two to one. Choices were thinned here too, though not as much, with nine open and closed factory styles ranging from a $3200 coupe to a $3900 convertible sedan. This would be the last year for separate chassis designations. Though the '35 Lincolns would still span two different wheelbases, all would be called Model K, and custom coachwork would be offered on the shorter platform for the first time.

Ford built 31,513 DeLuxe three-window coupes for 1935.

Some '35 Fordor sedans carried a built-in trunk.

The '35 coupe weighed in at 2647 pounds.

Ford built 4234 convertible sedans for 1935.

Compare this DeLuxe Phaeton with the car at the left.

didn't tilt open very far. This year's trunk was more useful, and added a mere $20 to the cost of the standard fastback sedans. The "trunkback" style, as it was first called, would soon prove enormously popular, not just at Ford but throughout the industry.

Ford's 1935 lineup was broadly the same as in recent years, but the Victoria departed, likely due to the new trunkback option. A newcomer, and the year's most expensive offering at $750, was the smart convertible sedan. Unlike its Model A predecessor, it had four doors instead of two, removeable centerposts, and no permanent side window frames. Still around were the glamorous DeLuxe Phaeton at $580, the rumble-seat Convertible Cabriolet at $625, and the youthful DeLuxe Roadster at $550. All open models now sported front-hinged doors, a definite safety plus, but sedan rear doors remained the rear-hinged "suicide" type.

According to Paul R. Woudenberg, author of *Ford in the Thirties*, this year's styling was largely the work of Phil Wright at bodymaker Briggs Manufacturing Company. "There were two styling sections at the firm," notes Woudenberg, "one headed by John Tjaarda being charged with experimental car-design exercises, while the [second] group did speculative designs for Briggs' regular customers, notably Ford and Plymouth. Phil Wright reportedly did the renderings for the 1935 Ford at his home, then showed them to his boss, Ralph Roberts, who in turn

showed them to Ford management including Edsel Ford. Ford officials were so pleased that the order went out to go right to a full-scale mockup of wood, rather than through the customary $1/24$ clay scale models. Famed stylist Bob Koto, a compatriot of Wright . . . was later assigned to facelift the '35s into the following year's 1936 Model 68."

Woudenberg also observes that by the end of the 1935 selling season, "Ford had decisively regained industry leadership in sales with 826,519 [units] compared to Chevrolet's 656,698 and Plymouth's 382,925." While the new styling surely played a part in this, so did a redesigned chassis. Responding to GM's new "Knee Action" independent front suspension, engineer Lawrence Sheldrick cleverly managed to relocate Ford's front transverse spring from behind the axle to in front of it. This permitted the engine to be shoved forward some 8.5 inches for extra interior space. More significantly, it allowed a longer spring, and prompted softer springs front and rear. The result for all passengers was what Ford termed the "Front Seat Ride." Compared to the Model 40 frame, the 1935 design "was much stronger, using more box sections and heavier bracing throughout," according to Woudenberg. "The car felt more solid, and the chassis racking, noticeable on Model 40 when negotiating sharp road angles, was gone."

The '35 Fords were introduced at the prestigious New York Auto Show in late December 1934. It had been 25 years since Ford had exhibited at that annual affair, and the company went all out to garner attention. Besides a bevy of sparkling cars, it had special "motion" exhibits on all three levels of the hall. Drawing throngs of admirers, they included a motorized "exploded" V-8 engine and chassis, and an engine assembly race against the clock by two workers from the big Rouge plant.

Ford also starred this year at Indianapolis, a sporty Convertible Sedan acting as pace car for the annual 500-mile racing classic. But the big event was the California-Pacific International Exposition in San Diego, where the company put on a huge show in a special building.

The 1935 models marked the end of several long-standing Ford features: standard wire-spoke wheels, external horns, and outside radiator cap. One item moved inside, though: the parking lamps, now housed within the headlamps.

And there was a first this year as Ford began manufacturing its own sub-assemblies for station wagon bodies. Previously, the Mingel Company of Kentucky had supplied the wood panelling, with Briggs or Murray in Detroit handling assembly. Hereafter, wagon panels would be fabricated in a plant at Iron Mountain on Michigan's upper peninsula, an ideal location because Ford owned nearby hardwood forest acreage that minimized transportation costs. Final assembly took place at the company's own branch assembly plants.

Lincoln was putting the final touches on its hoped-for salvation, the radical new unit-construction Zephyr, which would arrive in November as a "junior edition" priced thousands of dollars less than any previous Lincoln. Considered a 1936 model, it's covered under that heading.

Elegant: the 1935 Lincoln convertible sedan by Brunn.

Meanwhile, there was nothing to do but soldier on with warmed-over versions of the existing KA/KB cars, newly consolidated into a single line reviving the Model K designation of 1931. As before, there were 136- and 145-inch-wheelbase chassis. Total offerings continued to dwindle, but custom coachwork was now available on the shorter platform for the first time. These comprised a five-passenger convertible victoria by Brunn and three LeBaron styles—rumble-seat convertible roadster, five-passenger convertible sedan phaeton, and two-place coupe. All were pleasing combinations of fine styling and brisk performance, but production was slight: just 15 Brunns and only 73 of the LeBarons.

This year's factory coachwork consisted of two- and three-window four-door sedans and a five-passenger coupe on the short chassis, and the usual seven-passenger touring, sedan, and limousine on the extended platform. The Dietrich name now disappeared from the list of avail-

Judkins built only 13 three-window berlines on the 145-inch wheelbase Lincoln Model K chassis in 1935.

The Judkins two-window berline sold better: 34 units.

able long-chassis custom styles, and production of the survivors continued to decline. The LeBaron convertible sedan, for example, saw but 20 copies, and Brunn's two five-passenger cabriolets saw only 13 each. Curiously, Lincoln's output of "miscellaneous specials" on both chassis was up from 22 to 31, while rolling-chassis production fell from 33 units to nine.

Technical changes were few. The splendid 414 V-12 got a new camshaft for even smoother running, and a revised exhaust system aimed at improved performance, though engine output stayed the same. Also new were automatic spark control and needle-roller clutch bearings. Styling was again evolutionary, but bodies were moved forward 4.5 to nine inches in the interest of better weight distribution and a smoother ride.

After 1934's slight upturn, Lincoln's total 1935 model year volume of just 1434 units was a real disappointment—worse than even the dismal '33 figure. Short-wheelbase sedans and long-chassis sedans and limos accounted for most of this meager output. But the winds of change were blowing: the Zephyr was about to breeze in, a technical breath of fresh air that would lift Lincoln's fortunes like a hot-air balloon.

1936

Keeping to its two-year design cycle, Ford issued a mildly restyled 1936 lineup in mid-October 1935. Detailed to enhance the V-8 engine's growing reputation for performance, the new Model 68s sported a number of minor styling changes that, taken together, imparted a smart, graceful new look. Industry design practices of the day dictated hiding some previously exposed body components, so the horns were now placed behind "catwalk" grilles in the front fender aprons. The hood became longer and more pointed, and the radiator was more prominently

vee'd to match. Wheels were changed from wire-spoke to all-steel drop-center rims with full disc hubcaps.

For the first time, Ford fielded a two-series lineup, the previous DeLuxe offerings now set apart from base models prosaically labelled Standard. As had been the case since the first Model A, the main differences were fancier cabin trim and extra exterior chrome on the higher-priced DeLuxes.

This year's Standard models comprised five-window coupes with trunk or rumble seat, a four-door woody wagon, and Tudor and Fordor sedans in fastback and trunk-back form. Prices ranged from $510 for the trunked coupe to $670 for the wagon. The DeLuxe group included all but the latter, plus a brace of three-window coupes and no fewer than four different open styles, with prices starting at $560. Arriving in March was a new five-passenger DeLuxe Convertible Club Cabriolet, with a longer top to cover its back seat. The regular two-passenger DeLuxe cabriolet and roadster were still around for those who preferred rumble seats, though fewer people did by this time. Prices were $675, $625, and $560, respectively. Topping the line was the new $780 trunkback Convertible Touring Sedan. In fact, any '36 Ford save the roadster—and wagon, of course—could be ordered with the integral trunk at $25 additional.

Though not earthshaking, this year's engineering alterations were important in the neck-and-neck sales battle with Chevrolet, where every little talking point counted. Among them were an extra 3.5 inches of rear elbow room, new pivoting rear quarter windows for Fordors, reduced steering effort, and an increase in cooling system capacity and radiator area to alleviate the overheating problems that still dogged the V-8.

The pace of razzle-dazzle promotion quickened as Ford put on big shows this year at the Texas Centennial in Dallas, at the Atlantic City Boardwalk, and at the Great Lakes Exposition in Cleveland. Those attending saw a parade in which a float bearing a new roadster proclaimed the Ford ride as "The Car in the Clouds." Another crowd-pleaser was the "Human Ford," a '36 roadster that appeared on stage to answer audience questions in a "mystical" voice (no doubt that of a local ventriloquist).

Ford logged two production milestones in close succession during 1935-36. The 2-millionth V-8 car had rolled off the line in June 1935. Less than 12 months later, in May of this year, the 3-millionth was built. Though the country was now only inching its way out of the Depression—and slowly at that—Ford was rolling right along, surely a tribute to the inherent "rightness" of its cars. Nevertheless, the model year saw Chevy retake the number-one sales position, with 930,000 units to Ford's still substantial total of some 764,000.

At Lincoln, the big news was the all-new Zephyr, introduced in November 1935. Though entirely radical and eminently un-Lincoln, it was an instant success. A good thing, too, as Lincoln probably wouldn't have survived the Depression without it.

Like Cadillac's LaSalle, introduced back in 1927, and

Much sought after now: all '36 Ford open cars.

Only 5555 phaetons (list: $560) were produced in '36.

The '36 convertible trunk-back sedan sold for $780.

Buyers in '36 preferred Tudor sedans: 486,310 were built.

The DeLuxe three-window coupe went for $570.

Rare then, rarer today: a custom-bodied '36 Ford.

Only 4616 DeLuxe club cabriolets were built for 1936.

Unlike the Tudor above, this Ford has a built-in trunk.

Rare as hen's teeth: the '36 roadster (3862 built).

Clark Gable poses in a British '36 Jensen-Ford.

Packard's new 1935 One-Twenty, the Zephyr was a medium-priced "junior edition" designed to sell in high volume and thus keep its maker afloat until the luxury market recovered. And like the One-Twenty, it boosted its maker's annual production from a few thousand units to scores of thousands. But while Packard continued to pursue the mass market after World War II, both Lincoln and Cadillac abandoned "companion" cars and returned to the prestige class exclusively. Today we know which course was correct; back then, though, the choice was anything but clear.

The Zephyr was born in 1932 when John Tjaarda of Briggs Manufacturing Company, Ford's chief body supplier, sat down to talk with Edsel. But it was actually conceived long before. The Dutch-born Tjaarda (pronounced CHAR-dah) had worked for the tightly run Locke coachworks as well as Duesenberg and GM, but had left each in turn when it became apparent that they weren't interested in streamlining.

Tjaarda was. Independently, he'd created an advanced design concept that he called the Sterkenberg (after his family's estate in Friesland). The basic theme was a radical, teardrop-shape body built in unit with a sophisticated chassis featuring all-independent suspension and a rear-mounted engine. W.O. Briggs, one of the first industrialists to take Tjaarda's ideas seriously, suggested he show his sketches and a scale model to Edsel, the idea being to win a substantial new production contract to supplement Briggs' declining Lincoln orders.

"Ford's Lincoln business had practically come to a standstill," Tjaarda wrote later. "Relations between Briggs and [production boss] Charlie Sorensen were strained because Sorensen felt that Briggs paid more attention to their Chrysler business. . . . As far as Briggs was concerned, something had to be done [so they] hired me away from GM [to work on] Ford in particular." It was soon after that that Tjaarda met with Edsel.

Ford Motor Company's president was intrigued, and instructed the engineer to come up with a prototype suitable for volume production. Working in complete secrecy from both Ford and Briggs executives, Tjaarda devised a 125-inch-wheelbase car based on his Sterkenberg, a full-size wood mockup completed in October 1933 and shown the following year at Chicago's "Century of Progress" Exposition. Bearing a louvered fastback roof with a small dorsal fin, it weighed about 2500 pounds and carried a Ford V-8 in its tail. Top speed was estimated at 110 mph—unheard of for an 80-bhp car at the time.

The sedan delivery found favor with small businesses.

V-8 power made the '36 pickup a high-speed hauler.

FoMoCo in transition: current-era Ford (center), old-era Lincoln (right), new era Lincoln-Zephyr (left).

The classic Model K Lincolns for 1936: prices ranged from $4200-$6800, weight averaged 5200 pounds.

Ford's own design department then built a running, front-engine prototype in 1934. Tjaarda recalled that at least two more were built, though some sources say one was rear-engine. In any case, public response was overwhelmingly favorable wherever the prototypes went, which was enough for Edsel. However, only 50 percent of those polled indicated any interest in a rear-engine design, which was enough for Henry. But the old man insisted on making it even more conventional and, as usual, he got his way. The Zephyr thus emerged not only with the familiar front-engine/rear-drive layout but with Ford's traditional transverse leaf springs and solid axles at each end, plus a three-speed manual transmission instead of the automatic Tjaarda had envisioned—and Henry's cherished mechanical brakes.

Tjaarda's original snub-nose body design implied the compact Ford V-8, but Edsel thought that wasn't enough for a Lincoln, even a medium-price one. Lincoln's existing V-12 was too large, so he decreed a new engine for reasons of "prestige" and superior mechanical smoothness. His father didn't object but, ever the frugal tycoon, dictated the use of as many V-8 components as possible. The job was assigned to veteran engineer Frank Johnson, but the result wasn't one of his best. An L-head unit with four main bearings, it featured a monobloc casting with an exhaust core between the cylinders—more a "12-cylinder V-8" than a purpose-built twelve like Lincoln's. Displacement was 267.3 cubic inches on bore and stroke of 2.75 × 3.75 inches. Rated horsepower was 110 at 3900 rpm, a rather high power peak for the day, but the torque curve was quite flat, with at least 180 foot-pounds available from 3500 down to 400 rpm, which made for fine top-gear flexibility.

Though similar to the Sterkenbergs from the cowl back, the production Zephyr was more attractive, thanks to a longer, handsome new prow front grafted on by Ford designer E.T. "Bob" Gregorie, mainly to make room for the longer engine. Briggs built the unit body/chassis while Ford handled final assembly, adding drivetrain, front sheetmetal, upholstery, trim, and paint. Edsel told Tjaarda that Briggs might as well have done it all, since the Zephyr assembly line was only 40 feet long!

Initially, Tjaarda had mostly guessed at stress factors—crucial with unit construction—but the Zephyr was the

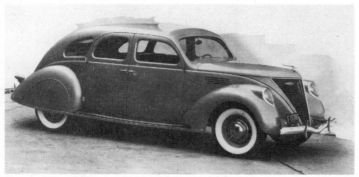
Streamlined and startling: the 1936 Lincoln-Zephyr.

Judkins built only 13 three-window berlines for '36.

The '36 Lincoln LeBaron coupe rode a 136-inch wheelbase.

first car subjected to aircraft-type stress analysis and it proved rock solid. Tjaarda later declared it "the strongest [yet] lightest car of its size ever built." Weighing about 3300 pounds at the curb, the Zephyr was 940 pounds lighter than a comparable Chrysler/DeSoto Airflow, yet could sustain nearly twice the impact loads of conventional body-on-frame cars. It was also aerodynamically efficient, though evidently not shaped with the aid of a wind tunnel like the Airflow. Neither car's drag coefficients look that great now, but the Zephyr's was later pegged at 0.45, the Airflow's at 0.50-0.53. Here too, Tjaarda had guessed right.

Arriving as a two- and four-door sedan priced at $1275 and $1320 respectively, the Zephyr offered typical Lincoln quality in a roomy, smooth-riding, and more manageable package with up-to-the-minute style and a down-to-earth

price. Predictably, it sold like hotcakes, at least by Lincoln standards. Accounting for better than 80 percent of total 1936 volume (14,994 units of 16,528), it lifted the make from 22nd to 18th place on the industry production list, the first time Lincoln had ever been in the top 20.

Zephyr was also the hottest Lincoln yet. Despite a mediocre power-to-weight ratio and a short, 4.33:1 final drive, it could do up to 90 mph and 0-50 mph in 10.8 seconds while averaging 16-18 miles per gallon.

The big Model K carried on much as before, though a few Zephyr-inspired styling touches were evident: more rakishly angled windshield; rounder, skirted fenders; steel wheels with disc hubcaps. Underdash handbrake, dual wiper motors, and all-helical-gear transmission were the chief mechanical changes. Model offerings and prices stood pat, as did production: just 1515 units.

But it didn't matter, because the Zephyr made this a watershed year in Lincoln history. With its new Depression-fighter, Lincoln proved that it not only deserved to survive but could still pioneer, much as it had in the Leland days.

1937

All-new styling and a number of new features made this a vintage Ford year. Billed by company publicists as the most stunning Ford yet, the '37 marked the start of another two-year design cycle—and a big departure from past design practice.

The '37 was more evidence of Ford's new interest in streamlining, pioneered within the '36 Lincoln-Zephyr. Headlamps were now firmly integrated with the "catwalk" areas, the prominently vee'd grille was stretched and sloped back, and fenders were more curvaceous. Slim louvers matching the fine horizontal grille bars adorned the sides of the pointed hood, which was newly hinged at the rear to open "alligator" fashion, as on the Zephyr.

It all added up to one of the decade's handsomest cars. Even President Roosevelt bought a '37 convertible sedan for use at his Warm Springs, Georgia, retreat. In a year of questionable styling for the industry as a whole, Ford was a standout—proof that streamlining didn't have to mean ugly. It might have been even lovelier had Henry Ford not personally ordered a 3-4-inch reduction in overall length from the original prototype, most of it ahead of the cowl. The trunkless "flatback" sedans probably suffered most from the resulting extra stubbiness.

Styling was one of Ford's few strong points by this time. Henry Ford, the rural inventor who had brought the automobile to the masses in his prime, was now a hardened old man in his middle 60s. On the one hand, he was a famous industrialist of stupendous achievement and beneficence;

on the other, a mean and curmudgeonly capitalist who once declared that the Depression might be "good for the country," particularly if it taught people to be more frugal and industrious. Though his son Edsel had been president since 1919, he still ruled Ford Motor Company with absolute authority, stifling new product developments with his stagnant attitudes, and fighting Edsel's ideas most every step of the way. He also remained adamant in his refusal to let workers unionize, and his right-hand man, Harry Bennett, employed a sort of private army to ensure they never would. This year saw men distributing union handbills take a brutal beating from Bennett's troops, which only further tarnished Henry's poor public image.

On a happier note, the 1937 Fords bowed in one of the splashiest extravaganzas ever seen. It was the morning of November 6, 1936, and some 7000 Ford dealers from all over the country had packed the Detroit Coliseum. The mood was one of excitement and anticipation: at long last, the nation seemed to be breaking out of its economic gloom. The auditorium darkened, and a slim shaft of light picked out a large V-8 emblem at the center of the elevated stage. There, golden-haired "elves" unwound themselves up from the floor and, rising one at a time, began tossing various car parts into a big cauldron. Steam began rising as engine components, wheels, radiators, and other bits and pieces were thrown into the brew. Then, in a fantasy of light and color, the fumes cleared, the elves disappeared, and a new 1937 Club Coupe rose up on a ramp, traversed the stage, and rolled down onto the main floor. It was a new way to introduce cars, one that would be widely imitated as the industry became increasingly enamored of such razzmatazz. Certainly, those dealers must have come away feeling that 1937 was going to be a banner year.

And in most respects it was. For the first time, closed body styles lacked the traditional fabric roof insert, as Ford followed GM's 1936 move to all-steel construction. Also new was a smaller, 136-cubic-inch version of the flathead V-8 (bore and stroke: 2.60 × 3.20 inches) rated at 60 bhp. Originally conceived for Britain and France, where it had powered locally built Fords for more than a year, it was prompted by European tax laws based not on vehicle size but engine displacement (in Britain, on bore). But here, this "V-8/60," as it was called, was marketed as an economy option, available only on Standard models as an appeal to buyers seeking a cheaper-to-operate full-size car. Alas, it offered too little power and thus failed to garner many sales, though it lowered list prices $10-$57. Ford would give up on it after 1940.

This year's other mechanical changes were more successful. The V-8/85 gained improved cooling via a larger, relocated water pump, plus larger insert bearings and new cast-alloy steel pistons. Ford still clung to mechanical brakes, but their old rod actuating system was discarded for a modern cable linkage housed in a protective conduit. Finally, steering ratio was again lowered to reduce effort at the wheel, though it made for an unseemly number of turns lock-to-lock.

Ford's streamlined look for '37 came from the Zephyr.

Skirts added to the speedy looks of this '37 Fordor.

The DeLuxe five-window coupe sold for $719 in 1937.

For 1937, headlights flared smoothly into the fenders.

Ford trucks served willingly back when coal was king.

Counting V-8/60 cars, this year's Ford line numbered 26 separate models in three series: V-8/60 Model 74 and V-8/85 Model 74 Standard and Model 78 DeLuxe. Body styles with clumsy side curtains continued to suffer dwindling sales throughout the industry as the decade wore on, so this would be the last year for the true Ford roadster, effectively supplanted by the more popular Convertible Cabriolet with roll-up glass. The DeLuxe Phaeton was still listed (at $750), but would last only through 1938. New to the catalog and also quite popular was a four-passenger five-window DeLuxe Club Coupe, priced at $720. Its roof length was halfway between that of the conventional Tudor sedan and the normal coupe, which acquired rear quarter glass to become a five-window style too. Still limited to Standard trim, the woody wagon again came with roll-down front door windows and side curtains in lieu of rear door and quarter glass. However, an "all-glass" wagon was available at only $20 more, $775 total. Repeating at the top of the line was the glamorous De-Luxe convertible sedan at $860.

In all, the more modern '37s lived up to customer expectations — aside from persistent comments that they would have been safer with hydraulic brakes like those on most competitors. The sales race saw Ford beaten by Chevrolet by a mere 2000 cars. However, Ford trucks sold better, which put Dearborn ahead in combined production. Alas, Ford wouldn't do as well for the next dozen years.

Lincoln's Zephyr sailed on with few changes but much higher sales. Production more than doubled in fact, to near 30,000 units, and Lincoln moved up two notches, to 16th, on Detroit's shortening list of makes.

Model offerings also doubled with the arrival of a close-coupled three-passenger coupe and a more deluxe four-door, the division-window Town Limousine. At $1165, the former was the cheapest Lincoln ever and the prettiest Zephyr to date, its foreshortened superstructure blending curvaceously with John Tjaarda's lower body lines. Helped by a $55 price reduction, the basic four-door remained the most popular Zephyr by far, accounting for over 23,000 deliveries. The two-door, now called coupe-

sedan, saw 300 fewer copies than in '36, about 1500 in all. Town Limousine production was a mere 139 units, an indication that the junior Lincoln really *was* built to a (medium) price. Evidently, Zephyr's market wasn't ready for a "loaded" version.

Designated Series HB (the '36s had been Series H), this year's Zephyrs were unaltered save for four evenly spaced double bars on their vee'd, horizontally ribbed grilles. Inside was a more elaborate instrument panel with a vertical extension running down to the transmission hump for housing a radio speaker. Speedometer and engine gauges were combined in a large central dial, flanked either side by a glove locker and ashtray, an arrangement that facilitated right-hand-drive conversion.

Lincoln built fewer than a thousand Model Ks for '37, but those few were impressive. Again reflecting Zephyr influence, headlamps moved from their traditional bullet-shaped pods beside the grille to fairings atop the front fenders, the big Lincoln's last major appearance change through its 1940 demise. This year also brought its last major mechanical change: hydraulic valve lifters for the superb 414-cid V-12, which rode further forward on redesigned engine mounts that eliminated what little vibration remained. Chassis were otherwise unaltered, with the same two wheelbases carrying a choice of 17 semi-custom bodies by Willoughby, Brunn, LeBaron, and Judkins. The Model K was now about as refined as it was possible to be, and future editions would differ only in detail.

1938

Ford adopted a new marketing ploy this year: different styling for Standard and DeLuxe models. The former, designated Model 82A with V-8/60 power and 81A with the V-8/85, were essentially warmed-over versions of the '37 Model 78 DeLuxe, though the upper horizontal grille bars were now swept back almost to the cowl, thus eliminating the separate hood louvers. This year's De-Luxe, also designated 81A, retained separate vents but got a longer hood that curved down into the grille, which was now rounded off at its upper corners. Broader market coverage prompted this split, as demand for cheaper, more austere standard cars was still sizable, and it would persist at Ford through 1940.

Engineering changes were almost nonexistent. The Standard line was down to the five-window coupe and brace of sedans. These were duplicated in the DeLuxe line, which added three convertibles, club coupe and, for the first time, the station wagon. The last got standard

At only 2743 units for '38, the convertible sedan was losing favor; the phaeton would be gone by 1939.

all-glass windows this year, while others came with built-in trunk. Accessory fender skirts were a new dressup item, and they suited the open cars particularly well, especially the romantic phaeton, which was in its final year.

This relative lack of change suggested that something was going on in Dearborn besides old Henry's usual railing against progress. And indeed there was: the company was busy preparing not only an all-new '39 Ford but a separate new "companion" make. In a way, then, this year's split was a preparatory move designed to provide an orderly price progression between the Ford line and the forthcoming Mercury. As we know now, the latter would be a slightly larger and more powerful version of the '39 Ford, intended to give Dearborn a more direct competitor in the medium-price field against Pontiac and Oldsmobile from GM, and Dodge and DeSoto from Chrysler.

A sharp, unexpected recession blunted the pace of the nation's economic recovery this year. But though car sales slipped industry-wide, Ford volume plunged to only about half its 1937 level, some 410,000 units in all. (Chevrolet also sank, but not as much.) In some respects, this reflected the fact that Ford was still behind the times, its old-fashioned transverse-spring suspension and mechanical brakes the most glaring anachronisms. But the old man was still in command and, ignoring all advice from Edsel on down, refused to follow what he considered engineering "fads." And though most everyone *but* Henry could see it, his intransigence had now set the company on a long, steady decline, one that would not be reversed until it was almost too late.

After its 1937 record, Lincoln fell to about 20,000 units, again reflecting the slack economy. Most were Zephyrs, of course, though there were fewer of them, 19,111 in all. Still, that was some 5500 ahead of LaSalle and, having fallen behind the previous year, Lincoln again moved ahead of the junior Cadillac in the volume race.

This year's Series 86H lineup was expanded by a new convertible coupe at $1700 and convertible sedan at $1790, but they accounted for only 600 and 461 units, respectively. The Town Limousine saw only 130. As usual,

Three generations of Fords: Henry II, old Henry, Edsel.

Recession year Ford: 1938 DeLuxe Fordor.

The '38 Standard was a warmed-over '37 DeLuxe.

Keeping watch over the Rouge: a '39 Ford fire truck.

Ford introduced the Cab-Over-Engine truck in 1938.

the workaday four-door was the big favorite: better than 14,500 units.

Zephyr's first facelift arrived this year, with reshaped rear fenders and new front sheetmetal accompanying a three-inch wheelbase stretch to 125 inches. Bob Gregorie's favored pointy nose and twin grilles appeared to further establish what was fast becoming the Ford family look, but the latter were set well down from the catwalk areas, thus predicting the horizontal-format fronts (emphasized here with thin horizontal bars) that would take hold in the Forties. Designers continued fiddling with the interior: larger, 18-inch-diameter steering wheel, new biscuit-pattern upholstery, and elimination of the previous chrome-tube seat frames.

On the mechanical side, an increase in rear spring base improved Zephyr ride, while the longer wheelbase allowed the engine/transmission assembly to be pushed further forward for more front cabin space. This, in turn, permitted a lower transmission housing, so the gearlever relocated to the console. The latter proved clumsy, though, and sales resistance led to another rethink two years later, when it went onto the steering column. The little V-12 came in for hydraulic lifters and reshaped combustion chambers, though rated outout was unchanged.

The original Zephyr's tapered tail had posed cargo-carrying problems for some owners, and some hasty, though clever, *post hoc* body engineering was required to minimize spare tire space intrusion. On the '36s, the luggage lid provided access only to the spare; to stow anything, you had to burrow it in from inside the car. The 1937-39 models put the tire on a swivelling bracket, which helped. Afterward, it was mounted under the trunk floor, where it should have been all along.

With sales down to a trickle, Lincoln's senior Model K was little changed. Coachbuilt offerings were broadly the same, but even the factory-built styles failed to exceed double-digit production. The two most numerous—if that's the word—were the standard 145-inch-wheelbase limousine (91 built) and seven-passenger sedan (78). Rarest were Willoughby's short-chassis coupe and long-wheelbase sport sedan, just four apiece.

1939

Overshadowed by the October 1938 introduction of the new medium-price Mercury were several significant developments for the 1939 Ford. Aside from pretty new lines on the Series 91A DeLuxe, the big attraction was hydraulic brakes. Old Henry had finally given in—three years after Chevrolet and 11 years after Plymouth. But though the new system answered one long-standing Ford

The '39 DeLuxe convertible coupe—10,422 were built.

After 1939 the convertible sedan would be discontinued.

criticism, the antiquated chassis was again untouched.

Ford's work on hydraulic brakes had begun in 1938 at Henry's direct order. But the aging motor magnate suffered a stroke soon afterward, and would be less and less involved in running his company and developing its products. Still, he continued to have the last word on important matters—and to rely less on son Edsel and more on Harry Bennett for advice.

Nevertheless, Mercury was mainly Edsel's idea. Though new from the ground up, it was really a "super deluxe" Ford, with scaled-up price, proportions, and power. At 116 inches, its wheelbase was four inches longer than Ford's, so it offered more interior room and a nicer ride. It should be noted, however, that some Mercury developments spilled over to this year's Fords, especially the DeLuxe. For example, Mercury's bored-out flathead V-8 had larger-diameter bearings, heavier rods and crankshaft, and other strengthened internal components, most of which were adopted for the Ford unit. Also, there was an obvious styling kinship between Mercury and the '39 Ford DeLuxe, especially at the front. Both wore low vee'd grilles, the former with horizontal bars, the latter with vertical bars. Headlamps on both were completely absorbed into the front fenders but retained the oval shape of previous years (circular sealed-beam units were on the way), while hoods were deeper and bereft of side louvers.

This year's Ford Standard was another mild rehash of the previous year's DeLuxe, with busier grille and hood detailing in contemporary fashion. The V-8/60 Model 92A Standard continued with the two sedans and five-window coupe from 1938, while the step-up V-8/85 line, also part of the Series 91A, reinstated the wood-bodied station wagon. The DeLuxe range contracted as the phaeton, club coupe, and convertible club coupe all disappeared. The lovely convertible sedan was in its final season and no longer alone at the top of the line: the DeLuxe wagon carried an identical $920 price. Curiously, the four-door convertible would resurface the next year—and that year only—as a Mercury.

New brakes aside, Ford engineering changes were few. The V-8/85 retained its customary power rating despite the stronger internals, though some tests suggested it was slightly more potent than before.

In what was expected to be a better sales year than it was, Ford sold over 481,000 cars, trailing Chevrolet by nearly 100,000 units. Worse, third-place Plymouth was closer than ever on the strength of its smart new '39 styling. There was also strong new competition in Studebaker's fleet, low-priced six-cylinder Champion, styled by Raymond Loewy. Ford was doing well enough, but so were most rivals.

Lincoln returned with much the same group of Zephyrs and Model Ks. Perhaps for this reason, production hardly budged, ending the year only a couple thousand units ahead of lackluster 1938. The little-changed senior line saw a mere 133 examples, with limos and long sedans again taking the lion's share.

This year's Series 96H Zephyr benefitted from the new hydraulic brakes but was otherwise unchanged mechanically. So, apparently, was styling, but there were actually a number of refinements. The front took on a more knife-edge look via recontoured prow and front fenders, while

The 1939 DeLuxe Fordor still rode a 112-inch wheelbase.

Majestic: the 1939 Lincoln Model K semi-collapsible cabriolet, by Brunn, one of only one built.

the front bumper was cut away in the center to accent a reshaped, vertical-bar grille. The vestigial running-boards, perhaps the Zephyr's most anachronistic feature, were newly hidden by extended lower-body sheetmetal. Sprucing up interiors were a revised dash and more color/trim choices. Closed models could be ordered with an expensive custom broadcloth option that included color-keyed instrument panel, window moldings, and control knobs. The leather-lined open cars were also more colorful inside, while bedford-cord upholstery was standard on the low-volume Town Limousine (95 built).

Zephyr production as a whole recovered slightly to reach 29,905 units this year. It might have gone higher had it not been for the new Mercury, effectively an intra-mural competitor with similar styling and more speed for less money. Predictably, it outsold the junior Lincoln by better than three to one, recording 75,000 units in its debut model year.

Mercury was way overdue. Conceived to fill the yawning price gap that had long separated Ford and Lincoln, it also reflected a certain Ford yearning to be a multi-make manufacturer like General Motors and Chrysler. Early ads said Mercury was "the car that dares to ask 'Why?'", implying a clean-slate approach. But as historian Beverly Rae Kimes later wrote: "Another question [was] why Ford Motor Company hadn't introduced [it] sooner. The answer to that one undoubtedly was that it had taken that long for Edsel to convince his father to build it."

Old Henry certainly wasn't chasing innovation as he had so successfully in the past. But his son was. Edsel knew that Ford needed a medium-price product for loyal customers looking to move up, an alternative to the popu-lar Pontiac and Dodge. Thus, Mercury was adroitly pitched just under Oldsmobile and DeSoto. While it didn't approach Pontiac/Dodge/Olds volume in the Forties, it usually matched or exceeded DeSoto's, averaging about 80,000 units a year, easily above the break-even point.

Dearborn's middle make arrived in a single Series 99A comprising convertible, coupe-sedan, two-door sedan, and four-door Town Sedan body styles. Prices ran around $1000, curb weights around 3000 pounds. As mentioned, power was provided by a larger, stronger version of the Ford flathead, with a wider, 3.19-inch bore (on the same 3.75-inch stroke) yielding 239 cubic inches and 95 horsepower. It would continue unchanged through 1948. Stylist Bob Gregorie used the longer wheelbase to make Mercury look more balanced and "important" than Ford. Interior appearance was similar, including dashboard with strip-type gauge cluster, but Mercury proudly touted its column-mount gearshift, then an innovation.

With its favorable power-to-weight ratio, Mercury soon became known as something of a hot rod. This befitted not only its name—after the winged messenger of Greek mythology—but the concept Edsel had thought right for it. Stock but well tuned, the early Mercs were quicker than comparable V-8 Fords. This year's debut models were capable of near 100 mph yet proved remarkably frugal, ads touting close to 20 mpg—except for leadfoot drivers.

Public interest in Ford Motor Company was heightened throughout the year by the firm's exhibit at the New York World's Fair. As in the past at Chicago, Dallas, and San Diego, the Ford story was showcased in a special building.

continued on page 129

bove and above left: With a face still known round the world, the Ford Model T remains among the most collectible of antique cars. Here, a 1911 example with touring bodywork, the most popular style throughout most of the Tin Lizzie's long life. Early Ts (1908-16) carried the square-cut radiator and open front and rear fenders shown here. **Below left:** By the time this 1926 Model T Fordor sedan was built, Lizzie had shed most of her "antique" appearance but remained a mechanical anachronism. U.S. production ended May 21, 1927, and close to 16 million Ts were built worldwide through the end of that year. **Below:** The T's handsome Model A replacement arrived to great acclaim in late 1928. Here, a beautifully restored 1929 cabriolet. Note the rumble seat, functional top irons, and folding accessory wood trunk rack.

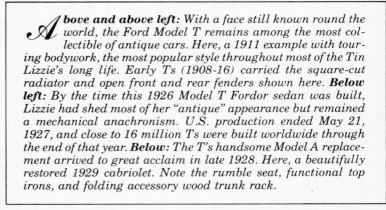

113

*T*his page, right: *Hard on the heels of the Model A came another historic Ford, the 1932 V-8 Model 18 and four-cylinder Model B. The latter, shown in popular Tudor sedan form, was identical with the revolutionary V-8 models save engine, of course, and lack of V-8 emblems on hubcaps and headlamp tie bar.* **Below:** *The first new Lincoln since the original Model L arrived in 1931 as the Model K. Here, an unrestored example of that year's factory-bodied Sport Phaeton.* **Opposite page, top:** *Ford's 1932 V-8 DeLuxe phaeton. Original list price was just $580.* **Center left:** *The '34 Fords brought further evidence of streamlining, with refinements to the new 1933 styling. Shown is the $590 convertible cabriolet.* **Center right:** *The '35s were sleeker yet, as this $595 DeLuxe three-window rumble-seat coupe shows.* **Bottom:** *Unit construction and fully streamlined styling made the '36 Lincoln Zephyr a milestone. Shown is the $1320 four-door sedan.*

*D*earborn engineering may have lagged during the late prewar years, but its styling was among the industry's best, as this sampling so beautifully illustrates. **This page, above:** The '37 Ford DeLuxe convertible sedan with optional rear fender skirts. Original base retail price was $859. **Right:** Lincoln's successful Zephyr received only a mild facelift for sophomore year '37, but this racy three-passenger coupe was one of two new body style additions. It sold for $1165. **Below right:** Zephyr added convertible coupe and sedan for '38. This 1939 convertible coupe sold new for $1747. Like all Zephyrs that year, it featured an improved V-12 with 120 horsepower, up 10 bhp from previous versions. **Opposite page, top:** Mercury made a successful 1939 debut as Ford Motor's entry in the medium-price field. Here, the $978 sedan-coupe from the little-changed 1940 line, identified by sealed-beam headlamps. **Center left:** Ford's 1940 shared similarly sweet Bob Gregorie styling, one reason it's still avidly sought-after. Five-window coupes like this V-8/85 DeLuxe later became popular as hot rods. **Center right:** Ford's 1940 V-8/85 DeLuxe convertible coupe went for $849. **Bottom:** The '41 Fords were longer, lower, wider, and heavier. Top of the line was this convertible coupe in the new Super DeLuxe line, priced at $946.

The immediate pre- and postwar years witnessed historic changes at Ford Motor Company. Here, a sampling of cars from this era. **This page, top right:** Rebodied for 1940, the Lincoln Zephyr changed little for '41. Shown is that year's coupe. **Center right:** The '41 Lincoln Continental was also little changed. Here, the $2778 cabriolet. **Bottom:** All Lincolns were facelifted for war-shortened 1942 like this $2150 Zephyr convertible. **Opposite page, center left:** Wood-trimmed Sportsman convertibles highlighted Dearborn's prewar-carryover 1946-48 products. This 1948 Ford Super DeLuxe saw but 2250 copies. **Top:** The all-new '49 Ford literally saved the company, and was improved for 1950. Here, the $1511 Custom V-8 Tudor. **Center right:** All-new '49 Mercury shared Lincoln's junior shell. This coupe sold for $1979. **Bottom:** Convertible was one of four Lincoln Cosmopolitans for '51.

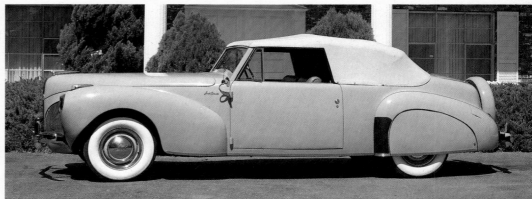

*T*his page, above: The 1951 Country Squire was Ford's last true woody wagon. **Above right:** Mercury's 1952 Monterey convertible. Price: $2370. **Right:** The followup '53 carried a bolder grille. **Bottom:** Ford also changed little for '53, the firm's 50th anniversary year. Shown is the $1941 Crestline Victoria hardtop. **Opposite page, top left:** The '54 Mercs like this Monterey hardtop had the make's first ohv V-8. **Top right:** Lincoln's 1955 Capri hardtop coupe sold for $3910. **Center:** Ford Thunderbird was new for '55. **Bottom:** $2712 Montclair convertible topped '55 Mercury line.

Opposite page, top left: Ford's 1955 Victoria hardtop coupe in the new top-line Fairlane series. *Top right:* Mid-range Ford Customline added a Victoria for '56. *Center:* Ford's most stylish '56s were the tiara-roof Fairlane Crown Victoria (**left**) and the followup Thunderbird, here with new porthole-window hardtop. *Bottom left:* Mercury's '56 Montclair Sport Coupe. *Bottom right:* The Fairlane 500 Town Victoria hardtop sedan from Ford's all-new '57 line. *This page, above:* Continental Mark II arrived for '56 at a lofty $10,000. *Left:* Tasteful '57 restyle marked Ford's final two-seat Thunderbirds. *Bottom:* Mercury's new '57 Turnpike Cruiser in hardtop sedan form.

Like other domestic auto-makers, Dearborn stumbled in the late Fifties, though its cars have become more appreciated in the years since. **This page, above:** New-for-'58 Edsel generated controversy with its "horse collar" vertical grille, but doesn't look too bad next to some contemporaries. Shown is that year's Pacer convertible. **Right:** Ford's '58 standards were facelifted to more closely resemble the new Thunderbird. Here, the Fairlane 500 Club Victoria hardtop coupe. **Bottom:** All-new '58 Lincoln adopted unit construction and massive size, as this Capri Landau hardtop sedan shows. **Opposite page, top left:** Edsel became more like Ford for '59, but retained unique grille. This is the Ranger two-door sedan. **Top right:** A big hit in debut '58, Ford's four-seat Thunderbird did even better for 1959. This rakish convertible sold at $3979. **Center:** After three years, Ford's innovative Skyliner came to an end with this '59 model due to management's turn from "gimmick engineering." Some 48,400 were built in all. **Bottom:** Edsel died after limited 1960 production as a badge-engineered Ford, which makes this Ranger ragtop a rarity.

*D*earborn produced some of its most memorable and successful cars in the early Sixties. Herewith, a sample. **Opposite page, top:** The 1961 Ford Galaxie Sunliner convertible, rarely seen today. **Center left:** Lincoln's handsome '61 Continental convertible sedan. **Center right:** 1962 Ford Galaxie 500 Sunliner. **Bottom:** Mercury's Meteor S-33 hardtop coupe, a rarity from '63. **This page, left:** 1962 Ford Thunderbird Sports Roadster recalled two-seater days. **Below left:** 1964 Ford Galaxie 500 XL hardtop coupe. **Below:** The '64 Ford Thunderbird convertible. **Bottom:** Ford started the ponycar stampede with the '65 Mustang, shown in hardtop form.

*F*ord Motor Company paced the American industry's model specialization in the Sixties. Here are three examples. **Top:** The first generation of Ford's highly successful Falcon compact concluded with the '65s. Here the Futura hardtop coupe. **Right:** Mercury's Comet bridged the size gap between compacts and intermediates. Shown is the 1965 Caliente convertible. **Bottom:** The popular Ford Fairlane was newly rebodied for '66. Sporty 500 XL bowed as hardtop (shown) and convertible.

Simplicity of line and elegance of design were hallmarks of the Continental, executed at Edsel Ford's request.

The Lincoln Continental was basically a chopped and altered Zephyr. Shown here the prototype.

The 1939 Lincoln Continental prototype, Edsel's own.

Mercury's first-year '39 Town Sedan sold for $957.

continued from page 112

But this time there was something quite extraordinary: the "Road of Tomorrow," an elevated highway completely encircling the structure, where visitors could take Ford's newest for a spin.

The decade coming to a close had been difficult for Dearborn, its technical advances with the Model A, flathead V-8, and the Zephyr offset by Henry's growing eccentricity and loss of low-price sales supremacy to Chevrolet.

Yet after several years of hasty, often confused new-model programs, Ford seemed to be sorting out its various problems, while looking forward to real national prosperity that, presumably, was just around the corner.

But the year movie buffs remember for *The Wizard of Oz* and *Gone With the Wind* brought the ominous rumblings of a new war in Europe. As the Forties opened, the question seemed not so much *if* America would get involved, but when.

129

1940

This year's Ford DeLuxe is still fondly remembered. True, it had few engineering refinements, save the addition of a front anti-roll bar or spring stabilizer. Workmanship, never a Ford selling point, was better, perhaps because the company was now producing all its car bodies, owing to labor problems at suppliers. Still, Ford trailed somewhat in fit and finish. But, oh, that styling!

And it *was* good—so good that these Fords remain some of the most desired cars ever built. Executed by Bob Gregorie with guidance, as always, from Edsel Ford, the DeLuxe was dominated by a crisply pointed hood meeting a handsome, chrome-plated vee'd grille composed of delicate horizontal bars and flanked by painted sub grilles. Headlamps—circular sealed-beam units for the first time—nestled in neat chrome nacelles. Fenders were artfully curved to complement the body contours, and the rear ones could be skirted for a more streamlined look. Distinctive chevron-shaped lamps adorned the beetle back. This deft facelift of the 1939 bodyshell worked amazingly well. Even the cheap Standards looked fresh and far less frumpy, distinguished by body-color headlamp housings and a '39-style vertical-bar grille with a simple chrome cap on the prow.

This would be the last year for Ford's old/new series split and the never-popular V-8/60. Unveiled in October 1939, the 1940 line continued with the price-leading, small-engine Standard series, designated O2A, and the V-8/85 series 01A comprising both Standard and DeLuxe models. The one remaining open body style was the rakish DeLuxe convertible coupe, priced at a reasonable $850. Demise of the convertible sedan left the wood-body wagon as the costliest '40 at $950. Club coupes were replaced by business coupes with fold-up rear jump seats and a large trunk. Sometimes referred to as the "opera coupe," it came in three versions: "60" Standard, "85" Standard, and DeLuxe at $640, $680, and $742, respectively. In future years it would be popular hot rod material. The three-passenger five-window coupe was still offered in these forms at $619, $660, and $721.

In April, the 28-millionth Ford car, a DeLuxe Fordor sedan, rolled out from the Edgewater, New Jersey assembly plant, then toured the country over the next few

This '40 DeLuxe Tudor lacks a bit of trim by the door.

Car collectors' delight: the DeLuxe convertible coupe.

The business coupe was priced at a modest $681 for 1940.

The 85-horse V-8 made this ragtop a sprightly auto.

The 1940 Fords remain among the most desired cars ever built. That's because the styling was so right.

months, stopping in major cities and state capitals to collect specially numbered license plates and celebrity signatures in its logbook. In June, Ford observed another milestone with completion of its 7-millionth V-8.

Ford's 1940 sales were encouraging, the total comfortably exceeding a half-million units, about 10 percent up on 1939. But Plymouth and Chevrolet had been busy, each scoring healthy gains. As ever, the Ford's problem was that it wasn't as up to date as the opposition.

Even more than this year's Ford DeLuxe, 1940 is remembered for the exquisitely styled, immensely romantic Lincoln Continental. Destined to become a Classic (as defined by the Classic Car Club of America), it remains an elegant tribute to the son forever in the shadow of his legendary father: the quiet enthusiast, pursuer of luxury, the great judge of excellence in both cars and people. Of course, the Continental wasn't Edsel Ford's only legacy, but it would have been enough to assure his place for all time in the annals of automotive greatness. It was certainly a brilliant followup to his successful new Mercury. Edsel, in fact, was now at the peak of his career. Sadly, it wouldn't last much longer.

As most enthusiasts know, the Continental originated in 1939 with a Zephyr-based custom that Edsel commissioned for his annual winter vacation in Palm Beach, Florida. Enamored of European design, he directed Bob Gregorie to create a car "thoroughly Continental"—hence the name—complete with Euro-style outside spare tire. (One of Gregorie's early ideas had omitted this feature but, as the designer recalled, Edsel turned it down flat: "It's very nice, but I want it to be strictly Continental.")

Gregorie, who admired the smooth shapes favored by John Tjaarda and others, was comfortable with this assignment. He'd already designed several cars for Edsel based on Ford chassis, with long curving fenders and tall peaked grilles. The "Continental" would be an extension of these themes. With '39 Zephyr convertible dimensions as a starting point, he eventually produced a scale model. Edsel liked everything about it except for the sloped Zephyr tail, which was awkward with the upright spare. So he had Gregorie raise the deck and square it up, resulting in a more finished appearance that looked "as if they planned it that way," as one Ford stylist later said. With this, Edsel told Gregorie to prepare the full-size car.

Like the scale model, Edsel's custom began as a '39 Zephyr convertible but with dramatic changes: 12 extra inches ahead of the cowl and suitably altered front fenders. It looked "sectioned" in profile because it was: four-inch horizontal strips were removed from each door and the doors welded together again, thus reducing their overall height. Other new body panels, like the deck, had to be hand-hammered over wooden forms by skilled sheetmetal workers. Not widely known is the fact that two more Continental prototypes were built for Edsel's eldest sons, Benson and Henry II, once 1940 Zephyr sheetmetal became available in mid-1939.

Completed by March 1 and bearing serial number H74750, Edsel's own car went down to Palm Beach with Eagle Gray paint and gray leather interior. It attracted scores of admirers, and Ford's president returned with over 200 requests that amounted to orders. Too astute to let them go, he ordered a run of 500 cars to see what would happen.

Scarcely four months later, the "Lincoln Zephyr Conti-

Much sought after today, only 350 Lincoln Continental coupes were produced for 1940.

Rarer still, only 54 cabriolets were built for 1940.

European-inspired styling shows on the Continental.

nental" went on sale following a massive effort by the production and body engineers. Besides the cabriolet, priced at $2840, the rakish newcomer was also offered as a club coupe at $2783. (A four-door had been sketched in September 1939, but would never make production.) Dealers now greeted customers who'd previously tram-

The 1940 Zephyr coupe featured a long, long rear deck.

pled the carpets only at Packard and Cadillac stores, and most of them could actually afford a Continental, unlike most exotic "traffic builders." Model year production totalled 54 cabriolets and 350 coupes. This was fairly low (except by Model K standards), but then these first Continentals were literally hand-built, basically Zephyr conversions that required a tremendous amount of cutting, welding, patching, refinishing, leading, and hand-forming. And that took time, even with the best will in the world.

It should be mentioned that the first production Continentals rode the Zephyr's 125-inch wheelbase. They also lacked any specific exterior identification, bearing Zephyr script only.

Another point of interest was the Continental's baked-enamel finish, the first time a paint other than lacquer had been used on a quality car. Ford chose it as "far more durable . . . due partly to its hardness and also to the methods used in its application." Continental historian OCee Ritch notes that "a huge sum [for the time] was expended . . . for installing the equipment necessary to use baked enamel instead of lacquer. . . . A total of seven coats was applied to each body." Manpower eliminated the "orange-peel" texture common to enamel: approximately eight times as much hand polishing as expended on an average car.

With its masterful styling, the Continental completely stole Ford Motor Company's 1940 show. Which is too bad, because this year's Zephyr was the best yet. Though it looked much like the '39, the Series 06H boasted a brand-new unit body/chassis minus runningboards, which allowed the bodysides to move outward for a corresponding gain in seat width. Other improvements included the corporation's new sealed-beam headlamps, increased glass area, a bigger trunk with underfloor spare, and a more conventional dash *sans* console, with column-mount gear-shift and the big combination instrument placed directly ahead of the steering wheel. The main mechanical change, also adopted for Continental, was a 1.13-inch bore increase, to 3.88 inches, that turned the V-12 from undersquare to oversquare (on the existing 3.75-inch bore). Displacement thus rose to 292 cid, and horsepower went up by 10 to 120.

Zephyr model offerings shifted as the convertible sedan vanished and a smart semi-fastback five-seat club coupe replaced the fastback sedan-coupe. Production again inched upward, reaching 21,765 units for the model year. Turning away from Model K coachwork, Brunn now offered special Zephyr Town Limousine and Town Car styles. The latter had an open chauffeur's compartment, while both had smaller tails and more squared-up roofs that looked incongruous with the aerodynamic body lines. Only about 10 of these cars would be built through 1941. Most went to company executives or members of the Ford family.

Lincoln's magnificent Model K, last link with the make's beginnings, was still technically available this year, though production had actually ceased during 1939. It was the end of an era—the line that had made Lincoln the "car of kings." Among the last of the custom-bodied Ks was the famous "King George Phaeton," built for the use of Britain's King George VI and Queen Elizabeth during their U.S.-Canadian visit of June 1939, and Franklin Roosevelt's "Sunshine Special" parade car, which was updated in 1942 with front-end sheetmetal from that year's Zephyr.

Mercury's 95-bhp, 239.4-cid V-8 was larger than Ford's.

Mercury was little changed, not unexpected for an all-new model in its second year. The one visible difference from '39 was the new sealed-beam headlamps in Ford-style nacelles. Joining the line was Ford's recently relinquished convertible sedan body style, but it was discontinued after only about 1000 were built, never to return. Mercury's total production advanced by about 6000 units to a little more than 81,000, good for 12th place in the industry standings.

1941

Despite the worrisome war raging abroad, many Americans were happy at the end of 1940. President Roosevelt and his New Deal had put many workers back on the job, and the country was hopeful that it could avoid the European conflict while enjoying renewed prosperity. A body painter at Ford Motor Company was making good wages for the time, $1.10 an hour; fender-stamping repair workers had the best pay, about $1.15.

It was into this optimistic climate that Ford rolled out its '41 cars at a big Dearborn press reception in September 1940. Henry Ford was 78 now, and this would be his last appearance at such an event. Reporters must have sensed this, for nearly 500 turned out to see and hear the industry's elder statesman. True to form, he had little to say. Instead, he escorted the party to a nearby site where his workers were erecting a huge new factory that would turn out fighter aircraft engines. Like many other companies, Ford was now involved in a growing number of defense projects as Washington geared up not to fight, but to supply European allies with war material.

The '41s were the biggest Fords yet: longer, lower, wider, flashier, and heavier. Wheelbase stretched by two inches, bodysides ballooned outward, interior space increased, and a stouter frame slid in underneath. Curb weights rose by an average of some 300 pounds over the lithe 1940s. Styling was evolutionary, marked by a rather busy front end with a vertical center grille flanked by low-riding "scoop" grilles, all with vertical chrome bars. Said *Ford News*: "Probably the most outstanding advancement in this year's car is improved riding, made possible by a number of factors including a wheelbase increased to 114 inches. That the 1941 Ford is a big car is indicated by the fact that the front seat in the Fordor Sedan is a full seven inches wider than in any previous Ford car. The front seat width is why so little runningboard shows outside. The unusually wide bodies, with doors that round out at the bottom to cover all but a narrow strip of the runningboards, are trim and sleek. Headlamps are mounted far apart on the massive front fenders to increase nighttime

The 1941 Ford was bigger—and better.

The Super DeLuxe Fordor listed at $859 for 1941.

Henry Ford takes a poke at a "soybean-plastic" decklid.

visibility, and the separate parking lamps are set high on the fenders."

Ford was right in step with its big new '41. Rivals Chevrolet and Plymouth had enlarged their cars substantially the previous year, a move that met with considerable buyer approval. If Dearborn had been behind the times, at least it was beginning to catch up. The '41's clean, ready-for-action look was quickly accepted as the latest in high-fashion motoring.

Ford's big engineering news this year was its first six since the Model K of 1906. An L-head design, it displaced 226 cubic inches and produced 90 bhp at 3300 rpm—5 cid and 5 bhp more than the V-8/85. Initial dealer reaction to the '39 Mercury was behind it, namely that a Ford Six would have been a better seller than a puffed-up V-8 car. Edsel Ford, always respectful of and often sympathetic to what his dealers had to say, promised them one. He even managed to get his father's approval in one of those strange turnabouts for which Henry was noted.

The new engine arrived as an alternative to the V-8/85 in a revised '41 line comprising Series 1GA Six and Series 11A V-8, each with the same body styles and trim levels. The former Standard coupe and Tudor/Fordor sedans were retitled Special, while DeLuxe was now the mid-level trim, adding business coupe and the wagon. At the top was a new Super DeLuxe group, with all the DeLuxe styles plus convertible coupe and a new two-door six-passenger sedan-coupe. With its more modern design and

greater power, the new six must have been a slight embarrassment to Ford, and buyers were quick to notice that it actually cost $15 *less* than the V-8 model for model. Prices ranged from $684 for the basic six-cylinder Special coupe up to $1013 for the V-8 Super Deluxe wagon. The latter marked the first time a regular-line Ford had exceeded the magic thousand-dollar mark.

Ford made up for lost time in another way this year. It may have been late with hydraulic brakes, but it now had the industry's largest—12 inches drum diameter. Other engineering alterations began with wider front and rear transverse leaf springs, which allowed softer spring rates for a more cushioned ride. Numerically higher gear ratios, borrowed from the previous V-8/60 transmission, were adopted for both six and V-8, mainly to make up for the expected performance losses from the new models' greater heft. The result was comparable low-end getaway at some expense in low-speed flexibility in second and third gears.

Ford again faced formidable competition this year, particularly the new '41 Chevrolet, still regarded as one of the best Chevys ever. Third-place Plymouth, fielding a restyled version of its new 1940 design, managed to pull within 100,000 units by some accounts, while Chevy outsold Ford by a 10-7 margin, far wider than usual. Overall model year totals were about 692,000 for Ford, slightly over a million for Chevy, and some 546,000 for Plymouth.

Dearborn recorded another milestone on April 29 this

Arguably the most beautiful of the Continentals, the 1941 model features pushbuttons for doorhandles.

year by building the 29-millionth Ford vehicle since the company's 1903 founding. It would be the last such production feat for several years: World War II was looming closer.

Lincoln made Continental a separate series this year, though it bore the Zephyr's internal designation (16H). Changes were few. The most visually noticeable were flush-mount pushbuttons instead of turn handles on the doors, and turn signals (something of a novelty) incorporated with parking lamps in housings atop the front fenders. With production bugs now sorted out, unit volume rose to about 100 a month, a total of 1250 for the model year. Prices were reduced some $100. The cabriolet came down to $2778, the coupe to $2727. The Continental remained a bargain. It would also be something of an investment, becoming one of the few used cars to see value appreciation within five or six years of production.

Zephyr returned with the same smart models, though this would be the last year for Tjaarda-like styling (the '42s would adopt Bob Gregorie's blowsy '41 Ford/Mercury lines). There were minor changes to bumpers, headlamp rims, and grille (with a slightly different texture than Continental's), and fender-top front parking/turn indicator lamps appeared here too. An inside hood release replaced the previous external latch operated via hood ornament. Like Ford, there were minor suspension tweaks including longer, wider springs that gave slower ride motions. Convertibles acquired a power top mechanism, and

a new deluxe radio with seek-tune foot switch became available at extra cost across the board. Another new option was Borg-Warner overdrive, an alternative to the two-speed Columbia rear axle offered since '36. A very few cars were built with both units.

Though much has been written of the Continental, relatively little has been said about the other limited-production Zephyrs of these years. As mentioned, the prestigious old firm of Brunn, Inc. began building town cars from Zephyr bits during 1940, which was quite a trick considering the unit body/chassis. The complete assembly was manhandled into the Brunn plant, and the work performed to designs sent along by Ross Cousins of Ford Styling. The results weren't very pretty—the town car configuration really wasn't suited to the Zephyr's sleek lines—and only nine to 11 were built. Edsel received the first, Henry the second; one of these was twice updated with new paint, upholstery and, finally, a 1948 Lincoln grille.

More numerous were this year's new 138-inch-wheelbase Lincoln Custom limousine and long sedan, further extensions of the luxury-Zephyr concept following the Continental. Replacing the Model K, at least in spirit, they were designed by Bob Gregorie and seen through to production by Henry Crecilius, former body engineer at the Brewster works, who'd helped spearhead the original '36 Zephyr.

Lincoln historian Jesse Haines has unearthed a bizarre

The '41 Continental coupe saw production of 850 units.

Continental's 292-cid V-12 put out 120 horsepower.

Interior shot of the $2812 Continental coupe.

story as to how the 138-inch wheelbase was selected: "Two driveshafts were used for the 1941 Zephyrs, standard and overdrive. The overdrive shaft was 13 inches shorter, so by making the Custom wheelbase 138 inches, or 13 longer than the Zephyr, the standard Zephyr driveshaft was used with Customs employing overdrive. Only Customs supplied with standard transmission required a specially long torque tube and driveshaft." Haines notes other money-saving details. Front doors came from the Zephyr club coupe, while the rear ones were elongated Zephyr sedan panels. From the cowl forward, the Custom body was the same as the regular Zephyr's except for a few details. The rear had a Continental bustle, more appropriate for a formal carriage, and it came off fairly well.

Though heavy-looking, the Custom was a decent stand-in for Lincoln's now-departed senior line, and cost considerably less. The sedan and limo arrived at $2704 and $2836, respectively; prices rose somewhat for 1942. However, production was never high enough to warrant their revival after the war. Fewer than 1000 were built, fully two-thirds of them limousines. An interesting sidelight is that a Custom won this year's Gilmore Economy Run.

Overall, Lincoln recorded a disappointing 18,244 units for the model year. Even poor Willys did better. Though few knew it at the time, Lincoln was now starting a long decline in both sales and market share. Much of this has been blamed on the Zephyr V-12's early history of rapid sludge buildup (due to inadequate crankcase ventilation), plus poor oil flow and too-small water passages that had led to overheating, bore warpage and ring wear. To some degree, these maladies were dealt with the first year, but the engine never shed its trouble-prone image, even the postwar versions that were actually quite reliable.

Equally serious was Lincoln's relatively weak dealer network (Ford dealers sold Zephyrs in some parts of the country), which wouldn't be rectified until Lincoln-Mercury Division was formed after the war. Then too, the Zephyr was aging, and many medium-price rivals had caught up with newer, more appealing designs. Thus, Buick, Oldsmobile, DeSoto, Chrysler, and even Hudson all notched '41 sales gains, most at the Zephyr's expense. But the real problem was Cadillac, which shrewdly abandoned its middle-class LaSalle after 1940 for the similarly priced Series 61, offering true luxury-car prestige for less cash than Zephyr. Also, Cadillac boasted more trim and body choices, plus improved steering, new self-shift Hydra-Matic Drive, bold new styling, and a smoother, quieter, more powerful engine. With all this, Cadillac nearly doubled its '41 volume over combined 1940 production, while Lincoln actually dropped by more than 2500 units.

To some extent, this reflected the problems of Ford Motor Company itself. The empire had gone to seed under the aging Henry, who had never allowed Edsel enough latitude or managerial control. Now, it was beginning to show.

After a good sophomore year, Mercury came back loaded for bear. Wheelbase extended two inches, to 118, thus maintaining its distance with Ford's, while the lineup

(Series 19A) was bolstered by new coupe-sedan, business coupe, and wood-wagon body styles. Appearance and engineering changes also paralleled Ford's, but the styling was chunky and not nearly as handsome as 1939-40, with more chrome, a wider divided grille, fender-mounted parking lights, and longer, higher, more squarish fenders. It had all the dash of a postwar Volvo 444 (and a lot of people compared the two). Perhaps due to the number of more attractive rivals—particularly from GM—production hardly budged in a year that saw sales gains throughout the industry, and Mercury dropped to 13th in the standings, behind Nash and DeSoto.

1942

Historically, a newly designed Detroit automobile is usually given only a mild reworking for its second year. The 1941 Ford was no exception, and the '42 edition was little changed in most important respects. But 1942 would hardly be the usual sort of model year at Ford or anywhere else in the industry. Less than three months after Ford introduced its '42s on September 12, 1941, the nation was at war.

It was inevitable that civilian car production would shut down after December 7. And when the spigot was finally turned off by government decree, automakers either hastily converted to war manufacturing or completed what efforts they'd already begun. Contrary to common belief, not everyone in Detroit had planned on America's entering the war—least of all Ford, which had geared up for a big 1942. But ever the pacifist, Henry had felt the winds of war blowing from Europe, so his company was also engaged in an increasing amount of war work long before the Japanese attacked Pearl Harbor.

Three days before that, on December 4, Ford and other automakers had been ordered to freeze all civilian projects and cut back on excessive use of brightwork. These restrictions were made all the more sober by the government's sudden war declaration of December 8, which implied the total mobilization of American industry. The implication became fact on February 10, 1942, when the government halted civilian car production for the duration. Only 43,307 Fords had been built since January 1, and the model year total of just 160,432 units would make the '42s the rarest Fords since 1910. They'd have to last, too, for there would be no more new cars for four very long years.

Mounting defense work in 1940-41 had left little time for Ford stylists and engineers to make anything but minor alterations on the '42s. Styling was marked by a more cohesive front end and runningboards newly concealed by extended lower-door sheetmetal. Now set in a chrome frame, the grille was lower, more horizontal, and close to

The 1942 Ford line boasted a bulkier-looking front end. The Super DeLuxe wagon weighed 3468 pounds.

V-8 power climbed to 90 bhp for '42, same as the six.

The '42 Super DeLuxe Fordor listed at $930.

full-width in line with industry trends. Above were square parking lamps mounted in what remained of the front fender "catwalks." The only vestige of '41's prominent central grille was a slim chrome strip running down from the hood.

This year's Ford lineup was unchanged except that the low-price Specials were now restricted to the six. As before, DeLuxe and Super DeLuxe could also be had with V-8. Ford dealers must have tired of explaining to customers why the six had more horsepower than the V-8, so the latter was now rated at the same 90 bhp even though it was mechanically unchanged. Prices *were* changed—up about $100 across the board—making the $1080 Super DeLuxe convertible the first Ford other than wagons to sell for more than $1000 since the Model A town cars of 10 years earlier.

Per Washington decree, Dearborn's final '42s were assembled with many parts painted instead of chromed, mainly because military applications now had priority over civilian ones for this and other metals. This makes the "blackout" '42s the rarest of a rare breed, something true of all Detroit cars built in the final days of this abbreviated model year.

Lincoln got most of the corporate emphasis for '42, with heavy facelifts and more horsepower for Zephyr, Lincoln Custom, and Continental. The last had become known as something of a "lead sled"—and there was plenty of it in those laboriously hand-formed bodies. For this and other reasons, the Conti was too heavy for its available power. So was the Zephyr.

Accordingly, the old "12-cylinder V-8" was punched out to 305 cubic inches via a 0.04-inch bore increase (to 2.94 inches) and gained improved manifolding and carburetion, all of which boosted output to a rated 130 bhp. Alas, the previous aluminum heads had been claimed by defense priorities, so cast iron was substituted. Due to its reduced heat dissipation properties, compression was eased from 7.2 to 7.0:1. Larger crank journals were also new.

But the V-12 really shouldn't have been bored. The inevitable core shifts during casting often made for off-center bores that, when machined, left cylinder walls either too thin or nonexistent, resulting in a raft of blown engines. (Lincoln would correct the problem postwar by reverting to the 292 block.)

And that's not the only reason for this engine's "trouble-prone" image. For one thing, it relied on no fewer than five filters; clog any one and they hindered instead of helped. We've already mentioned the inadequate crankcase ventilation and sludge build-up on early engines (see *1941*), but that was compounded by a unique Zephyr feature: an oil-level indicator that lulled owners into thinking that they didn't need to look at their dipsticks—and, as a result, their lubricant's condition. With the 305, more crankshaft oil passages were drilled to eliminate welch plugs and internal cavities, and a heftier oil pump was installed, but it was too late. People thought the V-12 was troublesome because it was. And though it's not clear whether this stemmed from faulty basic engineering or rushed production, the problems were real.

Because replacement V-12s were costly and hard to come by, a number of Zephyrs and a few Continentals were given engine swaps. Michael Sedgwick, the late British writer, branded the V-12 "lethargic and unreliable. Had it not been for the war, maybe the small-bore 12 would have got itself sorted out for keeps. But [it] did not truly succeed in its appointed class because Ford came up with something that didn't lend itself to American flat-rate over-the-counter service."

Nevertheless, given by-the-book maintenance and reasonable care, the V-12 was smooth, efficient and reliable.

Bulkier fenders and grille marked the '42 Continental.

British builders like Sidney Allard, George Brough, and the makers of the Atalanta certainly seemed willing to put up with its peculiarities in exchange for the performance it provided in their light, spare-bodied sports cars. It was certainly part of the Zephyr/Continental mystique. But its real significance lies in bringing more-than-eight-cylinders motoring to a segment of the American market that had never enjoyed it before—and never would again.

Common to all '42 Lincolns were longer front springs and a wider front track, aimed at improved ride. The old twin-speed Columbia axle disappeared from the options chart, but there was a new extra-cost transmission called "Liquimatic." Also offered on this year's Mercury, it was a hastily contrived reply to GM's Hydra-Matic, essentially a conventional overdrive transmission with fluid coupling. Unfortunately for Lincoln, the couplings seldom lasted more than 10,000 miles, and customer complaints eventually forced the factory to retrofit manual gearboxes free of charge. Needless to say, Liquimatic wouldn't return postwar.

Lincoln styling this year was nowhere near as memorable as 1940-41. Bob Gregorie dressed up the three-year-old bodies as much as he could to woo customers away from Harley Earl's sleek new Cadillacs, but the result was merely different, not better. Each end took on longer, higher, squared-up fenders that increased overall length. Height went down fractionally on all models, but weights were up. Front ends acquired broader grilles composed of stainless-steel horizontal bars that flared out to the sides and down to the bumper. Small sidelamps now flanked the headlights, while taillamps were shaped to match the fenders.

Lincoln mirrored Mercury in 1942 sales, which ran well through late 1941, only to be halted in February. The model year totals were tiny nevertheless: about 6000 Zephyrs, 336 Continentals, and 113 Customs.

Though the Zephyr name wouldn't return postwar, the basic 1942 design would. So perhaps it's useful at this point to pause and reflect on this historic car as well as its controversial engine.

Zephyr styling won wide acclaim in its day. It still does.

The last pre-war Lincoln moves off the assembly line.

With it, Ford proved conclusively that streamlining could be beautiful, especially next to opposing streamliners like the elephantine Chrysler Airflow. Thus, Zephyr won public and industry acceptance for "modern" design as we know it today. John Tjaarda, though understandably disappointed by some of the inevitable technical deviations from his original concept, loved the lines of the production car. "Foreign engineers and designers such as Dr. Porsche, Mathis, Rasmussen and Dolfuss called it the only car coming out of America to command their interest," he wrote. Later, the New York Museum of Modern Art cited Zephyr as "the first successfully designed streamlined car in America," a notable affront to Chrysler that was, some said, justified nevertheless.

A look at contemporary road tests confirms the worth of that slippery styling as well as the oft-maligned V-12. Especially with the optional Columbia two-speed rear axle (1936-40), the Zephyr was rapid for its time. Its 0-60

Only 113 Lincoln Customs were built for 1942.

FDR's "Sunshine Special" was given the '42 Zephyr look.

For $1215, one could own a 1942 Mercury convertible.

Mercury got a 5 horsepower boost to 100-even for '42.

The price-leader three-passenger coupe cost $995.

The most expensive '42 Merc: the $1260 station wagon.

mph time of 16 seconds was outstanding for a heavy pre-war sedan. So was its 75-mph cruising ability, not to mention a 90-mph maximum and fuel consumption of 15-18 mpg. All this for a thousand dollars or so made the Zephyr remarkable value.

Of course, the Zephyr will forever be remembered as the car that led to the Continental—and will be forever compared with it, which isn't fair. The Continental was an *objet d'art*; the Zephyr was a family hauler, albeit one designed by a genius who marched to the beat of his own drummer. Besides, many Zephyr fans see a better com-

The sedan delivery was a still-popular Ford in 1942.

parison. Says collector Chad Coombs: "A Zephyr really was the ultimate Ford. Throughout any Zephyr journey, one will be reminded of Ford V-8s. Zephyrs are certainly not delicate, specialist automobiles."

No, and they were anything but faceless. The Zephyr was a true pioneer: of streamlining and unit construction most successfully, cost-effective engineering to a lesser extent. But most of all, it pulled Lincoln through the most disastrous economic upheaval in modern history. Next to those accomplishments, siring the Continental seems almost superfluous.

Mercury was no bigger but a lot brighter for '42, at least the pre-blackout models. Though somewhat unexpected after the '41 makeover, this year's heavy restyle brought a Lincoln-like, two-tier grille composed of thin horizontal bars, plus double horizontal moldings on front and rear fenders. It was all part of an attempt to add "importance" (if not cleanliness) to the face that had launched 80,000 buyers a year, thus moving the medium-price make away from Ford and closer to Lincoln. Still on its year-old 118-inch wheelbase, the Merc was over 16 feet long and miles more impressive than a Ford, yet cost only a few dollars more. The '42s also cost a few dollars more than the '41s, the six-model lineup now ranging from $995 for the three-seat coupe to $1260 for the woody wagon. Ford liked to boast that Mercury had "made 150,000 owners change cars." What it didn't like was the fact that a lot of them had changed from Fords.

Mercury sales got off to a flying start, well ahead of the 1939-40 pace through the last quarter of 1941. But maybe people knew something, or had read about a Japanese gentleman named Tojo, because sales were up for almost everybody as Americans scrambled to buy 'em while they could get 'em. Sure enough, Mercury managed no more than about 22,000 units by the time civilian production was terminated.

1943-45

It hardly needs saying that Ford Motor Company was one of the nation's most important defense contractors during World War II. Though it had ceased to be the nation's top-selling automaker in the '30s, it remained a vast corporation with huge resources. Henry Ford saw to it that those resources were quickly mobilized.

Ford's war record was proud as any in American industry. Its huge new factory at Willow Run, Michigan, would turn out the famous B-24 "Liberator" bomber by the score. The company also stepped in to produce the Army's new light utility car, the Jeep, designed by the failing American Bantam Car Company of Butler, Pennsylvania, which proved unable to cope with the military's tremendous demand. Ford's other wartime production included a wide array of military vehicles, from amphibious and armored personnel carriers to light tanks and various conventional and all-terrain trucks. With government approval, the firm also built a limited number of 1942-style cars, mainly standard Tudor and Fordor sedans. Most saw service as military staff cars, but some remained stateside for "essential" civilian purposes.

The war years also witnessed a leadership crisis that would have a profound effect on the company, its operations, and products in the postwar period. Precipitating the upheaval was the untimely passing of Edsel Ford on May 26, 1943, at the age of only 50. Never a robust figure, he was claimed by a combination of fever, stomach ulcers, and cancer—hastened, perhaps, by Henry's continuing reliance on Harry Bennett, whose strong-arm tactics had produced labor unrest, and dissention among top company executives. But though overshadowed to the end by his legendary father, Edsel had emerged as his own man, an auto executive of rare taste and ability. In particular, he almost single-handedly established styling as a distinct and important function within the Ford organization. His absence would be keenly felt.

Shortly after this, in June 1943, Henry Ford was re-elected to another term as company president, a term he would not complete. Two months later, in August, President Roosevelt arranged an early discharge from the Navy for Edsel's son Henry Ford II, then only 25, with the express understanding that he was urgently needed to take over for his grandfather as head of one of the nation's most important businesses. Meanwhile, Clara Ford threatened to leave her husband if he continued to stand in the way of union organization. Old Henry finally relented, but not before he suffered further losses to his own prestige and in the loyalty of his employees.

Inevitably, this turmoil within the Ford family led to a breakup of the company's top managerial staff. Trouble had been brewing as early as 1939, but it didn't come to a head until several top designers walked out on March 4,

Even before the U.S. entered the battle, Ford was producing war material. Gliders were one of the products.

Ford's huge new factory at Willow Run, Michigan turned out the famous B-24 "Liberator" bomber by the score.

1944. Among them were engineer Lawrence Sheldrick and stylist Eugene T. "Bob" Gregorie. Their loss, wrote historians Allan Nevins and Frank E. Hill in *Ford: Decline and Rebirth*, were "body blows to the Ford Motor Company."

"Cast Iron Charlie" Sorensen was another crisis casualty. He'd become too ambitious. He wanted to be company president, and Henry wouldn't have it. Thus, Sorensen departed in March 1944 to head troubled Willys-Overland, about a month after Henry II became executive vice-president at Ford in late January.

The way now seemed clear for Bennett, but he hadn't counted on the close-knit Ford family. Again, Clara was the only one who seemed willing to tell Henry he was wrong. He must now resign, she told him, in favor of his grandson. The old man, wrote Nevins and Hill, "was peevishly reluctant." Ultimately, the scales were tipped by Edsel's widow, who took Clara's side: "If this is not done," she announced, "I shall sell my stock." Henry capitulated.

In August 1945, Henry II, still in uniform, was summoned to Fair Lane, his grandfather's Dearborn estate. He knew what he was up against: "I told him I'd take [over as president] only if I had a completely free hand to make any changes I wanted to make. We argued about that, but he didn't withdraw his offer." Thus, Henry Ford submit-

ted his resignation as president on September 20, 1945. The Board of Directors accepted it the next day and named Henry II to succeed him. Bennett stormed out that same day with the window dressing of a one-month directorship.

The leadership crisis, and the atmosphere of murky intrigue that pervaded Ford Motor Company in the mid-'40s, only made it more difficult to plan for the return of civilian production. But not impossible. In fact, proposals for a wholly revamped 1943 corporate line were well along before Pearl Harbor. And despite the press of military work, designers still found time during the war years to refine these ideas and develop new ones. Some of their efforts would be seen in the all-new 1949 Lincoln and Mercury, while others would appear in overseas products.

Gregorie recalled Ford's wartime activities in a 1970 interview with Michael Lamm, published that year in *Special-Interest Autos* magazine. Naturally, the outbreak of war left the 1943-45 models stillborn: "All at once, the whole company changed gears and got down to war work. . . . Yet in the backs of our minds we knew that after the war we were going to have to start building cars again. At the beginning, nobody knew whether the U.S. would win or not, but there seemed little point in planning on any assumption except that we would. So slowly, in between wartime assignments, this little skeleton group we held together would go back to the sort of nebulous business of designing after-the-war cars.

"The Ford lines were the ones we worked on most, because they were past due for a change. [Lincoln, having been heavily facelifted for '42, would have seen only detail alterations.] Edsel Ford was very busy with war production matters in 1942, but did spend what time he could with us on future planning. This lasted until his illness and death in the spring of 1943. The elder Mr. Ford took virtually no interest in design or styling activities, leaving this phase of operations to Mr. Edsel Ford and myself. There were no committees, etc., as is the usual practice. Decisions were quick and simple, which possibly accounts for some of the cleaner, simpler, straightforward styling we were able to accomplish. Mr. Edsel Ford and I were usually pretty much in agreement.

"What was intended as the larger Ford became the first all-new postwar Mercury," Gregorie continued. "At the time, we considered this design for the Ford of that era. Then, an entirely new Ford was developed, with lighter construction, new suspension, etc., and this became the 1949 Ford.

"One idea we had back then, and it came to fruition in 1949, was to associate the Mercury more closely with the Lincoln via certain body interchanges, as well as tie them together in advertising, sales, etc. Before, the Merc was based on the Ford. We figured the Mercury might gain some prestige by becoming a baby Lincoln, rather than a blown-up Ford. So during the war, our Lincoln designs did have some importance toward that end. We laid down the basic lines for what would become the 1949 Mercury in a painting that Ross Cousins did in 1943 . . . showing a five-passenger coupe driving past the Rouge plant. We called it a Lincoln, but the profile is very much what the 1949 Mercury became. Then too, all those early Lincoln clays show a lot more of what we had in mind for the Mercury, as well as the Lincoln Cosmopolitan.

"As for the Continental," Gregorie said, "we didn't know whether it would be continued after Mr. Edsel Ford's death in 1943. We made some renderings and full-size models of the Cosmo with a spare tire mounted on the trunk, but it was too ponderous and clumsy to project the true Continental image. I think the only reason Ford Motor Company kept the Continental after the war was because they already had the body tooling. If the 1946-48 Continental hadn't used 1942 tooling, it probably wouldn't have been built those years. With the strong demand for postwar cars, the Continental did sell, and it really carried Lincoln prestige into the postwar period and to later Continentals. After Mr. Edsel Ford's death, though, no one had the heart to come up with a completely new Continental design."

The upgraded Mercury to which Gregorie refers wasn't supposed to resemble the '49 Lincoln. Through early 1947, Ford planning envisioned no fewer than six distinct corporate platforms: a 100-inch-wheelbase compact to be built by a separate new division, a standard Ford on a 118-inch

Henry Ford II came home in 1945 to replace old Henry.

wheelbase (same as the 1941-48 Mercury), a two-tier Mercury lineup on wheelbases of 120 and 123 inches, a 125-inch-wheelbase Lincoln (perhaps continuing the Zephyr name), and top-of-the-line Lincoln Cosmopolitan and Continental on a 128-inch chassis. The erstwhile Zephyr would have had the baby-Lincoln styling Gregorie mentioned, while the '49 Mercurys would have continued as more luxurious Fords.

Dearborn wasn't the only Big Three producer with designs on a compact. GM and Chrysler had similar projects underway, stemming, like Ford's, from earlier studies done in response to the Depression. All the early-to-mid-'40s efforts were based on fears that a recession, like the one that had followed World War I, would make cheaper, smaller cars a necessity once peace returned.

Ford's postwar compact originated in 1942. First thoughts centered on a low-price four-cylinder car with the dimensions, power output, weight, and price of the prewar Willys-Overland. Later, some executives apparently wanted a size/price rival for Studebaker's Champion. Of course, the Champion had a six, and its dimensions had grown since Raymond Loewy's 1939 original. As it turned out, Studebaker fielded a warmed-over '42 Champion for 1946, then bowed dramatically styled all-new models for '47.

In late spring 1944, a group of Dearborn executives led by sales manager John R. Davis and production boss Mead L. Bricker came up with the idea of forming a separate committee to prepare new products for the postwar market. This became the Engineering Planning Committee, representing key departments from manufacturing to market research. Hudson McCarroll took the lead in defining these products and their technical makeup. Among them was what he saw as a new kind of economy car designed to sell at two-thirds the price of the standard Ford.

To this end, the committee reviewed Ford's last small-car project. Known as number 92-A, it was completed in 1938 by a team under Eugene Farkas, who'd played a big part in designing the Model A and the '32 Fords. This car was quite small, about 600 pounds lighter than the contemporary Ford, with a shorter wheelbase and a narrower track, and Farkas had cleverly proposed using the anemic V-8/60 rather than tooling up a new four or six. But in the end, 92-A was scrapped because of high production costs, which would have been too close to those of a standard Ford for the compact to have a significant price advantage and still be profitable. Now, in the mid-'40s, company planners realized that the cost/profit problem would be even more troublesome in the postwar world.

Ford had produced various smaller cars in Europe before the war, starting in 1932 with the four-cylinder British Model Y Junior, a Sheldrick design. But all were deemed too small for American buyers, and there was nothing technical that could be applied to a smaller U.S. model. Clearly, the new compact American Ford would have to be designed from scratch in Dearborn.

Frantic and furious work brought forth many ideas, some intelligent, others less so. For example, one proposal had front-wheel drive and a four-cylinder engine installed transversely ahead of the front wheel axis, a layout that's since become nearly universal. The radiator was placed slightly higher than the engine and behind it, backed by a cowl structure carrying the fuel tank, as on the Model A. The result was a short hood and a low, flat floor for unusually generous interior space. Also considered was a conventional rear-drive chassis with a longitudinal inline five, the elder Henry's doing. Though ostensibly not connected with product engineering by this time, the old man still maintained a private laboratory where he'd been toying with five-cylinder engines since about 1936.

Soon, the experimental department was humming with new powerplants, including air-cooled fours and sixes. Cast-aluminum blocks were tried for several water-cooled units, including the five-cylinder job, but were ruled out as too costly. A rear-engine layout wasn't even considered, perhaps because of Henry's objections to it on the original Zephyr prototype, and front drive was ultimately discarded because of its many unknowns as well as its higher cost.

As time went on, the small V-8 was increasingly preferred, along with other basic elements of Farkas' 1938 proposal, and a new prototype incorporating these features was completed in mid-1944. Then in September, Henry Ford II announced his company's intent to produce a smaller, lower-priced model for the postwar market.

By the time the Engineering Planning Committee ordered full-scale versions that winter, Gregorie had already been doing small-car sketches and clay models for about two years. A 98-inch wheelbase was selected, and a fastback two-door sedan was the first body style developed. What emerged was quite similar to the standard-size '42 Ford in overall proportions, but more modern-looking, with slab sides and a lower, wider grille. A continuing flow of fresh market information led to several more prototypes that differed from each other in many ways. These were further modified, and a 100-inch wheelbase was tried. Although the five-cylinder engine was still in the running at this point, the V-8/60 was more or less assumed.

By January 1945, a more precise package definition prompted planners to settle on the 100-inch platform. Within six months, the five-cylinder engine was scrapped and development proceeded around the V-8 alone. The frame would be a smaller version of the forthcoming '49 Ford/Mercury design, complete with its new coil-spring independent front suspension and parallel rear leaf springs, both firsts for Dearborn. Meantime, Clyde R. Paton, former chief engineer at Packard, was hired to direct the project through to the production-ready stage, with assembly slated to commence within six months after the war ended in Europe.

But he soon ran into the same snag that killed Farkas' project: cost. Hudson McCarroll, promoted to engineering director in 1945, didn't know what to do, and ended up listening to everybody. Sales manager Davis said he already had buyers for every standard Ford. Why put a lot of money into a compact that the public might not accept? He saw no need for a smaller car, even as a loss leader, until 1948-49 at the earliest. In that event, Paton thought an updated design might be needed, preferably with unit construction. With all this, the 100-inch-wheelbase prototype was shelved.

Paton and company then went to work on two larger versions of what was now being called the "Light Car": a 106-inch-wheelbase Ford and a 112-inch-wheelbase Mercury. To handle development and production, Ford created a new Light Car Division in April 1946. By this time, the program was seen as so important that no one questioned the need for a new corporate entity of this size.

But steel, copper, lead, zinc, and other metals were hard to come by even before the war ended, and Henry II knew it wasn't good business to add a whole new model line to vie for scarce resources with cars that were already selling well. Although management didn't officially curtail the small-car program in 1946, the Product Committee told the Light Car Division to defer production plans. The result was the same: the Light Car was dead in Ford's U.S. future. By then, the 106-inch-wheelbase version was fully engineered, effectively a production prototype.

Enter Maurice Dollfus, a prominent Paris banker and

president of Ford France, who'd long argued that the Light Car should be built in Europe. At last, he got his wish. The engineering department released all data and blueprints to him in June 1946, and the 106-inch-wheelbase prototype was redesigned at the Ford France factory in Poissy, near Paris, for production on metric tools, with specifications adjusted to accommodate locally produced components. Named Vedette, it started coming off the lines in the fall of 1948, but proved a sales disappointment due to relatively high fuel consumption and stiff competition from class rivals.

There was a funny thing about all these wartime machinations, and Gregorie sums it up perfectly: "It never dawned on any of us that, right after the war, anything on wheels would sell, whether it was restyled or not. We just never sat down and thought about it enough to figure that out. So we went right ahead as though the first thing we'd have to do . . . was restyle the Ford and Mercury, not realizing until the last minute that a suitable facelift would do as well. In fact, we had until about 1948-49 before we'd have to come up with anything really different."

Gregorie was only half right. The immediate postwar years did see an unprecedented seller's market in response to the huge demand for new cars resulting from the four-year production drought. And, like most everyone else except the independents, Ford got along fine by reprising its '42 models through 1948.

But by model year 1949, when the majors completed their postwar design overhaul, Dearborn was in serious financial trouble. Aside from impeding technical progress, old Henry had left his company in financial chaos, reflecting a long-time distrust of accountants. Thus, his grandson inherited not only an aging product line but a company laden with debt, fiscally out of control, and lacking broad, strong leadership in several key areas. Even worse, Chrysler Corporation had taken over as number-two in industry production behind General Motors.

As a result, 1949 would shape up as a do-or-die year for Ford. And strange as it may seem now, there were many at the time who didn't give Dearborn more than a 50/50 chance of making it.

1946-48

With the end of war in the Pacific theater, American industry turned rapidly from military to civilian production. For Ford Motor Company, this transition would be fraught with significance. The war years had seen the untimely death of Edsel Ford, the departure of the brilliant designers who had gravitated to him, and the

Henry and Henry look over the River Rouge plant layout.

end of his father's reign. Now, under the leadership of Edsel's son Henry II, the company was not only entering the bright new postwar world but embarking on a new beginning.

When Harry Bennett, the elder Henry's mercenary lieutenant, left Dearborn in 1945 because he was passed over as company president, he angrily told young Henry: "You're taking over a billion-dollar organization here that you haven't contributed a thing to!" But Henry II was about to start contributing. Aided by a bright young cadre of managers and accountants, he would quickly begin guiding Ford back to its late-prewar position as a near rival to the General Motors colossus.

During his first two years as president, Ford's losses ran as high as $10 million a month. Budgets and accounting procedures were either in total disarray or nonexistent. One department even calculated its due bills and receivables by measuring the height of the paperwork! Young Henry began looking for help, and in late 1945 he found it. Almost casually, Charles B. "Tex" Thornton had advertised the services of himself and a group of talented young officers just being discharged from the Air Force. Ford answered the ad, much to Thornton's surprise, thus bringing the "Whiz Kids" to Dearborn, the talented systems specialists that would help turn Ford's fortunes around.

Police received priority when assembly started for '46.

A new model: the '46 Ford Sportsman convertible ($1982).

The '46s sported a new grille; the rest was carryover.

The Super DeLuxe Tudor sedan sold for $1260 in 1946.

Then, in early 1946, HF II recruited Ernest R. Breech from the Bendix Division of General Motors. In much the same way that Harry Bennett had served his grandfather, he would be served by Breech—until he fired him unexpectedly in 1959.

Most U.S. automakers faced a dilemma toward the end of World War II: Should they return to civilian production with warmed-over prewar models or put the rush on new postwar designs? Studebaker, after a brief run of 1942 lookalikes labeled 1946s, did the latter; most everyone else did the former. Henry Ford II had no choice. Though financed to the tune of nearly $700 million, his company was heavily in debt, and faced the massive cost of winding down its war machine. Above all, Ford needed to get back to civilian production as quickly as possible.

Among the first product decisions made by the new man in charge were the Ford Sportsman and its second cousin, the Mercury Sportsman. HF II reasoned that if Ford's first postwar models couldn't be all-new, at least some of them could be strikingly different on the surface—enough to lure buyers into newly reopened showrooms with cars that were otherwise quite familiar. Paneling convertibles in maple or yellow birch with mahogany-veneer inserts seemed like a pretty good way to do that.

Before his departure (see *1943-45*), styling director Bob Gregorie had designed a convertible of this sort, and HF II liked it. Ford certainly didn't lack for wood. It had a massive timber forest and processing plant up at Iron Mountain, Michigan, which had supplied raw materials for station wagon bodies since 1936. And because the panels could be grafted right onto existing convertible bodies, building such a car would be no more difficult than turning out woody wagons. Not that Sportsman panels were mere appliqués. They were, in fact, structural body elements made from solid wood blocks, mitred together with handcrafted precision and handsomely finished with several coats of varnish.

Wood is nature's product, not man's, so no two Sportsmans were exactly alike. The Fords used three different types of trim during their two-year production run. Enthusiast Dr. Thomas B. Garrett noted that "Style A had horizontal pieces running full length across the doors and quarters. In the 'B' and 'C' styles, the full-length members ran vertically from top to bottom. All 1946 Sportsmans used the 'A' panels, whereas '47s were divided between all three." (Ford lists only 28 Sportsmans sold for 1948, all reserialed '47s.)

There was just one problem: the production '46 rear fenders. They wrapped around too much at the rear, which would have cut into the wooden trunklid. The solution was to use 1941 Ford sedan delivery fenders, with taillights, on both the Ford and Mercury versions. Naturally, they were the same as other models from the cowl forward. Like its non-woody linemate, however, the Ford came only in Super DeLuxe trim with the L-head V-8, the latter in deference to its greater weight. Exclusive standard equipment included hydraulic window lifts and vanity mirrors on both sunvisors.

Hollywood actress Ella Raines took delivery of the first Ford Sportsman on Christmas Day 1945, a scant three months after Henry II had assumed the presidency. Despite only incidental publicity, it was a fair success considering it cost $800 more than a comparable Fordor sedan and $500 more than the standard all-steel convertible. A total of 3487 were built for the three model years plus 205 Mercury Sportsmans, offered only for '46.

Performance was not a Sportsman asset. The Ford version, for example, weighed about 100 pounds more than the standard V-8 convertible and 200 pounds more than an equivalent Fordor, so it moved along well enough but wasn't sensationally quick. Typical figures for both models were about 85 mph maximum and a bit less than 20 seconds in the 0-60 mph dash. Either one had definite understeer, but handling was adequate considering their antediluvian front and rear transverse leaf springs. They even cope well with today's roads and traffic conditions, including 55-mph freeways. Most examples are unusually solid for convertibles, testifying to their careful construction. Altogether, the Sportsman is an entertaining piece of transportation and the most notable production Ford car of the early postwar years.

Aside from simplified frontal styling, the rest of the Ford line—including the Sportsman—was essentially the '42 package reborn. However, performance improved as the 221-cubic-inch V-8 gave way to the 100-horsepower, 239-cid unit borrowed from Mercury—to the detriment of

The '46 Continental wore a heavier grille and bumpers.

the latter's sales and "hot rod" personna. Ford's L-head six remained at its customary 90 bhp. The prewar Special series of low-priced sixes was eliminated, leaving six- and eight-cylinder DeLuxe and Super DeLuxe models as before. Body styles comprised Tudor and Fordor sedans, coupe, wagon, standard and Sportsman convertibles, and an "open express" pickup, a one-ton utility model with standard four-speed transmission.

The 1947-48 Fords were little changed: just reshuffled nameplates and lower-mounted round parking lights for '47, a six uprated to 95 bhp for '48. Prices *did* change,

Henry Dies: The First Era Ends

Ford Motor Company closed a momentous chapter in its history on April 7, 1947: Henry Ford was dead at the age of 83. Yet despite the bitterness and disappointments of his later years, his achievements were untarnished. And to the end, he remained irascible, unpredictable, enigmatic — and endlessly fascinating.

Not that Ford was simply characterized. Wrote Michael Lamm in the Ford 75th Anniversary Issue of *Automotive News* in 1978: "Almost anything anyone says about . . . Henry Ford contains a contradiction. Newton's third law of motion applies equally to physics and to the elder Mr. Ford. It seems that every action . . . had an equal and opposite reaction . . . [He] was an immensely complicated man, consistently inconsistent, and his personality changed not only from day to day but a good deal over the course of his long life. Men close to Ford could read his mood by the lines around

his mouth and the color of his complexion. When his face looked gray and furrowed, people tended to stay out of his way.

"It's hard to believe that a man enlightened enough to revolutionize labor via the $5 Day of 1914, revolutionize industry through the moving assembly line, who believed in lowering profits, who tried to stop World War I with the Peace Ship of 1915, who supported Wilson and the League of Nations and paid all bills for the Neutral Conference on Continuous Mediation; who founded schools, a hospital, an orphanage, and a museum; who ultimately gave away at least a third of his life's net income — it's hard to believe that [this man] would later harass his workers with a private police force; resist the National Recovery Act; come to despise Roosevelt; admire the Nazi government and accept a citation from Hitler in 1938; lash out at Jews, banks, and Wall Street and fire most of his closest colleagues." Hard to believe maybe, but that was Henry Ford.

If a folk hero can be said to have emerged from the ranks of the auto-

mobile industry, it was surely Henry Ford. Along with the Wright Brothers and his friends Thomas A. Edison and Harvey Firestone, he was an inspiration for millions — a symbol of the dreams, drive, and inventiveness that sparked America's unparalleled growth and prosperity in the first half of the 20th century. He had established his company purely on venture capital and an idea, and would see it blossom into a multimillion-dollar worldwide organization. He had taken just five years to produce a mechanical device that enabled a nation to conquer her vast size. No geographically large country had ever built a world-class economy before; for her's, America was in his debt. No less important were his manufacturing and product innovations, such as the simple, reliable Model A, and engineering benchmarks like the monobloc flathead V-8, which pioneered a whole new approach to affordable transportation.

For a man who once remarked "History is more or less bunk," Henry Ford certainly did more than enough to earn a permanent place in it.

Price had zoomed to $4392 for the '46 Continental coupe.

Lincoln built 265 Continental coupes for 1946.

The Zephyr name was gone, but it lived on as a Lincoln.

For $2722 one could buy a V-12 Lincoln four-door sedan.

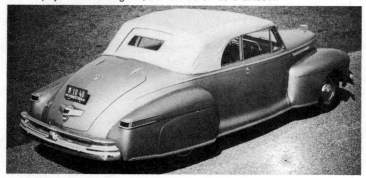

One of the best looking '46 Lincolns: the $3142 ragtop.

Lincoln's 292-cid V-12 put out 125 horses for 1946.

however, rising each year by an average $100, reflecting the influence of postwar inflation.

While all this sounds boring, no styling or engineering changes were really needed in the booming postwar seller's market. Ford output exceeded 429,000 units in 1947, then dropped to 236,000 in '48. This wasn't a sign of trouble (though it could have been), only an early end to 1948 production. Realizing the need for a truly modern product, Ford management had initiated work on an all-new design in early 1946. Set to debut for 1949, it would be a car of major importance to the still-struggling company—and the younger members of the Ford family now running it.

Shortly after he arrived, Henry Ford II also initiated a corporate reorganization along GM lines, no surprise with Breech around. One of its most lasting results was the 1947 formation of Lincoln-Mercury Division as distinct from the other car divisions (Ford and Light Car), with its

own engineering, purchasing, production, and sales departments, and a separate dealer network. This in turn prompted a new approach to product planning that would eventually see Mercury clones of certain hot-selling Fords, like the "glasstop" Sun Valley/Skyliner (1954), Comet/Falcon compacts (1960), the Cougar/Mustang "ponycars" (1967), and today's Cougar/Thunderbird. To some extent, competition between Ford and Lincoln-Mercury was now inevitable, but it was good, healthy competition. It still is, so long as Dearborn doesn't fall into GM's recent habit of badge-engineering exact copies of most everything in the corporate stable. (The design distinctions between today's Sable/Taurus and Mark VII/Cougar/Thunderbird suggest Ford recognizes the importance of avoiding that trap.)

Initially, divisionalization meant a closer design and engineering relationship between Mercury and Lincoln,

Production start-up was difficult after the war because of material shortages and labor unrest.

Mercury built 6044 convertibles for the '46 model run.

The '46 coupe-sedan was a good buy at $1495.

albeit within well-defined price sectors. But in 1946, this future tie-up was known only to a few upper-level managers, and both makes were still officially separate. The job at hand was getting cars built—and, like Ford, the quickest way to do that was to reissue what they'd been selling before the war: the '42s.

After the government allowed resumption of civilian production on a limited basis in early 1945, Ford produced about 34,000 cars, but Lincoln-Mercury managed only 10 percent of that. Volume rose slowly through early 1946, but the model year figures were encouraging: 86,608 Mercurys, 16,645 Lincolns. Mercury thus enjoyed a record total in its first full year back.

Like other makes, Lincoln took advantage of the opportunity to drop slow-selling prewar models, so its '46 lineup, bowing in September 1945, was somewhat simpler. Gone were the long-wheelbase Customs, the Zephyr name, and the three-passenger club coupe, leaving a standard 125-inch-wheelbase line (Series 66H) with five offerings, all simply called "Lincoln." Prices were up about $600. Mechanical specs stayed the same except that the thin-wall 305 V-12 was junked for the sturdier 292-cid block of 1939-41. Continental also returned (as Series 76H), priced at around $4400, but Edsel Ford's passing rendered it a token gesture, continued more out of respect for his memory than any real commercial benefit. Besides, Lincoln had neither the time nor staff to build them, as suggested by '46 production of only 201 convertibles and 265 coupes.

Lincoln's postwar restyle involved the same frontal lobotomy for both Continental and the standard line: a massive two-tier, die-cast checked grille, with a Lincoln emblem above and a winged globe as the hood ornament. Hoodlines were smooth and clean, though, and the curvy bodies still expressed John Tjaarda's original aerodynamic lines, sweeping back to a tapered rear deck on standard models. Retaining their exterior spare and high, square trunk, the Continentals were still impressive. Their only additional identification was modest script on each side of the hood near the rear. Body-color metal tire covers enhanced their cleanliness of line.

Mercury followed Lincoln in facelifting its '42s to get the greatest styling difference for the least money, though inner structure and sheetmetal were virtually untouched. The previous inboard parking lights and double-band fender moldings remained, but the '42's clean, Lincoln-like horizontal-bar grille was replaced by a vertical-bar

affair reminiscent of an electric razor. It was a pretty homely puss, but Mercury would stick with it for three years.

Of course, the words "Mercury Eight" were prominently displayed, signifying continuation of the familiar 239-cid flathead V-8. But since it now also powered V-8 Fords, the only thing Merc buyers got for their extra $200 in purchase price was slightly more elaborate trim and a gaudier grille. As mentioned, Mercury also fielded a wood-body Sportsman convertible (Model 71), effectively a replacement for the 1942 business coupe. The integral wood construction made it quite expensive—$2209—and quite impractical (the wood demanded frequent, meticulous care),

Sportiest—and rarest—Merc was the Sportsman: 205 built.

On the '47-'48s, parking lights moved down; prices moved up.

Postwar pickups looked just like the '42s.

Ford built 12,033 Super DeLuxe convertibles for '48.

Postwar Fords benefitted from Mercury's 239.4-cid, 100-bhp V-8.

The '48 Super DeLuxe station wagon listed at $1972.

all of which perhaps explains why so few were built. Only two are known to exist today; discovering another would be a major feat for some fortunate enthusiast.

Lincoln-Mercury Division began formal operations on April 1, 1947 (a date no doubt chosen unintentionally), and its basic organizational structure and chain of command were in place by May. Now, the formidable team assembled by Ernie Breech went to work determining the division's future. With Lewis D. Crusoe handling finance, Harold Youngren engineering, and Al Browning purchasing, Ford Motor Company was probably in more competent hands than it had ever been before. And it had to be: they faced a titanic job. Their cars were obsolete, even compared to the equally aged competition. The only way to regain market share—and build on it—was an entirely new corporate line.

At a Policy Committee meeting on August 23, 1947, Crusoe moved that the 118-inch-wheelbase Ford proposed during wartime should be the new Mercury instead. The planned Mercury, in turn, would become the new Lincoln, while Ford would be redesigned on its existing 114-inch wheelbase. As previously noted (see *1943-45*), consolidation was the order of the day at each end of the line, the compact Light Car being dropped from U.S. production and the Continental scheduled to disappear as of 1949.

Author OCee Ritch has suggested that the Continental's demise was caused by lack of "the decisive force of the man [Edsel Ford] who had instituted the car and kept it moving through its first years." But even Edsel might have been glad to see it go. "As Ford people analyzed it," Ritch continued, "the Continental would have to be, in 1949 or 1950, a completely new car with engine, chassis and body revisions of a major nature. More important, it would necessarily have to be compatible with lower-cost production methods. To undertake such a program, which would be extremely costly, merely to maintain a slim wedge in a small market did not make as much sense as concentrating on the bread-and-butter Ford/Mercury lines."

Continental was thus allowed to atrophy as body pressings and smaller components were used up through model year '48. The '47 was hardly different than the '46 except for a redesigned hood ornament and hubcaps at mid-year. Mechanically, only the starter drive gear and generator were improved.

Production also improved, and in a big way. Lincoln was turning out as many Continentals as its limited facilities would allow, and 1947 saw record model year production that wouldn't be topped until 1958 with the Mark III: 738 cabriolets and 831 coupes, a total of 1569, most of them just touching $5000 as delivered. At least part of this success reflected the spreading knowledge that the car wouldn't be around much longer, but pent-up postwar demand was the main reason.

The standard Lincoln also stayed mostly the same for '47, but sported the new Continental hubcaps (with "Lincoln" spelled out in script) plus pull-out exterior door handles and pocket-style interior armrests. Retained was the

The Continental ("Mark I") was phased out after 1948.

This 1947-48 Mercury wagon was kept for company use.

The all-new '48 Ford trucks debuted on January 16, 1948.

Ford claimed this F-1 half-ton model was "Bonus Built."

1946 lineup of sedan, convertible, and club coupe, along with the Custom interior option for closed models. Prices rose about $225 across the board, and production went up slightly, totaling 19,891 for the model year (excluding Continental). Lincoln remained well down in the volume race, however. Cadillac had doubled its model year production to more than 60,000 units, while the advent of the new Frazer and Kaiser had pushed Lincoln down to 18th place in the industry, just ahead of Crosley. All of which must have strengthened Crusoe's argument for an all-new Lincoln.

The '47 Mercury line, now *sans* Sportsman, was also little changed: new aluminum hood mascot, friction-lock pull-type vent windows, shorter belt moldings (ending just ahead of the hood break), and a new Mercury nameplate (forward of the moldings). Production bucked the opposition's rising tide: Mercury finished in 13th place as Chrysler, DeSoto, and Studebaker all shot past.

If Lincolns and Mercurys were among the least changed of early postwar cars, it might be due to Ernie Breech, who was adamant on the subject. Discussing plans for the '49 models, he told the Policy Committee: "I have a vision. We start from scratch. We spend no time or money phoneying up the old cars, because this organization will be judged by the market on the next car it produces and it had better be a new one." Historians Allan Nevins and Frank Hill have written that Breech claimed to have received divine guidance the night before when, after praying, he was inspired to "Start afresh!"

Of course, that's what they *had* to do—and the sooner the better. That's why the new '49 Lincoln and Mercury arrived in April 1948, months before the formal start of the model year. Meanwhile, the division could only ladle out another ration of its old-time religion, which makes model year '48 production misleading. The totals were 50,268 for Mercury (good for only 16th place in the industry), and 7769 for Lincoln (19th place and dead-last). But in terms of calendar year output, L-M was going hammers and tongs: for the 12 months, Mercury built a record 154,702 cars to finish a strong 10th, while Lincoln hit an all-time high at 43,938 units, good for 17th, if still far behind Cadillac (66,000). It only serves to illustrate the vast differences that often exist between model and calendar year production tallies.

With the final 1948 Lincoln Continental (numbered 8H182129), the curtain fell on one of history's most interesting cars and the first postwar car deemed a "Classic." Total series production since 1940 was 5324, including 452 cabriolets and 847 coupes for '48. The latter were completely unchanged from the '47s, including prices. Most dealers sold only one to three that year and some sold none at all, so few seemed to mourn their passing at the time.

But that would change, and the '48 wouldn't be the last Continental. Prosperity, and the new buyer's market it spawned in the 1950s, led Dearborn sales people to look for an edge, something to help them stem Cadillac's onslaught. By 1953, dealers and a good many would-be buy-

ers were clamoring for a new Continental. After all, the original had been nothing if not memorable. Moreover, values of used examples not only remained high but even began increasing at a time when you couldn't give away most 1940s cars. The 1940-48 Continental was thus one of the first cars to be "collected," and it remains as popular today among old-car enthusiasts as it ever was—maybe more so. Edsel Ford, concluded OCee Ritch, "had excellent taste. He was a person of refinement, of modesty and integrity. That an automobile could be at once utilitarian and reflect those qualities is sufficient tribute both to the man and the car he created."

The rest of Lincoln's '48 line was equally unchanged from '47. Of course, this was also the last year for the evolution of the Zephyr that had been so new and wonderful 12 years before, and Lincoln ads still extolled it—simple layouts on white backgrounds with elegant script proclaiming "Nothing Could Be Finer." But in fact, something was: Cadillac had stunned Detroit with sensational new styling for 1948, and was about to release the first of its high-compression overhead-valve V-8s for 1949. For the short '48 model year, then, Lincoln was just marking time.

Mercury was too, though there was one difference: the two-door sedan was dropped after seeing only 34 copies the year before, leaving convertible, woody wagon, coupe-sedan, and Town Sedan. The last two still garnered the most sales: about 17,000 and 25,000, respectively. Only 7586 convertibles and 1889 wagons were built for the model year, making these among the scarcest of the early postwar Mercurys.

1949

Ford Motor Company was a bit late with its first new postwar models, owing to the massive company reorganization carried out by Henry II and Ernie Breech. But it had been an all-out effort once plans were finalized, and management hustled the cars to market as soon as it could. Thus, Lincoln and Mercury went on sale in April 1948, Ford in June.

Yet because General Motors hadn't finished updating its fleet and Chrysler was still peddling prewar cars, Ford wasn't really too far behind, and in some areas it was ahead. The '49 Ford was out several months before this year's Chevy, and the new Mercury was available before the competing '49 Pontiac, Dodge, DeSoto, and Oldsmobile's 76/88. Lincoln trailed Cadillac, whose all-new '48 styling helped tighten its iron grip on the luxury trade, but closed the production gap with another model year record: 73,507 units, fewer than 20,000 units behind, though it was as close as Lincoln would come in the immediate future.

One cause for Cadillac's increasing lead was a Ford strike in May 1948, just when the company needed maximum '49 output. The union, complaining that management had perpetrated a "speed-up" at the Rouge and Lincoln plants, halted production for 24 days. Mercury was unaffected though, and would enjoy another record year. In fact, Dearborn's middle make soared in model year volume to 300,000 units, skyrocketing to 6th place just behind Pontiac. Mercury's calendar year output was 200,000-plus, but Lincoln managed only 33,000 cars.

It's difficult to overstate the importance of this year's Ford. It was, primarily, a design departure for Dearborn, the most dramatically different Ford since the Model A replaced the Tin Lizzie a generation before. Wrote veteran auto tester Floyd Clymer: "It is no more like the prewar Ford than day [is like] night. It does not operate like any previous Ford car; and in its roadability, ease of operation, and control, there is just no comparison between the new and old models." The '49 was also the car that literally saved Ford Motor Company. Had it not succeeded as it did, the firm might not have lived to see its 50th birthday.

The '49 Ford was the product of two key figures: design consultant George W. Walker and engineering vice-president Harold Youngren (the latter a Breech recruit from Oldsmobile who'd worked on its brilliant, overhead-valve 1949 V-8). Although wheelbase and engines stayed the same, the rest of the package was completely different from 1942-48: three inches lower, fractionally shorter and narrower, and much sleeker, thanks to new flush-fender styling. Despite the more compact dimensions, Youngren's people managed to increase seat width by half a foot, find more legroom, maintain headroom, and create a much larger luggage compartment, yet careful attention to detail kept curb weight below 3000 pounds as targeted; only the convertible and woody wagon were slightly heavier than before. By contrast, no 1948 Ford scaled less than 3000 pounds, and some were over 3500. Thus, the '49s were livelier despite their carryover engines.

The '49 Ford was also different underneath in a way that would have upset old Henry. First, his traditional beam front axle and transverse-leaf-spring suspension were finally discarded for Dearborn's first fully independent front suspension—via coil springs and unequal-length A-arms—and parallel, longitudinal leaf springs now supported the live rear axle, both arrangements long used elsewhere. Final drive was now of the hypoid type instead of spiral-bevel, and the heavy old torque tube was replaced by open Hotchkiss drive. The transmission was completely reengineered, and the old two-speed rear axle gave way to a modern optional overdrive. (Ford also planned to offer an optional automatic purchased from Studebaker, but South Bend's refusal forced Dearborn to develop its own, which wouldn't arrive until 1951.) Brakes remained hydraulically actuated drums all-round, but had greater swept area. Finally, the time-honored X-member chassis gave way to a lighter, more up-to-date

The 1949 Ford Custom convertible: 51,133 found buyers.

Most popular for '49: Custom Tudor, with 433,316 built.

Priciest '49 Ford was the two-door woody wagon: $2119.

Ford's Iron Mountain, Michigan plant did the woodwork.

The Lincoln Sport Sedan shared its body with Mercury.

Costliest '49 Lincoln: Cosmopolitan ragtop ($3948).

Lincoln's '49 convertible retailed for a lofty $3118.

Lincoln's 337.8-cid flathead V-8 developed 152 horses.

The Lincoln Cosmopolitan rode a 125-inch wheelbase.

Lincoln built 73,507 cars for 1949, a record.

Of the nine special limousines commissioned by the White House in 1950, this one got a "bubble-back" in 1954.

ladder-type frame except on the convertible, where X-bracing was retained for the greater structural rigidity demanded by that body style.

The '49 Ford was so desperately needed that Henry Ford II told development engineer Bill Burnett to forget last-minute efforts to reduce noise, and to concentrate on front-end geometry problems resulting from the new chassis' extreme forward engine location. But according to *Special-Interest Autos* magazine, the engineers "kept right on improving the car after introduction, insulating it, changing the fan pitch, the camshaft, body mounts, and exhaust system for less noise." By the time the facelifted '50 debuted, they had made it a very quiet automobile.

Consultant Walker usually gets credit for Ford's '49 styling, but it's not really his. Walker had ordered proposals from his various team members, and they produced at least a dozen. The one ultimately accepted was that of Richard Caleal, a freelancer then in Walker's employ and previously associated with the Raymond Loewy team at Studebaker. Caleal worked so hard to sell Walker that friends nicknamed him "the Persian rug salesman," and his scale model (reportedly cured in Mrs. Caleal's oven) was approved with only one change: Walker turned its vertical taillights horizontally and gave them accenting "pods" that ran forward along the rear fenders to add visual interest to the slab sides.

Studebaker influence was evident in Ford's new "bullet-nose" front, with a large central circle dividing a full-width horizontal bar that seemed to "float" in the grille cavity. Caleal later revealed that he'd asked former Loewy associates Bob Bourke and Holden Koto to help him meet Dearborn's tight deadline, which they did in their spare time. The result, as Bourke noted, "was similar to the component on Studebaker front ends for 1950-51," but not nearly so sculptured and far more pleasing.

The '49 Ford was an expensive program for an automaker trying to recover from a lot of lean years: 10-million man hours and $72 million. As noted, it debuted early because Ford literally couldn't afford to wait for the usual fall introduction. But the effort paid off, the firm recording a gratifying $177 million profit for calendar 1949. Even better, Ford bested Chevy in model year production by over 100,000 cars, nearly 1.12 million units.

To give the '49 Ford the big sendoff it needed, Henry II staged an extravagant six-day press party at New York City's Waldorf Astoria Hotel beginning June 8, 1948, just 10 days before the public unveiling. An estimated 300 reporters attended, brought in by car or train at company expense, along with almost every high-ranking Ford official. The resulting barrage of favorable publicity primed an already eager public, and an estimated 28.2 million visitors choked dealer showrooms in the first three days, more than 100,000 placing orders on the first day alone. For sheer impact, it was an introduction to rival the Model A rollout of 30 years before.

Ford still must have had a soft spot for limited-edition specials, because brief thought was evidently given to a new Sportsman. At least one '49 Tudor sedan was mocked

Ford designed a Sportsman for '49, but never built it.

up as such, with bold front fender script and a long wooden "frame" running from the rocker panel to about mid-body-side, split laterally by a thick chrome molding. It also wore rear fender skirts and a low-hanging windshield visor. Unlike the 1946-48 Sportsman, this one's wood trim was mere decoration, used only as a highlight or "outline," and the inserts were painted body color. This was no doubt a prelude to the spiffy Crestliner that would appear for 1950, but it would have made an interesting addition to the line.

What *was* offered for '49 were the usual sixes and V-8s in a two-tier lineup. The former comprised the base-trim series, officially nameless but sometimes called Standard, with Tudor and Fordor sedans, long-deck coupe, and stripped business coupe. The upper-level Custom V-8 group deleted the last but added convertible and a new two-door wagon, replacing the previous four-door style. Prices were up across the board, ranging from $1333 for the business coupe to $2119 for the wagon. The latter, incidentally, was identical from the cowl back with a new Mercury counterpart, both with partial wood construction at the rear.

This year's Lincoln and Mercury had originated with Bob Gregorie, but they didn't bow until after he'd left Dearborn a second time. As previously noted, what became the new Mercury had been Gregorie's proposed Ford; the standard '49 Lincoln was his intended Mercury, and his projected Lincoln became the Lincoln Cosmopolitan, a new top-line, long-wheelbase offering. This realignment dictated the crash effort that produced the eventual '49 Ford. Because Ernie Breech saw that car as crucial to the firm's future, he set up a design competition between Gregorie and George Walker. When the Policy Committee picked the Walker/Caleal proposal, Gregorie left again, this time for good.

The '49 Mercury and standard Lincoln emerged with shared sheetmetal from the cowl back and similar chassis with respective wheelbases of 118 and 121 inches. The decision that produced them was followed by a complete reorganization of the Lincoln-Mercury team. Youngren put in Earle S. MacPherson (inventor of the now-famous strut) as—eventually—chief engineer, with the rank of

1949

vice-president; John Oswald became chief body engineer, Bill Schmidt chief stylist, and Charles Waterhouse joined Schmidt's department. Overseeing all was Benson Ford, brother of the company president, named division general manager in January 1948.

The ultimate and final statement of Gregorie's design philosophy, the long, streamlined Cosmpolitan was equally a product of its time, from what Studebaker stylist Robert F. Andrews once called the "bar of soap school—you'd take a bar of soap and smooth off the edges." It might also serve as an example of what a later GM stylist termed "perceived aerodynamics." It wasn't actually tested for aero characteristics—the science was in its infancy then—but it looked smooth and slippery, and that was the idea.

In line with the larger Lincoln's upper-class image, Gregorie had penned smooth flanks with large chrome "eyebrows" over the front wheel arches, and stainless-steel window frames. Head- and taillamps were "frenched" or inset, a unique touch that made all '49 Lincolns immediately recognizable, and the grille was a development obviously taken from the lower half of the 1946-48 design. Prefiguring a trend, the Cosmo also had a one-piece windshield ever so slightly curved. Interiors were lavish amalgams of leather and Bedford-cord cloth, instruments a combination of round and rectangular ahead of a big steering wheel.

Designated Series 9EH, the Cosmopolitan was offered as a convertible and fastback coupe, plus notchback and fastback four-door sedans respectively called Sport and Town—curiously with rear-hinged "suicide" back doors. The public took a negative attitude toward "torpedoes" in these years, and the Town Sedan would be dropped for 1950. Prices were well up on those of recent Lincolns, ranging from $3186 for the coupe to $3948 for the convertible, meaning that they went for around $3500-$4300 delivered. Model year production was 35,123 units, close to half of Lincoln's total, somewhat surprising for what amounted to a reincarnation of the prewar Zephyr Custom. The Sport Sedan was the most popular single model.

Lincoln's smaller '49s (designated 9EL) bore no series name and can be more correctly compared to Mercury, which fielded a single, unnamed model group (Series 9CM) consisting of coupe, Sport Sedan, convertible, and two-door wagon. Neither line included a true fastback, and both were necessarily less elaborate than the Cosmopolitan, with conventional window frames and split windshields. Limited to coupe, convertible, and notchback Sport Sedan, the junior Lincoln saw production of 38,384 units for the model year, scarcely more than 10 percent of Mercury's volume. One reason was price: the Lincolns ran between $2600 and $3200, Mercurys $2000-$2700.

Powerplants were another key difference between these corporate cousins. Mercury now used a stroked version of the familiar flathead V-8 (3.19 × 4.00 inches), with 255.4 cubic inches and a rated 110 bhp, while Lincoln discarded its old V-12 for a new V-8 designed by C.C. Johnson. Writer Paul Woudenberg reported that work on this engine

began back in 1941, only to be halted by the war, though "a curious aluminum V-8 surfaced briefly in December 1943, with overhead cams driven by worm gears . . . disappointing in so many respects that it was destroyed [the following] January."

What emerged was thus fairly conventional: a heavy cast-iron "stroker" with cylinder dimensions of 3.50 × 4.38 inches, good for 336.7 cid and a rated 152 bhp gross. It was smooth and solid, however, with prodigious torque compared to the V-12: 265 foot-pounds against only 225. Understandably, Lincoln avoided mentioning that its new V-8 also powered Ford's F7/F8 trucks, where it produced less horsepower on lower compression. On the positive side, the truck version's early production start, in January 1948, allowed some 21 minor revisions to improve idling, valve and camshaft wear, and cylinder head stress before the Lincoln unit appeared. The result was a strong, reliable engine that would be around through 1951.

The '49 Lincoln/Mercury chassis was perhaps more interesting, being a new K-braced affair with heavy side rails, semi-floating Hotchkiss drive, and Ford-style independent front suspension with coil springs. Most customers noticed the improved ride right away, comparable with that of GM and Chrysler rivals, if not superior. Tidier handling was less appreciated but just as welcome, reflecting a much lower center of gravity conferred by the new chassis and the lower-slung bodywork.

Though the Continental was now history, Lincoln did consider one for '49. John Chika sketched a wood-trim convertible along Ford/Mercury Sportsman lines, and Martin Regitko did a huge phaeton. These may not have been intended as Continentals, but one idea definitely was: a special 128-inch-wheelbase model designed by Bob Doehler, who later won fame at Studebaker. It had all the familiar styling hallmarks: closed-quarter roofline, outside spare, high-riding trunkback deck, thin window frames. None of these saw production, of course. There just wasn't time—and, as Ford ultimately decided, sufficient demand—although nine long-wheelbase Cosmopolitan limousines were outfitted for the White House the following year.

These non-starters remind us that Lincoln was no longer vying for the limousine trade and other "professional car" business. The decision to abandon this field was deliberate, made in the face of a determined effort by Cadillac and even Packard, both of which had returned with long-wheelbase cars in 1946. To some extent, however, it would hurt Lincoln's image vis-à-vis Cadillac as time went on.

Mercury's promotion from "senior Ford" to "junior Lincoln" this year is significant, the first major change for Dearborn's middle make since its inception a decade earlier. Still, there were drawbacks. For example, its Lincoln-shared structure was somewhat sturdier than the '49 Ford's, reflecting longer development time, but this plus the heavier K-braced chassis increased the disparity in Ford/Mercury curb weights. Thus, respective four-door sedans tipped the scales at 3013 and 3386 pounds, versus

Out of 301,319 Mercs built for '49, only 8044 were wagons, which shared bodies aft of the cowl with Ford.

"Bathtub" 1949-50 Mercs symbolized the "Lost Generation."

Mercury built 16,765 ragtops (now at 110 bhp) for '49.

3266 and 3298 pounds for their 1948 counterparts. A standard rear axle ratio of 3.91, against Ford's 3.73, helped make up for the extra heft, so acceleration was pretty evenly matched. Transmission choices comprised standard three-speed manual with column shift or the same with Borg-Warner overdrive, a $97 option that brought a still-shorter, 4.27:1 final drive. But automatic was conspicuous by its absence, especially since rivals Buick and Oldsmobile both offered one.

The Mercury dash was flashier and less unified than the '49 Ford's, though it wasn't bad. The driver faced a pudgy little box mounting five round dials, with a large, central speedometer flanked by fuel and oil pressure gauges on the left, temperature gauge and ammeter on the right. The old manual choke was gone, much to the regret of many buyers, but interiors were handsomely done. Coupes and sedans wore simple broadcloth upholstery; convertibles were trimmed in genuine leather. Besides overdrive, accessories included custom steering wheel, grille guard, windshield sunvisor, rear fender skirts, engine compartment lamp, backup lights, and a little-known set of fitted luggage.

Though Ford Engineering was still pretty agricultural in this period, Harold Youngren did what he could to make the Ford/Mercury flathead V-8s more competitive. The cooling system, a bugbear since 1932, was a major focus of his attention. Water was now pumped from the radiator straight to the back of the block without any baffle detours. This, plus a larger radiator, lowered running temperatures by 12 degrees, but still didn't eliminate the familiar overheating and vapor-lock problems. The old camshaft-driven "crab" distributor was relocated for easier servicing, though not necessarily longer life, mounted above the head on the right front cylinder bank to be shaft and gear driven. Of course, this was all patchwork stuff. What Mercury *really* needed—as did Ford and Lincoln—was a modern ohv engine, but it was still a few years off.

Nevertheless, the so-called "bathtub" Mercs inaugurated with the '49 are still fondly remembered today, though less for what they were meant to be than what they became: a symbol for the Lost Generation. Discovered by the "Kalifornia Kustom" crowd, and popularized by James Dean's tail-draggin' modified in the film *Rebel Without a*

157

Cause, the 1949-51 design would achieve a kind of cult status among the car-crazy youth of mid-Fifties America, who saw its slightly sinister styling as the perfect canvas for a personal automotive statement. The result was the genre we now call the "Lead Sled," typically with a chopped and lowered body, special grille, cruiser skirts, wild paint job, tuck-and-roll interior, and other individual touches. Remarkably, people are still building these one-of-a-kind creations, and even restoring the original customs of more than 30 years ago. So in this respect at least, Mercury remained a "hot rod" in the best tradition of the 1939 original and the early V-8 Fords.

1950

Advertised as "50 Ways New . . . 50 Ways Finer," the 1950 Fords bore little outward change. A simple crest replaced block letters over the bullet grille, and the same basic model lineup returned: six-cylinder DeLuxe (*nee* Standard) sedans and business coupe; Custom V-8 coupe, sedans, convertible, and semi-wood wagon, now called Country Squire in some ads.

The all-new '49 design's tremendous tooling costs precluded an immediate Ford response to a new body style from GM that year, the pillarless "hardtop convertible." This rakish innovation had found immediate buyer favor among GM's senior nameplates as the Buick Roadmaster Riviera, Cadillac Series 62 Coupe deVille, and Oldsmobile 98 Holiday. More important for Ford was the fact that Chevy had one for 1950, the stylish Bel Air. What to do? Why not a spiffy Tudor sedan with the look, if not the function, of a hardtop? George Walker's design staff went

to work, and the Crestliner bowed late in the season as an addition to the Custom V-8 series.

The Crestliner's colorful styling was influenced by Gordon M. Buehrig, famed designer of Classic-era Auburns, Cords, and Duesenbergs. Buehrig, at this time a member of the Dearborn design staff, likened the new model's two-tone paint treatment to the dashing "LeBaron sweep" of the custom-body era. This referred to the unique, elliptical chrome moldings that delineated the contrast color area. Crestliner also wore a vinyl roof covering, emphasizing its "convertible" aspect, and rear fender skirts. Final touches included anodized-gold fender nameplates and a luxurious color-keyed interior.

At $1711, the Crestliner was Ford's priciest '50, some $200 above the Custom Tudor. Despite that and its late start, this "factory custom" scored respectable sales of 17,601 units. Today, it's a highly prized collectible.

All Fords got a number of detail revisions this year because the '49 had been a rush job and management knew certain things still needed fixing. Among these changes: new pistons, three-blade cooling fan, new-design emergency brake lever, larger defroster vents with greater air flow, water-resistant brake drums, increased use of sound-deadening material, wider sunvisors, higher-capacity heater, and a new gas filler tube and cover.

Benson Ford, Henry's younger brother, enjoyed his most successful season since being appointed vice-president in charge of Lincoln-Mercury Division. The postwar seller's market reached its peak this year, with unprecedented buyer demand fired by all-new models from virtually every make. With most of the nits picked from its '49 cars, L-M also reached a peak. Mercury's calendar year production soared to a new high of 334,081 units—four times its previous level. Lincoln didn't do nearly as well, its 35,485 units being about level with its annual output since 1947. By contrast, Cadillac was up over the 100,000 mark; Packard, aided by its line of medium-price Eights, was at about 72,000.

It marked the start of what would be a topsy-turvy decade for Lincoln. Its '49 styling, which had seemed so

The 1950 models got new parking lights and Ford crest.

Ford's answer to Chevy's Bel Air hardtop: the Crestliner.

Ford convertible production reached 50,229 for 1950.

Lincoln entered the 1950 model year with a new grille.

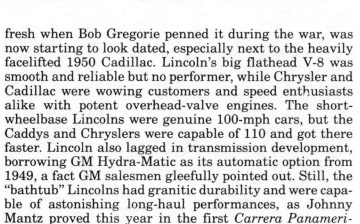

Only 1824 Cosmopolitan coupes were built for 1950.

Output of '50 Mercury soft tops was only 2.84 percent of production.

fresh when Bob Gregorie penned it during the war, was now starting to look dated, especially next to the heavily facelifted 1950 Cadillac. Lincoln's big flathead V-8 was smooth and reliable but no performer, while Chrysler and Cadillac were wowing customers and speed enthusiasts alike with potent overhead-valve engines. The short-wheelbase Lincolns were genuine 100-mph cars, but the Caddys and Chryslers were capable of 110 and got there faster. Lincoln also lagged in transmission development, borrowing GM Hydra-Matic as its automatic option from 1949, a fact GM salesmen gleefully pointed out. Still, the "bathtub" Lincolns had granitic durability and were capable of astonishing long-haul performances, as Johnny Mantz proved this year in the first *Carrera Panamericana*, the fabled Mexican Road Race.

The great open-road contests are gone now, victims of a sensible public demand that cars not kill innocent bystanders, which happened regularly in the *Carrera*, the *Mille Miglia*, and *Targa Florio*. But many remember the cars and their drivers boring down long straights lined with cheering spectators, and skimming along precipices at speeds no sane mortal would ever dare. While they lasted, these were memorably exciting contests.

When the *Associacion Mexicana Automovilistica* announced an open road race the length of Mexico along the new Pan American highway, scores of Europeans and Americans scurried to enter. Lincoln may have been

known for luxury, but rock-solid construction and a durable drivetrain gave its 1949-50 models definite competition appeal. Thus it was that no fewer than 15 Lincolns set forth from Juarez, bound for the Guatemala border 2178 miles away. Mantz, driving a standard sedan entered by Los Angeles dealer Bob Estes, finished 11th overall, averaging as high as 91 mph over some sections and actually leading the vaunted Olds 88 of Herschel McGriff for 11½ minutes. Though no one quite understood it at the time, this was a forecast of much greater things to come.

Back home, where customers knew little about such shenanigans and cared less, Lincoln fielded a group of modestly revised '49s with unchanged mechanicals on the same two wheelbases. Common to all models was a handsome new dash by former coachbuilder Tom Hibbard, an attractive rolled affair with an oblong glass-covered gauge cluster, a motif Lincoln would retain through 1957. The junior convertible and Cosmo Town Sedan were scratched, but two new sport coupes arrived: the Capri in the Cosmopolitan series (0EH) and the Lincoln Lido in the short-wheelbase line (0EL). As stopgap replies to GM's '49 hardtops, they were upmarket counterparts to the Ford Crestliner and thus followed the same formula: padded top outside, convertible-like decor and bright colors inside. Both arrived quite late (on July 5, 1950) and their numbers were trifling (though exact figures are unavailable, being combined with those for the standard coupes).

Rare: only 1746 Merc wagons went out the door in 1950.

Neither was a strong response to GM's initiative, but they were the only "sporty" cars Lincoln had for the moment, though Hibbard was already working on an entirely new entry for 1952.

Lincoln's "carriage trade" days were recalled this year in nine special Cosmopolitan limousines on a stretched, 145-inch platform, commissioned by the White House as lineal successors to the famous "Sunshine Special" used by Presidents Roosevelt and Truman since 1939 (and now on view at the Henry Ford Museum). Built by the Henney Body Company of Freeport, Illinois, these were huge cars weighing nearly three tons, comprehensively equipped with writing desks, vanity cases, telephone, and gold-plated hardware, plus bulletproof glass throughout and runningboards for security outriders per Secret Service requirements. The first also sported fitted lizardskin parcel cases in the armrests, thermos bottles, even a tobacco humidor. One of these cars would see long service, lasting through the memorable 1963 European tour in which President Kennedy proclaimed "Ich bin ein Berliner" before the Berlin Wall. It was the same one fitted with an all-weather clear-plastic rear "bubble" at President Eisenhower's request in 1954.

Lincoln's individual 1950-model production figures are interesting. The short-wheelbase Sport Sedan tallied 11,741 units against 5748 coupes and Lidos; the Cosmopolitan saw 8341 sedans, again the most popular offering by far, against only 536 convertibles and 1824 coupes and Capris. Prices were little changed; the Lido/Capri arrived about $200 upstream of their standard-trim counterparts.

This year's Mercury line (Series 0CM) was also mostly a '49 rerun. Larger parking lamps were newly integrated with the outboard ends of the barrel-shaped vertical-bar grille, while the separate "Mercury" hood letters were now encased in a wide chrome strip to emphasize the horizontal. Advances in glassmaking technology brought a new one-piece rear window to replace the previous three-piece affair on coupes and sedans, a change also shared with Lincoln. Inside was a new, cleaner dashboard similar to Hibbard's Lincoln design, with a plexiglas-covered strip running about ⅝ of the way across and housing crescent-shaped speedometer, minor gauges, and optional radio.

Mercury also gained a pair of coupes this year: a stripped $1875 economy version to compete with the cheaper Dodges and Pontiacs; and the Monterey, available with either canvas or vinyl roof covering at $2146 and $2157, respectively. The latter, of course, was yet another counter to GM's '49 hardtops, which were imitated this year not only by Chevrolet but Pontiac, Chrysler, DeSoto, and Dodge. Like Lido/Capri, the Monterey came with a luxury interior that hopefully reminded you of a full-blown convertible's. Again, individual production figures aren't available, but the Monterey was certainly more salesworthy than its Lincoln relatives. In today's money it would be a $15,000 car, not too much to pay for its aura of exclusivity.

While Mercury had long been known as something of a "factory hot rod," the heavier '49s weren't as quick on the stock-car tracks, eating Ford dust in early NASCAR competition. But the '50s held their own, thanks to a slight cam change and other minor mods, though rated power was unchanged. Mercury also turned in a sterling performance in the first *Carrera Panamericana* to recapture some of its performance reputation. Five out of 11 entries finished the gruelling event, a higher proportion than most makes. Symbolic of its prowess, Mercury was selected pace car for the Indianapolis 500. Finally, an overdrive-equipped Sport Sedan won the Grand Sweepstakes in this year's Mobilgas Economy Run, recording the best weight-to-mileage figure of any car entered.

The last involved an 18.5-hour trek from Los Angeles to the south rim of the Grand Canyon, a total 751.3 miles. Temperatures ranged from 29 to 68 degrees Fahrenheit, altitudes from 178 feet below sea level to 7005 above, conditions from LA freeways to semi-desert highways, Death Valley to the mountains. Entered by Long Beach dealer Art Hall and driven by Bill Stoppe and Clay Smith, the winning Merc averaged 26.52 mpg, beating a Cadillac 60 Special and Series 62. Significantly, it tallied the highest actual mpg among the class winners, beating such presumed misers as the Willys Jeepster, Kaiser Special, Studebaker Land Cruiser—and the six-cylinder Ford. Amazingly, Stroppe drove the first 180 miles without using overdrive.

Motor Trend magazine tested a similar car for its May 1950 issue. Wrote editor Walt Woron of the economy champ's dynamic qualities: "The suspension, like [that of] most domestic cars, is quite soft, providing the comfortable ride to which we have become accustomed. Naturally, this detracts somewhat from the car's cornering ability . . . however, there is not at any time the feeling that the car is laying over excessively. The steering system provides for extreme ease in handling and parking, although a faster ratio would be an advantage from the standpoint of giving quicker control." Woron commented little on performance, as the test figures spoke for themselves: 0-60 mph in 15.98 seconds, top speed of 83.75 mph.

By available model breakdown, Mercury ran off 132,082 copies of its popular four-door Sport Sedan. The four coupe models accounted for 151,489 units, the convertible for 8341, and the station wagon 1746. As in '49, the last suffered from having only two doors when an increasing number of wagon buyers wanted four. Management considered such a development, but decided to hold off until the corporate-wide redesign scheduled for 1952.

As a whole, Mercury was still doing just fine. Though it slipped to ninth in the model year production race, volume was second only to record 1949, remaining solidly in six-figure territory at 293,658 units. Included was a milestone: the millionth Mercury built since the make's 1939 debut.

1951

Just when it seemed that Ford Motor Company was on the move, the Korean War intensified and Washington ordered production cutbacks that immediately affected the firm's building program. For example, a proposed Lincoln-Mercury assembly plant in Wayne, Michigan, was turned over to Westinghouse for Navy jet-engine manufacture. Then came the materials and market-share allocations, which Ford felt were biased in favor of Chrysler and the independents, the former being awarded a 21.76-percent market share to Ford's 21.43. But as Ford vice-president Bill Gossett remarked: "If the controls were lifted, we would very quickly demonstrate who is entitled to the second place." He was right. Even in 1952, with the controls still on and Chrysler overselling its quota, Dearborn would outproduce Highland Park, and Chrysler has yet to regain second place to this day.

Nevertheless, the semi-war footing meant lower production for all Ford makes. It was probably just as well: the 1949 designs were in their final year, and the great seller's market was beginning to wane.

The sales picture was predictably mixed. Ford closed its model-year gap with Chevy by about 73,000 cars, but both were down about 200,000 from their 1950 totals. Worse, after losing to Ford for '49, GM's breadwinner had returned to the number-one spot, and repeated this model year. Mercury fell off to 239,000 units for calendar '51 and was passed by Dodge, but model year volume was up to over 310,000 units and Mercury resumed 6th place, ahead of Dodge and Oldsmobile. Alas, Lincoln was still mired in the industry cellar: only 25,000 units for the calendar year (just sufficient to best the fast-expiring Crosley Company). But it, too, was up on a model year basis at some 32,500, a gain of more than 4000 units over 1950. Not that it made much difference, for rival Cadillac also improved to better than 110,000 for the model year, its second consecutive record.

Highlighting this year's mildly facelifted '51 Ford line

Ford's real answer to the Bel Air: the '51 Victoria.

Ford-O-Matic transmission was finally offered in '51.

All 1951 Fords sported a new "double-spinner" grille.

Ford's cheapest 1951 model: the $1324 business coupe.

With new grille and taillights, the Lincoln Cosmopolitan Sport Sedan rode into 1951 on a 125-inch wheelbase.

was a true pillarless hardtop called Victoria, available only in the upper-level Custom V-8 series. With its dashing appearance, developed by Gordon Buehrig, and plush, convertible-like interior, it was a smash. Altogether, 110,286 were sold, beating both the Chevrolet Bel Air (103,356) and Plymouth's new Cranbrook Belvedere (about 30,000) in this first year of the battle of the low-priced hardtops. Naturally, the Victoria and its success rendered the Crestliner redundant, so the latter was dropped after sales of only 8703 units.

All '51 Fords had a new face courtesy of a thick horizontal grille bar with two smaller bullets at its outboard ends instead of the one big central bullet. Inside was a handsomely redesigned, asymmetrical dash. There were no mechanical changes save the addition of three-speed Ford-O-Matic Drive, the company's new automatic transmission, thus answering Chevrolet's new-for-'50, two-speed Powerglide. Ford Customs retained their classic, monobloc flathead V-8, still at 100 horsepower; the cheaper DeLuxe models continued with the 95-bhp, 226-

The '51 Cosmopolitan Capri coupe wore a vinyl roof.

Rare then and now: '51 Cosmo ragtop (only 857 built).

Lincoln's Mercury-based, vinyl-topped coupe: the Lido.

The '51 Merc got a new grille; 3812 wagons were built.

cubic-inch L-head six. Model offerings stayed the same, but the two-door Custom wagon was now officially called Country Squire, spelled out in bodyside script.

Victoria was billed as the "Belle of the Boulevard . . . smart as a convertible . . . snug as a sedan." The brochure also pointed out that it was the only such car in its price range with a standard V-8. Popular when new, the '51 Victoria is now treasured by collectors, though its road manners and performance pale by modern standards. The seats provide little lateral support, the large steering wheel with its inverted-V spokes can be slippery, and exuberant cornering brings out considerable body roll and great howling from the optional 6.70 × 15 four-ply whitewall tires. Yet performance is sprightly if not dramatic, the ride comfortable, engine noise low. In one respect, the Victoria is literally head and shoulders above most newer cars; its interior is positively cavernous, with a flat floor and lots of stretch-out space for tall adults. As a roomy, handsome touring car, it was hard to beat. No wonder it sold so well right off the bat.

Lincoln reprised its 1950 lineup with more obvious appearance changes. Fewer (five) but more prominent vertical teeth appeared above the horizontal grille bar, parking lamps moved further outboard, and bumpers were reshaped. Cosmos lost their chrome wheelarch "eyebrows," while juniors took on extended rear fenders like this year's Mercury. All models wore full-length bodyside moldings with flashy little "sails" sticking up above on the front fenders, ahead of "Cosmopolitan" or "Lincoln" script. L-M Division was still without a hardtop, so the Lido and Capri continued as stand-ins—and in very low demand. Production divided almost equally between the 121-inch-wheelbase standard line (Series 1EL) and the 125-inch Cosmpolitan (1EH), with sedans dominating. Lincoln built only 857 Cosmo convertibles this year, while coupe production totalled 4482 juniors (including Lido) and just 2727 Cosmos (including Capri).

Mechanical changes were nearly nil, though detail internal mods had coaxed two more horses from Lincoln's 337-cid flathead V-8, now rated at 154 bhp. Still, it was probably a bit more efficient. As proof, Les Viland drove a standard '51 Sport Sedan with overdrive and 3.31:1 final drive to a class victory in this year's Mobilgas Economy Run, averaging 25.448 mpg over 840 miles from Los Angeles to the Grand Canyon. It was an astonishing performance for a heavy, large-displacement machine, though 14 competitors bettered it, two of them with V-8s.

Mercury's "bathtub" generation bowed out with a new transmission and the same sort of style changes applied to the little Lincolns. The "economy" coupe was gone, but the rest of the lineup returned, including the two Montereys (as Series 1CM). This year's facelift was as radical as they could make it: a big semicircular crest above a toothier new convex grille, still-larger parking lamps wrapped around the front, vertical taillights, and extended, more upright rear fenders with rounded corners dropping straight down to the bumper. Paralleling Ford-O-Matic was Mercury's first self-shift transmission. Called Merc-

O-Matic, it was a two-speed torque-converter unit developed in cooperation with the Warner Gear Division of Borg-Warner. Priced at $159 extra, about $70 more than the optional overdrive, it proved highly popular in a slow sales year.

Once more, Mercury's four-door production was just ahead of coupe output, by a ratio of about 15-14, while the convertible saw but 6759 copies and the wagon only 3812. Like Lincoln's, the Mercury V-8 gained two horsepower, now 112 bhp total, again through detail adjustments. Mercury also followed Lincoln by taking class honors in the Mobilgas Economy Run, but didn't repeat as the Grand Sweepstakes winner.

L-M cars were again favored in this year's Mexican Road Race, though the factory had yet to mount a formal effort. There was still only one class, as in the 1950 inaugural, but the event was now open to outright sports cars, which naturally cleaned up. The Ferraris of Taruffi and Ascari finished 1-2, followed by Bill Sterling's hemi-engine Chrysler. But Troy Ruttman's Mercury was right behind, and Ray Crawford took eighth overall in his Lincoln Sport Sedan.

Ruttman's Merc was a predictive *Carrera* car in that it was tuned by Clay Smith, soon to become a legend in Lincoln circles. (Amazingly, it was a used '49, purchased for about $1000.) In all, three Lincolns entered but only Crawford finished; Mercury had four starters and two finishers. These weren't bad survival rates. The car-beating '51 *Carrera* saw just 34 finishers out of 91 starters, and even the mighty Hudson Hornet, soon to be America's stock-car champion, managed only four out of 11.

1952

This year saw a resurgent Ford Motor Company carry out its second corporate restyle in only three years and its second since the war, thus one-upping Big Three rivals. Significantly, all makes shared the same general look, basic body structure, and chassis design, good for production economics if not make distinction and image, especially Lincoln's. Ford and Mercury also shared bodyshells, thus returning the latter to its original status as a "senior Ford," though with its extra wheelbase length now entirely ahead of the firewall.

Proclaimed as the "big" '52, Ford was an inch longer between wheel centers, 115 in all. It was also lower and wider than the 1949-51 models, yet its boxy new styling somehow contrived for a smaller look (also true of Lincoln and Mercury). At least it was clean and trim. More important, it was fresh at a time when Chevy and Plymouth were still peddling tired, 1949 designs.

All new for '52: Ford jumped ahead of Chevy and Plymouth with clean, neat, evolutionary styling.

The Ford grille reverted to the familiar center-bullet theme, but the solitary horizontal bar was now slotted instead of solid. Discreet bulges around the rear wheel openings helped relieve the slab sides, and their thrust-forward leading edges (decorated with moldings suggestive of air scoops) imparted a sense of motion. Rear decks were squared up and flanked by small round taillights, a Ford hallmark for the next several years. A neat touch was a fuel filler relocated from the left rear fender to the lower rear valance panel, hidden behind a pull-down license plate holder.

Ford now listed 11 models in three series instead of two. Mainline and Customline replaced the previous DeLuxe and Custom series but offered the same basic choices. Most were powered by Ford's first overhead-valve six, a new 215.3-cubic-inch unit rated at 101 bhp. Victoria hardtop coupe, newly named Sunliner convertible, and a new

Ford's first all-steel wagon, here the Country Sedan.

four-door Country Squire wagon were grouped into a special top-shelf series called Crestline. All came with the time-honored flathead V-8, mechanically unchanged but packing 10 more horsepower, 110 total, probably a paper increase. The V-8 was also standard for the new four-door Country Sedan wagon in the Customline series. All wagons, including the Mainline two-door Ranch Wagon, now employed all-steel construction, new to Ford but old hat at GM and Chrysler. Squire side/tailgate trim was now simply a metal frame with decal inserts resembling wood.

Underneath Ford's new bodies was an equally new chassis. Called the "K-bar" frame, it had five cross-members welded to box-section side rails, and was claimed to be more rigid than the previous ladder chassis. At the rear were longer and stronger "Para-Flex" multi-leaf springs, and shocks resited to reduce side way in turns. Brake seals were redesigned for better protection against dust and water. At the front were "Hydra-coil" springs that allegedly made for easier steering and more precise handling. Altogether, the new chassis/suspension package provided what was described as "automatic ride control," aided by a lower center of gravity and wider track front and rear. Extra weight may have helped: up by about 100 pounds on the Victoria hardtop, for example, and 70 pounds on the convertible.

Inside, the driver peered through the first one-piece windshield on a postwar Ford and operated brake and clutch pedals with suspended instead of floor-mounted pivots, features also new to this year's Lincoln and Mercury. The Ford dash was restyled but still pleasingly simple, with speedometer and engine gauges mounted in a small pod on top. Passenger room was about the same as before, seating similarly upright.

The continuing Korean conflict led to further industry-wide production declines this year. Ford was no exception,

Lincoln was also all-new in '52, carrying the corporate styling theme and FoMoCo's first overhead-valve V-8.

its model year total falling from slightly over a million units to about 672,000. Front-running Chevy dropped by about the same amount.

Back in 1950, a reporter had asked Harold Youngren when he thought there would be a new Lincoln. The engineer replied, "Soon, please God." The "bathtub" generation's much-needed successor finally arrived this year, and for the Fifties it was remarkable. Styled by George Walker with assistance from Bill Schmidt and Don De-LaRossa, it was clean, smooth, curvy in the right places, and with a minimum of decoration—*too* little, said some salespeople, to satisfy chrome-happy Americans. Following a trend started by the '51 Packard, the hoodline sat a bit below front-fender level, giving excellent forward visibility. For visual interest, rear fenders bore a forward-raked dummy scoop, echoing Ford, and large, three-way-visible taillights above a body-hugging rear bumper. Glass

area was ample if not abundant, and backlights were more noticeably wrapped. There were new features galore, including optional four-way power seat and factory air conditioning (one of the first systems affording fresh-air ventilation with the compressor engaged instead of simple recirculation). Fabrics and leathers, fit and finish were all to high standards.

All '52 Lincolns rode a new 123-inch wheelbase, an apparent compromise between the previous 121/125-inch lengths, but there were still two series. Cosmopolitan now denoted the standard line, while the upper-class cars took the Capri name from the 1950-51 limited-edition Cosmo coupe. Both lines listed the usual four-door sedan and, at last, a true pillarless hardtop. Called Sport Coupe, the latter sold 10,000 copies in all. The convertible was a Capri exclusive and Lincoln's costliest '52 at $4045. This year's price leader was the $3517 Cosmo sedan.

The '52 Lincoln Capri, powered by the 160-bhp, ohv V-8.

Only 1191 Capri convertibles were built for 1952.

Mercury built only 2487 wagons for '52; wood was fake.

Merc, still on a 118-inch wheelbase, upped bhp to 125.

Four-door sedans were the most popular Mercs in '52.

With a man like Earle MacPherson in charge of engineering, the '52 Lincoln stood to be a fine-riding road car. It was. Ed Sullivan probably did more than anyone in those days to make Americans conscious of "ball-joint front suspension" (Lincoln-Mercury sponsored his weekly TV variety show at the time), but what Mac had actually done was to use rotating sockets instead of conventional kingpins and bushings. This eliminated lots of unsprung weight (and, incidentally, 12 of 16 grease fittings), as "buff" magazines were quick to notice. Said *Motor Trend*: "It doesn't heel excessively on sharp, high-speed turns, and it doesn't feel like you're guiding a couple of sponges around a turn." In time, ball joints suffered certain fail-

ures in the field, so they needed improving, but they certainly gave Lincoln a handling edge over just about everything else in its class. Other engineering highlights included recirculating-ball power steering, oversize drum brakes (the first *good* Lincoln brakes anyone could remember), more and better body mounts, and lots of insulation for quietness and solidity.

But the capper was a brand-new V-8, Lincoln's first valve-in-head powerplant and superior to most rivals in many ways. Its crankshaft, for example, had eight counterweights instead of the usual six, plus oversize intake valves for better breathing and more output per cubic inch. Also featured was a deep-skirted crankcase extending below the crank centerline for an extremely stiff shaft support.

Like GM's ohv V-8s but unlike its flathead forebear, the new Lincoln unit followed modern practice with short-stroke, oversquare cylinder dimensions (3.80 × 3.50 inches). Displacement thus worked out to 317.5 cubic inches and horsepower to 160 at 3900 rpm with standard four-barrel carburetor and 7.5:1 compression. (By contrast, Lincoln's last 337 V-8 yielded 8 bhp less on 20 more cubes.) Your one and only transmission choice was GM's dual-range (four-speed) Hydra-Matic.

Such a fast, roadable, and solid package seemed tailor-made for competition. And it soon was, thanks to tuning ace Clay Smith. Dearborn helped with a binful of heavy-duty "export" components, a well-known industry euphemism for racing parts. Included were stronger suspension pieces, Ford truck camshafts, mechanical valve lifters, special front spindles and hubs, and a variety of rear axle ratios, the lowest of which gave the Smith Lincolns a stupendous 130-mph top speed. Lincoln had suddenly become race-conscious, at least where the high-visibility *Carrera Panamericana* was concerned, and it went to Mexico in November of this year determined to win.

It didn't, of course, at least not overall; Europe's thoroughbred sports cars were clearly going to dominate the Mexican donnybrook, as they had in '51. But the sponsors had created an "American Stock" class which was supposed to be just that. The only allowed mods were oversize brakes, suspension stiffeners, electric fuel pumps, special wheels, a .020-inch overbore, and removal of mufflers and rear seat. These rules were loosely enforced, however, and Lincoln, among others, took great liberties.

Undeniably, though, it was a great performance. The first six finishers were all sports cars: Mercedes, Ferraris, a lone Lancia. But after them came three Clay Smith Lincolns and a private entry. Lincoln had finished 1-2-3-4 in class! National stock-car champion Chuck Stevenson drove the winning Lincoln, which put out 205 horsepower with "factory" modifications and Smith's expertise. It was a fantastic coup that hardly anyone expected—except Mr. Smith perhaps.

Still, it's long been axiomatic that racing doesn't help sell luxury cars, so Lincoln's *Carrera* win probably had little to do with its '52 fortunes. Still, Lincoln deserves credit for the car itself: a monumental improvement and exactly what the public wanted. In a declining year for the industry as a whole, still beset with allocations and material shortfalls, Lincoln was one of only two makes to see a sales increase. (The other was Willys, which had just introduced an entirely new line.) In model year production, Lincoln narrowed Cadillac's lead by some 5000 units, although its own volume was down about that much compared to 1951. But this is misleading, since the '52s didn't go on sale until January and were gone by September.

Mercury was fully redesigned along the same clean lines as Lincoln and Ford, and by the same people. Wheelbase and drivetrain were unchanged, but chassis developments paralleled Ford's and higher compression boosted horsepower to 125 bhp. There was now a genuine hardtop here too, called Monterey, as were this year's convertible and a new deluxe-trim four-door sedan. All fell within a single series (2M) that also included a pillared sport coupe, two- and four-door sedans, and the new four-door wagon with six- or eight-passenger seating. The Montereys accounted for the bulk of production, more than 100,000 units. But Mercury was well down for the model year at just over 172,000 units, dropping two spots on the industry list to 8th, behind Buick, Pontiac, Olds, and Dodge.

1953

Ford Motor Company celebrated its 50th anniversary this year by making no major changes to its cars but making a lot more of them. The government now eased Korea-prompted production allocations, and Dearborn made the fateful decision to "blitz" its dealers in an all-out bid to out-sell GM, shipping cars in record number without regard for orders. This combined with increasing competition in the middle- and high-price segments to create a surfeit of Mercurys and Lincolns, though not for long. The public had liked the all-new '52s; the '53s were just more of the same good thing.

The "blitz" was primarily intended to benefit Ford in its perennial battle with Chevrolet, and to some extent, it worked. The division built nearly 1.25 million of its '53 cars, up nearly 50 percent from '52 and less than 100,000 behind Chevy. The effort peaked in 1954, when swamped dealers again advertised new Fords at "less than cost."

Trouble was, the onslaught didn't at all damage Chevrolet, which simply cut prices in reply, but it mortally wounded Chrysler and the independents, which couldn't afford to discount nearly as much. Today, the Ford/GM price war is generally regarded as one of the key factors in the independents' postwar decline. In particular, it precip-

Ford's 50th anniversary 1953 models, here a Victoria.

itated Packard's ultimately fatal acquisition of Studebaker, and the Nash/Hudson merger that formed American Motors, both in 1954. It also hastened the demise of Kaiser-Willys, which abandoned the U.S. market late that same year.

Ford styling stayed mostly the same, predictable for an all-new design in its sophomore year. The main distinction was a reworked bullet-nose grille with a slimmer crossbar. Mechanical changes were equally minor, but 1953 marked an important milestone: the last U.S. Fords powered by the flathead V-8 introduced more than two decades before.

Lincoln advertised its bhp per cubic inch this year, and it certainly looked respectable. Leaping from 160 to 205 bhp, the 317 V-8 now cranked out 0.64 horsepower per cubic inch, against 0.63 for Cadillac and 0.54 for the Chrysler hemi. The car around it was little changed: gold "V" decorating grille and rear fenders, block hood lettering, one-piece rear windows. Oddly, overall width slimmed an inch (to 76.2 inches), and there were minor front suspension adjustments. This year's model mix was the previous blend of Cosmopolitan hardtop and sedan at about $3500, and Capri hardtop, sedan, and convertible at $3700-$4000 delivered.

Lincoln had another big year in Mexico. Its obvious flaunting of the '52 stock-class rules invited closer scrutiny now, so only "dealer options" were allowed, but it didn't matter: Lincoln had already "prodified" most of the necessary items. Once more, the *Carrera Panamericana* was a Lincoln parade, with Stevenson, Walt Faulkner, Jack McGrath, and Johnny Mantz finishing 1-4 in class and 6-9 overall against a host of Detroiters—everything from hemi Chryslers to Henry Js. But the death toll was high, including three drivers. The Italians charged the race committee with negligence for not insuring safer road conditions, and local resistance stiffened to what was now being called "La Carrera de la Muerte" (race of death), a big event for foreigners at the expense of Mexican lives. The '54 *Carrera* would thus be the last.

Mercury shuffled models into its first two-series lineup: a base Custom group with hardtop coupe and two sedans, and a Monterey quartet of convertible, hardtop, wagon, and four-door sedan. Monterey sedans were luxuriously

William C. Ford piloted the Ford pace car at the Indy 500 in 1953. Bill Vukovich won the race at 128.740 mph.

Horsepower went up by 45, to 205, on the '53 Lincoln.

Mercury built 8463 ragtops for '53, at $2490 each.

The Capri four-door sedan sold for $3453 in 1953.

Cosmopolitan sold for $200 less than Capri in 1953.

Lincoln built 2372 top-shelf '53 Capri convertibles.

The '53 Mercury Monterey hardtop found 76,119 buyers.

1954

The wagon (7719 built) was Merc's rarest '53 offering.

Mercury's price leader at $2004, the Custom two door.

Dearborn bid farewell to its 22-year-old flathead V-8, as Ford and Mercury were finally treated to new overhead-valve replacements. Actually, these were the last of three such engines stemming from a project initiated in early 1948 under company engineering director Harold T. Youngren. The idea was to develop a common block that could serve as the basis for a new Ford six, a small Ford/Mercury V-8, and a larger Lincoln V-8. All were needed in the shortest possible time, and the program was completed with remarkable speed. Test engines were on the dynamometer by late '48, and final specifications were approved by mid-1950. Ultimately, some 400 prototypes were run the equivalent of nearly a million miles in the laboratory and on the road. As previously noted, two of the three—the Ford six and Lincoln V-8—debuted for 1952. For a variety of reasons, the Ford and Mercury V-8s had to be delayed another two years.

But they were worth the wait. Though both were about the same size as their predecessors—239.4 cubic inches for the new Ford unit, exactly 256 cid for Mercury's—they were much more efficient, had lots of room to grow (the flathead had reached its size limit), and arrived with five-main-bearing crankshafts for greater reliability and smoothness. Both were modern short-stroke designs like their Lincoln relative, and featured the same deep crankcase that gave them a distinctive Y-shape in head-on view, hence their family name "Y-block" (the six was called "I-block").

The new Ford V-8 had an initial bore and stroke of 3.50 × 3.10 inches, good for 130 horsepower on 7.2:1 compression. This proved short of expectations, though, so an increase to 254 cid was ordered for 1955. Then Ford learned that Chevy would have a 265 V-8 that year, so it bored and stroked to 3.62 × 3.30 inches for 272 cid and a handsome 162/182 bhp. There was also a 292 rendition for the '55 Mercury and Ford's new Thunderbird, with bore stretched to 3.75 inches. The '54 Mercury engine shared the Ford's stroke but used the 3.62-inch bore. Power output was 161 bhp gross with standard four-barrel carburetor, up 25 percent from Mercury's previous flathead.

Victor G. Raviolo handled the Y-block's principal engineering. In determining cylinder spacing, he'd aimed for a displacement range of 230 to 320 cubic inches. As it turned out, that wouldn't be enough to keep pace in the Fifties "horsepower race," and it led to yet another new engine family for 1958.

Despite its ultimate size limitations, Ford engineers were quite proud of the Y-block. It exhibited no valve bounce below 5500 rpm, while hard tappets, fully pressure-lubricated rocker arms, umbrella-type valve guides, and dampening coils on valve-spring ends contributed to quiet running and low oil consumption. Following Ricar-

upholstered in quality broadcloth; convertibles and hardtops had leather and vinyl. Solid colors were used for sedans, but hardtops now had standard two-tone paint, with the roof finished in a contrasting color. Styling revisions were modest here, too: four vertical teeth in the upper grille cavity, new—and prominent—bullet front bumper guards, a reshaped dummy-scoop hood ornament, full-length bodyside moldings, and three chrome "windsplits" on the leading edges of the rear fender bulges. Like Lincoln, sedans and hardtops now sported one-piece wrapped backlights. Retained from '52 was the interesting "aircraft-inspired" Mercury dash, a convex ensemble with a half-moon gauge cluster atop a flat pod holding horizontal levers (with large knobs) for heating/ventilation, lights, and wipers, plus other ancillaries.

In all, 1953 was a vintage L-M year. Lincoln output was at record levels again: 40,000-plus for the 12 months and nearly 41,000 units for the model year, the latter up more than 13,000 on '52. Mercury built a near-record 320,000 units for the calendar year and was sixth in volume behind the low-priced three, Buick, and Pontiac. The model year tally wasn't as good: nearly 306,000 units, enough for only 8th on the industry roster.

But it was bonanza time for Lincoln. Assembly plants in New Jersey, Missouri, and Michigan ran double shifts, and May's 5009-unit volume was the highest one-month total in Lincoln history. The "Master of Precision" would have been proud.

do principles, combustion chambers were kidney-shaped, with the larger ends away from the spark plugs. Combustion thus began there, progressing to the smaller areas where the mixture was cooled by head/piston contact. It was quite a contrast to the symmetrical combustion chambers of Chrysler's hemi-head V-8s.

It bears mentioning that Chevrolet and Plymouth would trail Ford by a full year in offering high-compression V-8s. And as the low-priced three were all essentially styling and engineering carryovers for '54, the new ohv unit was undoubtedly a key factor in putting Ford on top in the industry production totals. Its margin over Chevy was slim to be sure—less than 23,000 units for the model year—but it was an important moral victory and an indication of just how far Ford Motor Company had come in a very short time. In fact, Dearborn was again solidly entrenched as the industry's number-two, having passed Chrysler Corporation in volume—this despite only three makes to GM's and Chrysler's five. Much of this success came on the strength of the Ford line.

Ford had something else for 1954, though not nearly so significant: a brace of hardtop coupes with a novelty heretofore seen only on show cars—a see-through top. Designers had been thinking about "bubbletops" since the late Thirties, when technical advances in the infant plastics industry began yielding stronger materials that could be used structurally, not just decoratively. The first such application was executed by John Tjaarda for Briggs, a one-piece plastic top for a 1939 Plymouth convertible sedan. By the end of World War II, the public had been titillated with promises of radical see-through cars from a number of companies, but nobody ever built a production bubble-top until Ford.

The new Ford Skyliner and Mercury Sun Valley likely gained impetus with the arrival of Gordon M. Buehrig, who'd come to Dearborn in 1949 to design the Ford Crestliner and '51 Victoria. He also helped develop the all-steel '52 Ford/Mercury wagons, and would later handle body engineering for the beautiful Continental Mark II. Buehrig had previously worked at Studebaker with Raymond Loewy, a leading proponent of the see-through top, then became a freelance designer and created the stillborn TASCO car, which had hinged roof sections of transparent plastic, an idea he patented. (Buehrig was later moved to take issue with General Motors when it showed something similar on an experimental Corvette. "But I settled," he said. "They were too big to sue.")

A more direct Skyliner/Sun Valley forecast was the fiberglass-bodied XL-500 show car of 1953, with a clear plastic top and pillars raked forward to form a "basket handle" roof band. The idea resurfaced two years later on the experimental Mystere, where the up-and-over pillars served as the only structural roof members.

The production bubbletoppers were considerably less radical, of course: just the ordinary pillarless coupes with Plexiglas inserts ahead of where B-pillars would be, tinted deep green to ward off heat and glare. The Skyliner listed at $2164 with standard six, $109 more than the

The 1954 "bubble-top" Skyliner: Ford's newest model.

The '54 facelift hid Ford's all-new overhead-valve V-8.

The $2209 Ranch Wagon had "ball-joint" suspension.

normal Crestline Victoria. Mercury's $2582 Sun Valley cost $130 more than the equivalent Monterey. Aside from the half-plastic roof and minor identifying trim, both were virtually identical with their steel-roof counterparts.

Ford described the Skyliner in rather flowery prose, claiming for it "a freshness of view, a new gaiety and glamor, vast new areas of visibility, a whole new concept of light and luxury . . . You're comfortably 'out of doors' all year long . . . with that wonderful feeling of being fashionably first." This happy puffery wasn't entirely accurate. The green tinting made for a kind of bilious, slightly weird interior ambience. As *Motor Trend* magazine's Walt Woron quipped: "It may cause many a young lady to check

The mildly facelifted '54 Lincoln Capri ragtop: $4031.

Lincoln's '54 price leader: Cosmopolitan sedan, $3522.

Lincoln built 36,993 '54s; here a Cosmopolitan hardtop.

gave up after 1955, while Ford persisted with the same decreasing success through '56. At least Dearborn was trying to give the public something it couldn't get anywhere else.

Of course, it's that low production that has since made these cars hot—figuratively, that is—as collector's items. The '54 Sun Valley is especially prized for its greater rarity (the successor '55 was even scarcer and is hardly seen anymore). It was a pretty car, typically finished in black over yellow or mint green and distinguished by gold-anodized front fender script.

Bubbletoppers aside, both Ford and Mercury retained their '53 model offerings and settled for only minor appearance alterations (a heavy facelift was coming for '55). Ford shuffled trim and complicated its horizontal grille bar a bit. Mercury followed suit, but also reshaped rear fenders, capped them with wrapped vertical taillamps, and cleaned up its face by adopting a double-bar front bumper, the upper one ribbed between the two bomb-like guards. It all added up to the best-looking Merc of this period. Besides the new ohv engines, Ford and Mercury belatedly adopted another engineering feature first seen on the '52 Lincoln: an improved version of its ball-joint front suspension.

With the Ford "blitz" in full swing, Lincoln-Mercury again met with mixed sales success this year. Mercury finished a notch higher on the model year production board, beating Dodge for 7th, but tallied 50,000 fewer units, just over 259,300. Lincoln did comparatively better, marching from 17th to 15th but down fewer than 3000 cars to near 37,000 in all.

Lincoln facelifted more heavily than Merc, and many judged it the best-looking Lincoln since the war. Brightwork was heavier, lending a "richer" appearance. A new V-cradled crest rode above a heavier-looking grille, with two slim uprights behind a pair of massive horizontal bars, the lower one dipped between large, canted bumper guards. The rear bumper moved away from the body, helping boost overall length an inch (to 215), and carried the Lincoln name in block letters. Width returned to 77.4 inches overall. All models exchanged their dummy rear fender air scoops for bright gravel guards ahead of the wheelarches, with a slim chrome strip trailing behind. Offerings stayed the same: sedan and hardtop coupe in Cosmopolitan and Capri trim, plus the low-demand Capri convertible (just 1951 built this year). The major mechanical change was higher, 8:1 compression, which swelled torque output on Lincoln's 317 V-8 to 305 footpounds. Horsepower, though, remained at 205.

Lincoln base prices now ran $3500-$3600 for the Cosmos and from $3700 to $4100 for Capris, reasonable but misleading, as Lincolns didn't carry as many standards as they do now. Not included were items like power steering ($145), radio ($122), heater ($113), power brakes ($40), power windows ($65), power seat ($165), and whitewall tires ($37), all of which totaled nearly $700; air conditioning added another $647. Thus, a Capri hardtop could easily cost $5200, definitely in the full-luxury category.

her makeup. She might as well switch to green lipstick."

A more serious problem was perspiring passengers. Though desert tests showed that the steel-roof hardtops were only about five degrees cooler inside, the bubbletoppers undoubtedly felt much warmer on sunny days than that difference implied. And as air conditioning cost upwards of $600 extra in those days, not many of the cars had it. What they did have was an interior sunshade (snapped onto the headliner around the transparent section's perimeter), but it provided only partial relief.

Interesting though they were, the Skyliner and Sun Valley were predictably poor sellers. The former saw only 13,344 copies this year, the latter a mere 9761. Mercury

Merc's Skyliner equivalent was the plexi-top Sun Valley.

Under the Monterey ragtop's hood lurked 161 horsepower.

Mercury for 1954: an effective facelift and a new V-8.

The '54 Mercury Monterey wagon saw 11,656 copies built.

The fifth and final running of the *Carrera Panamericana* saw Lincoln's third consecutive sweep, with Ray Crawford and Walt Faulkner finishing 1-2 in the International Stock Class behind a pack of sports cars. Crawford's was a private entry, however. Clay Smith had unexpectedly died, and while Bill Stroppe capably relieved him, the factory team wasn't as successful against this year's tougher opposition. They covered the gruelling 1983 Mexican miles in about 21 hours, but were closely followed by a pair of very strong Cadillacs. Of 14 Lincolns entered, half by the factory, only four finished, including two privateers. For Lincoln, it was perhaps fortunate that the Mexican Road Race ended when it did.

The last *Carrera* also saw a not altogether successful attempt to tighten the rules. Technical director Pedro Vivao de la Prida made it clear that "heavy-duty packages, severe-usage and police kits and export kits" were strictly prohibited, regardless of whether they were in the manufacturer's catalog. This was vague enough to circumvent, since the difference between dealer and factory options was hazy, and most stock-car contenders did so. This year's purse was the largest yet—$117,000—but local opposition was higher than ever. So, tragically, was the number of lives lost.

Despite this, Smith's death, and the increased competition, the '54 *Carrera* Lincolns were formidable. Three of them sped nose-to-tail at 130 mph along the 300-mile straightaway running north from Mexico City. Interestingly, the previous aversion to automatic transmissions had vanished, most drivers using them like manual gearboxes, Lincoln's among them. They certainly knew their business. Said Pete Molson of the Lincoln team: "They all have so much experience in driving or as mechanics, or both, that it's staggering. Many come from the aircraft industry, whose standards of accuracy are second to none. All are perfectionists, without the neurotic overtones that sometimes accompany this attitude. To them perfectionism means something very simple: if the job isn't perfect, they just keep at it until it is. That's why they had a better chance to win than anyone else."

While Lincoln had impressed enthusiasts with its Mexican exploits, and had smartly improved production—not to mention its cars' design and engineering—Mercury offered even greater potential in the opinion of Benson Ford: "From the viewpoint of the total Ford Motor Company, what should Ford owners graduate to? The next logical step would be a Mercury." But according to authors Nevins and Hill in their seminal company history, Benson "had inherited a difficult situation. He had to sell in the medium-priced and high-priced field two models that had never become outright successes, although the Mercury had shown high promise. Benson was assisted by Stanley Ostrander, but [L-M] Division lacked an official who could push a point of policy against [executives] like J.R. Davis, Breech or Henry II. Nevertheless, the Lincoln-Mercury Division held possibilities through the improvement of existing models or the creation of a new one ....Other possibilities lay in the Lincoln Continental...." Dearborn was now on the brink of its fateful decision to form a multi-division structure in an effort to overhaul General Motors itself, a drama that would unfold in 1955-56.

It's not easy to buy the Nevins/Hill thesis that Mercury hadn't been an outright success up to this time—unless by that they mean that it had yet to outsell, say, Buick. Since the war, Mercury had often exceeded 300,000 cars a year and placed sixth in the industry, remarkable next to its prewar performance. The '54 did well in a lackluster year for the industry as a whole, and a newer, larger and more impressive design was in the works for 1955.

But the medium-price field was growing in '54, and Ford had only one contender to GM's and Chrysler's three. That irked the pride of Dearborn managers, who longed for another make no matter how well Mercury might do. Thus, within the division's inner sanctum, Lincoln-Mercury began studying prospects for a new car—not the compact planned for postwar sale but a companion for Mercury, with a strong, well-defined image and, perhaps, a slightly higher price. Robert S. McNamara, then assistant general manager at Ford Division, asked a sensible question of the Executive Committee: "What is the new car intended to offer the car-buying public?" Their ultimate answer wasn't fully considered. Insiders called it the "E-car," but they soon nicknamed it after the first Henry's fondly remembered son: Edsel.

1955

Ford dealers got their first companion model this year: the sleek, two-passenger Thunderbird, a "personal" car with sports car overtones. The standard line was hardly ignored, however, being restyled stem to stern and packing more power than any previous Ford. The traditional Ford/Chevy sales battle was especially fierce in the industry's best-ever year. Ford again claimed second spot on the sales chart, but enjoyed unprecedented model year volume of over 1.4 million cars. Robert S. McNamara, one of the "Whiz Kids" hired by Henry Ford II shortly after the war, was elevated to division general manager in early '55, and his influence would be felt well into the next decade.

The 1955 Ford Fairlane featured new styling, more go.

Ford's costliest '55 model was the $2392 Country Squire.

Ford Motor Company's steadily improving fortunes since '49 had been accompanied by management's steadily increasing desire to take on General Motors product-for-product. For example, Jaguar, MG, and other sports cars began selling consistently in the late Forties and early Fifties, though hardly in large numbers. Several American producers decided that homegrown models would do much better, owing to customer loyalties and the easier parts and service availability domestic makes enjoy. Thus arrived the 1951-54 Nash-Healey and '54 Kaiser-Darrin, neither of which sold more than a handful. At first, the same was true of Corvette. But as a Chevrolet, it was a challenge Ford couldn't ignore.

Impetus for the Thunderbird came from two directions. Ford styling director Franklin Q. Hershey, assisted by young William P. Boyer, had been rendering sports cars since 1950, hoping to interest management in a production model. Nothing much happened until Ford Division chief Lewis D. Crusoe went to the 1951 Paris Auto Show with George Walker, still an outside consultant. Crusoe yearned for a Ford reply to the sporty two-seaters he saw there: the Spanish Pegaso, a revived Bugatti, the Jaguar XK-120, and GM's LeSabre show car. Turning to Walker, he reportedly asked, "Why don't we have something like that?" "Oh, but we *do*," replied Walker—who then grabbed a phone to tell the folks back home to get a sports car going. Both Walker's and Hershey's staffs started drawing up ideas, but there wasn't much urgency until the Corvette's 1953 debut, underlining Henry Ford II's

1955

The '55 Crown Victoria ($2202) saw 33,165 units built.

determination to match GM in every market sector.

Designed by Boyer under Hershey's direction, the production Thunderbird moved rapidly through the usual stages of renderings, clay models, and steel prototypes, during which its basic lines were gradually refined.

Among discarded notions were canted fins and taillights; a wide, eggcrate grille and high-set bumper; numerous scoops and scallops; and a bolt-on hardtop patterned on the roofline of the locked-up Continental Mark II. Scrubbed before production was a sweepspear side molding similar (but not identical) to that of the '55 Ford Fairlane, shown in two early ads. The result was a timeless look that could hardly be improved upon.

Thunderbird production began September 9, 1954, and the new model received generally favorable reviews. The only thing it had in common with Corvette was two seats. A boulevard tourer rather than all-out sports car, it shunned snap-in side curtains for more convenient roll-up windows, fiberglass bodywork for traditional steel, and a six-cylinder engine for a potent V-8, this year's new 292-cubic-inch Mercury engine with 193 (stickshift) or 198 (automatic) horsepower. With its good looks and ample zip, the T-Bird sold a respectable 16,155 units for the model year. More important in Ford's eyes, it soundly trounced Corvette.

But in the end, it didn't sell in sufficient volume to

Everybody loved it: a 1955 Ford Thunderbird prototype.

This T-Bird prototype uses '55 Fairlane side sweepspear.

The '55 T-Bird, which started at $3000, sold 16,155 copies, way ahead of Corvette's 674 units.

satisfy company accounts—or Bob McNamara. It thus became something quite different: the post-1957 four-seat "Squarebird." According to Boyer and others, the transformation was underway even as the first two-seaters were being sold. It proved correct. Though the early Birds outsold Corvette, the four-seaters did far better—enough to make money, which was what McNamara cared about. As almost everyone knows now, the change rendered the two-seaters "instant classics" that remain highly prized—and high-priced—collector's items.

Ford's '55 passenger cars boasted a number of new features and a heavy Hershey facelift of the 1952-54 bodyshell. Design highlights comprised trendy wraparound windshield, full-width concave mesh grille, hooded headlamps, artful sheetmetal "speedlines" around the wheel openings, and modestly finned rear fenders. The lineup now comprised four series, with wagons as a separate group for the first time. Replacing Crestline at the top was the new Fairlane (named after the Ford estate in Dearborn) identified by full-length side moldings running from atop the headlamps and saucily dipped at the A-posts.

Fairlane arrived with two sedans, Sunliner convertible, Victoria hardtop, and the new Crown Victoria, a hardtop-inspired two-door sedan available in steel- and Plexi-top form, the latter replacing the Crestline Skyliner. Its distinctive roof came from L. David Ash, a young designer working under Hershey, who had created the X-100 and Mystere show cars. These undoubtedly inspired the production model's "basket handle" top, with a wide, raked-forward chrome band wrapped up and over to conceal the B-pillars. It looked like a rollbar but didn't function like one, and engineer Harold Youngren thought body flex was enough to warrant the stiffer X-braced convertible frame—which made Crown Vics unusually tight and solid-feeling. Like Skyliner, the bubbletop version had a 1/4-inch-thick Plexiglas half-roof (forward of the band).

As the star of the new top-shelf series, Crown Victoria was typically well-equipped and finished in bright two-tone color schemes. It added zest to an already impressive Ford line. But like the Skyliner before it, the Plexi-roof version found far fewer takers than its steel-top sibling: 1999 against 33,165. Both returned for '56, but only 603 and 9209 were built, respectively. With sales like that, the Crown Vic was dead (though it was briefly considered for the all-new '57 line).

Ford answered Chevy's new '55 V-8 with a pair of larger engines. First came a bored-and-stroked version of the previous 239, a 272-cid unit rated at 162 bhp with two-barrel carburetor or 182 with extra-cost four-barrel and dual exhausts. Raiding the parts bin produced an optional 292, a bigger-bore 272 with the same 198 bhp as in the T-Bird and '55 Mercury. Late in the year, a special 205-bhp "Interceptor" 292, ostensibly for police use, appeared on the list, an outgrowth of the factory's efforts in NASCAR stock-car racing. Here, Ford was attempting not only to match its chief rival in the horsepower race but to prevent defection by speed merchants and hot rodders who quickly

The '55 Lincoln got a tasteful facelift, more power.

Lincoln built only 1487 Capri ragtops; list was $4072.

Base Lincoln for 1955 was the $3563 Custom four door.

This '55 Capri was air conditioned—find the two clues.

acclaimed the Chevy V-8 for its freer, higher-revving valvetrain and superior hop-up potential. At the other end of the spectrum, Ford's basic ohv six was rated at 120 bhp, up five from '54.

Ford stressed "Torque-Tailored" axle ratios this year, final gearing matched to body style, engine, and transmission for "brilliant response at all driving speeds." Transmission choices were the usual three-speed manual,

Mercury's 1955 flagship series was the Montclair. The two-door hardtop, as shown, listed at $2631.

For '55, Montclairs had 198 bhp, lesser Mercs got 188.

Mercury's mid-price 1955 series was the Monterey.

The Custom two door was Mercury's price leader at $2218.

Prototype '55 wagon: note taillights and front chrome.

manual with overdrive, and "speed-trigger" Ford-O-Matic. The last referred to full-throttle kickdown into Low (manually selected on earlier Ford-O-Matics, which started in Second). Said the brochure: "For a real 'speed-trigger' start, just press the accelerator to the toeboard and you'll flash away in low gear."

Chassis alterations included a slight rearward tilt on the ball-joint front suspension so that road shocks were absorbed from the front as well as vertically. Brakes were enlarged by about 10 percent, and had harder linings that lasted 40-50 percent longer.

A typical bit of period kitsch was Ford's new "Astra-Dial" instrument panel. Three circles low down in the center contained (left to right) heater controls, radio, and

clock. The driver faced a semicircular speedometer mounted atop the dash in a housing with a little window in front "for daylight illumination."

In all, this was a good Ford year. Though not appreciated as much as Chevy's '55 passenger models, the Fords are worthy collector cars in their own right. The fast-looking Fairlanes, especially, had a lot going for them, and their values seem destined to climb as the years pass.

Having delivered the Thunderbird, Lew Crusoe moved from Ford Division in early '55 to become executive vice-president of the Car and Truck Division, responsible for assembly and distribution of all Ford products. Here he picked up Francis C. "Jack" Reith from Ford France, who set to work on new-model planning. One of Reith's first actions was to greatly enlarge the developing '57 Mercury (soon nicknamed "Reith's Merc" within certain corporate circles).

This was in line with a new overall product strategy predicated on rapid growth. Reith told the board of directors that population and per-capita income were soaring, which implied an expanding car market. To capture a larger share of it, Ford needed a broader range. "Too large a percentage of our business [is] in one car and one price bracket," he said. At the time, the Ford shell accounted for 97.7 percent of the company's output. The forthcoming "E-car," initiated in '54, should be slotted in *below* Mercury, not above, said Reith, with a wheelbase of 118-120 inches, versus the 122 of his '57 Mercury. There should, however, be some overlap for the sake of the dealers.

Reith's basic plan, which was accepted, contemplated not two shells but four: low-line Ford; E-car/Ford Fairlane; standard Mercury and perhaps a higher-priced E-car; Lincoln and a new "super Mercury" (the last would materialize for '58 as the Park Lane.) Ford would thus compete as usual against Chevrolet and Plymouth; the basic E-car against Dodge and Pontiac; the standard Mercury and higher-priced E-car against Olds, Buick, and DeSoto; the "super Mercury" against Chrysler and Buick Roadmaster; Lincoln against you-know-who. Wrote Nevins and Hill: "The plan seemed so convincing that no one was prepared to offer what might appear petty objections."

Accordingly, Lincoln-Mercury was split into two divisions in mid-April 1955. Ben Mills took over Lincoln, while Mercury was put under . . . F.C.Reith. (You couldn't say he didn't have the courage of his convictions.) The E-car project was handed to Dick Krafve at Special Products Division, where a talented team of stylists and engineers had been working on a reborn Continental since 1952 as "Special Product Operations." That program, with most of its staff, was now transferred to a separate new Continental Division. Overseeing all these activities was newly named group director Benson Ford. While separate dealers were sought for the E-car, Lincoln-Mercury agencies were dualed as before, selling an all-new Mercury and what many consider the most beautiful Lincoln of the Fifties.

Alas, Lincoln was a sales disappointment. Calendar year volume went up but slightly in a year that saw huge gains by other makes. Lincoln was also one of the few to tally lower model year volume than it had in '54 (the others were fast-fading Hudson, Willys, and Kaiser). Though strictly a hindsight observation, the factors behind this were the very ones collectors admire today: high quality, tremendous roadability, and clean, uncluttered styling. The last was a particular drawback in 1955, when buyers wanted acres of chrome on lower-longer-wider bodies. For example, Lincoln was the only make other than Kaiser-Willys without a faddishly wrapped windshield and knee-banging "dogleg" A-pillars—impractical but almost mandatory in '55. Cadillac had ballooned into a tail-finned, 129-inch-wheelbase cruiser bedecked with chrome

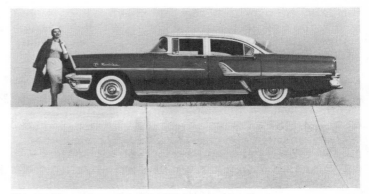

This '55 Montclair predicted the '56 four-door hardtop.

and stainless steel, while Chrysler had launched an ornate new Imperial as a separate make on a 130-inch platform. By contrast, Lincoln merely facelifted its aging 123-inch-wheelbase '52 platform.

But, in retrospect, Lincoln was easily the best of the three: crisp and elegant yet somehow eager, thanks to a smooth new bumper/grille, "boomerang" accents on the aft flanks, and shapely, extended rear fenders. Interiors were as luxurious as ever. Sharing in the corporate muscle-building program, the Lincoln V-8 was bored to 3.94 inches for 341 cid and a rated 225 bhp (both Cadillac and Imperial had 250, though). An important image point was the belated arrival of Lincoln's own automatic, three-speed Turbo Drive, replacing the Hydra-Matic transmission imported from GM. Model offerings stayed the same, but the base Cosmopolitan twosome was now called Custom. Weight changed little (one of the few '55s that didn't heavy-up a lot), as did prices. Only around 3500 Customs were called for. Most buyers preferred the fancier Capri, which sold only some 23,500 units, including 1487 convertibles. But the low totals were just temporary: Lincoln would bounce back with a trendier '56 car.

Mercury looked a sure winner in expansive '55, and it was. Like Ford, there was dramatic new styling on the basic 1952-54 shell and larger, more potent V-8s, but Mer-

Ford called the 1955 F-100 pickup a "Money Maker."

cury also grew an inch between wheel centers, to 119 inches, the first such increase since 1942. Reith's game plan was starting to look exactly right, because Mercury built a whopping 435,000 cars for the calendar 12 months, 100,000 more than its previous best. Model year volume rose by some 70,000 units to near 330,000, though Mercury remained 7th in the industry. The only other disappointment was the bubbletop Sun Valley, which tapered off to just 1787 units and would never be seen again.

This year's Mercs certainly reflected the unbridled optimism of Crusoe, Reith, and the Executive Committee. Not only were they longer, lower, wider, and faster, but there were more of them than at any time in the make's history: three series (up one from '54) spanning 14 models ranging in delivered price from $2700 to $4000. With industry sales at record levels, it was exactly the right formula.

Topping the line was the new Montclair, offered as a sedan, hardtop coupe (with or without Sun Valley treatment) and convertible. Like all '55s, it had an evolutionary form of the '54 grille, but was distinguished by a thin color panel under the side windows, color-keyed to the roof on two-tone models. Next came the Monterey sedan, hardtop, and wagon, followed by a base Custom series with the same styles plus a price-leader two-door sedan. Like Ford, all wore newly wrapped windshields and sported more "important-looking" lower-body sheetmetal. Unique to the Montclair sedan was a more rakish, hardtop-style roofline, really a forecast of the pillarless hardtop sedans to come.

Also like Ford, Mercury bored and stroked its V-8, reaching 292 cid (shared with the Thunderbird, as mentioned). Custom and Monterey packed 188 bhp with 7.6:1 compression. Standard for Montclairs and optional on others was the high-compression (8.5:1) 198-bhp version teamed with Merc-O-Matic.

In all, the '55 was one of Mercury's best efforts to date—arguably *the* best in some ways. But after more of the same for '56, the next Mercs really worth remembering would be a long time coming.

1956

Dearborn's big event this year was the return of the fabled Continental. The famous effort of William Clay Ford and his star-studded team—Gordon M. Buehrig, John Reinhart, and Harley F. Copp—began in 1952 with a committee called Special Product Operations, set up by Ernie Breech. It was the first company assignment for young Bill Ford, then only 26. By December, an initial design had been completed for a long-hood/short-deck coupe inspired by Edsel Ford's 1940 original. But as the

The '56 Customline wore a new grille, splashier trim.

Ford built 58,147 Sunliners for the 1956 model year.

New for '56: Fairlane Town Victoria four-door hardtop.

story goes, Bill's brother Henry II took one look, said "I wouldn't give a dime for that," and sent Bill back to work.

SPO tried again four months later. But this time, management looked at 15 different designs—each shown in front and rear ¾ views—submitted in a contest between five different teams: Walter Buell Ford, Grisinger-Miller Design, Vince Gardner, George Walker, and SPO's Reinhart/Buehrig. The last won unanimously with a proposal that combined the imposing front end of one SPO design with the semi-continental spare tire deck outline of another. With that question resolved, Special Products began finalizing the details.

"They used to call us the 'country club boys,'" John Reinhart remembered, "because for competitive comparisons we'd drive prospective rivals like Packard Caribbeans and Cadillac Eldorados. [But we] had never worked so hard in our lives . . . These were the kind of people we had—they would literally die for this damn automobile."

By now they'd agreed to call it Continental Mark II, and

its engineering was as interesting as its styling. To provide chair-height seating within a planned package height of only 56 inches overall, Copp devised a new steel-rail chassis dipped low between wheels with a base of 126 inches. This "cow-belly" design left no room for exhausts, so he routed them through the frame rails. Locomotive and aircraft controls influenced the ultra-clean dash design. Lincoln's newly enlarged 368-cubic-inch V-8 was specified, but Continental engines were to be specially selected from the regular assembly line, then individually balanced and tested. Completing the driveline were Lincoln's three-speed Multi-Drive automatic transmission, also new for '56, and a 3.07:1 rear axle. With elegant "modern formal" styling, marked by a wide-quarter roofline and the trademark spare-tire motif, the Mark II was one of the most beautiful cars ever produced. For mid-Fifties Detroit, it was unbelievable.

Priced at a breathtaking $10,000, the ultra-deluxe Mark II hardtop coupe (a convertible was planned but only one prototype was built) met loud acclaim from press and public alike. Here at last was a serious Cadillac challenger, perhaps a new Standard of the World. "What we had going was a revival of the Duesenberg concept," said one designer, "a no-holds-barred, all-out luxury car of impeccable design and exquisite taste."

But with that tall price, the Mark II sold sparingly: only 1325 were built this model year. Of course, it was never intended to be a high-volume item. But with such low sales—and losses of about $1000 a car—management began wondering whether the price of this boost to corporate prestige wasn't perhaps a little *too* high.

Ford moved in two different directions this year: safety and performance. All models wore a conservative rehash of their '55 styling. Passenger cars received larger parking lights and taillamps, plus a grated grille insert. Following GM's lead at mid-1955, Ford bowed pillarless hardtop sedans, called Town Victoria, in the Customline

T-Bird gained a larger trunk by booting the tire out.

and Fairlane series. Priced about $75 above the renamed Club Victoria two-doors—$1985 and $2249, respectively—they enjoyed strong sales of over 65,000 units.

As elsewhere in the industry, Ford horsepower continued to climb. Joining the 272 and 292 Y-blocks was a new 312-cid enlargement (bore and stroke 3.80 × 3.44) with 215 bhp in standard two-barrel form or 225 bhp with four-barrel carb, the latter limited to Ford-O-Matic. At mid-year, a twin four-barrel setup with 245 bhp was announced as a Thunderbird option. The standard Fords weren't mentioned, though a few may have been built with it.

Dearborn tried selling safety this year by standardizing impact-absorbing dished steering wheels, breakaway rearview mirrors, and crashproof door locks throughout its corporate line and offering factory seatbelts and padded dash and sunvisors at extra cost. At first, the public took to these "Lifeguard Design" features in a modest way, but the rush to install seatbelts overtaxed Ford's supplier, and only 20 percent of its '56 cars were so equipped. Ford would continue to stress safety for another

Porthole windows were a new option on the 1956 Thunderbird, as was a 312-cid V-8 of 215 or 225 horsepower.

The award-winning 1956 Lincoln: seven inches longer, 60 horsepower stronger. Production doubled.

few years, but a lot of dealers said performance was more important.

The most marked difference in this year's Ford Thunderbird was a "continental" exterior-mount spare tire, a last-minute change likely made more to increase trunk space than to enhance styling, though it came off well visually. So did the now-famous porthole windows, a new option for the accessory hardtop. Though they didn't relate to any other line on the car, they improved over-the-shoulder vision, which may explain why buyers preferred them four-to-one over the blind-quarter hardtop. Finally,

The plush '56 Premiere outsold the Capri five-to-one.

front fenders now sported flip-open ventilators, answering complaints of excessive engine heat in the '55 cockpit. The 292 V-8 returned with 202 bhp as standard with manual transmission, while the new 312 engine offered 215 bhp with optional stick-overdrive and 225 bhp with Ford-O-Matic.

Writer Karl Ludvigsen judged the '56 Thunderbird better balanced than the '55, mainly due to the more equal front/rear weight distribution from slinging the spare out back. Nevertheless, the early Birds were not genuinely sporting handlers. The quick steering and fairly stiff rear springs from '55 were respectively slowed and softened for '56, because most buyers wanted them that way. Thus, the '56 (and '57) plowed a bit more through corners, and steering response was rather vague, though not completely robbed of feel by excessive power assist. The all-drum brakes were adequate for normal driving if not track work. Still, the two-seaters seem entirely up to date today, giving away little in comfort or driving pleasure to cars several decades younger.

Despite their expected disadvantages as competition cars, early T-Birds not only raced but did surprisingly well. In fact, they were far more capable than many appreciated. At the 1955 Daytona Beach Speed Weeks, for example, a car sponsored by Tom McCahill of *Mechanix Illustrated* magazine and driven by Joe Furguson swept all honors among American production sports cars, averaging 124.633 mph on a two-way run to best every Porsche and Austin-Healey and all but one Jaguar XK-120M.

This year, Ford hired ex-racing driver Pete DePaolo to prepare a flock of T-Birds for Daytona. Chuck Daigh's carefully set-up '56 won the production-class standing mile at 88.779 mph, very nearly beating a modified-class Corvette driven by Zora Arkus-Duntov (89.735 mph). But the Birds weren't entered in the long-distance race, a Chrysler 300 won the Grand National stock-car event, and the car wasn't competitive in road racing because of its soft suspension and indifferent brakes.

In the all-important sales race, Ford pulled a lot closer to Chevrolet, building a bit more than 1.4 million cars for the model year compared to Chevy's 1.56 million. Thunderbird output eased to 15,631 units, perhaps reflecting slightly higher prices. Now all that remained was to pull ahead of its perennial rival and stay there. Ford wouldn't do that, but it would again outsell Chevy in '57.

While the new Mark II was a model of studied restraint in this chrome-happy year, the all-new '56 Lincolns took the opposite approach. Ads called them "Unmistakably Lincoln," but you had to look twice for any vestige of '55. The short wheelbase, conservative styling, flat windshield, and year-old 341 engine were all gone. In their place came a three-inch-longer (126-inch) wheelbase and a 368 V-8 (bore and stroke: 4.00 × 3.66 inches) belting out 285 horsepower—60 more than the year previous. Bodies added seven inches in overall length, three inches in overall width. Model offerings were unchanged, but Capri was demoted to lower-line status and the upper series was called Premiere.

Lincoln's '56 styling had been started by Bill Schmidt before he left to join Packard and, like his previous work, was simple and tasteful. What distinguished it from '55 was not glitter but size. Details and surface development were deftly handled and fit the larger proportions extremely well. As possible proof, the '56 Lincoln was cited for excellence in automotive design by the Industrial Designers Institute.

Certain elements, especially the bodyside and rear fender shapes, had been previewed on the '54 Mercury XM-800 show car. The grille was composed of slim horizontal bars behind a full-width bumper bar with wide oval parking lights at its outboard ends, integrated with a broad U-shaped bumper below. Headlamps nestled under large, thrust-forward hoods. Rear fenders were straight-topped but angled forward at the trailing edges to house rakish vertical taillights above long exhaust ports. The last flanked a dummy grille duplicating the frontal motif. Two-toning was still confined to the roof, not blasted haphazardly around the lower body. The dash represented an idea John Reinhart had wanted to use on the Mark II, and had been using on Lincolns since 1949: a central bar bisecting a rectangular panel containing instruments (above) and control switches (below), with toggle levers for heating/ventilation and a garish steering wheel. There were 17 basic body colors, 35 two-tone combinations, and 29 upholstery choices.

With one of the year's few new designs, Lincoln did well for '56. Calendar year output rose to near 50,000 units and model year volume nearly doubled, also to 50,000, good for 14th place, up two spots from '55.

Mercury, on the other hand, was in a facelift year and, like most rivals, saw far fewer sales: about 250,000, down some 180,000 from 1955. However, model year production eased by less than 1000, though it seemed Mercury was stuck in 7th. Styling changes involved a wide "Big M" hood emblem, a revamped upper front-bumper bar with "Mercury" in block letters, more prominently bulged rear

The elegant Continental returned for 1956 as the Mark II. It met with acclaim but—at $10,000—sold sparingly.

Among the seven '56 Mercury Customs lurked a two door.

Merc built 10,083 Custom and Montclair ragtops for '56.

Mercury listed four four-door Phaeton hardtops for '56.

This bottom-of-the-line Medalist was priced at $2389.

Not all Medalists carried the front fender/door trim.

Ford trucking in '56: new grille, wrapped windshield.

fenders with reworked taillamps, and full-length Z-shape bodyside moldings on returning Custom, Monterey, and Montclair models. The area below the moldings could be keyed to roof color with optional two-toning, though a conventional roof/lower body contrast was also available.

To attract buyers at the low end of the medium market, Mercury added a new cut-rate Medalist series comprising sedans and hardtops with two and four doors. But inflation was starting to run, so they actually cost more than the previous year's Customs. Nor were they priced far enough below *this* year's Customs to offset their cheaper

appearance (no Z-trim at first, for instance) and reduced standard equipment. Dealers tried but sold only about 46,000 Medalists, while the other three lines at least doubled that figure.

Like Ford, Mercury went in for four-door hardtops this year, called Phaeton and offered in all four series. Sales seemed proportional to price: most popular in the Montclair series, least in the Medalist line, where it was probably a contradiction in terms. Mercury also fielded a second convertible, in the Custom series. Priced at $2712, it wasn't nearly as popular as the $2900 Montclair ragtop, respective production being 2311 and 7762 units.

Maintaining power/displacement distance with Ford, Mercury dropped the 292 V-8 for three versions of the new 312: two-barrel/210 bhp for Medalists and manual-shift Customs, four-barrel/225 bhp for Monterey and Custom automatics, and four-barrel 235 bhp for Montclair and Monterey automatics. A fourth version arrived late in the season with 260 bhp, courtesy twin four-barrels and higher, 9.7:1 compression.

Of course, all this was necessary to keep pace with Detroit's "horsepower race," and Mercury moved to the fore this year by setting 20 new world records at Kingman, Arizona, in NASCAR-sponsored speed trials. Mercury also won its class in this year's Grand National contest at Daytona. So for all its many changes over the years, and despite being overshadowed by Lincoln's prowess in the Mexican Road Races, Edsel Ford's factory hot rod remained just that.

1957

Ford pulled out all the stops for 1957, still considered by many enthusiasts as Detroit's vintage year of the decade. Ford Division certainly contributed its share of the harvest: a line of totally restyled standard cars, a handsome facelift for the last of the two-seat Thunderbirds, and V-8s ranging from a mild 190-horsepower "300" powerplant to a supercharged 300-bhp 312.

A massive product overhaul coming only two years after major model revisions would be unheard of—and prohibitively expensive—today. But most anything was possible in this extravagant era, and the huge '57 investment paid off. The race with Chevrolet, which fielded only heavily facelifted cars, was hard-fought as always. Some figures showed Ford ahead in calendar year output for the first time since 1935, but the final tabulation had Chevy the winner by a scant 130 units. However, Ford scored a substantial victory margin in model year production: better than 170,000 units. Its grand total of 1.67 million cars was a new high, and would not be surpassed until well into the Sixties.

A big factor in Ford's '57 popularity was its line of powerplants, one of the industry's broadest. At the bottom was the ohv six, the base engine for all passenger models save one, rated at 144 bhp. V-8 offerings began with the 190-bhp 272, followed by a 212-bhp 292, standard for Thunderbird. Then came a raft of 312s, commencing with a four-barrel 245-bhp version and extending through twin-four-barrel 270- and 285-bhp units. At the top were two supercharged 312s, rated at 300 and 340 bhp on 8.5:1

Ford for 1957 was truly new—and on two wheelbases.

The '57 Victoria hardtop sedan found 68,550 buyers.

Fairlanes (including 500s) rode a 118-inch wheelbase.

The 1957 Ford Fairlane Town Sedan listed at $2286.

compression. While the latter's production is doubtful, the former found its way into a few Thunderbirds.

Standard Fords gained all-new bodyshells atop a Continental-style cow-belly chassis spanning two different wheelbases, and model offerings were rearranged into five separate series. On the shorter, 116-inch platform were the bottom-end Custom and flashier Custom 300 sedans (replacing Mainline and Customline, respective-

Ford built 77,726 Sunliners for '57; price was $2505.

Top model: the $2942 Skyliner steel-top convertible.

Country Squire wagons continued with fake wood in '57.

At $2301, the '57 Ranch Wagon was Ford's bargain wagon.

This Custom 300 two-door rode a 116-inch wheelbase.

The '57 T-Bird cost $3408; a record 21,380 were built.

Horsepower ranged from 212-300 bhp on the '57 T-Bird.

ly), plus two-door base and Del Rio Ranch Wagons, a brace of four-door Country Sedans, and the woody-look Country Squire. Also included was the Ranchero, a new wagon-based pickup (and thus technically a product of Ford Truck Divsion) prompted by the growing postwar demand for plusher, more car-like commercial vehicles. A new 118-inch wheelbase was reserved for two Fairlane series: a four-model standard line of two- and four-door hardtops and sedans, and a new 500 group with these styles plus Sunliner convertible and the unique Skyliner retractable hardtop/convertible.

Ford's '57 styling was particularly clean for the period: full-width rectangular grille, rakish side moldings, small tailfins, large, round taillamps. Windshields wrapped more via pulled-back A-posts, and a switch from 15- to 14-inch wheels and tires, in line with an industry trend, contributed to a three-inch reduction in overall height. Overall length and width were noticeably greater, approaching Mercury dimensions of only a few years earlier.

Skyliner, reviving the '54 "bubbletop" name, was the year's most interesting Ford by far, the world's first retractable hardtop produced in significant volume. Introduced slightly behind the rest of the line, it didn't look that different from the Sunliner in top-down form, but its rear fenders were three inches longer and somewhat higher, resulting in an ungainly "bustle" look. Still, it was the ultimate expression of Fifties gadgetry, and Ford advertising played on it with a legitimate point: "How can it be a 'hardtop *convertible*' if the top doesn't go down?"

The retractable concept was broached in Dearborn by stylist Gilbert Spear, whose designs convinced William Clay Ford, then head of Special Projects Division, to earmark $2.2 million for development as part of the Continental Mark II project. Cost escalation precluded it, however, so the idea was turned over to Ford Division in 1955, though only after another $18 million had been set aside for testing. As the all-new '57 line was less than two years away by then, a crash program was instituted to get the Skyliner out in time.

Most of the work went into the rear structure, of course, to make room for the roof (shorter and squarer than that on standard hardtops but still plenty big) and its hardware. The decklid was hinged in the only possible way, at the back, and the top was hinged 10 inches from the front to create a space-saving flap that folded under as it slid back. The convertible chassis was modified with closer-set side rails to leave room for the top's control linkage. Remarkably, little leg space was lost in back. The gas tank took up valuable real estate under the trunk floor, so it moved aft of the back seat (an "accidental" safety benefit for rear-end collisions) and the spare was put in its place. To compensate for the extra weight, the base 272 V-8 option was made standard.

The Skyliner's "nervous system" comprised 600 feet of wiring and no fewer than 10 power relays, eight circuit breakers, 10 limit switches, three drive motors, and a safety interlock that prevented anything from happening without the transmission in Neutral. It was complicated,

The Ranchero was a pickup based on the two-door wagon.

This deluxe '57 Ranchero looks ready for the country club.

Lincoln sprouted fins, inspired by the 1955 Futura show car.

The '57 Premiere coupe was Lincoln's most popular model.

Only 4436 Capri four-door sedans were built for 1957.

The ill-starred Continental Mark II lasted only two years; 1957 was its last year on the market.

Mercury added three inches to its wheelbase for 1957, and adopted all new styling. Here the Turnpike Cruiser.

but more reliable than generally believed.

Here's how it worked. Pressing a steering-column switch with the ignition on (and, preferably, with the engine running, to minimize battery drain) activated two (1957-58) or three (1959) switches to start the deck motor, which lifted the long lid via twin shafts at each edge. Once the deck locked fully open, it tripped the switch for another motor (behind the rear seat) that raised the package shelf to deck level. This started another motor that unlocked the top, after which two more motors (one on the '59) raised the roof and sent it back into the open trunk cavity. A separate servo folded the hinged flap as the roof eased its way down. A dashboard warning light glowed throughout, then extinguished when the sequence was completed, though the operation could be reversed at any time. In case of failure, the point at which the sequence stopped told a mechanic where the trouble was.

Arriving $437 upstream of the Sunliner at $2942, the

Skyliner sold respectably for a specialty item appealing mainly on novelty value, 20,766 units for the model year. That nearly equalled this year's record two-seat Thunderbird volume and was more than twice the number of Corvette sales through 1960. Still, the Skyliner was doomed by inconvenience and high cost. Its price premium over the Sunliner, which had the same open-air appeal, grew each year; other Fords went up too, but not as much. Worse, there was no luggage space with the top down, only 6.5 cubic feet with it up, and the only access was from over the high sides. But the most telling factor was division chief Robert S. McNamara, who deplored "gimmick engineering" and steadily turned Ford toward no-nonsense products as the Sixties approached. Thus, Skyliner was ditched after 1959 and 48,394 units.

Rumors of a new, larger Thunderbird started circulating this year. Some suspected the two-seater was dead, while others hoped it would continue as a companion to the "family" Bird. The former view proved correct, but at least Ford saved the best of the two-seaters for last. A serious facelift brought a bold bumper/grille (proposed by Bill Boyer for 1955 but deemed too radical and costly then) plus modest blade tailfins, similar to the standard Ford's, flanking a longer rear deck. "We extended the trunk largely to get rid of the spare tire," Boyer remembered, so the '57 ended up four inches shorter than the '56. (An optional exterior spare was listed, but found few takers.) Inside were a handsomely redesigned dash with telescoping steering column (revived from '55) and modified door panels with repeating T-Bird logo.

The '57 was the most "styled" two-seat Bird, but designers resisted attempts to gook it up with extra chrome, two-tone paint, and sheetmetal creases. They deserve a lot of credit, because the result was good and still looks good today. Production ran longer than usual due to '58-model delays, so the '57 was the most numerous of the two-seat generation at 21,380 units.

Among Thunderbird mechanical changes were a larger fuel tank (20 versus 17 gallons) and a new rear axle with straddle-mounted pinion gear. The strong frame and coil-spring front suspension were retained, but engineer Bill Burnett substituted five-leaf rear springs (as on the '55) for the '56's six-leaf, and wheel/tire diameter shrank from 15 to 14 inches. Considered but rejected were Edsel-style pushbutton automatic transmission controls. Transmission choices stayed the same, but engine options expanded to include the aforementioned supercharged mills.

The Paxton-McCulloch supercharger was supplied at the behest of driver Pete DePaolo, who'd learned that Chevy might have a blower on its '57 Corvette. A $500 option, this centrifugal unit delivered up to 6 psi of compressed air to a sealed carburetor, and it worked wonders for performance. While the 245-bhp setup would turn 0-60 mph in 10 seconds and 115 mph tops, the blown car would see 125 mph and well under 7 seconds. (The editors timed a Ford-O-Matic "F-Bird" at 5.5 seconds to 60 mph but didn't correct for speedometer error, which couldn't have been much.) Just 208 blown Birds were built, plus another 1500 with the twin-four-barrel 270- and 285-bhp engines.

Of course, Ford wasn't doing this for fun but for Daytona, and 15 of the 300-bhp Birds were run off to qualify as "stock" in time for February's Speed Weeks. Chuck Daigh scored 93.312 mph in the standing mile, and a private entry ran the flying mile at 146.282 mph one-way, 138.775 mph both ways. But shortly afterward, the Automobile Manufacturers Association decided to deemphasize competition, and the T-Bird's racing career was nipped in the bud.

After only a year on the market, the Continental Mark II bowed out with 1957 production of just 444 units. Changes were minor: higher compression (from 9.0 to 10.0:1) and 300 bhp, a switch from Holley to Carter carburetor, newly optional "Directed Power" limited-slip differential, and removal of the central frame member (to reduce weight). Left stillborn were three proposed "line extensions": soft-top and retractable convertibles and

Turnpike Cruiser's rear window retracted for ventilation.

The ragtop Cruiser was called the Convertible Cruiser.

Mercury's first four-door hardtop wagon, the Colony Park.

This '57 Montclair nudged two tons, listed at $3236.

Gordon Buehrig's limousine-like Berline sedan. For a luxury leader intended to lose money for the sake of publicity, model proliferation didn't make sense. And in the end, the whole Mark II idea made no sense to Dearborn managers hungry for volume. A new Continental was coming, but it would be a vastly different car.

Lincoln returned with a wild "taillift" of its '56 styling, plus new four-door hardtops, named Landau, in both Capri and Premiere series. The Premiere convertible still topped the line, at $5381; only 3676 were built. Designer L. David Ash grafted on huge canted fins, while four headlamps arrived (a "first" shared with Nash and Cadillac's Eldorado Brougham this year) in twin vertical stacks. Engine changes were the same as Continental's.

Lincoln had come within a third of Cadillac's sales volume in 1956; Ash's styling was an attempt to keep it there, an appeal to what seemed to motivate luxury car buyers (more available now that the big Packards were gone). So were features like power vent windows, electric door locks, six-way power seats, low-fuel warning light, automatic headlamp dimmer, remote-control rearview mirrors, and more efficient air conditioning. But the '57 failed its assignment. Output dropped by about 10,000 units to 37,500, while Cadillac rose to well over 150,000

units. Lincoln still wasn't cutting it.

But bigger things were coming—literally. The divisionalization of 1955 simultaneously decreed larger-than-ever Lincolns, which had been evolving ever since. As for 1957, one division manager said, "All we could [do] was hang on and try to promise the dealers a more competitive product the following year. You can better understand the decision to downgrade the Continental when you consider the failure of Lincoln Division to handle Cadillac."

Mercury now showed the public what Jack Reith had wrought back in 1955: bigger, flashier cars on a 122-inch wheelbase, longest in Merc history. Styling was completely different, announced by a concave grille and a front bumper with two, huge oblongs. Rear fenders were topped by long, concave projectiles ending in canted, wedge-shape taillamps. The rear bumper echoed the front. Custom and Medalist disappeared, but Monterey and Montclair returned along with a new station wagon series listing no fewer than six models, all with hardtop-style pillarless rooflines, at delivered prices approaching $5000. Topping the line ($3700 base) was the posh wood-trimmed nine-passenger Colony Park four-door, followed by two- and four-door Voyager wagons, all trimmed like Montclair. Commuter wagons carried Monterey trim and

Mercury built 21,567 Montclair four-door hardtops for '57.

The "Mermaid" was a stock-car racing Mercury in 1957.

The $2576 Monterey two-door sedan was the price leader.

One of Ford's Fifties big trucks: the "Big Job" C-900.

the lowest prices, offered as a nine-passenger four-door and six-passenger two- and four-door versions.

The "Big M" was now very big indeed, tipping the scales at up to two tons in wagon form. Horsepower kept pace. A single 312 V-8 returned as standard but now packed 255 bhp, 20 more than the top '56 unit, while this year's Lincoln 368, detuned to 290 bhp, was standard for the new Turnpike Cruisers and optional for other models.

Billed as "a dramatic expression of dream car design," the well-named Turnpike Cruiser was as close as Reith got to a "super Mercury" (his planned Lincoln-based model wouldn't materialize), arriving above Montclair as a hardtop coupe and sedan. It had, he said, just about everything the well-heeled '57 buyer could want: quad headlamps (where legal), "skylight dual curve windshield," a reverse-slant backlight that retracted for flow-through ventilation, a forward-facing air intake over each A-pillar with a protruding radio antenna, and "Seat-O-Matic" memory power seat, which automatically assumed one of 49 preset positions at the twist of a dial. The Cruiser also had pushbutton controls for its standard Merc-O-Matic transmission, following Chrysler's lead for '56. Celebrating Mercury's selection as pace car for the Indianapolis 500 was the mid-year addition of a Convertible Cruiser, supplied with replica pace-car regalia.

For all its novel glitz, the Turnpike Cruiser was a sales dud, perhaps a forecast of 1958's unpleasant surprises, though it was too late by now to change those plans. The '57 series saw only 8305 four-door hardtops, 7291 two-doors, and a mere 1265 convertibles.

Overall, Mercury volume was up by about 10 percent from '56, but that was small compared to most other gains, Chrysler Corporation's in particular. For the model year, the Big M slipped to eighth place behind Dodge, GM's B-O-P trio, and Chevy/Ford/Plymouth.

1958

Divisionalization and Jack Reith's master plan reached fruition this year—and ran head on into the worst economic slowdown since World War II. A sharp recession, beginning in late 1957, put a big damper on everyone's sales, but Ford Motor Company was particularly hard hit. No wonder. Aside from Mercury and the standard Ford, everything in the corporate fleet was new. And the fleet was larger now with arrival of the long-rumored "E-car," named Edsel. The one bright spot in Dearborn's dismal '58 picture was the new four-seat Thunderbird, the only car line besides American Motors' Rambler to score higher sales than it had in '57.

We should first dispense with some hoary old myths

Edsel debuted on September 4, 1957, the first '58 model out.

The top-of-the-line Citation had a 410-cid, 345-bhp V-8.

about the Edsel—starting with the fact that it wasn't a complete disaster. Close to 60,000 were produced before the end of 1957, and the model year output of 63,110 was respectable for any make in its first year. It was also better than that of several well-established brands, including DeSoto, Studebaker, and Lincoln.

Trouble was, the market had contracted almost overnight. As one latterday auto writer put it, Edsel's "aim was right, but the target moved." What moved it, of course, was the sudden recession, which dramatically altered buyers' perceived needs. Volkswagen and Rambler cashed in, the latter doubling its volume, mostly at the expense of the mid-priced stalwarts that had carried Detroit for years. DeSoto and Packard never recovered, while Lincoln and Imperial were severely wounded. By contrast, Rambler would rise to third place by 1961, behind Chevy and Ford.

A key Edsel marketing mistake was the name itself, which by then was little recognized. The new division's ad agency had come up with 6000 possibilities, four of which generated good vibes in consumer testing: Ranger, Pacer, Corsair, and Citation. But they didn't satisfy somehow, so more radical alternatives were considered. Division manager Dick Krafve even hired poetess Marianne Moore to conjure a few, and she produced some stunners: Mongoose Civique, Turcotinga, and Utopian Turtletop among many. Board chairman Ernie Breech, who liked neither the agency's nor Moore's ideas, casually said, "Let's call it the Edsel." When advised that the company president was

1958

Edsel offered two convertibles for 1958: a 118-inch wheelbase Pacer for $3028, and a 124-inch wheelbase Citation for $3801.

Edsel built 4959 Pacer four-door hardtops for 1958.

The '58 Edsel Pacer four-door sedan listed for $2375.

Edsel offered five wagons, all on Ford's 116-inch wheelbase.

The $3247 nine-passenger Bermuda was Edsel's costliest wagon.

Only 1876 Edsel Pacer convertibles were built for 1958.

The Ranger series lacked front fender/door bright trim.

190

against naming the car for his father, Breech replied, "I'll take care of Henry." He did.

But the agency names survived as series designations. With four model groups, 18 different offerings, and nearly 100 color/trim combinations, it was an expansive lineup reflecting Krafve's confidence that Edsel was just what the public wanted. Ranger and Pacer rode a 118-inch wheelbase (wagons 116), basically the '58 Ford Fairlane/Fairlane 500 chassis, while Corsair and Citation used a 124-inch platform derived from that of the new Mercury Park Lane (which was an inch longer between wheel centers).

The junior Edsels differed considerably from the seniors in size and drivetrain (361- vs. 410-cid V-8s, c. 3800 vs. c. 4200 pounds) but basic styling themes were the same. The one that got all the attention, of course, was the infamous "horse collar" vertical grille (a motif that, ironically, became accepted in the Sixties). Also shared were large, elliptical rear fender indentations; flat, finless rear deck with depressed center section; and "boomerang" horizontal taillights (which one cynic said looked like ingrown toenails). Inside were a rotating-drum speedometer that glowed red when a preset speed was exceeded (a Thirties idea), wild duotone pastel color schemes, and extra-cost "Teletouch Drive" automatic transmission with pushbuttons in the steering wheel hub. Other interesting options included compass, indoor/outdoor thermometer, and a tachometer, the last furthering Edsel's intended image as a posh performer for the rising "young executive."

Alas, there were numerous problems that went beyond the '58 recession. One was price structure. Instead of slotting all models under Mercury, Edsel Division pitched Corsair and Citation above. This led to hesitation among buyers raised on the Al Sloan/GM maxim of "a car for every price and pocketbook." (It still does, witness the confusion over today's various GM clones.) Quality nits were more plentiful than usual, and breaking into the hotly competitive middle-priced field was tough even in a good year. Then too, Ford abandoned advertising when sales started slowing early in the model year. With 20-20 hindsight, it's easy to see that Edsel arrived with too many models spanning too wide a price range. The mistake was corrected for '59, but by then it was too late.

The standard Fords faced the recession with a heavy facelift. Quad headlamps and a big-mouth bumper/grille gave an obvious familial relationship with this year's new T-Bird, while extra flash was provided by broader anodized-aluminum side trim, nine longitudinal roof grooves (to strengthen the weak '57 panels), and a blunted tail with four oval lamps and scalloped trunklid. Model offerings were unchanged save for higher prices. The fascinating Skyliner "retrac" still topped the bunch at $3163 basic, $513 more than the soft-top Sunliner and a whopping $728 above the fixed-roof Fairlane 500 Club Victoria. Only 14,713 were built, some 6000 fewer than in '57.

A happier development was Ford's first "big-block" V-8s in 332- and 352-cid sizes. Part of the new FE-series devised principally by Robert Stevenson, chief engineer at

The restyled '58 Ford sported a Thunderbird-style grille.

Fairlane 500 Skyliner production was down to 14,713 for 1958.

The Custom 300 two door was Ford's most popular '58 model.

Even the lowly Custom models used quad headlights for '58.

First of the "Squarebirds" was the new four-passenger 1958 Thunderbird. Prices started at $3631.

Ford Engine & Foundry since '57, they were derived from the Y-block and incorporated all its lessons. Bore centers were chosen for maximum enlargement to 425 cubic inches, an arbitrary figure so far above forseeable needs that long production seemed assured. (It would be.) The main improvements were bigger valves and bearings, the latter prompting a low-cost, precision-cast crankshaft. Combustion chambers were fully machined and located in the head (as opposed to the block), while overheating and valve warpage were minimized by having no two exhaust valves adjacent. Cylinder heads were smaller but intake manifolds larger than usual, which allowed manifold passages of about equal length for more even fuel distribution. A bonus was added engine rigidity and elimination of separate tappet chamber covers.

Besides the two Ford versions, the FE-series also appeared as this year's Edsel 361 and Mercury's new 383. As installed in the Thunderbird, the 352 was rated at an even 300 bhp with four-barrel carburetor and 10.2:1 compression.

Ford's other big mechanical news was Cruise-O-Matic, a new three-speed torque-converter automatic based on Ford-O-Matic. It offered so-called "dual-range" drive, with first-gear starts in position D1 and second-gear take-

offs in D2, plus a hill-holder that obviated the need for applying the brakes to keep the car from rolling backward when stopped on an incline. Like the FE-series V-8s, it would be around a long time.

In retrospect, T-Bird's transformation from two-seater to four-seater seems perfectly logical in view of its surprising success in a bad sales year—up over 50 percent from '57 and nearly 100 percent better than first-year '55. It also pioneered the personal-luxury concept that would be widely imitated in a few years. But back in '55, when the decision was made, few knew for sure whether it would "play in Peoria."

Product planner Thomas Case had recommended retaining a two-seater "to add some spiff to the ['58 program. It was not set up to be a profit program per se, although it turned out to be. . . ." But McNamara wanted the T-Bird to pay for itself, and Case got a "chewing out" when McNamara heard he was angling to keep the two-seater: "Tom, it's dead. I don't want anybody to do any more about it." Still, the Thunderbird might have died altogether without McNamara's support. Recalled stylist Bill Boyer: "He thought it was a good concept; he went in and fought for it [with the board of directors] and won." Of course, part of his pitch was that a four-seater would make *real* money—which it did.

Styling work began during 1955. Boyer stretched the proposed wheelbase from 108 to 113 inches, and development focused strictly on a low-slung hardtop coupe. A "formal" wide-quarter roofline was adopted to keep decklid height down for the ultra-low stance the sales department wanted. Setting off the blocky lower body—hence the "Squarebird" nickname later given this generation—were a gaping mesh-filled bumper/grille, quad headlamps nestled under "gullwing" hoods, prominent side sculpturing, and a broad deck terminating in two wide rectangles, each holding a pair of large circular taillamps. Surprisingly, a convertible wasn't approved until May 1957 and didn't get to dealers until June '58.

The new Bird's main innovation was unit construction,

Although T-Bird sales took off, only 2134 ragtops were built.

The 131-inch wheelbase Continental Mark III was marketed as a separate nameplate in 1958, but only 12,550 were built.

used by European producers since the Twenties and by Ford itself for the original Lincoln Zephyr (see *1936*). Inspired by aircraft practice and also known as the monocoque principle, it does away with the traditional separate frame and results in a tighter, lighter platform. As unit construction was also ordained for this year's Lincoln and Continental Mark III, Ford erected a new factory at Wixom, Michigan, to build all three, which made sense. Though low-volume luxury models, they generated

enough volume between them to keep one plant busy. This also made unit construction economically feasible, since their lower individual unit volume would have made separate frames far costlier than for a mass-market car like the standard Ford.

Despite the '58 T-Bird's fairly revolutionary nature, Ford Division allotted only $5 million for styling and body/chassis/engine engineering and $45 million for tooling. To economize on R&D, management farmed out body en-

The Continental convertible saw production of 3048 units.

The Lincoln Capri Landau sedan sold for $4951 in 1958.

This '58 Premiere was as big as a Lincoln would ever get.

Lincoln boasted 375 bhp, but also weighed 5000 pounds.

The 1958 Mercury Park Lane rode a 125-inch wheelbase, three inches more than lesser Mercs, and got a 430-cid V-8.

The Turnpike Cruiser returned for '58 as a Montclair.

Mercury built only 2864 two-door Turnpike Cruisers for '58.

The '58 Mercury Park Lane Phaeton sedan retailed for $3944.

Mercury built 5012 Montclair Phaeton hardtop sedans for '58.

Monterey was easily Mercury's best-selling line for '58.

Top of Mercury's 1958 wagon line was the $3775 Colony Park.

gineering to the Budd Company and the convertible to Wettlaufer Engineering. The latter arrived with a manually operated rear-hinged decklid that completely concealed the stowed top, which was lowered by a complex mechanism similar to the Skyliner's. However, the system was made fully automatic late in the '59 model run, via a single dashboard pushbutton.

T-Bird's '58 engineering was rapid-fire and often clever. Body engineer Bob Hennessy recalled that when the planned overall width was discovered to be insufficient for rear wheel movement, "we were about two-thirds into engineering with die models. [So] we literally split the drawing down the centerline [and] spread it apart." The interior package envisioned a car 10 inches lower than the standard Ford and was surprisingly roomy. But "with a five-inch ground-to-floorpan height, 2½ to three inches for a seat track and electric seat motor, plus four inches of actual seat height, the driver's fanny was only 12 inches off the ground. This left us with a high tunnel on the inside and, of course, the main integral frame sill section above the floor on the outside....The front seats were literally in a deep well." Boyer took advantage of it by creating the first tunnel control console. It's been *de rigueur* for personal + luxury cars ever since.

The 1958 Thunderbird was such a success that Ford had to put Wixom on heavy overtime to keep up with demand. "We were making money so fast we didn't know what to do with it," said engineer John Hollowell. "It came ... to somewhere around $1000 per car." Hardtop production totalled close to 36,000, while late introduction held the ragtop to just 2134 units. As author Tim Howley observed in *Collectible Automobile®* magazine, what Ford had created was "a latterday Continental," with the same kind of sporty elegance at less than half the price of a Mark II ($3631 for the hardtop, $3929 for the convertible). No wonder it did so well. Yet despite that, Ford Division finished the model year some 160,000 cars adrift of Chevrolet, which fielded an all-new (but one-year-only) design that cost almost as much to bring out as the Edsel.

Dearborn's other newcomers, the Continental Mark III and a completely redesigned Lincoln, proved almost as disappointing as Edsel. Here too, the heady atmosphere of 1955 had encouraged drastic changes. But like Edsel, the exigencies of Detroit's usual three-year lead time left these cars out in the cold of the withering '58 market.

Continental Division, established to wrest luxury leadership from Cadillac, even if it lost money, was now pressed to shore up faltering Lincoln Division with a higher-volume product. "Reith sent over a Mercury cost analyst," designer John Reinhart remembered. "You can't hold it against him: he was only doing his job. He had been ordered to make the '58 model profitable, and he succeeded—but at the cost of the original concept. [From our original] modern Duesenberg ... we ended up with something much less....It was a project that for a time broke Bill Ford's heart, and I guess you could say that in many ways it broke ours too."

It also marked the end of Continental Division, which

To spur sales, Merc reintroduced the bottom-line Medalist.

The Medalist two-door sedan was Merc's cheapest '58 at $2547.

The '58 Ford Ranchero: Chevy would field its version in '59.

was merged in January 1958 with Mercury, Edsel, and Lincoln to form the short-lived M-E-L Division that lasted through November 1959, after which Lincoln-Mercury Division was reinstated. The car itself was little more than a top-line Lincoln, with minor styling differences on the same new unit platform striding an enormous 131-inch wheelbase. Prices were dropped to the $6000 level in a search for sales, and the customary hardtop coupe was joined by a convertible, pillared sedan, and Landau four-door hardtop. It all worked as intended—over 12,500 were built—but it was mere "badge engineering" and hardly memorable.

Though the "jumbo Mark" handily outsold the Mark II and earned a tidy profit, Lincoln floundered as a whole. The division's 12-month production fell to 26,000 units, including Continental, while the standard line managed only a bit more than 17,000 for the model year. Both Lincoln and Continental had everything the planners thought they'd need back in '55: a six-inch longer wheelbase; Gigantus-Enormous styling (sharp tailfins, pointed front fenders, slant-eyed quad headlamps, huge grilles front and rear); and a 350-bhp 430 V-8 (bore and stoke: 4.30×3.70 inches), largest in the industry. Yet Cadillac, relatively unaffected by the economic malaise, turned out 125,000 of its facelifted '58s, and even Imperial was selling at Lincoln's rate.

At Mercury this grim year, things were, as they say, "the same, only more so." The Big M gamely hung onto eighth place, but volume tailed off by over 40 percent for the second year in a row. The Turnpike Cruiser, *sans* convertible, snuck quietly into the Montclair line, but Reith's "super Mercury" found new expression in the 125-inch-wheelbase Park Lane. It arrived mid-year in convertible, hardtop coupe, and hardtop sedan form, powered by the Lincoln 430 and priced from $3870 to over $4000. Montclair and Monterey shared a new 383-cid big-block (bore and stroke: 4.30×3.30 inches) with 312 or 330 bhp. Undermining the junior Edsels was the return of the lowline Medalist with a 235-bhp 312. A desperate effort to garner more buyers, it failed to impress once more, and sales were low. The wagon group was still there but did even worse—only 568 Voyager two-doors, for example.

Very simply, the bottom had dropped out of the medium market, evident in Mercury's maintaining industry production rank on scarely more than half its '57 volume. On the other hand, getting clubbed on the head gets attention, and it got Mercury's. The course was now clear: pare down the overlapping biggies and, above all, get going on a version of the new compact developing at Ford. Mercury would do both within two years.

1959

After the doldrums of 1958, this year almost seemed a relief to Ford Division—but not Edsel, Lincoln, or Mercury, the only makes in the entire industry to produce fewer '59s than '58s. Edsel, of course, was destined for oblivion. In fact, production ceased in November after just 3008 of the Ford-clone 1960 models.

In belated realization of its overly wide price spread, the Edsel lineup was pared to Ranger, Corsair, and a station wagon series, all sharing basic structure with this year's Fords but riding a two-inch-longer, 120-inch wheelbase.

The "horse collar" was toned down, flanked by horizontal mini-bars running outboard to the quad headlamps, while the rear deck/fender area was less sculptured and the previous gullwing taillamps gave way to conventional three-light clusters moved down into the back panel. Spear-like double-bar bodyside moldings enhanced the illusion of greater length while forming a contrast color area that could be painted to match the roof on two-tone models.

Edsel engine choices expanded from two to four, but three were smaller than '58 offerings, dictated by the move downmarket—and the public's recession-inspired economy consciousness. The 410 "Super Express" was dropped, an unchanged 361 V-8 (Edsel's only '59 engine requiring premium fuel) returned as a line-wide option, and Ford's 145-horsepower, 223-cubic-inch six was offered as a credit option for all but Corsairs. In between were the 200-bhp Ford 292 as standard for Ranger and wagons and the 225-bhp 332 for Corsair, optional on the rest. The complex "Teletouch Drive" pushbutton linkage had been troublesome, so conventional column control was substituted with automatic, standard on Corsairs.

Most '59 Edsels were cheaper than equivalent Mercurys, ranging from $2629 for the Ranger two-door sedan to $3072 for the posh Corsair convertible (the only soft-top in the line). But the public knew about the sudden drop-off in '58 sales and, believing the make was about to disappear, continued to stay away in droves. It was a classic vicious circle: Edsel wasn't selling because people thought it would be dropped, and it was more likely to be dropped because it wasn't selling. Thus, only some 45,000 of the '59 models were called for. Tellingly, over 28,000 were bottom-line Rangers while fewer than 9000 were Corsairs, suggesting that Dearborn marketers were off the mark in positioning Edsel, regardless of whether "the target moved."

Among this year's low-priced three, buyers had a clear styling choice: Chevrolet's radical new "bat-fin" design, Virgil Exner's "shark-fin" Plymouth, or Ford's conservative, squared-up look. Though Chevy emerged the winner in model year production, by slightly less than 12,000 units, it's clear the public preferred Ford, which outsold its perennial rival for the calendar year by about the same margin.

Mechanically, Ford's '59 standards were similar to the '58s, but all now rode the longer, 118-inch wheelbase. Engine offerings shrank from five to four with cancellation of the 265-bhp 332 V-8. Again, the 200-bhp 292 was standard for the Skyliner retractable, appearing for the last time. Exactly 12,915 of the '59s were built.

Big-Ford appearance alterations involved cylindrically shaped upper rear fenders, simpler but broader side trim, flat hood/front fender treatment, set-in "Flying V" back panel, and a simple rectangular grille filled with floating, star-like ornaments. Shared with Edsel were raised windshield headers, with the glass almost wrapped up into the roof. At mid-year, the Thunderbird's fashionable, wide-quarter squared roof was borrowed for a new line of hard-

Ford Motor Company offerings for 1959 (top left, clockwise): Edsel, Lincoln, Mercury, Ford, Thunderbird.

tops and sedans called Galaxie. (At the same time, the new name substituted for Fairlane 500 on Sunliner and Skyliner rear fenders, forecasting a shakeup in the 1960 line.) It proved a popular move, and would be used again to enhance the appeal of some smaller Fords in the Sixties.

Thunderbird was refined with minor trim changes, a new engine option, and a redesigned rear suspension. The last was dictated by a change in company plans. Ford had planned to offer air suspension, called "Ford Aire" on the '58 T-Bird, and had engineered complex coil-spring/trailing-arm rear geometry to accommodate it. The option was

Edsel built only 1343 Corsair convertibles for 1959.

The '59 Corsair four-door hardtop sold for $2885.

Production run for the Edsel Villager wagon was 7820.

The $2691 Edsel Ranger hardtop coupe found 5474 buyers.

Ford returned to big round taillights for 1959.

All '59 Fords could be ordered with a 300-bhp 352-cid V-8.

This prototype '59 Galaxie carries Fairlane 500 badging.

Ford built 12,915 Skyliners for '59, its last year.

also slated for the '58 standards, but proved so trouble-prone (only about 100 standard Fords were so equipped) that it was withdrawn before the new T-Bird went on sale. Thus, the '59 reverted to conventional rear leaf springs. More minor mechanical modifications included a new auxiliary coolant tank and radiator fan and a relocated windshield washer system. The new engine was Lincoln's big-block, 350-bhp 430-cid V-8, largest member of the

"MEL" family introduced the previous year. The 300-bhp 352 remained standard.

Externally, the '59 T-Bird was freshened with thin-horizontal-bar inserts on grille and taillight appliqués (the '58s had a honeycomb pattern), plus front fender ornaments, pointed chrome moldings on the lower-bodyside "bullets" (instead of the previous hash marks), relocated name script, and revised wheel covers. White replaced

The 1959 Thunderbird differed from the '58 only in detail, but production continued to zoom, reaching 67,456.

Continental became a Lincoln for '59, and a Mark IV, too.

The '59 Lincoln's front fender scallop extended into the door.

The mid-range Premiere hardtop sedan sold for $5594.

All 1959 Lincolns were powered by a 430-cid 350-bhp V-8.

black on instruments, and there were the usual trim/color shifts. Prices rose by about $50, to $3695 and $3979 for the hardtop and convertible, respectively.

Though the "Squarebird" was more luxury-liner car than performance car, it was quite fast. With the 352, it hit 60 mph from standstill in 11-12 seconds, while the big 430 reduced that to about nine seconds—and hiked fuel consumption to about 12 miles per gallon. Though smaller and lower than most all contemporaries save Chevy's Corvette, it was no handler, with lots of plowing and body roll in corners. Braking and steering also left something to be desired. But the car itself was very desired, witness model year production that moved up smartly to near 67,500 units, nearly double the '58 tally.

While competition exploits had never been a factor in T-Bird sales, the "Squarebird" carried Ford's colors this year in NASCAR events, though for some reason it was considered a separate make, not a Ford. At the inaugural Daytona 500, run on the then-new International Speedway in late February, Johnny Beauchamp's Bird was declared the winner in a three-way photo finish with Lee Petty's Oldsmobile and a Chevrolet. But the victory lasted just three days. After examining a photo of the finish, the judges decided that Petty should get the trophy instead. The followup Firecracker 250 on July 4 saw Fireball Roberts' Pontiac in Victory Lane, but six T-Birds were among the top nine finishers. For the season, the "Squarebird"

racked up six NASCAR wins to Chevrolet's 14, Plymouth's nine, and eight for the standard Fords. Dearborn had better weapons for 1960 and beyond, but privately entered "Squarebirds" still managed an occasional first in minor, usually short-track races over the next few years.

For Lincoln, 1959 and '60 were a pair of very grim years. The huge, ornately styled cars of 1958 had been generally unsuccessful, but their design and construction had to be amortized over at least two seasons: In other words, Lincoln was stuck with them.

Now officially a Lincoln, not a separate make, Continental returned with detail trim changes and six models designated Mark IV. The two newcomers were a $10,230 limousine and a $9200 formal sedan, Lincoln's attempt to return to the "professional car" business it had abandoned after the war. Actually, they were nothing more than conversion jobs that could be built in very low volume at something approaching a profit, riding the same wheelbase as other Marks and thus not genuine competitors for the Cadillac Seventy-five. Production was 49 limos and 78 formals. About 10,000 "standard" models were built, with the four-door hardtop dominating sales as usual.

Downmarket at least $1000 from the Mark IV were the similarly unchanged Lincoln Premiere and Capri, the former now bereft of its convertible. Prices were again competitive (the Capri four-door started at only $5090), but neither impressed the public and output was almost ludi-

199

Mercury built 1254 big Park Lane convertibles for 1959.

The Colony Park wagon saw production of 2496 units for '59.

The Mercury Montclair hardtop coupe listed for $3357 in 1959.

Commuter wagons were more popular; over 16,000 were built.

The Monterey four door was Mercury's best seller (45,570).

For $2768 one could own a '59 Monterey two-door sedan.

crously low: 7000 Capris, about 7500 Premieres. Underlining its sales crisis, Lincoln was outsold by Imperial, and would be again for 1960. A new smaller Lincoln was already taking shape under stylist Elwood Engel but was still two years off. All dealers could do in the interim was to keep treading water.

Mercury also issued slightly quieter styling for '59, albeit on a huge, new (and still exclusive) platform with longer wheelbases than ever: 126 inches for Monterey, Montclair and station wagons, 128 for the top-line Park Lane. The last, returning from '58 in the same three body styles, delivered for close to $5000 but was evidently not what the public wanted: only about 12,000 were built, including just 1254 convertibles. Monterey models stood pat, but the mid-range Montclair was down to just three with demise of its convertible and the ill-starred Turn-

pike Cruisers. The Medalist also disappeared—again—and station wagons withered to four.

Mercury's '59 styling was unmistakable: gigantic compound-curve windshields, blocky front ends, big missile-like upper-bodyside sculptures running aft from the A-posts, and sharply creased rear fenders ending in large pie-wedge taillamps above a dummy back panel "grille." Engines were about the same but had lower ratings. The great "horsepower race" was over, at least temporarily. Montereys carried a 312 V-8 with 210 bhp standard, 280 optional; Park Lane still had the Lincoln 430, newly downgraded 15 bhp to 345; Commuter wagons packed a 280-bhp 383, and a 322-bhp version was standard for other models.

This year saw the arrival of none other than James Nance, fresh from failure at Studebaker-Packard, to head up the newly formed Mercury-Edsel-Lincoln Division. Nance had had many good ideas at S-P, but had tried to do too much too soon and without enough capital. Now he had plenty of capital but a negative mandate: consolidate, don't expand. "It was a difficult position," he said, "because we had to merge three formerly separate divisions into one, and inevitably that meant laying off a lot of people." No sooner had this been accomplished than Nance left to run a bank. ("One thing I learned from the auto industry: you can't do anything without money!") With Edsel's demise in November, Dearborn's senior division reverted to being just plain old Lincoln-Mercury. It's been that way ever since.

1960

Edsel expired early this model year, production ceasing in late 1959, blamed partly on the steel strike that fall. Ironically, some of its styling hallmarks would be seen on far more successful cars in the decade ahead. For example, the vertical grille and the split motif that replaced it for 1960 were both used by Pontiac, while Chrysler's chiseled, 1965-66 lower body owed much to this year's Ford/Edsel design (possibly because the same man styled both). But the hard fact was that Dearborn had failed in its attempt to conquer fortress GM by expanding to five separate divisions.

The last Edsel retained a 120-inch wheelbase but was even more Ford-like than the '59, sharing basic body/chassis design, most outer sheetmetal, even instrument panels. Engines, still borrowed from Ford, comprised standard 185-horsepower 292 V-8, optional 300-bhp 352, and credit-option 223-cubic-inch six. The lineup thinned again, to five Rangers and six- and nine-passenger Villager wagons. Prices were held at around $3000. Production (at Ford Division's Louisville, Kentucky plant) stopped barely a month after the '60s were announced, resulting in some real rarities that have since garnered collector interest. For example, there were only 295 Ranger hardtops, 135 hardtop sedans, and just 76 convertibles. At 59 units, this year's nine-seat Villager became the rarest Edsel of all.

According to John Brooks in *The Fate of the Edsel and Other Business Adventures*, Ford spent $350 million on the E-car project, though $250 million is the sum traditionally bandied about. George Dammann, in *Fifty Years of Lincoln-Mercury*, says that the tooling bill alone came to $24,000 per car, but that multiplies to over $2.5 billion, which seems excessive.

Still, Edsel was a costly marketing mistake—or was it? If nothing else, the cars and the experiment that spawned them taught Ford an important lesson: not even number-two could compete with General Motors on the same broad, diverse scale. Ford learned that lesson and would never again stray from its two-division structure, thus avoiding the "corporate clone" sales hazard that plagues GM a quarter-century later. To have learned that lesson in 1960 was probably worth $350 million. And as Nevins/Hill observed: "That the [firm] took the adventure in stride is proof of its sound financial condition." Even so, as

Second rarest of all Edsels, the 1960 Ranger convertible saw production of only 76 units. It sold for $3000.

For its final season, Edsel built 275 station wagons.

The 1960 Ranger four-door sedan carried a sticker of $2697.

Only 295 Edsel Ranger hardtop coupes were built for '60.

Another rare Edsel: the Ranger hardtop sedan, 135 built.

Lee Iacocca wrote in his autobiography: "Looking around Dearborn for someone to admit responsibility for the Edsel project today is like old Diogenes with his lantern, searching for an honest man."

Edsel had another lesson, for Ford and every other automaker, summed up nicely by Art Railton of *Popular Mechanics*: "Motivation research doesn't tell what's to come, only what has been." Yet the end brought a solid consolation, something long overlooked by most historians. Gearing up for Edsel had boosted Dearborn's total production capacity; now, that extra volume was freed to the benefit of Ford's important new 1960 compact, which largely explains Edsel's abrupt demise. A good thing, too, as the Falcon was a big hit right off the bat, helping to ease the embarrassment of the Edsel fiasco. Coming hard on the heels of the successful 1958-59 "Squarebird," Falcon proved that Dearborn hadn't lost its marketing touch.

Mention of Lido Anthony Iacocca reminds us that he took over as Ford Division general manager this year. A born car salesman with a keen sense of what turned on the public, he would be the driving force behind the Mustang, Ford's most successful car of the Sixties, and spearheaded the memorable Total Performance campaign that injected excitement into most every Dearborn car of this decade. All this helped propel him into the president's chair by 1970 but, as most everyone knows by now, he was booted out after eight years by the temperamental "Henry the Deuce" and rode off to rescue Chrysler Corporation,

an achievement not Iacocca's alone but certainly equal, if not superior, to anything he did for Ford.

Falcon was born in 1957 under the code name "XK Thunderbird," one of several small-car projects then in progress throughout the worldwide Ford organization (another was a front-drive model that would culminate in 1962 with the stillborn Cardinal, later transplanted to Germany). Completed in a remarkably short 19 months, it arrived with Chevrolet's Corvair and Chrysler's Valiant as a response to the growing popularity of small imports like the Volkswagen Beetle and to the economy-car craze spawned by the '58 recession. It was deadly conventional next to Corvair: live-axle rear suspension and a front-mounted, water-cooled straight six, versus all-independent suspension and air-cooled flat-six at the back. About

The Galaxie Victoria hardtop sedan sold for $2675 in 1960.

Ford's modern day Model T: the successful 1960 Falcon.

Falcon sales proved sensational, almost 436,000 '60 models.

Falcon had a 109.5-inch wheelbase and a 90-horse six.

For 1960, the Ranchero moved from full-size to compact.

the only things they had in common were four wheels, drum brakes, and unit construction. But while Corvair's unusual specifications appealed mainly to car buffs, Falcon's anvil simplicity proved far more saleable, and the little Ford quickly ran away with the compact market.

Riding a 109.5-inch wheelbase, Falcon bowed as a two- and four-door sedan, supplemented by wagon versions later in the year. (The Ranchero car/pickup also moved to this platform in a search for sales, where the full-size-

based 1957-59 models had been something of a disappointment.) Styling was simple, almost severe, with a large concave grille and dual headlamps, attractive bodyside creases, rounded corners and fenders, and an unadorned rear with big round taillamps. At 181.2 inches overall, it was more than two feet shorter than this year's full-size Fords yet surprisingly roomy inside. Power was supplied by a 144-cid (3.50 × 2.50) pushrod six developing 90 bhp, hooked to three-speed manual or two-speed auto-

The '60 Ford Starliner proved popular, with 68,461 built.

The Country Squire was Ford's costliest model at $2967.

Ragtops still sold well in 1960: Ford built 44,762 Sunliners.

Ford built 104,784 mid-line Fairlane 500 four doors for '60.

The workaday two-door Ranch Wagon sold for $2586 in 1960.

Ford built 92,843 T-Birds for '60, its best showing yet.

matic transmissions with column shift. Interiors were plain (some said stark), but it was all part of the plan.

In a sense, the Falcon was a latterday Model A: simple and reliable, easy to buy and cheap to own. Reported fuel economy was upwards of 27 mpg, and prices ranged from just $1912 for the two-door sedan to $2287 for the four-door wagon (the Falcon Ranchero listed for a low $1875). There weren't many options available (though there would soon be), but that was part of the plan too. And the plan worked beautifully. Corvair scored a quarter-million sales for the model year, which wasn't bad, but Falcon saw nearly 436,000, which was stupendous.

Thunderbird was left pretty much alone in this final year for the original four-seat design. New to the options list was a sliding metal sunroof, a first among postwar American cars. Styling changes were confined to hash marks on rear fenders, cleaner side trim, a large horizontal grille bar with three vertical dividers and square mesh behind, triple-taillight clusters, standard outside rear-view mirror, polarized day/night inside mirror, revised interiors with built-in armrests, and new color combinations. Prices were up to $3755 for the hardtop, $3967 for the sunroof hardtop, and $4222 for the convertible. Nevertheless, popularity reached a new high with model year production of nearly 93,000 units, a record that wouldn't be broken until 1964. Included were about 2500 special high-trim models with gold-colored vinyl top. Again this year, most T-Birds carried the standard 300-bhp 352 V-8; only about 3900 were equipped with the big-block Lincoln engine. Both units were unchanged.

Now that compacts were here, auto writers coined a new term for the largest U.S. cars like the Ford Galaxie: full-size. And for 1960, the big Fords grew even larger, gaining a much longer, lower, wider bodyshell. Wheelbase grew an inch, to 119 inches, where it would remain for the rest of the decade, but overall length was up 5.7 inches and width swelled by five inches to a massive 81.5 overall. The new styling seemed a hastily contrived reply to the bat-wing '59 Chevrolet, but lead times made any similarity quite coincidental.

And the Fords were prettier. Headlamps moved down into a wide U-shape grille announcing a lower, broader hoodline. The old dogleg A-pillars gave way to straight posts and a taller windshield. Bodysides gained discreet contouring below a shallow, full-length beltline overhang swept back into modest horizontal fins and a flat rear deck. Altogether, Ford was the best-looking of this year's Big Three standards.

Big-Ford model offerings didn't change much, but series names were reordered to read (from the bottom) Custom 300, Fairlane, Fairlane 500, and Galaxie; as before, the separate Station Wagon series paralleled these in trim and equipment. An attractive newcomer to the Galaxie line was an airy hardtop coupe called Starliner (an old Studebaker name), with gently curved roofline that almost qualified as a fastback. Of course, there was more to it than looks: the sloped top was aerodynamically superior to the Galaxie's boxy, T-Bird-style roof on the NAS-

The Lincoln Continental Mark V coupe cost $6598 in 1960.

Lincoln built only 1703 Mark V hardtop coupes for 1960.

The '60 Lincoln Landau sedan came in at $5441.

Unfortunately, only 4397 went out dealer's doors that year.

CAR supertracks, and winning races seemed the Starliner's main mission. But with more than 68,000 sales, it was one of this year's more popular big Fords. It wouldn't hang around long—only two years—but as one enthusiast observed, it was "the kind of car you never forget."

Engine choices still involved the familiar 292 and 352 V-8s. After a few dormant years following the AMA's 1957 "anti-racing" edict, the Big Three were beginning to resume their race-track skirmishing, and Ford's maximum 300 bhp wasn't enough. Accordingly, the division released its first performance engine in three years. Dubbed "Interceptor 360," it was a tuned 352 initially restricted to three-speed manual transmission, and pumped out the expected 360 bhp with single four-barrel carburetor and 10.6:1 compression. *Motor Life* magazine got hold of an Interceptor-equipped Starliner prototype in the summer of '59 and was startled to find that the 4141-pound car would do 0-60 mph in 7.1 seconds and an honest 150 mph. A "new bomb," said the editors. (By contrast, *Motor Trend*'s 300-bhp/automatic Starliner needed 11.7-seconds 0-60.) Perhaps the best thing about the Interceptor was its price: just $150 extra. The Total Performance era had begun.

Lincoln, struggling to maintain volume with its definitely dated, three-year-old design, saw only 13,734 units for the model year, the lowest since 1948 and far down from halcyon 1956. Retitled Mark V, this year's Continen-

tal accounted for almost as many sales as the standard Lincoln (*nee* Capri) and Premiere combined, thus fulfilling its assignment of stemming losses as much as possible. Model lineups were unchanged. Again, only a few "professional" Continentals were built: 34 limousines, 136 formal sedans.

All 1960 Lincolns picked up revised grille inserts and front bumper, the massive guards moving inboard of the canted headlights. Non-Marks gained new tail/backup lights set into the rear "grille" instead of the fender edges, reshaped rear roof and backlight, and full-length bodyside moldings to heighten the impression of length. Standard equipment now included dual-range Turbo Drive automatic, self-adjusting power brakes, power steering, heater/defroster, whitewalls, undercoating, clock, windshield washers, radio, remote-control driver's door mirror, padded instrument panel and sunvisors, backup lamps, parking brake warning light, and full wheel covers. Premieres and Mark Vs also came with standard power seats and windows and a rear compartment reading light.

Mercury cleaned up its '59 big cars and entered the compact market with the pretty little Comet. The latter, planned as an Edsel, was essentially Ford's new Falcon with squared-up sedan rooflines and different sheetmetal at each end, including a longer rear deck with shapely canted fins. It was exactly right for compact-happy 1960, and it scored close to 120,000 despite a late, mid-model-

Lincoln-Mercury dealers got their first compact as a '60½ model.

Comet sedans rode a 114-inch wheelbase, 4.5 inches longer than Falcon.

Comet station wagons rode Falcon's 109.5-inch wheelbase.

Mercury simplified both its lineup and its styling for 1960.

The '60 Mercury Park Lane Cruiser retailed for $3794.

Over 22,000 Mercury station wagons were sold for 1960.

year start. It wasn't as popular as Falcon, but then Comet was an upgraded compact, with better trim and a 4.5-inch-longer wheelbase. In fact, it was more of an "intermediate" by Detroit's contemporary definition, and would remain so for most of its life. When Ford brought out its successful mid-size Fairlane for '62, Mercury's counterpart Meteor was a slow seller partly because of showroom competition from the cheaper Comet.

Despite its more deluxe makeup, the average 1960 Comet only cost about $100 more than corresponding Falcons. Models were the same: sedans and wagons with two or four doors. The sedans took the vast majority of sales, over 92,000 for the model year. Naturally, Comet was heavier than Falcon and thus somewhat slower with the same 90-bhp six. But that didn't matter much. Gas mileage was the thing in 1960 and Comet performed well, returning 20 mpg for most drivers.

The big Mercurys did an abrupt about-face. Analyzing

the changing public taste of 1957, management decreed much more conservative styling for 1960. Then, a little closer to deadline, they yanked the long wheelbase, putting Park Lane on the standard 126-inch chassis. They also rationalized body choices in line with a new price structure. Thus, all Park Lanes were pillarless, Montclair had pillarless sedans and hardtops plus a pillared sedan, and the bottom-end Monterey added convertible and a price-leader ($2700) two-door sedan. Wagons contracted to just Commuter and Colony Park, both four-doors. Merc wagons had never been strong sellers, but a small market remained and more than 22,000 were retailed.

"Big M" styling changes were both dramatic and welcome. The '59's sharp creases were shaved off, bodysides ironed smooth, rear sheetmetal reshaped and simplified, and the grille remade with closely spaced concave vertical bars *a la* Comet and widely spaced horizontal quad headlamps. Fewer engines with lower compression, two-barrel carburetors, and less horsepower answered buyers' economy concerns. Monterey and Commuter still ran a 312 V-8, but output dropped by 5 bhp to 205, while the 280-bhp 383 returned as an option. Standard on others was the Lincoln 430, down a whopping 35 bhp to 310. A more positive engineering feature was new printed electrical circuits for instruments, one of the first examples of this technology.

The result of all this was a strong upsurge in demand and a nice, solid 360,000-car year. Mercury rose from ninth to eighth and passed a faltering Buick, which had failed to react as rapidly to the new demand for efficiency and clean styling. Of course, Edsel's demise helped by leaving Mercury a slightly wider market.

1961

Ford's sporty 1961 Starliner hardtop sold for $2599.

Starliner's popularity was down for '61; 29,669 were built.

Headlining this year's Ford news was the third-generation Thunderbird and a trimmer, restyled big car. The division offered more horsepower up and down the line, from a larger Falcon six to a brawny new 390 V-8. These and a raft of mechanical and cosmetic refinements helped Ford slip past Chevrolet in model year production by over 20,000 cars. The grand total was close to 1,339,000.

The new 390 V-8 was essentially an enlarged 352, created by stretching bore 0.05-inch (to 4.05 inches) and lengthening stroke 0.28-inch (to 3.78). Dubbed "Thunderbird Special," it produced the same 300 horsepower as the previous 352, but packed more torque (427 foot-pounds versus 381 ft/lbs, both at a lazy 2800 rpm). In this form, the 390 was the standard—and only—powerplant for the new Thunderbird and the largest big-Ford option. All Ford V-8s now bore the Thunderbird name regardless of whether they were available in the T-Bird. This applied to the 352, still around as a regular-fuel 220-bhp option, and the 292, now at 175 bhp.

Two other 390s were also available: a police-only 330-bhp Interceptor engine and a "Thunderbird 390 Super" conservatively rated at 375 bhp. At mid-year, the single four-barrel engine initially offered was supplemented by one with triple two-barrel carbs and higher compression, good for a mighty 401 bhp.

In *Fearsome Fords*, author Phil Hall notes that the 390s differed internally from the smaller FE-series engines: stronger castings, thicker main-bearing webs, enlarged oil passages, larger intake manifolds. However, they retained the cast-iron exhaust headers of the 352 Interceptor and its larger dual exhaust outlets. The 375-bhp unit could be ordered in any full-size '61 Ford except wagons and was strictly for performance: power steering, power brakes, and automatic weren't available. With all this,

Best seller among the full-size Fords: Galaxie four-door sedan.

Ford built 44,614 Sunliner convertibles for the '61 model run.

At $3013, Country Squire was Ford's costliest full-size car.

207

With 87,933 built, '61 Falcon four-door led in wagon sales.

Ford's most popular '61: Falcon four door (159,761 built).

Thunderbird was restyled for 1961; prices started at $4172.

Official pace car for the '61 Indy 500 was the Thunderbird.

Ford was firmly in the big-brawn league with Pontiac's 389 V-8 and the new Chevy 409.

None of this mattered much to Thunderbird fanciers, who were too busy drooling over this year's swoopier interpretation of the personal-luxury theme so successfully established by the 1958-60 design. "Unique in All the World," said the ads, and it was.

Thunderbird had been following a three-year design cycle, so a new '61 was no real surprise. Two clay mockups were in contention: one by long-standing Bird designer Bill Boyer, the other by Elwood Engel, both working under vice-president for styling, George Walker. Engel's crisp, angular proposal was eliminated when Robert McNamara, then Ford Division general manager, decided it should be the basis for the new "compact" Lincoln Continental, so Boyer's work was again the starting point for a new-generation Thunderbird.

Boyer remembered his model as "very rocket-like in concept—very much aircraft-oriented, with big round 'flowerpot' taillights. It had what I called a 'fleet-submarine bow.' We wanted to keep the thing very youthful, and of course that meant aircraft and missile-like shapes—a model as aerodynamically aesthetic as possible. In contrast, Elwood's was a very formal job, [thus] perfectly suited to Lincoln." But they had much in common: "Both featured very highly integrated bumper/grille combinations," said Boyer. "There was much similarity in the windshield and side glass, a lot of interchangeability." The T-Bird tapered cleanly in plan view and bore only a suggestion of tailfin, while the "Squarebird" roofline was retained but a bit more rounded. The front end was a bit chromey, and remained so through 1962-63 grille insert revisions.

Interior design proceeded under 40-year Ford veteran Art Querfeld: "I wanted to emphasize and delineate the positions of the driver and front seat passenger, [so] I conceived of two individual compartments separated by a prominent console [that] swept forward to the dash [and] curved left and right, meeting the doors and continuing around on the door panels." This was finished in brushed aluminum with horizontal lines. Stuart Fry of the packaging team created a unique "Swing-Away" steering wheel that moved laterally 10 inches to the right (with the transmission in Park) to assist entry/exit. Pop-up roof panels were considered but rejected due to complexity and high cost.

Dimensionally, the third-generation Bird was not greatly changed from 1958-60. The customary hardtop and convertible retained their 113-inch wheelbase and 52.5-inch height but were half an inch shorter and about an inch narrower. Body construction followed the "dual unitized" principle, with separate front and rear sections welded together at the cowl. The cowl structure itself was shared with the new Continental, which held down tooling and production costs and afforded greater rigidity than in previous models.

Most of the new Bird's engineering work involved a completely redesigned chassis featuring "controlled wheel recession," lots of rubber bushings to allow fore/aft as well as up/down movement. Then familiar Mercedes-Benz practice, it was another T-Bird "first" in U.S. production. Front suspension employed coil springs located above the upper wishbones. The lower control arm was now a single bar instead of a wishbone, with a strut running from its outer end to a body-mounted bushing. At the

Lincoln's all-new, smaller Continental bowed for '61. Its clean and elegant design makes it a collectible car today.

Only 2857 Continental four-door convertibles were built for '61.

The Continental sedan sold for $6067, a stiff tariff in 1961.

rear, forward spring mounts were also carried in rubber, with arms from the leaf shackles to each bushing permitting fore/aft movement. Stability was improved by increasing track an inch at the front and three inches in back. A quicker steering ratio reduced turns lock-to-lock to 3.5 and allowed use of a smallish, 16-inch-diameter wheel. The power-assisted, self-adjusting brakes had 14 percent more lining area than in 1960.

This thoroughly overhauled chassis gave the '61 Thunderbird much better handling than its predecessor. It took high-speed turns with little body lean, plowing heavily only in tight corners. The quicker steering was more responsive, the enlarged brakes had better stopping power, and "controlled wheel recession" made for the smoothest T-Bird ride yet. It was certainly the most comfortable American car on a wheelbase under 115 inches—and the best-engineered Thunderbird to date. Ford sold 73,051 of them, of which 10,516 were convertibles.

A heavy facelift left this year's full-size Fords slightly lighter and shorter than the '60s. Changes included a concave grille, abbreviated rear deck, and large circular taillamps topped by subtle blade fins. The model line stayed basically the same. All closed Galaxies save Starliner continued with squared-off wide-quarter rooflines *a la* Thunderbird, which buyers definitely preferred. Starliner declined to under 30,000 units for the model year

and wouldn't return; only the Galaxie two-door sedan was less popular among non-wagons.

Ford began stressing reduced maintenance this year by extending big-car lubrication intervals to a full 30,000 miles, made possible by a special new molybdenum-disulphide lubricant for key points, now protected by polyurethane caps or liners. Normal grease fittings were eliminated, replaced by threaded plugs that could be removed if necessary. Oil-change intervals also lengthened, to 6000 miles. Other mechanical changes comprised thinner main leaves for the semi-elliptic rear leaf springs, recalibrated shock absorbers, and standard self-adjusting brakes. Less welcome was a 50-percent reduction in steering effort with optional power assist.

Falcon entered its second year with the same models, a convex grille, and a bit more chrome. Responding to Chevrolet's mid-1960 Corvair Monza was the "1961½" Futura, a more uptown version of the standard two-door, boasting bucket seats separated by a mini-console, plusher carpeting, higher-grade vinyl trim, and special emblems. Floorshift manual transmission was optional. The Futura pointed the way to success in the compact class, notching close to 45,000 sales despite its abbreviated selling season. Newly available for all '61 Falcons was a stroked, 170-cid version of the pushrod six with 101 horsepower. It would linger through the early Seventies and Falcon's spiritual successor, the Maverick.

For those who planned and sold Lincolns, 1961 must have seemed like a banquet after a long fast. For the first time in anyone's memory—possibly since the original Zephyr—Lincoln had come up with a car so advanced that it left the rest of the industry gaping. And like the Zephyr, it rallied the marque after too many years of decline. Sold only as a four-door in hardtop or convertible form, the magnificent new Lincoln Continental saw 25,164 sales, Lincoln's best model year tally since 1957. Even better, at least 10,000 represented "conquest" sales from Cadillac.

For the first time since the war, the "Standard of the World" had what looked like a serious rival.

Indicative of its design excellence, the '61 Continental received the Industrial Designers Institute Bronze Award, one of the few cars so honored. The citation recognized six Ford stylists: Gene Bordinat, Don DeLaRossa, Elwood Engel, Gayle Halderman, John Najjar, and Bob Thomas. Thus, the car was evidently a committee project, but this particular group was laden with talent and couldn't have worked better together.

Heart of the '61's crisp new shape was the cowl-forward

Mercury moved back to the Ford body shell for 1961, but its 120-inch wheelbase measured one inch longer.

Top-of-the-line Monterey hardtop sedan sold for $2943 in '61.

Mercury built 7887 Colony Park wagons for the '61 model run.

Meteor joined the '61 Mercury lineup; here an 800 two door.

Bargain-basement full-size Merc: Meteor 600 sedan ($2589).

structure that housed its mechanical heart—electrics, air conditioning, powerplant—and was inherently the most expensive to create. As mentioned, this was shared with the new Thunderbird, a handy way of halving development and tooling costs for two relatively low-volume cars. Component-sharing wasn't new, of course, but it was a radical step here, since these cars were so different in size and style, even to the number of doors. It limited the Lincoln's size in only one critical dimension, overall width at the front door post—but that only dovetailed with the objective of a relatively compact luxury car, a complete reversal of past Lincoln practice.

"We had just come out of the flamboyant age," said Bob Thomas. "We wanted the car to be a statement of elegant simplicity . . . like a girl in a simple black dress with her jewelry no more complicated than a diamond necklace." But the task of making it appear substantial and stable within the smallest practical dimensions was a challenge that required extremely close attention to detail. "By creating the top edge of the body side and defining it with thick chrome trim," added John Najjar, "the appearance of stability and width was achieved. An additional benefit of this clearly defined longitudinal edge appeared from the driver's seat: the fenderline was visible from front to back. [The "wide shoulders" also helped make the greenhouse look "nestled," adding further to the impression of stability.] By introducing curved side glass, we were able to achieve what was probably the greatest angle of tumblehome [inward curvature] on a car of this type."

The new convertible sedan, a style not seen in U.S. production since the 1951 Frazer line, was adopted to one-up Cadillac with what was seen as a more saleable soft-top. No fewer than 11 mechanical and hydraulic relays were needed to open its rear-hinged deck, unlatch its top, and lower it into the trunk. But because the top did fold flush, the stylists were able to bring the flat rear deckline right to the passenger compartment, much as Dutch Darrin had done with his memorable '54 Kaiser-Darrin. The lack of B-pillars above the belt prompted the use of throwback center-opening doors, with the rear ones hinged at the back.

Aside from its classy styling, the 1961 Lincoln was renowned for its high-quality workmanship, largely promulgated by Harold C. MacDonald, chief engineer of the Car and Truck Group. Shunning rampant innovation, he concentrated on proven techniques: the most rigid unit body/chassis yet produced, the best sound insulation money could buy, extremely close machining tolerances, an unprecedented number of long-life components, sealed electrical system, extra rust and corrosion protection. These cars also received the most thorough testing yet seen in Detroit. For example, each engine was run on a dynamometer at 3500 rpm (equal to 98 mph) for three hours, then torn down, analyzed, and reassembled. Every transmission was tested for 30 minutes before installation, and each finished car took a 12-mile road test, during which it had to pass 200 individual checks. Black light was used to visualize a fluorescent dye in lubricants to

Mercury Comet prices started at $2000 for this '61 two door.

The Comet wagon needed the new 170-cid, 101-bhp engine option.

Mercury built 85,332 Comet four-door sedans for '61.

Falcon-based Econoline van joined Ford's '61 truck lineup.

Restyled '61 Ford pickups looked lower, wider, and longer.

check for leaks. Backing it all up, Lincoln offered an unprecedented two-year/24,000-mile warranty.

Public response was immediate and satisfying. Though the new Continentals didn't appear until quite late in 1960, sales exceeded 25,000 units, putting Lincoln ahead of Imperial for keeps. Note that this was accomplished with just two models to the Chrysler make's six. The hardtop predictably accounted for the bulk of production; convertible output was just 2857. Against Cadillac, Lincoln had essentially one model to counter 12, hardly a toe-to-toe match, but the Continental was so good that it outsold all but one of the Caddys and stole at least 10,000 sales from the GM division.

Mercury spread its big cars downward to cover some of the price territory formerly claimed by Edsel. They even rode the same 120-inch wheelbase as the last Edsel and were just as Ford-like, cost considerations dictating that Mercury now lose its unique body/chassis platform and share the junior make's. The big Park Lane and Montclair were dropped along with the 430 V-8 (and the Cruiser name from hardtops). Monterey resumed its position as top of the line and a new Meteor series was slotted in below, comprising a brace of basic "600" sedans (starting at just $2535) and more luxurious "800" sedans and hardtops ($2800-$2900).

Aside from a similar concave grille, big-Merc styling was even cleaner than '60, with gently curved bodysides, Ford rooflines, longer-than-Ford rear deck, triple-element taillamps, and much less brightwork. Naturally, the engine lineup followed Ford's: standard 175-bhp 292 V-8, optional 220-bhp 352 and new 300-bhp 390 V-8s. Commuter wagon and Meteor buyers could order the 135-bhp six as a reduced-cost option. In all, this more attractive mix proved successful: Meteor and Monterey sold over 50,000 each, while the Commuter and Colony Park wagons added over 15,000 between them.

Mercury's compact Comet again proved extremely popular, notching close to 100,000 units for the model year. The main styling change was a busier grille, while the Falcon's new 170-cid six delivered more performance for a few dollars extra. Mid-model year brought a Comet cousin to the Falcon Futura, the good-looking S-22 sport coupe. The 1960 Corvair Monza had proven that bucket seats, center console, and deluxe interiors were sure-fire sales boosters. What's more, they were simple and inexpensive to add to a largely unchanged design. The S-22 offered all these features plus padded-vinyl dash, deluxe steering wheel, and the 170 engine at an attractive $2284, about $300 more than the ordinary two-door. It found 14,004 buyers.

With its little-changed Comets and smaller but more practical big cars, Mercury had a reasonably good year. Sales ran about 10 percent ahead of 1960, and production exceeded 300,000 units for the second 12 months in a row. It was quite an accomplishment in an overall market that had leveled off. Mercury returned to sixth for the first time since 1953 while outproducing both Plymouth and rival Buick.

1962

Dearborn's stable became even more specialized with arrival of the intermediate Ford Fairlane/Mercury Meteor, and the first of its big performance cars, the Ford Galaxie 500XL and Mercury Monterey S-55. The year also brought an important new small-block V-8 and a near-revival of the two-seat Thunderbird. In model year car production, Chevrolet outpaced Ford by 500,000 units, partly on the strength of its new conventional compact, the Chevy II. Still, Ford's total was better than 150,000 units higher than the 1961 tally, nearly 1.5 million.

Ford began the industry's swing to intermediates with an all-new Fairlane sized between Falcon and its standard cars. A kind of grown-up compact, it was six inches longer than Falcon in wheelbase (115.5 inches), 16.5 inches longer overall, and 500 pounds heavier. However, it employed the same sort of unit construction, conventional engineering, and conservative styling, even the Falcon's optional 170-cubic-inch six as its standard engine. Models were initially restricted to two- and four-door sedans in standard and ritzier 500 trim.

Coincidentally, Plymouth and Dodge fielded smaller full-size cars of similar dimensions. Whether because of their size or oddball styling, they didn't sell well, and Chrysler hurriedly revived the big Dodge at mid-season. Fairlane had no such difficulty, however, selling more than 297,000 for the model year. Even better, most of it represented additional business that didn't come at the expense of other Fords. Some auto writers observed that the Fairlane marked the return of a size not seen in a U.S. car since 1955. Its success wasn't lost on GM, which fielded '55-size cars of its own just two years later.

Fairlane was well along in 1960 when Ford product planners determined that it would need an engine larger than the Falcon six as an extra-cost option. Unfortunately, none of the firm's existing powerplants would fit the in-between package. The big Ford's 223-cid six was getting old, while the smallest FE-series V-8, the 292, was too thirsty. Accordingly, engineering director Harold C. McDonald convinced management to authorize $250 million for developing a new "small-block" V-8 of 220-230 cubic inches. The project was handed over to a team headed by George F. Stirrat, who joined Ford in 1949 and had worked his way through the ranks at the company's Engine & Foundry operation.

Stirrat's major objectives were 20 inches maximum block width and an installed weight of 450 pounds. He went to new extremes for the compact block, selecting a 3.50-inch bore and a short, 2.87-inch stroke, plus short connecting rods and low-height pistons. The block extended only as far as the crankshaft centerline, which

Introduced as one of "The Lively Ones," Ford's 1962½ Galaxie 500 XL came with bucket seats and V-8s of 170-401 bhp.

Ford wanted this "Starlift" roof for racing; NASCAR said no.

Mercedes currently uses the "Starlift" concept on its 560 SL.

Ford built 174,195 Galaxie four-door sedans for 1962.

The '62 Country Squire nine-seater wagon retailed for $3088.

The 1962 bucket-seat Falcon Futura coupe returned from mid-1961.

The '62½ Futura featured a T-Bird style roof; 17,011 were built.

213

Ford's '62 Fairlane started the stampede to "intermediates."

The Fairlane 500 four-door sedan saw 129,258 units built.

T-Bird Sports Roadster was always rare; 1427 were sold in '62.

didn't leave enough crankcase room for full counter-weighting, so 30 percent of the engine's total unbalanced forces had to be handled by external masses. Bore-center spacing was 4.38 inches, which allowed considerable freedom for later enlargement beyond the initial 221 cid. On 8.5:1 compression, the new engine delivered 145 horsepower at 4400 rpm.

The small-block's valvegear design was new to Ford but familiar Pontiac/Chevrolet practice. Rocker arms were mounted on ball-studs that eliminated the need for rocker shafts, while valves were conventionally sized relative to bore, with head diameters of 1.59 inches for the intakes and 1.39 inches for the exhausts. Timing was fairly conservative. The weight target was met with thin-wall, high-precision casting techniques developed by Harold C. Grant, a leader in nodular-iron castings and the shell-molding process using resin-filled cores. This dealt a knockout blow to the aluminum-block engines then built

in America. Buick's 215-cid V-8 and American Motors' six were lighter but cost more to build, as did Chrysler's heavier, 225-cid six. Ford's cast-iron small-block sent these and other rivals scurrying to the foundries to copy its construction.

A step down the ladder, the compact Falcon carried on with an "electric shaver" grille, Deluxe-trim editions of all body styles, and a new Squire wagon with the same sort of imitation-wood side panelling found on the big Country Squire. The Falcon name also appeared for the first time on two passenger versions of the Econoline forward-control van.

The big Fords, still on their 1960 platform, were thoroughly restyled again, gaining more rounded sheetmetal and a bulkier look. The lineup contracted to make room for the new Fairlane. Galaxie was now the base series, a new Galaxie 500 line was added above with a full range of body styles, and the complementary wagon line returned minus the two-door. Engine availability at the start of the model year was unchanged: standard 223-cid six, now at 138 bhp; optional 170-bhp 292 V-8, 220-bhp 352, and 390s with 300, 340, and 375 bhp.

A marketing technique favored by division chief Lee Iacocca was the "half" model year, special trim and/or mechanical options to give familiar models added zest for the spring selling season, traditionally the year's busiest. Iacocca continued the practice this April with three "1962½" offerings marketed as "The Lively Ones" and keyed to the growing buyer interest in bucket seats, console, floorshift, and other youthful features popularized by Chevy's Corvair Monza. The trio comprised a revised Falcon Futura two-door with squared-off T-Bird-type roof; a Fairlane 500 Sports Coupe, the pillared two-door with buckets and special trim; and the similarly outfitted Galaxie 500 XL Victoria hardtop coupe and Sunliner convertible with standard 292 V-8. Some thought the letters on the last stood for "Experimental Limited," but they meant nothing more than "extra lively."

Accompanying the XL was Ford's largest V-8 yet: a bored-out 390 (by 0.08-inch) with 406 cid. Optional only in the full-size line, it was offered as a 385-bhp "Thunderbird High-Performance" unit with single four-barrel carb, and the "Thunderbird Super High-Performance" with three two-barrel carbs and a rated 405 bhp, nearly 1 bhp per cubic inch. The latter was clearly not for the faint-hearted and cost a sizable $380. Still, the 406 gave the big bucket-seat Fords the go-power to match their sporty pretentions. Contemporary road tests showed 0-60 mph acceleration times ranging from the mid-6s to a bit over 7 seconds—fantastic for quiet, smooth-riding freeway flyers weighing nearly two tons.

The 406 Galaxie would have been a fine stock-car racer but, aside from heft, it had a problem. As writer Phil Hall explained: "When the Starliner was dropped, so were Ford's superspeedway chances. The squared-off sedan roof just didn't cut through the air as quickly as the sleek Starliners." Ford attempted to recoup with the Starlift, an optional accessory hardtop that turned the big convertible

Lincoln Continental greeted 1962 with a revised grille, more insulation. Only 3212 convertibles were built that year.

into something resembling the now-departed Starliner. Though ostensibly available to the public as well as race teams, few were actually built, and NASCAR banned it as "not production" after only one race. Ford would improve full-size aerodynamics with racing in mind, but not for another year.

Also new for mid-'62 was a more potent small-block as an option for the Fairlane/Meteor. Called "Challenger 260," it put out 164 bhp via a 0.30-inch bore increase and higher 8.7:1 compression. Of course, it only hinted at the little V-8's development potential, which would be realized soon enough.

The third-generation Thunderbird was little changed in its sophomore year, but there were two interesting developments. One was the optional M-series 390 V-8, with triple two-barrel carbs, 10.5:1 compression, and 340 bhp. So equipped, the Bird could do 8.5 seconds in the 0-60 mph dash and top 125 mph.

Equally exciting was the Sports Roadster, a spiritual successor to the two-seat T-Bird. Ever since the final '57 models, Ford had received a steady stream of inquiries from dealers and customers who, although happy with the four-seater, longed for a new "little Bird." Iacocca was sympathetic but knew a separate model would cost too much. Stylist Bud Kaufman provided the solution: a fiberglass tonneau (with faired-in front seat headrests) to cover the existing convertible's rear seat area. Through careful attention to detail, it didn't interfere with raising or lowering the top, and the front seats were still free to hinge forward so luggage could be stuffed in underneath, but it was too big to carry in the trunk, so you had to leave it at home if you wanted to travel four-up. This and a tall price—about $5500—limited sales to only 1427 for the model year.

Still, the Sports Roadster was dramatic, set off by Kelsey-Hayes wire wheels and skirtless rear wheel openings. (The spinner hubs made the wires too bulky to fit under the normal T-Bird skirts, and they were too pretty to hide anyway.) Rarity makes this the most desirable Sixties T-Bird today. The rarest, of course, are those with the M-series engine, a mere 120 of the '62s.

Thunderbird had a second new "package" model this year. Called Landau, it was a high-line hardtop with vinyl roof and dummy rear-quarter landau bars, a Bill Boyer flashback to the Classic era. Priced at $4398, only $77 more than the standard model, it accounted for about a fourth of '62 T-Bird hardtop volume.

With one exception, this year's Lincoln-Mercury line was based entirely on the successful '61 range of compacts and standards. The exception, of course, was Fairlane's kissin' cousin, the Mercury Meteor, offered in the same five variations including a mid-season bucket-seat job called S-33. Meteors weighed less than 3000 pounds, and all but the S-33 started below $2500. Styling followed that of this year's Monterey, with a barrel-shaped, vertical-bar grille, and taillights sprouting from small vestigial fins. The excellent small-block V-8 was optional, of course.

But Meteor lagged way behind Fairlane in sales: fewer than 70,000 this year and under 50,000 for '63. The reasons weren't difficult to fathom. Meteors cost a couple hundred dollars more than equivalent Fairlanes and $400 or so more than comparable Comets, which were about the same size overall on a wheelbase only 2½ inches shorter. On a small scale then, this Meteor was a repeat of the Edsel mistake—trying to fill a market gap that didn't exist—and L-M decided to kill it even before 1962 was out. Still, it made a small profit, selling about twice as well as Edsel over roughly the same amount of time.

215

The '62 Mercury Monterey Custom ragtop found 5489 customers.

Mercury built 8932 Monterey Custom hardtop sedans ($3037).

The '62 Comet two-door sedan started at a modest $2084 . . .

. . . while the deluxe Comet Villager wagon sold for $2710.

Mercury's intermediate Meteor rode a 116.5-inch wheelbase.

The $2428 Meteor Custom four-door sedan weighed 2964 pounds.

Passenger versions of the '62 Econoline wore a Falcon badge.

By 1962, diesels powered many of Ford's heavy-duty trucks.

Comet's model year production was up to a solid 150,000 units, largely reflecting a lineup expanded from five to 10. The newcomers were posh Custom versions of the basic two/four-door sedans and wagons, plus a handsome four-door wagon called Villager (resurrecting a name from Edsel days) with pseudo-wood trim. At $3000 delivered, the Villager was this year's costliest Comet and garnered only 2318 sales, but it helped build showroom traffic, which was the idea. There were still no floorshifts or V-8s to jazz up the S-22 (or the Falcon Futura, for that matter) but the bucket-seater sold briskly nonetheless. All models were little changed in appearance—just a busier grille and round taillights—or mechanicals.

Like Fairlane, the Meteor nameplate had been pried from a big car, so Mercury shuffled its full-size line like Ford. Monterey became the base series, offering sedans and hardtops with two and four doors, while a new Monterey Custom group listed all but the two-door sedan for a few hundred dollars more. The latter also included Mercury's only '62 convertible.

As at Ford, mid-year brought a brace of big bucket-seat Mercs, the S-55 convertible and hardtop coupe in the Monterey Custom series. Like the XLs, they followed contemporary trends with a big center console *mit* shift lever for the standard automatic, thick carpets, vinyl trim, and an optional tachometer. The latter replaced the standard clock, mounted down on the console where you didn't have to look at it. Not that there was much need with engines as large as the 406 available. But the S-55 wasn't cheap. Few were delivered for under $4000, and that limited production to just 2772 hardtops and 1315 convertibles—which makes them desirable collectors items today.

Mercury also approximated Ford in big-car engine choices. The base Montereys and Commuter wagons carried the 223 six. Customs, including S-55s, and Colony Park wagons came with the 170-bhp 292, optional for the lower-line models. All could be ordered with the 220-bhp 352, 330-bhp 390 and, at mid-year, the 406s.

Lincoln laid back with a mild facelift: a cleaner grille with narrower central crossbar, higher-mounted headlamps, more conventional front bumper. Still more body insulation was added, increasing weight by about 45 pounds. Several pre-1961 features returned, including standard automatic headlamp dimmer and padded sunvisors. There was also a new remote-control rear deck release, then a novelty. Model year production totalled a bit more than 31,000 units, 90 percent of which were sedans. The limitation of just two body styles precluded pulling closer to Cadillac, but this was satisfying volume compared to 1958-60 levels.

By this time, another Lincoln Presidential limousine had surfaced in Washington, built on an extended, 156-inch-wheelbase '61 chassis by Hess & Eisenhardt of Cincinnati. The rear seat had a hydraulic lift for parade purposes, and there were several roof configurations. The forward section was finished in stainless steel; interchangeable rear portions gave either formal closed motoring or "fishbowl" viewing via a transparent plastic bub-

ble, the latter having its own black covering. Painted navy blue, the 9000-pound special was vastly strengthened underneath and throughout the chassis. Runningboards for Secret Service agents were added front and rear, and a big outside spare tire evoked memories of the Marks I and II.

Lincoln listed four extended chassis built in 1961, but Hess & Eisenhardt also crafted special limousines on the standard chassis. After the Kennedy assassination in 1963, the Presidential model was refitted with a bullet-proof-glass bubble and returned to White House service. It remained in the Presidential fleet through 1978, when it was presented to the Henry Ford Museum after logging more than a million miles.

1963

Total Performance was in full swing at Ford Division this year, with larger V-8s and new body styles for Falcon, Fairlane, and Galaxie. Much of this activity was reserved for mid-year introduction. Ford built over 1.5 million cars for the model year—its best total since 1957 and a new record—but trailed Chevrolet by a significant 600,000 units.

Per now-standard Ford practice, the '63 line bowed with engines from the end of the preceeding model year. The Galaxie's chart was revised by cancelling the 292-cid Y-block. A single 352 and a brace of 390 and 406 V-8s were the initial options, offering respective horsepower of 220, 300/330, and 385/405.

All Ford lines were facelifted. Falcon sedans adopted the squared-up roof from the mid-'62 Futura, and all models displayed slightly pointier front fenders and a more pleasing convex grille. Futura replaced the previous Deluxe as a separate series, with two- and four-door sedans and a pretty new convertible identified by spear-like side trim. Galaxie was fractionally longer and wider, marked by a handsome concave grille, more prominent round taillamps, and twin bodyside moldings on Galaxie 500s. A square-roof hardtop sedan joined the bucket-seat XL subseries. The mid-size Fairlane was slightly restyled to more closely resemble the big cars, with a similar concave grille, and added two new body styles: a trio of four-door wagons, including a fancy Squire with imitation-wood side trim, and a 500 hardtop coupe. Thunderbird acquired flat-top wheel openings, modest horizontal creaselines in doors and front fenders, plus the usual trim shuffles.

Ford saved its most interesting developments for mid-season. Starting with Falcon, a graceful semi-fastback two-door hardtop arrived in Futura and new Futura Sprint form, the latter also offered as a convertible. Be-

The 3599-pound Galaxie 500 hardtop coupe cost $2674 in 1963.

A Galaxie 500 hardtop sedan joined the XL subseries for '63.

Ford built 33,870 Galaxie 500 XL "slantbacks" for 1963.

For '63, Fairlane added hardtop coupes: regular or sporty.

Costliest '63 Fairlane was the $2781 Squire station wagon.

sides bucket seats, Sprints came with floorshift four-speed manual transmission, dash-mount tachometer—and the dull 170-cubic-inch six. But they could be made into honest performance machines with the 164-bhp Challenger 260 V-8, a first-time Falcon option.

Car Life magazine called the V-8 Sprint "Le Petite Sport," noting that its power-to-weight ratio was only 21 lbs/bhp versus 31.4 for six-cylinder models. The editors described the 260 as "a willing engine. If it seems unaware of the choking restrictions of its single two-barrel carburetor, it is because of somewhat generous valve sizes and relatively clean intake and exhaust designs. Its ability to readily surpass the 5000-rpm redline would have one believe it is fitted with mechanical lifters, but, of course, it isn't. The engine is completely devoid of fussiness, and exhibits a surprising amount of torque from rather ridiculous rpm levels. [It's] much happier in Falcon surroundings than it ever seemed to be in the Fairlane. . . ." As proof, *CL*'s four-speed test car recorded 0-60 mph in 12 seconds, the quarter-mile in 18 seconds at 75 mph, and a top speed of 105 mph.

As agile as its name, the Sprint had all the makings of a potential rally winner, and Ford knew it, sending a trio of specially modified hardtops to contest this year's Monte Carlo Rally. Prepared by the Holman & Moody works of stock-car-racing fame, they featured a tuned, 260-bhp version of the 260 V-8, close-ratio four-speed gearbox, abbreviated Galaxie rear axle with 4.51:1 final drive, big Bendix/Dunlop front disc brakes, and heavy-duty suspension. The teams comprised Bo Ljungfeldt/Gunnar Haggbom, Anne Hall/Margaret McKenzie, and Peter Jopp/Trant Jarman. The results were mixed. Veteran Erik Carlsson was the outright winner in his two-stroke Saab 96 and Hall/McKenzie didn't even finish. But for the first time in the Monte's 32 years, one car won all the special stages: the Ljungfeldt/Haggbom Sprint. Icing the cake, Jopp/Jarman won the big-engine class and finished 35th, eight spots ahead of their teammates. Ford reaped a lot of "Total Performance" publicity from this and other Falcon successes. For example, a factory-sponsored production car won the manufacturer's trophy in this year's Shell 4000 Trans-Canada Rally, though a Chevy II was the overall winner.

Fairlane kept pace for excitement with a more potent small-block option. Another bore increase (to 4.00 inches) yielded 289 cid and 271 bhp with four-barrel carb and 11:1 compression. (There was also a 195-bhp version that replaced the 260 as base power for the big Galaxie at midyear.) Heralding the 289 was a bucket-seat special, the Sports Coupe hardtop, offering center console and deluxe wheel covers with simulated knock-off spinners.

In June 1962, Ford had declared it would no longer adhere to the AMA racing "ban" of 1957. Evidence of this in production appeared for 1963½ in the form of the new "slantback" Galaxie 500 Sports Hardtop. Sitting about an inch lower than its square-top counterpart, it had sloping rear roof pillars and a smallish backlight—not as smooth as the old Starliner but a step in the right direction for

Of 455 Sports Roadsters for '63, only 37 had the 340-bhp V-8.

The $4548 T-Bird Landau saw production of 14,139 units.

stock-car racing, as events would prove. In fact, Ford enjoyed one of its best NASCAR seasons this year. Commencing with Dan Gurney's win at the Riverside 500 in January, Fords were in the winner's circle at every 500-mile event and took 23 Grand Nationals in all. The big XL was also a winner, with 12,596 copies of the square-roof four-door hardtops, 29,713 of the two-doors, and 18,551 convertibles. The new slantback was most popular of all, with 33,870 XLs and another 100,000 in Galaxie 500 trim.

Matching competitors' moves in the big-inch wars, Ford again bored its FE-series block, this time by 0.10-inch, bringing displacement up to 427 cid. Output with single four-barrel carb was 410 bhp, and a new twin-four-barrel setup (plus aluminum intake manifold) pushed that up to 425, both on tight, 11.6:1 compression. Price was discouraging—the 410 cost $405 additional—but a beefed-up chassis and suspension and bigger brakes and tires were included. A four-speed manual transmission, which had first appeared as a late 1961 option, was a mandatory extra with both.

Ford also cooked up a limited-production 427 for the dragstrip, with 12:1 compression and a nominal 425 bhp, the latter mainly to satisfy the rulebook. By now, lighter mid-size cars were beginning to rule the quarter-mile circuits, but Ford tried to keep its big cars competitive by offering an S/S kit, with fiberglass body panels and other

changes that lightened the front end by some 160 pounds. The factory also built a handful of S/S cars with stripped interiors. Still, the smaller Plymouths and Dodges were faster in Super/Stock action, and the typical XL rolled out the door with the 390 and automatic.

The same applied to the interesting Thunderbird Sports Roadster, which saw a mere 455 copies in this, its second and final year. Personal-luxury buyers were now clearly moving away from open cars. Consider that Ford built 10,516 of the '61 T-Bird ragtops, 7030 of the conventional '62 convertibles, and just 5913 of the '63s. Sales would bounce back a bit with the advent of 1964's fourth generation, only to decline the next two years. With the fifth-generation, 1967 design, the convertible would be gone. It hasn't reappeared since, but there must be many Bird lovers who hope that Ford will yet revive it.

The times were a-changing in other ways, and a small but growing number of buyers no longer perceived the annual model change as necessarily a good thing. Lincoln was one of the first to recognize this and, beginning with the '61 Continental, announced a new policy of making only minor year-to-year refinements. So it was again for '63. Later this year, Lincoln ads promised that "the classic look" would continue with the '64s.

Prices rose slightly, about $200 per car, but there was little to distinguish the '63s from the 1961-62 models: slightly raised rear deck for a bit more luggage space; finer eggcrate grille insert; matching dummy rear grille; and a new four-barrel carburetor that boosted the big 430 V-8 to 320 bhp. Detail revisions included an alternator to replace the generator, new power-vent windows, six-way power seat, and new audio equipment. For exhaust system longevity, more stainless steel and a freer-flow design were employed; U-joints were strengthened to cope with the increased power and had an extended, 30,000-mile service interval. Aluminum front brake drums had worked well on previous convertibles and were now adopted for sedans.

Despite its considerable bulk (the sedan weighed 6300 pounds, the convertible nearly 7000, some 400 more than comparable Cadillacs despite a six-inch-shorter wheelbase) this Continental was surprisingly quick. Pressed

Falcon came to life with the '63 V-8-powered Sprint hardtop.

Lincoln Continental gained 20 bhp, received new grille for '63.

Continental convertible production held steady for '63: 3138.

hard, the sedan could sprint from rest to 60 mph in 10 seconds, and would run all day at 110 mph. Fuel mileage was predictably meager, about 10-12 miles per gallon.

Lincoln finally made a serious return to the professional-car business this year. In May, the Chicago coachbuilding firm of Lehmann-Peterson announced a 160-inch-wheelbase division-window limousine with options such as rear-facing jump seats, bar, television, and secretary's desk. Ford cooperated by honoring the normal two-

year/24,000-mile warranty and lending its Dearborn test facilities for evaluation. The base price, however, was a tall $13,400, well above that of the Cadillac Seventy-Five, and at that level the L-P Continentals could not challenge Cadillac for volume. But at least Lincoln was back in the "carriage trade" after almost 20 years.

Without changing wheelbase, Mercury reskinned its full-size Monterey, Monterey Custom, and Colony Park wagons (the Commuters were dropped), making them

S-33 was Mercury Meteor's bucket-seat, sporty coupe for 1963.

Most-purchased Meteor for '63 was the $2428 Custom four door.

The $2605 Mercury Comet Custom hardtop weighed 2572 pounds.

The '63 Comet S-22 convertible cost $2710; 5757 were built.

Big Mercurys received a major facelift for 1963: new concave grille, triple taillights, and "Breezeway" rear window.

boxier and larger (the latter mostly via increased rear overhang). Sedans and hardtops now bore "Breezeway" rooflines, another fling with the retractable, reverse-slant rear window first seen on the 1958-60 Marks. Styling highlights included an attractive full-width concave grille, Lincoln-style chrome-edged beltline, new lower-body creases (above the rocker panels), and reshaped tail with triple lamp clusters.

As with Ford's XL, the bucket-seat Monterey Custom

Econoline could be had as a van or light-duty pickup in 1963.

Basically unchanged, '63 Ford trucks wore a new grille.

S-55 hardtop and convertible were joined by a new hard-top sedan and a mid-season slantback rocket, the $3650 Marauder. The latter also appeared in non-bucket form at some $570 less. Here too, the slantbacks were intended as alternatives to the square-cut standard rooflines as an appeal to the sporty set, and they did make a dramatic difference in appearance. The ultimate S-55 Marauder added all-out performance to the formula, packing a standard 300-bhp 390 and offering optional bhp to 425. A racing version driven by Parneli Jones gave Mercury its first NASCAR Grand National win since 1956, launching a skein of stock-car victories that would last into the 1970s.

Comet sales were down this year, primarily because Mercury's compact was largely unchanged for the fourth straight year. Not that there wasn't some sprucing up. Like Falcon, the Comet line picked up its first convertible, available in Custom and S-22 trim. They differed little apart from badges and trim, and together accounted for over 12,000 sales. A corresponding pair of slant-roof hard-tops arrived at mid-year, with the Custom version called "Sportster." The peppy 221 and 260 small-block V-8s were new to the options list, as were four-speed gearbox and power steering. Styling, on the other hand, was another mild facelift, chiefly a revised grille and new chrome trim highlighting the bodyside character lines.

Mercury's mid-size Meteor got the same mechanical and model adjustments accorded Ford's Fairlane, plus a busier grille and the expected trim shuffles. The S-33 switched from two-door sedan to hardtop coupe configuration. Yet despite more available power and a design that was still quite fresh, this year's nine-model line garnered fewer sales than the five-model '62 group.

With its aging big cars, disappointing Meteor sales, and a slowdown in Comet demand, Mercury's model year production dropped by some 40,000 units, to near 302,000, putting the make back to ninth place behind Plymouth, Buick, and Dodge. Lincoln, on the other hand, held up well with its still-popular and good-looking Continental twosome, running off a bit more than 31,000 units. In all, 1963 was a good but not great L-M year. The time had come for something new, and both marques would have it for '64.

1964

Dearborn's biggest success of the decade arrived this year with the Mustang ponycar. Reflecting another of Lee Iacocca's favorite marketing schemes, it was an early offering for '65, and is thus covered in the next section.

But Ford Division had a lot to show for '64 proper: a brand-new Thunderbird, thoroughly revamped big cars, and facelifted Falcons and Fairlanes. They made a very good year, car production rising by well over 60,000 units. But Chevy did considerably better, topping the two-million mark for the third straight model year and up more than 160,000 over 1963. The gap with Ford was better than 700,000, but Mustang would close that up substantially for '65.

Though you wouldn't think it from looking at them, the full-size 1961-63 Fords employed the inner structure introduced with the 1960 line. Ford now reskinned this platform one last time, achieving a distinctive if rather busy look compared with earlier models. Highlights included

"pontoon" bodyside sculpturing, longer rear deck, rounded nose, and a horizontal-bar grille with three distinct vertical peaks. The previous Galaxie and 300 names were replaced at the bottom of the line by Custom and Custom 500, while Galaxie 500 and its XL sub-series continued at the top. There were no major changes in drivetrain specs or availability.

The big '64 Ford may not seem historically significant—just a five-year-old design set to be phased out—but it's perfect for collectors. Author Tim Howley declared in *Special-Interest Autos* magazine that it "stands quite alone as the ultimate Total Performance Ford." *Motor Trend* magazine evidently agreed, naming the entire Ford line "Car of the Year." Though mechanical specs were basically the same as in 1963, Howley notes that big-Ford "styling had been carefully dictated by the aerodynamics of racing. Even the body panels were designed to be lighter than the '63s."

As before, there were three 500XLs: convertible and two- and four-door hardtops, the latter now with the slantback roofline from 1963½. Production totaled 58,306 two-doors, 15,169 convertibles, and 14,661 four-doors. Thanks to a strong quality-control effort begun in 1961, XLs and other big Fords wore like iron. Observes Howley: "All too many of them were driven for 10 years or 200,000

The heavily restyled 1964 Fords featured new sheet metal.

This Galaxie 500 hardtop sedan was powered by the 390 V-8.

The 1964 Sunliner retailed for $3495; 15,169 were built.

Rare: the $2671 Falcon Sprint ragtop saw only 4278 produced.

miles, and they just don't show their age. Rare is the low-mileage '64XL, as this was not the kind of car you bought to put away in your garage." Economy was hardly impressive, but performance definitely was. In a contemporary comparison test, a 390-equipped XL did 0-60 mph in 9.3 seconds, which was fair going, while a 427 clocked it in 7.4 seconds—remarkable for a two-ton luxury liner.

While the lighter and more competitive Fairlanes now carried Ford's drag racing colors, the big cars still did very well on Grand National stock car circuit. Chrysler Corporation brought back its fabled hemi-head V-8 for the '64 campaign, planning to beat back any Ford or GM threat. Ford cried foul; if the hemi was legal, Ford ought to be allowed to run its overhead-cam 427. Not quite, said NASCAR, but the pushrod 427 could use a high-rise manifold and a higher rev limit, both of which Ford quickly attended to. The hemis grabbed the limelight: Plymouth won the Daytona 500, the World 600 at Charlotte, and finished 1-2-3 at the Darlington 500. But when the smoke cleared, Ford had 30 NASCAR victories.

Falcon entered its fifth year with new lower-body sheet-metal and an extra engine option, the 200-cid ohv six introduced with the '63 Fairlane. Even pointier front fenders flanked a thrust-forward grille, bumpers were bulkier, bodysides were etched with prominent full-length character lines, and rear ends were squared up. The result was not altogether pretty; the hardtops and convertibles probably looked best. The sporty Sprint hardtop saw more than 3000 additional copies this year, 13,830 in all, but the convertible dropped from 4602 to 4278 and would fall even further for '65. Too bad, because the light and lively 289 small-block was now available, making these the fastest Falcons ever.

No fewer than eight Falcon teams contested this year's Monte Carlo Rally, and the results were better. New competition from Plymouth's V-8 Valiant prompted Ford to split its entries, half in the under-2500cc class, the remainder in the over-2500cc category. The latter ran tuned, 285-bhp 289 V-8s (two two-barrel carbs, 10:1 compression) and used more lightweight body components than the '63 factory cars but were otherwise similar. The Austin Mini-Cooper S of Paddy Hopkirk/Harry Liddon was first, due partly to rules changes that favored small-displacement machines. But Bo Ljungfeldt was again fastest on all the timed stages (though he tied one with Hopkirk) and he finished second overall and first in the upper division. Anne Hall capped the proceedings by taking the GT class. Rally rulemakers then banned the Sprints, but the point had been made: the Falcon was as much a "Total Performance" car as any Ford.

Fairlane was freshened up by being shorn of its tiny fins and adorned with oversize bull's-eye taillamps. Rear flanks picked up barrel-like sculptures terminating in chrome-capped, raked-forward dummy scoops; a large bulge appeared in the hood; and the grille insert was a bit more complicated. Model offerings stayed the same. Sales eased, but Ford's mid-size was still generating healthy sales volume of some 200,000 units a year.

A drag-racing Thunderbolt cost only $3980 in 1964.

Ford built 21,431 Fairlane Sport Coupes, priced at $2504.

The reskinned '64 Thunderbird set a new sales record: 92,465.

To lead its quarter-mile assault against the mid-size Plymouth and Dodge, Ford trotted out the mid-year Thunderbolt, a special factory drag car superficially resembling the workaday Fairlane two-door. According to Phil Hall in *Fearsome Fords*, some 54 were built by Dearborn Steel Tubing, then one of Ford's contractors for special projects like this. Thunderbolt's heart was a fortified "High Riser" version of the already potent 427, boasting stratospheric 12.7:1 compression, two four-barrel Holley carbs on an aluminum high-rise intake manifold, plus high-rise heads, machined combustion chambers, domed pistons, high-lift cam, and a modified Galaxie driveshaft mated to a Detroit "locker" differential. The big-block V-8 was physically too big for the stock engine compartment, so the Fairlane's front suspension and much of the 427 exhaust system had to be modified and/or custom-fabricated. Weight was removed wherever possible: fiberglass

The 1964 Lincoln Continental sported a three-inch-longer 116-inch wheelbase, which provided more rear seat legroom.

The Continental convertible sold for $6938; 3328 were built.

"Fastback" styling spread to four-door models on the '64 Merc.

hood, front fenders, and doors; gutted interior; Plexiglas rear and side windows. Two transmissions were available, a very heavy-duty four-speed with Hurst linkage or three-speed automatic.

As Hall points out, the amazing thing about the Thunderbolt was that "you could order [it] through your dealer, race ready, for about $3900. Considering what you got, it was stealing." Of course, few knew about it except those who wanted to put Ford on the National Hot Rod Association throne. Their efforts were generally successful, though the automatic proved a handicap against the MoPar four-speeds. Highlighting the year was Butch Leal's Super/Stock class win at the Labor Day NHRA Nationals at Indianapolis Raceway Park. In what some said was the closest competition in memory, his Thunderbolt blasted through the quarter in just 11.76 seconds at 122.78 mph. With this and other successes, Ford won the NHRA Manufacturer's Cup.

By contrast, this year's new fourth-generation Thunderbird made absolutely no gesture toward "Total Performance." The Sports Roadster was gone (though some dealers fitted leftover tonneaus and wire wheels to 45-50 standard '64 convertibles). So was the M-series engine. The plain 390 V-8 was again the only powerplant listed, with the same 300 bhp it had three years earlier.

Planning for the third-series four-seater evidently took note of the competitive challenge from Buick's Riviera,

which Ford knew about some time before GM launched it for '63. Thus arrived completely new sheetmetal with busy bodyside sculpturing, bulged hood, and drop-center rear deck. Wheelbase remained at 113 inches, but there was more emphasis on luxury and refinement. For example, the hardtop roofline retained its formal air but now incorporated "Silent-Flo" ventilation. Flicking a console-mounted lever activated a servo that opened a full-width vent beneath the backlight to pull air through the car from the cowl into the slipstream behind.

Overshadowing the new Thunderbird's exterior styling was a jazzy interior dominated by a dash that would have done justice to an airplane. No serious driver liked the ornate speedometer with its red-banded drum pointer, or the chrome-trimmed minor gauges, or the plethora of highly styled buttons, knobs, and levers. But Ford would have Mustang for the enthusiast crowd; Thunderbird owners simply loved their cars. Despite strong rivalry from the elegantly muscular Riviera, the '64 broke 1960's sales record with 92,465 units, a mark that wouldn't be bettered until the LTD II-based 1977 model. The '65 sold 74,972 copies; the '66 scored 69,176. No three-year generation did better.

Advertising said these Birds were "Begadgeted and Bedazzling," a fair description, but they weren't simply luxurious bombs. For example, Car Life thought the '65 Landau near-ideal in high-speed motoring: "So quiet and effortless was the running that the . . . speedometer too often crept well past the 80-mph mark. . . .This is precisely the type of service for which the Thunderbird was designed—covering vast distances between two points in the shortest legal time with the least extraneous intrusions upon the passenger's serenity." The magazine's test car ran 0-60 mph in 10.3 seconds, did 115 mph maximum, and scored 13-16 miles per gallon.

Road & Track, long a champion of sports cars and small imported sedans, was less sanguine than its then-sister publication, saying the '65 Thunderbird had "more symbolism than stature. Only the blessedly ignorant view it as anything more than what it is: a luxury-class car for those who want to present a dashing sort of image, who worry about spreading girth and stiffening arteries, and who couldn't care less about taste." But it misrepresents *R&T* to quote out of context. "Even when viewed in that light," the editors continued, "the Thunderbird must be admired. It is extremely well done for its purpose. Its roofline, its bucket seats, and console have inspired dozens of lesser imitations which, by their very imitation, proved the Bird a better beast."

With an eye to additional conquest sales from Cadillac, Lincoln-Mercury Division released the first significantly changed Continental in three years. Wheelbase stretched three inches, to 126, but weight was little changed from 1961-63. Though overall length now measured 216 inches, the Continental was still shorter than this year's Cadillac and Imperial, and Gene Bordinat, now director of design, wisely maintained the styling continuity that had won the car so many adherents.

The extra wheelbase length showed up mainly in rear seat legroom, something of a sore point among sales personnel. It also meant three-inch-longer rear doors, which benefitted entry/exit ease. Further enhancing aft cabin space was a front seat moved two inches further forward. To compensate for the diminished room that resulted, the dashboard was redesigned with a shallower contour and the steering wheel set closer to it. Detail features included a low-fuel warning light, tilt steering wheel, auxiliary map light, and automatic parking brake release.

That the Continental would change in such an evolutionary way was an article of faith among buyers, particularly those who had crossed over after being turned off by Cadillac's constant revision. The '64's faithfulness to 1961-63 styling convinced even more to come over. Cadillac finished the year 10,000 units down while Lincoln went up about 4000. It was still a huge spread, thanks to Cadillac's broader lineup and bigger dealer network, but the difference was smaller than it had been for quite awhile and Lincoln planners were cheered.

Another rival's '64 restyle underlined the basic sense and elegance of Elwood Engel's original design. Engel had left Ford in 1961 to head Chrysler styling, and this year's Imperial was his first complete car since taking over at Highland Park. Not surprisingly, it closely followed his Continental formula: chrome-edged fenderlines, formal rear roof, even a demi-spare tire outline on the trunklid.

Elwood thus proved that good styling works regardless of badge: Imperial recorded over 23,000 sales for '64, the best since its all-time, 1957 record.

Not to be ignored—which was impossible—was this year's handsome Continental Town Brougham show car, named for the 19th century aristocrat who conceived a semi-closed carriage with open chauffeur's compartment. L-M designers used a special 131-inch-wheelbase chassis and decked it out in English Traditional: walnut appliqués, deep pile carpets, dummy landau bars on a vinyl-covered rear half-top, thick broadcloth upholstery, even a magazine rack. Telephone, radio, and chauffeur's intercom were provided—as mockups. Painted Plaza Blue Pearl, the Town Brougham was strictly for show and, despite wide display, not meant to be driven.

Other interesting '64 customs included a special parade limousine for Pope Paul's American visit, and a new Presidential limo for the White House. The Papal Lincoln had a retracting roof section surmounted by an auxiliary wraparound windshield; the Presidential featured an open landau-type rear roof with Plexiglas cover and a deck bulge that actually housed a spare.

In partial observance of its 25th birthday, Mercury reverted to its four-series big-car lineup of Monterey, Montclair, Park Lane, and Commuter/Colony Park wagons, thus spanning a broader market. The first included Breezeway two- and four-door sedans and hardtop coupe plus Marauder hardtop coupes and sedans; Montclair deleted the two-door sedan, Park Lane added a Breezeway four-door hardtop, and convertibles were reserved for Monterey and Park Lane. Marauders with the 427 V-8 were still tremendous performers, rocketing to 60 in as little as seven seconds. A mild facelift brought sculptured, Lincolnesque bodysides and front/rear cavities with typical Mercury dental work.

With Meteor's demise, Comet was reworked to cover both the compact and intermediate segments. Like this year's Falcon, styling was squared-up and more "important," again with Lincoln-like knife-edge fenderlines and a convex, fine-mesh grille. Extra rear overhang extended length to 195 inches overall, though wheelbase remained at 114 inches (wagons still rode the Falcon's 109.5-inch span). Broader market coverage prompted an expanded, four-series lineup: 202 and 404 sedans and four-door wagons; posh Caliente four-door sedan, convertible, and hardtop coupe; and the new Cyclone hardtop. The last was Mercury's first serious salvo in the sporty compact wars and the hottest Comet to date, with Ford's impressive 210-bhp 289 small-block as standard equipment. It was also nicely turned out at around $3000 delivered, with vinyl top, buckets-and-console cabin, simulated chrome-reverse wheels, and bright rocker moldings. With all this, Comet sales rallied slightly; the Cyclone was peripheral though, accounting for just 7454 copies.

Like its Falcon sister, Comet had developed a reputation as a "throw-away" car that wore out after three or four years. Attempting to beat down this image, Mercury sent a four-Comet team to Daytona, where they ran

1965

Comet's sporty V-8-powered Cyclone coupe: 7454 were built.

At $2655, Cyclone out-priced all '64 Comets, except Villager.

The $2636 Caliente convertible saw production of 9039 units.

Comet's best sellers were four-door sedans, such as the 404.

With 10 million cars, 1965 was the American industry's biggest year in a decade and its greatest ever. Dearborn accounted for over 2.5 million of them, but the ghost of F.C. Reith might have commented that Ford was still too dominant at close to 2.2 million cars. By contrast, Mercury production was 350,000, Lincoln's 45,000. Furthermore, Lincoln was nearly 150,000 units behind resurgent Cadillac, although Mercury had passed Rambler to resume its accustomed eighth place.

If this lopsided situation led product planners to wonder about the wisdom of abandoning the five-division structure back in 1959, developments were about to confirm that decision. Harder times were at hand. A generation of young people would soon vanish from the market, their outlook altered by an unpopular war; with them would vanish the muscle cars and ponycars starting to make sales history. The government would begin demanding safety and emission equipment, contributing to inflation-fed price escalation. And a new threat of unprecedented proportions was already on the horizon: Japan, Inc.

Yet none of this loomed large in 1965. Toyota was then a sideshow. Gas still sold for 30 cents a gallon. The Viet Nam conflict remained comfortably distant for most Americans. Ralph Nader hadn't finished writing *Unsafe at Any Speed*. Watergate was just the name of a new hotel in Washington.

Without question, 1965's most significant automotive story was the phenomenal success of Ford's Mustang, first of the new sporty compacts that would soon be dubbed "ponycars" in its honor. Introduced at the New York World's Fair on April 17, 1964, it made more news than Barry Goldwater's sewing up the Republican Presidential nomination. America went wild over this affordable new personal car with lithe, long-hood/short-deck proportions. Ford had projected first-year sales of 100,000 units, but the model year total (through December 1965) was an astounding 680,989. A legend had been born. And its base price was only $2368 f.o.b. Detroit.

The Mustang itself was born during 1961 in meetings of the Fairlane Group, an informal eight-man executive committee headed by Lee Iacocca that met regularly at the Fairlane Inn in Dearborn. The division chief wanted a new youth-oriented car to capitalize on growing buyer interest in bucket-seat compacts with four-on-the-floor. Working under project code T-5, the group considered a 1955-57 Thunderbird revival (called "XT-Bird") and a production version of the experimental Mustang I, a light, open, mid-engine design with all-independent suspension and Triumph/MG dimensions. But both were rejected and for the same reason: only two seats. The team shrewdly realized that such a car would have limited sales appeal—none for young couples with children, or anybody else who

around the clock for 100,000 miles at an average 105 mph, setting over 100 new speed and endurance records. The bodies might rust away before the Comet owner's astonished eyes, but the 289 drivetrain was strong and reliable, as this feat proved. Mercury also sent Comets to the dragstrips, developing a special A/FX package for the Caliente hardtop. Included were the 425-bhp 427 V-8, heavy-duty four-speed transmission, beefed-up standard-wheelbase chassis, and lightweight body panels (aluminum bumpers, fiberglass hood, fenders, and trunklid). In the hands of drivers like "Dyno" Don Nicholson and Bill Shrewsberry, they did so well that Mercury refocused its competition program from stock-car to quarter-mile events.

The most influential car of the Sixties: the 1965 Mustang.

The '65 Mustang ragtop sold for $2614; 101,945 were built.

With 501,965 built, Mustang's hardtop was its best seller.

Mustang's fastback coupe listed at $2589; 77,079 were built.

Only 2806 Falcon Sprint hardtops were produced for 1965.

The '65 Futura convertible ($2481) was Falcon's last ragtop.

occasionally needed a back seat. Thus, the decision was made to go with the "median sports car," a four-seat proposal that established the new model's basic package. Now, all the stylists had to do was develop an appropriate look for it.

They produced scores of proposals beginning in late '61. The one that ultimately impressed Iacocca was a white-painted clay model dubbed Cougar, a low, sleek hardtop by Joe Oros, Gale Halderman, and L. David Ash of the Ford Division studio, one of several teams competing in the intramural design contest. Their mockup prompted a running prototype called Mustang II, with evolutionary styling that closely resembled that of the forthcoming

production car. By the time it was first shown, at the United States Grand Prix in autumn 1963, the production model was largely locked up. All indications were that it would meet Iacocca's goals: 2500-pound curb weight, a base price not more than a dollar a pound, and looks that said "young."

The Mustang was mainly a body engineering project, as Iacocca had directed that running gear and chassis components be off-the-shelf Falcon and Fairlane bits to keep development costs down and thus retail price. At 181.6 inches overall, the Mustang was as long as a '64 Falcon, but its 108-inch wheelbase was 1.5 inches shorter. Hardtop coupe and convertible body styles were designed early

At $3498, the Galaxie 500 XL convertible was Ford's costliest full-size offering for 1965; 9,849 units were built.

The '65 Galaxie 500 XL hardtop rode a 119-inch wheelbase.

The '65 LTD forced Chevy to respond later with its Caprice.

on to accommodate the 170-cubic-inch Falcon six as well as the efficient 260-cid Fairlane V-8. Besides the six, standard equipment would include three-speed manual gearbox with floorshift, full wheel covers, padded dash, bucket seats, full carpeting, and a color-keyed interior.

A key part of the Mustang concept was a smorgasbord of options so buyers could personalize their cars to taste. On the menu were self-shift Cruise-O-Matic, four-speed manual, and three-speed-with-overdrive transmissions;

If bigger is better, then here's the best 1965 Ford of all!

three different V-8s; limited-slip differential; "Rally-Pac" gauges (tachometer and clock in a small pod atop the steering column); handling package; power and front-disc (late 1965) brakes; power steering; air conditioning (except with the Hi-Performance 271-bhp V-8); center console; deluxe steering wheel; vinyl roof covering; pushbutton radio; knock-off style wheel covers; 14-inch styled steel wheels; and whitewall tires. Then came the *packages*: Visibility Group (mirrors and windshield washers); Accent Group (striping and rocker moldings); Instrument Group (needle gauges and round speedometer); GT Group (disc brakes, driving lights, special trim). Air conditioning was the costliest individual extra at $283, but others were bargain-priced: handling package ($31), disc brakes ($58), Instrument Group and Rally-Pac ($180).

Engine determined a Mustang's personality, and offerings changed a bit during the long, 20-month '65 model run. The smaller V-8 for the debut "1964½" cars was the 164-horsepower 260-cid small-block. Derived from it was the 289 delivering 195 bhp with two-barrel carburetor and 210 with optional four-barrel or 271 bhp in "Hi-Performance" guise. After September 1964, the 260 was discontinued, a two-barrel 200-bhp 289 became the base V-8, and the four-barrel unit was boosted to 225 bhp. The four-barrel 289 cost $162 extra, the "Hi-Po" engine $442.

Developing 0.95 bhp per cubic inch and 312 foot-pounds of torque at 3400 rpm, the 271 featured high-compression head, high-lift cam, free-breathing intake manifold, free-flow exhaust, solid valve lifters, low-restriction air cleaner, and chrome-plated valve stems. Dealer parts counters offered even more go: $73 Cobra "cam kit" (306-degree-duration cam with 0.289-inch lift), $222 "cylinder head kit" (stock heads with extra-large intake and exhaust valves plus heavy-duty springs and retainers), $343 "engine performance kit" (matched pistons with the cam and head kits). A big-port aluminum manifold cost $120 with single four-barrel carb, $243 with dual four-barrels, and $210 with triple twos. As a final touch, a dual-point centrifugal distributor was available for $50. Front disc brakes—one-piece Kelsey-Hayes cast-iron units with 9.5-inch-diameter rotors—arrived late in the run at $58 and were worth every penny.

Mustang wasn't exotic, but it looked right. The most criticized styling elements were the dummy "scoops" ahead of the rear wheel openings, and the shallow, high-set grille. Space utilization was poor for the wheelbase length, with only marginal rear seat room for adults. Some "buff books" also took issue with the driving position, the sloppy standard suspension, and the Falcon-like dash.

But properly optioned, the Mustang was a horse of a different color. *Road & Track* magazine's 271-bhp car did 0-60 mph in 8.5 seconds, the standing quarter-mile in 15.6 seconds at 85 mph, and 120 mph tops. Its optional handling package (larger front anti-roll bar, 5.90×15 Firestone Super Sports tires, quick steering ratio) "eliminated the wallow we experienced with previous Mustangs [and tied] the car to the road much more firmly, so on a fast run the point of one's departure into the boondocks is delayed very considerably. . . . There is a certain harshness to the ride at low speeds over poor surfaces . . . a small price to pay for the great improvement in handling and roadholding." In all, the Mustang 271 was "a big step in the right direction." But *R&T* was the harshest, and most other publications liked Mustang as much as the

public. *Motor Trend*'s 271 did 0-60 mph in 7.6 seconds, and ran the quarter-mile slightly faster. It was obvious that with the right equipment, Mustang could be very satisfying.

In autumn '64, Ford added a Mustang fastback called "2+2" to mark the start of the official 1965 model year. Priced about $200 above the hardtop and mere pocket change below the convertible, it had even less rear legroom but looked slick. Rear quarter windows were omitted for vents that functioned as air extractors for flow-through ventilation. The 2+2 sold over 77,000 for the model year, against 102,000 convertibles and—the really stupendous figure—over half a million hardtops.

Arriving about a year behind Mustang was a limited-production, high-performance offshoot, the memorable Shelby GT-350, a fastback heavily modified at Ford's behest by former race driver Carroll Shelby. One of the few truly dual-purpose American production cars, it was brilliant on the street, superb on the track. The impetus behind it was Ford's desire that Mustang have a solid performance image. And what better way to do that than by taking the Sports Car Club of America's B-Production championship from Chevy's Corvette?

The GT-350 easily accomplished its mission: Jerry Titus won the B-Production national crown in 1965. Walt Hane won it again—with the same car—in 1966, and another GT-350 owned the class in 1967. The GT-350 was also successful on the dragstrips. It was, in a word, a thoroughbred. Today it stands as one of the most coveted Fords of all—surely one of the hairiest.

Shelby, of course, was the man behind the equally memorable Cobra, the light and lovely British A.C. Ace roadster adapted for Ford small-block power (the 260 V-8 initially, later the 289). Introduced in 1962, it partly realized his dream of building the world's fastest production sports car (ultimately fulfilled in the brutal 427 models). Built in tiny numbers, the Cobra was never important to Ford commercially, but its numerous race wins had tremendous publicity value. Moreover, it established Shelby as a manufacturer. Indeed, he'd opened a small-scale as-

Priced at $4486, the 1965 T-Bird coupe weighed 4470 pounds.

Ford built 6846 Thunderbird soft tops for the '65 model run.

Continuity of styling marked the 1965 Lincoln Continental.

Even the price was unchanged: $6292 for the Continental sedan.

sembly operation in Venice, California by 1962. Thus, when Iacocca decided Mustang needed an extra dose of excitement, Shelby was an obvious choice.

Shelby's assignment was deceptively simple: turn the Mustang into a race car capable of winning the national B-production crown. There were just two requirements. First, it had to be identifiable *as* a Mustang for Ford to realize any sales benefit (SCCA rules tended in this direction). Second, it would have to see at least 100 copies annually to race as a "production" model. The latter prompted Shelby to devise two versions: street machine and ready-made racer. Both would be available through

the network of Ford "performance" dealers Shelby had knit together to sell the Cobra.

Each GT-350 started out as a white fastback from Ford's San Jose, California plant, with the 271-bhp 289 and Borg-Warner T-10 four-speed transmission. Shelby added High-Riser manifold, big four-barrel carb, hot cam, and free-flow exhaust headers, bringing output to 306 bhp at 6000 rpm. A factory-installed Galaxie rear axle (replacing the stock Falcon unit) was located by trailing arms and brought 10×3-inch drum brakes that Shelby fitted with metallic linings. Koni shocks were used all around. The front suspension's forward mounts were relocated

Mercury's '65 Comet Caliente convertible: $2664, 6035 built.

Comet's top-line Caliente four-door sedan weighed 2659 pounds.

Best-selling Comet hardtop for 1965 was the $2403 Caliente.

Rarest of the '65 Comets was the Villager wagon: 1592 built.

and the optional disc brakes installed, along with quick-ratio steering box, a large anti-sway bar for extra roll stiffness, and a heavy steel-tube brace linking the tops of the front shock towers to eliminate body flex under high cornering loads. Shelby's own 15×6 cast-aluminum wheels were shod with Goodyear high-performance tires. The result of all this was near neutral handling instead of the standard Mustang's strong understeer.

Outside, the standard Mustang's prancing pony was plucked from the GT-350 grille, the steel hood replaced by a fiberglass replica with functional intake, and the dummy bodyside scoops eliminated. Bright blue racing stripes appeared along the rocker panels, and a pair of much wider stripes was applied longitudinally to hood, roof, and deck. Inside, the street Shelby was stock Mustang apart from three-inch-wide competition seatbelts, mahogany-rim steering wheel, full instrumentation, and no back seat. The last was prompted by the way SCCA defined a production "sports car." For those who occasionally needed to carry rear riders, a kit was available with a small bench seat that put the spare back in the trunk.

The full-race GT-350R was a more highly tuned street car set up for the track. Its engine was the same except for special heads, basically the Cobra racing unit rated at 340-460 bhp. To save weight, the transmission got an aluminum case and the interior was stripped except for a racing bucket seat, rollbar, safety harness, and necessary instruments. A heavy-duty suspension was used along with racing tires. The final touch was a new fiberglass nose *sans* front bumper, leaving a rudimentary air dam with a large central slot that acted as an air intake for an oil cooler. Some cars also had four-wheel disc brakes. Curb weight was only 2500 pounds compared to 2800 for the street machine.

The GT-350 was duly homologated for B-Production, which included small-block Corvettes, Sunbeam Tigers, Jaguar E-Types, and the occasional Ferrari or Aston Martin. Out of 562 completed as '65 models, no more than 30 were built to racing specifications. But since all the special parts were available over the counter (per Shelby philosophy), anyone could turn the street car into the racer—as some did.

Arriving at $4547, about $1000 more than a standard V-8 Mustang and an equal amount less than a Corvette, the GT-350 was in the middle of the performance market but ahead on the road. With 0-60 mph times averaging 6.5 seconds, a top speed of 130-135 mph, and race-car handling and braking, it drew rave reviews. Predictably, the first-year Shelby-Mustang would be the purest of the breed, and is thus most highly prized today. Beginning with the '66s, it was progressively softened into a plusher, more stylized version of the production Mustang, something completely different from Shelby's original concept.

Mustang seemed born to race, and did even before it went on sale. In late winter of 1963-64, Ford prepped a team of rally Mustangs to take over for the newly banned Falcon Sprints, but their only major win came in the Tour de France, where Peter Proctor and Peter Harper finished

one-two in class. There was more success on the drag-strips, where 2 + 2s stuffed full of 427 racked up numerous wins in NHRA's A/FX class and, less often, as "funny cars." The factory got into the act for the '65 season, fielding wild altereds with two-inch-shorter wheelbases. At the Pomona Winternationals in February, Bill Lawton's Mustang outlasted and outpaced a pack of Comets, Mustangs, and Mopars to win A/FX. Les Ritchey did the same at the Labor Day Nationals in Indianapolis, beating famed dragster Gas Rhonda.

Meantime, the big Fords were giving the division its best-ever year in NASCAR, winning 48 of the 55 scheduled events. Although a rules dispute kept the factory Plymouth and Dodge teams out for most of the season, these and other makes were still represented by intermediates—which makes the big Ford's record all the more impressive. Veteran Ford pilot Fred Lorenzen won this year's rain-shortened Daytona 500 at an average 141.539. Bobby Johns placed third, also in a Galaxie.

But the stockers bore little resemblance to the all-new showroom models, now billed as being "quieter than a Rolls-Royce." Pride of the line was the limousine-like LTD, and all big Fords acquired more square-cut body lines. Yet the 500 XL hardtop retained its semi-fastback roofline from 1963-64, and this undoubtedly contributed to Ford's supertrack victory streak.

Beneath its new styling and luxury demeanor, the full-

Wheelbase stretched to 123 inches on the big Mercs for 1965.

Mercury built 4672 Monterey ragtops for '65; price was $3230.

Note the similarity between this stretched Mercury Park Lane and the Ford LTD on page 228 (both non-factory).

Mercury's top-line Park Lane hardtop sedan listed at $3442.

Breezeway styling appeared only on four-door sedans for 1965.

size '65s were the most changed Fords since 1949. Author Phil Hall summarized their new engineering in *Fearsome Fords*: "The frame and concept were new. There were now coil springs front and back. The front units were redesigned for strength utilizing the experience from stock car racing. Conventional coils were still between the upper and lower control arms. The design was so strong that it became the standard for NASCAR stock cars, regardless of make . . . right into the 1980s. . . . The rear coil springs were mounted just ahead of the rear axle with two control arms anchoring the axle and springs to the body. A third member was attached to the right-hand side of the differential. There was also a Panhard rod from the right side of the axle to the left frame member. . . .Frames contained torque boxes for added strength. In addition, the bodies were strengthened similar to unitized bodies [and] the number of frame attachment points was reduced. . . . While this had little to do with performance, it did make for a quiet ride. . . ."

As before, the big-Ford line comprised Custom and Custom 500 sedans, the full-range Galaxie 500 series, and parallel Station Wagon offerings. Styling was cleaner and more stately, announced by a horizontal-bar grille flanked by stacked quad headlamps. The fussy pontoon bodysides of 1964 gave way to more flowing sheetmetal, while upper-end models abandoned round taillights for large, roughly hexagonal lamps. There were few changes in the engine department, but a new 240-cid "Big Six" replaced the base 223-cid unit that had been around since

1952. No fewer than six V-8s were available, with horsepower ranging from 200 to 425 bhp, including two 427 big-block mills.

The posh LTD's mid-season debut forecast the future and hastened the demise of the overtly sporting XL, which declined to only 37,990 units from its high of nearly 95,000 just two years before. By contrast, the LTD two- and four-door hardtops scored over 100,000 sales. Ford's overall full-size sales were up for the third year running (to 978,519), but buyer interest in bucket-seat biggies was waning. From here on, the emphasis would be on luxury.

Fairlane was in the last year of its original 1962 design and, as so often happens in Detroit, got a bevy of alterations to keep customers interested. A lower-body reskin produced a more square-shouldered look, with some attempt at aping the new big-car appearance. Wheelbase grew half an inch (to 116) and there were minor increases to rear track, overall length and width—and weight. The standard 200-cid six was reworked with seven main bearings and gained 4 bhp (120 total). Optional engines comprised three 289 V-8s, with the high-performance 271 still top dog. New to the list was a 225-bhp version with 10:1 compression and four-barrel carb. Despite all this, Fairlane production dropped to a new low, 223,954 units.

Falcon retained its basic '64 styling and model choices. The Sprint convertible and hardtop remained the most interesting variants but weren't popular in what would be their final season: respective production was only 2806 and a mere 300. However, they were still fine buys at

$2337 and $2671. Falcon finally got the 289 V-8 (the 260 was dropped), but it was just the easy-going 200-bhp version.

Thunderbird was only mildly facelifted for the fourth-generation's second year. A Bird emblem replaced block letters on the nose, chrome "C-spears" adorned front fenders, and taillamps were segmented into thirds for sequential turn indicators, a new gimmick. More significant was standardization of front disc brakes, something this weighty personal car had long needed. Added in late March was a fourth model (actually a trim package) called the Limited Edition Special Landau, with "Ember-Glo" metallic paint and matching wheel covers, parchment-color vinyl top, pseudo-wood interior trim, color-keyed carpeting and vinyl upholstery, and a console plaque bearing the owner's name. Priced less than $50 above the regular Landau, it saw only 4500 copies. Thunderbird model year production slid by some 18,000 units to about 75,000.

Like most automakers, Lincoln-Mercury Division wasn't quite ready for the unprecedented seller's market that suddenly rared up in the autumn of 1964, after Lyndon Johnson swamped Barry Goldwater on the irresistible platform of peace and prosperity. As planned back in '62, the big Mercs now followed Lincoln's upsizing, switching to a 123-inch wheelbase (wagons shrank to the big Ford's 119 inches) and adopting a crisp, if conservative, new look "in the Lincoln Continental tradition." The Marauder name was dropped, though hardtop coupes retained slantback roofs, and Breezeway offerings thinned to a single pillared sedan in each series. The losses were an apparent gain, however, because Mercury production topped 350,000 units for the calendar year, up over 50,000 from '64, with the full-size line accounting for most of it. Model year volume was up to near 347,000.

Many thought the big '65 the best-looking Mercury in years, relative to class rivals. Dearborn styling chief Gene Bordinat decreed an "extruded" look, announced by a clean grille with protruding center section, and it worked well with the longer wheelbase. Besides Breezeway sedans, the upper-crust series included pillarless coupes and sedans and the $4000 Park Lane convertible. Monterey, which still started well under $3000, also listed a convertible and Mercury's lone full-size two-door sedan. Commuter and Colony Park wagons continued in six- and nine-passenger form. Chassis changes mimicked the full-size Ford's, while engine offerings continued to center on the workhorse 390 (250, 266, 300, and 330 bhp) and the 425-bhp 427.

The unchanged Comet line held at 150,000, but the cars looked more Ford-like, with stacked quad headlamps flanking a simple grille, plus reshaped tails and more complicated bodyside creases (still adorned with Buick-like portholes on some models). Cyclone returned with the 289 V-8 in standard 200-bhp tune and could be ordered with the 225-bhp "Cyclone Super" version. Sales soared to over 12,000 units, which means the musclebaby was now actually making a bit of a profit. Following up 1964's

Daytona durability run, a trio of '65 Caliente hardtops trekked uneventfully from Cape Horn to Fairbanks, Alaska.

Lincoln, riding high on its longer '64 platform, was much the same car—and one of the few '65s whose price wasn't raised by so much as a dollar. Base list was $6292 for the sedan, $6938 for the convertible, though they went out the door for closer to $7000 and over $7600, respectively. Model year production topped 40,000, the first time Lincoln had done this well since memorable 1956.

Styling changes were as mild as ever: horizontal-bar grille (again with center bulge) and wraparound parking/turn signal lamps visible from every angle except dead-rear. Vinyl tops were more popular at only about $105 extra and looked quite handsome, unlike the overstuffed versions of later years. The sedan accounted for most of this year's production gain; the convertible had been around 3000-3300 per year since 1962. Air conditioning, which now reached a 90-percent installation rate, was the only major option ($505) except for individual power front seats ($281). The 320-bhp 430 V-8 was untouched for another year.

Lincoln continued its profitable, image-building relationship with Lehmann-Peterson, whose Executive Limousine had grown to 21 feet overall and $16,500. L-P also built another Town Brougham show car this year, the standard platform with dummy landau bars over a vinyl-clad rear roof, plus the usual open chauffeur's cab and flush-mount side carriage lamps. It's too bad this Classic-era throwback wasn't offered for sale on at least a limited basis, as it would have done wonders for Lincoln's luxury image.

1966

In an ad claim with some justification, Ford Division modestly touted 1966 as "the greatest year yet for Total Performance." The same might be said for the corporate fleet. Heading the list were a totally redesigned Ford Fairlane, an upgraded Mercury Comet and Ford Falcon, plus a smoother and larger new Lincoln Continental. The year also brought the largest extension of the venerable FE-series V-8, still going strong after eight years, and a hulking new Lincoln powerplant. Ford Division had a very successful season, tallying some 2.2 million cars to shade Chevrolet by over 6000 units. Much of this reflected continuing strong demand for Mustang, the mainstream big cars, and the new intermediates.

Pontiac had created the muscle car back in '64 with the GTO, basically that year's mid-size Tempest LeMans stuffed full of 389 V-8. It was an instant hit, so copies were

Special stretched LTD was continued for 1966. It was probably the world's only pillarless hardtop limousine.

Ford Galaxie 500 soft top sold for $2934; 27,454 were built.

The '66 Country Squire started at $3182; 69,598 were built.

not long coming. Oldsmobile, in fact, fielded its 400-cid 4-4-2, a heated up F-85 Cutlass, that same year, and Chevrolet dropped a 396 into its Chevelle during 1965 to produce the SS-396. But Ford had to sit on the sidelines because the original Fairlane hadn't been designed with sufficient underhood room for anything larger than a small-block. While that provided fine performance and made more sense from a weight/handling standpoint, the Fairlane was simply outclassed by GM's more muscular middleweights.

Ford finally caught up with this year's new second-generation Fairlane. Though dimensionally similar to the 1962-65 models, it could accommodate any big-block mill the engineers wanted to shove in. The new GT hardtop and convertible were the muscle models, packing a 335-bhp 390 with higher-lift cam, larger four-pot Holley carb, and a lower-restriction air cleaner than the 315-bhp unit, next step down on the '66 chart. Standard gearbox was a three-speed manual, but most buyers opted for either floorshift four-speed or new "Sport Shift" Cruise-O-Matic, the latter denoted by special "GT/A" badges on trunklid and front fenders. Sport Shift referred to a new-design range selector (with console mount) that permitted holding first or second gear to maximum rpm as with a manual.

By contrast, other Fairlanes seemed pretty tame. They

carried a modest 120-bhp 200-cid six, with options of 200-bhp 289 V-8, a 390 with 265 or 275 bhp depending on transmission, and the 315-bhp 390. Aside from the GTs, model choices comprised the usual body styles in base and 500 trim plus a new 500 convertible. The last was also available with a two-door hardtop as the new 500/XL, with center console and all-vinyl front bucket seats as on the GT. The new platform was also adopted for the Ranchero car/pickup, replacing the 1960-65 Falcon-based design.

Fairlane's '66 styling was clean and contemporary, a complete break with the previous dowdy look. A new front-end appearance was achieved by stacking the quad headlamps either side of a wide, horizontal-bar grille, much as on the big '65 Ford. Fall-away front fenders swept back past a broad, flat hood to mildly kicked-up "Coke bottle" rear fenders that terminated in a shortish rear deck with neat vertical taillamps. Hardtops were graced by a nicely integrated, semi-fastback roofline.

These hotter, smoother Fairlanes seemed to be the muscle-car warriors Ford needed, but competitors hadn't been idle. Pontiac, for example, offered up to 360 bhp in this year's GTO, and Chrysler had a street version of its fabled 426-cid hemi V-8—with 425 *very* strong horses—as the top power option for its mid-size Plymouth Belvedere/ Dodge Coronet. Ford responded by running off about 70

Fairlane two-door sedans with the mighty 427, still rated at 410 bhp with single four-barrel carb or 425 bhp with twin quads. These cars also carried special fiberglass hoods with functional air scoop, and were destined solely for dragstrip service. Interestingly, no GTs were built this way.

Despite lacking the ultimate power of its rivals, Fairlane scored near sensational sales. Production totalled over 317,000, second only to the 1963 figure and an impressive 42 percent above lackluster '65. The GTs proved quite popular, outselling the tamer, less expensive XLs by some 8000 units, though the GT ragtop saw only 4327 copies.

Falcon was now more mid-size than compact, because planning had decreed that Mercury's Comet would share Fairlane tooling for '66. As a wholly separate compact would have been too costly, the second-generation Falcon became a short-wheelbase version of the new intermediate and lost its hardtops and convertibles, the latter transferring to Ford's mid-size line. It was thus nearly identical to the new Fairlane from the cowl back, but had different front and rear styling. While Falcon and Fairlane wagons shared a 113-inch wheelbase, Falcon four-door and "club coupe" two-door sedans rode a 110.5-inch span, an inch longer than before but 5.5 inches shorter than the non-wagon Fairlane measure. The previous powertrain lineup returned without change. With the Sprint's demise, the most interesting '66 Falcon was the bucket-seat Futura Sport Coupe. In all, Ford's latest compact combined mid-size interior room and comfort with more manageable exterior size, but it wasn't that much cheaper than Fairlane and was eclipsed by the intermediates in both marketing emphasis and sales.

With its overwhelming 1965 success, Mustang didn't need to change, but some minor alterations appeared on this year's sophomore models. The horizontal grille bar was ditched and thin bars replaced the previous honeycomb as a backdrop for the galloping-horse emblem. Windsplits decorated the simulated bodyside scoops (except on GT-equipped cars), and fuel filler cap and wheel covers were restyled. Inside, the standard Falconesque gauge cluster with strip speedometer gave way to the more comprehensive five-dial instrumentation formerly listed as an option. Engines were reduced to standard 200-cid six (the 170 was dropped) and 289 V-8s with 200, 225, and 271 bhp. The option list lengthened to include a stereo tape system and deluxe seatbelts with reminder light.

Mustang model year sales were down because early introduction had made the '65 season longer than usual, but the '66s actually sold better for comparable 12-month periods—by some 50,000 units. There were still no direct competitors for Ford's ponycar. Chevy was a year away from launching its Camaro and Corvair sales were dwindling, while Plymouth's hastily created Barracuda was just a fancy Valiant with a glassy fastback and lagged way behind. Meantime, Ford happily counted the proceeds from selling 35,000 fastbacks, 70,000 convertibles, and nearly a half million hardtops.

Why tinker with a winner? The '66 Mustang changed little.

The '66 Mustang 2+2 listed at $2607; GT option was extra.

Ford built 72,119 Mustang convertibles for the 1966 model year.

The 1966 Ford Fairlane 500 hardtop coupe retailed for $2378.

To move up to the Fairlane 500 XL hardtop cost another $155.

The new Falcon Futura put on an added 200 pounds for 1966.

Ford's 345-bhp, 428-cid V-8: a new option for the '66 T-Bird.

Thunderbird's price leader for '66 was the $4483 hardtop.

Dealer and customer feedback prompted most changes to this year's Shelby GT-350. The most obvious ones were external: fixed Plexiglas rear side windows in place of the stock fastback's air-exhaust vents, side scoops for rear brake cooling in place of the windsplits, and the thin-bar production-'66 grille (still minus the galloping pony). Also, the 15-inch mag wheels (actually aluminum centers with steel rims) were replaced by 14-inch rims in no-charge choice of chrome styled steel or cast-aluminum alloy.

Otherwise, there's no clear distinction between 1965 and '66 production. Shelby didn't always incorporate changes at the start of a model year, preferring to use up parts on hand (shades of Model A days). Thus, some 250 early '66s were actually leftover '65s with the new cosmetics and the previous suspension, interior, and blue-on-

white paint scheme. When actual production began, colors were expanded to red, blue, green, and black, all with white stripes; the stock 2+2's optional fold-down rear seat became available; and batteries were left in their stock, underhood location. The '66 also used heavy-duty Ford-installed shock absorbers but retained the special Pitman and idler arms that gave the 1965 its sharp steering. All '65s and early '66s used rear traction bars that ran from inside the car to the top of the rear axle; late '66s used Traction Master underride bars. Early cars also had lowered front A-arms that altered the steering geometry for improved cornering, but this was later discontinued as not cost-effective. Drivetrains remained the same, but the Detroit "Locker" rear end was made optional, as was automatic transmission. Ol' Shel also offered a Paxton centrifugal supercharger as a new option (a special GT-350 "S" was envisioned but never actually released), claimed to boost horsepower "up to 46 percent."

Shelby planned increased '66 production so that every dealer who wanted cars could get them. He also sold a fleet of special GT-350H models to the Hertz company, finished in black with gold stripes. Hertz rented them at major airports, but many returned from a weekend's use with definite signs of having raced. Naturally, Hertz found this a mite unprofitable and soon bailed out. Total '66 Shelby-Mustang production was 2380 units, including 936 Hertz cars and six specially built convertibles that Carroll gave away as gifts at the end of the model year. No racers were constructed, though a few leftover '65s were registered as '66s. Shelbys continued to race and win, though they were essentially the same cars that had run and won the year before.

Detail appearance changes marked Ford's full-size '66s. Taillights squared up, the grille and hood were pushed forward a bit, and rear wheel arches were a bit bigger. Pride of the line was the new Galaxie 500 7-Litre convertible and hardtop coupe, named for the metric displacement of their standard 428 V-8. This new engine was created by combining the 406's 4.13-inch bore with the Mercury 410's 3.98-inch stroke. Displacement actually worked out closer to 427 cubes, but Ford called it a 428 to avoid confusion with the high-performance big-block. Despite 10.5:1 compression, a big four-barrel carb, and hydraulic lifters, the 428 wasn't a muscle mill but a torquey, low-revving slogger designed to keep pace with big cars growing ever heavier with the addition of more and more power accessories. Output was 345 bhp in standard tune, and a 360-bhp police version was theoretically available to civilians.

Despite its heft (over two tons at the curb), the 7-Litre was quite fast. *Car Life* magazine's automatic car ran the 0-60 mph dash in creditable 8.0 seconds. But this was really a luxury liner with just a hint of sport—much like the XL, in fact (even interiors were shared)—and would thus find a limited audience: only 8705 hardtops and a mere 2368 drop-tops. XL sales continued to decline: 25,715 hardtops and only 6360 convertibles. By now, buyers seeking *real* performance looked to the mid-size mus-

For 1966, Lincoln brought out its first hardtop coupe since 1960. It retailed for a "low" $5485 and 15,766 were built.

The '66 Continental sedan outsold its stablemates two-to-one.

Continental soft top output remained steady at 3180 for '66.

cle brigade, not big-inch, standards. But if the 7-Litre wasn't a success, its engine was. The 428 was optional for other full-size Fords as well as the '66 Thunderbird, and would continue as such for several years. Other power-teams remained as before.

As a group, the big Fords did quite well, production topping the 1-million mark for the first time in six years. As usual, the mid-line Galaxie 500 sedan and hardtop coupe were far and away the best-sellers.

A mild restyle and a couple of new options marked the last of the fourth-generation Thunderbirds. The former brought a reshaped checked grille with a wide-winged Bird emblem, and taillamp lenses spread completely across the back, still with sequential turn signals. Joining the lineup were the Town Hardtop and Town Landau, the latter with dummy, S-shaped landau bars on the rear roof quarters. Both differed from the normal hardtop in having C-pillars extended forward to the doors (eliminating the small, triangular rear quarter panes) and a standard warning-light console (optional on the base hardtop) above the windshield header. The new roof made for bulky-formal looks—more so with accessory rear fender skirts—but proved popular with the style-conscious. Combined Town volume was well over 50,000 units; the plain hardtop tallied only a little over 13,000 sales.

The trusty 390 remained standard T-Bird power, now rated at 315 bhp; the 345-bhp 428 arrived at a modest $64.30 extra. Another new feature was a cruise control

system with buttons mounted in the steering wheel spokes for convenience. Ford called it "Highway Pilot Controls"; later, "Fingertip Speed Control." Leather upholstery with reclining front passenger seat arrived ($147) along with a combined AM radio/eight-track stereo tape player ($81.55).

Significantly, this would be the last year for the factory-built T-Bird convertible. Buyers in this market had long shown a preference for the greater comfort of closed models with air conditioning, reflected in '66 ragtop production of only 5049 units. Overall Thunderbird sales dipped to near 69,000 units, down some 5000.

Though 1966 was almost as lucrative as '65 for most of the industry, it was a veritable bonanza for Lincoln, which saw a record 52,000 units for the model year. Much of the improvement can be credited to a heavily revised Continental blown out four inches in length and again wearing curved side glass (it became flat in 1964) for a smoother look. A two-door hardtop was offered for the first time since 1960, and one can only guess why it took so long to revive this perennially popular body style. The hardtop usually delivered for under $6000, making it this year's least expensive Lincoln, and registered an impressive 15,766 sales, about half the sedan's total but five times the convertible's volume.

In view of what *hadn't* been done in recent years, Lincoln's '66 styling represented a substantial change. Elwood Engel's straight-edged front fenders were retained,

Rare: only 669 S-55 ragtops were built by Mercury for 1966.

The '66 Montclair hardtop coupe sported new grille, taillamps.

Mercury offered two '66 Breezeways: Monterey and Montclair.

Most popular Park Lane was the hardtop sedan: 19,204 built.

but the rears were now slightly upswept just ahead of the wheel arches. Grille and hood were more prominently "domed" in the center. Parking lights returned to the front bumpers, designers not anticipating the federally required side marker lamps for '68 (when the parkers reverted to the fenders). Taillights received the same treatment. There was a new deeply hooded dashboard, and braking power improved with standard front discs for the first time.

Another aid to Lincoln's greatly improved sales must have been the much-improved performance from this year's huge new 462 V-8: 0-60 mph in close to 10 seconds. The coupe had a top speed of 125 mph (it was the lightest model but still came in at 5000 pounds). The 462 would be Lincoln's last and most powerful pre-emissions V-8, with 340 gross bhp (it would reach 365 before being detuned) and a monumental 485 lbs/ft of torque. It weighed an equally monumental 750 pounds and, until Cadillac topped it for '68, was the industry's biggest powerplant. Based on the 430, it was bored and stroked (to 4.38 x 3.83 inches), and had a larger bell housing. Cylinder heads and intake manifold were completely redesigned, and water passages around the exhaust valves and plugs were nearly twice as large as before. Still, it was an understressed engine capable of far greater power had that been required (it produced only 0.73 bhp per cubic inch). But because it powered a Continental, it was designed for smooth, quiet cruising above all, as witness the long-striding final drive ratio of only 2.80:1. Even with that, however, few '66s returned better than 10 miles per gallon.

Among the year's more curious automotive artifacts was a trio of stainless-steel Continental convertibles built by Ford's steel supplier, Allegheny-Ludlum of Pittsburgh. A-L had been fiddling with stainless bodies since 1936 when it built six rustless Ford V-8s, and had turned out a pair of stainless '60 Thunderbirds. The first of these Continentals was used to celebrate the record 50,000th Lincoln for the model year, but the whole exercise was academic. As the DeLorean would prove 15 years later, stainless steel is far from ideal for car bodies. It's almost impossible to repair by the usual mode of panel-bashing, and it's hard to paint. It may resist rust, but so does cement.

Lincoln-Mercury division got a new general manager this year. E.F. "Gar" Laux had very definite product ideas that would have to be cycled through the usual three-year process, but he liked performance and knew he could get some more into production without such a long wait. Accordingly, he made Mercury's big S-55 a separate series and expanded Comet Cyclone offerings by adding a convertible and two trim variations.

His Cyclones couldn't have been better timed, because Comet not only received its long-awaited restyle but graduated to full mid-size status by switching to the new '66 Fairlane platform. This underlined a basic marketing distinction: Comet buyers were wealthier than Falcon buyers. And while Ford still had a "less compact compact" this year, Mercury didn't. Laux probably could have had one if he'd wanted it. But he didn't, and he probably didn't need one.

While the second-generation Comet shared Fairlane's

Top-of-the-line '66 Comet Cyclone GT hardtop sold for $2891.

The Comet Caliente convertible cost $2735; 3922 were built.

Mercury produced only 3880 Comet Villager wagons for 1966.

Comet's price leader and best seller: 202 two door ($2206).

116-inch wheelbase (wagons 113), it offered a more complicated lineup of 13 models (up from 11) arrayed in 202, Capri, Caliente, and Cyclone series in ascending price-and-plush order. Styling was similar to Fairlane's, with stacked quad headlamps and the same curvaceous flanks, but a body-color horizontal bar added distinction up front, while horizontal taillamps emphasized the wider new bodies.

Cyclone remained the most exciting Comet but was now equivalent to Fairlane's 500/XL, with hardtop and convertible in basic or GT trim. "GT" meant a thumping 335-bhp 390 as standard—too much power, really, but that was the muscle car game—plus hood scoops, body striping, black-finish grille, appropriate emblems, heavy-duty suspension, dual exhausts, power-booster fan, and three-speed manual transmission. "Sport Shift" automatic was optional here too, and a lot of drag racers found that it gave away little to a stick on the strip. In all, this new Cyclone was a fine package. Indy 500 officials recognized it as such by selecting a GT convertible to pace this year's edition of the Memorial Day classic.

Mercury's full-size cars got a very mild facelift. The front end exchanged its domed effect for a flat hood and simple thin-bar horizontal grille, and the rearranged body trim was as restrained as in '65. Montclair substituted a conventional-roof four-door for its Breezeway sedan, leaving just the Monterey and Park Lane models. Mercury wasn't finished with this gimmick, but it would look very different for '67.

This year's S-55 convertible and fastback hardtop delivered at around $4000-$4500, packed the new 345-bhp 428,

and stood apart with slim full-length body moldings, chrome-trimmed rockers, the familiar buckets-and-console interior, dual exhausts and special i.d. But while Cyclone racked up close to 25,000 sales—double its '65 volume—the S-55 was evidently too big for the sporty car crowd. Model year production ended at just 2916 fastbacks and a mere 669 convertibles. S-55 would merge back into the Monterey series for '67, when even fewer were built, then vanish.

Mercury's 335,000 cars and eighth-place finish was a near-repeat of its 1965 performance, but sales fell behind the '65 pace at mid-year, and the usual Spring spurt didn't materialize. The slide would continue into 1967 but would be shortly halted by the Cougar, a very different sort of cat for L-M.

1967

For this final year before the onset of federal safety and emissions regulations, Dearborn presented a totally new Thunderbird and a second ponycar, while Mustang and the big Fords and Mercurys were restyled from the waist down. The new-for-'66 Falcon and Ford Fairlane/Mercury Comet got only minor touch-ups, though the latter now offered their most powerful engines ever.

Mustang demand remained strong despite new Chevy and Plymouth competition, and the new T-Bird turned in a better sales performance than its 1966 predecessor. But declines in mid-size and big-car sales brought Ford Division's total way down. Model year car production plummeted by half a million units to a little more than 1.7 million, while Chevy maintained its previous volume.

Ford had been debating a Thunderbird sedan since the early Sixties. By mid-decade, division chief Lee Iacocca and others were satisfied that the Bird no longer needed to make even a token gesture toward sport, especially since Mustang and the new Fairlanes would cater to the younger, performance-oriented crowd.

Such was the rationale behind this year's new fifth-generation Thunderbird. Perhaps the purest expression of the personal-luxury idea yet seen, it firmly fixed the Bird's shape, size, and character for the next decade, being larger, heavier, and plusher than any previous model. Replacing the convertible was a new four-door Landau sedan built on a 117.2-inch wheelbase—nearly as long as the full-size Fords' Base and Landau hardtop coupes, with wide C-pillars and tiny quarter windows that slid back into them, returned on a 114.7-inch chassis, up 1.5 inches from the 1964-66 wheelbase. Powerteams stayed the same: standard 315-horsepower 390 V-8 or optional

Ford built 197,388 Galaxie 500 hardtop coupes for 1967.

Only 7053 Falcon Sports Coupes ($2437) were built for 1967.

Fairlane GT/A: GT model combined with automatic transmission.

Ford Fairlane GT convertible was priced at $3064 for '67.

Ranchero continued on the Fairlane chassis for 1967.

Ford built 356,271 Mustang hardtops for the '67 model year.

345-bhp 428. Both were available only with Cruise-O-Matic, now with the manual-hold feature—renamed "SelectShift"—as introduced on the '66 Fairlane.

Thunderbird returned to body-on-frame construction for the first time in 10 years, a move dictated by cost considerations. The '67 frame consisted of side rails joined front and rear by torque boxes. Rigidity lost through departure of the unit body was largely replaced by stiffening ribs, sheetmetal crossmembers, and a full-length tunnel stamped into the floorpan. There were no fewer than 14 body mounts, located ahead of and behind the passenger compartment to reduce noise and vibration within.

In appearance, the '67 Bird was quite fresh, though vestiges of the past could be seen in the sail panels and at the rear. The drop-center decklid returned in muted form and taillights still stretched all the way across the back, but rear fenders had fashionable hippy contours, bodysides were more massive, and hidden headlamps appeared for the first time in a massive, "wide-oval" grille.

Long-time T-Bird stylist Bill Boyer recalled that the '67 design was actually the work of two separate studios, joined together: "It was a compromise in a way . . . [L. David] Ash had at that time what I think was called the Corporate Projects Studio, which was in competition with the Thunderbird Studio. [We] essentially did the roof, backlight, and rear half. . . . Dave was responsible for the front end. He had a design that he considered a giant Ferrari. Management liked [this] front end and our rear end with its hopped-up rear quarter. What we ended up with was an amalgamation, I would say just about down the middle. . . . The four-door just sort of happened. . . . We did a rendering in black cherry with a black vinyl roof, a four-door with center-opening doors and a "sail" on the rear door where it hinged to the body. Iacocca saw this and just about flipped. 'Let's get that four-door nailed down,' he said."

The '67 T-Bird sold well, mainly on the strength of its new looks and greater size. Interesting gimmicks also helped, like the new Tilt-Away steering wheel that moved out of the way laterally like the 1961-66 Swing-Away wheel but also tilted up to the right. The two-door Landau was the most popular model, but the new sedan scored respectable sales of nearly 25,000 for the model year. However, this would be the highest it would ever achieve, its popularity falling with each passing year until the body style was dropped with 1972's sixth-generation.

Ford's full-size platform got a heavy, "mid-life" redo to carry it through two more years. While still massive, the new look was more flowing, with hopped-up rear fenderlines, elliptical wheel openings, and a two-element horizontal grille. Hardtop coupe rooflines took on a faster slope. The LTD version had very wide C-pillars with vertical leading edges, while Galaxie 500 and XL hardtops had larger, triangular rear side windows and correspondingly slimmer pillars.

Powerteam availability for the 18-model big-Ford line was unchanged, but the 7-Litre hardtop and convertible were transmogrified into an XL option package. Priced at

$515.86, it included the 428 V-8, uprated suspension, and power brakes with front discs. The 427 was still available, but on a more restricted basis. New big-Ford features included Fingertip Speed Control, eight-track tape player, and SelectShift Cruise-O-Matic. The XL's standard engine remained the 200-bhp "Challenger" 289, but equipment now ran to "leather-smooth" all-vinyl trim, Thunderbird bucket seats, and "command" console with T-bar shift lever.

Big-Ford production declined 15 percent for the model year but XL sales hit a new low: barely 23,300, including a paltry 5161 convertibles. By contrast, the luxury LTD, now a separate series and bolstered by a new sedan,

Mustang convertible production was down to 44,808 for 1967.

A '67 prototype is pictured; $2698 bought a production model.

The sleeker '67 Mustang 2 + 2 fastback outsold the convertible.

A first for Thunderbird: the 1967 Landau four-door sedan.

scored over 110,000 sales. Once again, the most popular single big-car offering was the Galaxie 500 hardtop coupe, over 197,000 units.

The hot-selling Mustang ponycar finally got some competition this year. Chevrolet fielded its similar Camaro, and Pontiac debuted its Camaro-clone Firebird at mid-year. Plymouth's Barracuda, which arrived as a "glass-back" version of the Valiant compact at about the time Mustang bowed, received a handsome new look all its own, plus coupe and convertible body styles. Of course, Ford knew something of these plans, and had readied some new Mustang features for '67. Chief among them was a bold engine option: the broad-shouldered four-barrel, 320-bhp Thunderbird 390. With the carryover 200-cid six and the 289 V-8 trio, available powerteams now numbered 13.

Though Mustang retained its customary 108-inch wheelbase, new lower-body sheetmetal imparted a beefier look. Overall length went up by two inches, width by 2.7 inches and—to make room for the new big-block—front track was wider by 2.6 inches. (It also improved handling response.) The 2 + 2 became a true fastback, with a sweeping roofline instead of the previous semi-notch effect. Other changes were a concave tail panel and a few extra inches in the nose to match a more aggressive grille. And, oh yes: the single three-element taillamps were now three separate units. Engineers pitched in with new rubber bushings at suspension attachment points for reduced noise and vibration, and a general front suspension re-work decreased understeer without stiff springing.

Mustang shed another vestige of its Falcon origins with

a new "twin-cowl" dash dominated by a pair of large, circular dials in front of the driver, surmounted by three smaller gauges. The optional tachometer eliminated the ammeter and oil pressure gauges in the starboard slot, a retrograde step. A new Competition Handling Package (stiff springs, thick front anti-sway bar, Koni shocks, limited-slip differential, quick steering, 15-inch wheels) was available with the GT Equipment Group and not commonly specified, making it quite rare today. Still restricted to V-8s, the GT package comprised front foglamps, rocker stripes, dual exhausts, power brakes with front discs, and fat wide-oval tires. You could also get an Exterior Decor Group with thin bars on the back panel and turn signal repeater lights in a twin-scoop hood. And, as on the Fairlane, combining the GT group with automatic got you "GT/A" badges on the lower front fenders. The T-Bird's Tilt-Away steering wheel was optional across the board.

It was almost a foregone conclusion that Mustang sales would decline in the face of competition, and they did—by about 25 percent. The hardtop sustained most of the loss, but convertibles also suffered, trailing fastbacks for the first time. Yet the model year total of 474,121 units led the ponycar field by a wide margin. Interestingly, that was more than *double* the most optimistic estimates of Ford's marketing mavens for Mustang's *first* year.

The '67 GT-350 was markedly altered along the lines of Mustang's restyle but, in typical Shelby fashion, Carroll went Ford one better with an even larger big-block: a warmed-up 428 with an advertised 355 bhp but closer to 400 by most estimates. As installed in the new GT-500, it had an aluminum intake manifold and a matched set of

600-cfm Holley four-barrel carbs. The GT-500 proved popular, outselling the smaller-engine GT-350 two to one. The latter still carried the Hi-Performance 289 with the usual Shelby tweaks save the steel-tube exhaust headers. Quoted power remained at 306 bhp, but it must have been less without the headers and straight-through muffler.

To keep weight down and appearance distinctive, Shelby stylists created a fiberglass front end to complement the stock Mustang's longer hood and put two high-beam headlamps in the center of the grille. (Some later cars have these outboard to comply with state motor vehicle requirements for minimum headlamp distance.) Added were larger hood scoop, sculptured brake cooling scoops on the sides, and another set on the rear roof quarters for interior air extraction. The rear end received a spoiler and a bank of large taillights. In all, it was stunning. Customer feedback and the '67's extra weight prompted addition of power steering and brakes as mandatory options, and there were some special interior appointments not shared with the production Mustang: racing steering wheel, additional gauges, and a functional rollbar with inertia-reel shoulder harnesses.

Shelby-Mustang production forged ahead to 3225 units for the model year, much of it due to the new GT-500. The '67s saw little track action, though, and for a good reason: they were about equal parts luxury and performance, while the 1965-66 cars were more like thinly disguised race cars that could be used on the street.

But it should be noted here that Mustang won the SCCA's new Trans-American Sedan Championship in its first two years. Created for ponycars as well as domestic and imported compacts, the series was staged on road courses, and quickly earned a wide fan following. The initial 1966 schedule comprised six races, four of which went to Shelby-prepped Mustangs. The sophomore '67 season saw serious competition from the Roger Penske Camaros and Bud Moore's Mercury Cougars, but Ford again won the manufacturer's crown as Jerry Titus took Mustangs to four wins.

Ford's mid-size Fairlane received only detail refinements. Exterior trim shuffles were confined to badges, taillights, wider bodyside moldings, and a reworked grille with a chrome horizontal divider bisected by three vertical bars. Engineering changes were minimal, but 390 V-8 offerings were cut to 270-bhp two-barrel and a four-barrel rated at 320. The high-performance 427 was ostensibly available to give Ford an edge in advertised horsepower over the Pontiac GTO, Buick GS, Olds 4-4-2, and

The Lincoln Continental four-door sedan sold for $5795 in 1967.

Lincoln built 11,060 Continental hardtop coupes for 1967.

Lehmann-Peterson converted a number of Continentals into stretch limousines; this '67 reposes on Chicago's North Side.

Mercury's answer to the "ponycar" craze was the 1967 Cougar. It shared parts with Mustang, but rode a longer wheelbase.

Mercury's new *grand luxe* coupe for '67 was the $3989 Marquis.

Most popular big Merc for '67 was the Monterey hardtop coupe.

Output of 145 makes this S-55 convertible very rare indeed.

The top-line Park Lane Brougham sedan sold for $3896 in '67.

Chrysler's hemi-engine intermediates, but few were actually installed. Fairlane production fell by nearly 25 percent, landing not far above the 1965 nadir at 238,668. The 500XL and GT convertibles were quite scarce: only 1943 and 2217, respectively. The hardtops were more numerous, with respective totals of 14,871 and 18,670.

Falcon also flew along with few changes. A new "crosshair" grille bar marked the front, and Futura back panels gained a brushed-metal applique. The one new engine option was a four-barrel 289 packing 225 bhp.

This year's new 111-inch-wheelbase Cougar was probably the most interesting Mercury of the Sixties, though it's been long overshadowed among collectors by the Mustang that spawned it. Built to give Lincoln-Mercury a toehold on the apparently limitless ponycar market, it premiered as a hardtop coupe in three different trim/equipment levels: standard, GT, and XR-7. At $2851, the base Cougar cost some $350 more than Mustang, but came with a 200-bhp 289 V-8 and such premium features as hidden headlamps in a distinctive "electric shaver" grille, matching taillamps with sequential rear turn signals, vinyl bucket seats, "sport" steering wheel, deep-loop carpeting, and floor-mounted three-speed stick. The $3175 GT added the 390 V-8, commensurate handling mods, wide-oval whitewall tires, serious-sounding low-restriction exhaust system, power front disc brakes, and special identification. Compared to Mustang, Cougar was 6.7 inches longer overall, a bit wider, and 200 pounds heavier, the last a partial consequence of its more generous equipment.

Perhaps the nicest Cougar was the pretty XR-7, a mid-year addition intended to get a few poeple out of imported sports cars. C-pillars crests were its only exterior i.d., but the cabin was decked out in contemporary Euro-style, with leather-surfaced buckets and a woodgrained dash containing genuine needle instruments. Base price was only $3081 and most XR-7s delivered for around $3600, making it a price rival for open two-seaters like the Sunbeam Tiger and big Austin-Healey, and rather cheaper than a Corvette. It was a satisfying car, especially with the "Hi-Po" 225-bhp 289, and its appeal was proven by sales, which totaled close to 28,000 for the model year despite the late introduction. Overall, Cougar did about what management expected, selling upwards of 140,000 units, about 30 percent of Mustang volume.

Mercury's mid-size Comet returned with minor change-for-change-sake appearance alterations and slightly higher prices. The only lineup revision was breaking the 202 Voyager and Capri Villager wagons into a separate series. Comet was competing in a very populated field, so sales were generally down. Those who might have bought a Cyclone before now tended to want Cougars; those who might have bought a 202 or Capri marched to their Ford dealer for a Falcon or Fairlane.

In fact, despite the new Cougar, 1967 was a year of reverses for Mercury. The make remained eighth on the industry volume list but dropped about 50,000 units from 1966—good training for the hard days ahead.

The big Mercurys got new outer sheetmetal like this year's full-size Fords and stuck to the chiseled look, but were somehow clumsier. Front and rear overhangs were more massive than ever, domed hood/grille ensembles returned, and huge vertical taillamps appeared in chrome housings integrated with the back bumper. Per division chief Gar Laux's policy of keeping distance with Ford, the Monterey and Montclair stayed with their basic '66 offerings, while S-55 again became a Monterey sub-series, and the Park Lane added luxurious Brougham four-doors with and without B-pillars. There was also a new *grand luxe* hardtop coupe in a one-model series, the $3989 Marquis, distinguished by its "fast," vinyl-clad wide-quarter roof. These three ultra-luxury Mercs typically carried $4500 stickers but, again, they were competing in a crowded field and sales were slow. Monterey proved to be Mercury's only real volume full-size: Montclair, Park Lane, and the Marquis sold no more than 500 a month of any one body style.

Speaking of bodies, the Breezeway sedan was still

Mercury built 3419 Comet Cyclone GT hardtop coupes for 1967.

The 1967 Comet Villager station wagon listed at $2841.

Most popular Comet for '67 was the bottom-line 202 two door.

around. In fact, there were four of them now with the new Park Lane Brougham model and a reinstated Montclair. All looked more like the workaday Monterey/Montclair four-doors, with a conventional roof and a slightly recessed backlight that lowered only an inch or two, replacing the distinctive reverse-slant styling of yore. Significantly, the Monterey model was outsold nearly three to one by the non-Breezeway sedan. Montclair/Park Lane margins were closer, but the trend was clear: the Breezeway wouldn't last much longer.

Lincoln fell back to its pre-1965 production rate this year, perhaps because there was nothing new. The drivetrain was unchanged, the model lineup was as before, and you had to look twice to discern styling change. This would be the final year for the interesting four-door convertible, abandoned as unprofitable—it had never sold more than 3500 annually—despite a long run as the "ultimate Lincoln." Its '67 volume was the lowest ever: 2276 units.

1968

A soon-to-be-famous, soon-to-be-quoted ad slogan arrived this year: "Ford has a better idea." Actually, what Ford Motor Company had was a lot of little ideas and two big ones: revamped intermediates and a new Continental Mark. The government had a few ideas too, and they were quite visible. Like other automakers, Ford now had to fit certain "passive" safety items like shock-absorbing collapsible steering column, front and rear side marker lights, anti-glare interior trim, and non-protruding, tougher-to-open inside door handles. Of course, the list would lengthen in future years. Also, exhaust emissions standards now applied to all 50 states, not just California, and Ford was scrambling to find the best way(s) to meet them like everyone else.

Ford Division did well in what would be the American industry's best year yet. Model year production rose some 534,000 units despite a lengthy strike and a considerable drop in Mustang sales, but Ford still trailed league-leading Chevrolet by a healthy margin.

Mid-size cars took the '68 limelight, with each of the Big Three issuing newly styled and/or engineered editions of these increasingly popular models. Like Mercury, Ford introduced a new name for its high-trim intermediates: Torino, after the famous Italian city. It graced a six-model group comprising standard formal-roof hardtop coupe, four-door sedan and Squire wagon, plus GT hardtop, convertible, and a new fastback hardtop. The Fairlane name returned on a lower-priced companion line with the same body styles in base and 500 series. Chassis design and the 116-inch wheelbase (113 on wagons) carried on from 1966-67, but overall length grew by about four inches, width by a half inch, and weight by around 120 pounds.

With dimensions that now approached the full-size class, the new Fairlane/Torino was styled to bear an obvious relationship with the big Fords. Rear fenderlines had the now-obligatory hop-up, and bodysides were more radically tucked under, as on Mustang. Front and rear ends were pleasingly simple. Quad headlamps reverted to side-by-side placement within a recessed grille cavity, and front fenders jutted slightly ahead to house combined

Big Fords sported new sheet metal; this '68 LTD cost $3153.

Ford built 50,048 XL fastback coupes for '68, this one a GT.

Prices started at $3108 for the 1968 Galaxie 500 convertible. Ford cranked out 11,832 of them for the model year.

Most popular LTD was the hardtop sedan; 61,755 were built.

Output of Ford's Country Squire reached 91,770 for 1968.

parking/side marker lamps. The new fastback hardtop was a real head-turner, its roofline taken directly from the Mustang 2+2. But unlike previous sloped-roof intermediates such as AMC's Marlin, this one avoided looking fat and heavy via an upswept rear side window line and a deep backlight.

Fairlane/Torino engine selections were the usual array, but there was a new number among V-8s: 302, simply the 289 with a longer, 3.0-inch stroke. Rated at 210 bhp and

engineered with emissions standards in mind, it was standard for Torino GTs at the beginning of the year, then became an option at mid-season, replaced by a two-barrel 289. That engine lost 5 bhp to 1968 emissions tuning (down to 195 bhp), as did the optional two-pot 390 (now 265). The four-barrel 390 gained five ponies (for 325 total). Standard for non-GTs was the sturdy 200-cid six. It, too, fell victim to emissions controls at 115 bhp, five fewer than before.

The Falcon Futura wagon retailed at $2728 for 1968.

A 302-cid V-8 was the largest engine ever offered in a Falcon.

Ford built 5310 Fairlane Torino GT convertibles for '68.

Most popular Torino was the hardtop, with output of 35,964.

247

Ford's intermediates were rebodied for '68, and grew a bit bigger and heavier. Here a Torino GT fastback with the 390 V-8.

Torino got extra exposure by pacing the 1968 Indy 500.

Mustang convertible production dipped to 25,376 for 1968.

Here a '68 Mustang GT/SC prototype (later, California Special).

Ford built 42,581 '68 Mustang fastbacks, some with GT option.

Performance mills also changed during the year. At the start was one 427, a single four-barrel unit rated at 390 bhp thanks to a milder cam profile and first-time use of hydraulic lifters. But it was available only with automatic, not what the drag set wanted. Accordingly, it was phased out by spring in favor of the 428 Cobra Jet, a huskier version of the T-Bird/big-Ford engine. For drag racing and insurance purposes it was advertised at 335 bhp on 10.7:1 compression, but was undoubtedly much stronger.

After a lackluster '67 NASCAR season, Ford roared back, notching 20 wins—more than any other make and twice as many as it had in each of the previous two years. David Pearson won the championship. The new mid-size fastback was a big help, its superior aerodynamics having been conceived with an eye to long-haul superspeedway events. It was the same story in USAC, with A.J. Foyt's Fairlane on top, and Benny Parsons was king with his

Torino in ARCA (Auto Racing Club of America). There was only one problem: the rival Mercury Cyclone—faster still in long-distance sprints because of its smoother front end, a fact Cale Yarborough and company rubbed in every chance they got.

Of course, the race that mattered most to Dearborn accountants was the sales race, and here the new Fairlane/Torino was a champ. Production climbed better than 50 percent over '67 to a record 372,000 cars. Significantly, the most popular single offering was the slick GT fastback at 74,135, and more than 32,000 of the Fairlane 500s were sold. Convertibles, by contrast, were falling out of favor: just 5310 GTs and a mere 3761 Fairlane 500s.

Mustang sales dipped to about 300,000, good but not great next to earlier years. The likely reasons were continuing strong competition—and more of it now, with AMC's handsome new Javelin—and familiarity. Considering there were more engines and other options than

The 1968 Thunderbird wore a "bold" new grille and a two-piece wraparound front bumper. Bucket seats were optional.

The $4845 Landau coupe was Thunderbird's most popular 1963 model.

The T-Bird four-door Landau saw production of 21,925 units.

ever, this decline was a bit worrisome.

Since a major facelift had been just carried out, Mustang's '68 changes were limited. The grille was more deeply inset and the crossbars omitted, leaving the horse to "float" in its chrome frame, and the grid-pattern dummy rear fender scoops were erased. A new option was a distinctive C-stripe tape treatment, so-called because it started at the front fenders and swept back to the rear fender indentations, where it looped around and ran forward. Compression drops took 5 horses from the base six and optional two-barrel 289, but the 390 rose by 5 to 335 bhp. Transmission choices stayed the same except that sixes could no longer be teamed with four-speed manual. The 390 was still available with heavy-duty three-speed. The 289 was ousted at mid-year by a 220-bhp two-barrel 302. As in the Fairlane, it was a reasonable performance/economy compromise between the base six and the high-power V-8s, and reasonably priced at about $200. A

250-cid six with 155 bhp, lifted from the Ford truck line, was added at the same time.

To counter Chevy's growing escalation of the horsepower war, Ford offered its mighty 427 V-8 as a new Mustang option. Running on 10.9:1 compression, it packed the same wallop as in the mid-sizers but was also restricted to Cruise-O-Matic. Still, typical 0-60 mph times were in the neighborhood of six seconds, making this the fastest showroom-stock Mustang yet. But the engine's heaviness (which tended to overwhelm the front suspension) and a formidable $755 surcharge kept it from being very popular.

As with Fairlane/Torino, the 427 was hastily retired from the Mustang program at mid-year and the 335-bhp 428 Cobra Jet substituted. A quarter-mile zip of 13.56 seconds at a trap speed of 106.64 seconds caused *Hot Rod* magazine to sing its praises. Also announced was a fortified 302 with high-compression heads, larger valves,

Lincoln built its 1,000,000th car on March 25, 1968 in its Wixom, Michigan plant. Behind it is a 1925 Lincoln Town Car.

wilder cam timing, and a pair of four-barrel carbs. Humorously rated at a 240 bhp, it was clearly developed for Trans-Am racing, but Ford had trouble getting it into production after getting SCCA's okay, and few were actually made. It didn't matter: Mark Donohue's Camaro won 10 events to Mustang's three, and Chevy collected the manufacturers' trophy.

New to Mustang's lengthening options list was the Sports Trim Group, with woodgrain dash, two-tone hood paint (also available separately), Comfort-Weave vinyl seat inserts, and wheel lip moldings on sixes, plus styled-steel wheels and larger tires with V-8. A spring/summer Sprint package offered GT C-stripes, pop-open gas cap, and full wheel covers plus, with V-8, styled wheels and wide-oval tires. The GT Equipment Group remained essentially the same. Despite all the go-go goodies, withering installation rates suggested buyers were shifting from

The 1968 Lincoln Continental Coupe retailed for $5736.

pure sport to a combination of sport and luxury. Other new extras included rear window defogger and Fingertip Speed Control.

Appearing this year only was a somewhat rare, limited-production Mustang called the California Special and available primarily to Golden State buyers. Styled along Shelby lines, it was basically the standard hardtop with a ducktail spoiler above wide taillight clusters, plus mid-bodyside tape stripes and a plain grille cavity with foglamps and no Mustang emblem.

The real Shelby-Mustangs got another facelift: more conventional front, segmented taillamps incorporating sequential turn indicators, and new convertibles with built-in rollbar. The 302 small-block became standard GT-350 power, and luxury options like air conditioning, tilt wheel, tinted glass, and AM/FM stereo now outnumbered performance items. At mid-year, the GT-500's 428 V-8 was superseded by the new Cobra Jet for the retitled GT-500KR ("King of the Road"). Again, the big-blocks proved more popular, outselling the GT-350 two to one. Model year production rose for the third straight year, reaching 4450 units. Convertibles were predictably much rarer than fastbacks. The totals were 404 GT-350s, 402 early GT-500s, and a mere 318 KRs.

A more important change for Shelby was the late-'67 production shift from Carroll's Los Angeles facility to Michigan, where the A.O. Smith Company converted stock Mustangs under contract. From here on, Ford would handle all Shelby promotion, advertising, and model development.

The encore fifth-generation Thunderbird saw minor

trim shuffling and a new engine. Sales dipped some 13,000 units to 64,931, the lowest since 1963. At the start of the season, the familiar 315-bhp 390 was standard and a new 429 the lone option, but only the larger V-8 was being fitted by the new year.

One of the "385-series" engines (so-called because of the first design's 3.85-inch stroke), the 429 was a cousin to Lincoln's big 460, also new this year. Both would soon spread to lesser Ford/Mercury models, including intermediates, because of their greater adaptability to emissions control. With bore and stroke of 4.36 × 3.59 inches, the 429 arrived with 360 bhp, and would continue powering T-Birds well into the Seventies.

This year's full-size Fords were mechanically unchanged apart from emissions-tuned engines. Another round of lower-body surgery plus fresh nose and tail grafts yielded a more massive, yet still flowing, appearance. Sail panels on formal notchback hardtops became less imposing (and obstructive to driver vision), while LTD, XL, and the Country Squire wagon acquired headlamps hidden behind retracting lids, matched to a special cross-hatch grille. The hoary old 427 V-8, considerably tamer than before, remained the top power option throughout the model run.

Ford's big XL fastback and convertible lost their standard bucket seats at mid-year, but putting in a front bench and deleting a few standard items allowed a price cut. The 7-Litre package was replaced by a $205 GT Equipment Group tied to the 390 or 427 V-8s, with heavy-duty suspension, the requisite stripes and emblems, power front disc brakes, and wide-oval tires. While big-Ford sales dropped fractionally as a whole, XL demand shot up to its highest level since 1964: more than 56,000. The convertible accounted for only 6066 orders.

Falcon was largely ignored. The only cosmetic change of note was a new twin-element mesh grille that would continue through the compact's demise in 1970. As elsewhere at Ford, the 302 V-8 was an extra-cost alternative to the base six and optional two-barrel 289, and the automatic transmission got SelectShift manual override.

By any measurement, 1968 was a vintage year for Lincoln-Mercury, both makes setting new production records. Dominating headlines was the return of the Continental Mark. Logically, it should have been called Mark VI, a designation that actually finished first in public-opinion surveys. But since this was a lineal successor to the Mark II, the embarrassing 1958-60 Marks III/IV/V were forgotten and the newcomer arrived as the Mark III.

Officially part of the Lincoln line, this second Mark III is the Ford product most closely associated with Edsel's son, Henry Ford II. Just as he'd rejected the first Mark II design ("I wouldn't give a dime for that"), the outspoken board chairman is said to have okayed the Mark III by saying, "I would like to drive that one home." But its basic concepts and premises are more correctly credited to Lee Iacocca, not yet company president but already playing an important role.

Like the Mark II, the '68 Mark III was the work of a

Mercury built 3248 Montego MX convertible coupes for 1968.

The 1968 Mercury Cyclone fastback retailed for $2768.

Output of '68 Cyclone fastbacks (including GTs) reached 12,270.

Buyers preferred the Montego MX, especially with Brougham trim.

Mercury produced 9328 Montego MX station wagons for 1968.

1968

The 4122-pound Mercury Park Lane convertible listed at $3822 in 1968. Only 1112 were built for the model year.

Two-door Park Lanes offered simulated wood trim in 1968.

Mercury boasted about its "relationship to the Continental."

Mercury built only 3965 Marquis fastback coupes for 1968.

Compare the roofline of this Montclair and the Marquis (left).

stellar team, headed by L. David Ash, with Art Querfeld assisting and Ralph Peters the product planner. Also involved was Hermann C. Brunn, son of the late Hermann A. Brunn, the coachbuilder who produced most of Lincoln's prewar custom bodies. The project began in September 1965, entrusted to the Special Development Office at the Dearborn Design Center.

Iacocca insisted that, unlike the II, this new Mark must be a profitmaker. The first production cars delivered for about $7000, about 30 percent below the Mark II's price. (Given the rate of inflation, the $10,000 Mark II would have been about $11,000 in 1968 dollars.) So this was very much a volume luxury car, as sales soon confirmed: 7770

for the abbreviated '68 model year, 23,088 for '69, and about 25,000 annually for 1970-71.

(There is some confusion about model years. Introduced in April 1968, the Mark III was ostensibly a '69 model, but Ford records break out 7770 as '68s. This probably represents sales through the normal new car introduction month of September.)

Though Iacocca likes to take credit for it, the Mark III's design theme was self-evident: a modern interpretation of the early, close-coupled Continental coupe, with similar long hood/short deck proportions, wide-quarter roof, and some vestige of the trademark outside spare tire. By the time of the final clay model in October 1965, designers had settled on a squarish, "classic" grille flanked by panels hiding the headlamps, and clean, chiseled lines flowing back to a short deck on which the spare tire outline was even more pronounced than the Mark II's. The hood was the longest of any American car. Parking lamps and taillights were neatly set into the fender edges. Wrapping it up was a choice of 26 colors, including four new "Moondust" custom finishes with aluminum flake pigmentation, hand-rubbed to produce a deep, rich metallic finish. Counting the various interiors, three vinyl-roof colors, and eight accent stripes, Mark III trim combinations numbered no fewer than 4752. Hermann Brunn contributed a five-pod dash with woodgrain accents and easy-to-reach controls, plus large, comfortable seats. The latter, he noted, "have wrinkles. We put them in deliberately because we think they denote comfort and luxury."

The Mark III rode a 117.2-inch wheelbase, about nine inches shorter than the Mark II's and the same as the four-door Thunderbird's. In fact, it was a T-Bird underneath, sharing basic structure and suspension. As it turned out, the Mark III wheelbase was also exactly the same as that of Cadillac's new front-drive '67 Eldorado. Although the latter was more technically advanced, the Continental seemed to have more magic in its name. Despite Cadillac's big distribution/production advantages, the Mark almost matched Eldo production in its four-year lifespan, and never trailed by more than 2000 a year.

With demise of the four-door convertible, Lincoln's senior Continental line was back to two models, hardtop and sedan. Another detail touch-up brought side marker lamps to front and rear fenders and a temporary end to the standup Continental star hood mascot, both per federal requirements. Emissions standards prompted adoption of the new 385-series V-8 in 460-cubic-inch form. Despite a smaller bore and shorter stroke (4.36 × 3.75 inches), it produced 15 more horsepower than the superseded 460, a total of 365. Helped by the Mark III, Lincoln model year production reached a new high: 64,000 units.

Mercury developments generally paralleled those of equivalent Ford lines—with some interesting differences. Comet, for instance, was reduced to just a single price-leader hardtop ($2477 base), and the newly named Montego and Montego MX stepped in for the Capri and Caliente series, as well as corresponding wagons. Following big-car practice, the Montego MX sedan and hardtop could be ordered in fancy Brougham versions, distinguished mainly by vinyl roof, special insignia, and nicer cabin appointments. Cyclone lost its convertibles but gained the new fastback, offered along with a notchback hardtop coupe in base and GT form. All the mid-size Mercs wore Fairlane/Torino styling, but stood apart with their domed noses and unique taillamps and body trim.

Cougar continued with standard and XR-7 hardtops as individual models, but the GT option returned along with a new GT-E package. The latter, identified by twin dummy hood scoops and silver-grey lower body, included beefed-up suspension and tires, power brakes with front discs, SelectShift Merc-O-Matic and, new to Cougar, the

This 1968 Cougar prototype varied a bit from the final version.

The Cougar 7.0 Liter GTE put out 390 horsepower in 1968.

big 390-bhp 427 V-8. Thankfully, the handsome styling was left alone apart from the mandatory side marker lamps. Interim engine changes paralleled Mustang's. A '68 rarity—only 300-400 built—was the XR-7G, the letter honoring race driver Dan Gurney, captain of the short-lived Cougar Trans-Am team. Officially a separate model and similar to the mid-'67 Dan Gurney Special, it boasted foglamps, special hood with scoop and racing-style lock pins, chrome wire-spoke wheels, and a vinyl top with power sunroof. Yet despite all this variety, Cougar sales were on a five-year slide. The '68 total was down about 41,000 from 1967's nearly 151,000.

Apart from meeting "fed regs," Mercury's full-size line mostly marked time, though the sporty S-55s departed for lack of sales, and Breezeway ventilation was now an option instead of a body style. Following L-M's newly established divisional look, the hood/grille ensemble was more prominently domed, and parking/turn indicators moved into the front fender edges *a la* Lincoln. Wagon-style simulated-wood bodyside panelling was an odd new option for two-door Park Lanes, and didn't find many takers.

As management had intended, the big Mercs were now firmly in the upper end of the medium-price field. Over 99 percent were sold with power steering and automatic this year, while 60 percent had air conditioning. Sales were good throughout the line. The palatial and pricey Colony Park wagons accounted for 20,000 units alone, and total big-Merc deliveries passed 120,000. The intermediates added another 120,000 and Cougar 112,000, making Mercury's grand total about 360,000 for the model year. Sales jumped again when the '69s arrived late in the year, boosting calendar '68 volume to over 420,000. Mercury was still eighth in the industry but, for the moment at least, it could apparently do no wrong.

1969

Ads said Ford was "The Going Thing" this year. There certainly was a lot going on at Ford Division: a new-generation Mustang, a larger small-block V-8, the last of the Falcons, and larger, redesigned big cars. Also, some *very* hot intermediates arrived to carry Dearborn's performance colors on and off the track, while the Shelby-Mustang was about to depart. Two significant executive shifts were in place by new model announcement day. In a move that sent shockwaves through the industry, chairman Henry Ford II appointed recently resigned General Motors executive vice-president Semon E. "Bunkie" Knudsen as the firm's new president in early 1968. Also, John B. Naughton was promoted to the general manager's post at Ford Division.

In production, Ford's model year total improved by about 75,000 units to a bit beyond 1.8 million (not counting 3150 Shelby-Mustangs), the full-size line accounting for slightly more than a million. Chevrolet lost about 25,000 but still tallied a bit more than 2.1 million cars.

Knudsen's defection astonished Detroit. There probably hadn't been such a startling shift since the Twenties, when Bunkie's father, William S. "Big Bill" Knudsen, left Ford after an argument with the elder Henry. He went to Chevrolet and built it into a Ford-beater. Now his son was trying to make Ford more competitive with Chevy for the Seventies.

Much of that involved performance. Knudsen wanted lower, sleeker cars, with particular emphasis on fastbacks. In fact, he said that while "the long hood/short-deck concept will continue . . . there will be a trend toward designing cars for specific segments of the market." While he denied Ford had any intention of building a sports car, he did hint that an experimental mid-engine car was being developed. (This turned out to be the Mach 2, a design exercise begun in 1966, making liberal use of Mustang components in a curvy two-seat coupe package.) He also assured the press that Ford's stock-car racing effort would continue.

The compact Falcon celebrated its l0th birthday this year but was virtually unchanged. Models stayed the same, and deleting the four-barrel 289 V-8 left the 220-horsepower 302 as the most powerful engine option. Production dropped as buyers deserted compacts for the slightly more costly intermediates or lower-priced smaller imports. But Ford had sensed the shift and was readying a new compact. Falcon would hang on, unloved and unpromoted, through the end of calendar '69, when it was unceremoniously dropped.

Few changes attended this year's Thunderbird. Besides the usual trim shifts, the Landau hardtop lost its vestigial rear-quarter side windows, creating one of the all-time great blind spots. Minor chassis tuning gave two-doors

flatter cornering and a slightly lower ride height. The year's major new option was one that would soon spread through the U.S. industry: an electrically operated sunroof, harking back to the 1960 Bird. Bucket seats had moved to the options column for '68, and Landau sedan and hardtop buyers continued to show a marked preference for the now-standard front bench. Overall T-Bird production declined by about 15,700 units for the model year to slightly more than 49,000—the lowest since the abbreviated 1958 run. The picture wouldn't change much for the next few years.

Ford now filled a rather obvious displacement gap in its corporate engine lineup with a new 351-cubic-inch V-8, basically a 302 redesigned by Phillip A. Martel, who'd come to Ford from GM back in 1950. (He was also responsible for the big 385-series engines of 1968.) Directly de-

Most popular LTD for '69 was the hardtop sedan (113,168 built).

Wheelbase stretched to 121 inches on the big Fords for 1969.

Ford's XL SportsRoof with "tunneled backlite" sold for $3069.

scended from the original 1962 small-block, it used the 302's 4.00-inch bore and a half-inch-longer stroke (3.50 inches). As author Phil Hall observed in *Fearsome Fords*, actual displacement was 351.86 cid, but the company called it "351" to avoid confusion with the earlier 352 Y-block. It was optional in 1969 intermediates, full-sizers, and ponycars except the new Mustang Mach 1 and Cougar Eliminator, where it was standard.

It should be noted that the 351 we're talking about here is the "Windsor" unit, not the more famous "Cleveland" engine. The former got its nickname from the Canadian plant that built it starting in the fall of 1968, a full year before Cleveland production began (in Ohio). While both had the same bore/stroke dimensions, the Windsor featured increased bulkhead strength, a deck height raised 1.27 inches, and a new crankshaft with larger main and

crankpin journals. Its intake manifold was of drop-center design, and its valvetrain included "positive-stop" rocker arm studs. Its 4.38-inch bore spacing, as in the original Fairlane 221, was retained for the Cleveland, which became the basis for nearly all of Dearborn's high-performance cars from 1970 through 1974. That relegated the Windsor to a secondary role, used mainly with low compression and two-barrel carburetion.

Ford spent some $100 million in tooling the Cleveland. Its block casting was unique, with an integral timing chain chamber and water crossover passage at the front. Its deck height was exactly one inch higher than the 302's block. Cylinder heads differed dramatically from the Windsor's, with valves canted 9.5 degrees from the cylinder axis for modified-wedge-type combustion chambers. In addition, the intakes were tilted 4 degrees, 15 minutes

The Galaxie 500 wore exposed lights, simpler grille than LTD.

The '69 Mach I started at $3139, offered engines up to 355 bhp.

The '69 Mustang Boss 429: exotic engine, limited production.

The legendary Mustang Boss 302 saw only 1934 built for 1969.

Mustang's posh model for 1969: the $2866 Grande (22,182 built).

The street version of the 1969 Boss 302 sold for $3720.

Only 5931 Falcon Futura Sports Coupes were produced for 1969.

Falcon Futura four door listed at $2498; 11,850 were built.

Falcon's priciest 1969 model was the four-door wagon ($2771).

Thunderbird's $4964 two-door Landau was its best-seller in '69.

With 15,695 built, four-door Landau was losing popularity.

forward and the exhaust valves 3 degrees backward for shorter port areas with more direct gas flow. The widest possible spacing was chosen for maximum valve size. Intakes had a 2.19-inch head diameter, while the forged-steel exhausts were 1.71 inches across their aluminized heads.

This year's big Fords were fresh from the tires up. Basic chassis and suspension changed only in detail, but wheelbase stretched two inches, to 121 (where it would remain through 1978), the first such increase since 1960. Overall length went up too, and there were fractional gains in track and overall width. The 21-model lineup began with Custom and Custom 500 sedans and wagons, progressing through seven Galaxie 500s, two XLs, and the posh LTD sedan, hardtops, and Country Squire wagons.

Styling was a nice mixture of Lincoln-Mercury pretense and the svelte brawn of recent big Fords. Hoods were longer, rear decks shorter, bodysides more shapely. Headlamps were again concealed behind flip-up doors on LTDs, Squires, and XLs, which shared an imposing, full-width eggcrate grille with protruding center. Lesser models had a flatter, plainer face. The fastback hardtop coupe, offered as a Galaxie 500 or XL, was renamed "SportsRoof"—as were all Ford fastbacks this year—and acquired tunnel-roof or "flying buttress" styling, with a near-vertical backlight flanked by sloping outrigger sail panels. Inside was what Ford called its "front room," a cockpit-style dash curved in front of the driver and swept away to the right to give passengers, as the brochure boasted, "more room than Ford has ever offered before."

A redrawn big-Ford engine chart scratched the old 427 as the top option for two versions of the 429 "Thunder Jet": two-barrel 320 bhp and four-barrel 360 bhp, both running 10.5:1 compression and requiring premium gas. The 150-bhp 240-cid "Big Six" was base power for all except the LTD and Country Squire, which had a 200-bhp 302. Also available were a two-barrel, 265-bhp 390 and, at mid-season, the new 351 Windsor in 250-bhp two-barrel form. Four-speed manual gearbox was still optional, but only with the four-barrel 429.

A new Mustang had been planned long before Bunkie Knudsen arrived. While he wouldn't have much influence on this or any other Dearborn product until the '71 models, he was able to make a few last-minute changes for '69. He also lured stylist Larry Shinoda from his former employer to head Ford's Special Design Center. Working under GM design vice-president William L. Mitchell since the early Sixties, Shinoda had been involved with such stunning show cars as the 1960 Sting Ray racer, Corvette Mako Shark, and Corvair Monza GT and Super Spyder. He favored wind-cheating shapes and eye-catching aerodynamic addenda: spoilers, front air dams, low-cut noses, voluptuous lines. These and other GM characteristics would show up on a variety of Dearborn cars.

The '69 Mustang was mostly finished when Shinoda arrived, with dimensions that marked a departure from

continued on page 273

Mustang was undoubtedly Ford's biggest success of the Sixties, a spectacular seller that opened up an entirely new market. Many enthusiasts still consider the initial 1965-66 models the best of the breed. Left: The debut-year convertible listed at $2614 without options, which were plentiful. This profile view highlights the graceful long-hood/short-deck proportions that would become synonymous with the breed named in Mustang's honor as "ponycars." Bottom: Appearance changed only in detail for '66, as on this hardtop, which had a suggested base retail price of $2416. Engine choices comprised 200-cid six and Ford's delightful 289-cid small-block V-8 with 200, 225, or 271 horsepower. Center: Recognizing Mustang's potential in production sports car racing, ex-Ferrari driver Carroll Shelby offered specially tuned and tweaked versions of the Mustang fastback as the GT-350 beginning in 1965. Shown is the "street" '66 with a nominal 306 bhp from its 289 V-8. Shelby also offered a race-ready model with 350 bhp and more mods.

*T*his page, above: The Thunderbird Town Landau hardtop for 1966, the last year for the third-generation four-seat design. **Right:** 1966 Ford Falcon Futura Sport Coupe. **Below:** Ford's '67 Fairlane 500 Sport Coupe. **Opposite page, top:** Like all '67 Mustangs, the convertible sported a more aggressive look. **Center:** The rare '67 Mercury Monterey S-55 convertible. **Bottom left:** The '68 Mustang GT/SC was only for Southern California. **Bottom right:** Mercury's new-for-'69 Marauder X100 hardtop.

*R*ight: *1968 Ford Galaxie 500XL Sports-Roof hardtop coupe.* **Below:** *Buick-like sweepspear sculpturing marked 1969 Mercury Cougars like this convertible.* **Bottom left:** *1968 Mercury Cougar hardtop coupe.* **Bottom right and opposite top:** *Ford Torino Talladega arrived for 1969 to qualify the slippery fastback for NASCAR racing.* **Opposite center:** *Mercury's hottest '69 Cougar was the Eliminator, here in hardtop form.* **Opposite bottom:** *1970 Cougar Eliminator hardtop with 351CJ engine was a rare animal.*

260

*T*op: Cyclone Spoiler was Mercury's mid-size 1970 performer. Only 1631 were built. **Above left:** Ford's new-for-'70 Maverick subcompact beat Mustang's first-year sales record with nearly 579,000 units. This two-door arrived first. Initial base price was a low $1995. **Above right:** Mercury unleashed a bigger, plusher Cougar for '71. Here, the $3629 XR-7 hardtop. **Right:** The rare big-block 1970 Mustang Boss 429. Just 498 were built. **Opposite page, top:** 1972 Mercury Montego MX Brougham hardtop coupe. **Bottom:** The new-for-'72 Continental Mark IV poses with **(left to right)** the '68 Mark III, '56 Mark II, '48 "Mark I."

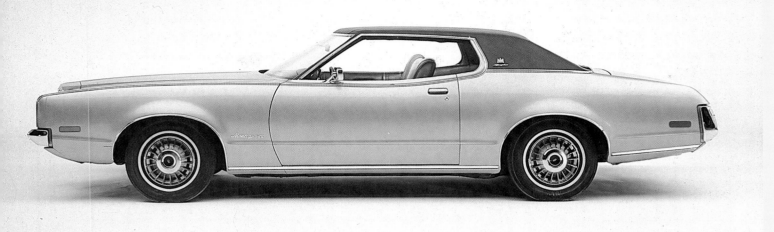

This page: Like Cougar, the fourth-generation 1971-73 Mustangs were as big as Ford's ponycars would ever get. *Right:* The '73 Grandé hardtop. *Below right:* The '73 convertible. *Below:* Downsized Mustang II began a successful new chapter in ponycar history. Here, the debut '74 Ghia coupe. *Bottom left:* Ford's Gran Torino hardtop coupe for '73. *Bottom right:* New-for-'75 Mercury Bobcat was a spiffier Pinto. Here, the '78 Runabout hatchback. *Opposite page, top:* LTD II succeeded Torino as Ford's '77 mid-size. This is the '78 Brougham pillared hardtop coupe. *Center left:* The impressively sized 1978 Lincoln Town Coupe. *Center right:* Lincoln Continental Mark V was base-priced at $12,318 for '78. *Bottom:* Replacing Maverick for '78, the Ford Fairmont introduced the "Fox" platform that would be used for a number of Dearborn's future cars. Initial offerings comprised two-door sedan *(foreground)*, wagon *(left, with Squire option)*, and four-door.

264

261

Top: Cyclone Spoiler was Mercury's mid-size 1970 performer. Only 1631 were built. Above left: Ford's new-for-'70 Maverick subcompact beat Mustang's first-year sales record with nearly 579,000 units. This two-door arrived first. Initial base price was a low $1995. Above right: Mercury unleashed a bigger, plusher Cougar for '71. Here, the $3629 XR-7 hardtop. Right: The rare big-block 1970 Mustang Boss 429. Just 498 were built. Opposite page, top: 1972 Mercury Montego MX Brougham hardtop coupe. Bottom: The new-for '72 Continental Mark IV poses with (left to right) the '68 Mark III, '56 Mark II, '48 "Mark I."

This page: Like Cougar, the fourth-generation 1971-73 Mustangs were as big as Ford's ponycars would ever get. *Right:* The '73 Grandé hardtop. *Below right:* The '73 convertible. *Below:* Downsized Mustang II began a successful new chapter in ponycar history. Here, the debut '74 Ghia coupe. *Bottom left:* Ford's Gran Torino hardtop coupe for '73. *Bottom right:* New-for-'75 Mercury Bobcat was a spiffier Pinto. Here, the '78 Runabout hatchback. *Opposite page, top:* LTD II succeeded Torino as Ford's '77 mid-size. This is the '78 Brougham pillared hardtop coupe. *Center left:* The impressively sized 1978 Lincoln Town Coupe. *Center right:* Lincoln Continental Mark V was base-priced at $12,318 for '78. *Bottom:* Replacing Maverick for '78, the Ford Fairmont introduced the "Fox" platform that would be used for a number of Dearborn's future cars. Initial offerings comprised two-door sedan *(foreground)*, wagon *(left, with Squire option)*, and four-door.

*T**his page, top left:** Companion to Fairmont, the 1978 Mercury Zephyr in Z-7 coupe form.* ***Top right:*** *1978 Grand Marquis pillared hardtop sedan headed Mercury's last traditional full-size lineup.* ***Above left:*** *The 1978 Mercury Monarch sedan.* ***Above right:*** *The Mercury Cougar XR-7 for '78.* ***Right:*** *1978 Lincoln Versailles.* ***Opposite page, top:*** *Ford's newly downsized '79 LTD Landau coupe and Country Squire wagon.* ***Center left:*** *Ford's 1980 Fairmont Futura coupe with the rare turbo engine option.* ***Center right:*** *A cleaner and lighter new Mustang bowed for '79. Here, the standard coupe with optional 5.0-liter V-8.* ***Bottom:*** *Downsized 1980 Continental Mark VI offered a new four-door to supplement the traditional coupe.*

This page, right: Ninth-generation 1980 Thunderbird was the second to be downsized. Here, the ritzy Town Landau coupe. **Below left:** Mercury 1981 Cougar LS sedan. **Below right:** Smaller new Continental sedan bowed for '82. **Bottom:** Ford's '82 Escort three-door and wagon were joined by a new five-door sedan **(foreground)** and the sporty EXP coupe **(background)**. **Opposite page, top left:** 1983 Mercury Capri GS. **Top right:** Mercury's Escort-based '83 Lynx RS three-door. **Center:** 1983 Thunderbird, the first "aero" Ford. **Bottom:** 1983 Mercury Cougar LS.

270

Opposite page, top left: 1983 Mercury LN7, cousin to Ford's EXP. Top right: Aero-styled front-drive Tempo succeeded Fairmont as Ford's compact. Here, the '85 GLX coupe. Upper center: Merkur XR4Ti arrived for '85 from Ford Germany. Lower center left: Ford's potent '84 LTD LX sedan. Lower center right: From '85, the Ford Thunderbird 30th Anniversary edition. Bottom left: 1985 Ford EXP. Bottom right: The mid-'85 turbocharged Mustang SVO. This page, left: Lincoln's 1986 Continental Mark VII LSC. Below left: 1986 Mercury Sable wagon. Below right: Ford's slick new '86 Taurus sedan in LX trim. Bottom: 1987 Mercury Cougar XR-7.

*F*ord Motor Company speeds towards its 100th anniversary with solid commitments to quality, efficient aerodynamic design, and driving fun. **Top:** New-for-'87 Thunderbird LX offers traditional luxury, contemporary styling. **Right:** Turbo Coupe remains the sportiest T-Bird for '87, but packs more punch than its predecessors by adopting the intercooled turbocharged four from the Mustang SVO. The TC's standard anti-lock brake system, also new to Thunderbird, is a significant safety advance in this price class. **Below:** On sale since 1983, the Mustang convertible returns for '87 in high-performance GT trim (shown) and four-cylinder LX form. Like T-Bird, all Mustangs gain a different appearance via redesigned, low-drag noses with Euro-style flush headlamps.

Standard engine for the '69 Torino Cobra was the 335-bhp 428.

Ford built 2552 Torino GT convertibles for the '69 model year.

Torino GTs started at $2840; this one has 428 Cobra Jet power.

Weight was up to 3128 pounds on the Torino four-door sedan.

continued from page 256
the original ponycar concept. It retained the customary 108-inch wheelbase but emerged four inches longer (most of it in front overhang), about a half-inch wider, and some 140 pounds heavier. Unit construction was retained for the all-new bodyshell, which continued successful appearance themes. There was a more prominent "mouth" grille with eggcrate insert that carried two extra headlamps at its outer ends in place of the optional (and mostly ineffective) foglamps of previous years. The old side sculpturing was erased, but rear fenders now bulged noticeably above the wheel arches. Taillights were still vertical clusters but no longer recessed in the back panel, which was flat instead of concave. The same three body styles returned, and the SportsRoof fastback acquired flip-out rear side windows. Driving range was increased by enlarging fuel tank capacity from 17 to 20 gallons.

Dimensional increases were also evident inside: 2.5 inches more front shoulder room and 1.5 inches more hip-room, thanks to thinner doors; a modified frame cross-member under the front seat added a significant 2.5 inches to rear legroom. Trunk capacity was enlarged "13

Even at $6873, the 1969 Continental Mark III found 23,088 buyers. Power was supplied by a 365-bhp 460-cid V-8.

Mark III rode same wheelbase as the T-Bird four-door Landau.

The 1969 Continental coupe sold for $5830; 9032 were built.

to 29 percent," but it wasn't much of a gain because there hadn't been much space to begin with. A Mustang trunk could still just manage a two-suiter and little else.

Mustang model permutations expanded by four, two appearing at mid-season. Priced about $230 over the standard hardtop was the Grande, aimed at personal-luxury ponycars like Cougar and Firebird. Features ran to vinyl roof with identifying script, twin color-keyed door mirrors, wire wheel covers, pinstriping just below the belt-line, and bright wheel well, rocker panel, and rear deck moldings. Dash and door panels were trimmed in imitation teakwood, a good copy of the real thing, and some 55 extra pounds of sound insulation were added. More exciting was the $3139 Mach 1 fastback. Encroaching on Shelby territory, it boasted simulated rear-quarter air scoops, decklid spoiler, flat-black hood with NASCAR-style tiedowns, and a functional "Shaker" scoop that sat atop the air cleaner and stuck up through a hole in the hood (and earned its name by vibrating madly).

Mustang engine availability also expanded. The hardy 200-cid six was standard for all but Mach 1, while the 155-bhp 250 six cost $39 extra. V-8 offerings ranged from the 220-bhp 302 to the 335-bhp 428 Cobra Jet, available with or without Ram Air induction. Mach 1 came with the new 351 in two-barrel, 250-bhp regular-fuel tune, optional for other models, as was a high-compression four-barrel unit with 290 bhp. Rounding things out was a four-barrel 320-bhp 390 with 10.5:1 compression.

For all-out performance, the Cobra Jet was king. Devel-

oped by Ford's Light Vehicle Powertrain Department under Tom Feaheney, it was thoughtfully combined with a tuned suspension engineered by Matt Donner. Beginning with the heavy-duty '67 setup, he mounted one shock ahead of the rear axle line and the other behind it to reduce axle tramp in hard acceleration. Result: a street machine that handled like a Trans-Am racer. The big-engine Mustang still exhibited final oversteer, but it was more easily controlled with the accelerator. "The first Cobra Jets we built were strictly for drag racing," Feaheney recalled. "Wheel hop was damped out by staggering the rear shocks. It was not a new idea, but it worked." As for straightline performance, a Cobra Jet Mach 1 would run the quarter-mile in about 13.5 seconds, making it one of the world's fastest production four-seaters.

Mid-model year brought two very exotic Mustang fastbacks: the Boss 302 and Boss 429, both created to qualify for racing. The latter was ostensibly to satisfy NASCAR officials, but it was actually conceived for the dragstrip. Priced at $4798, it carried a modified 429 V-8 with thin-wall block and semi-hemispherical combustion chambers ("crescent-shaped" in Ford parlance), plus aluminum heads, beefed-up main bearings, and cross-drilled steel-billet crankshaft. There were two versions: hydraulic-lifter "S," fitted to the first 279 cars, and the later "T" unit, with different rods and pistons and either mechanical or hydraulic lifters. Both were nominally rated at 360 bhp in street form or 375 bhp in race trim.

To accommodate the big-block mill, the stock Mustang front suspension was heavily modified, the battery relocated to the trunk, and an oil cooler added to prolong engine life. Outside, the Boss 429 wore a discreet "chin" spoiler, large hood duct, Magnum 500 chrome wheels with massive F60 × 15 tires, and small front-fender i.d. lettering. As a "homologation special," the Boss 429 was too involved for Ford to produce economically, so construction was contracted to Kar Kraft, a Brighton, Michigan firm specializing in such small-scale projects. Even so, Ford lost money on every one. After a slow start, some 852 of these monster Mustangs were completed for the year.

The Boss 302 was created to challenge the Camaro Z/28 in SCCA's Trans-Am series. To qualify as production, Ford had to build at least 1000 copies for sale, but 1934 of the '69s were completed. Among its design touches were matte-black hood finish and rear window slats, jazzy body striping with "Boss 302" lettering, and spoilers at each end (the rear one an adjustable, inverted airfoil). The latter resulted in a gain of perhaps 2.5 seconds per lap at Riverside Raceway in California with no increase in engine power.

But of course, there *was* more power: up to 400 bhp by some estimates, though the Boss 302's V-8 was advertised with 290 bhp at 4600 rpm so as not to arouse the insurance companies. Features encompassed "Cleveland" heads with oversize intake valves and huge 1.75-inch-diameter exhausts (inclined in the big ports to improve fuel flow), aluminum high-rise manifold, Holley four-barrel carburetor, dual-point ignition, solid lifters, bolted central main bearings, forged crankshaft, and special pistons. To guard against accidental over-revving, an ignition cutout interrupted current flow from the coil between 5800 and 6000 rpm. Chassis hardware included ultra-stiff springs, staggered shocks, four-speed gearbox, power brakes with 11.3-inch front discs and heavy-duty rear drums, and F60 × 15 Goodyear Polyglas tires. Ford hadn't missed a trick: even the wheel wells were radiused to accept racing rubber. Alas, the Boss 302 bowed to Penske, Donohue, and Chevrolet in this year's Trans-Am series, winning but a third of the dozen events.

Car Life magazine tested both Boss Mustangs and found the little guy quicker to 60 mph—6.9 seconds versus 7.2. But the 302 lost in the quarter-mile at 14.85 seconds and 96.14 mph compared with 14.09 seconds and 102.85 mph for the 429. Top speed for both was shown as 118 mph. Axle ratios on both ranged from 3.50 to 4.30:1. The magazine also discovered that the Boss 429 was actually slower than a 428CJ Mach 1.

Mustang's reach into the luxury and performance ends of the ponycar field showed interesting results. Of 184,000 cars delivered in the first half of the model year, only about 15,000 were Grandes but close to 46,000 were Mach 1s. On cue, division general manager John Naughton predicted "heavy emphasis on performance" for what he (or his press writers) saw as the "Sizzlin' Seventies."

Because Mustang changed, so did its Shelby GT cousins. Styled in Dearborn, the '69s were somewhat more rakish than the new Mustangs, marked by a longer hood with a prominent bulge and NACA-type scoops, a loop bumper/grille with single headlamps instead of the production car's quads, the customary rear brake cooling scoops, a fiberglass spoiler, taillamps *a la* Mercury Cougar, and center-mount twin exhaust outlets. GT-350 was upgraded to the 351 Windsor V-8, while the 428CJ continued in the GT-500 (no longer "KR"). As usual, fastbacks way outsold convertibles and the GT-500 maintained its lead over the GT-350. Model year production totalled 3150 units, including just 194 GT-350 convertibles and 335 of the GT-500s.

By this time, Carroll Shelby had had enough. The cars bearing his name were being designed by committees instead of engineers, had become too soft and plush to be raced, and were being crowded by Ford's own Bosses and Mach 1. On October 4, 1969, Shelby announced his retirement as race car developer and team manager; soon afterward, executive vice-president Lee Iacocca agreed to terminate the Shelby-Mustang program. Cars stranded in the pipeline—a little over 600—were given Boss 302 front spoilers, black-finish hoods, and 1970 serial numbers, thus ending one of the most remarkable chapters in high-performance history.

Ford's middleweight Fairlane/Torino returned with only minor trim changes and optional availability of the new 351 V-8, but there were two hot newcomers. One was the Cobra, a very different animal from Carroll Shelby's like-named sports car. This was a no-frills muscle machine answering Plymouth's popular '68 Road Runner,

offered as a two-door hardtop in SportsRoof and formal notchback form. Exact production isn't available (body designations were shared with corresponding Fairlane 500s), but most were probably fastbacks. Prices were attractive: $3164 for the notch, $3189 for the fastback. That got you the 335-bhp 428, four-speed manual transmission, heavy-duty suspension, six-inch-wide wheels, and F70 × 14 wide-oval belted tires, plus taxicab-plain interior. The outside was devoid of doodads save small, cartoon snakes (decals on early cars, emblems on later ones) on tail and front fenders. Options included a wide choice of axle ratios, Cruise-O-Matic, Ram Air induction with broad hood scoop, bucket seats, console, tachometer, front disc brakes with power assist, and limited-slip differential.

The Cobra lived up to its name on the dragstrips, proving to be the fastest mid-size Ford ever. Typical quarter-mile time was 14.5 seconds, and the 0-60 mph run took a mere six seconds flat. Fuel economy was only 8 mpg or so, but who cared when gas cost but 30 cents a gallon? The Cobra boosted Ford's performance image among the street-racing crowd. And most professional road testers agreed that of all '69 supercars, it was the tightest, quietest, and best built.

Ford had its last big season in NASCAR stock-car racing, thanks partly to the new limited-production Torino Talladega. Named for the 2.66-mile Alabama superspeedway that opened this year, it featured body mods designed to solve the aerodynamic problems that had hampered the fastback Torino stockers the previous season. It was also Ford's weapon against the still-slippery Mercury Cyclones and Dodge's new winged warrior, the Daytona. The key differences were at the front: a six-inch-longer nose curved gently to meet a simple, flush-mount grille (taken from the Cobra) above a sectioned Torino rear bumper. Developed with the aid of wind tunnel tests, these changes reduced air drag and made for higher speeds with no more horsepower.

Even so, Ford sought approval for its semi-hemi 429, but NASCAR disputed how "production" it was. As the rules didn't say that an engine had to be sold in the model being raced, Boss Mustang installations counted toward certifying the 429 Talladega. The rules also required a minimum of 500 cars, and Ford scrambled. While the 429 wasn't approved until late in the season, Ford built the requisite number of cars in time for the Daytona 500 in late February.

They proved formidable. After a 10-year association with Plymouth, driver Richard Petty was enticed to the Dearborn camp and won with the Talladega his first time out, at the Riverside 500. Lee Roy Yarborough was victorious at Daytona despite being forced to run the old 427 wedge. David Pearson ended up with the NASCAR crown and Ford with 26 Grand National wins.

Altogether, 754 Talladegas were completed, including prototypes. The street models, built at Ford's Atlanta facility, had the 428 Cobra Jet and Cruise-O-Matic, power steering and brakes (with front discs), competition suspension, and F70 × 14 tires on six-inch-wide styled steel

Cougar offered its first convertibles for '69, regular or XR-7.

Cougar Eliminator, with up to 360 bhp, came out in April, 1969.

Mercury built almost 10,000 Cougar soft tops for 1969.

Stripes and spoilers were part of the Cougar Eliminator package.

wheels. All had white bodies and flat-black hoods.

Dearborn design director Gene Bordinat was so fond of the Continental Mark III that he had its grille made into a clock for his office wall. Nobody at Rolls-Royce would have done such a thing, but Gene had these cute ideas from time to time. Still, R-R's famous "parthenon" design had undoubtedly influenced the Mark III radiator. Though it wasn't nearly as much a hand-crafted job, it became a badge of sorts and survived until the 1984 Mark VII, where it was reformed in the interest of better aerodynamics.

"We did not design [the Mark III] to offend anybody," Bordinat told the press. "Some will respond to this sort of thing. . . . Others wouldn't touch it with a ten-foot pole. The buffs may not like it, but the people with money will." Uncommonly honest, that, but quite accurate: the Mark

III was a big factor in Lincoln's vast production surge, which reached a new high this year by just eclipsing the '68 figure.

The senior Continentals were as strong as ever, with '69 sales almost exactly the same as '68's. Per established policy, design alterations were few. A revised grille was the main one, surmounted by the Continental name in block letters and still prominently domed to match the hood. A new Town Car interior option arrived for the four-door model (last of the Continental sedans with center-opening doors), comprising "unique, super-puff leather-and-vinyl seats and door panels, luxury wood-tone front seatback and door trim inserts, extra plush carpeting, and special napped nylon headlining." Though prices still started around $6000, government-required safety equipment was multiplying. Among this year's items was a

Cyclone "Cale Yarborough Special" honored the famed race driver.

Mercury built a total of 9143 Cyclone fastbacks for 1969.

The full-size Mercury Monterey hardtop coupe listed at $3237.

Merc's top mid-size street machine: Cyclone CJ 428 (335 bhp).

This '69 Montego MX wagon wore optional "Yacht Deck Paneling."

Mercury built 10,590 Montego MX station wagons for 1969.

dual-circuit brake system with failure warning light, which Lincoln might have thought of itself. Senior models still rode the 126-inch wheelbase of 1964, but had grown to 224.5 inches overall. The Mark III, meanwhile, stayed absolutely the same.

Year-to-year changes in various Mercurys would continue to follow those in counterpart Ford lines, always with a few differences dictated by recent sales results and changing buyer tastes. This year was no exception.

Like the full-size Fords, the big Mercs were completely revamped, becoming as large as they'd ever get, though nobody knew it then. Wheelbase went up an inch, to 124, except on wagons, which shared the 121-inch Ford span. Styling, mainly Dave Ash's work, still hewed to Lincoln themes: domed hood and grille, chrome-edged fenderlines, and vast acreage aft.

Seeking better coverage at the low end of the medium market, Mercury divided full-size offerings for the first time since 1961, giving each a somewhat different face. Monterey returned as the "price-leader" with sedan, wagon, hardtop coupe and sedan, and convertible. All but the last were duplicated in the spiffier Monterey Custom line, replacing Montclair and sharing the standard series' big loop bumper/grille with exposed headlamps. Taking over for Park Lane was a full-range Marquis group with convertible and woody-look Colony Park wagon, plus a sedan and the two hardtops in standard and Brougham trim, all marked by a two-tier grille and hidden headlamps.

Mercury also fielded a bucket-seat biggie, curious in view of declining demand for such cars. Reviving the Marauder name, it was a cousin to Ford's XL SportsRoof hardtop, with the same "flying buttress" sail panels and

The 1969 Montego MX convertible rode a 116-inch wheelbase.

Montego MX Brougham emphasized luxury; it cost $2808 in 1969.

Mercury's big sportster for 1969: the $4091 Marauder X-100.

Mercury produced 14,666 Marauder hardtop coupes for 1969.

Even at $3895, Mercury moved 25,604 Colony Park wagons.

For 1969, Marquis expanded to become an eight-model line.

Big Mercs (except wagons) rode a 124-inch wheelbase for 1969.

121-inch wheelbase but sporting the handsome Marquis front end. Offered in base and uplevel X-100 guise, it looked a little like the '68 Dodge Charger. And with a standard 360-bhp four-barrel 429, it really *was* a charger, scaling 0-60 mph in eight seconds or so. Helping it stand out from the herd were styled steel wheels, rear fender skirts, a choice of three seat/trim packages (including leather-and-vinyl bench or vinyl buckets with console), and optional "sports tone" matte-black deck finish. A burly, attractive package, the X-100 didn't sell at close to $5000; production was an anemic 5635 units for the model year. The base Marauder wasn't much higher at 9031.

While it's easy to mock these big cruisers with the benefit of hindsight, nobody worried much about a dearth of petroleum or razor-edge handling in 1969—at least nobody in the big-car market, where Mercury still did most of its business. And business was better for '69. Mercury production set a record at 398,000 overall. This was a strong dose of optimism-juice for the product planners, who happily put more ornate biggies into the design mill for the coming decade. But 1970-model sales lagged late in the year, and overall volume, while still strong, did not approach that of vintage 1968.

Mercury's mid-sizers changed in the same ways as Fairlane/Torino, again with most of the action—literally—in the muscle ranks. Cyclone offerings expanded with the CJ 428, a high-performance/low-cost fastback named for its standard Cobra Jet engine. Equivalent to Ford's Cobra, it delivered the same blistering go and slightly fancier surroundings for $2754 suggested base. Not to be outdone by the junior division, L-M also fielded a smooth-nose NASCAR special, the Cyclone Spoiler II. Sold in equally limited numbers—519 total—it was virtually identical with the showroom Talladega apart from special striping and "Cale Yarborough" signature decals, the latter honoring the winningest Merc driver in history. There was also a Dan Gurney Special with the stock Cyclone nose, airfoil deck spoiler, and blue/white paint.

Like Mustang, this year's Mercury Cougar was rebodied on its existing wheelbase and grew slightly larger. Models proliferated here too, as convertibles joined the line in standard and XR-7 trim, along with the racy Eliminator hardtop, inspired by "Dyno" Don Nicholson's world-record-setting Cougar funny-car dragster. Styling remained recognizably Cougar but was somehow less distinctive. The previous split grille gave way to an uninspired full-width affair (still with hidden headlamps), while Buick-like sweepspear character lines appeared on bodysides and the rear fenders got Coke-bottle contours, all rather derivative.

The hotshot Eliminator, ostensibly a separate model but actually composed of two option packages, could be ordered with most any engine in the book except a six (the two-barrel 351 was now base Cougar power). Naturally, it sported a big hood scoop, color-keyed racing mirrors and rear spoiler, styled-steel wheels with fat tires, tape stripes (surprisingly modest), more complete instrumentation, and other obligatory "performance car" goodies. There were also Cougar equivalents of Mustang's Boss 302 and Boss 429, though production of the latter is unclear.

What *was* clear was that Cougar was still slipping. Model year production now dropped below 100,000 units, of which fewer than 10,000 were convertibles. At least Cougar wasn't alone. The ponycar market had peaked, inflation was pushing up prices, and emission controls and rising insurance rates were cooling demand for hot cars like ice on a burn. It was a portent of things to come.

1970

Number Two touched three very different bases this year, unveiling a new compact Ford, heavily restyled intermediates, and a redesigned senior Lincoln. After working briefly with a presidential troika following Bunkie Knudsen's abrupt dismissal in 1969, chairman Henry Ford II appointed former Ford Division chief Lee Iacocca as overall president (Iacocca had headed North American Automotive Operations in the interim).

The new compact, called Maverick, bowed well ahead of the model year, on April 17, 1969, a date likely chosen for luck (five years to the day since the launch of the phenomenally successful Mustang). Billed as "the first car of the '70s at 1960s prices" it was much the same package as the first Falcon, with resolutely ordinary engineering and a similar, $1995 price (the original Falcon two-door sold for $1912), the only Ford listing below $2000. It also had a similar mission: to counter small imports, sales of which had been creeping steadily upward since the mid-Sixties.

Predictably, Maverick was pitched as a roomier, more powerful, more trouble-free import alternative. Its simplicity certainly implied reliability. The 103-inch-wheelbase chassis had a typical leaf-sprung live rear axle, twin-arm front suspension with coil springs, recirculating-ball steering, and all-drum brakes. Under the hood it was 1961 all over again. Standard was the same 170-cubic-inch cast-iron six (rated at 105 horsepower) that had been optional in that year's Falcons, and its 200-cid enlargement was optional. "Three-on-the-tree" manual transmission was standard, Cruise-O-Matic optional. Curb weight was in the vicinity of 2500 pounds, making Maverick quite a bit heavier than most rival foreigners.

Arriving as a two-door fastback sedan, Maverick was contemporary if a bit overdone in appearance. *Road & Track* magazine opined that "it looks like an American car. That isn't necessarily bad . . . and the overall impression is detracted from only by the tiny tires [6.00-13s were standard], its fat-hipped look, and the rather unattractive grille. . . . The vogueish blind-rear-quarter routine makes all three rear windows too small from both the visibility

and styling standpoint." Trim and equipment were kept basic to keep price down. There were no instruments apart from speedometer and fuel gauge, for example, and a European-style under-dash shelf filled in for a glovebox. However, the plain bench seats were covered in a spunky tartan-plaid cloth, and armrests and full carpeting were standard. Interiors were color-keyed to five whimsically named exterior hues: Anti-Establish Mint, Hulla Blue, Original Cinnamon, Freudian Gilt, and Thanks Vermillion. It was all part of the attempt to make this an economical "fun" car for those on a budget—or those who didn't like imports.

And in that, Maverick succeeded admirably. Production for its extra-long 1970 model year was nearly 579,000 units, reflecting just how right it was for the market. Though it would be refined and modified as time went on, Maverick would continue to appeal principally to mainstream buyers and, on that basis, must be considered one of Ford's more successful products.

Maverick's debut signalled the end of Falcon. The '69 models carried on this year virtually unchanged, then disappeared after 15,700 had been built. However, the nameplate would return briefly on stripped versions of the mid-size Fairlane/Torino for "1970½."

All-new styling "shaped by the wind" marked the 1970 mid-size Fords. Wheelbases grew an inch, to 114 on wagons and 117 inches on other body styles. Width increased two inches, overall length by four. Interiors were redone, trim upgraded, and comfort and convenience options pro-

First of the '70s, Ford's Maverick bowed on April 17, 1969.

Ford built 578,914 Mavericks for 1970—all two-door sedans.

Ford built 6348 full-size 1970 XL convertibles ($3501 list).

The 1970 LTD Brougham was "Built for quiet inside and out."

An LTD Brougham four-door hardtop listed at $3579 in 1970.

Ford built 50,825 Galaxie 500 tunnel-roof hardtops for 1970.

liferated. Basic engineering was untouched. A new topline Brougham series was added in line with the move upmarket. The GT convertible and "SportsRoof" fastback hardtop and the Cobra fastback remained the hottest of this clan. The latter continued as Ford's budget muscle car, with standard four-barrel 360-bhp 429 V-8. GT and Cobra power options ran to the 370-bhp Cobra Jet 429 with or without Ram Air induction. Cobra appearance was highlighted by NASCAR-style hood lock pins, black-finish hood and grille, and fat glass-belted tires. "Sports slats," backlight louvers *a la* Mustang Boss 302, were optional for hardtops. GTs could be dressed up with hidden headlamps, "laser" bodyside stripes, center console, and spoked road wheels.

These mid-size Fords could be blistering street performers. A 300-bhp GT could touch 60 mph from rest in about 8 seconds; the 370-bhp Cobra would do it in a mere 6 seconds. But the new styling proved less aerodynamic in superspeedway racing than that of the 1968-69 Torinos. The hardtop's concave backlight was said to be one of the problems. Ford had little choice but to run the older models in NASCAR this year, this time without the services of Richard Petty, who returned to the Chrysler camp. Ford took just six big-track events, and by year's end would abandon the Grand National and most of its other racing programs, including the Trans-Am and international endurance events.

Now touted as the number-one ponycar, Mustang faced more competition than ever. The beefy new Dodge Challenger and a completely redone Plymouth Barracuda companion appeared to do battle, followed at mid-season by the handsome second-generation Chevrolet Camaro/Pon-

Falcon entered the 1970 model year virtually unchanged. . .

. . . but became a stripped down Fairlane/Torino at mid-year.

tiac Firebird. Despite an exciting lineup, Mustang model year volume fell alarmingly to 190,727 units, down from nearly 300,000. Though this partly reflected the shrinking demand for ponycars in general, Mustang's design familiarity was also to blame.

As expected, 1970 Mustang changes were evolutionary. All seven models continued with a tasteful facelift of the new 1969 design, marked by a return to dual headlamps, minor ornamentation shuffling, and recessed taillamps. Powerteams stayed basically the same, and mechanical changes were few. The hot Boss 302 remained a limited-production Trans-Am special: output was just 6319 units for the model year. The high-performance Mach 1 got its own grille with built-in driving lamps, plus standard rear stabilizer bar. New appearance options for fastbacks included backlight louvers, adjustable rear spoiler, and distinctive C-stripe tape treatment. Optional Hurst shift linkage was new to Ford Division this year. The 250-bhp two-barrel 351 was now base Mach 1 power, but options still ran to the big 335-bhp Cobra Jet 428. The incredible Boss 429 was still around, though not often: only 505 were built, all before the end of December 1969.

Thunderbird got some radical sheetmetal surgery, but its basic 1967 body/chassis engineering was left substantially the same. New frontal styling reflected the influence of the now-departed Knudsen/Shinoda regime, with a longer hood terminating in a prominent, forward-thrusting vee'd snout. The effect was strikingly similar to the 1969 Pontiac Grand Prix—and must have confused some buyers. Headlamps were exposed for the first time since 1966, and hardtop coupes got "faster" rooflines. Production ran marginally ahead of '69 levels, but the Landau sedan faded, scoring only about half as many sales.

Detroit tradition dictated few changes for the just-renewed big Fords. Appearance was altered via grille inserts and new rear bumpers with integrated horizontal taillamps, and the lineup swelled with new Brougham sedan and two- and four-door hardtops. The XL convertible and "tunnel-roof" fastback, last of the sporting full-size models, made their farewell appearance. Big-Ford sales were strong (though not as much as Chevrolet's), with the Galaxie 500s and standard LTDs again far and away the most popular.

Lincoln turned 50 this year but, curiously, the milestone was all but ignored. Instead, L-M Division trotted out a completely revamped big Continental. Wheelbase went up a token inch, to 127 total, and other exterior dimensions stayed roughly the same. Styling was clean, if bulky, and maintained the traditional look despite a number of departures: hidden headlamps *a la* Mark III; hidden wipers; much hippier, newly skirted rear fenders; and a sharply etched "coffin nose" that may have owed something to the classic late-Thirties Cord 810/812. (Coffins were big at the Dearborn Design Center this year). Hardtop coupe and pillared sedan returned, but the latter forsook its unique center-opening doors for conventional rear-hinged back portals.

That implied a major structural change: the end of the

Torino was restyled for 1970, and grew bigger and heavier.

Only 7675 Cobra fastback hardtop coupes were built for 1970.

Priced at $3212, Ford built 3939 Torino GT soft tops for 1970.

Ford's first mid-size Torino four-door hardtop bowed for 1970.

long-running "Wixom" unit body/chassis (named for the plant where it was first built) that had come in with the revolutionary '61 Continental. In its place was a separate body resting on a box-rail perimeter frame similar to the Mark III's. According to Paul Woudenberg, author of the excellent *Lincoln & Continental: The Postwar Years*, Lincoln chief engineer Fred Bloom had "concluded that a

T-Bird's new nose was called the "Bunky beak" by some wags.

The 1970 T-Bird Landau coupe cost $5104; 36,847 were built.

Mustang Mach I came with a 351 V-8; 335-bhp 428 was optional.

Grande, Mustang's 1970 luxury offering, found 13,581 buyers.

Boss 302 took 1970 Trans-Am racing honors; output was 6319.

Mustang Mach I was popular for 1970 with 40,970 units built.

return to body-frame construction was needed" because it provided "greater interchangeability of underbody and chassis components with other Ford products." As a result, the Continentals of the Seventies would be much less unique than those of the Sixties—more closely tied to the big Mercurys, which in turn were becoming ever more like the full-size Fords.

Still, this was one instance where new really *was* better—or at least no worse: the 1970 seniors sold at about their 1968-69 volume, accounting for about 35,000 of Lincoln's total model year output. The standard equipment list continued with all the usual items plus pinstriping, padded inside windshield posts, multi-adjustable map and reading lights, and woodgrain dash and door panel appliqués. There were no drivetrain changes.

Having proved the success of its formula, the Mark III was left generally alone and again saw better than 20,000-unit sales for the model year. Following a fad, L-M gave it hidden wipers, which cleaned up exterior appearance—and posed the wintertime challenge of having to

dig frozen blades out from under the snow that was invariably trapped by their hiding place. Parking lamps now doubled as running lights, and the "electric chronometer" bore the name of Cartier Jewelers. Vinyl roof, spare tire cover, fiber-optic rear lamp monitors, and a "walnut dash panel" were all standard.

Despite a cornucopia of no-cost conveniences, the Mark III could be ordered with a good many wallet-lightening extras, such as "Moondust" paint ($131), six-way power seat with reclining passenger backrest ($280), and AM radio with Stereosonic 8-track tape and power antenna ($300). Although 96 percent of this year's models were sold with air conditioning, it remained an accessory item—and an expensive one at $523. Finally, an important new feature: the 1970 Mark III was the first American car with standard steel-belted radial tires.

Meanwhile, Lehmann-Peterson continued building Lincoln limos in small quantities, and another Presidential carriage had been delivered to the White House in 1968. Likewise, show cars weren't entirely dead. Appearing in 1969 was a new one-off town brougham called the Lincoln Town Sedan, with Mark III-style hidden headlamps. More interesting was this year's exotic Mark III Dual Cowl Phaeton, put together for the annual Chicago Automobile Show in February. The name was inappropriate, as this was neither true phaeton (meaning extra-roomy convertible) nor a genuine dual-cowl (there was only one cowl, up front as usual). But there was a second, auxiliary windshield, a clever piece of design by body engineer Stuart Frey, with two panes of glass, one attached to the back of each front seat. When a seat was folded forward, the glass moved with it. The special was also bumperless, the front protected mostly by an extended grille. Styling was very crisp. Needless to say, it was never contemplated for production.

Mercury, like Ford, changed its mid-size models most this year, but seemed overrun with big cars and big power. Consider that the 1970 engine chart listed just a single six, the 155-bhp 250, standard on Montego (the price-leader Comet was dropped). Cyclones, Cougars, and V-8 Montegos could all be ordered with 351s, while the 390 was the smallest available in the full-size line. From there the list ran to the 335-bhp 428 as an option on Cougar (making it a nose-heavy beast) and five different 429s from 320 to 375 bhp, the latter available with Ram-Air induction for the new Cyclone Spoiler, now a regular-production model. All very impressive, but not sales-building material.

Like the big '69 Mercs, this year's revamped Montego/Cyclone became as large as they would ever be. Wheelbases increased per Fairlane 500/Torino, contours were swoopier, and a hardtop sedan was a first-ever mid-size offering. The Mercurys' one distinction—if you can call it that—was a radically sculptured nose with a center proboscis big enough to frighten an anteater. On Cyclones it wore a chrome square with a "gunsight"—most curious, and no compensation for loss of the pretty 1968-69 fastback styling. All models gained hidden wipers and all but base Montegos had hideaway headlamps.

The Montego MX Brougham had not sold well, so it's difficult to understand why the series now expanded to include the new four-door hardtop (production 3685), only one in the line. All told, MX Brougham accounted for only about 50,000 sales, not to be sneezed at but hardly sensational for this high-volume league. Similarly, the base Cyclone and the $3800 Cyclone Spoiler were way outsold by the mid-range GT; respective model year production was 1695, 1691, and 10,170 units. Besides its giant engine, the Spoiler sported "semi-functional" airfoils front and rear, plus *really* functional hood scoop, racing mirrors, high-back bucket seats—and a not-so-functional 3800-pound curb weight. The last explains why Mercury also ran its 1968-69 stockers on the NASCAR circuit.

Cougar carried on with its four-model range of standard and XR-7 hardtops and convertibles, all modestly facelifted. The split grille and vertical-bar motif returned, only the center divider was another nasal protrusion with matching "grille-let." Engines stayed mostly the same,

After almost 10 years, Continental was totally restyled for 1970.

Lincoln built 9073 Continental coupes for the 1970 model run.

The Continental Mark III saw output of 21,432 units for 1970.

The 1970 Mark III started out at $7281, but options abounded.

though the 429 was less available. The Eliminator was demoted to option status but could still be combined with the Boss 302 engine—not that many were. In fact, Cougar sales seemed to vary inversely with rising prices and new government regulations, and this year's volume dropped to about 72,000 units, less than half the 1967 total. Con-

Second year (1970) was also the last year for Marauder X-100.

Largely unchanged Mercury Cougar offered four models for 1970.

The '70 Mercury Marquis Brougham hardtop sedan sold for $4500.

Cougar saw production of only 4299 convertibles for 1970.

Merc built only 1357 Monterey Custom hardtop coupes for 1970.

The Mercury Cyclone Spoiler sported spoilers front and rear.

Hidden headlights came standard on the Montego MX Brougham.

Mercury began importing the made-in-Germany Capri in 1970.

vertibles were particularly scarce—2322 standards and 1977 XR-7s—and they'd become scarcer still.

The jumbo Mercs were largely reruns. Full-size convertibles were making their final bow at L-M Division, and the '70s were even scarcer than corresponding Cougars: 1233 of the posh Marquis and a piddling 581 Montereys. Also making a final stand was that belated bucket-seat biggie, the Marauder; only 2646 X-100s and 3397 standard models were sold. However, overall big-Merc production held about even with '69.

While Mercury would soon have its own version of the Maverick, a more interesting new small car arrived in L-M showrooms this spring. Borrowing Lincoln's old Capri name, it was a shapely, semi-fastback coupe on a 100.8-inch wheelbase, conceived by Ford Europe as a Mustang for that burgeoning market. Ford had been peddling "captive imports" in the U.S. with varying degrees of success since the early Fifties, mostly workaday, indifferently built British sedans that looked like shrunken versions of its domestic designs. But the Capri was different: Mustang-sporty yet decidedly European, thriftier, and a lot more agile.

A sort of early, small-scale "world car," Capri was built in both Germany and England, where it was sold (as a Ford) with a wide array of engines and option "packs." What Americans got was a hybrid: a German-built car powered by the 71-bhp 1.6-liter pushrod four from British Cortina sedans. There were reasons for this. German workmanship was superior, and the crossflow engine was already emissions legal (Cortinas had been sold in the U.S. since 1964).

In initial U.S. form, Capri was more penny-pincher than hotshot, averaging an easy 25 mpg thanks largely to a svelte, 2100-pound curb weight. There was just one trim level, but it included vinyl interior with front buckets, plus full carpeting, four-speed floorshift, and styled wheels with radial tires. This combination of sportiness, economy, and low price—just $2295 P.O.E.—proved immensely appealing, and L-M sold 156,000 Capris during the long introductory model year. Encouraged by the strong reception, division planners decided to order up bigger engines and more equipment from the European catalog.

It was a timely move. Capri was just right for a market seeking more rational substitutes for overblown ponycars and overpowered muscle machines. In fact, it was probably ahead of the market, as events would soon prove.

1971

A new minicar, restyled full-sizers, and the largest-ever Mustangs and Cougars made this a busy Dearborn year. Ford Division was fresh from its best sales performance since 1966, recording over 1.8 million registrations for calendar 1970 against 1.6 million for archrival Chevy. Lincoln would set another production record for model year '71, and Mercury was up too.

The perennial Ford/Chevrolet sales fight now extended to the increasingly important subcompact arena. Ford's contender was the Pinto, a chunky two-door sedan on a 94-inch wheelbase, Dearborn's smallest car yet. It arrived not coincidentally with Chevy's Vega, a slightly larger small car with typically GM lines and a 2.3-liter (140-cubic-inch) overhead-cam four of unusual construction. Both had resulted from programs started in the mid-Sixties to develop direct domestic competitors for various small economy imports. Led by the quirky VW Beetle, import sales had climbed up to 15 percent of the total U.S. market by 1970, too large a slice for Detroit to ignore. Pinto and Vega were intended to get some of it back.

Developed as project Phoenix, the Pinto stemmed from

Ford debuted its import fighter, the Pinto, as a '71 model.

Two-door sedan was the only Pinto model initially available.

Mid-year Runabout offering added to Pinto's versatility.

an earlier program that envisioned a more radical mini. According to author Jan Norbye, this G-car, as it was called, "had VW exterior dimensions and [would have been] powered by a transversely positioned inline four-cylinder water-cooled engine in the rear. The chassis configuration was [ultimately] discarded, but the G-car body was adopted for a new project . . . using a front engine and live rear axle." Phoenix envisioned use of certain components, mainly engines and transmissions, from Ford's German and British subsidiaries in a package sized to compete head-on with the Beetle. Those ideas survived.

The result was a conventionally engineered Euro-American hybrid. Pinto's standard engine was a cast-iron, 1.6-liter ohv four from the British Ford Cortina and L-M Division's newly imported Capri, rated at 75 horsepower. Optional (at $82 extra) was a 2.0-liter 100-bhp overhead-cam four from the German Ford Taunus (and newly available this year in U.S. Capris). Its standard four-speed manual gearbox and optional three-speed automatic were imported, too.

Comparisons between Pinto and Vega were inevitable. *Road & Track* magazine said that while the Chevy is "by far the more interesting design . . . Pinto happens to be the more pleasant car to drive in everyday use—base model for base model—and carries a price tag some $172 less. To be sure there is 'less car' in the Pinto; where the Vega has disc front brakes, it has drums; the Vega coil-and-link rear suspension, the Pinto simple leaf springs; it is somewhat less roomy, and in standard form it's not as quick as a standard Vega. But, thanks to a quieter and smoother engine, a superior gearbox, somewhat greater comfort for the driver and better finish throughout, it is

subjectively the nicer car." Even so, Pinto lagged behind Vega and many imports in several key areas. *R&T*'s initial 1.6-liter test car needed 20 seconds to reach 60 mph, versus 16.5 seconds for the Chevy and a brisk 13 seconds for the lighter Datsun 510. Also criticized were Pinto's sparse instrumentation, lack of back seat and trunk space, the long stopping distances and poor directional control of its all-drum brakes, and the tendency of the lightly loaded back end to hop around.

But it wasn't all bad. Said *R&T*: "Pinto is maneuverable and handles pretty well. Its rack-and-pinion steering . . . is not very quick . . . but it's a far cry from the wheel-twirling of the Maverick. Out on the road we found good cornering adhesion, at least in the dry (with the optional A78-13 tires on 5-in. rims), and steering characteristics close to neutral. . . . Mind you, it's no sports car, but for the

Ford claimed its 1971 full-size design looked "crisper."

Ford built 43,303 LTD Brougham hardtop coupes for 1971.

Grabber sported stripes and scoops—and Maverick's economy.

Mustang was new for '71; it grew as big as it would ever get.

The 1971 Mustang Boss 351 was discontinued at mid-year when Ford got out of racing. An estimated 1800 were built.

economy-car class the handling can't be faulted." And economy was pretty good: 22 mpg in the *R&T* test versus 18.6 for the four-speed Vega, though both trailed the sprightlier, 25.3-mpg Datsun.

R&T later sampled a 2.0-liter with the $32 front-disc brake option and liked Pinto even more. The engine, they said, "makes it a proper car . . . smooth and quiet, much better than the Vega in these respects." The 0-60 mph performance improved to a more reasonable 11.4 seconds, and there was no mileage penalty, the larger-engine model actually proving 0.5 mpg thriftier than the 1600. As for braking, the car "stopped in less distance from 80 mph than the drum-brake Pinto did from 70!" Fade resistance was 50 percent better.

Over 350,000 buyers liked Pinto enough to buy one this model year, a fine performance achieved in spite of a recall to fix carburetors on early cars, prompted by a rash of underhood fires, and short 1.6 engine supplies due to a strike in Britain. At mid-model year, Ford brought out an identically styled three-door hatchback sedan, with standard fold-down back seat and cargo area carpeting. Called Runabout, it answered at least one Pinto failing, poor trunk space.

Pinto would have a long, 10-year production run and would remain a consistently good seller despite emission controls, weighty safety equipment and, later, a fuel tank design proven unsafe. Moreover, it would always outsell Vega. Pinto wasn't enough by itself to stem the import tide, but it served Ford well through a difficult decade.

Mustang was all-new this year and as big as it would ever get. Its larger dimensions stemmed from Ford's belief that sales would improve with more passenger room, presumably the reason compacts were generally outstripping ponycars. Accordingly, overall length ballooned eight inches, width by six inches, and curb weights by some 600 pounds. The familiar long-hood/short-deck proportions were retained on an inch-longer, 109-inch wheelbase, but the car was more "styled" than ever, aping Ford's GT Le Mans racers and the tastes of Bunkie Knudsen and Larry Shinoda. Most noticeable were a sweeping, almost horizontal, fastback roofline, plus full-width grille and Kamm-style back panel inspired by the Shelby-Mustangs. Models stayed the same except for the new Boss 351, replacing the Boss 302/429, powered by a tweaked four-barrel Cleveland 351 V-8 with 330 bhp. Lesser models started with a modest 250-cid six and base-option 302 V-8, the latter now standard for Mach 1; two- and four-barrel 351s and the 429 Cobra Jet were available for leadfoots. Appearing later in the year was a 351CJ with 280 horses.

Naturally, these "fat" Mustangs weren't as agile as their predecessors and, with their greater weight, they needed larger engines just to maintain previous performance levels. *Motor Trend* magazine's Chuck Koch found the Boss 351 quicker in the quarter than the automatic 429 Mach 1 (13.8 versus 14.5 seconds) and slower from rest to 60 mph (10 flat versus 6.5). But the Boss handled better on its standard competition suspension: beefier springs and shocks, staggered rear shocks, and stabilizer

The '71 Torino Brougham two door cost $3175; 8593 were built.

Torino's youthful GT fastback found favor with 31,641 buyers.

Ford built 4408 Torino Brougham hardtop sedans for 1971.

Base '71 Thunderbird hardtop sold for $5295; output was 9146.

The $5438 Landau was more popular; production reached 20,356.

The 1971 Mark III was little changed, but 27,091 were built.

Lincoln celebrated its 50th anniversary one year late in 1971.

Continental sedan, with 27,346 built, barely edged the Mark III.

Continental coupe weighed in at 5032 pounds, listed at $7172.

bars at both ends. The "cooking" 302 wasn't in the same league, but could deliver 0-60 mph in about 10 seconds with 2.79:1 axle and automatic—and up to 17 mpg—making it the best all-round choice.

Though it doesn't seem so bad now, the '71 Mustang got a lot of poor press when new and didn't prove nearly as popular as earlier models, production falling to below 150,000 units. The ponycar market was fading fast, and greater size, copious options, and fresh looks just weren't enough.

The full-size Fords received a mid-life restyle, introducing a basic look that would continue through 1978 along with an unchanged, 121-inch-wheelbase chassis. A massive bumper/grille, again reflecting Knudsen's influence, featured deeply inset quad headlamps either side of an eggcrate center section, and sharp horizontal creases appeared above elliptical wheel arches. Hardtop and sedan backlights were slightly curved; hardtop coupes had bulky sail panels terminating just behind the door glass, where tiny vertical panes filled the gap. A new instrument panel put controls in a large pod jutting out from the cowl. With the XL's demise, the convertible moved to the LTD series and both "Sportsroof" fastbacks were dropped. The engine chart remained the same apart from a new 400-cid V-8, basically the 351 with a larger, 4.00-inch bore. A relatively efficient engine with torque and emission characteristics suitable for family-car applications, it would appear in a variety of Dearborn cars in the years ahead.

Maverick broadened its appeal for this sophomore year with a four-door sedan and a sporty two-door. The latter, modishly called Grabber, had a jazzy two-tone hood with fake scoops and partial matte-black finish, extra lamps in the grille and no round emblem, plus dual racing mirrors, reflective bodyside tape stripes, and flat hubcaps with wheel trim rings. Floorshift and high-back bucket seats were new options for Grabber and the base two-door. More practical folk were interested in the new sedan, built on a longer, 109.9-inch wheelbase, making it about the same size as the last Falcons. Both Maverick sixes lost 5 bhp to emissions tuning, but a 250-cid unit with 145 bhp was newly optional. Other changes included larger, 14-inch wheels and tires, extra-cost vinyl roof, and new colors.

After a decade, the Fairlane name was retired from Ford's U.S. lineup as Torino 500 became the middle series in the intermediate line. The cars weren't changed much apart from split grilles and minor trim twisting, but Cobra lost a lot of its bite, downgraded to a standard, four-barrel 285-bhp 351 V-8.

Thunderbird also sailed along with few significant changes. Two-door rooflines reverted to the huge, blind C-pillars of 1966-69, and all models displayed more restrained, horizontal-bar fronts. Sales continued at their previous pace, but the four-door hit a new low of only about 6500 units. New to the options slate was a Turnpike Convenience Group combining cruise control, reclining front seat backrest, and Michelin steel-belted radial tires. High-back front bench or bucket seats were available.

The 1971 Canadian Meteor Rideau 500 looked for all the world like a U.S. Mercury Monterey—and it was, save for badging.

The 1971 Mercury Marquis Brougham sported a "halo" vinyl roof.

Mercury produced 20,004 Colony Park station wagons for 1971.

Lincoln set another model year production record with 62,642 units, and calendar year output was fast moving toward an unprecedented six-figure total. More heartening, Mark III began grabbing some Eldorado sales to trim Cadillac's huge lead from some 200,000 cars in 1970 to only 120,000. With all this, 1971 seemed like a good year to party, and Lincoln duly celebrated its "Golden Anniversary"—actually its 51st (the company historians were apparently on vacation).

With a new Mark IV scheduled for '72 and its seniors only a year old, Lincoln confined alterations to trim and equipment this year. Included were two new metalflake paint colors and standard air conditioning, tinted glass and, for the big cars, steel-belted Michelin tires. Engineers were mainly occupied with meeting government regulations. Smog-prone California had now mandated oxides of nitrogen (NOx) levels requiring additional engine controls, so "49-state version" became part of the

Cougar grew bigger for 1971; 25,416 XR-7 hardtops were built.

The '71 Cougar XR-7 sported a three-quarter length vinyl roof.

Cyclone Spoiler charged into 1971 with a "gun-sight" grille.

The Montego MX Brougham was one of 12 mid-size '71 Mercurys.

Mercury's "new" 1971 compact Comet was a Maverick in disguise.

Comet came as two door, four door, or GT, with sixes or 302 V-8.

Ford's '71 pickups sported a bolder grille, started at $2904.

technical lexicon. Retarded low-rpm spark timing helped sanitize Lincoln's 460 V-8. It hurt acceleration but not gross bhp, still 360. Mark III's most noticeable change was a high-back split front bench seat with individual armrests, but final drive was lowered to 3:1 in line with the emission-based engine mods. Nearly 90 percent of the '71s were ordered with "Traction-Lok" limited-slip differential. A power sunroof had joined the option list for 1970, and one in four cars had it this year.

Despite lacking a convertible like Eldorado, the personal-luxury Lincoln now almost matched its rival's production and actually led in coupe volume by about 7000. Cadillac dealers were finding this year's bulkier, heavier Eldo—built on a new GM E-body platform along with Buick Riviera and Oldsmobile Toronado—wasn't as saleable as its slick 1967-70 predecessors. Lincoln-Mercury couldn't foresee this when designing the Mark III's somewhat larger successor back in '69, but they stuck pretty much to its styling, which would prove advantageous.

Mercury ran ahead of its 1970 sales pace despite some questionable product moves this season. Cougar, for example, widened its gap with Mustang in size, price, and equipment by becoming a virtual intermediate. Restyled on a two-inch-longer, 113-inch wheelbase, it continued to share much of the Mustang's underbody structure but grew so large (196.9 inches long) and heavy (3300-3900 pounds) that it could hardly be called a ponycar. Styling was more ponderous, too: three-element grille with a high, squarish center flanked by oblongs and newly exposed headlamps; bulged bodysides; and a "flying buttress" hardtop roof large enough to land a helicopter. The same four models continued, but the Eliminator option was eliminated and engines centered solely on the 351 and 429.

Originally conceived "for the man on his way to a Thunderbird," Cougar was on its way to *being* a Thunderbird. Of course, this transformation was dictated by the rapidly changing market, but it didn't bring more sales, which now bottomed out. Convertible demand continued withering as fast as the ponycar market itself: just 1723 standard models and 1717 XR-7s.

A more successful development was the return of a true Mercury compact, this time based on the popular Ford Maverick but still called Comet—to no one's surprise. Except for a prominently bulged front-end ensemble, Montego taillamps, and somewhat more deluxe trim, it was exactly the same package but priced a few dollars higher per Merc tradition. There was even a GT equivalent to the two-door Maverick Grabber. Comet would never outsell its Ford cousin, but it did bring in over 80,000 sales in its first year, sales that might have otherwise been lost.

It also gave L-M dealers a second small car to supplement the German-made Capri. And there's reason to think that part of Comet's mission was to act as a hedge against currency fluctuations and supply problems that might affect the import's sales. (They'd surface soon enough.) The Capri itself was outwardly little changed, but Pinto's 2.0-liter (122-cid) engine became optional.

Mercury's mid-size Montego returned in the same array with eggcrate grille inserts and detail cosmetic touch-ups. Also little changed were the companion high-performance Cyclone hardtops, which were fading fast (a lot of their would-be buyers were plodding through Southeast Asian jungles) and would not be renewed for another season. Production was paltry indeed: 444 base models, 2287 GTs, and only 353 Spoilers.

With big-car sales sluggish, Monterey Custom was folded into the base series as a trim variation, and all models took on more voluptuous lower-body contours. Front ends were more sharply peaked than before, and grilles now wrapped into the front fender edges along with bumpers. Monterey still wore a lower-profile grille than Marquis and had exposed headlamps. Like the big Fords, this basic '71 styling would persist for most of the rest of the decade.

1972

Ford Division presented two completely new car lines for the second year in a row, while Lincoln-Mercury unveiled a new mid-size generation and a successor to the Mark III. Quipped *Motor Trend* magazine: "The Ford Motor Company executive who claimed 'the annual model change is dead' must be joking. Either that or he didn't get a good look at the company's plans. . . ."

Except for engines, Ford's Torino was all-new from road to roof, switching from unit to body-on-frame construction for the first time. The idea was that the frame be fairly flexible, thus effectively becoming part of the suspension to isolate road shocks from the rigid body. Accompanying this change was a new four-link rear suspension with coil springs instead of the previous semi-elliptics. Front disc brakes with new single-piston calipers were now standard, and there was a new steering linkage, integral with the boost mechanism with power assist. Front suspension remained much as before: upper control arms, coil springs mounted on lower lateral arms.

Following GM's practice since 1968, Ford split its mid-size line along different wheelbases: 114 inches for two-doors, 118 for four-doors. Overall width grew by 2.5 and 4.6 inches, respectively. Front and rear track also increased, as did weight, thanks to the separate frame and added sound insulation. With all this, Torino was now about as large and weighty as a full-size late-Sixties Ford.

Styling, needless to say, was dramatically different. Front fenders were pointed, wheel arches bulged, beltlines higher, rear fenderlines humped, bodysides more heavily sculptured. Gran Torinos carried a distinctive "mouth" grille nestled above a scooped-out bumper and flanked by quad headlamps; others carried a full-width

For 1972, Ford praised LTD's new grille and "long elegant look."

All seven big Ford wagons claimed a 96-cubic-foot cargo area.

Maverick sedan yielded six inches more rear hiproom than coupe.

V-8 power became available on the 1972 Maverick Grabber.

Pinto enlarged its hatchback glass by lowering it eight inches.

Red, white, and blue Mustang Sprint models debuted in mid-1972.

Spring 1972: sporty Sprint Decor Option debuts on small Fords

Mustang convertible production reached but 6401 for 1972.

The luxurious Mustang Grande fared better—18,045 were built.

Base Mustang prices ranged from $2729 to $3053 in 1972.

face. Sports wore a simulated hood scoop.

A slimmed-down model platoon listed base Torino and new Gran Torino and Gran Torino Sport series, the last replacing GT and Cobra. Convertibles were gone, and four-door hardtops were now "pillared hardtop" sedans. Exclusive to Sport was a full-fastback pillarless Sports-Roof. Remaining offerings comprised three notchback hardtop coupes, two four-door sedans, and a trio of five-door wagons. The last had the two-way "Magic Doorgate" pioneered by big-Ford wagons way back in 1965. Special hinges allowed it to open laterally like a door or to swing down like a conventional tailgate. Existing powerplants were detuned where necessary to run on regular gas, a sign of the times. A 250-cid six and 302 V-8 were standard depending on model. A brace of 351 V-8s, one 400, and one 429 were the extra-cost choices. Most Torinos rolled out with SelectShift Cruise-O-Matic, but four-speed manual was available with the four-barrel 351.

Options availability revealed that these new Torinos were aimed more at comfort and smooth-riding quietness than sporty performance. The one vestige of the "muscle" era was a $443 Rallye Equipment Group for Sports only, with full instrumentation including tachometer, plus higher-rate springs and shocks, rear stabilizer bar, 14 × 6-inch wheels mounting G70 wide-oval tires, and manual transmission with Hurst linkage. The four-barrel 351 V-8 cost $127 extra. The 429 was $100 if you ordered it with the Rallye package. But brochures stressed the new Torino's kinship with the big LTD in matters of ride, luxury, and room, and this year's Sports would be the last "interesting" mid-size Fords we'd see in this decade.

Ford seemed to be right on the money with its tarted-up Torinos. The intermediate's model year tally was up by some 170,000 cars over 1971, to about 496,000, and the Gran Torinos accounted for about half. At 60,794 units, the Sport fastback was the third most popular model in the line. Some of this initial success may have come at the expense of the big Ford, which sagged by about 100,000 units. And some of it was no doubt due to lack of new competition from GM, whose mid-sizers were now five years old. GM had intended to introduce new designs for '72, but delays forced a one-year postponement. Even then, Torino sales were hardly affected, and they remained strong through "energy crisis" 1974.

Sloganeers billed the personal-luxury Ford as "More Thunderbird Than Ever," and they weren't kidding. In fact, the Bird was now a close relative of this year's new Continental Mark IV, sharing basic body structure, a new perimeter chassis, even one engine. There was also "more" to its price, now almost $5400 basic.

This largest T-Bird yet resulted from a series of decisions made shortly after Lee Iacocca moved into the president's chair at Ford's "Glass House" World Headquarters. The main ones were more conservative styling, dumping the slow-selling sedan, and enlarging the two-door to share more Mark tooling. The last would spread production costs over higher volume than either model would generate alone, thus improving their profitability.

All this came to pass, with the mainstay two-door put on a 120.4-inch wheelbase, 5.7 inches longer than before and the same as the new Mark's. Overall length stretched to 216 inches, some four inches less than the Mark IV measure. Though center body sections were identical, Ford stylists played variations on familiar themes at each end of their car: restrained horizontal-bar grille and squared-up front fenders housing the parking lamps; flared wheel arches accented by slim, full-length moldings about half-way up the bodysides; and the now-traditional full-width taillamp treatment. Though it looked heavier, the new Bird actually weighed a bit less than its immediate predecessor.

Beneath the larger body was a new chassis. All-coil suspension was retained, but the rear employed new four-link geometry, with the upper links (now made of drawn rather than stamped steel) mounted outboard and splayed inward, assisted by an anti-roll bar. Power front-disc/rear-drum brakes were standard, and there was a new option called "Sure Track," an anti-skid device that acted on the rear wheels to prevent premature lockup in hard stops. Not many were ordered, though it was highly beneficial and much less costly than the Bendix all-wheel electronic

Torino was all-new for '72: here the racy Gran Torino Sport.

Torino's 1972 wagons featured a three-way "Magic Doorgate."

The '72 Gran Torino four door found favor: 102,300 were built.

system on Chrysler's Imperial. The 429 big-block remained standard power, rated at 212 bhp by the SAE net method adopted throughout the industry this year. Lincoln's 460 was the lone option, packing 212/224 bhp (net) and available only with air conditioning. Both engines were teamed with SelectShift Cruise-O-Matic, of course.

Buyers responded to the new T-Bird with enthusiasm. Model year sales leaped 60 percent above the '71 total to near 58,000—putting Ford's flagship firmly ahead of the Buick Riviera and Oldsmobile Toronado. Road testers found little to get excited about, but the package would prove good enough to last five full years. Though the Middle East oil embargo crippled big-car sales in 1974-75, Thunderbird maintained a solid lead against the aforementioned rivals.

A little Pinto wagon trotted out in April, identical with the two- and three-door sedans ahead of the rear wheels but with 10 extra inches aft for good cargo space. Appropriately, it came with the optional 2.0-liter four as stan-

Thunderbird shared Mark IV's 120.4-inch wheelbase for 1972.

The '72 T-Bird grew in every direction; a 460 V-8 was offered.

Output of the '72 Lincoln Continental Mark IV zoomed to 48,591.

dard, and could be ordered with plain sides or as a woody-look Squire, the latter earning the nickname "Country Squirt" in some quarters. A string of detail running changes begun in 1971 continued for all Pintos this year. Included were an eight-inch deeper rear window for the Runabout hatchback, standard carpeting on the two-door, and newly optional vinyl roof and Accent exterior moldings. Sales improved by about 130,000 units, topping 480,000 for the model year.

Though described as "virtually unchanged," Ford's compact Maverick had a few new items. Notable was first-time availability of the small-block 302 V-8. It was an especially good choice for the bestriped Grabber, but you still couldn't get a four-speed or disc brakes. Arriving in time for spring was a new Luxury Decor Option (LDO) for both body styles, with copper-color vinyl top and bodyside moldings, matching wheel covers, whitewall tires, and low-back bucket seats with reclining backrests. Despite

Although the 1972 Mark IV shared many pieces under the skin with the new Thunderbird, it still looked every bit a Mark.

all this, Maverick sales slipped by about 17,000 units for the model year.

Heavily revamped for '71, the big Fords stayed pretty much the same. Appearance was altered slightly with simpler grilles bisected by a new front bumper cross-piece, and rear bumpers were extended up to the trunk sill on all models (except wagons, of course). The main new option was an electric sliding sunroof to make up for the now-departed convertible. The "Big Six" and 302 V-8 were scratched from the chart, leaving a two-barrel 351 as the base engine.

There's nothing to do with a one-year-old design but live with it, and that's what Ford did with this year's Mustang. The main news concerned powerplants, down to five with cancellation of the 429. Though still running a standard 302, Mach 1 was now the hottest of the herd, as the Boss 351 was also deleted. Convertibles—all 6401 of them—gained a standard power top mechanism. The disheartening sales trend continued, production sinking to just under 125,000, a 20-percent decline and Mustang's lowest yearly total yet. Attempting to perk things up, Ford offered two "Sprint" option packages at mid-year, featuring white paint with red accent striping, broad blue hood stripes and rocker panel paint, and stars-and-stripes shields on rear fenders. A complimentary color scheme was used inside. The better group included Magnum 500 road wheels shod with 60-series raised-white-letter tires.

Gar Laux, Gene Bordinat, and Henry Ford II were quite sincere about "never changing" the Mark III. But no design lasts forever, and it was time for an update, which they decided to call Mark IV. This was not a return to the annual model change that had seen three "Marks" in a row back in 1958-60. Like its T-Bird companion, the Mark IV would be around for five years—and not much altered in any of them.

The design assignment was handed to Wes Dahlberg, with the Cadillac Eldorado his ever-present target. Beat the Eldo, Wes was told—any way you can. Work began in 1969, when the Eldorado was on a 120-inch wheelbase; Dahlberg chose a 120.4-inch spread, aiming for more back seat room rather than outdistancing Cadillac. But '71 brought a second-generation Eldo on a whopping 126.3-inch span, so the Mark still trailed, though the designers were able to give it a more spacious interior—and a more substantial profile. The IV also had a slightly wider track, giving it a small handling edge over the III if not the bloated Eldo.

Dahlberg didn't, or couldn't, change the Mark's big square grille. Gene Bordinat had one on his wall, for heaven's sake! But he did make it more prominent by scooping out the front bumper so that it looked, and was, taller. Equally apparent were the more abrupt rear-fender kick-up, and broader roof sails relieved by oval "opera windows." The latter, a Bordinat idea probably inspired by the "porthole" T-Birds, may have been a gimmick, but they proved just as popular as they had back in 1956 and soon became a Mark IV trademark—as well as *de rigueur* all over Detroit. They also served the practical purpose of

The 1972 Continental sedan sold for $7302; 35,561 were built.

The Lincoln Continental coupe weighed in at 4906 pounds in '72.

making over-the-shoulder vision much better than it would have been without them. They were sure timely, as Cadillac had oblong ones on this year's Eldorado, which had been styled after the Mark III and looked more like a Lincoln than ever.

As expected, the Mark IV chassis was basically the same as the new Thunderbird's, engineered for a smoother ride and improved handling. Detail niceties included intermittent windshield wipers and—at the behest of Your Friends in Washington—steel beams within the doors to resist intrusion in side impacts.

The senior Lincolns weren't forgotten, picking up a rich-looking crisscross grille, full-length fender moldings and a stand-up Continental "star" hood ornament (also found on Mark IV), spring-loaded so as not to impale hapless pedestrians. The grillework and mascot aped Mercedes-Benz, a common tactic in the 1970s. More original were neat, extra-cost "mini-vent" front side windows, small triangular sections that lowered (electrically) before the main door glass for "no-draft" ventilation like in the old days. The feature also surfaced on various big Fords and Mercurys.

Emission controls meant serious detuning and lower compression for Lincoln's 460 V-8, and the resulting performance loss was underlined by the industry's shift to SAE net instead of gross horsepower ratings. They were more accurate but did nothing for sales. Official bhp was now 224, 212 for California.

Much has been made of Lincoln's tremendous production upsurge in 1972 but, when the figures were in, Cadillac had increased its lead. While Lincoln's model year production was up by 32,000 units, Cadillac's improved by 37,000. The problem was that Cadillac still had many

The Mercury Marquis Brougham hardtop sedan for 1972: $5034.

Monterey front-end styling continued to differ from Marquis.

Mercury touted the 1972 Cougar's "classic vertical grille."

Cougar convertible production was down to only 3169 for 1972.

At $3438, the Villager was Montego's priciest 1972 offering.

With 28,417 built, MX Brougham coupe was Montego's best-seller.

Mercury built 20,192 Colony Park station wagons for 1972.

Montego MX easily outsold the base version, which is shown here.

more models and wider distribution. Nevertheless, Lincoln's record performance was something to cheer about.

Likewise Mercury's, which broke all previous model year records at 441,964 units. The big cars had recovered considerably, especially the premium models: this year's Marquis output was the best in that nameplate's history. The deluxe Marquis Broughams garnered nearly 75,000 sales, and the wood-trimmed Colony Park wagons saw

about 20,000. Most of these cars delivered for well over $5000 now, but Mercury customers seemed to prefer them to the less-posh Montereys at $500-$800 less. Styling helped. The Continental look was still in vogue, Marquis gaining a bold eggcrate grille, Monterey a waffle pattern. Both had full-length bodyside moldings. The Marquis' long list of standard equipment—power disc front brakes, power steering, thorough sound insulation, umpteen

A 429-cid, 205-bhp V-8 was biggest engine for Montego in '72.

The 1972 Comet sold well, with prices beginning at $2342.

Like the Maverick, Comet was available as a four-door sedan.

The imported Capri offered a peppy 120-bhp V-6 for 1972.

courtesy lights, thick carpeting, power ventilation—also appealed to buyers this year.

Elsewhere at Mercury, the mid-size Montego was revamped along the lines of Ford's new Torino—and ended up looking a lot like it, with the same sort of square, central grille and hunky-chunky bodywork. Model offerings were the same as before, aside from convertibles and the MX Brougham hardtop sedan. Cyclone was also gone

with the wind. In its place was a pillarless Montego GT fastback at $3346 basic.

Comet and Cougar were largely carryovers. The former acquired Maverick's new four-door style and optional small-block V-8, while the latter suffered further drops in horsepower and production. For the record, 1972 Cougar convertible output was 1240 standards and 1929 XR-7s. Hardtops sold about 20 times better.

L-M's sprightly imported Capri also got another engine option and it was a goodie: a 2.6-liter (156-cid) V-6 from Ford Cologne with 120 horsepower. The Euro-Mustang now had the performance its looks implied, *Road & Track* magazine recording a brisk 10.4 seconds 0-60 mph. Even better, you got tach and full engine instrumentation plus larger, 185 × 13 radial tires, all for a base list of $2821 P.O.E.—America's lowest priced V-6. At the same time, the little 1.6 was phased out in favor of the 2.0-liter engine as standard. In V-6 form, Capri was a standout in the growing "supercoupe" ranks that included GM's German-built Opel 1900 Rallye and a Japanese newcomer, the Toyota Celica. It was, perhaps, a bit odd to find such a spirited enthusiast's car among the big Marks and Marquises in L-M showrooms, but dealers didn't complain a bit as their cash registers jingled.

1973

Aside from new lower-body sheetmetal on full-size cars, this was a quiet Dearborn year. Most engineering efforts went into meeting another round of federal requirements, the most visible of which was heavier, bulkier front bumpers for the 5-mph impact protection rule (front only) that took effect this year. This also meant recalibrating suspensions throughout the line to compensate for the new bumpers' greater weight—not to mention hard styling work to make the things look acceptable.

Ford Division's sales results were mixed. Despite some 80,000 more registrations for the calendar year, its market share dropped below 19 percent for the first time in recent memory.

A below-the-belt reskin made the full-size Fords appear more substantial and "important." All wore flatter, more muted noses and deeper-section front bumpers that increased overall length by about three inches. LTDs had three-element grilles filled with little rectangles, while Galaxie and Custom 500s had a full-width ensemble. Bodyside creaselines were toned down, wheel arches took on a rounder form, and taillamps were set above the bumper, with the trunklid curved down in the center. Though not immediately apparent, sedans and wagons got new greenhouse styling with deeper windows. Sub-

The 1973 Ford LTD Brougham hardtop sedan listed at $4157.

All '73 Torinos wore five-mph, impact-absorbing front bumpers.

A 351 V-8 was standard fare on this $3771 Galaxie 500 sedan.

Ford built 51,853 Torino Gran Sport models ($3154 list) for 1973.

tracting the LTD convertible and base Custom sedan and wagon left the model count at 16. Engines stayed the same except for addition of the four-barrel 460-cubic-inch Lincoln-Mercury V-8 as the top option. Inside, the "front room" curved instrument panel was abandoned for a more conventional dash with radio and climate controls on the driver's right. New options included factory-fitted alarm system, power "mini-vent" front windows on four-doors, and steel-belted radial tires. In a year when rival makes had little new, big Fords picked up about 40,000 sales.

Thunderbird output hit 87,269 for 1973, a very good year. Heft and price escalated 150 pounds and $1100, respectively.

This 1973 Pinto features the popular Sports Accent Option.

Best-selling '73 Pinto was the wagon; 217,763 were produced.

Ford boasted that Pinto was America's most popular subcompact.

For $2343, the 1973 Pinto wagon offered a roomy cargo area.

Thunderbird was facelifted with a busier egg-crate grille flanked by headlamps in square chrome nacelles, and small parallelogram "opera" windows were a new option (at $80, vinyl top mandatory). Buyers responded to the more glittery package in record numbers, production soaring to over 87,000, the second highest total in T-Bird history after record 1964. Base prices jumped substantially to a bit over $6400, and it didn't take much to run that up to $7500 or more.

Only minor changes marked the last of the "fat" Mus-

Except for the new Federal bumpers, the '73 Maverick was largely unchanged. This one sports the Luxury Decor Option.

Last of the "big" Mustangs, the '73 Mach I listed at $3088.

Mach I production totalled 35,440 for the 1973 model year.

Output of the Mustang convertible climbed to 11,853 for 1973.

The '73 Ranchero car/pickup was based on the Torino chassis.

tangs, which increased sales by a bit less than 10,000 over 1972. Convertibles scored the largest percentage gain—100 percent, to nearly 12,000—but this was partly because of Ford's announcement that the ragtop wouldn't be around for '74. (This year's Mustangs and Cougars were thus Dearborn's last "factory" convertibles for the next decade.) Faces altered with vertical instead of horizontal parking lamps and a nicely integrated safety bumper with an optional body-color polyurethane cover, as used on the '72 Mach 1, for an even cleaner appearance. Mechanical mods were practically nil. As was true throughout the corporate line, final drive choices thinned due to the high cost of certifying each engine/transmission/ratio combination for emissions compliance under the Environmental Protection Agency's mandatory 50,000-mile durability test. Radial tires were newly optional, as was a "dual ram induction system," a special hood with twin air scoops, black or argent paint, decals, and twist-type hood locks, available with the extra-cost two-barrel 351 V-8. A two-tone hood with the locks and dummy scoops was also offered. Prices, which had been cut to spark '72 sales, remained fairly stable. Mach 1 now listed at $3088, the V-8 convertible at $3189, and the base six-cylinder hardtop at $2760.

Pinto sauntered on with a beefier front bumper backed by a reinforced structure to better absorb impact loads, revisions that added only about 40 pounds and 1.5 inches in length. Standard tires were upgraded to A78-13 bias-

plys, and air-conditioned cars got an extra pair of dash vents. New options included AM/FM stereo radio, forged-aluminum road wheels, and a handling package. Model year production breezed past the half-million mark as Pinto continued to outsell the rival Chevy Vega by a comfortable margin. The wagon accounted for nearly 40 percent.

Maverick's main improvement was 35-percent greater lining area for the all-drum brakes, which had been roundly criticized for lack of stopping power. The standard 170-cid six was replaced by the 200-cid unit, which was switched from four to seven main bearings for smoother

Continental Mark IV sales zoomed in 1973; 69,437 were built.

The 1973 Lincoln Continental Town Car featured power mini-vent windows as standard. Weight: 5049 pounds. Price: $7474.

running and gained six horsepower. All models now wore the richer-looking Grabber/LDO grille, and wheelarch and greenhouse moldings became standard along with full carpeting and nicer cabin trim. New options included "halo" vinyl roof for two-doors, AM/FM stereo, and forged-aluminum wheels. Overall length increased by four inches, all of it in the front bumper.

One of the less successful bumper grafts appeared on this year's Torino, bringing wider grilles on upper-line models (lesser cars retained a full-width treatment). A new Brougham hardtop and sedan arrived at the top of the line, with cloth and "leatherlike" vinyl upholstery,

pseudo-wood interior appliques, electric clock, and other amenities. Engines were detuned, but availability was unchanged.

This was the last model year before America's first "energy crisis." Middle East nations, acting under the Organization of Petroleum Exporting Countries cartel (OPEC), turned off the oil spigot during the winter of 1973-74, touching off political forces that would alter American life and its auto industry more dramatically than at any time since the great Depression.

Lincoln-Mercury Division was probably in better shape than most Detroit producers to weather this unexpected

Lincoln built 45,288 Continental sedans for '73, a new high.

This Continental was a prototype for the new 1973 Town Coupe.

storm. The Maverick-clone Comet had given it a contender in the high-volume compact field, while most of its Mercury Marquis and Lincoln Continental customers could well afford 80-cent-a-gallon gas. Looking ahead, the division would not have a really bad sales year until 1980.

That old Yankee expression, "If it works, don't fix it," also applies to cars. Lincoln's Mark IV and restyled senior cars had been tremendously successful in 1972 despite government decrees, so they stayed pretty much the same. The former, offered with a choice of 23 standard and four "moondust" colors, now enjoyed the best volume of its five-year run, helping Lincoln exceed the 100,000 mark for the first time ever. Nearly 70,000 Mark IVs rolled out of L-M showrooms despite a price that, since 1971, had nudged rather close to $10,000. This year's changes were trifling: a more solid die-cast grille shortened by the heavier new "crash" bumper, which also prompted taller fender-mount indicator/side marker lamps. A noticeable

rolling gait had caused some criticism of Mark IV handling, so shock absorbers were mounted vertically instead of at an angle, had firmer valving, and contained a bag filled with non-foaming freon. Rear drum brakes were enlarged slightly, the front discs improved, and larger standard tires were specified.

That bumper was a makeshift item, jutting out like the prow of a battleship and adding 130 pounds. The 5-mph thing was a "dog's breakfast" regulation that Congress would later repeal after discovering that the bumpers' presumed savings in body repairs for the average U.S. car were amply exceeded by their extra cost and the loss of gas mileage occasioned by the weight and wind resistance they added. More appropriate were the emission requirements, which now saw the 460 engine acquire closed-crankcase ventilation, lower compression, revised ignition timing, and exhaust gas recirculation. All this dropped bhp slightly to 219 federal, 208 California.

Comet prices started at $2432 for 1973. LDO trim was extra.

The 1973 Comet four-door sedan weighed in at 2904 pounds.

Full-size Mercurys were reskinned for 1973. The Marquis Brougham hardtop sedan listed at $5206; 10,613 were built.

Monterey again sported its own grille, exposed lights in '73.

car-nut named Leonid Brezhnev, thus helping relieve the shortage of decent limousines in that classless society.

Mercury responded to federal edicts in the same ways as Ford, and revamped its full-size fleet *a la* Galaxie/LTD. The new "cowcatcher" bumper helped the latter look more like the big Lincolns than ever, especially the hidden-headlamp Marquises, which continued to outsell the cheaper Monterey/Monterey Custom. Comet was still rocking along at about 80,000 units annually, with two-doors outpacing four-doors by some two to one. Cougar, on the sales skids since '68, finally showed an upturn, production rising from 1972's all-time low of just under 54,000 units to near 61,000. There were even a few more convertibles: 1284 standards, 3165 XR-7s. Of course, Capri was now L-M's *real* ponycar—and still selling briskly at $3175 for the 2.0-liter four-cylinder version or $3470 with 2.6 V-6. It, too, wore a front "battering ram," plus a nicely restyled dash with standard full gauges regardless

The senior Continentals shared the Mark IV's mechanical changes—one hesitates to call all of them improvements—and carried its name in separate letters on the hood. As a goodwill gesture, President Nixon presented one of these rolling monuments to capitalism to a Soviet

Monterey prices started at $3961 in 1973, but most buyers paid $700 extra for the more "Lincolnesque" Marquis models.

Mercury built 35,110 XR-7 coupes for '73, Cougar's sales leader.

MX Brougham hardtop was Montego's best-seller (40,951 built).

1974

Capri received a new dashboard and stronger bumpers for 1973.

Ford pickups for '73 featured an all-new cab and disc brakes.

Econoline Club Wagon registrations reached 20,942 in 1973.

Econoline E-100 vans offered wheelbases of 106 or 124 inches.

With one major exception, Ford Motor Company marked time this year, marred by the Middle East oil embargo that began in late 1973 and led to panic fuel buying and long lines at gas pumps, plus a big drop in big-car demand toward the end of the model year. Among new federal mandates were rear bumpers able to withstand 5-mph shunts, and the starter interlock. The latter prevented the engine from being started unless the driver's seatbelt was fastened, and it proved so irksome to so many people that it was soon scratched from the books.

Ford's Division's main product news was the smaller, lighter Mustang II, a return to something like the original ponycar concept. It arrived almost simultaneously with the "energy crisis," though it had been in the works long before. Still, this fortuitous timing undoubtedly contributed to strong sales: close to 386,000 for the model year, a figure within 10 percent of the original Mustang's 12-month production record of nearly 419,000.

That car's "father" was the driving force behind this new Mustang. But while Lee Iacocca had only guessed the first time, he knew *in advance* that Mustang II would hit it big: "When I look at the foreign-car market and see that one in five is a sporty car, I know something's happening." By 1972, cars like L-M's Capri, the Opel Manta from GM Germany, and Japan's Toyota Celica were running at around 300,000 annual sales, and 1974 projections put them at over 400,000. Mustang II was assigned to capture a big slice of this "mini-ponycar" pie.

Once again, Dearborn's army of stylists and engineers worked from parameters Iacocca had clearly defined: sporty appearance, wheelbase of 96-100 inches, standard four-speed gearbox, four-cylinder or small six-cylinder engine. Most important, "it must be luxurious—upholstered in quality materials and carefully built . . . a 'little jewel.'" What he got was the familiar long-hood/short-deck styling themes reinterpreted on a reduced scale—smaller even than the original. Against the '73, the II was 20 inches shorter, four inches narrower, an inch lower, 400-500 pounds lighter, and nearly 15 inches shorter between wheel centers.

Intramural competition again produced a new Mustang design, this time between the divisional Ford and Lincoln-Mercury staffs and the Ghia studios, the renowned Italian coachbuilding house Dearborn had recently acquired. The choice came down to five clay models, a pillared notchback hardtop and four fastbacks. The one selected as the basis for production styling—and surprisingly little altered— was a fastback from the L-M group. Iacocca had decided "the convertible is dead and can be forgotten," leaving hardtop and fastback. There were plain and fancy versions of each, the latter being the Ghia

of engine. Montego saw few changes other than those required, but the sporty GT fastback found fewer takers: 4464 versus 5820 for '72.

An indication of the change in Mercury's market orientation was its engine lineup, which had been dominated by big-inch V-8s just a few years before. There were still a few of those, including the Lincoln 460 (optional for the first time on Monterey and Marquis), but there were also three sixes and the nice little 302 V-8 for Comet/Montego, while most larger Mercurys used the old reliable 351.

Mustangs had gotten too fat, Mrs. Anna Muccioli protested, so Henry Ford II showed her the downsized 1974 Mustang II.

Lee Iacocca poses with early Mustang (in back) and Mustang II.

The 1974 Mustang II offered a hatchback model, Mustang's first.

1974

Mustang II's luxury model was the Ghia, offered only as a sumptuous two-door coupe; 89,477 were built for '74.

Mach I, the performance Mustang II, came with a 105-bhp V-6.

Heaviest Mustang II was the $3480 Ghia coupe at 2820 pounds.

Ford built 74,799 Mustang II three-door hatchbacks for 1974.

Mustang II hatchbacks started at $3328, weighed 2734 pounds.

notchback (replacing Grande) and the Mach 1, which along with the standard fastback gained a new lift-up rear hatch "door." The interior package included a neatly styled dash with standard tachometer, plus plush pleated cloth, vinyl, or optional leather upholstery. Rear seat room was limited, mainly because Mustang II was seen as a fun car for one or two adults.

In line with Iacocca's instructions, there was no thought of a V-8, a first for Mustang. Instead, engineering proceeded around a new 2.3-liter (140-cubic-inch) overhead-cam inline four to be built at Lima, Ohio. The only option would be a 2.8-liter (171-cid) ohv V-6, an enlarged version of the Capri's 2.6-liter unit. The "Lima" four was the first American-built engine using metric-measure compo-

306

nents—no surprise, as it was actually a bored and stroked derivative of the European 2.0-liter four first seen in the Pinto. The standard four-speed gearbox was a strengthened rendition of Pinto's British-built transmission. The standard vacuum-assisted brake system consisted of 9.3-inch discs in front and 9 × 1.75-inch drums at the rear.

With so many shared components and an identical 94.2-inch wheelbase, some observers suggested that Mustang II was really just a rebodied Pinto. Although they *did* have a lot in common, Pinto was actually upgraded for '74 by taking advantage of some parts and features designed for Mustang II. Both had unit construction and a front suspension with unequal-length upper and lower arms and coil springs; however, the lower arm attached to a rubber-mounted sub-frame on Mustang II, while on Pinto it bolted directly to the main structure. The Mustang sub-frame carried the rear of the engine/transmission assembly, and was designed for more precise steering and a smoother ride than Pinto. It also better isolated drive-train vibration but was costlier, though company cost accountants allowed it because Mustang II would sell for more than Pinto. Rack-and-pinion steering was also shared, but Mustang's steering gear was mounted differently, again to minimize shock. Also, Mustang could be ordered with power steering, but not Pinto. Mustang's rear leaf springs were two inches longer than Pinto's and its shock absorbers staggered as in recent high-performance Mustangs. Spring rates were computer-selected according to each car's equipment, weight, and body style. The optional competition suspension had the stiffest, along with a thicker front anti-sway bar, a rear bar, and Gabriel adjustable rear shocks.

In ride and handling, the "cooking" Mustang IIs and the top-line Ghia were typically American. The Mach 1, with its standard V-6, radial tires, and optional competition suspension, was more capable. Acceleration on any model was brisk but no more. Mustang II was heavy for its size (2650-2900 pounds curb weight), so a four-speed/V-6 needed 13-14 seconds 0-60 mph and topped out at only 100 mph.

Mustang II wouldn't change significantly over what would turn out to be a five-year model run. The four-cylinder and V-6 Ghia as well as the Mach 1 were available throughout, and Ford continued to add options (and more model variations). The '75 list showed air conditioning, a variety of radio and tape players, vinyl top, sunroof, forged-aluminum wheels, and many other goodies.

Apart from those already mentioned, this year's Pinto changes were minor. Stronger roof rails and underbody crossbars strengthened the unit structure. They added weight, of course, which together with tightening emissions controls rendered the original 1.6-liter engine too weak to provide decent performance, so the 2.0-liter four became standard.

This year's big Fords were mainly carryovers. LTDs received a new fine-checked grille insert and standup hood ornament, along with standard steel-belted radial tires. Solid-state ignition was now fitted on all optional

Ford LTD Brougham got a spring-loaded, stand-up hood ornament.

It took $4647 to buy an LTD Brougham four-door sedan in 1974.

The fuel embargo of late 1973 helped Maverick sales for 1974.

Basically unchanged, '74 Maverick wore a heavier rear bumper.

Pinto Runabout listed at $2676 for 1974; 174,754 were built.

T-Bird sales were down, but prices went up to $7330 for '74.

V-8s, but the big 429 engine was no longer listed.

Mid-size Fords were likewise little changed. Gran Torinos got vertical grille bars, with the parking lights at the outboard ends of the opening. Rear fender skirts were a new option for Gran Torinos, and hardtop coupes could be ordered with Thunderbird-style rear opera windows.

Thunderbird was little altered too. A new styling fillip was segmented taillamps incorporating a large, central backup lamp with stylized Bird logo. The 460 V-8, now with solid-state ignition and rated at 220 bhp net, was made standard, along with vinyl roof, opera windows, manual air conditioning, power windows, and tinted glass. Two of this year's new options would later show up on Dearborn's less expensive cars. One was "Autolamp," which used a photocell receptive to changes in ambient light levels to switch the headlamps on or off as needed. It also incorporated a delay timer that would extinguish the lights a few seconds after switching off the ignition, thus lighting the way for occupants from car to doorstep. Also new was the "moonroof," a tinted glass panel that retracted electrically, a descendant of the Fifties "bubbletop" idea. The fuel shortage put a crimp in sales, T-Bird production crumbling to about 58,500 for the model year.

Predictably, the compact Maverick benefited from the gas scare, production rising by about 10,000 units. The '74 models were substantially the same as the '73s, identifiable only by their deep-section rear bumpers.

The oil embargo didn't start clobbering sales until about the middle of model year '74. And since we're mainly recounting model years here, it must be said that this was a pretty good one for the industry as a whole and Lincoln-Mercury in particular. Sales were down compared to high-rolling '73, but not by much. Lincoln's output returned to its '72 level, which was hardly bad. Mercury's 404,650 units was down substantially but still one of its best-ever totals. The problem, of course, was that a six-million-car year was not the boom it had been in the Fifties. Detroit was now geared to produce 10 million units annually, and when sales didn't match, the moguls began muttering.

All 1974 Thunderbirds were powered by a 220-bhp, 460-cid V-8. Federal mandates helped push weight up to 4825 pounds.

Introduced as a 1974½ model, the Gran Torino Elite was brought out to do battle with Chevy's high-flying Monte Carlo.

Opera windows and skirts were options on this '74 Gran Torino.

Gran Torino wagon listed at $4017; 29,866 were built for 1974.

Base price of the Mark IV topped $10,000 for first time in 1974, but sales remained strong even during the fuel crisis.

Least bought '74 Lincoln was the Continental coupe (7316 built).

Output of the $8238 Continental sedan was 29,351 for 1974.

Besides the mandated rear safety girders, both Lincoln lines got rub-strips on each giant bumper. New standards for roof crush resistance were also in effect now but did not affect the Mark, with its large, strong C-pillars. Seniors received a more Mark-like face, with a squarish vertical-bar grille, wrapped parking lights, and plain headlamp doors. It was well that they had dropped the four-door convertible, which would never have met the roof-crush test; even so, pillars had to be reinforced, giving the cars a more tank-like look. All this fiddling cost

weight as well as dollars, the Mark IV, to take the worst example, now nearly 10 percent heavier. Its price, meanwhile, had shot from the previous year's $8984 base to $10,194, same as the old Mark II, albeit in depreciated dollars.

Ironically, Lincoln's most important safety development this year was *not* federally required: a power brake system drawing its energy from the power steering reservoir. Since the latter stored fluid under pressure, this meant the brakes had some assist even when the engine

Mercury's new mid-size luxo-cruiser was the 1974 Cougar XR-7.

The 4092-pound Mercury Montego MX sedan sold for $3478 in '74.

Best-selling Montego was the MX hardtop coupe (20,957 built).

Comet prices started at $3008 for 1974; sales skyrocketed.

wasn't running, where conventional systems were virtually dead. This notable improvement made Lincoln brakes a near-rival to Imperial's and distinctly better than Cadillac's, worst in the luxury field.

As at Ford, electronic ignition came to L-M's 460 and 400 V-8s in all applications. This was another important technical improvement in that it extended tune-up intervals, though it was dictated more by the need to meet stiffer emission standards.

This year's Mercury lineup was mainly a rerun, with beefed-up back bumpers and associated minor styling changes for the compact Comet, mid-size Montego, and full-size Monterey and Marquis. The exception was Cougar, which became a high-line Montego on the 114-inch two-door wheelbase, distinguished by standard rear-quarter "opera windows" and, inevitably, a higher price ($4706 base retail).

For once, Mercury had opted out of cloning a new Ford, in this case the Mustang II—odd considering that L-M's proposal was the one chosen as the basis for it. Ford Design Center photos show that some consideration was given to a Mustang II-based replacement for the European Capri (and bearing that name). But the import was selling too well, and Mercury marketers likely wanted a more direct competitor for GM's personal-luxury middleweights, the popular Pontiac Grand Prix and Chevrolet Monte Carlo. The obvious strategy was to upgrade Cougar, and it paid off. Production jumped to over 90,000 for the model year, up over 30,000 from '73.

Meantime, the Torino-twin Montego went well down in sales, and would continue languishing until its 1976 demise. (Its basic platform would survive in an expanded Cougar line for 1977-78.) The larger and more expensive Marquis didn't do much better, though the immensely profitable top-line Broughams and Colony Park wagons took the lion's share. As the gas spigots dried up, so did Monterey sales, and the mid-range biggie would disappear for '75.

Comet, on the other hand, enjoyed even greater success, running up close to twice as many sales as it had in any of its first three seasons. Capri was still doing good business too, with an enlarged, 119-bhp 2.8-liter V-6 as its main attraction. But it was getting expensive—up to $3566 in base form, $3807 with V-6—thanks to inflation, which was starting to gallop, and currency fluctuations that were beginning to price most German cars right out of the market.

Nobody who lived through the winter of 1973-74 will forget that time when gasoline, always assumed to be almost as plentiful as water, suddenly became a much

Big Mercury's grille looked even more Lincoln-like for 1974.

Colony Park wagons exceeded $5000 in 1974; output was 10,802.

Only 4510 Monterey Custom hardtop coupes were built for 1974.

The Capri 2800 V-6 four-passenger coupe sold for $3807 in '74.

The compact four-wheel-drive 1974 Ford Bronco listed at $3635.

This 1975 Thunderbird carried the Copper Luxury Group option.

more expensive—and, occasionally, a black-market—commodity. Drivers got up at dawn to grab position in gas lines that stretched for blocks as dinosaurs bred three to five years before queued for a suck at the life-giving pumps. Some owners even resorted to carrying a spare set of license plates in places where gas was rationed according to odd/even numbers, and locking gas caps sold like crazy as protection against fuel thieves with syphons.

Lincoln-Mercury was pretty well prepared for this unexpected vision of the apocalypse, and would bolster its Capri and the thrifty Comet with the mid-size Monarch and Pinto-based Bobcat for '75. All of them were exactly the right products for an automotive world that would never be the same again.

1975

Thunderbird marked its 20th birthday in a busy model year that saw introduction of a new mid-size Ford/Mercury, a restyled big Continental, a junior T-Bird, and a spate of lesser changes in other lines. The U.S. auto industry was still in a sales slump following the Middle East oil embargo. Ford Division's market share reflected this, dropping more than two points for the calendar year to slightly below 18 percent despite the broadest range of models, sizes, and prices since the mid-Sixties.

Buyers had lately shown increasing preference for well-equipped, more luxurious smaller cars, and the 1973-74 gas panic only accelerated their desire. Ford's response was the Granada, trumpeted as the "car designed for the times." Actually, it had been designed to replace Maverick. The original plan called for a plusher, slightly larger compact of more formal appearance and essentially the same chassis and running gear. But with sales consistent-

ly strong, Ford felt it couldn't afford to drop the old compact. Accordingly, the plan changed: Maverick would continue, while its intended successor would be an addition to the line, occupying a size and price niche halfway between Maverick and the mid-size cars.

Though its 109.9-inch wheelbase was shared with the Maverick four-door, Granada emerged 10 inches longer, an inch wider, and several hundred pounds heavier. Suspension was also shared and typical Detroit, but Granada was blessed with standard front disc brakes, more body and suspension bushings, and softer springs and shocks, the last in the interest of a "big car" ride. There were no powertrain surprises. Base engine was Maverick's standard 200-cid, and options were the same 250-cid six and 302 V-8, plus a two-barrel 351. Three-speed manual transmission was standard, automatic optional, and floorshift available for both.

Granada also offered two- and four-door body styles like Maverick, but that's where the similarity ended. Where Maverick looked American, Granada struggled to be European. Styling, supervised by design vice-president Eugene Bordinat, was an unabashed imitation of certain upper-class imports. Mercedes-Benz, in particular, had every reason to be flattered, and Ford advertising hammered away at the size and styling similarities with M-B's junior "New Generation" sedans. (TV commercials showed passers-by mistaking Granada for the Mercedes.) The four-door was unquestionably more handsome than the two-door, which was afflicted with opera windows that looked out of place with the Mercedes-like rectangular grille and similarly boxy body. The interior could have come from Lincoln. While a few European touches were available on the costlier Ghia models—individual front seats with reclining backrests, grab handles, map pockets, and the like—instrumentation was next to nil and the dash slathered with "test tube" wood.

Enthusiasts were disappointed by Granada's handling and performance. *Road & Track* magazine reported that "the car doesn't handle badly; it corners quite flat . . . and on the skidpad it got around only slightly slower than the vaunted Brand M. . . . But Ford's power steering still has little road feel . . . and we found ourselves too concerned with just staying on course. . . . The live axle, not particularly well controlled since it's on simple leaf springs, is quite susceptible to bumps and loses traction easily." With 302 V-8, automatic, and 3.00:1 axle ratio, *R&T*'s tester ran 0-60 mph in a respectable 12 seconds and returned a not-so-respectable 12.5 mpg in normal driving. But the editors praised brakes, driving position, and quietness, as well as the more intelligent design. "If we had expected it to be a surrogate Mercedes . . . we'd be disappointed. But if we look at the moderate price tag [around $3700] and think of the Granada as a reasonable-size interpretation of the traditional American car with a little inspiration from Europe, there's no problem liking it."

A good many buyers liked Granada—nearly 303,000, a model year total that outnumbered Maverick's nearly two to one. Again, Ford had read the market correctly, and Granada's strong initial acceptance showed clearly that the way to future sales success was upmarket, not down.

Other '75 Fords changed but mildly. Special "MPG"

Pinto and Mustang II models arrived at mid-year with that new emissions cleanup device, the catalytic converter. By obviating the need for much of the add-on emissions hardware of past years, it allowed engines to be retuned for greater efficiency, thus boosting fuel economy—which hadn't been that spectacular of late in Ford's smallest cars. The 2.3-liter "Lima" four was now standard Pinto power, while the 302 V-8 became optional for Mustang II (automatic only), answering cries for more go. Mustang II notchbacks gained an optional power moonroof at $454, and a Silver Luxury Group arrived for the Ghia, with cranberry-color crushed velour upholstery and silver paint and vinyl top. Pinto and Maverick acquired standard steel-belted radial tires and solid-state ignition. F-O-R-D letters appeared on Maverick's trunklid and hood, a proper glovebox was added to Grabber and the LDO package, and a heavy-duty suspension option was a new—and overdue—extra for Grabber.

While Torino went virtually untouched, mid-year 1974 had seen an interesting line expansion called Gran Torino

New for 1975 was the Ford Granada, an up-scale compact with Mercedes-like styling; model year output hit 302,652.

Top-of-the-line 1975 Granada Ghia four door listed at $4283.

Least expensive Granada, the two door sedan, started at $3698.

The LTD Landau became Ford's plushest full-size offering in 1975. The two door weighed 4419 pounds and retailed at $5484.

Ford built 32,506 four-door LTD Landaus for the '75 model year.

Best-selling full-size '75 Ford: LTD coupe (82,382 produced).

Elite. Ford called it "Thunderbird-inspired," but actually it was a pillared coupe on the beefy Cougar XR-7 chassis. Its mission was to take sales away from the fast-selling Chevrolet Monte Carlo. For 1975, the name was shortened to Elite, but it kept the body structure, dimensions, and interior appointments of the Torino, as well as its two-barrel 351 V-8 as standard. Styling hallmarks included an aggressive eggcrate grill, dual (instead of quad) headlamps in square nacelles, wide body moldings, and two slim opera windows per side. Production hit over 96,000 in

Maverick soldiered on in 1975 with output of 162,572 units.

its short debut season, and increased to 123,000 for 1975, a good start for a new nameplate.

The big Fords were given a modest restyle, with flatter and more rectangular grilles, raised and planed rear decks, and slim vertical windows cut into the B-pillars of two-door "hardtops." Series hierarchy changed, with the new LTD Landau (identified by hidden headlamps) at the top, followed by LTD Brougham and plain LTD.

Marking 20 years of Thunderbirds were two new luxury option packages for the otherwise unchanged cruiser. One was done in silver, the other copper, both color-keyed to a fare-thee-well. Though not many people knew it, four-wheel disc brakes had been a T-Bird option since '72, and were now included with the extra-cost Sure-Track antilock system. Sales sank to 43,000, down about 16,000 from 1974.

If Ford could have a Cougar, Mercury could have a Granada. It duly arrived as the Monarch, virtually identical apart from grille texture and minor ornamentation. Mercury described it as "precision-size," but it was just a more sensible intermediate and thus more appropriate for the changing times. Still, Granada/Monarch was the forerunner of a whole new Detroit generation patterned on the junior Mercedes, which for some reason was deemed the

A Silver Luxury Group option adorns this 1975 Mustang II Ghia.

Price was up to $3938 on the '75 Ghia; note new opera window.

Steel-belted radial-ply tires and solid state ignition became standard on all 1975 Mustang IIs. Mach I listed at $4188.

key to design salvation in mid-Seventies Detroit. Mercedes is a great car in many ways, but to set it up as a design ideal is to pursue a phantom. It is, perhaps, better now than it was then—boxy and unslippery, with tortured metal at the corners and curious castbacks like a standup hood ornament.

One thing Mercedes did have, though, was a knack for

extracting maximum interior space from a given exterior package, and Granada/Monarch was similarly good, particularly for a mid-Seventies American. Likewise engineering, sturdy if hardly as elegant as Stuttgart's. Most Monarchs sold this year with the larger six or a 302 V-8, and those sales were good indeed: close to 150,000.

Mercury had another newcomer that was an even bet-

Pinto Runabout upped heft to 2528 pounds and price to $2984.

The 1975 Gran Torino Brougham four door retailed for $4805.

1975

Lincoln boasted that the 1975 Continental, "more than any of its predecessors, has the look and feel of a limousine."

The 1975 Continental sedan sold for $9656; 33,513 were built.

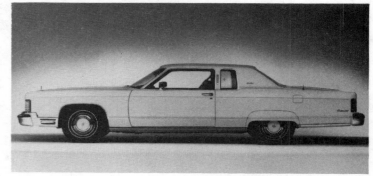

Continental Town Coupe for '75 adopted fixed quarter windows.

ter bet for the oil crisis. Called Bobcat (since Cougar, L-M dealers had hung out "the sign of the cat") it was an upmarket Pinto distinguished mainly by a mock-Mark vertical-bar grille that looked a bit pretentious on such a small package. Mercury eschewed Pinto's basic two-door, offering Bobcat as a Runabout hatchback and as a pseudo-wood-trim Villager three-door wagon. They were good little cars, but buyers apparently couldn't figure them out and first-year sales totalled only 34,000 units.

Elsewhere, Mercury's Montego was little changed. Ditto Comet, but production dropped by more than half—to below 54,000 units—probably reflecting showroom com-

petition from Bobcat. Cougar was another carryover with lower volume, a bit over 60,000. As for Capri, its sales were suspended once leftover '74s had been cleared. But L-M wasn't abandoning the "Sexy European," merely clearing the decks for something better: the Capri II, which arrived late in the model year as an early-'76 entry (and is thus covered under that heading).

All the big Mercs were now named Marquis and received a modest restyle, including a grille that was a dead-ringer for the '75 Lincoln's. Pillarless sedans fell victim to threatened government rollover standards that never materialized, leaving four-door sedan and hardtop

Four-wheel disc brakes became standard on the 1975 Mark IV.

Mercury built 62,987 Cougar XR-7 personal-luxury coupes for '75.

Mate a Lincoln-style grille to a Pinto and—voilà—a Bobcat!

From here, the Bobcat Villager looked just like a Pinto Squire.

Bobcat production for 1975 amounted to a modest 34,234 units.

Comet output skidded 60 percent when the '75 Monarch appeared.

coupe in base, Brougham, and new Grand Marquis guise, plus standard and woody-look Colony Park wagons. Grand Marquis, latest in a long line of "super Mercs," weighed two and a half tons and usually sold for well over $7000. Boasting standard deep shag carpets, map reading lamps, vinyl top, extra trim, and the Lincoln 460 V-8, it found nearly 20,000 buyers this gas-short model year. Amazingly, Marquis as a whole managed a slight volume gain, reflecting the start of a big-car sales rebound at about mid-season.

Conceptually—and perhaps socially—Lincoln's restyled seniors were about as wrong as they could be for their time—bulkier and thirstier, though on the same wheelbase. But wrong was often right in their particular price class, and they led Lincoln to more than 100,000 units for the second time in its history. Rooflines were redone in GM's "Colonnade" style—windows with rounded upper corners, more prominent B-posts, big opera windows on the coupe—again in anticipation of the government's never-to-be roof standards, and the grille was reworked into six vertical oblongs, each filled with six small, vertical bars. Lincoln wrung out 21,185 coupe sales—better than the old pillarless model had ever done—and rather more four-doors to boot. Less welcome

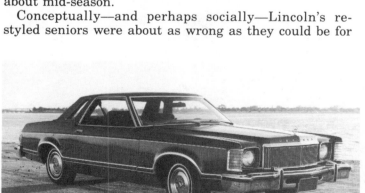

Monarch, Mercury's Granada-clone, sported a "European look."

Mercury pegged the Monarch Ghia four door list price at $4349.

317

Flagship of the Mercury lineup for 1975, Grand Marquis bore "a strong kinship to the Lincoln Continental."

Montego replaced the standard 302-cid V-8 with a 351 for 1975.

The Montego MX Brougham sedan weighed 150 pounds more in 1975.

An all-new Capri II hatchback bowed late in '75 model year.

Ford built 34,709 Club Wagons during calendar year 1975.

was the frameless side glass, which made for rattles and drafts as time and miles passed.

Mark IV was again unchanged, though there was a new Landau roof option with frenched, oval opera windows and a chrome "tiara" roof band that owed something to Ford's 1955-56 Crown Victoria. A further engineering improvement was standard four-wheel disc brakes for the first time. Again reflecting the market, Lincoln's finest fell by about 10,000 units, to 47,145.

Despite this, "there was no panic move to replace the Mark IV with a downsized successor," according to a former Dearborn stylist. "The Mark V was the same car with modest changes, and had been planned for 1977 in 1974—it stayed in the saddle. We had been attempting to outsize Cadillac with both the Mark and the Continentals for some time, and especially after the 1975 market recovery, this still seemed to us the right way to proceed."

Sure enough, it proved the right way once gas started flowing again in mid-1974. And right it remained for some years, at least for Lincoln. Cadillac, ever the great rival, changed the game a bit this year with its new compact Seville, which prompted a Lincoln response but not an immediate change in the Continental or Mark.

1976

America's Bicentennial year was not a memorable one for Dearborn product developments. Worse, Ford Division's market share dropped yet again. Despite recent attention, the big Fords ran a poor fourth in the sales race, trailing the full-size Chevrolet, Oldsmobile, and Buick. But there were bright spots. Mustang II, for instance, was second among domestic subcompacts, bested only by Chevy's new-for-'76 Chevette—and then by less than 400 units. And Pinto, despite its five-year-old design, was still hanging in there, a solid fourth. Granada quickly captured top spot among compacts, leading a redesigned Chevy Nova and Plymouth's new Volare by very comfortable margins.

Most Ford changes this year involved the smaller models. In further pursuit of sport—or what was left of it—a new Stallion trim package arrived for Pinto, Maverick, and Mustang II. Content differed, but all involved silver body paint set off with lots of black on hoods, grilles, and greenhouse, plus bold front-fender decals emblazoned with a fiery steed. More functional but slightly outrageous was the new Cobra II option group for Mustang II hatchbacks (including Mach 1). Intended to evoke memories of the great Shelby GT-350/500, it had the requisite rocker-panel stripes, plus black grille, styled steel wheels with trim rings, flip-out rear quarter windows with louvered covers, a front air dam, ducktail rear spoiler, and simulated hood scoop. You also got radial tires, sports steering wheel, dual remote-control door mirrors, brushed-aluminum dash and door panel trim, and Cobra II emblems. It was initially available with the traditional white paint and blue striping, but other color combinations were added for '77.

Pinto got a minor freshening via a close-checked grille housing square parking lamps, and a no-frills Pony two-door appeared to battle budget import rivals. Options expanded with a half-vinyl roof for sedans and pseudo-wood Squire bodyside appliqués for the Runabout. The aging Maverick also got a new grille, a split horizontal-bar affair, and front disc brakes became standard at last. The

The little-changed '76 Granada—America's best-selling compact.

New for the '76 Granada was a Sport Sedan Option, as pictured.

This '76 Granada Ghia four door sports the Luxury Decor Option.

It took $5613 to buy a 1976 Ford LTD Landau two-door sedan.

Although full-size Ford sales were slipping, 29,673 LTD Landau two-door sedans found buyers in 1976.

Four-wheel disc brakes were offered on 1976 full-size Fords.

This '76 Maverick was optioned with the Stallion trim package.

In addition to a new grille, Runabout offered a Squire option.

The 1976 Maverick received a new grille with divider bar.

highly successful Granada continued with no appearance changes. A new Luxury Decor Option for the Ghia four-door offered two-tone black/tan exterior and lacy-spoke aluminum wheels plus color-keyed tan interior with crushed-velour upholstery. The standard two-door could now be dressed with a "Sports Sedan" group comprising special paint, color-keyed road wheels and pinstripes, floorshift, and leather-rim steering wheel. Other new options included a power moonroof and, interestingly, all-disc power brakes. Headlamp dimmer switches were com-bined with the turn signal stalk on both Granada and Mustang II.

Ford's mid-size Torino and Elite were practically un-changed, the latter now a separate, one-model series. The Gran Torino Sport hardtop disappeared, but Elite filled the gap with bucket seats and console with floorshift as a new option. There were no appreciable changes to the big LTDs, but optional four-wheel power disc brakes showed up here too, along with a half-vinyl top for two-doors. Thunderbird's only alteration was another round of trim

The Stallion trim package was also available on Mustang II.

A revised Luxury Decor Option became available on '76 Mavericks.

This '76 Mustang II Ghia has the "silver blue luxury option."

Scoops and stripes went into making the 1976 Mustang Cobra II.

Pinto got its Stallion package for the 1976 model year, too.

With optional V-6, the Pinto Stallion had some get up and go.

Output of Mustang II hatchbacks increased to 71,544 for 1976.

Elite was no longer a Gran Torino for 1976; 146,475 were built.

and paint packages—Creme and Gold, Bordeaux (as in wine), and Lipstick (a bright red). Besides coordinated colors, each included half-vinyl top, thicker carpeting, special upholstery, and body accent stripes. T-Bird sales recovered somewhat to nearly 53,000 for the model year as the curtain rang down on the big seventh generation.

That meant that the Continental Mark IV was also in its last season. Again, it was practically unchanged. The senior Lincolns continued having good success with the Town Car option package, which had been around for the four-door since the beginning of the decade: leather seat inserts, wood-like panels on front seatbacks, deep pile carpeting, soft nylon headliner, all carefully color-keyed in a variety of fairly conservative hues. The idea was extended to the '73 two-door to create the Town Coupe. These popular sub-models prompted Lincoln to try something a bit more radical on the final Mark IV: the "Designer Series."

American Motors had done something similar a few years earlier with its Gucci Hornet and Pierre Cardin

321

Ford's Gran Torino Brougham four-door pillared hardtop for '76.

Better gas mileage was a selling point for the '76 Gran Torino.

Thunderbird production bounced back up to 52,935 for 1976.

A power lumbar seat was a new option for the '76 Thunderbird.

Javelin. But as a luxury make, Lincoln was in a far better position to cash in on the snob appeal of such high-fashion names. These extra-cost couturier groups were done up inside and out with colors and materials chosen by four famous designers. The schemes would vary somewhat from year-to-year, but were always striking and usually pleasing. Perhaps the most consistently tasteful was the Bill Blass edition, a nautically inspired blend of navy blue paint and eggshell-white vinyl top outside, combined with navy velour or dark blue-and-cream leather upholstery inside. There were also versions by Givenchy (usually turquoise or jade), Pucci (maroon and gunmetal grey), and Cartier (champagne/gray). The latter, of course, was not a designer per se but the famous jeweler.

Holding the line with America's largest cars, Lincoln cashed in with its second-best model year volume ever:

With styling unchanged, T-Bird promoted three "new colorful luxury groups" in 1976: Creme and Gold, Bordeaux, and Lipstick.

Although the Lincoln Continental Mark IV was in its last year, output increased to 56,110 for the 1976 model year.

Continental featured "an understated contemporary look" in '76.

Total Continental output rebounded to 68,646 units for 1976.

124,756 units. And Mercury was up strongly overall as the market recovered to pre-embargo levels, again producing at its record 1973 pace.

This year's Mercury lineup was a near-duplicate of 1975's, and styling changed only in detail across the board. One new addition was the ultra-luxe Grand Monarch sedan, done up *a la* the big Grand Marquis and base-priced at close to $6000. Both Monarch and Cougar had

good years, but Comet and Bobcat showed little improvement. "People really want big cars," said Henry Ford II. "Give them the option and they'll go for big ones every time."

With that attitude at the top, Dearborn's advance-design department certainly felt no pressure to rush out smaller intermediate and full-size cars in the wake of the energy crisis. Contrary to popular belief, Ford had a few

Cougar XR-7 pushed luxury options in 1976, which often inflated the $5125 base price. Nonetheless, 83,765 were built.

The 1976 Runabout sported a simulated-cherry woodgrain option.

Mercury offered a "new tu-tone group" on the '76 Grand Marquis.

The cargo capacity of the Bobcat Villager was 58 cubic feet.

Mercury's top-of-the-line compact: 1976 Grand Monarch Ghia.

Bobcat prices started at $3338 for the base hatchback in 1976.

Montego MX Brougham featured a low-back flight-bench seat.

Comet sales dropped again in 1976; output was down to 36,064.

Mercury marketed eight Montego models in '76, here an MX coupe.

Mercury Grand Marquis four door listed at $6528; 17,650 were built.

Sportiest Capri II for 1976 wore the black and gold "S" option.

All 1976 Capri II models came with the 2.8-liter V-6 standard.

A newcomer to the 1976 Ford truck line was the F-150 4 × 4.

such projects in the works, but the prevailing opinion—or was it a hope?—seemed to be that it would be big-car business as usual just as soon as buyers got used to higher gas prices. Of course, HFII hadn't reckoned on a challenge to Detroit's "bigger is better" tradition—least of all by that bastion of bigness, GM. But it hit like a bomb for '77, rattling the "Glass House" like nothing since the Edsel.

A more enlightened attitude was evidenced by this year's new Capri II, an updated version of the appealing Euro-Mustang. Wheelbase stayed the same but overall length went up seven inches (to 174.8), most of it in rear overhang to accommodate a roomier luggage compartment accessible via a lift-up hatch. With its attendant structural reinforcements, the new body configuration swelled curb weight to near 2600 pounds, but performance remained respectable despite minor horsepower losses to emissions tuning. Sensibly, the four was discontinued, leaving the 2.8-liter V-6 as the standard and only engine.

Styling was cleaned up by simplifying the grille and erasing the fussy bodyside character lines, but familiar Capri "cues" persisted: elliptical rear side windows, domed hood, close-coupled proportions. Base, luxury Ghia, and sporty "S" models were now listed, the last available with a striking black-and-gold color scheme (later called "Le Cat Black") reminiscent of the treatment used on contemporary Lotus Grand Prix racers. Interiors continued with front buckets, console-mount shift, and well-arranged, fully instrumented dash, with a newly available fold-down back seat for extra practicality.

Unfortunately, a strengthening Deutsche mark lifted Capri II into an altogether different price class from the one its predecessor had occupied—up to Monarch/Montego territory, in fact: around $4100 this year, escalating to near $4600 for the '77 Ghia. Capri was still a fine enthusiast's coupe, but fewer buyers saw much reason to prefer it over the mechanically similar Mustang II, not to mention a few Japanese sportsters that cost considerably less. Predictably, then, Capri II withered rapidly through the little-changed 1977-78 models, after which it was ousted from the L-M stable by a ponycar of a different color. However, an evolution would continue in Europe (as the Capri III) all the way through 1986, a remarkably long production run that testifies to the durable popularity of Capri's basic design.

1977

Responding to GM's downsizing initiative, Dearborn realigned its intermediates and fielded a new, but less than brilliant, "baby" Lincoln. Topping the corporate fleet was a totally redesigned Continental Mark, the first in five years.

Attempting to shore up its relatively weak position in the increasingly important mid-size field, Ford Division abandoned Torino for the LTD II, styled like the Elite but with crisper front and rear sheetmetal. The Elite itself was also cancelled, replaced as the "premium" intermediate by a much cheaper Thunderbird on the same platform. Likewise, Mercury junked Montego for a full range of Cougars, with a T-Bird-like XR-7 coupe leading base and Brougham sedans and coupes, plus standard and Villager wagons. Despite all the name switching and appearance alterations, these "new" cars were essentially the old ones underneath, retaining body-on-frame construction, the same suspension design, and most running gear. Someone in Dearborn had evidently been thinking of the Edsel, for this was nothing more than an attempt to improve sales

Maverick, now in its final year, saw 1977 ouput slip to 98,506.

The 302 V-8 put out 139 horses in the '77 Mustang II Cobra II.

A new option for Mustang II hatchbacks in 1977 was the T-top.

Buyers could also choose a Rallye Appearance Package in '77.

Granada prices started at $4118 in 1977; this Ghia cost $4452.

The '77 LTD wagon came with engines of 351-460 cubic inches.

A restyled Torino became the LTD II for the 1977 model year.

The $4785 LTD II hardtop coupe saw production of 56,704 units.

Stacked rectangular headlights were featured on the '77 LTD II.

via more popular names. Fortunately for all involved, it worked.

Described as "a sporty new trim-size line in the LTD tradition," the LTD II arrived with an Elite-type nose, checked grille and—something new—rectangular headlamps, stacked in pairs. Overall appearance was straighter and starchier than Torino's, but marked similarities in the greenhouse area were there for all to see. Cougar was scarcely different apart from horizontal lamps, a different grille cap, and minor trim. Thunderbird got its own eggcrate frontispiece flanked by flip-up doors concealing the headlamps, plus a "basket handle" roof with wrapover chrome bands defining body-color B-posts. The latter had tiny "coach" windows, trailed by large rear quarter panels and slim C-pillars aft.

LTD II continued Torino's nine-model line of wagons and pillared hardtops and sedans, arrayed in base (called "S"), standard, and Brougham series. There was only one T-Bird initially, but the Town Landau name was resurrected in January for a second version with an arm-long list of comfort and convenience equipment. Respective base list prices were $5063 and $7990. The 302 V-8 was standard for federal versions of both LTD II and T-Bird; Californians got the optional 351 at no charge. SelectShift Cruise-O-Matic was the one and only transmission, and the largest available engine was the corporate 400 V-8 in two- or four-barrel form.

This reorganization produced some interesting sales results. The LTD II failed to match Torino's performance, slipping from sixth to seventh among intermediates. The new T-Bird, however, captured fifth, outselling the entire LTD II line by some 80,000 units—more than 318,000 in all. Part of this was doubtless due to the magic of the Thunderbird name, but dramatically lower prices didn't hurt: down some $2700 for the base offering compared with its '76 counterpart. Cougar was less impressive, but the story was the same. At 125,000 units, the posh XR-7 outpulled the rest of the line better than two to one.

The Ford Granada/Mercury Monarch was largely unchanged for its third season aside from several new options. These included a four-speed overdrive manual transmission, basically the old three-speed with a high-geared ratio tacked on, plus four-way manual driver's seat (up/down as well as fore/aft), leather upholstery for Ghia four-doors, and big-car features like illuminated entry system, thermostat control for heating/air conditioning, and front cornering lamps. Meanwhile, the old-soldier Maverick/Comet returned one last time with fewer options and no styling or mechanical changes.

Pinto got another front-end redo plus larger sedan taillamps. The new sloped-back "soft" nose had taller headlamp buckets and a narrower chrome grille flanked by twin vertical parking lamps. A new Runabout option was a frameless, all-glass hatch, providing a different look outside and a better view from inside. Other first-time extras: the Mustang/Capri II 2.8-liter V-6, bronze-tint flip-up sunroof, four-way manual driver's seat, and a Sports Rallye Package consisting of tachometer, extra engine gauges, sport steering wheel, and front anti-roll bar. Also new was the Cruising Wagon, a youth-oriented version of the regular Pinto wagon, with front spoiler, styled wheels, and blanked-off rear quarters containing glass portholes. It also had all the Sports Rallye features plus a fully carpeted rear deck and interior side walls, the latter an appeal to the van set. All Pintos now wore front bumpers made of aluminum instead of steel, which together with a lighter energy absorbing system reduced total weight by about 80 pounds. For all this, Pinto waned in popularity, sales falling by over 50,000 units, though it remained fourth in the subcompact class.

Biggest change on the 1977 Pinto was a new front end design.

Pinto taillights were bigger; all-glass hatch was an option.

The 1977 T-Bird was downsized to the Torino/LTD II platform.

Engines for the 1977 Thunderbird ranged from 130-173 horsepower.

Mercury's Bobcat looked the same but added a plain-side wagon, bringing models to three, and offered some of this year's new Pinto features. The latter included the lightweight bumpers and optional sunroof, all-glass Runabout hatch, and four-way driver's seat.

"Continental Mark heritage takes a step forward," Lincoln boasted in 1977. The new Mark V stands in the foreground.

The '77 Continental Mark V set a production record of 80,321.

A Continental Town Car hallmark was the oval opera window.

Prices started at $9636 for the 1977 Continental four door.

Continental output reached 95,600 for '77; here a Town Coupe.

Despite some 34,000 fewer sales, Mustang II now headed the subcompact list, handily outpacing Chevy's less sporting, less expensive Chevette by nearly 20,000 units. Much of this came on the strength of new options. Among them were T-bar roof with lift-off glass panels for hatchbacks; flip-up/removable glass sunroof for hardtops; a new Rallye Appearance Package, replacing the Stallion option; two-tone paint; and a color-keyed Sports Appearance Group for the Ghia. The Cobra II package picked up tricolor tape striping and black side window and backlight louvers late in the season. Engine outputs fluctuated a good deal on most cars of the Seventies and Mustang II was not immune. This year's 2.3-liter four was rated at 92 bhp, the extra-cost 2.8-liter V-6 at only 93, and the 302 V-8 at 139, all SAE net.

This was the year GM introduced its first downsized cars, smaller renditions of its full-size models. Ford advertising was quick to seize on this, and the mostly unchanged LTD was promoted as "the full-size car that kept its size." Obviously, the appeal was to those buyers who didn't think smaller big cars were such a good idea. To a degree, it worked: LTD sales moved up by about 24,000. But all big cars scored increases as memories of the energy crisis dimmed, and Chevrolet, Buick, and Oldsmobile scored healthy gains with their trimmer '77s to remain ahead of Ford.

Mercury used a similar tactic with its seemingly changeless Marquis, which also rebounded as one of L-M's "Ride Engineered" '77s (signified by a little dashboard plaque). The implication, of course, was that Buick-Olds-Pontiac weren't—or at least that their downsized models didn't ride as well because they didn't have as much "road-hugging weight." Auto writers properly took Ford to task for equating poundage with ride comfort, and the notion still draws the occasional barb *in memoriam*. What's often overlooked is the fact that many buyers bought that argument at the time—and bought LTDs and Marquises.

There was another reason for Mercury to push its bigger wares this year: dwindling demand for its small cars. The two Comets and three Bobcats managed just over 50,000 units combined, a scant 1/9 of the make's total model year volume. Escalating prices didn't help. A bare-bones Bobcat Runabout now listed at $3438, and most models, as well as the Comets, delivered for well over $4000.

Lincoln's big news was the Mark V. "It will run five years unchanged," said one promoter—and looked like it would: large, luxurious, quiet, and smooth as ever. Yet it seemed little different from the Mark IV. The Designer Series returned, wheelbase was unchanged, styling was similar, and the big 460 was still available—and more powerful: now at 208 bhp (up from its 194-bhp 1975 nadir through an interim 202 bhp).

But a closer look revealed a crisper, lighter appearance. And appearances weren't deceiving. Despite retaining its predecessor's 120.4-inch wheelbase and general size, the Mark V was some 500 pounds lighter at the curb. It also

Unlike Pinto, the Mercury Bobcat saw few changes for 1977.

It took $3438 to buy a '77 Bobcat hatchback; 18,405 were built.

The 1977 Mercury Monarch Ghia four door retailed for $4722.

Total Monarch Ghia production for 1977 came to 27,596 units.

A four-speed overdrive manual was standard on the '77 Monarch.

Comet's final year was 1977. Output slumped to 21,545 units.

Prices started at $3544, but this '77 Comet had many extras.

Cougar boasted a full lineup of intermediate models for 1977.

Mercury built 8569 Cougar Villager station wagons for '77.

Cougar base prices ranged from $4700 to $5363 for 1977. Pictured here an XR-7 hardtop (left) and a four-door Brougham.

Mercury built 20,363 Colony Park wagons for model year 1977.

At $6975, this Grand Marquis was 1977's costliest Mercury.

The 1977 Capri II came with a 2.3-liter four or a 2.8-liter six. It was sold as a base model, sporty "S," or posh Ghia.

boasted 21 percent more trunk space—which seems like a large gain only because the IV had so little. Engineers had also paid attention to economy by specifying the corporate 400 V-8 as standard, not only for the Mark V but the big Continentals as well. The old-standby 460 continued as a 49-state option (it couldn't meet California emissions requirements).

Despite a $330 stiffer base price—now a towering $11,396—the Mark V recorded a smart sales gain, up from a little more than 56,000 for the final Mark IV to just over 80,000. Alas, that would prove to be its peak.

Lincoln's senior pair also peaked, attracting close to 96,000 buyers, versus fewer than 67,000 the year before. Mechanical alterations were few aside from the smaller

Ford's 1977 "Custom Cousins": Cruising Van and Cruising Wagon.

"Fancy Truckin' " is how Ford referred to the '77 Ranchero GT.

Ford C-8000 diesels were serviced by tilting the cab forward.

This Ford F-600 Crew Cab chassis rode a 176-inch wheelbase.

The LTL-9000: 154.3 inches from bumper to back of sleeper-cab.

The Ford high-tilt WT-9000 was phased out on June 28, 1977.

A Styleside eight-foot box mates with this Ford Ranger F-150 4x4.

This '77 U-1000 Bronco Wagon sports the Special Decor Group.

standard engine, but a slimmer, taller grille and recontoured front fenders provided a closer-than-ever family resemblance with the Mark. Oval opera windows furthered the relationship on the Town Coupe/Town Car, as had been the case since '75.

If imitation be the sincerest form of flattery, then Lincoln paid Cadillac a big compliment with its new Versailles, the first addition to the Lincoln line in years and the make's second attempt at a more compact luxury car (after the 1961-63 Continental). Yet this hastily contrived reply to Cadillac's remarkably successful Seville was little more than a gussied-up Granada/Monarch. Of course, it carried a Continental-style square grille, standup hood ornament, and humped trunklid, plus gobs of standard equipment. The last was necessary because, again aping Cadillac, Lincoln priced Versailles at the top of the line: $11,500 base list, costlier than even the new Mark V.

But while Cadillac somehow managed to get away with marketing Seville on this "less for more" basis, established Lincoln buyers looked askance at Versailles—though perhaps without much surprise, as it inevitably sat cheek-to-jowl with Monarch. Delivering at near $13,000, the Versailles at least competed on price with Seville, which had also been evolved from a rather ordinary car: the Nova. But somehow, Bill Mitchell's styling came off better on an uprated Chevy than Gene Bordinat's did on an uprated Ford, perhaps because the former was more cleverly disguised. The Seville was a melting pot of new ideas, whereas the Versailles was a catch-all for every Continental styling cliche of the past 20 years, yet was still quite obviously a Granada in drag.

You can fool some of the people some of the time, but few were fooled by Versailles, which would go down as one of Lincoln's bigger marketing mistakes in this period. Model year '77 production ended at just 15,434 units, a third of Seville's total.

1978

Past, present, and future seemed to coalesce as Ford Motor Company celebrated its 75th anniversary. A limited-edition Diamond Jubilee Thunderbird and Mark V arrived to honor the past. For the present, all Detroit was obligated to meet the government's Corporate Average Fuel Economy requirements that took effect this year. Under CAFE, the fuel economy of all cars sold by a given manufacturer had to average at least 18 mpg on a "sales-weighted" basis; the target would then rise in steps to 27.5 mpg by model year '85. Part of the company's response was a new compact advertised as "The Ford in your future," a twist on an old slogan. The words were prophetic:

The 1978 Fairmont four-door sedan, shown with optional vinyl roof, wire wheel covers, flow-through ventilation louvers.

The $4044 Fairmont Futura coupe debuted on December 2, 1978.

Ford expected the '78 Fairmont to be its best-seller. It was.

Fairmont offered an ES (Euro-Sport) option in November '78.

Fairmont prices started at $3624 for the base two-door sedan.

Top-of-the-line '78 Fairmont Squire wagon retailed for $4428.

With 80 cubic feet of cargo area, Fairmont wagon found favor.

Ford LTD Landau sedan, little changed, listed at $6055 for '78.

Fiesta, Ford's German-built mini, made a 1978 American debut.

Among Fiesta's four 1978 models was the Sport, as shown here.

Fiesta pictured here shows the side stripes offered in 1979.

in its engineering and much of its hardware, Fairmont would be the literal foundation for a new Dearborn design dynasty.

Fairmont and Mercury's near-identical Zephyr originated in the "Fox" program, initiated in the early Seventies to develop an eventual Ford Maverick/Mercury Comet replacement. Significantly, it had been started at about the time of the first energy crisis, which dramatically highlighted the need for smaller, lighter, more economical cars. Efficiency was the overriding concern. "The initial objective was an overall body design that would enhance performance and fuel economy through minimized weight [plus] aerodynamic refinements," said a company publication. "Once these goals were achieved, the challenge was to design an efficient interior package that would make optimum use of available space." Though certain existing components like engines, transmissions, and suspension pieces might be used, the plan was to combine "the economy and maneuverability of a compact with the interior roominess and comfort of a mid-sized car."

Fox broke fresh engineering ground for Dearborn in several areas. For example, it was the firm's first car designed with the aid of computers as well as three-dimensional scale models and full-size prototypes. Through the use of mathematical models like the so-called "finite analysis" technique, engineers could "pinpoint where the car's structure may require additional strength, or where it can be lightened without decreasing strength or durability." Now called computer-assisted design (CAD), it would prove a great time- and money-saver and, beginning with Fairmont/Zephyr, would figure in the development of all Dearborn products.

The Fox program also envisioned greater use of lightweight materials like aluminum, high-strength steel, and reinforced plastics than any previous project, again to save weight in the interest of fuel economy. And despite its conservative, boxy appearance, Fairmont/Zephyr was Dearborn's first car styled with an eye to aerodynamics to reduce fuel-wasting air drag as much as possible. Both ⅜-scale and, later, full-size prototypes spent more than 320 hours in wind-tunnel testing. Ford noted that "although almost imperceptible, [the resulting] minor refinements were responsible for an approximate 13 percent reduction in drag from the first clay models to the finished vehicle."

What emerged was thoroughly modern and a definite advance on Maverick/Comet. There were now three body styles: two- and four-door sedans and, something sorely needed, a practical five-door wagon. Mid-year brought a brace of coupes with T-Bird-style rooflines, the Fairmont Futura and Zephyr Z-7. Both were initially popular, reflecting renewed interest in sporty domestic compacts.

Riding a 105.5-inch wheelbase, Fairmont/Zephyr was 4.5 inches shorter than the Maverick/Comet four-door, yet interiors were roomier in every dimension. Space-saving features helped, like thinner front seatbacks and doors. So did the pleasingly simple styling, with lower beltline, higher roof, and much greater glass area contributing to

The '78 Granada offered two ESS (European Sport Sedan) models.

A split opera window was but one change for Granada in 1978.

The '78 LTD II looked as before, but lost its station wagons.

Every LTD II had a V-8 in '78: 302, 351, or 400 cubic inches.

improved outward vision and a feeling of greater spaciousness. Sedan trunk room increased by a healthy three cubic feet. The logically organized dashboard boasted European-style steering-column stalk controls for headlamp dimmer and windshield wipers and washer. In overall appearance and packaging, Fairmont/Zephyr was "close to European middleweights," as Ford put it, cars like the Audi 100LS and Volvo 240. *Car and Driver* magazine even called it "an American Volvo."

The Fairmont/Zephyr chassis was, again, conventional but contemporary. Up front was a modified MacPherson-strut suspension, with coil springs mounted on lower A-arms instead of encircling the struts. This, said Ford, meant less noise and harshness, and also saved some weight. Steering was by the more precise rack-and-pinion mechanism favored in Europe instead of recirculating ball as on Maverick/Comet. At the rear, antiquated leaf springs gave way to coils, and four links tied down the live axle more securely. The springs and the two lower links were mounted outboard and behind the axle, which Ford said minimized axle tramp and side-to-side shake and also improved ride control.

Pinto prices started at $3139 in 1978; the stripes cost extra.

Most popular '78 Pinto was the hatchback; 74,313 were built.

An extra $1300 transformed a Mustang II into a King Cobra. A 302 V-8 and handling suspension made it decent for its day.

This '78 Mach I (list $4430) is optioned with V-8 and T-top.

Cobra II kit provided the show; a V-6 made it go (V-8 optional).

Ford built 34,730 Mustang Ghias for the 1978 model year.

A 1978 Mustang Ghia could be had for $4149, up $30 from 1977.

With its light but strong construction, Fairmont/Zephyr weighed up to 300 pounds less than a '77 Maverick/Comet, which allowed the use of smaller engines for better fuel economy with little, if any, performance penalty. Thus, standard power was the 2.3-liter ohc "Lima" four from Pinto/Mustang II, the first four ever seen in a postwar Ford compact. Optional were the familiar 3.3-liter/200-cid six and small-block 302 V-8. The latter required optional three-speed automatic transmission, as did the six in California and high-altitude areas. Otherwise you got a four-speed manual with floorshift.

Fairmont/Zephyr was greeted with almost unqualified praise. In *Auto Test 1978*, the CONSUMER GUIDE® staff declared it "head and shoulders above the General Motors and Chrysler compacts. It is efficient . . . has more room for passengers than any of its competitors, just as smooth a ride, superior handling, and the look of a more modern car. The improvement over the Maverick . . . is substantial." Their six-cylinder/automatic test car returned an average 21 mpg (versus the 19 city/26 highway EPA ratings), and the only gripes were the awkward, stalk-mounted horn button and unsupportive seats. They rated it the Best Buy in its class. So did a good many buyers. Fairmont easily captured the top spot in compact sales with over 312,000 deliveries, easily surpassing all rivals. Zephyr tallied another 152,000. As a final "vote of confidence," readers of *Car and Driver*, mainly enthusiasts not inclined to notice family models, voted Fairmont the most significant new car of the year in the magazine's annual poll.

Ford Division's other '78s were overshadowed by Fairmont and its great success. The reason: not much changed. The mid-size LTD II was left alone except for cancellation of wagons, while the full-size LTD stood pat because a downsized successor was on the way. The little Pinto also carried on with few changes, the most notable being standard "bucket-look" rear seat cushion and newly optional variable-ratio power steering.

Granada was updated with a new grille and dual rectangular headlamps (the latter shared with Fairmont/Zephyr) and upgraded to the 250-cid six as standard; the optional 351 V-8 was deleted. New to the options list were CB and AM/FM/cassette stereo radios along with an ESS (European Sports Sedan) package for base models. The latter included black exterior trim, hood and rear deck paint stripes, color-keyed racing mirrors, deluxe bucket-seat interior, and heavy-duty suspension. Opera windows on two-doors got a vertical chrome rib to become "twindows."

Mustang II was in its final season but offered some new options. Packing every racy styling touch a kid could want, the new King Cobra package offered front air dam, a huge "snake" decal for the hood, tape stripes and name decals everywhere, plus snazzy cockpit trim. Unlike Cobra II, however, this group also had some functional features, like the 302 V-8, power steering, "Rallye" handling package, and 70-series tires. Though hardly a muscle car, the typical King Cobra could run the quarter-mile in about 17 seconds, not bad for the times. An appeal to women was the Fashion Accessory Package for the standard hardtop, offering door pockets, striped-cloth upholstery, lighted vanity mirror, and four-way manual driver's seat. As on Pinto and Mercury's Bobcat, variable-ratio power steering was newly available across the board.

T-Bird was mechanically untouched but pushed opulence to new heights with a special Diamond Jubilee Edition listing near $10,000. It came with a whole slew of extras plus, as a personal touch, your very own monogram on each door and your name on a 22-carat-gold dash plaque. Lesser Birds could be ordered with the inaccurately named Sports Decor Group, with light tan vinyl roof and spoked road wheels plus matching imitation "luggage straps" for the rear deck, a tacky throwback to the Thirties. Thunderbird continued to sell well at over 350,000 units and moved up two notches in the mid-size class to third, trailing only Oldsmobile's Cutlass and the Chevro-

T-top and T-Bird: this '78 has the optional Sports Decor Group.

Thunderbird had its best year yet in 1978—352,751 were built.

Even at $12,318, the 1978 Lincoln Continental Mark V sold well.

Mark V Diamond Jubilee Edition had beveled-glass opera windows.

Versailles, the "compact" Lincoln, found 8931 buyers in 1978.

The Cougar XR-7 outsold its plainer stablemates three-to-one.

A 1978 Lincoln Continental sedan retailed for $10,396, up $760.

Top-line Cougar for 1978 had the Midnight/Chamois Decor Group.

let Malibu, both newly downsized this year.

Lincoln-Mercury was in the second of three record years in a row. While its 1977-79 performance hasn't been equalled in the Eighties, there are signs—mainly the slick Mercury Sable—that the Division may yet see more 800,000-unit seasons. Of course, the end of 1979 ushered in the worst recession since the 1930s, and U.S. car sales plunged to levels from which they have yet to completely recover, though at this writing, profits have never been better.

Lincoln planners who'd scoffed at the idea of a glorified

Monarch now nodded knowingly, pointed to dismal Versailles sales, and said they were right all along. While Cadillac's Seville soared to new heights, Versailles volume dropped to below 9000 for the model year. Product changes were almost undetectable.

But Lincoln wasn't finished with "precision size" cars. In fact, plans were afoot to radically downsize the big Lincolns for the first time. Even the recalcitrant HFII couldn't ignore CAFE and its threat of heavy per-car levys for makes that didn't meet the standards. Versailles gave Lincoln breathing space, but it was only a warmup

Who needed a Continental when a Grand Marquis cost $3000 less?

The '78 Mercury Zephyr started at $3777; a sporty ES cost more.

Mercury marketed four Zephyr models in 1978, three of them pictured here. Production totalled 152,172 that year.

for the slimmer, less-thirsty generation of Continentals and Marks to come.

Further efforts to curb Lincoln's drinking habits were seen in this year's smaller and/or detuned engines. Versailles switched from the 351 to the 302 V-8 as base power, though there was little horsepower change (135 versus 133, respectively). The big cars retained the 400 but carried a two-barrel version with less horsepower (166 bhp SAE net, down from 179). Taller gearing was another weapon in the economy quest, now 2.75:1, which would have been laughable five years before. The 460 remained

a 49-state option on Mark V and Continental and actually gained a bit (from 208 to 210 bhp net). By law, all three engines were cleaner-running. The 302 took on electronic controls, the fuel/air mixture being adjusted in response to input from sensors that kept tabs on speed, throttle and crank positions, coolant and incoming air temperatures, manifold and barometic pressure, and EGR. The result was enough plumbing for the World Trade Center. As Paul Woudenberg wrote: "It was a hard challenge for local dealer's mechanics, and ruled out the home tinkerer for good." Somehow it's hard to imagine Continental owners

Most popular 1978 Zephyr was the four-door sedan ($3863 base).

Ranchero entered 1978 almost unchanged; sporty GT sold well.

Bronco lost its identity in 1978—it became a shrunken pickup.

Wheelbase on the new Bronco went up by a foot to 104 inches.

The Free Wheeling option made this a "Poor Boy's Cruising Van."

Ford called the 1978 Pinto Panel Delivery a "Little Hauler."

as shade-tree mechanics, but it's not hard to imagine their reaction when one of the new widgets broke.

Engineers were still whittling away at weight—one area where they could improve mileage for relatively little money—with more lightweight materials like plastics, aluminum, and low-alloy steel, plus thinner glass. This year's big Lincolns were thus slimmer by 100-130 pounds, the Versailles by 40, and the make's EPA ratings inched up from around 12 to near 14 mpg.

Lincoln styling hardly changed this year apart from the usual color and minor trim shifts. The Mark Designer Series was back in a new round of hues: cordovan (Bill Blass), silver/red/grey (Pucci), "Midnight Jade" (Givenchy), "light Champagne" (Cartier). Mark Vs carried a "miles-to-empty" indicator (using speed/fuel level sensors), a token gesture to economy, while all models could be ordered with Citizens Band receivers. As a final touch, in celebration of Ford's 75th Anniversary, Lincoln released 5159 copies of a Diamond Jubilee Mark V, done up in Diamond Blue Metallic or Jubilee Gold with a matching interior. Most Mark options were standard at its lofty $20,529 price.

Zephyr helped Mercury to record model year volume of 635,051 units, though Monarch continued to do well (near 92,000) and Marquis enjoyed excellent sales in its final

season on the huge 124-inch-wheelbase platform. Monarch mimicked Granada changes (including the new ESS package), and Cougar copied LTD II in losing wagons. As before, the fancy XR-7 way outsold both plain Cougars combined, this year by a four-to-one margin. The little-changed Bobcat was down to a bit more than 32,000 units and looking terminal, though, like Pinto, it still had two more years to run.

1979

Dearborn product developments this year comprised a new-generation Mustang and a downsized, thoroughly redesigned Ford LTD and Mercury Marquis. But reporters covered a very different development shortly after they saw the '79s in the summer of '78: a big shakeup at World Headquarters. In a surprise move, chairman Henry Ford II fired president Lee Iacocca in what most observers labelled a personality clash. Philip Caldwell succeeded Iacocca, who would go on to become president of moribund Chrysler Corporation and, soon afterwards, its chairman.

Though few could have predicted it, this would be Detroit's last year for "business as usual." Total production went up by more than a half-million units, a model year figure topped only by record 1973, and sales remained strong, though down slightly from '78. Unfortunately, a big drop was just around the corner.

Redesigned for the second time in only five years (and now minus the Roman numeral II), the fifth-generation Mustang originated in 1976 as a spinoff of the just-completed Fox platform, which was ultimately shortened 5.1 inches in wheelbase. Mustang II power units—"Lima" four, 2.8-liter V-6, and 302 V-8—would be retained along with Fox suspension. As with the original Mustang, curb weight was pegged at a comparatively low 2700 pounds, and the interior package was planned to accommodate two adults comfortably, four in a pinch.

Once more, a new Mustang's styling was selected from proposals submitted by competing teams working with the same package. The one ultimately chosen came from a group headed by Jack Telnack, then executive design director for North American light trucks and cars, the same team that had created the prototype for Ford Europe's pretty front-drive Fiesta. Like the original Mustang but unlike the II, a notchback body style was designed first and a fastback derived from it. Quarter-scale clays were subjected to 136 hours of wind-tunnel tests, the industry having rediscovered aerodynamics as a key to improved fuel economy.

What emerged was a sort of notchback wedge, with a rather high cowl (actually an inch above that of Fairmont/Zephyr) to "get a faster sloping hood . . . to pivot the hood over the air cleaner," according to Telnack. This dictated special inner front fender aprons and radiator supports instead of Fairmont/Zephyr pieces, but their extra expense was approved in the interest of fuel economy. Aerodynamic considerations also prompted a slight rear-deck lip and the front bumper with integrated mini-spoiler.

"One of the basic themes for this car was 'form follows function,'" said Telnack in June 1978, "and we wanted to be as aerodynamically correct as possible before getting into the wind tunnel. In the past we have designed cars and then gone into the tunnel mainly for tuning the major surfaces that have been approved. . . . With the Mustang, the designers were thinking about aerodynamics in the initial sketch stages, which made the tuning job in the tunnel much easier. Consequently, we wound up with the most slippery car ever done in the Ford Motor Company: a drag coefficient of 0.44 for the three-door fastback, 0.46 for the two-door notchback. [Aerodynamics is] probably the most cost-effective way to improve corporate average fuel economy. We know that a 10 percent improvement in drag can result in a five percent improvement in fuel economy at a steady-state 50 mph. . . . That's really worthwhile stuff for us to go after."

A base Fairmont four-door sedan retailed for $4220 in 1979.

Production of '79 Fairmont four doors amounted to 133,813 units.

Ford pushed "luxury-car options" for the Fairmont Futura coupe.

The 1979 Ford Granada Ghia four door listed at $5157 base.

Granada ESS (European Sport Sedan) cost a bit more: $5317.

The downsized full-size Ford LTD shed over 500 pounds for 1979.

Cargo capacity of the new big Ford wagons was 91.7 cubic feet.

LTD trunk offered 23.3 cubic feet of space, .7 more than before.

Stylist Jack Telnack poses with the restyled 1979 Mustang Cobra.

As with the Fox program, Mustang body engineering envisioned lightweight materials wherever possible, so plastics, high-strength/ low-alloy (HSLA) steel, and aluminum figured heavily. The most significant use of plastics was the reaction-injection-molded [RIM] soft urethane bumper covers. The number-three frame crossmember and the rear suspension arms were made of HSLA steel, while aluminum was found in drivetrains and the bumpers of some models. Thin but strong glass and thinner door design also saved weight. So although the '79 was slightly larger than Mustang II in every dimension, it weighed an average of some 200 pounds less, a notable achievement.

Telnack's quoted 0.44 drag figure sounded good in '78 but seems mediocre today. Ford's 1983 Thunderbird, for example, arrived at an altogether more impressive 0.35. While that difference may not seem dramatic, it represents a reduction of over 20 percent and shows just how radically standards can change in a few years.

Interior design received equally careful attention. Total volume rose by 14 cubic feet on the notchback and by 16 cubic feet on the hatchback. The thinner door construction yielded 3.6 inches more shoulder room and 2.0 inches more hiproom in front. Back-seat gains measured 5.0 and 6.0 inches, respectively, while rear legroom expanded by over five inches. Cargo volume enlarged by two cubic feet on the notchback and four cubic feet on the hatchback. European practice was evident in such features as the standard full instrumentation and fingertip stalks for turn signals/headlight dimmer/horn and wiper/washer (shared with Fairmont/Zephyr). A third lever (on the right) was provided for the extra-cost tilt steering wheel. A new option was a console-mount graphic display for "vehicle systems monitoring," with a profile outline of the car and appropriately placed warning lights for low fuel and washer fluid, and failed headlights, taillights, and brake lights. The display could be tested by a pushbutton, and included a digital quartz clock that showed time, date, and elapsed time.

Mustang's new all-coil suspension was borrowed from Fairmont/Zephyr, with modified MacPherson struts in front and four-link rear geometry. V-8 models had a standard rear anti-roll bar, more for lateral location than sway control, but it also effectively lowered the roll center, thus allowing lower-rate rear springs for a commensurately softer ride. Rack-and-pinion steering returned with optional power assist and 1978's variable-ratio rack. Brakes remained front discs and rear drums, with standard vacuum boost.

Like past Mustangs, the '79 was to have broad market appeal, and planners ultimately settled on three suspension setups: standard, "handling," and "special," each tuned for and issued with specific tires. The first came with conventional bias-plys. The second, limited to 14-inch radials, included higher-rate springs, different shock valving, and stiffer bushings, plus a rear stabilizer bar with optional V-6. The "special" suspension, conceived around Michelin's recently developed TRX radials (with

Mustang II became Mustang again for 1979. It rode an eight-inch-longer 104.4-inch wheelbase, but weighed 200 pounds less.

"Intermediate" size LTD II now weighed more than the "big" LTD.

This 1979 LTD II hardtop features the "Sports Touring Package."

The turbocharged '79 Mustang Cobra boasted 140 bhp.

Mustang Cobra (foreground) sported a snake decal on its hood.

As in the past, '79 Mustang came in coupe or hatchback form.

an unusual 390mm/15.35-inch diameter dictating like-size wheels), featured specific shock valving, high-rate rear springs, larger (1.12-inch-diameter) front stabilizer bar, and a rear bar.

Besides Mustang II engines, the '79 offered an intriguing new option: a turbocharged version of the standard four, delivering claimed 0-55 mph acceleration of 8.3 seconds with four-speed, plus mid-20s fuel economy. The 302 V-8 was revised with low-restriction exhaust system, more lightweight components, and a ribbed V-belt for the accessory drive. The V-6 was in short supply, so it was replaced late in the model year by the old 200-cid inline six. Optional with both six and V-8 was a four-speed overdrive gearbox similar to the one developed for Granada/Monarch, with direct third (1:1 ratio) and mildly overdriven fourth (0.70:1). Final drive ratios were 3.08:1 for automatics, four-speed/V-6, and normally aspirated four, 3.45:1 for all other drivetrains.

Mustang was chosen as the Official Pace Car for the 63rd Annual Indianapolis 500 Mile Race, which was run on May 27, 1979.

Powerteams naturally determined '79 performance, just like previous Mustangs. With 0-60 mph in about nine seconds, the V-8 car was a dragster by late-Seventies standards, while the turbo-four needed 12-12.5 seconds with four-speed, the V-6 about 13-14 seconds. Some writers thought the V-8 overpowered and out of step with the fuel-short times, but the turbo 2.3 generated favorable comment, John Dinkel telling *Road & Track* readers that it "would seem to be an enthusiast's delight. I just hope that the design compromises dictated by costs and the fact that Ford couldn't start with a completely clean sheet of paper don't wreck that dream. . . . There's no doubt the new Mustang has the potential to be the best sport coupe Ford has ever built, but in some respects [it] is as enigmat-

Ford's German Fiesta Sport offered a sunroof on the '79 model.

Ford built 53,846 Pinto station wagons for the 1979 model run.

Pinto got new front-end styling for '79; here with ESS option.

Cruising Package was continued, but modified for 1979 Pintos.

Thunderbird output, down for '79, was still strong at 284,141 units. Prices ranged from $6328 to a towering $11,060.

ic as its predecessor."

Nevertheless, this "whole new breed" Mustang turned on a lot of buyers, quickly rising to number-two in the compact class (after Fairmont) where it now competed by dint of its larger interior. Overall model year sales were well over 300,000, making it the seventh most popular car in the land.

This year's downsized Ford LTD and Mercury Marquis were less successful in their field, which was curious. Developed as the "Panther" project, they were fully a match for GM's smaller full-size cars, which had enjoyed great success since their '77 model year debut. Despite a seven-inch shorter wheelbase, now 114.4 inches, the new LTD/Marquis offered more claimed passenger and trunk space than their outsize predecessors, plus superior visibility and better fuel economy. Styling was up to date—boxy but cleaner—and ride was more competent thanks to the new all-coil suspension with short-arm/long-arm front geometry and a four-link rear end with the shocks mounted ahead of the axle.

With all this, sales should have gone up, yet LTD fell by some 80,000 units for the model year, to nearly 246,000, barely enough to beat the full-size Oldsmobile and far behind Chevy's Caprice/Impala. Marquis also declined, though by less than 5000. Aside from GM's two-year head start, the problem seemed to be the sudden economic downturn that began this spring, bringing inflation, soaring interest rates, and rising gasoline prices that knocked the entire market for a loop, especially the full-size segment. LTD/Marquis would enjoy a sales resurgence, but not before the U.S. industry passed through some of its bleakest years ever.

The popular Ford Fairmont/Mercury Zephyr returned with few changes apart from new options: tilt steering wheel, speed control, more comprehensive "performance instrumentation," and remote decklid release. A standard four-speed overdrive manual replaced the three-speed

transmission with the optional six, and was extended to the V-8, which was previously restricted to automatic. All top-trim models now wore the badge of Ford's Italian design house, Ghia. Fairmont remained the nation's favorite compact, though model year sales were off by some 63,000 units.

Dearborn's wee ones, Pinto and Bobcat, got what would be their final facelift, with rectangular headlamps flanking more coherent grilles (horizontal slats on the Ford,

Lincoln built 92,600 Continental coupes and sedans for 1979.

Prices started at $12,093 for the '79 Lincoln Continental sedan.

Output hit 75,939 in 1979 for the Lincoln Continental Mark V, now in its last year. It took $13,593 to buy the base model.

thin vertical bars on the Mercury). Standard equipment was upgraded to encompass power front disc brakes, electric rear window defroster, tinted glass, and AM radio. New Pinto ESS/Bobcat Sport appearance options offered black grille and exterior moldings, and Pinto's extra-cost Cruising Package was extended to the Runabout. By now, the unsafe fuel tank and filler neck on pre-1977 sedans had been highly publicized, and Ford would be forced to defend itself in a series of class-action product liability suits arising from several horrendous collision-related fires. But sales weren't affected much. Pinto remained at about 187,000 units for the second straight year, and Bobcat jumped by better than 12,000 to near 45,000 units.

Granada, now promoted as "An American Classic," soldiered on with the same styling and minor interior revisions. Mercury's Monarch followed suit. The four-speed overdrive manual gearbox was made available with V-8, and the extra-cost all-disc brakes disappeared for lack of interest.

The mid-size Ford LTD II/Mercury Cougar were little changed in this, their final year—and still languished on the sales charts. The optional 400 V-8 was discontinued,

and front bumper systems were lightened in a futile attempt to improve mileage. A new option highlighted their relatively poor economy: a larger 27.5-gallon fuel tank.

With a redesign scheduled for 1980, Thunderbird and Cougar XR-7 were also little altered. T-Bird's grille gained a broad crisscross pattern set ahead of thin vertical bars, and full-width taillamps gave way to dual units separated by a central backup lamp. XR-7 grilles tacked on body-color tape stripes, and taillamps turned horizontal. Both also lost their optional 400 V-8. Thunderbird's Diamond Jubilee Edition returned as the Heritage, with the same blanked-off rear roof quarters and full-luxury treatment. Sales dropped by nearly 80,000 units to a bit more than 284,000, yet Thunderbird continued to far outpace LTD II, ending up 12th on the overall industry roster. XR-7 lost a bit less than 3000 units, but its near 164,000 units again far outpaced the standard Cougars, which mustered a mere 8400.

Lincoln-Mercury as a whole was still rocketing upward, however. In fact, this was its greatest model year ever: 670,000 Mercurys, 190,000 Lincolns.

Besides the downsized Marquis, already described, L-

The '79 Versailles sported a longer roofline, halogen headlamps.

Bobcat got a new front end, its first styling change since '75.

The Capri was Lincoln-Mercury's most aerodynamic car in 1979.

Mercury built 110,144 Capris for '79; here the sporty RS model.

M's big news was a second-generation Capri. Division planners had been denied a version of the Mustang II, getting the imported Capri instead. This time they got a Mustang clone—but only in hatchback form—and even put on Mercury nameplates (the German-built Capri nev-

er had them) to ensure that no one would think this another "sexy European." Not that most people would. Styling was all-American and very similar to Mustang's. Its main distinctions were a blunt grille with horizontal bars, prominent bodyside bulges around the wheel openings

Mercury Zephyr prices started at $4253 in 1979. A new four-speed manual, full instrumentation, and a 302 V-8 were available.

Zephyr had a good year in 1979—output reached 125,377 units.

Cougar XR-7 listed at $6430 in 1979; 163,716 units were built.

The 3110-pound Monarch two-door coupe retailed for $4735 in 1979.

Monarch listed two engines for '79; 250-cid six and 302-cid V-8.

Mercury noted that Grand Marquis was 17 inches shorter for 1979.

Marquis price range in '79 was $6292 to $7909; V-8 came standard.

The 1979 Captain's Club Wagon sported rectangular headlights.

Ford marketed "trend-setting 'youth' packages" for the Econoline.

(amazingly predictive of the later Porsche 944), and slightly different taillamps with horizontal instead of vertical ribs.

Naturally, Capri shared the new Mustang's chassis, running gear, interior layout, even dashboard. Model selections were also similar: base, luxury Ghia, and sporty RS, the last an option package with fortified underpinnings and available with the turbocharged engine. The base model listed about $200 upstream of its Mustang sister, but Ghia hatchback prices were within a few dollars of each other. Though Capri would never outsell Mustang (and wouldn't last as long, either), its first-year reception was good at some 110,000 units, 15 percent of which were Ghias.

Desperately trying to get some mileage out of the poor Lincoln Versailles, designers tried to lionize it by lengthening the roof eight inches, padding the rear half, and adding a Crown Victoria-style wrapover band at the B-pillars, complete with coachlamps. Though the result looked more like a Mark V, it was, in the opinion of one stylist (who shall remain diplomatically anonymous), "the goddamndest thing you ever saw." There wasn't much substance behind the glitter, but it sold—not well, but better than before—despite a price hike of about $1000 that put it almost level with the Seville. Versailles' model year total: 21,007 units. By contrast, Cadillac held price and sold more than 53,000 Sevilles.

The Continentals and Mark would never be so enor-

A Ford pickup could be purchased for as little as $5297 in 1979.

Ford registered 1,122,656 trucks during calendar year 1979.

Bronco continued its winning ways with 90,922 built for 1979.

nentals painted Midnight Blue or white, with Midnight Blue interior and all the Town trim save nameplates and the oval opera windows. Collectible they may yet be, but at this writing they're still depreciating from their original list prices of well over $22,000. Even the standard Continentals were averaging an easy $13,000 as delivered, but plenty of buyers rushed to save one of these dinosaurs: 92,600 for the model year.

The Mark V also went out in style, led by another rash of Designer Series models with sticker prices over $14,000, and a $20,000 "Collector Series" successor to the '78 Diamond Jubilee Edition. The latter, trimmed like its senior counterparts, helped push production up to nearly 76,000, not far off the record '77 pace. It would be a long time before the Mark or Lincoln as a whole would generate numbers like that again.

1980

It was a year of "stagflation"—the combination of a stagnant economy and double-digit inflation that clobbered the U.S. auto market beginning in the spring of '79—and the second great fuel crisis, initiated by the Iranian revolution and an oil cut-off at the behest of an America-hating Ayatollah. Lines reformed at gas stations and fuel prices doubled. Though gas wasn't as hard to come by as in 1973-74, its higher cost intimidated hundreds of thousands of new-car buyers, already suffering "sticker shock" from soaring, inflation-fueled prices. The market flip-flopped almost overnight, some 40 percent of it switching from full-size cars to compacts. For Detroit, it was the start of a long nightmare.

As if that weren't enough, this year's Corporate Average Fuel Economy mandate was 20 mpg, up 1 mpg from '79, and it would go to 22 mpg for 1981. Worse, the import invasion was now an all-out assault, aided by "Energy Crisis II," vastly more competitive Japanese products, and new buyer awareness that Detroit "quality control" was a contradiction in terms. Back in 1974, imports had captured some 1.4 million sales in a total market of about 8.7 million. By 1979, the number had grown to over 2.3 million in a U.S. market that had peaked in '78 and was declining to similar volume.

While Chrysler Corporation's cliff-hanger existence made most of the headlines, Ford Motor Company was in similarly dire straits. Echoing the late Forties, the firm was facing another historic change of leadership. Chairman Henry Ford II had announced his intention to resign, but his erstwhile heir was trying to keep Highland Park from becoming a ghost town, and some wondered whether Ford's new guard could do the same. The company cer-

mous and lavish as they were in 1979. Town Car packages continued for senior coupe and sedan, still with oval portholes on the four-door's rear roof quarters. The Designer Series lived on, and there was even a "Williamsburg" Town Car, with a velour interior and two-tone paint. Though the Continental was set for a vast downsizing in 1980, weight paring went on and—believe it or not—the '79 was the lightest Lincoln since '57. Also in the interest of meeting CAFE, the 460 engine did not return after a long and satisfactory run of 14 years.

Since it was broadly known that this would be the big Lincolns' last year, division marketers decided to cash in with a fond farewell to these "traditional size" cars. They did it with a pair of late-season "Collector Series" Conti-

1980

The newly named 1980 Crown Victoria two-door, priced at $7070, poses with the Country Squire, which listed at $7426.

tainly needed turning around. Though sales had been good in recent years, profits were dwindling due to the high cost of the massive product overhaul, begun with the '79 Fairmont/Zephyr, necessary to stay competitive in the Eighties. When the bottom dropped out of the market, this shortfall mushroomed into a major cash crisis.

Such was the backdrop for FoMoCo's 1980 rollout. And a very different group of cars it was, with a new Panther-based Continental and Mark, and a realigned Ford fleet that hinted at the significance of the sensible "Fox" plat-

Top-line Crown Victoria sported a rear-half padded vinyl roof.

A four-speed automatic was a new feature on the '80 big Fords.

Fairmont was available with a 2.3-liter turbo engine for '80.

The "classically styled" Granada would be downsized for 1981.

350

form in the firm's near-term plans.

Heading the Ford line was the 25th edition of the Thunderbird, an all-new car built on what was essentially an elongated Fairmont chassis. Compared to the eighth-generation models, it was nearly 16 inches shorter overall, 4.5 inches shorter between wheel centers, and slimmer by more than four inches. Unit construction returned for the first time since 1966, and chassis specifications were identical with Fairmont's. Weight came down dramatically from 1977-79—the division said more than 700 pounds—just the ticket for boosting Bird mileage and thus the division's fleet-average fuel economy.

Smaller powerplants and higher gearing also played a part. The base engine was a newly debored derivative of the 302 V-8 displacing 4.2 liters (255 cid), also offered optionally for Mustang and Fairmont. The lone option was the 302 itself, which could drive through a new four-speed automatic with a tall (0.67:1) overdrive top for economical low-rpm highway cruising. Axle ratios were numerically lower, again to promote good mileage.

Work on the new T-Bird had begun in 1976. The aim was a four-seater of sporty shape and contemporary size retaining such hallmarks as wraparound parking lights and prominent B-pillars. As with the '79 Mustang, aerodynamics was a prime consideration, and over 400 hours of wind-tunnel testing reduced drag coefficients from 0.58 on the first clay model to 0.48 on the final fiberglass model, versus 0.55 on the production '79. Even so, the styling was more throwback than predictive: very blocky and not well received. Ford no doubt felt it crucial to preserve traditional appearance "cues," but they just didn't fit the smaller package.

Fortunately, downsizing made for a more habitable cabin (as luxurious as ever) and markedly better handling. Said Rich Ceppos in *Car and Driver* magazine: "If the truth be known, the new car does an infinitely better job of carrying four [adults] than the old one did. According to Ford, no interior room was lost up front . . . though rear hiproom is down about five inches. But more important is the increase of 2.8 inches in rear knee clearance. . . . The Thunderbird still floats along as if it were in dreamland. The [overdrive automatic] shifts as smoothly as any conventional automatic. And little if any of the [previous car's] bank-vault quietness was lost. . . . About the only changes in [its] unenthusiastic road manners are positive ones: a welcome increase in steering effort and precision, and a touch of nimbleness that the engineers couldn't filter out. . . . An optional handling package—recalibrated shocks, alloy rims, and the largest Michelin TRX tires to date, 220/55R-390s—works small wonders."

Despite its better mileage and handier size, the new Bird failed to make the impression Ford marketing types expected. Model year sales dropped by over 40 percent, and T-Bird slipped from 12th to 19th place in the domestic model rankings. The grand total, a bit more than 156,000 units, was split among base, Town Landau, and mid-year Silver Anniversary offerings.

Mustang received only detail styling refinements and

The little-changed Fiesta was Ford's German-built "Wundercar."

Fairmont: "America's most successful new car nameplate."

Mustang's 1980 Cobra kit was much toned down from earlier days.

This '80 Mustang sports the diamond-grain Carriage vinyl roof.

Pinto, in its last year in 1980, offered a Rallye Pack option.

Pinto's priciest '80 model was the $5320 Squire station wagon.

The Cruising Package was available for Pinto wagon or Runabout.

Thunderbird prices started at $6816 for 1980; sales were slow.

As a Town Landau, T-Bird sold for $10,424; 255 V-8 was standard.

Thunderbird was 16 inches shorter, 700 pounds lighter for 1980.

an expanded options list. The '79 had paced the Indianapolis 500, and the division had sold about 6000 mid-year replicas. That model's appearance features—horizontal-bar grille, fore/aft spoilers, integral front fog lamps, hood bulge—plus special TRX suspension returned for this year's edition of the sporty Cobra package. The driveline chart now listed the 255-cid V-8 as the largest available engine, and four-speed overdrive manual was a new extra on six-cylinder cars. Other first-time options included genuine Recaro front bucket seats, roof-mounted luggage carrier and, for hardtops, a vinyl "Carriage Roof" that simulated the look of a true convertible. Equipment and trim were mildly revised, and all Mustangs acquired more effective halogen headlamps. Ford's ponycar remained 7th in the domestic sales race but, as with most other U.S. models, saw much lower volume. The year-end total was

about 75,000 short of the previous year's.

Numerous minor changes marked other 1980 Fords and most Mercurys, none of which changed appreciably. With cancellation of LTD II, Granada was now the division's sole representative in the mid-size field and continued to trail the Chevrolet Malibu/Monte Carlo and Oldsmobile's Cutlass/Cutlass Supreme. Likewise returning for the last time was Mercury's Monarch, as little changed and down to about 31,000 units, less than half its '79 level. The subcompact Pinto, also in its final year, lost two spots on the sales chart and its optional 2.8 V-6. Similarly the Bobcat, only it saw a third fewer sales.

Fairmont moved up from 5th to 3rd place despite few changes. The 255 V-8 took over from the 302 as the top power offering. Ford also listed the Mustang's turbo-four as a Fairmont option, but few cars got it owing to persis-

Prices started at $16,291 for the downsized 1980 Mark VI coupe.

Top-line 1980 Mark VI four-door Signature Series cost $22,243.

Shrunken Continental saw output of only 31,233 units for 1980.

The 1980 Lincoln Continental four-door sedan listed at $13,593.

The Lincoln Versailles sold for $15,664 in 1980, its last year.

Production for the 1980 Versailles was a dismal 4,784 units.

tent mechanical bugs. Replacing both Ghia models at mid-year was a Futura four-door wearing the coupe's cross-hatch grille and spiffier interior. Mercury's companion Zephyr made the same alterations to engines but not models. All recorded slightly lower sales except the Z-7 coupe, which plunged by more than 50 percent.

Advertising again compared the big Ford LTD with Rolls-Royce for ride and quietness. The one significant mechanical change was availability in most areas of the overdrive automatic with the standard 302 and optional 351 V-8s. A fleet-market "S" sedan and wagon joined the lineup. The premium series, previously called LTD Landau, was rechristened LTD Crown Victoria, reviving a mid-Fifties name. Sales, as a whole, were not great, down by more than 100,000 units, good for only 16th place among domestic nameplates. Mercury Marquis was even

further down the list, suffering big volume drops across the board.

On paper, Lincoln was fairly well prepared for the second energy crisis, unveiling a downsized Continental and a new Mark, the VI, that were more alike than ever. Each line retained its traditional appearance "cues" but not big-block engines. Instead, they carried a standard 302 with a newly developed throttle-body electronic fuel injection system. Output was a lowly 129 horsepower. The familiar 351 was optional but had scarcely more muscle, a rated 140 bhp. It was all for the sake of CAFE. The new corporate OD automatic also aided efficiency.

Underneath was the body-on-frame "Panther" platform of the '79 LTD/Marquis, with the same wheelbase for the Mark VI coupe and a three-inch-longer span (117.3 inches) for other models. Compared to their immediate

The 1980 Mercury Cougar XR-7 shared its body shell with T-Bird.

The XR-7 weighed 3191 pounds, cost $7045; 58,028 were built.

Mercury built 33,650 Bobcats for 1980, its sixth and final year.

Capri prices started at $5672 for '80, shown here with RS option.

Favorite big '80 Merc was the Grand Marquis sedan (15,995 built).

Only 30,518 Monarchs were built for '80; prices started at $5628.

Mercury produced 19,486 Zephyr Z-7s; only a few had the turbo.

Zephyr prices started at $5041 for 1980; Z-7 went for $5335.

predecessors, the '80s were some 10 inches shorter in wheelbase and about 800 pounds lighter yet almost as roomy, thanks to their taller, boxier bodies. They also handled better on the Panther's all-coil suspension, and refinement benefitted from retuned body mounts and sus-

pension bushings, plus standard high-pressure radial tires.

Thus Lincoln had come full circle—and back to its old image problem of the Fifties: too much like a Mercury, let alone a Ford. History-wise observers would have realized that the 1958-60 experience proved the inappropriateness of Mark sedans, yet here was four-door Mark VI virtually identical with the Continental sedan. The main differences were hidden headlamps (Contis reverted to exposed lamps, albeit rectangular, horizontal quads), fancier trim, and the expected opera windows and humped trunklid. Both Marks were available in base and upmarket "Signature Series" guise, the latter with much the same equipment as the previous Collector package.

The lackluster Versailles, now in its close-out year, cost a minimum of $15,664 but usually went out the door for much more. That was a jump of almost $2000, and made life even tougher for dealers still trying to give it away: model year production totalled just 4784. Relative to the Mark VI, the standard Continental coupe and sedan were just slightly detrimmed but still very expensive ($13,250 and $13,650, respectively), though $2000 below Versailles.

Rounding out the Mercury line were a Capri with Mustang's revised mechanicals and options (though they didn't attempt the Carriage Roof, thank goodness) and a lone Cougar XR-7 sport coupe cloned from the new Thunderbird. The latter was good strategy marketingwise, leaving Capri to handle the ponycar business. At 58,000 units, Cougar sales were well down, though perhaps not as much as some sales people feared. Capri was another story, model year volume sinking by 30,000 units to near 80,000.

Of course, everyone was hurting now, but L-M Division seemed to suffer more than most. Mercury production stopped at 347,711 units—a hefty 48 percent below model year '79 volume. Lincoln's output was down a whopping 60 percent, to 74,908, its worst since 1971. Even American Motors beat Lincoln this year. And things were not going to get better right away.

1981

If '80 had been dismal, '81 was grim, particularly in Dearborn. For the model year, Ford dropped to less than a million cars for the first time since 1958, and was almost passed by Oldsmobile. While Mercurys sold a bit better, avoiding the massive factory layoffs of most other makes, Lincoln took another plunge, ending below 70,000.

The deep recession continued to dampen car sales generally and U.S. car sales in particular. With inflation pushing prices ever higher and interest rates soaring to unbelievable levels, many Americans could no longer afford a new car—or at least to buy one as often as they used

In an otherwise dismal year, the 1981 Ford Escort sold well.

Introduced on October 3, 1980, Escort prices started at $5158.

This $6939 Escort GLX four-door wagon carries the Squire option.

Escort's standard overhead-cam, 1.6-liter four developed 65 bhp.

Fairmont entered 1981 little changed; prices started at $6091.

The $6735 Futura station wagon was a new Fairmont model for '81.

Granada shared a 105.5-inch wheelbase with Fairmont in 1981.

The base Granada L four-door sedan retailed for $6633 in 1981.

to. Dearborn's share of this shrinking market was itself shrinking, hitting an all-time low of 16.5 percent at the end of 1980. Worse, the general slump came at a time when the firm could least afford it. Ford was irrevocably committed to a multi-billion-dollar program that would overhaul its entire product line, and the sudden sales drop only accelerated the drain on the company's capital reserves. As model year '81 opened, some old hands may have had dark thoughts about the similarly tough times of the late Twenties and late Forties.

Nevertheless, this was a significant Dearborn year. The reason was the Ford Escort and its near-identical Mercury Lynx twin, the all-new "world car" replacement for the subcompact Pinto/Bobcat. And it *was* a big departure

from previous domestic practice: front-wheel drive, all-independent suspension, overhead-cam four-cylinder engine of advanced specification, a truly international package size. As Dearborn's first direct challenger to a hoard of small imports—mainly Japan models—Escort/Lynx was commercially crucial. It was also something of a symbol: a measure of the U.S. industry's ability to fight back against the strongest overseas onslaught ever.

Escort/Lynx was the end product of the "Erika" project that had originated back in 1972 when a powertrain development team within the Engineering and Research Staff began exploring engine designs for the much smaller cars that might be needed in the Eighties. Meanwhile, Ford of Europe had embarked on a new front-wheel-drive

Priciest full-size Ford for 1981 was the $8775 Country Squire.

Full-size '81 Ford sedans were 209.3 inches long (wagons 215).

Mustang lineup for 1981: T-top, two door, and three-door hatch.

prompted valve stems slanted at 45 degrees, which in turn allowed relatively larger valve faces, plus separate cam lobes for both intakes and exhausts and crossflow breathing. Two displacements were planned, 1.3 and 1.6 liters, but only the latter was ultimately built in the U.S. The CVH also featured a machined aluminum cylinder head, and a block made of reliable cast iron.

To save space up front, the compact engine was mounted transversely, as was becoming common small-car design practice. The standard four-speed manual transaxle was a wide-ratio unit with a slightly overdriven top gear. The new automatic transaxle (ATX) featured a "splitter" gearset within the torque converter that apportioned torque between the converter and a direct mechanical drive to the halfshafts, thus reducing frictional loss from converter rotation for better fuel efficiency.

Dimensionally, Erika was to match the rear-drive Escort, next-to-smallest model in the European line, but would be narrower and shorter than the domestic Pinto. A three-door hatchback sedan would be offered everywhere. Americans would also get a five-door wagon, while Europeans could choose from a five-door sedan and three-door wagon as well. Styling was a separate, though coordinated, effort. Partly because of U.S. safety requirements, the American Escort/Lynx wasn't as smooth as its overseas cousin, though Dearborn touted its sedan's 0.40 drag coefficient—quite good for a short, boxy car all things considered. An aerodynamic aid common to all sedans was a tiny back bustle (called a "decklid kicker") that helped lower drag and rear-end lift by minimizing turbulence.

By coincidence, the U.S. Escort/Lynx emerged on a 94.2-inch wheelbase, same as that of the old Pinto/Bobcat, and also used rack-and-pinion steering. Everything else was different. Front suspension was by MacPherson struts instead of A-arms, with lower control arms, anti-roll bar and, of course, coil springs. The rear was fully independent—much more modern than Pinto's leaf-sprung live axle—comprising one-piece forged spindles mounted laterally, pivoted inboard on the rear crossmember, and acting on vertical shock/struts. Coil springs were positioned between the arms and longitudinal chassis beams above. A tie rod ran from the hub carrier on each lateral arm to a forward mounting point. In all, it was an elegant, low-cost irs arrangement, and gave Ford a class exclusive among domestics, not to mention many imports. As in the later Pinto/Bobcat, the front brakes were discs; drums were used at the rear. Power assist was available at extra cost for both brakes and steering.

Though three inches narrower outside, the "world cars" were much roomier than Pinto/Bobcat inside, thanks to thinner, space-saving doors and the compact power package. In overall length, the Escort/Lynx three-door was some seven inches shorter than the Pinto/Bobcat Runabout, the wagon a full 15 inches trimmer than its predecessor. Escort/Lynx were also several hundred pounds lighter, had higher seats, and much more cargo space and glass area. All of a sudden, Dearborn had not only a genuine import-fighter but America's up-to-date subcompact.

car to replace rear-drive designs in the British and German lineups. This became the Fiesta, which bowed in the fall of 1976 and was also sold in America through 1980. It was such a success that European executives decided to offer a slightly larger car of similar design as the next step up the range. This idea dovetailed neatly with U.S. plans for a smaller successor to Pinto/Bobcat. By mid-1977, the two efforts had been brought together and the "world car" was born.

Complicated but sensible, the Erika project envisioned a single basic package designed for high-volume production to realize cost savings through "economies of scale" but tailored to suit buyer preferences in each market. Components would be a mixture of local and imported, again to cut costs. Early on, it was decided that Erika's engine would be developed and engineered in Europe but built on both sides of the Atlantic, while manual transaxles and other running gear would come from Japanese affiliate Toyo Kogyo (Mazda). Because American demand would be higher, the optional automatic transmission would be developed in Dearborn. Body design would be a joint effort facilitated by computer hookups and frequent on-site personnel exchange.

Erika's heart was a clean-sheet overhead-cam four dubbed "CVH" for Compound Valve Hemispherical, a reference to its valve and head layout. Engineers had determined that, for a variety of reasons, a hemispherical combustion chamber shape was the best choice for both efficiency and performance, and that spark plugs should be placed as close to the chamber center as possible. This

357

Top-of-the-line '81 Thunderbird was the $11,561 Heritage V-8.

Standard engine for T-Bird was the 200-cid, 88-bhp inline six.

Escort/Lynx was greeted with enthusiasm, if not always the highest praise. CONSUMER GUIDE® magazine's initial test car ran 0-60 mph in 15.4 seconds with four-speed—nothing to get excited about—and returned a creditable 25.5 mpg in demanding city/suburban driving. Though we thought it a great advance over Pinto, we concluded that, compared to foreign rivals, the Escort "sadly lags behind in ride and handling control, interior design, and workmanship. Still, Ford's billion-dollar baby has a lot of potential. All it needs is detail refinement to stand up fully to the best in its class. Then, it would be a 'world car' in the true sense of the term." Evidently, Ford took such comments to heart, because running changes were instituted almost as soon as sales began. By the end of the model year, Escort/Lynx had become more pleasant, better-riding, and smoother-running. And such "fine tuning" would continue; in fact, Escort is still being refined at this writing.

Considering the gloomy national economy and the depressed car market, Escort sold exceedingly well in its debut season. More than 60,000 were retailed between October and the end of December 1980, and the model year total was over 320,000, making it the second most popular car in the country (after Chevrolet's Chevette). Lynx did only half as well—near 112,000—though that was far above its predecessor's best. Competitive prices helped—as little as $5158 for the base Escort three-door—as did a choice of four trim levels in each line.

Pushed out of the limelight by Escort was a new Ford Granada. Actually, the '81 version of Ford's erstwhile intermediate was less new than it appeared, for it was essentially a restyled Fairmont—two- or four-door sedan—with softer chassis settings and plusher interior trim. Still, a reconstituted Fairmont wasn't a bad thing to be. It weighed some 350-400 pounds less than the 1975-80 models, offered more room inside, a better control layout, more precise steering, greater maneuverability, and somewhat better ride control. Fuel economy was also improved even if performance wasn't. While this bit of badge engineering made economic sense for Ford, the Fairmont remained a better buy in the opinion of CONSUMER GUIDE® magazine's editors. Nevertheless, model year volume rose by some 30,000 units, to more than 121,000, arrayed in L,

mid-range GL, and plush GLX trim levels.

During 1980, Ford had given every indication that it was about to get its performance act back together and put it on the road. And Mustang would definitely be the star of the show. A tantalizing "concept car," the Mustang IMSA, toured the auto show circuit that season. Powered by the turbocharged four, it sat astride massive Pirelli P7 tires nestled under outlandishly flared fenders. Also featured were deep front air dam, rear "loop" spoiler, and pop-riveted plastic covers for side windows, taillight panel, and headlamps. In name and appearance, it hinted strongly that Ford was more than just thinking about a return to competition—and about the International Motor Sports Association GT series in particular.

Then, in September, Ford announced formation of the Special Vehicle Operations department. Significantly, it was headed by Michael Kranefuss, newly arrived in Dearborn from his post as competition director for Ford of Europe. The purpose of SVO was to "develop a series of limited-production performance cars and develop their image through motorsport." It quickly got down to business with a turbo Mustang to be driven in selected '81 IMSA GT events by former Porsche pilot Klaus Ludwig. Other Mustangs receiving similar direct factory help were a Trans-Am car for Dennis Mecham and an IMSA Kelly-American Challenge racer for Lyn St. James.

As if to signal its return to the track, Ford debuted the

The McLaren Mustang, with turbo power, was a Ford "concept" car.

McLaren Mustang in late 1980. The work of designers Todd Gerstenberger and Harry Wykes, it was a heavily modified Mustang with enough built-in potential to make it easily adaptable for racing. The formula was quite similar to the IMSA show car's: grille-less nose above a low-riding skirt spoiler, functional hood scoops, tweaked suspension (mostly a mixture of heavy-duty off-the-shelf components), bulging fender flares, and delicate-looking BBS alloy wheels wearing broad-shouldered 225/55R-15 Firestone HPR radial tires. The turbo-four was used again but carried a new variable-rate boost control providing a maximum 5-11 psi range, versus the stock engine's fixed 5-psi pressure. At 10 psi, output was 175 bhp at 2500 rpm, a considerable jump over the stock mill's, usually pegged at 131 bhp (Ford never released official ratings for this engine). Price was $25,000, quite reasonable for a custom "cafe racer," but only 250 (including the prototype) were built.

All this muscle flexing came too late to affect the '81 Mustang, however, which was little changed visually or mechanically. Reclining backrests were now standard for the factory bucket seats, while options now included power side windows and a T-bar roof with twin lift-off glass panels. An optional five-speed overdrive manual gearbox had been announced for both fours in mid-1980, and this became more widely available for '81. It came with a shorter 3.45:1 final drive (versus the normal 3.08:1 cog) for better off-the-line snap, and fifth was geared at 0.82:1 for economical highway cruising. But all was not bliss. The CONSUMER GUIDE® staff objected to the "linkage—stiff, yet vague—and its shift pattern [with 5th] awkwardly located . . . to the right of and opposite 4th. . . . Why Ford did it this way is a mystery. . . . Our guess is that the engineers wanted to prevent inexperienced drivers from accidentally engaging overdrive. . . ." The factory's official explanation was that the U-shaped shift motion would better emphasize the economy benefits of the overdrive fifth gear. Whatever the reason, it didn't work.

The rest of the Ford line saw few changes apart from engine availability. The 4.2-liter/255-cid V-8 took over as standard in the full-size LTD, the 302 moving to the options column. The 351 Windsor V-8, now in its last year, returned as the top option, rated at 145 bhp. The standard three-speed automatic transmission was phased out in favor of the four-speed OD unit introduced as a 1980 option. There were almost no alterations to appearance or equipment availability. The compact Fairmont returned with no styling modifications, but the lineup expanded with addition of a Futura station wagon. The 4.2-liter V-8 replaced the 5.0-liter engine at the top of the chart, and the turbocharged 2.3-liter four was officially cancelled. New options included a Mustang-style diagnostic graphic display and digital clock with console, plus Michelin TRX wheels/tires and an illuminated entry system *a la* Thunderbird and the full-size Fords.

Thunderbird continued with little change. Ford had made history at mid-1980 by making the 3.3-liter/200-cid

The 1981 Mark VI highlighted an electronic instrument panel.

Lincoln Continental became a Town Car for '81 (list: $14,423).

Mark VI rode the same 114.3-inch wheelbase as the full-size Ford.

Capri for '81 came only as a hatchback; prices started at $6745.

six a $76 credit option, a first for the Bird. Now the six was standard, with the 4.2- and 5.0-liter V-8s optional. External identification was provided by removing the below-bumper grille extension, and all models acquired the former extra-cost Exterior Luxury Group trim. In a move that paralleled 1978-79, the 1980 Silver Anniversary model returned as the Heritage but was otherwise the

Mercury's "Class Cat," the new Cougar, expanded its 1981 lineup.

Cougar's '81 prices started at $6694 (with four-cylinder engine).

Mercury built 53,653 Cougars and 37,275 Cougar XR-7s for 1981.

Cougar XR-7 sold for $8005, but came with standard 200-cid six.

same. Its roof treatment was now applied to the middle Town Landau model, with smaller "coach" rear side windows framed by a wrapover roof band, plus rear-half vinyl top, bodyside striping, and nighttime coach lamps. Alas, model year production dropped by nearly half, to 86,700.

In fact, aside from Escort and Granada, Ford Division suffered lower production across the line. Mustang dropped by near 89,000 units, the full-size line managed just over 78,000, and Fairmont sank by more than 73,000.

Lincoln unceremoniously dumped its poor Versailles, but a better "baby" was in the works for '82. Continental

Mark VI continued with coupe and sedan in base and Signature Series trim, plus the usual quartet of Designer Series package options. Styling carried over, but the 351 was dropped, leaving the injected 302—now with 130 SAE net horsepower—as the standard and only powerplant. The corporate four-speed OD automatic returned with a longer-striding 3.08:1 final drive for better highway fuel economy. New options included wire-spoke aluminum wheels and puncture-resistant, self-sealing tires, and a "mix" mode was added to the standard automatic-temperature-control climate system.

Mercury sold its version of the new front-drive Escort as the Lynx. Base prices ranged from $5199 to $6070 for 1981.

This '81 Mercury Marquis is highlighted by a "Formal Coach Roof."

The 1981 Zephyr Z-7 listed at $6355 with four-cylinder engine.

Output of the little-changed Zephyr was down to 52,276 for '81.

Ford Bronco for '81 had an independent front suspension system.

A big sales disappointment despite its more appropriate size, the Mark VI was nevertheless a better car than the V. Ride, quietness, and interior comfort were all as good, while handling and fuel efficiency were better. But its styling seemed contrived and overdone, beset with cliches, while Cadillac's new second-generation Seville had a talking point in its standard diesel V-8, troublesome though it was.

Continental came in for the Mark's mechanical updates and a new name: Town Car, previously a trim package. Twin-Comfort Lounge front seat with six-way power was

now standard, and the Signature Series option group was continued. Despite downsizing, this was still a 4000-pound-plus car, so the newly standard 302 gave only leisurely performance.

Mercury's Capri shared Mustang's drivetrain revisions and newly optional T-top and power windows. Not shared was the new $609 "Black Magic" trim option, basically black body paint with gold-color wheels and body accents. Cougar XR-7 picked up T-Bird's mechanical changes, deleted the under-bumper grille extension, and picked up restyled taillamps and slim moldings below the door win-

The '81 Econoline featured a posh "King of Clubs Wagon" option.

The Ford pickup truck was America's best-selling vehicle in '81.

dows. The previous Decor, Luxury, and Sports Groups were deleted for GS and LS trim/equipment packages, essentially sub-models identified by appropriate badges. The big Marquis and compact Zephyr were general hold-overs too, except for the more economical standard engines described for their Ford counterparts.

Vying for attention with Lynx was Mercury's other '81 newcomer, a redesigned mid-size called . . . Cougar. (As Ronald Reagan would say, there they go again.) Of course, it was just a slightly more upmarket version of the new Fox-based Granada, though exterior appearance was, as expected, a bit more ornate and Lincoln-like. Running gear and the unit body/chassis were taken from the Fox-hole too. At least it weighed 350-400 pounds less than the now-deposed Monarch. Options were extensive: various power assists (steering, brakes, seats, windows, door locks), air conditioning, choice of four different factory-installed sound systems, tilt wheel, cruise, flip-up glass sunroof and upgraded suspensions including the premium set-up with Michelin TRX tires and special metric-size wheels. Like XR-7, GS and LS option packages were also offered.

Overall, Mercury was the only Dearborn make to score higher '81 volume, tacking more than 58,000 units onto its 1980 total. Most of it was due to Lynx, far and away the make's best-selling line. However, the new Cougar sedans did 23,000 units more than the last Monarchs (no big deal, that), about 54,000 in all, while Marquis was up fractionally. XR-7 was down about 21,000. Capri and Zephyr also declined. Interestingly, the ponycar outsold the higher-volume compacts 59,000 to about 53,000.

1982

Reborn ponycar performance, a surprise two-seater, and a new compact Continental highlighted an otherwise forgettable Dearborn year. The U.S. industry, still reeling from the nationwide recession, suffered its worst sales in 20 years. Ford was not immune. The company's market share held at just under 16.5 percent, production was down for every nameplate, and total volume was off by more than 230,000 cars.

But there were bright spots. Escort, voted "Most Significant New Domestic Car" for '81 in the annual *Car and Driver* readers' poll, now shot to the top of the sales charts, ousting Chevrolet's antiquated Chevette by close to 75,000 units. Among compacts, Mustang remained a solid fourth, and Fairmont was right behind in 5th despite a now five-year-old design. Unfortunately, Granada was well down among mid-sizers, Thunderbird was even further behind, and the full-size Ford continued to trail the big Oldsmobile, Chevrolet, and Buick.

Enthusiasts cheered the newly fortified 302 V-8 that arrived as an across-the-board option for Mustang and Capri. Ford left no doubt about its mission by calling it "high output," which meant a special camshaft adapted from a marine version of the small-block, larger two-barrel carb, bigger and smoother exhaust system, and low-restriction twin-snorkel air cleaner. Offered only with the wide-ratio four-speed overdrive gearbox, it was capable of 0-60 mph in less than eight seconds—closer to seven by some magazine accounts. "The Boss is back!" said Ford ads. And so it seemed. Output was a muscular 157 bhp at 4200 rpm, with peak torque of 240 lbs/ft at a low 2400 rpm.

Elsewhere on the ponycar front, the turbo-four was discontinued after compiling a poor reliability record, though it would return in a considerably altered state in about a year. Mustang model nomenclature was revised to read L, GL, GLX, and GT in ascending order of price and sportiness. Capri offered base, L, GS, sporty RS, and Black Magic models, all three-doors. The new GT kept the low-slung front air dam, integral fog lights, and rear lip spoiler from the previous Cobra, but gaudy decals were gone. Both GT and RS rode a beefed-up chassis with stiffer front and rear anti-roll bars; wider, 185-section radial tires, and specially calibrated springs, bushings, and shocks. All models got a larger gas tank (15.4 gallons) for longer cruising range, while base cars received wider wheels and tires and left remote-control door mirror. Other drivetrains continued as before, but the optional 4.2-liter V-8 got a lockup torque converter, effective in all forward gears, for its "mandatory option" SelectShift automatic.

The more powerful Mustang GT/Capri RS signalled a performance revival in Detroit after a dull decade in which all U.S. automakers had learned to cope with government safety, emissions, and fuel economy mandates. Of course, Ford wasn't alone in swinging back to excitement. At mid-year, GM rolled out its totally restyled third-generation Chevrolet Camaro and Pontiac Firebird. With their 5.0-liter V-8s, tuned chassis, and race-inspired styling touches, the Dearborn duo was quickly matched up with the Camaro Z-28/Firebird Trans Am in comparison tests. While the GM cars won points for their superior handling and arguably more modern styling, Mustang/Capri was conceded more practical for everyday use—and discernibly quicker than their overweight foes. *Car and Driver* clocked 0-60 mph in 8.1 seconds with its GT against 8.6 seconds for the injected V-8 Camaro with automatic, and a comparatively sluggish 10.6 seconds for the carbureted V-8 Trans Am with four-speed. Editor Don Sherman noted that ". . . in terms of sheer visceral appeal, [the Mustang] is right up there with the Porsche [928]."

Not all was sweetness and light. In testing the Capri RS, the CONSUMER GUIDE® staff found the power steering irritatingly vague, overly light, and lacking in feel. Wet-weather traction was also a problem because of ample V-8 torque. While test conditions precluded a full

Harold Poling, Don Petersen, and the 1983 Mustang convertible.

Fairmont production declined to 127,739 for the '82 model year.

The $7387 Ford EXP offered an optional 80-bhp HO engine for '82.

Fairmont's top-line Futura series sold for $6419 as a four door.

Ford's Escort lineup for 1982 highlighted the new five-door sedan. EXP (rear) came out as an '82 model in mid-'81.

handling evaluation, we found it possible to light the back tires easily in a brisk take-off from a stoplight, accompanied by rear-end jitter that prompted concern about hard cornering on bumpy surfaces. Despite such faults, Ford's latterday muscle cars had much to recommend them. Compared to Camaro/Firebird, they offered more interior and luggage room, lighter shift action (with a more com-

fortably placed shifter), and a more comfortably upright driving posture—in all, a far better compromise for the daily drudgery of stop-and-go traffic. There was still work to do, but the extra dose of performance pizzazz was heartening indeed.

Pizzazz of a different sort arrived in Dearborn's first production two-seater since the '57 Thunderbird. In the

Ford experimented with alternative fuels in the early Eighties.

The '82 Granada wagon (its first) held 74 cubic feet of cargo.

Base prices for the '82 Granada ranged from $7126 to $8399.

tradition of two best-selling Fords of the past—Maverick and the original Mustang—the new EXP and its Mercury LN7 companion were announced about six months ahead of the model year, in early 1981. They were just sporty coupes derived from the Escort/Lynx platform, planned around a more rakish body with reworked interior dimensions. In other words, they were to the "world cars" what the original Mustang had been to the Falcon.

EXP/LN7 (the designations signified nothing) shared the 94.2-inch Escort/Lynx wheelbase, plus suspension, running gear, and instrument panels. They measured about 6.5 inches longer overall, nearly three inches narrower, and more than two inches lower. Styling drew sharp love/hate reactions. Like Escort/Lynx, they offered

hatchback convenience, but EXP wore a notchback profile while LN7 was saddled with a large (and heavy) "bubbleback" rear window. Also common were large wrapped taillamps, prominent lipped wheelarches, and wide bodyside moldings about a third of the way up from the rockers. "Faces" were dominated by single rectangular headlamps in large nacelles faired into the hood and front fenders. These flanked a sloped center section running down to a "grille" composed of two wide air intakes on EXP, 10 small slots on LN7. They certainly looked different, but there were those who said the styling vaguely recalled an Escort with adenoid trouble.

Underneath, EXP/LN7 differed from the Escort/Lynx in using stiffer springs and shock valving for flatter cornering response. Initially offered for the coupes and later extended to the sportier sedans was an optional setup designed around Michelin's premium TRX tires in a new-to-America P165/70R-365 size. This comprised harder pivot bushings for front and rear lateral control arms, harder rear tie-rod bushings, even stiffer shock valving all-around, higher-rate front springs, larger-diameter front anti-roll bar, and variable-rate instead of constant-rate rear springs. With either suspension, power steering came with higher-effort valving for more precise steering control and better road feel than on Escort/Lynx.

The coupes also carried more standard equipment than the sedans in keeping with their higher list prices—$7387 for the basic EXP against $5518 for the least expensive Escort. Included were power brakes, electric rear window defroster, full carpeting, tachometer and extra engine gauges, electric hatch release, digital clock, and a handy roller-blind shade to hide cargo from prying eyes.

Early road tests found a lot to like in the new little sportsters—except performance. The reason was that the sedans' 70-bhp CVH four had to pull about 200 extra pounds. Additional sound insulation and the extra comfort/convenience features accounted for some of the difference, but most of it was in the extra body bracing needed to support the heavy hatchback, especially on the glassy LN7.

Ford recognized the problem and, as an interim step, made a shorter 4.05:1 final drive ratio a no-cost option with manual gearbox at the start of the formal 1982 model year. Testing an LN7 so equipped (the Mercury got more press play than EXP, probably because of its more radical shape), *Road & Track* magazine recorded 15.0 seconds 0-60 mph, about a second adrift of the lighter sedan. CONSUMER GUIDE® got a lackluster 15.8 seconds, while an automatic EXP proved even slower at nearly 18 seconds.

Embarrassed by such reports, Ford offered a close-ratio gearset with 3.59:1 final drive that accomplished much the same thing as the wide-ratio gearbox with 4.05 gearing. Then, in March 1982, came a high-output CVH with 80 bhp at 5800 rpm, a 14 percent increase. The extra horses resulted from higher compression (from 8.7:1 to 9.0:1), larger air cleaner intake, free-flow muffler and twin-branch exhaust manifold, higher-lift camshaft, and

Mustang sizzled in 1982; the GT model had a five-liter HO V-8.

Ford announced the Mustang convertible early; it bowed for '83.

larger carburetor venturis. All this knocked about a second off the acceleration times—but it also magnified the noisy gruffness inherent in the "world car" engine.

As for roadability, most reviewers found the EXP/LN7 quite capable with the TRX package. Quantitatively, *R&T* ranked it up with such nimble handlers as the VW Scirocco. Qualitatively, the story was different. Nobody liked the power steering—too insensitive and overassisted—or the ride—an unhappy combination of overly stiff springs and overly soft shocks. CONSUMER GUIDE® critics found the ride harsh, choppy, and irritating, but found the car fun to drive on twisty, smooth roads. And compensating for the Milquetoast performance was very good mileage: a genuine 28 mpg in our test versus the government's 27-mpg city estimate.

Ford has often been accused of overdoing its market research, and this may have been the new two-seaters' biggest problem. EXP/LN7 was aimed at a new sort of buyer: young, mainly single people seeking something sporty, personal, and fun for errand-running or the occasional cross-country trip with a favored companion. What

they got was an economy coupe with no back seat and somewhat dubious styling (Ford's promise of an optional rear jump seat never materialized). To date, neither of these cars has been a sales winner. Despite an extra-long model year, EXP failed to crack 95,000 units; LN7 did even worse, and would be gone after '83.

Elsewhere, the story was mainly one of refinements to improve fuel economy. A new engine was part of the plan, Dearborn's first domestic V-6. At 3.8 liters or 232 cubic inches, it was about the same size as the successful Buick V-6, by now a workhorse throughout GM. However, the Ford unit was far lighter; in fact, it weighed only four pounds more than the "Lima" four thanks to the use of aluminum for cylinder head, front cover/accessory drive, and intake manifold. Bore and stroke were 3.87 × 3.44 inches, and initial power output was 112 at 4000 rpm, with peak torque of 175 lbs/ft produced at 2600 rpm. An important powerplant in Ford's future, it was initially offered as Granada's top power option and the step-up choice for Thunderbird.

As expected, Escort added five-door sedans but saw few

A new Continental four-door sedan debuted for 1982, replacing the Versailles. Lincoln built 23,908 of them for the model year.

The $21,302 base Continental out-priced the Town Car by $5000.

Like Escort, Mercury's Lynx added a five-door sedan for 1982.

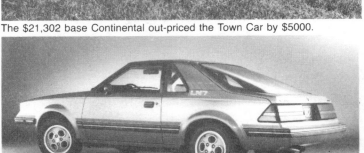

The '82 Mercury LN7 sported a "bubble-back" rear window. Styling was controversial, sales slow; it was soon discontinued.

other changes. Identifying all '82s front and rear were blue oval emblems bearing the famous "Ford" script. It was the first time in years that the insignia had been used, and was adopted throughout the Ford line. Escort's five series returned minus the base and sporty SS wagons, but the new five-doors in L, GL, and GLX trim brought the model count to 11. Standard equipment changes included wider radial tires, power front disc brakes for wagons, larger-diameter exhaust system and, with air conditioning, an accelerator switch that interrupted the A/C drive at full throttle.

Ford's middleweights changed little. All Fairmonts were now called Futura as the two-door sedan departed

The Capri RS: hood scoop, 157-bhp HO V-8, and 17 mpg city (EPA).

and the wagon was restyled as a Granada. Reshaped fuel tanks in Fairmonts and Granada sedans permitted the center trunk floor to be dropped slightly for extra cargo space. Gas caps with plastic tethers to prevent loss during fillups were new to these models as well as other '82 Fords. Fairmont's most powerful engine was now the 200-cid six, still in production after some two decades. A new option for the ex-Fairmont wagon was a rear window that could be flipped up for loading or unloading small items without having to open the tailgate. The new 3.8 V-6 took over from the 4.2-liter V-8 as the top Granada engine.

Still seeking better fuel economy, Ford added a lockup torque converter clutch to its three-speed automatic in this year's six-cylinder Fairmont, Granada, and Thunderbird. Unlike GM's system, however, this one was effective in all forward ratios, not just top gear. The lockup clutch provided direct mechanical drive from crankshaft to propshaft, thus eliminating the inherent torque-converter slip that eats up fuel. It was one of many subtle extremes Detroit engineers turned to in the face of tightening corporate average fuel economy targets. The '82 mandate was 24 mpg.

A practical demonstration of Ford's work in automotive electronics appeared in a new option for Thunderbird and LTD, which were otherwise virtual reruns. The '81 Thunderbird and Cougar XR-7 had offered an optional electronic instrument cluster with digital speedometer and bar-graph read-outs for fuel level and coolant temperature. This year's new "Tripminder" was the next logical step. A sophisticated quartz clock with trip odometer, it kept tabs on fuel flow, vehicle speed, and real or elapsed time, from which it would calculate such information as instantaneous or average miles per gallon, fuel used, average trip speed, trip mileage, and journey time.

Lincoln-Mercury finally fielded a "proper" luxury compact in this year's new Continental sedan, boasting an impressive array of no-cost standards, and bustleback styling that was clearly a take-off on Cadillac's successful, second-generation Seville of 1980. Underneath was the stretched, 108.5-inch-wheelbase Fox platform used for Thunderbird/Cougar XR-7. That meant the same suspension, of course, but spring/shock rates differed and Lincoln claimed two firsts in the Continental's standard gas-pressurized shock absorbers and self-sealing radial tires. Hydraulically assisted four-wheel disc brakes and the four-speed overdrive automatic completed the picture. Standard power was the venerable 302 V-8 (in 130-bhp carburetor form). The 3.8 V-6 (112 bhp) was a credit option, but few were ordered and it was soon dropped.

Though there was only one body style, Lincoln's new "baby" was offered in lush Signature Series and Givenchy editions that cost a cool $3000 more than the base version—up to $24,800. That was a lot, but everything was included: cruise control, variable-ratio power steering, air, electronic instruments, and a complicated travel computer with alpha-numeric "message center." Options ran to a garage door opener, power moonroof, wire-spoke wheel covers, and oversize fuel tank. Weighing in at 3600 pounds, the Continental was altogether the most efficient package Lincoln had sold in eons. And at near 24,000 copies, it sold respectably all things considered.

Rapidly changing standards made the senior Lincolns seem as big now as their predecessors were in the late Seventies. Still, sales fell by only 7000 units or so—again, not bad. Changes were few. The Town Coupe, never a big seller, was dropped, leaving Town Car and Mark VI sedans and the short-wheelbase Mark coupe. Understandably, the baby Continental got most of Lincoln's merchandising emphasis this year, while most testers found little to choose between the Town Car/Mark VI and their Cadillac rivals. "Trouble is, a growing number of buyers are finding big luxury liners quite distasteful," as CONSUMER GUIDE® observed. On a more positive note, the Mark coupe was at least "its own car" again, a unique body on a relatively close-coupled wheelbase in the grand tradition first conceived by Edsel Ford in 1939. On the other hand, what had seemed somewhat revolutionary just two years before was now looking obsolete. A ground-up Mark VII would be needed soon.

Mercury's market-straddling lineup stood mostly pat despite a flood of new models from domestic and foreign opposition. Cougar added wagons (GS and Villager) like Granada; Lynx gained five-doors like Escort; Zephyr offerings thinned; and other lines followed Ford's moves in running gear and equipment. The lack of change probably accounted for this year's mild sales drop of some 47,000 units, to just under 326,000.

Still, Mercury could claim a pyrrhic victory, moving

A new 3.8-liter V-6 was standard in the 1982 Ford F-100 pickup.

past Plymouth up to sixth place—but only because Plymouth was doing much worse. Lincoln, however, rallied on the strength of the new Continental which, if smaller than Versailles, had none of its heavy-handedness. People responded to it despite high prices, which only proved that good design will win out. Lincoln finished the model year at 85,313, a decent improvement of near 16,000 units. It would do even better for '83.

1983

The market had bottomed out in 1982, but the comeback was going to be a long, hard slog. While every domestic except—ironically—Chevrolet and Pontiac enjoyed better sales this year, Ford was swamped by a surging Oldsmobile, whose Cutlass helped it slash into second place in the U.S. production race. It was the first time since 1905 that Ford had *not* been one of the top two. In fact, Ford was number four, behind Buick, despite building nearly 35,000 more cars for the model year. (Ford remained second in sales, however, partly because of the large number of Escorts assembled in Canada.) The senior division did better. Mercury rallied to near-1981 levels, while Lincoln racked up its first 100,000-unit model year since '79.

The U.S. industry had been through some very rough times of late—and they weren't over despite faint signs of a general economic recovery as the model year opened. Some critics suggested that the events of the early Eighties, the result of a complex set of forces, were forever changing the way American cars are designed and manufactured. They certainly were, and Ford was in the vanguard of what amounted to nothing less than an industry-wide renaissance. All very fitting as the firm observed its 80th year in business.

Especially since something else was staging a comeback: "Total Performance." Ford fielded one of its most exciting lineups in years, with an unusual number of new

Spoilers, fog lamps, and black-out trim were part of the GT package.

The '83 Escort GT did 0-50 mph in 8.5 seconds according to Ford.

The 3748-pound Ford LTD Crown Victoria listed at $10,094 in '83.

A 1983 LTD Brougham four cylinder, four door sold for $8165.

Like the Fairmont and Granada, LTD rode a 105.5-inch wheelbase.

or heavily revised models, plus a new emphasis on fun combined with practical high technology. Nowhere was there a better expression of Detroit's new way of doing business—or its determination to survive in the face of unprecedented foreign competition and an economic crisis of historic proportions.

A perfect example of the new order was this year's dramatically restyled Thunderbird. Though mechanically and structurally similar to the 1980-82 models, this 10th-generation design signalled a complete break with established styling philosophy. Familiar fripperies once used to imply luxury and status—half-vinyl tops, standup grilles, opera windows, and all the rest—were consigned to history. Henceforth, aerodynamic considerations would make Dearborn design "functional" and "organic"—a new aesthetic that relies on form for attractiveness instead of tacked-on glitz.

Design development for the '83 Thunderbird and its Mercury Cougar companion involved more than 500 hours of wind tunnel tests with ⅜-scale and full-size clay models beginning in early 1979, and eventually led to more than 850 changes. The result was sleek, even daring: far more distinctive than the square-cut Chrysler Cordoba/Dodge Mirada and more contemporary than mid-size GM coupes like Olds Cutlass Supreme and Buick Regal, which had received an "aerodynamic" facelift for '81.

As before, Thunderbird/Cougar shared roughly the same sheetmetal, but contours were rounded now, decoration minimal. In plan view, their bodies tapered markedly toward the front to minimize frontal area, a key factor in reducing air drag. A "fast" 60-degree windshield angle was adopted for the same reason, the steepest slope ever used on a Dearborn production car. The main difference was in rear rooflines: Cougar went "formal," with a near-vertical backlight and upswept rear side window line; Thunderbird had a more rounded backlight and a smoother window-to-deck transition. Wind tunnel results favored the Ford, which registered an impressive 0.35 drag coefficient at the Lockheed facility in Georgia. The Mercury's 0.40 Cd didn't look so hot by comparison, but that didn't matter to the product planners. Let Cougar appeal to traditional mid-size coupe buyers; Thunderbird would be aimed at trendier types.

Underneath, much was familiar. Thunderbird/Cougar continued to employ unit construction for what Ford now called its "S-shell," one of several spin-offs from the rear-drive "Fox" platform, but the '83s were detectably smaller. Notable were a 4.4-inch cut in wheelbase (to 104.0 inches), a 2.8-inch chop in overall length (now 197.6 inches), and 3.0 inches less width (to 71.1 overall). Overall proportions were much the same but rear overhang was trimmed, which exchanged about three cubic feet in trunk space for a slightly tighter turning circle. Despite this shrinkage, interior space was about equal to 1980-82 except for 1.2 inches less rear legroom.

Predictably, the '83 chassis retained all-coil suspension with modified MacPherson-strut geometry and anti-roll bar in front and a four-link live-axle in back, plus standard rack-and-pinion power steering and power front-disc/rear-drum brakes. One new wrinkle was standard nitrogen-pressurized shock absorbers as introduced on the '82 Continental sedan, claimed to improve handling response with no penalty in ride comfort.

Bird buyers found a few surprises on the '83 model and engine charts. The Town Landau was dropped for an equally well-equipped base model. Heritage returned as the most expensive offering, with standard amenities like power windows, tinted glass, electronic instrumentation, velour upholstery, and illuminated keyless entry system. The standard powertrain for this pair was the 3.8-liter "Essex" V-6 with three-speed Select-Shift automatic. Op-

All Fairmonts became Futuras for '83; here the $6666 coupe.

Most Fairmonts were equipped with the extra-cost 200-cid six.

Mustang soft top, the first in 10 years, finally bowed for '83.

The aero-look '83 T-Bird expressed Ford's new design philosophy.

Look Ma, no whitewalls! The 1983 Thunderbird sported a European look and listed at $9197-$12,228; 121,999 were built.

tional was a new version of the venerable 302 V-8, with "central" or throttle-body-type electronic fuel injection, available only with the corporate overdrive automatic (extra cost with V-6).

But the real excitement was the mid-year Turbo Coupe, the sportiest T-Bird since the last two-seater and the first ever powered by a four-cylinder engine. With specially uprated chassis, mandatory five-speed manual transmission, and multi-adjustable bucket seats, it made even jaded enthusiasts take notice.

The Turbo Coupe engine was actually a reengineered version of the blown 2.3-liter ohc four last offered for the '81 Mustang/Capri, and was optionally available in their '83 descendants. Mechanical changes involved junking the carburetor in favor of Bosch port electronic injection and positioning the turbocharger upstream of the induction system to "blow through" it rather than "draw down" from it. Ford's latest electronic engine control system, EEC-IV, governed injector timing, idle speed, wastegate operation, supplementary fuel enrichment, engine idle, and emissions controls. Other changes included forged-aluminum pistons, valves made of a special temperature-resistant alloy, lighter-weight flywheel, die-cast aluminum rocker cover, and an engine-mounted oil cooler. Per usual turbo practice, compression was lowered from 9.0:1 to 8.0:1, and premium unleaded fuel was recommended for best performance. The result of all this was a healthy 145 bhp at 4600 rpm—better than the magic "1 horsepower per cubic inch" ideal—and 180 foot-pounds torque peaking at a relatively low 3600 rpm.

For the road manners enthusiasts demand, Ford developed a special Turbo Coupe handling package. Optional for other models, it comprised P205/70HR-14 Goodyear Eagle HR performance radials on distinctive aluminum wheels, plus firmer springs and shocks. Unique to the TC was an extra pair of rear shock absorbers mounted horizontally to resist axle patter on bumps and tramp in hard acceleration. Traction-Lok limited-slip differential with 3.45:1 final drive was also standard.

Distinguishing Turbo Coupe externally were black-finish headlamp surrounds and greenhouse moldings, and a pair of fog lamps in the under-bumper front valence panel. Inside were contoured Lear-Siegler bucket seats with sphygmomanometer-type inflatable lumbar support, adjustable thigh support and side bolsters, reclining backrests, and open-mesh head restraints. Unfortunately, the Turbo Coupe dash was shared with lesser Birds and not ideal for an enthusiast's machine, though tachometer and turbocharger "on-boost" and "overboost" warning lights were provided.

Announced at a base price of slightly under $12,000, the Turbo Coupe was roundly applauded by the "buff books" and even CONSUMER GUIDE® magazine, though our critics did find a few faults. The main ones were undue high-rpm engine harshness, an irritatingly narrow power band, ill-placed shifter, overassisted power steering, and that unhappily incomplete instrumentation. We also wondered about the turbo engine's long-term reliability—and

TC sales, as the proven V-8 offered similar performance (albeit at the expense of extra front-end weight that upset handling agility).

But there was no disputing Turbo Coupe performance: 0-60 mph in just 9.6 seconds and an honest 23 mpg in demanding city/suburban driving. For a large, posh, emissions-controlled coupe weighing almost 1.5 tons, the TC represented an amazing balance between performance and economy.

It also proved that Ford was serious in saying "Quality is Job 1." In fact, the newer Dearborn products sampled by CONSUMER GUIDE® magazine's test team continue to show excellent quality control. Bodies are tight and rattle-free, panels properly aligned, and interiors neatly finished with good-looking, apparently sturdy materials. Even paint finish, once a literal Detroit blotch, stands comparison with the best. We know. By chance, our '83 Turbo Coupe arrived while we were evaluating a Mercedes-Benz 380SL, and there wasn't that much difference in exterior finish. Considering the Turbo Coupe sold for about a fourth as much, it was heartening to see.

Elsewhere at Ford, the original ponycar was treated to its first major appearance change since 1979, and a Mustang convertible returned to the herd after a 10-year absence. All models now wore a sloped, slightly vee'd horizontal-bar grille that reduced air drag 2.5 percent, and restyled taillights. The 4.2-liter V-8 was dropped, and the "Essex" V-6 replaced the 200-cid straight six as the step-up option. Continuing as standard power was the 2.3-liter four, with one-barrel instead of two-barrel carb, plus long-reach spark plugs for fast-burn combustion, a move aimed at reducing emissions while improving warmup and part-throttle response. Manual-shift models came with a new Volkswagen-style upshift indicator light. This signalled the driver when to shift to the next higher gear for economy, based on the fact that an engine is most efficient at relatively low revs on wide throttle openings. Other changes included revised seat and door trims, standard roller-blind cargo cover for hatchbacks, easier-to-read gauge graphics, and less interior brightwork. A new extra-cost sport seat with mesh-insert headrests replaced the optional Recaro buckets, which hadn't sold well. Again reflecting aerodynamic concerns, hatchback liftgate louvers and rear window wiper and the notchback's Carriage Roof were all scratched from the options sheet.

Mustang chassis and engine revisions were designed to keep pace with Chevrolet Camaro/Pontiac Firebird in the renewed ponycar performance wars. First, the GT's standard handling suspension got a thicker rear anti-roll bar, softer rear spring rates, stiffer front-control-arm bushings, and revised shock valving, plus higher-effort power steering and optionally available 220/55-390 Michelin TRX tires. Next, the H.O. V-8 was booted to 175 bhp at 4000 rpm via four-barrel carb (replacing two-barrel), aluminum intake manifold, high-flow air cleaner, enlarged exhaust passages, and a modified valvetrain. Borg-Warner's new T-5 close-ratio five-speed gearbox (also used in the Turbo Coupe) arrived as an option to answer gear-

Lincoln Continental production was down to 16,831 for 1983.

The Lincoln Continental Givenchy retailed for $22,576 in 1983.

Three designers series '83 Continental Mark VIs were offered.

Mark VI production increased a bit to 30,856 units for 1983.

Least expensive '83 Lincoln, the Town Car, started at $16,923.

Cougar shared T-Bird body shell, but with squared-off roofline.

spacing complaints on the previous wide-ratio four-speed, backed by a shorter final drive (3.27 versus 3.01:1) for better takeoffs. Returning as a late-season option was the revitalized turbo-four, tuned as in the Turbo Coupe and available with five-speed only (though not, unfortunately, with air conditioning).

This year's most glamorous Mustang was the new convertible, offered only in top-line GLX trim. A number of conversion specialists had been prospering by snipping the tops from Mustang notchbacks (and other cars) to satisfy a small but steady demand for top-down motoring. Ford apparently decided it was time to get in on the action, too. Unlike the Buick Riviera and Chrysler LeBaron ragtops announced at about the same time, the Mustang was a regular assembly line model. Interior trim and top installation were carried out by Cars & Concepts of Brighton, Michigan; Ford did the rest. Roll-down rear side win-

dows and tempered-glass backlight were included, and the convertible could be had with any drivetrain save the base four-cylinder/automatic combination.

Among Ford's Escorts, the sporty GT three-door was revised to more closely approximate the handling, performance, and appearance of the European XR3 model. Included were port electronic fuel injection for the 1.6 "CVH" four, plus a new five-speed overdrive manual transaxle pulling a shorter 3.73:1 final drive. Suspension was specifically tuned for TRX tires. New appearance touches included front and rear spoilers, under-bumper fog lamps, and "spats" around wheel openings, while standard full instrumentation with special graphics, floor console, and new sport bucket seats with cloth upholstery and mesh-type headrests featured inside. It was a zippy little package, and attractively priced at $7339.

The new five-speed and EFI engine were optional for

The mid-range 1983 four-cylinder Capri GS listed at $7914.

Capri production slipped to 25,376 for the 1983 model year.

Lynx RS sported electronic fuel injection and five-speed manual.

The LN7 was in its second—and last—year of production in '83.

The aero-look Marquis saw production of 67,358 units for 1983.

other Escorts as well as EXP. The latter packed 88 bhp at 5400 rpm, compared to 80 bhp for the high-output four (still available) and only 72 for the base engine. Other changes included upshift indicator light on manuals, larger fuel tank, standard all-season radial tires, and a fourth speed for the heater fan. Base Escorts were dropped. A locking fuel filler flap with inside release was a new standard for all but L models.

Recalling 1977, Ford applied the LTD badge to a second model line, essentially a reskinned Fairmont with slant-back six-window greenhouse and aero-look lower-body sheetmetal, taking over for Granada as the division's mid-size contender. There were no major mechanical changes to this latest version of the Fox except for gas-pressurized front struts and rear shock absorbers and availability of the corporate four-speed OD automatic. Engine choices comprised standard "Lima" four and optional straight and V-angle sixes, plus a propane-fuel version of the four, offered on a limited basis mainly for high-mileage fleet users. Sedan and wagon body styles continued as before. Fairmont was a carryover and making its final appearance. Reason? A smaller, front-drive replacement was on the way.

To avoid confusion with the "little" LTDs, big-Ford sedans were renamed LTD Crown Victoria and the wagon became LTD Country Squire. Standard and "S" models were dropped, a more open eggcrate grille appeared, and the only drivetrain now was the new fuel-injected 5.0-liter V-8 with overdrive automatic.

Overall, 1983 was a disappointing year for Ford. Escort was no longer the nation's top-selling line, EXP was still going nowhere, Mustang was down nearly 10,000 units, Fairmont dropped by almost 47,000, and the big cars slipped slightly. The bright spots were the slicked-down T-Bird at nearly *triple* its '82 volume, and the little LTD, up over 35,000 from Granada.

Some of Lincoln's success reflected the start of a general market recovery, as its basic range was much as before. The best-selling Continental now acquired the 5.0-liter V-8 with Ford's new throttle-body electronic fuel injection as in the senior Lincolns. There was still no diesel, but the need was less acute as gas prices began levelling off, then fell following the President's decontrol of oil. (The move was criticized at the time as inflation- and recession-bait, but the critics haven't been heard from much lately. Neither has OPEC.)

The little bustleback Conti remained a very nice car, put together with care, its body rock-solid, its paint and trim properly applied, its sound-deadening the—ahem—standard of the world. Of course, it wasn't front-drive like Cadillac's Seville, but that really wasn't a factor in this field (and still isn't). And the Lincoln was arguably the better buy because of its simpler rear-drive layout and associated lower service costs. Who needed a Mark VI? Why, you could even get the compact Continental with swanky Givenchy or Valentino trim packages. If it took 14 seconds to scale 0-60 mph and failed to average 20 mpg, at least it rode and handled well and served its primary

Grand Marquis, at $10,654 to $11,209, was Mercury's flagship.

The Zephyr GS four door sold for $7311 in model year 1983.

Ford's little Ranger pickup offered four-wheel drive in 1983.

Club Wagons accounted for 30,446 truck sales in calendar 1983.

purpose competely. It was the best Lincoln of the early Eighties.

Mercury gave Capri a modified grille, "bubbleback hatch" *a la* LN-7 (the latter aesthetically dubious), and Mustang's fortified H.O. V-8 option. Great in a straight line, a bit twitchy in curves, Capri recalled the hot pony-cars of the late Sixties—a bit crude, maybe, but effective. The rest of the Mercury line saw minor facelifts and trim/drivetrain shuffles per corresponding Fords. Like Fairmont, Zephyr was on the way out, while Mercury switched mid-size names like Ford did, fielding an aero-look Marquis twin to the "little LTD" and calling its big cars Grand Marquis. The latter now included upmarket LS coupe and sedan. Lynx RS was Mercury's version of the hotshot Escort GT.

Of course, Mercury's main focus was the sleek new Cougar. It's already been described, except to point out that it had no Turbo Coupe equivalent. What it *did* have was a different styling feel and image, as Dearborn rediscovered the sales importance of emphasizing make identity via styling if not model and mechanical variations. As shown by recent sales of certain front-drive GM cars, people still have ideas about what various makes stand for, and they don't take kindly to Cadillacs that look like Oldsmobiles that look like Pontiacs that look like Chevys. Thanks to the Edsel fiasco, ironically enough, Dearborn has more successfully avoided that pitfall between Ford/

Mercury twins, and these days is making its corporate designs even more distinct. Cougar was one of the first clones to go "back to the future."

Curiously, a rival aero-engineer claimed the notchback Cougar was more slippery than the fastback Bird: "We put both of them through our new wind tunnel," he told the editors at the GM Tech Center in 1983. "There was a definite advantage for the Cougar—less turbulence aft." This worthy then coined an interesting description of Ford Motor Company's new fling with slippery shapes:

Ford registered 942,568 trucks in 1983, 37,896 more than Chevy.

"perceived aerodynamics." (He hadn't yet seen the Taurus/Sable.)

Perceived or not, the '83 Cougar was slick and novel, and it performed like no Cougar before. The standard V-6 and three-speed automatic delivered sedate acceleration (though more power was on the way), but cars with the upgraded suspension option handled well and had a nicely controlled ride. The interior was restful and plush, construction quality was good, materials of high quality. Nor was Cougar particularly pricey, as prices went in '83. The standard model came in at $9500—as usual, a few hundred more than the corresponding T-Bird. In all, the '83 Cougar pointed toward the direction Lincoln-Mercury was going—and going fast, as customers became serious about aerodynamics for the first time in the history of the domestic auto industry.

1984

Once again, Dearborn jumped the gun on a busy model year by announcing the first of its '84s in May 1983: the all-new Ford Tempo/Mercury Topaz, successor to Fairmont/Zephyr. These were important products, the company's first front-drive entries in the high-volume family-compact market then dominated by GM's X-car quartet (Buick Skylark, Chevrolet Citation *et al*) and Chrysler's popular Dodge Aries/Plymouth Reliant K-cars. Their mission was simple if difficult: win back sales lost to these competitors while further polishing Ford's image as a builder of modern, high-technology cars with advanced aerodynamic styling.

Tempo/Topaz emerged as one of the few American cars that honestly deserved to be called "all-new," and Ford took great pains to point out that it was *not* simply a puffed-up Escort. Work on project "Topaz" had been initiated in late 1979 to develop a larger running mate for Escort/Lynx, incorporating some of its design principles but not necessarily hardware. Unlike Erika, Topaz was strictly an American effort. The goal was to use front-drive's packaging advantages to preserve Fairmont/Zephyr interior space in a smaller, lighter car. That implied a purpose-designed engine, as the 1.6-liter CVH was judged too small. Body design would reflect all Ford had learned about aerodynamics, not just for distinctive appearance but for enhanced fuel economy and reduced wind noise. Of course, the company would hedge its marketing bets by effectively continuing Fairmont/Zephyr in its plusher, restyled LTD/Marquis guise.

Dearborn engineers again went to the wind tunnel, spending more than 450 hours on scale and full-size clay models that led to more than 950 separate design changes.

Interestingly, this work started a full year before Topaz got management's formal go-ahead, and continued until quite late in the game, March 1981. Tests with production-approved prototypes followed in 1982. Only coupe and sedan were planned, both notchbacks to separate the compacts from Escort/Lynx. A wagon was deemed unnecessary, strange considering the popularity of Chrysler's K-wagons. Evidently, product planners felt their Erika and Fox wagons catered adequately to those seeking a smaller hauler.

Styling was definitely from Dearborn's new "jellybean" school: chunky and rounded, with a shortish, sloped nose and abbreviated bustle tail. At least it was different from the boxy GM and Chrysler compacts. A 60-degree windshield slope (as on T-Bird/Cougar) helped cheat the wind, while drip rails were hidden in "aircraft-style" door openings cut into the roof. Rooflines differed markedly. The four-door Tempo had the "six-light" styling so favored in Europe, while the Topaz sedan used solid quarters. Coupes had rather thick A- and C-posts, like the sedans, but their long rear side windows made them altogether sportier. Grilles differed too: narrowish body-color slats on Tempo, a broader black-finish ensemble for Topaz. It was further evidence of Dearborn's return to more distinct Ford/Mercury identities.

The wind tunnel work paid off. Tempo's drag coefficient came in at 0.36 for coupe and 0.37 for sedan. Significantly, the vaunted Mercedes-Benz S-class also claimed 0.36. Since achieving low Cd is much more difficult on a shorter car, the Tempo/Topaz design was even more impressive than the bald numbers suggested.

Dimensionally, Tempo/Topaz fell about halfway between Escort/Lynx and Fairmont/Zephyr. The 99.9-inch wheelbase and 176.2-inch overall length were 5.5 and a whopping 20 inches less than on F/Z, and the new front-drivers were a significant 400 pounds lighter. All this put them quite close to Chrysler's 99.6-inch-wheelbase K-cars. Compared to GM's X-body, Tempo/Topaz had similar interior space despite a four-inch-shorter wheelbase.

Chassis specs were bang up to date. Front suspension was by MacPherson struts with coaxial coil springs (as on Escort), an anti-roll bar was standard, and steering was Escort/Lynx rack-and-pinion. Instead of its competitors' beam rear axle, Tempo/Topaz boasted fully independent "Quadrilink" geometry. It was similar to Escort's but used twin, thin lateral arms either side of the hub carrier instead of a single arm pivoted at the center. The carriers, in turn, acted on vertical shock/strut units, again with coaxial coil springs, and connected to tie-rods running forward to the chassis rails. Brakes were front disc/rear drum with standard power assist. Tires were a new all-season radial design in a P175/80R-13 size.

Under the hood was the first in a promised family of "fast burn" powerplants. Though roughly the same size as the overhead-cam "Lima" four, it was actually a reengineered version of the old 200-cid ohv six, with the same 3.68-inch bore, longer 3.30-inch stroke, and two fewer cylinders. Called 2300 HSC (for High Swirl Combustion), it

The 1984 Ford Escort GT sold for $7585, or $8680 with turbo.

The EXP weighed in at 2212 pounds for '84 and sold for $6645.

Ford produced 213,742 mid-size LTDs for the 1984 model year.

Prices ranged from $8596 to $9093 for the 1984 Ford LTD.

The Ford LTD and Crown Victoria could be optioned with Brougham roofs for a "richer, more formal appearance for 1984."

featured wedge-shaped combustion chambers with shrouds around the intake valves to speed up ("swirl") the incoming mixture for faster, more complete burning. Ford claimed this promoted lower emissions levels and provided more torque at low rpm. The latter was a key consideration in handling the optional automatic transmission that most buyers were expected to order. Engine ancillaries were carefully placed to keep the entire package as compact as possible. Intake manifold, water pump, and front cover were made of aluminum to save weight. On a fairly high 9.0:1 compression ratio, the two-barrel HSC produced 85 bhp at 4400 rpm and 125 foot-pounds torque peaking at a low 2400 rpm.

Initially, the standard Tempo/Topaz transaxle was either a wide-ratio four-speed overdrive manual or a closer-ratio five-speed. The former was part of a special Escort-style Fuel Saver package but wasn't available with air conditioning, so most manual-shift cars had the five-speed. As with Escort, both manuals came from Toyo Kogyo (Mazda) of Japan. Optional at extra-cost was an American-made three-speed automatic (ATX) similar in principle to Escort's.

At the start of the formal model year, a 2.0-liter four-cylinder diesel, also supplied by TK, became optionally available with five-speed only. Ford stressed that it wasn't simply a converted gas engine but had been designed *as* a diesel. Features included belt-driven overhead camshaft, aluminum cylinder head, altitude-compensated fuel injection pump, swirl-type combustion chambers, and precisely "square" bore and stroke (3.39 × 3.39). Besides the now-customary quick-start glow plugs, this diesel had an "after glow" device that kept the plugs lit even after the engine was running to burn off excess hydrocarbons and particulates visible as white smoke.

The '84 Mustang SVO wasn't cheap ($15,585), but it sure could go!

Mustang quickly became America's best-selling convertible.

Production of the Thunderbird rose to 170,551 for the '84 model.

Highest flying Thunderbird for '84 was the posh Fila ($14,046).

Ford said that the '84 Tempo, introduced in May, 1983, proved that "family transportation need not be boxy or boring."

Ford had long since mastered the art of merchandising-with-options but, except for the basic L versions, Tempo was quite well-equipped. The upper-level GL and GLX models boasted such niceties as full carpeting, padded door panels with armrests, intermittent wipers, sound insulation package, and individual front seats with reclining backrests. Options were extensive: electronic radios, extra gauges, Fingertip Speed Control, air conditioning, power windows, and tilt steering wheel. Topaz came in GS or LS trim levels, and Mercury developed some unique marketing techniques, making Tempo's extra-cost handling suspension standard and offering a Special Western State Package (for California, Oregon,

Washington, Alaska, and Hawaii) that added to standard equipment.

With its handy size, rakish looks, and five-speed gearbox, the Tempo/Topaz two-door would have made a dandy sports coupe. Ford lent credence to the idea with an optional TR Handling Package with the special Michelin tires, metric-size cast-aluminum wheels, and uprated steering and suspension pieces. It did wonders for transient response, but these just weren't cut out to be enthusiast's cars. Even with five-speed, CONSUMER GUIDE® magazine's test two-door needed about 14 seconds in 0-60 mph acceleration—adequate but hardly exciting.

Several other Dearborn products definitely were. The

most striking of this year's performance models was the long-rumored Mustang SVO, a limited edition developed by Ford's Special Vehicle Operations section around the turbo-four hatchback. Its lengthy list of modifications read like a hop-up artist's wishbook. Notable were an air-to-air intercooler and the first-ever use of electronic control to vary the amount of boost, which ranged up to 14 psi, the highest on any production turbo engine. These and other changes produced a claimed 20 percent more horsepower—up to a remarkable 175 bhp at 4500 rpm—and 10 percent more torque—210 ft/lbs at 3000. Other mechanical features included a cockpit selector switch that "tuned" engine electronics to the grade of fuel being used, and special dampers to resist drivetrain rocking under full power. Putting that power to the ground was a five-speed manual gearbox with special Hurst linkage, and standard Traction-Lok limited-slip differential with 3.45:1 final drive ratio.

SVO chassis revisions were equally thorough. In place of the stock 9.0-inch rear drum brakes were beefy 11.25-inch-diameter discs working in concert with front discs enlarged from 10.06 to 10.92 inches. Tires were European V-rated Goodyear NCT radials on fat, 16 × 7-inch cast-aluminum wheels, later switched to P225/50VR-16 Goodyear Eagle GT50s with unidirectional "gatorback" tread (as on the '84 Corvette). Spring rates and bushings were stiffened, Koni adjustable shocks replaced the stock dampers, the front anti-roll bar was thickened from 0.94 to 1.20 inches, and a rear bar was added along with an extra inch of front wheel travel. Mustang's power rack-and-pinion steering was retained, but with a quick constant ratio instead of variable-ratio, and high-effort valving for better road feel.

Setting SVO apart from lesser Mustangs were a distinctive "biplane" rear spoiler of polycarbonate plastic, grille-less nose, a large hood scoop feeding the intercooler, and dual square headlamps instead of the normal Mustang's smaller quads. A wide air slot sat above the front bumper, and the deep front air dam incorporated standard fog lamps. Small "spats" or fairings were fitted at the leading edges of the rear wheel openings to smooth airflow around the fatter tires. Inside were such driver-oriented accoutrements as left footrest, brake and accelerator pedals spaced for easier heel-and-toe shifting, 8000-rpm tachometer, turbo boost gauge, and multi-adjustable seats like those in the T-Bird Turbo Coupe. Other standards included rear-window defroster, tinted glass, AM/FM stereo radio with speaker/amplifier system, leather-rim tilt steering wheel, and center console with graphic warning light display. Only a few major options were listed: air, power windows, cassette player, flip-up glass sunroof, and leather upholstery.

The SVO was perhaps the closest thing to a European-style GT yet seen from America, and the best-balanced high-performance Mustang ever. Handling was near neutral, cornering flat and undramatic, steering direct and properly assisted, braking swift and sure. Performance was exhilarating: 0-60 mph in about 7.5 seconds, the

quarter-mile in just under 16 seconds at near 90 mph, top speed approaching 135—real muscle car stuff. "Buff books" applauded this sophisticated screamer, but buyers didn't. At over $16,000 out the door, the SVO was expensive next to the V-8 Mustang GT, which delivered similar style and sizzle for a whopping $6000 less. As a result, Ford retailed fewer than 4000 SVOs for the model year (though it had capacity for 15,000 annually).

Between them, the V-8 and SVO killed off the Mustang Turbo GT after fewer than 3000 hatchbacks and about 600 convertibles had been run off for 1983-84. Changes to other Mustangs this year were comparatively minor. A base-trim hatchback joined the existing two-door, a new LX series was combined from the former GL and GLX offerings, and the fun-loving convertible was available with GT equipment as well as in LX trim, bringing total ragtops to three. Interiors were spruced up, and automatic was extended to the H.O. V-8, in which case you got the injected engine. Ford's throttle-body EFI was also applied to the 3.8-liter V-6 option, now listed only with Select-Shift. And as with EXP and Escort, a clutch/starter interlock was standard with manual transmission.

Mustang celebrated its 20th birthday this year (how time flies when you're having fun), and Ford ran off 5000 copies of a special edition to mark the occasion. Reviving the hallowed GT-350 designation, it was basically a trim package for the convertible and hatchback, finished in "Shelby White" with maroon rocker panel stripes but little different from the normal Mustang GT. It was a nice remembrance, but the legal department forgot to check with Mr. Shelby, who claimed he owned "GT-350" and had been promised that Ford wouldn't use the name without his okay. Carroll, by now, was working again with his old friend Lee Iacocca at Chrysler, and was, perhaps, thinking of it for one of the hot Dodges he was building at his small-scale production facility in California. In any case, he was miffed enough to hit Ford with a copyright infringement suit. Sometimes, it just doesn't pay to be sentimental.

Another hot tip was a blown edition of the 1.6-liter "CVH" four. Like its 2.3-liter brother, it featured a blow-through turbo system and electronic port injection. Also included were high-lift cam (from the H.O. 1.6), high-flow air cleaner, EEC-IV electronic engine controls, and a turbo wastegate integral with a new bifurcated low-restriction exhaust manifold. At its maximum 8-psi boost, the little puffer spun out 120 bhp and 120 lbs/ft torque.

This engine was the heart of a new turbo package option for the two-seat EXP, and was extended to the three-door Escort/Lynx at mid-year as the Turbo GT/RS. The former got an uprated suspension with Koni shock absorbers, higher-rate front springs, P185/65R-365 Michelin TRX tires on newly styled cast-aluminum wheels, and front ride height lowered 0.75-inch (to reduce half-shaft angles and thus torque-steer in hard acceleration). Completing the package were five-speed MTX (automatic was *verboten*), front air dam, "teatray" rear spoiler, and black lower-bodyside paint with "Turbo" lettering.

Improved suspensions for the 1984 Continental and Town Car prompted Lincoln to boast that "High tech meets high fashion."

The Mark VII was the smallest Mark yet—and costliest ($21,695).

Lincoln called the '84 Mark VII a driver's car—and rightly so.

Mercury cancelled the LN-7 this year due to slow sales, but EXP picked up its taillamps and "bubbleback" hatch, and the normally aspirated H.O. 1.6 returned from '83 as base power. Other changes included a redesigned instrument panel, fold-down center armrest, and roof-mounted console with map light and digital electronic clock/stopwatch. Electronic radios, graphic equalizer, and tilt steering wheel arrived as options. With all this, Ford was effectively reintroducing its odd little coupe after suspending production in '83 (at just 2250 units; LN-7 saw but 699). To some extent, it worked: model year volume jumped to around 23,000. But the new Turbo was crude-running, rough-riding, and not very attractive against sporty import rivals that, admittedly, cost more.

Escort suffered no such problems, recording a smart production gain to near 332,000 units. All models received EXP's redesigned dash and many of its new options. Also newly available was Tempo's 2.0-liter diesel four, again limited to five-speed manual. Replacing the three top-line GLX models were the LX five-door sedan and wagon, with standard fuel-injected engine, TR suspension package, black-finish exterior trim, luxury cloth upholstery, floor console, overhead console, and tachometer. Rear seatbacks got a two-stage folding mechanism to replace the former flop-down arrangement for a flatter cargo deck, and standard split backrests on all but the basic L models. Power door locks, tilt steering wheel, and electronically tuned radios joined the options list.

Though brand-new for '83, Thunderbird boasted embellishments like a Tempo-style "A-frame" steering wheel with hub-mounted horn hooter (except Turbo Coupe) and amber instead of clear parking lamp lenses. Powerteam revisions comprised electronic injection for the base V-6 (thus eliminating carbureted T-Birds), availability of three-speed automatic with that engine nationwide, and optional automatic for the Turbo Coupe. The top-trim Heritage was renamed Elan, and a new Fila "designer" model (named for the Italian sportswear maker) arrived in white over dark charcoal with red and blue pinstripes. Exclusive to Turbo Coupe were viscous-clutch drive for the radiator fan and an oil-temperature warning switch.

Ford's Crown Victoria/Country Squire continued without change except for addition of a plain-side wagon. Full-size sales were on a general rebound as buyers took advantage of declining fuel prices to grab what they feared would be Detroit's last biggies. Unlike GM, Ford saw no reason to change its full-sizers as long as they continued selling, having mostly written off their tooling costs. And sell they did, model year volume leaping by nearly 50 percent to 169,000. Every one represented almost pure profit—and a handsome one at that—which delighted cash-starved dealers to no end.

Having enjoyed a good first-year reception, the mid-size LTD returned with more of the same and higher production (near 214,000). The faithful 200-cid six was retired after more than 20 years, leaving standard "Lima" four and the optional 3.8 V-6 in its new fuel-injected form. Amber parking light lenses and hub-mount horn buttons featured here too, along with standard power steering. A return to the bad old styling days was a standard cloth roof cover for the upscale Brougham sedan, with blind sail panels and a smaller "frenched" backlight. To get it without the fancy top, you had to order the base sedan with the Interior Luxury Group, also available for the wagon.

A far more interesting LTD was the mid-season LX. Ford president Donald E. Petersen, a car nut in the best tradition of Lee Iacocca, got the idea for it from the Bob Bondurant high-performance driving school, which had adapted Mustang GT components to the LTD sedans that Petersen and other Ford executives had recently trained in. Included were the 165-bhp 302 V-8, fortified suspension, Traction-Lok axle with 3.27:1 final drive, and P205/70R-14 Goodyear Eagle GT tires. Transmission was limited to four-speed automatic, but tachometer, shift console, blackout exterior, and plush bucket-seat interior were all included for a modest $11,100. It was a timely response to the growing hoard of domestic sports sedans like the Dodge 600ES Turbo and Pontiac 6000STE—and a rapid one: 0-60 mph in an easy nine seconds, 16.8 seconds at 81.3 mph in the standing quarter-mile. Alas, it went nowhere with the public, and production stopped after just 3260 had been built through model year '85.

But overall, Ford Division had reason to be pleased with '84. At 1.19 million units, it outstripped all of Chrysler Corporation in model year production and pushed aside a faltering Buick to take third place in the industry. Escort remained the division's outright volume champ, but Tempo scored an impressive 214,000 units and Thunderbird rose to better than 170,500. Sales hit 1.3 million that year, a quarter-million less than Chevy, but an equal amount above third-place Oldsmobile.

Lincoln-Mercury was also up, notching close to 633,000 units (up from 461,000) on the strength of good gains by Cougar, mid-size Marquis, Continental, and Lincoln Town Car, not to mention Topaz (better than 59,000). Lynx, Capri, and Grand Marquis were down, though not by much.

Sharing the divisional limelight with Topaz was the long-awaited new Continental Mark VII, which prompted a significant model alignment at Lincoln. Now built on the 108.6-inch-wheelbase Continental sedan platform but offered only as coupe, it left the Town Car as Lincoln's sole big car. Model choices comprised base, Bill Blass and Versace designer editions, and the LSC (Luxury Sport Coupe), the last audaciously targeted at the likes of the $55,000 Mercedes-Benz 500SEC—and a much stronger rival than Europhiles liked to admit. While the LSC wasn't quite as sophisticated as the SEC, it was very close not only in workmanship—a surprise in itself—but roadability. Best of all, it sold for less than half as much.

Motor noters were quick to paint the LSC as the "hot rod Lincoln" of pop-song fame, though few Lincoln or even Mercedes owners ever drive anywhere near their cars' limits. Still, Mark VII arrived with the capable Thunderbird/Cougar suspension, augmented by new electronically controlled Goodyear air springs with automatic leveling (shared with this year's Continental). In standard form it allowed substantial body lean, and the tires howled through any moderately fast corner. But the firmer LSC setup provided noticeably improved cornering, with

Ford of Germany's Scorpio was chosen European "Car of the Year."

Mercury's Grand Marquis soldiered on little changed.

The Mercury Marquis had standard automatic transmission.

For 1984, Capri offered a 205-bhp V-8 with 265 lbs/ft of torque.

The 1984 Grand Marquis was powered by a 5.0-liter, 140-bhp V-8.

XR-7—running a 2.3-liter turbo four—rejoined the Cougar lineup.

Mercury sold an '84 four-cylinder Marquis that ran on propane.

Topaz output nudged 120,000 units for the long '84 model year.

Topaz coupes and sedans cost the same; here the LS ($7872).

The '84 Bronco II, shown in XLS trim, rode a 94-inch wheelbase.

New to Ford's F-Series trucks was the F-250 heavy-duty SuperCab.

quicker response, less lean, and great stability.

Mark VII also borrowed much from T-Bird/Cougar styling (it used the same bodyshell, in fact) but was very different in detail. A low-profile but recognizable Mark grille adorned the front, and the obligatory outline of the old spare tire was on the deck. Bodysides were sculptured, with prominent full wheel cut-outs (reminiscent of the first Olds Toronado) imparting an aggressive, road-hungry stance. Base-priced around $24,000, the LSC cost $2000 more than the base car but added performance axle ratio, leather-covered console/steering wheel/gearshift knob, hide seat trim, dark charcoal lower-bodyside paint, and the all-important handling suspension. Alas, power was provided by the same mildly tuned 5.0-liter V-8, with throttle-body electronic injection and 140 bhp, though more muscle was coming. Belatedly chasing the oil-burner market, Lincoln also offered a 2.4-liter (149-cid) turbodiesel-six, made to a BMW design by Steyr of Austria, in package similar to the LSC. But V-8s were back in vogue with gas becoming cheaper again, and the smoker would be withdrawn after only a few thousand installations.

Overall, though, the Mark VII was a fine development by any standard, and helped pace Lincoln to a full recovery. At 157,434 units, model year output was the third best in the make's history. More significantly, it amounted to 54 percent of Cadillac volume, the best Lincoln had done ever against its old foe. If Cadillac keeps building dull clones of lower-priced GM makes, the day may come when Lincoln at last overhauls the one-time standard of the world.

Mercury enjoyed another fine season with close to half a million '84 sales. Like Lynx versus Escort, Topaz was less successful than Tempo and the reasons weren't hard to find. It faced a lot of competition, and its styling somehow had a "senior-citizen" look that not everyone admired. But everyone agreed that Cougar deserved more power, and it duly appeared in the form of a revived XR-7, a counterpart to the Thunderbird Turbo Coupe. Careful development drastically improved ride and handling, and even the base model was more competent.

Elsewhere, L-M had little to talk about. Lincoln's Continental sedan was rounded off at each corner, giving it a smoother look more in line with that of the new Mark—

and it nearly doubled sales, to 30,000 plus, despite few other changes. Gas-pressurized shocks and larger tires were the only updates for the big Town Car, which rolled on as a single four-door sedan in base, Signature, and premium Cartier trim as a glitzmobile with plenty of appeal to tradition-minded buyers—this year, nearly 94,000 of them.

But Capri was waning, trimmed to GS, RS, and RS Turbo models, the last abruptly cancelled along with its Mustang counterpart. Ditto Lynx, which added a Euro-style LTS five-door at $7879, with blackout exterior and sporty cabin. It went nowhere. Marquis shared mechanical changes with LTD (but not a planned LTS equivalent to the hot LX) and Grand Marquis was as much a rerun as Crown Victoria.

1985

After the long dry spell of 1981-83, Detroit was suddenly awash in money again, with record 1984 profits and—controversially—record executive bonuses. Japan's self-imposed quotas on U.S. car exports were still in effect, but the market was tougher than ever and overall industry volume eased from 8.1 million to 7.9 million cars. Included were over 200,000 domestically built Japanese models —Honda Accords, Nissan Sentras, and Chevrolet Novas, the last the Corolla clone resulting from GM's historic joint venture with Toyota.

Such Oriental "transplant" operations only added to a worsening production capacity surplus in the U.S., the impact of which has yet to be fully felt. Meantime, domestic makers strengthened their ties with various Japanese companies (if you can't beat 'em ...) while extending their "outsourcing" of key components, necessary to cut manufacturing costs in an increasingly price-competitive market but, understandably, not at all popular with unions.

Like its Big Three rivals, Ford Motor Company had already forged links with a Japanese "affiliate": Mazda. This relationship ripened as plans formed for future models, including a smaller, Mazda-designed Mustang for the Nineties, and an Escort successor based on the next generation of Mazda's front-drive 323 subcompact. Old Henry wouldn't have believed it.

Still, Dearborn was prospering in the general recovery, back to its traditional 20 percent of the market but aiming to capture more. That wasn't necessarily evident in this year's corporate offerings, though it would be in a bold new '86 product. For now, both Ford and Lincoln-Mercury Divisions were content to refine the good stuff they'd offered for '84.

Ultra-sleek Taurus: early '85 showings avoided shocking mid-America.

Taurus bowed on December 26, 1985, besieged with customer orders.

Gas-filled shocks came standard on the 1985 Ford Crown Victoria.

The sporty V-8-powered LTD LX served as a "four-door Mustang."

The two-seater EXP borrowed LN7's bubble-back window for 1985.

Escort adopted upgraded insulation and revised shift pattern.

Intercooled turbo kicked horsepower of '85½ Mustang SVO to 205.

Meanwhile, tweaks to the Mustang GT V-8 resulted in 210 bhp.

Tempo got electronic fuel injection and a new dashboard for '85.

There was an interesting newcomer, though. Called Merkur XR4Ti, it was an Americanized version of the German-built Sierra XR4i, hotshot of Ford Europe's family-car line. People were slow to recognize the name—pronounced mare-COOR, the German word for Mercury—but Dearborn intended that they should. You see, this was the first in a promised fleet of upmarket Teutonic Fords that would battle Audi 4000, the BMW 3-Series, Saab 900, and similar cars in the lucrative, so-called "yuppie" market. Some 800 Lincoln-Mercury dealers signed up to sell it.

Though close to Tempo/Topaz in overall size, XR4Ti rode a longer, 102.7-inch wheelbase and drove its rear wheels, not the fronts. Only one model was offered, a sporty three-door hatchback sedan bearing yet another interpretation of the corporate "jellybean" aerodynamic styling, created under Ford Europe design chief Uwe Bahnsen. The all-coil suspension with gas-pressurized shocks employed modified MacPherson struts, lower control arms, and anti-roll bar in front, while the rear relied on BMW-style semi-trailing arms. Power rack-and-pinion steering and assisted front-disc/rear-drum brakes were on hand as expected. But instead of the Germans' 2.8-liter V-6, Merkur had the blown, port-injected 2.3-liter four from the Thunderbird Turbo Coupe (hence the "T" in the designation). Reworked to produce 175 horsepower with intercooler, it mated to a five-speed overdrive manual transmission or optional three-speed automatic (145 bhp without intercooler).

With a curb weight just over 2900 pounds, the XR4Ti carried only about 16 pounds for each net horsepower, which meant 0-60 mph in about eight seconds with manual. Despite marked body roll in tight turns, it exhibited balanced, agile handling—quick to the helm and somewhat less twitchy than a small Bimmer, though damp surfaces demanded right-foot restraint to avoid kicking in the blower at the wrong moment, thus spinning the wheels and precipitating a tail slide. The styling drew mixed reviews (especially the biplane backlight spoiler) but most everyone acknowledged the first-rate workmanship, good ride, and well-planned "driving environment."

Priced at near $16,400 but boasting an impressive list of standard equipment, the XR4Ti gave Lincoln-Mercury a strong alternative to established Euro-sedans. Why, it was even made in Germany just like Audi, BMW, and Mercedes (a fact proclaimed on Merkur badges with the legend "Ford Werke Koln"). Alas, buyers wanted the automatic and leather upholstery more than L-M thought they would, and this put such a damper on sales that Ford was later forced to deny that it was planning to dump the entire Merkur program. L-M tried to perk up interest by putting XR4Ti's into various car-rental companies, which seemed to help, though sales remain below expectations at this writing.

Changes among Dearborn's domestic products are more easily summarized by considering the various Ford/Mercury pairs. Starting with the least changed, the mid-size LTD/Marquis got revised grille inserts, all-season tires a

John J. Telnack, Jr., Ford chief design executive, poses with a 30th-anniversary '85 T-Bird and a first-year '55 two-seater.

size larger than the previous standard rubber, and a slightly punchier, slightly thriftier 2.3-liter base engine with low-friction piston rings and higher compression. Both versions saw fewer sales, LTD skidding by 8000 units, Marquis nearly 4000. But it didn't matter: this would be the last year for these Fairmont/Zephyr descendants. Something far different was on the way.

Equally minor changes attended the big LTD Crown Victoria/Grand Marquis: standard gas-pressurized shocks, ignition diagnostics added to the EEC-IV engine controls (shared with the mid-sizers), and the usual trim/color shuffles. Sales went down, but only slightly.

The successful Tempo/Topaz compacts returned with new-design dashboards, an optional 100-bhp version of the four-cylinder HSC overhead-valve four, a more convenient shift pattern for the now-standard five-speed manual transaxle, larger fuel tanks, and more no-cost extras. A newly optional sports performance package nodded to the enthusiast set with uprated suspension, larger tires, bucketier front seats, and special trim. Thanks to the somewhat softer market and class competition that remained intense, Tempo dropped about 12,500 units from its '84 volume, but Topaz tacked on some 1500.

Dearborn's ponycars got a more powerful carbureted V-8 courtesy of low-friction roller tappets and new high-performance camshaft. Horsepower now read 210, up 35 bhp. As before, this engine was available only with five-speed (the injected unit was still restricted to automatic), which came in for revised internal ratios and a more precise, redesigned linkage. Beefier P225/60VR-15 "Gatorback" tires on seven-inch-wide cast-aluminum wheels

(borrowed from the slow-selling SVO) were now standard for the muscular Mustang GT/Capri RS. Capri appearance was virtually unchanged, but Mustangs acquired a new front-end cap with integral air dam and a simple air slot above the bumper. The SVO itself returned at mid-season with flush-mount headlights, newly allowed by the government (and pioneered by Ford among domestics with the '84 Mark VII), and an air-to-air intercooler that added 30 bhp to the turbocharged four, now rated at 205 bhp. Mustang GT continued to trade points with Camaro/Firebird in magazine showdown tests, while Capri was all but ignored, dwindling to less than 19,000 units for the model year. By contrast, Mustang attracted about 15,000 additional buyers, some 156,500 in all.

The '85 Continental was a carryover, but now listed at $23,086.

Lincoln's Mark VII and Continental, both built off Ford's ubiquitous "Fox" platform, got ABS (anti-lock brakes) for 1985.

The Lincoln Town Car, with prices ranging from $19,458 to $24,091, saw output of 119,878 units for the 1985 model run.

There were no major mechanical changes for the svelte Ford Thunderbird/Mercury Cougar, but engines were easier to get to thanks to counterbalanced hoods that did away with the clumsy old prop rods. Cougar gained a very Mercedes-like grille, while T-Bird's revised insert was barely noticeable. New for the sporty Turbo Coupe and XR-7 was a complete set of analog gauges set in a revised instrument panel. The standard cluster on lesser models combined analog fuel and temperature dials with an LCD digital speedometer, and a new all-electronic display was available at extra cost. Standard tires were upped one size across the board, while graphic equalizer and power front seat recliners joined the options list. Production was off here too, though not drastically. T-Bird fell to about 152,000 units, Cougar to 117,000.

Escort and Lynx were carryovers to mid-model year, when they were freshened with tidier grilles and flush headlamps. At the same time, the turbo engine was dropped, and the base and H.O. 1.6-liter units gave way to a 1.9-liter enlargement offering 86 bhp with two-barrel carburetor or 108 bhp with port fuel injection. The only other alteration was a rearranged five-speed shift pattern with more conveniently sited Reverse. These updates evidently had appeal. Escort volume went up more than 32,000 units, Lynx's by over 13,000, and even EXP did better—though not much, up about 3500.

At the top of the heap, the winning Continental sedan and Mark VII coupes saw only minor trim changes but, curiously, no longer wore Lincoln nameplates. The big Town Car was unchanged in most respects save one: a reworked rump with rounded corners, matched by smoother front fender edges. Evidently, even this blocky barge wasn't immune from the aero-fever raging throughout the Dearborn Design Center. The Mark VII LSC became more of a "hot rod Lincoln" with a more powerful 302 V-8, basically the previous Mustang GT unit with throttle-body injection and new tubular exhaust headers but tuned for a milder 180 bhp.

But the year's most significant mechanical news by far was the arrival of European-style anti-lock brakes as

Mercury produced only 18,654 Capris for 1985, a disappointment, but it continued to improve hand-in-hand with Ford's Mustang.

Cougar continued its winning ways in 1985, with 117,274 built.

Prices for a four-cylinder Marquis started at $9188 in 1985.

standard equipment for all V-8 Designer Series Continentals and Mark VIIs, and all V-8s sold in the five Pacific states. Jointly developed with the Alfred Teves company in Germany, it employed a computer that modulated line pressure in response to signals of imminent lockup from any of three wheel-mounted sensors, thus providing rapid "cadence" braking to avoid a skid. It was a first for the American industry, and an important safety feature that would soon be picked up for other Dearborn cars.

The Town Car, throwback to the past though it was, remained important in the L-M sales picture, particularly now that gas was cheap and plentiful again. Many Americans were still thinking big-car, and division product planners probably congratulated themselves for having resisted the urge to downsize the jumbo Lincoln. Besides this year's "taillift," changes included single-key lock system and, as elsewhere in the Dearborn fleet, shifting the horn button from the turn signal stalk back to where it belonged, on the steering wheel hub. Standard equipment expanded. In fact, the Town Car was now quite elaborate-

ly equipped, with backrest recliners, twin remote control outside mirrors, cruise control, tilt wheel, intermittent wipers. New options this year were automatic leveling for the rear suspension and air adjustable shocks, as well as a mobile telephone permitting hands-free operation.

Lynx was facelifted and given a 1.9-liter engine for 1985½.

The bi-plane spoiler on the rear deck provided the show—a 2.3-liter turbocharged four gave the 1985 Merkur XR4Ti its go.

Mercury Topaz GS Sport boasted a 100-bhp 2300 HSC engine for '85.

"Bronco II's toughness shows itself on the trails," Ford claimed.

Ranger hit its stride in '85 with 264,769 built, including 4x4s.

Ford produced 49,261 Aerostar vans during calendar year 1985.

The Town Car was hard to beat for luxury and comfort, especially since it seemed to lose competition every year. By 1985 there were very few alternatives to a car of its size and weight (219 inches long, over 4000 pounds). It was, perhaps, like a stopped clock, held up vainly but stubbornly in the face of the changing times. Yet there were still many buyers who had not been "born again," not yet convinced that value wasn't measured in inches and pounds. Like Cadillac's Fleetwood Brougham, the Town Car mocked Detroit's new religion, and dealers in both were glad they had them.

Especially Lincoln dealers, as the Town Car was their best-seller by a wide margin this year. Nearly 120,000 were retailed, compared to about 29,000 Continentals and some 20,000 Mark VIIs. Which only proves that it doesn't usually pay to be too hasty with design changes in the conservatively minded luxury market.

Still, the Mark VII's disappointing sales must have bothered Dearborn product planners, committed as they were to "aero styling" up and down the line. And that probably explains their extraordinary decision to preview an important new family car a full six months before it went on sale—a story that unfolds in the next section.

1986

By now, Detroit styling leadership rested firmly in Dearborn, thanks to the revolutionary changes fostered by design chief Jack Telnack and his team. General Motors, the arbiter for half a century, didn't seem to care anymore; Chrysler hadn't had the initiative since 1957 and was still a long way back.

Of course, Ford Motor Company had its share of leading-edge designs—the first and second Continentals, the Lincoln Zephyrs and '61 Continental four-doors, the '55 and '58 Thunderbirds, and the original Mustang, to name a few. But never had its lineup been so replete with state-of-the-art styling.

Dearborn advanced the art even further with this year's new Ford Taurus and Mercury Sable, the sleek, front-drive replacements for the mid-size LTD/Marquis and among the most daring American cars in years. The sedans had a drag coefficient of 0.32, one of the best in the world. But while "aerodynamic" cars are often ugly, these were beautiful. There was hardly a bad angle or panel anywhere, and there certainly shouldn't have been: the development price came to just about three *billion* dollars.

Likewise, Taurus/Sable demonstrated Ford's canny understanding that it just doesn't pay to build "corporate cars" differing mainly in nameplates. Front sheetmetal was shared, but faces were very different. Taurus was simpler, with a body-color insert between flush-fit headlamps; Sable was jazzier, with a full-width "light bar" incorporating nighttime running lamps. They were different aft of the cowl too. Taurus had the more conventional greenhouse, a European-style six-window treatment; Sable's was smooth and glassy, with a backlight artfully wrapped around to conceal the C-pillars. Other distinctions were rear wheel openings (rounded on Taurus, flat-topped on Sable) and taillamps. There were fewer differences between the five-door wagons, the only other body style offered, but they were Detroit's most exotic-looking "estate cars" yet.

Like the Tempo/Topaz before it, Taurus/Sable was new from the ground up. Nary a screw, molding, or fixture was carried over. Oh, they did have unit construction like their predecessors, but wheelbase was a tad longer at 106

The aerodynamic Ford Taurus finally became a reality for 1986.

Despite shortages, Taurus sales hit 267,506 by the end of 1986.

With new-found power, '86 Escort GT did 0-60 mph in 10 seconds.

GT's 1.9-liter HO engine put out 108 bhp and 114 lbs/ft torque.

As Taurus production increased, the 1986 LTD was phased out.

After a shutdown in production, EXP was given a new lease on life in mid-1986 with a new front end and Escort GT's HO engine.

EXP came as a Luxury Coupe or a Sport Coupe (pictured) for 1986½.

Tempo received a facelift, and went on to sell 251,618 '86s.

inches, and the mechanical layout was, of course, entirely different: front drive with transversely mounted engines. Initially all models were built with a new 3.0-liter (183-cubic-inch) "Vulcan" V-6, an oversquare overhead-valve design with port electronic fuel injection and a rated 140 horsepower, teamed exclusively with a new-design four-speed overdrive automatic transaxle. Arriving a bit later was a 2.5-liter (153-cid) ohv four, essentially an enlarged version of the Tempo/Topaz engine, available with three-speed automatic. Weighing around 3100 pounds at the curb, the V-6 models provided adequate acceleration, but no more, though quiet highway cruising and excellent directional stability were strong suits. The four-cylinder jobs were mainly for fleet duty and predictably slower.

Ford put great effort into chassis development, and it showed. All models employed MacPherson struts, lower control arms, and coil springs for the front suspension, plus power rack-and-pinion steering and front-disc/rear-drum brakes. Rear suspension was also independent, but each body style had its own geometry. Sedans rode on MacPherson strut/coils plus twin parallel arms. Wagons had the coils between double wishbones, an arrangement deemed more suitable for the heavier loads they might carry, and used shorter shock towers to maximize cargo space. Regardless, ride was compliant thanks to ample wheel travel and well-judged spring/shock rates, body lean modest even in hard corners.

High-tech styling, front drive, all-independent suspension. It sounded like the makings of a premium European sports sedan. Yet Taurus and Sable were actually high-volume family cars, competing against the likes of GM's square-lined A-bodies at prices starting around $11,000. Their sophisticated styling was a bold departure for this market, especially after the innocuous LTD/Marquis, and Ford knew it. Accordingly, Taurus and Sable made their public debut at the Chicago Auto Show in February 1985—more than six months before they went on sale—to give middle-of-the-road buyers time to adjust to their

Mustang underwent further fine-tuning for 1986. The 5.0-liter HO V-8 now put out 200 horsepower and 285 lbs/ft torque.

While Thunderbird offered the performance-oriented Turbo Coupe, the Ford LTD Crown Victoria featured comfort and luxury.

striking aero looks. At the same time, pre-production cars went out to major magazines for preliminary assessment.

But the product people needn't have worried. Helped by glowing published reports, Taurus and Sable were hot sellers from day one, and the two plants building them (Atlanta and Chicago) went on overtime to meet the demand. The styling was definitely a plus. By coincidence, Taurus/Sable bore more than a passing resemblance to the futuristic but flawed Audi 5000, already embraced by trendy, upwardly mobile types as *the* status car of the day. Though they shared not a single line between them, Taurus and Sable were undoubtedly viewed as sort of bargain-basement Audis, offering the same "with it" looks and similar roadability for thousands less. As such, they seemed like bargains—which, of course, they were: solidly built, understated, refined, well-equipped.

More than a few GM folks must have been worried by Taurus/Sable and its enthusiastic response; if they weren't, then GM was in more trouble than most people

thought. In a wider sense, though, Taurus/Sable is solid evidence that the American industry is still capable of producing world-class automobiles, and that's about the best news since the Model T proved that cars were for everybody.

At the opposite end of the conceptual spectrum, the big Ford Crown Victoria and Mercury Grand Marquis continued to fill any residual need for Sixties-style land cruisers, necessary for a certain conservative market group that remained important. The main changes on this year's models were an overhauled version of the venerable small-block V-8, with port electronic injection (replacing throttle-body), new-design fast-burn combustion chambers, higher compression (8.9:1), roller tappets, low-friction piston rings, and a viscous radiator fan clutch. The resulting output gains were modest, up to 150 bhp and a sizable 270 lbs/ft peak torque.

Tempo and Topaz, meanwhile, lost some of their initial clumsiness via new grilles with flush-mount "aero" head-

Lincoln Town Car sales continued at a high level for 1986: 119,180.

Anti-lock brakes were standard equipment on the 1986 Continental.

Mark VII's multi-port fuel-injected engine was an industry first.

As it turned out, 1986 was the last year for the little-changed Capri.

The 1986 Sable wagon provided a roomy 82 cubic-foot cargo area.

During the first nine months of '86, Mercury sold 70,563 Sables.

Sable's "light bar" front end differentiated it from Taurus.

The 1986 Cougar XR-7 Turbo, as pictured, retailed for $14,377.

Mercury's counterpart to the Escort GT was the $8193 Lynx XR3.

Topaz received a mild facelift for '86; prices started at $8085.

lamps, plus revised bumpers and taillamps. Detail updates comprised larger (14-inch) standard wheels and tires, optional 15-inch roadwear with the extra-cost sport packages, relocated switchgear (including a retrograde, dash-mount wiper/washer control), single-key lock system, and miscellaneous trim and equipment alterations. Tempo's top GLX series was renamed LX.

Escort/Lynx were unchanged from their "1985½" makeover apart from addition of a budget-price Escort Pony three-door (at a competitive $6052) and reconfigured sporting models called Escort GT and Lynx XR3. The latter featured a more potent 1.9-liter four with 108 bhp, P195/60HR-15 tires on six-inch-wide aluminum wheels, fortified suspension with rear stabilizer bar and larger front bar, plus asymmetric grilles, fore/aft spoilers, and rocker panel skirts, all in body color. The little two-seat EXP got the same treatment, save for a Tempo-style nose with slat grille.

Back at the horsepower war, Mustang/Capri discarded the old carbureted and TBI V-8s in favor of a new 200-bhp small-block with sequential port electronic injection, accompanied by a stronger rear axle. V-8 and V-6 now sat on viscous mounts, introduced on the mid-1985 Mustang SVO, and all models got one-key locking and more sound insulation.

T-Bird and Cougar were largely reruns, but V-8 efficiency and driveability improved a bit with adoption of the 150-bhp port-injected unit from Crown Victoria/Grand Marquis. Standard tires again went up one size, the T-Bird Fila was deep-sixed, and a power moonroof gave buyers a new way to spend their mad money.

The big Lincoln Town Car continued to satisfy both Dearborn accountants and its remarkably loyal public. It was, incidentally, the best-selling of Lincoln's three lines by a country mile, running off an effortless 100,000 units a year, some three times more than either the mid-size Continental or the Mark VII. It was even a preferred car of the rental companies, according to writer Tom Bonsall: "One Ford official went so far as to describe the Town Car to me, bluntly, as a 'fleet' car. Reportedly it is all but sold out two years in advance." Little news was again good news: standard 150-bhp port-injected V-8, and a newly optional Ford/JBL audio system with power amplifier and no fewer than a dozen speakers.

Continental and Mark VII returned wearing Lincoln badges again (why they were removed on the '85s remains a mystery). More significant was adoption of the Ford/Teves anti-lock braking system as standard. The optional turbodiesel six disappeared, and the 150-bhp V-8 was now the one and only engine for all models except LSC.

But the "hot rod Lincoln" wasn't ignored, picking up the port-injected, 200-bhp Mustang GT/Capri RS V-8, plus a new analog gauge cluster where other models had electronics. The latter was clearly a hasty afterthought. Then again, in the old days, Ford likely wouldn't have bothered improving such a marginal seller. Clearly, the "Glass House" was still populated with genuine enthusiasts who appreciated the fact that there's more to running a car

company than just the bottom line. Much like the hallowed Mark II of the Fifties, the LSC was a labor of love, a goodwill ambassador whose main mission was casting an aura of class over the rest of the line. In that, and as a satisfying road car, it was superb. We predict it'll be a sought-after collector's item in not too many years.

1987

Ford Motor Company's 1987 fleet elegantly disproved the hoary old myth that Detroit builds the cars it wants to build and forces them down our throats. The wide, traffic-choked avenues of Southern Michigan are hardly the best places for evaluating—or enjoying—a Taurus, Sable, Cougar, or Thunderbird, but that environment alone didn't spawn such cars. Ford people have been out driving the twisty lanes of New England, the high-speed byways of California, the desert wastes of Nevada, the mountain routes of West Virginia—and it shows. As a whole, Ford, Mercury, and Lincoln are delivering what

Thunderbird Turbo Coupe received new styling, 190 bhp for 1987.

"Ordinary" '87 T-Birds still sported a shiny grille up front.

1987 Mustang GT convertible sported aero headlamps.

Mustang GT took on wilder styling and 225-bhp HO V-8 for 1987.

Prices for the 1987 Ford LTD Crown Victoria started at $14,355.

Ford Escort GT: performance and economy for 1987.

Both Escort GT and EXP adopted 15-inch aluminum wheels for '87.

Americans want, perhaps more effectively than at any time in their history.

Having seized the design initiative among U.S. producers, Dearborn targeted engineering leadership for '87: specifically, extending its use of anti-lock brakes, and pioneering four-wheel drive among high-volume cars. The latter arrived this year in the form of a new "All-Wheel-Drive" option for Tempo/Topaz. A part-time system intended for use in slippery conditions, not on dry pavement or off-road, it was teamed with a higher-output (94-horsepower) 2.3-liter four and a new three-speed automatic transmission with so-called "fluidically linked" torque converter (FLC) that obviated the need for converter lockup. For convenience, it incorporated a "shift-on-the-fly" capability, meaning you could shift into or out of 4WD without stopping. Unlike some 4WD conversions, this one brought little detectable change in ride height, and there were no major suspension changes save appropriate spring/shock tuning.

Some of this reflected Ford's European work with the purpose-built, mid-engine RS 200 rally car and the high-performance Sierra XR4×4 and 4WD Granada/Scorpio. But, coming as it does in the family market, the All-Wheel-Drive Tempo/Topaz represents not only a price breakthrough but the first domestic challenge to a growing number of workaday Japanese 4WDs. It also indicates that Ford still isn't afraid to try something different, especially if it upstages General Motors or Chrysler.

GM, in fact, paid Ford a compliment by offering anti-lock brakes on some of its upmarket front-drive cars during '86, albeit on a halting, limited basis. Not to be outdone, Dearborn also brought this significant feature to a lower price bracket by extending its Teves system from the Mark VII/Continental to this year's Thunderbird Turbo Coupe as standard equipment—and throwing in rear disc brakes for good measure.

Ford didn't rest on its styling laurels either, reskinning T-Bird/Cougar and facelifting Mustang. The former retained their trend-setting aero silhouettes, but side glass was now flush-mounted to reduce turbulence even more, and lower beltlines combined with reshaped windows for improved outward vision. The changes were especially noticeable on Cougar, marking its milestone 20th anniversary. Front ends were also freshened, with fresh grilles and trendy flush headlamps; rear ends were similarly cleaned up. Mustang's restyle, the ponycar's first major sheetmetal change since '79, involved new flush headlamps, grille-less nose, and revamped back panels, plus lower front air dam, prominent rocker-panel skirting, cooling scoops ahead of each wheel, and a big hatchback spoiler for the muscular GT.

Speaking of muscles, Mustang returned from the Dearborn gym with revised induction and cylinder heads that extracted 225 bhp from its port-injected 5.0-liter V-8, thus matching output of the newly available 5.7-liter engine in the rival Chevrolet Camaro/Pontiac Firebird. The high-tech Mustang SVO was dropped for lack of interest (as indeed was Mercury's Capri), but its intercooled, port-injected turbo-four now powered the T-Bird Turbo Coupe and Cougar XR-7. However, it was slightly detuned, in the interest of durability and refinement, to "only" 190 bhp and 240 lbs/ft torque (150 bhp and 200 lbs/ft with optional automatic). Even the unblown 2.3 and base Escort/Lynx 1.9-liter engines were more powerful, both up to 90 bhp thanks to adoption of throttle-body fuel injection. And with that, Dearborn completely banished carburetors from its passenger cars.

Refinement was the word elsewhere. Ford Crown Victoria and Mercury Grand Marquis, still much as they were when downsized nine years before, added standard air conditioning and tinted glass. They were still selling well enough to warrant an aero makeover, confirmed for 1990 or so. Sable separated a bit from Taurus by dropping the base four, leaving 3.0-liter V-6/four-speed overdrive ATX as the one and only drivetrain. The four-speed automatic replaced the three-speed as an option on the four-cylinder Taurus, which was still available with five-speed manual transaxle in sporty MT-5 trim, a Euro-sedan in every way except for decidedly sluggish performance.

Among the smaller cars, EXP was still hanging in there, part of a rejiggered Escort line comprising base Pony and top-trim GT three-door sedans, and GL three-door, five-door, and wagon. Lynx retained base L, midrange GS, and sporty XR3, but only temporarily, for reasons we'll get to shortly. Tempo/Topaz was little changed aside from the All-Wheel-Drive option, but the front-drive models also got the new fluidically linked converter.

The latest Federal mandates decreed that each manufacturer (not make or model line) install passive restraints on 10 percent of its 1987 production. Ford had already offered a driver-side air bag as a limited option for the '86 Tempo/Topaz. Only about 100 were ordered, though Ford promised to promote it more for '87. Meantime, Escort/Lynx was tapped for the 10-percent solution, adding motorized front belts that automatically pivoted around occupants on closing the doors. The previous year had brought the government-required central high-mount stoplamp (CHMSL), and Ford continued to satisfy this rule on most of its cars with a lot more elegance than some rivals displayed.

And that was pretty much it—at least for the first half of '87. Like everyone else in Detroit, Ford had long ago realized the value of not introducing new designs until they were right, and this year was no exception. Even so, "1987½" announcements were more plentiful—and significant—than usual.

Unfortunately, not everything was known about them at this writing, but the most interesting will undoubtedly be the eagerly anticipated, Taurus-based replacement for the Continental sedan. Likely to ride a wheelbase of around 109-110 inches, it's bound to be as sleek and purposeful as Taurus/Sable, with all the opulence expected of a Lincoln and road manners that haven't been experienced since the Mexican Road Race days (Mark VII LSC excepted). Powered by a 3.8-liter Essex V-6 reengineered for front drive and installed transversely, it stacks up as

Ford Tempo offered an All-Wheel Drive system on 1987 models.

The '87 Taurus rode a 108-inch wheelbase, was 188.4 inches long.

Taurus prices started at $10,491 (sedan) and $11,722 (wagon).

Lincoln's '87 Town Car was "enhanced" with a compact disc player.

Lincoln priced the Mark VII LSC coupe at $25,863 for 1987.

1987

another Dearborn challenger to the great European road cars, especially if/when a rumored supercharger option materializes. L-M hopes the new Continental will perk up interest in the Mark VII, which also comes in for smoother styling and more LSC power. For those who can't—or won't—move with the times, the familiar Town Car is on hand as always.

Also coming is a second Merkur based on the German-built Scorpio five-door sedan (and likely to retain that name), voted Europe's 1986 Car of the Year. Again, it's a rear-drive design in the "jellybean" mold but more attrac-

tive to most eyes than the Sierra-based XR4Ti. It's also comparable in size with an existing U.S. product, in this case Taurus/Sable. Specifically, it's three inches longer between wheel centers (108.7 inches), but less overhang at each end leaves it about 4.5 inches shorter overall (186.4 inches). Power will be supplied by a new-design, 2.9-liter ohv V-6 with about 145 bhp in emissions-legal U.S. tune, with the usual five-speed manual/four-speed automatic choices. Scorpio was supposed to debut during 1986, but was put back several times for unexplained reasons.

The 1988 Lincoln Town Car is notable for continuity of styling.

Continental featured 140-watt, 12 speaker audio system option.

Mercury Sable offered GS and LS series (all V-6 powered) for '87.

The 1987 Mercury Sable station wagon weighed in at 3228 pounds.

Mark VII enters 1988 with new grille, subtle exterior changes.

After some delay, the German Merkur Scorpio debuted in 1987.

Mercury priced the 1987 Lynx GS five-door hatchback at $7308.

Grand Marquis LS ($15,621) continued as Mercury's flagship model.

"World cars" are still very much a part of Ford's future, and the future arrives in early '87 with a pair of newcomers that illustrate just how small the automotive world has become. First up is the Mercury Tracer, replacing the languishing Lynx and essentially a restyled derivation of Mazda's popular 323 subcompact. Offered as a three- and five-door sedan and five-door wagon, it's fractionally longer than the 323 in wheelbase (94.7 inches) and overall length (162.0/171.4 inches) but runs the same 1.6-liter overhead-cam four with port fuel injection and 82 bhp, mated to five-speed manual or three-speed automatic transaxle. Chassis specs are the same too: all-coil, all-independent MacPherson-strut suspension; front-disc/rear-drum brakes; rack-and-pinion steering. Appearance is pleasingly chunky and quite distinct from the 323's. Perhaps the most significant thing about the Tracer is where it's built: Ford's new highly automated facility in Hermosillo, Mexico. It underlines the growing importance of "third world" countries in determining the winners and losers in today's high-stakes auto business.

Equally international is Ford's new Festiva, a petite three-door sedan with boxy "phone booth" styling on a 90.4-inch wheelbase. Like Tracer, it's a Mazda design and, in light of today's fierce cost/profit squeeze, it's also built in a country with much lower labor rates than either the U.S. or Japan. In this case it's South Korea, with assembly carried out by Kia Motors, in which both Ford and Mazda have a financial interest.

Measuring just 140.4 inches long, Festiva drives its front wheels with a 1.3-liter carbureted four. The base L model has a four-speed transaxle, while a five-speed features on the better-equipped LX. Chassis engineering is similar to Tracer's, while styling is more rectilinear, though recognizably Ford, with "aero" headlamps and smooth, wraparound bumpers. Festiva will be Dearborn's "entry-level" car, a competitor for low-price minis—as in minimal—like the Japanese-built Chevy Sprint (which the company claims Festiva beats in outright interior volume by 11.3 cubic feet).

From all this, it's clear that Ford intends to remain a major player on the international automotive stage—as well it should. With the possible exception of General Motors, no other automaker can claim more worldwide manufacturing experience.

Controversial best-sellers notwithstanding, history and past accomplishments count for much less in today's rapidly changing world than they used to, as the "Japanization" of America so pointedly reminds us. But as the automobile enters its second 100 years, it's appropriate to note that Ford has been a giant for most of the first 100. The accomplishments chronicled here, both good and bad, testify to that.

Today, leading-edge products and sensible cooperative ventures aggressively pursued by forward-thinking management suggest that the company Henry Ford built will not only survive but thrive past its own centennial in 2003. So perhaps now more than ever it may be truly said of Ford that the best is yet to come.

Cougar XR-7 for '87 took on new sheetmetal and the 5.0-liter V-8.

Merkur XR4Ti added larger 15-inch wheels and tires for 1987.

The Ford F-150 pickup was redesigned for 1987.

The F-150 SuperCab standardized rear anti-lock brakes.

Full-size Bronco shared the pickup's aero-look styling for '87.

INDEX

INDEX

INDEX